AXIOMATIC FORMAL ONTOLOGY

VOLUME 264

UWE MEIXNER
University of Regensburg,
Regensburg, Germany

AXIOMATIC FORMAL ONTOLOGY

KLUWER ACADEMIC PUBLISHERS
DORDRECHT / BOSTON / LONDON

A C.I.P. Catalogue record for this book is available from the Library of Congress

ISBN 0-7923-4717-X

Published by Kluwer Academic Publishers,
P.O. Box 17, 3300 AA Dordrecht, The Netherlands.

Sold and distributed in the U.S.A. and Canada
by Kluwer Academic Publishers,
101 Philip Drive, Norwell, MA 02061, U.S.A.

In all other countries, sold and distributed
by Kluwer Academic Publishers,
P.O. Box 322, 3300 AH Dordrecht, The Netherlands.

Printed on acid-free paper

Printed in the Netherlands

To my teacher
Franz von Kutschera

TABLE OF CONTENTS

PREFACE ix
INTRODUCTION 1

I: THE ONTOLOGY OF STATES OF AFFAIRS 23
I.1 The Central Axioms for the Part-Concept "P" 24
I.2 Concepts based on "P" and Elementary Theorems 29
I.3 The Concept of State of Affairs 34
I.4 Functional Terms Definable by "P" 42
I.5 The Conjunction Axiom 46
I.6 The Exhaustion Axiom 53
I.7 The Connection Axiom 56
I.8 Theorems for Negation, Conjunction and Disjunction 67
I.9 The Big Disjunction 69
I.10 Possible Worlds and Elementary States of Affairs 73
I.11 Possibility and Necessity 80
I.12 The World and the Truth 88
I.13 The Law of Non-Contradiction 93
I.14 The Law of Excluded Middle 97
I.15 Laws of Truth and Falsity 103
I.16 Contingency 109
I.17 A Further Examination of Axioms AP7 - AP9 114
I.18 The Hierarchies of States of Affairs 118
I.19 The Discreteness of "P*" 123
I.20 The Cardinality of the Universe of States of Affairs 126

II: ONTOLOGY OF PROPERTIES AND MEREOLOGY 131
II.1 Intensional Parthood between Properties 132
II.2 New Readings of Predicates and Functional Terms, and Inherence 137
II.3 Actual Existence for Accidents and Substances 145
II.4 Real Subsistence as a Property? 150
II.5 Laws of Actual Existence 154
II.6 Laws of Inherence, and Superessentialism 158
II.7 Leibniz's *Principium* 165
II.8 Once More: Real Subsistence as a Property? 169
II.9 The Philosophy of Leibniz and the Ontology of Properties 175
II.10 Meinongian Objects in the Ontology of Properties 181
II.11 Time-Free and Momentary Material Individuals 189
II.12 The Mereology of Gorups 206

III: FULL ONTOLOGY LIMITED TO PROPERTIES OF INDIVIDUALS 219
III.1 Categorial Predicates, Language LPT1, System PT1 220
III.2 Saturation and Extraction 225
III.3 Parthood and Identity for Properties 231
III.4 Important Singular Terms for Properties 234
III.5 The Principle of Property-Quanta and the Exhaustion- and Connection-Principle for Properties 239
III.6 Properties by Conjunction and Properties by Extraction 243
III.7 Essential and Accidental Properties 245
III.8 Maximally Consistent Properties and the Property Specific to an Individual 251
III.9 <0>-Exemplification 253
III.10 The Relationship between Maximally Consistent Properties, Individuals and Possible Worlds 255
III.11 Individuals and Leibniz-Individuals 259
III.12 Counterpart Theory 265
III.13 Actual Existence for Individuals and Leibniz-Individuals 271
III.14 The Modelling of Sets and Extensions 280
III.15 Predicates and Properties 285
III.16 Modalizers and Quantifiers 288
III.17 Conceptions of Properties, and their Number 296

IV: UNIVERSAL INTENSIONAL ONTOLOGY 299
IV.1 The System IOU: First Stage 300
IV.2 The System IOU: Second Stage 308
IV.3 The System IOU: Third Stage 312
IV.4 Actual Existence, Identity, and the Fundamental Status of States of Affairs 320

EPILOGUE 323

APPENDIX: PRINCIPLES, PROOFS AND DEFINITIONS 325
System P 325
A Variant of System P 346
The Leibnizian System 351
The Mereology of Momentary Material Individuals 353
System PT1 354
System IOU 375

INDEX OF SUBJECTS 379
INDEX OF NAMES 388
LITERATURE 390

PREFACE

The contents of this book are set out in the introduction. Here a few words remain to be said about the general intentions pursued by its author.

The book is intended as a fairly comprehensive systematic treatise on ontology (*metaphysica generalis*). "Part" and "intension" are the core-concepts around which the work is organized. Formal methods are used throughout; the subject is treated axiomatically *more geometrico* on the basis of first-order predicate logic. Philosophy *more geometrico* is an old ideal, to which many philosophers have aspired - with dubious success, to say the least. I hope, I have done better, sacrificing neither conceptual clarity nor logical stringency to philosophical depth. Certainly these three values ought not to be *a priori* inimical to each other.

I also hope that the use of formal methods has not overly impaired the readability of the book. To aid readability I have presented the formulas in the book in semi-formal fashion - they are composed out of abbreviated and standardized elements of ordinary language. In addition, I have banished all the proofs - with some exceptions - to the appendix, where a listing of axioms, theorems and definitions can also be found.

The general philosophical climate has changed considerably since the days of Carnap; unfortunately, it has changed also with respect to the use of formal methods. One can witness a diminishing patience with logical formulas in philosophical writings, and the qualities of clarity and logical precision are beginning to disappear from philosophical publications, even if they are written from the point of view of analytic philosophy (strangely contrasted by speakers of English with "continental philosophy," as if there were no analytic philosophers on the Continent). To reassert the power and beauty of the use of formal methods *in philosophy* (aside from formal logic) is thus one of the additional aims of this book.

There has been more appreciation of such methods in philosophy in Poland than anywhere else, and hence it is surely no accident that it was Jan Woleński who first suggested to me that this book be published by Kluwer. I am greatly indebted to him for making this opportunity of reaching a greater audience available to me. I also would like to thank Barry Smith for his editorial help.

INTRODUCTION

Every science has a field of reference and a point of view from which this field is examined. The point of view determines a selection of facts from the totality of facts pertaining to the corresponding field of reference; the point of view can be identified with the set of scientific interests, by which the science is guided. There are scientific interests which are shared by all sciences, others which are restricted to specific sciences. Every science aims at cognizing facts (in its field of reference) that lend themselves well to deductive systematization, that is, to theory-construction. Such facts are, in particular, general facts; they are not however arbitrary general facts, but only those which can be expressed by employing certain selected terms. Every science aims at choosing such terms as can be brought into a definitional system. But most of all its selection of terms is determined by the scientific interests and the field of reference which are *specific* for it.

The field of reference of the science of ontology consists of *everything there is*. It comprehends everything that can be named, in other words: *everything*, that which is only possible (if such there be), as much as that which actually exists. Hence the field of reference of ontology is universal: we may call it "the totality of being." But not all facts with respect to this field form part of the *subject-matter* of ontology. Ontology does not of course attempt to be a universal science. Ontology examines being *qua* being, as Aristotle says. It aims at cognizing those facts of all the facts there are about everything there is which are the *fundamental* facts.

Every entirely precise delineation of what is a fundamental fact about the totality of being is certainly bound to be to some degree arbitrary; but such a delineation can nevertheless be made in a rough and ready manner which will be sufficiently precise and natural for our purposes. The fundamental facts with respect to the totality of being are those facts which concern the fundamental distinctions and relations in that totality. We may expect that these are mirrored in the core structures of (descriptive) language, the language we use to speak about everything there is. This follows from the following consideration: (1) language [*1] is the main tool of cognition, and (2) a tool, if it is to be useful, must fit what there is; but (3) language, in fact, *is* useful for the cognition of what there is.[*2] Hence, if we ask what it is in the totality of being that corresponds to this central linguistic distinction (for example, that between sentence and predicate), or to this central linguistic relation (for instance, predication), then we are led to the fundamental distinctions and relations in that totality. These distinctions and relations are fundamental, since the core structures of a language must precede every instance of concept- and theory-construction by means of a language. The core structures of our natural languages have been what they are now as far as we can look back in history; they are what a child first grasps when she learns to speak a language.

That the science of ontology exists is beyond question. Since the time of Parmenides, philosophers have more or less continuously directed their attention to the fundamental facts about the totality of being, often taking as their starting points certain central linguistic phenomena. To be sure, ontology has not been pursued in a purely ontological manner. Ontological considerations were mixed with theological, cosmological and psychological factors to form the conglomerate we call Western metaphysics. This science - in part because of Kant's criticism and in part because certain philosophers with other sorts of ambitions usurped its name - has not been in good repute in recent times. The word "metaphysics" is even today widely used as an epithet for groundless and even meaningless speculation, where the expression of vague emotions only too often replaces theses which are capable of being true or false. This devaluation of metaphysics is not only a vast injustice, it has also blocked for many people - since ontology is considered to be a part of metaphysics - the appreciation of the results of ontological enquiry, which in their way are no less eminent than those of other sciences.

There has been scientific progress in ontology. Plato first distinguished (albeit not perfectly) attribute and individual, and he formulated the first theory of exemplification (in order to explain linguistic predication); no less important is his first analysis of the different meanings of "to be" (in the *Sophistes* in reaction to Parmenides). Aristotle developed an alternative theory of exemplification and therewith a new account of attribute and individual; he created the first comprehensive system of ontological concepts (in the *Categories*), and he is the first who discerned the concepts of possibility and relation.

The Middle Ages saw a flowering of ontology (it is possible that there were at no other period more people working in the field). In addition to the systematization of traditional ontological ideas, the medieval philosopher-theologians have to their credit notable achievements in the field of the theory of dispositions and potentialities and in the field of the theory of individuation. The three main positions in the controversy about the status of universals - realism, conceptualism, and nominalism - were discussed in a most subtle manner during the Middle Ages. A central methodological principle of ontology known as "Ockham's Razor" is (in its most familiar form) also of medieval origin (Ockham, however, can hardly be said to be its inventor).

Leibniz constructed the first algebra of (first-order monadic) attributes that went beyond syllogistics. He made use of the concept of possible world in order to produce a definition of modal concepts, and he explicated the general laws of identity, which is one of the most important ontological concepts.

With Bolzano's "*Sätze an sich*" the ontological category of state of affairs began to emerge into the light of explicit ontological attention. (It was already known to Abelard, and it had been more or less implicitly present all the time since at least the time of the Stoics. Even when they were not the objects of attention states of affairs themselves were nonetheless mentioned almost as often as individuals: every "that"-phrase - that I am sleeping, that 2+2=4 - at least purports to denote a state of affairs or something rather similar to a state of affairs.)

Frege was the first to classify attributes according to their *types*. His ontology of objects and functions (in which attributes figure as special functions) is the first ontological theory that fits simultaneously very many of the core structures of language and it played a key role in the development of modern logic. Frege's semantic distinction - foreshadowed in the *Port Royal Logic* - between sense and "Bedeutung" (the tranlation true to Frege's intentions is "reference" or "denotation,") is also of fundamental importance. On the ontological level it leads to the distinction between intensional entities (such as properties and states of affairs) and extensional entities (such as sets and individuals). The work on set theory that was initiated by Cantor ultimately produced a widely accepted ontological theory that in precision and systematic power (for both deductive and definitional purposes) surpasses every such theory there has been so far. Mathematics can be developed within it. If it is extended by the concept of possible world (or by that of possible individual in general), intensional entities can be modelled within it. Numbers, properties, states of affairs - all these are sets according to (possibilistically extended) set theory. But set theory is recommended more by its efficiency than by its naturalness; its primitive concepts "set" and "element" appear to be derivative of other ontological concepts, above all the concept of property and of exemplification. Although *set* in a sense marks a fundamental distinction in the totality of being, and *elementhood* a fundamental relation, there seem to be even more fundamental distinctions and relations which are also more clearly manifested in the cores structures of language; but more on this anon.

From this rather cursory presentation of the history of ontology it can be gathered that ontology is closely related to two other sciences: formal logic and (general) semantics. Today the term "logic" is frequently taken in such a wide sense as includes ontological as well as semantic inquiries (usually it is then called "philosophical logic"). Formal logic, strictly speaking, is, however, the science whose field of reference is restricted to the set of inferences, where an *inference* is a finite sequence of sentences whose last member - the conclusion - is connected to its preceding members - the premises - by a term such as "hence", "ergo", "consequently". Formal logic is not interested in all the facts about inferences so conceived; like other sciences it has its own specific point of view. It aims at cognizing the laws pertaining to the formal validity of inferences, where an inference X is (standardly) *formally valid* if and only if for every inference having the same logical form as X, it is in the strictest sense impossible that its conclusion is false while its premises are true. The *logical form* of an inference, in turn, is its syntactically standardized version, taken in abstraction from the meanings of the non-logical words occurring in it.

Given the specific interest of formal logic in formally valid inferences, and on the basis of the definitions which determine that interest more closely, it becomes clear that the concepts of formal logic - "sentence", "predicate", "variable", "the conjunction", "sentence-connective," etc. - have mainly to do with the description of the logical forms of inferences. Consider the following two examples of laws pertaining to the formal validity of inferences. (A, B, C, X, Y, Z in what follows stand in for sentences.)

LL1 If the inference of C from XYZ and A is formally valid, and so also is the inference of C from XYZ and B, then the inference of C from XYZ and the disjunction of A and B is also formally valid.

LL2 The inference of the disjunction of A and B from A is formally valid.

In formal logic no derivation of the correctness of the basic laws is sought. The correctness of such laws is simply declared, perhaps on the basis of some logical intuition (which is not an ability in any way mysterious, but simply a special case of the ability to understand linguistic utterances). Starting from the simple basic laws, other more complex ones, where logical intuition does not help, can be deductively established. Hence, like every science, formal logic cannot do without logic. There is no vicious circle in this; formal logic is not aiming at constituting its subject-matter *ex nihilo*, but only at comprehending it systematically.

But there is also a way of supplying derivations of the basic laws of formal logic; these are given via semantics. According to the procedure that is in general use - the orthodox ("Tarskian"), or "normal" semantic procedure - the central step in deriving the correctness of logical laws consists in laying down the following criterion for formal validity:

C1 An inference is formally valid if and only if there is no *interpretation* of its *logical form* in which its premises are true and its conclusion is false.

The logical form of an inference formulated in English or in any other natural language can be identified for our purposes with the counterpart inference formulated in an *artificial language*. For the logical constants in the "natural" inference certain symbols are used, for example "&" for "and", "∨" for "or"; the non-logical words in the original version are replaced in a standardized manner by letters meaningless in themselves. Which inferences turn out as formally valid according to the criterion C1, and which laws of formal validity hold, depends on how the concepts of interpretation and of truth in an interpretation are defined. Precisely those inferences ought to be formally valid according to C1 which are formally valid in the intuitive sense given above; and it is to ensure this that the concepts of interpretation and of truth in an interpretation are normally defined. But however they are defined, according to the orthodox semantic procedure they are always defined in set-theoretical terms. The derivation of the correctness of the fundamental laws of formal logic then consists in their deduction from the definitions of interpretation and of truth in an interpretation, making use of the criterion C1.

The fundamental laws of formal logic can thus be justified in a semantic manner according to the orthodox procedure (though logical intuition alone would be sufficient justification - "1+1=2", too, is a sentence that does not require for its justification to be derived in set theory: intuition is enough). But, in addition, laws of formal logic, although they can be generated from the fundamental ones, can often be ascertained much more easily in this normal semantic manner than via a deduction from the fundamental laws. Moreover, the normal semantic approach to formal validity makes it possible to capture certain instabilities in our logical intuitions in a precise way by producing alternative definitions of the concepts of interpretation and of truth in an interpretation. And last but not least the semantic approach also yields answers to questions like: Does a given class of fundamental logical laws capture a certain subclass of the laws of formal validity *completely*, or not? (Are all the laws in the subclass deducible from the ones in the given class, or not?)

Let this suffice as a description of the connection between formal logic and semantics as it presents itself according to the usual semantic procedure. (More detailed information can be found in a standard textbook on formal logic.) However, there is also a procedure quite different from the one just described to justify the fundamental laws of formal logic "semantically." It starts with a rather different criterion of formal validity:

C2 An inference is formally valid if and only if the generalization of its *ontological interpretation* is an ontological law.

Here the importance of semantics is greatly reduced. Semantics now has merely the auxiliary task of saying what the ontological interpretation of an inference is (it is assumed that every inference has precisely one such interpretation), that is, of bridging the gap between the linguistic and the ontological level. According to this approach, the non-conditional laws of formal logic (those that do not have the form "if such and such inferences are formally valid, then also such and such") are mirror images of ontological laws, not the consequences of the set-theoretical definitions of the concepts of interpretation and of truth in an interpretation.

To substantiate all this, let us consider as an example the following simple inference:

(I) Jack is travelling to Spain or to Portugal.
Jack is not travelling to Spain.

Hence: Jack is travelling to Portugal.

This inference can be immediately seen to be formally valid in the sense of our intuitive definition of formal validity; for every inference that has the same logical form as (I) it is evidently in the strictest sense impossible that its premises be true while its conclusion is false. But if we want to, we can also derive the formal validity of (I) within formal logic. To this purpose we derive

LL3 The inference of B from the disjunction of A and B and the negation of A is formally valid

from the basic laws of formal logic. We then simply subsume (I) under LL3. The derivation of LL3 might look like this: The inference of B from B is formally valid (*trivial inference*), hence so also is the inference of B from the negation of A and from B (*monotonicity*). The inference of B from the negation of A and from A is also formally valid (*ex contradictione quodlibet*). Hence the inference of B from the disjunction of A and B, and from the negation of A is formally valid (by LL1 and *interchange of premises*).

Alternatively, we can derive the formal validity of (I) according to the orthodox semantic procedure: The logical form of (I), represented as an inference in a familiar artificial language, is:

$$R(a,b) \vee R(a,c)$$
$$\neg R(a,b)$$

$$R(a,c)$$

(I) is formally valid, for there is no interpretation of its logical form which makes all its premises true, but its conclusion false. Assume that V is an interpretation of the logical form of (I) according to which $R(a,b) \vee R(a,c)$ and $\neg R(a,b)$ turn out to be true sentences (of the artificial language), but $R(a,c)$ a false one. Hence by the definition of the concept of truth in an interpretation $R(a,b)$ or $R(a,c)$ is true in V, and $R(a,b)$ is false, that is, not true in V; consequently $R(a,c)$ is true, that is, not false in V, which is a contradiction.

Alternatively, we can also justify the formal validity of (I) in the *ontological* way mentioned above (using semantics merely as a bridge). The ontological interpretation of (I) is as follows: the conjunction of (1) the disjunction of the states of affairs expressed by "Jack is travelling to Spain" and "Jack is travelling to Portugal" with (2) the negation of the state of affairs expressed by "Jack is travelling to Spain" (intensionally) contains the state of affairs expressed by "Jack is travelling to Portugal." The generalization of the ontological interpretation of (I) is: For all states of affairs p and q: the conjunction of (1) the disjunction of p and q with (2) the negation of p contains q. (I) is a formally valid inference, for the generalization of the ontological interpretation of (I) is indeed an ontological law. (The non-conditional law of formal logic LL2 is, according to this approach, the mirror image of the following ontological law: for all states of affairs *p* and *q*: *p* contains the disjunction of *p* and *q*.)

After these necessarily short expositions, I leave for the time being the connection that obtains between formal logic and ontology; in the course of this work this connection, call it "mirroring," will become quite apparent also for fields of formal logic much richer than mere truth-functional propositional logic. For first we need some further elaboration of ontology, not only with respect to states of affairs, but also with respect to individuals, properties and relations (as intensions). ("State of affairs", "property", "individual", "relation" are core concepts of ontology, the science of the fundamental facts about the totality of being.) Our elaboration of ontology is effected step by step, and reaches its culmination in part IV of the book. Set-theoretical concepts and arguments are avoided throughout, even - except for heuristic purposes - in the meta-language. Nothing whatever is systematically based on them.

Rather, all systems in this book merely presuppose elementary predicate logic with identity and definite description. This is fitting; for ontology speaks about everything there is in the very same manner. Consequently there is only one type of variable, one type of name, one type of predicate in the language in which ontology is formulated; it is a straightforward first-order language. Hence ontological categorial distinctions are not represented *implicitly* in the syntactic structure of the language (as is done in the language of the theory of types), but *explicitly* by predicates of it.

Within the framework of the fully developed ontology it is possible to formulate explicit definitions of the concepts of set and elementhood, even to the degree of generality required for general axiomatic set theory. Before we come to this, however, we will already have shown how to define the primitive concepts of what might be called "basic" set theory, in which all sets are sets of individuals, and also those of the set theory which comes in the guise of the so-called "standard theory of types" [*3]. Thus, set theory will here be accorded the place properly belonging to it in the theoretical presentation of ontology. The theory of states of affairs, properties and relations is not constructed, in what has come to be seen as the orthodox manner, on the basis of set theory (extended by admitting possible individuals, at least possible worlds); rather, the procedure is here the other way round: set theory is founded definitionally on the theory of states of affairs, properties and relations as basic intensional entities. (For a similar attitude towards set theory see G. Bealer, *Quality and Concept*, chapter 5.)

Moreover, the concept of possible world can also be defined in the intensional ontology that will be defended here, and indeed it turns out to be much more primitive than the concept of set. It will turn out to be possible to justify the fundamental theses of possible worlds ontology by deriving them as theorems (for example, that "coarse-grained" properties - of individuals - are identical if and only if they apply to the same individuals in every possible world). This result is important, since in recent times a reaction against possible worlds ontology has set in. It has been criticized - even from the realist side - because of its allegedly problematic ontological commitments (to sets and to possible worlds), and because of its artificial flavor. But its ontological commitments can be justified; whoever accepts properties and states of affairs (and there is a very good case for such acceptance) must also accept sets [*4] and possible worlds, or at least entities that are structurally completely identical to sets and possible worlds (and once you allow possible worlds, it seems arbitrary - to say the least - to deny that there are merely possible individuals). The only charge that can fairly be raised against possible worlds ontology is that it perverts the order of presentation and begins with what comes epistemologically, and perhaps also ontologically, later (hence the artificiality of its constructions). It is indeed a curious fact that people believe that they understand possible worlds and sets better than states of affairs and properties, especially considering how recently sets were explicitly conceptualized, and how much effort was spent on finding an intuitively satisfactory way of avoiding the set-theoretical antinomies (their first appearance came as a shocking surprise). We might mention also the strangeness of the concept of possible world which strikes everyone not inured to contemporary philosophical writings (its strangeness, however, is the very source of the fascination exerted by the concept). But the perversion of the order of theoretical presentation in no way impairs *the essential correctness* of the results of possible worlds ontology. For considered in itself it is of no importance how one begins, whether with sets and possible worlds (and possible individuals), or with states of affairs and properties; the investigations in this book will, among other things, demonstrate the equivalence of the intensional and the extensional approach in ontology.

In possible worlds ontology no claims are made to the effect that entities of this or that kind are the semantically adequate *meanings* of certain linguistic expressions. Such claims are *semantic* claims; their possible incorrectness cannot be blamed on possible worlds ontology. In fact, as everyone knows, it is at most a good approximation (and strictly speaking incorrect) to say, for example, that the meaning of a monadic predicate is a property (in particular, a coarsely individuated property). It can be at most a good approximation; for the meaning of an expression (the totality of what is *expressed* by it) is not only co-determined by the syntactic structure of the expression (as Carnap knew, who proposed to capture the concept of synonymity - identity of meaning - via the concept of intensional isomorphism; see *Meaning and Necessity*, p. 56ff), it is also not separable from the expression at all (hence there cannot be a perfect translation from one language to another). Properties (in any sense whatever) are, however, entities without linguistic constituents; in particular, predicates with which they are semantically correlated by convention are not constituents of them; they are not language-dependent at all. Hence, without qualification one can only claim that the *intensions* (*not* the meanings) of monadic predicates (that what they "intend," so to speak) are properties.

One of the fundamental questions of ontology - the science which is concerned with the fundamental facts about everything there is - is what fundamental kinds of entities - *ontological categories* - there are. On the face of it, this question is ambiguous. It can be understood as a question about which kinds of entities are fundamental kinds of entities; and it can be understood as a question about which fundamental kinds of entities are *non-empty*. But only non-empty kinds of entities are fundamental kinds of entities; therefore the ambiguity is only apparent.

To find out about the fundamental kinds of entities, one must look at the core structures of language, as has been urged generally for finding out about the fundamental facts about everything there is. (One will certainly not find out anything about them by merely staring at the world and forgetting about language.) No other linguistic distinctions are so central as those between declarative sentences, names and predicates. However, it is an old objection of the nominalists that the realists naively project non-empty linguistic kinds onto the totality of being, thus producing fictions of non-empty ontological kinds. This objection has some justice to it. It is quite true that language supplies the phenomena that ontology must come to terms with, just as experience (whether unaided or aided by instruments) supplies the phenomena for the theoretical efforts of physics. Just as experience is the phenomenal basis for physics, so language is this basis for ontology.[*5] But the *objectivity* of experience is not beyond criticism, nor is the objectivity of language. Both experience and language comprehend deceptive phenomena that do not reveal the objective fact of the matter, but rather disguise it. For example, there is in fact no single ontological category that would correspond to the linguistic category of names (just as the apparent movement of the sun around the earth points to no objective movement); for everything whatsoever can be designated by a name, no matter to what ontological category it belongs. The category of names is defined by the intended (main) semantic function of the expressions belonging to the category, namely the function of referring to some entity for purposes of predication; it has no categorial ontological significance at all. (Generally speaking, a system of categories for entities X is formed by a finite or denumerably infinite number of non-empty monadic predicates each of which applies only to X, but none of which applies to all X, that effect on a fixed number of different levels a complete and disjunctive classification of X such that each succeeding level of classification is obtained by a subdivision of the classification on the preceding level. Notice that two categories never overlap, except in case one of them contains the other.)

It is the central ontological mistake of Frege to have overlooked this. He thought that everything that is designated by a name is a *Gegenstand* (an "object," which means for Frege: a *saturated* entity), and therefore not a

Begriff (not a "concept," which means for Frege: not a language-independent, extensional concept, and hence, surely, not a property or a relation). This got him into the difficulty of having to hold that the name "the concept *horse*" does not refer to a concept. "Eine freilich unvermeidbare sprachliche Härte [a quite unavoidable infelicity]" says Frege ("Über Begriff und Gegenstand," p. 170). But worse: it made him believe, at least at the time of writing of his *Grundgesetze der Arithmetik*, that the entities that are designated by the names "0", "1", "2", "3", etc. are objects, in other words: that (natural) numbers are objects, while according to his careful argumentation in *Die Grundlagen der Arithmetik* they ought to be second-order concepts. Since numbers needed to be objects, he introduced the *Wertverläufe* (graphs of functions) in order to get from second-order concepts to objects, and the naive conception of the *Wertverlauf* (no more and no less naive than Cantor's conception of set) led to his overloading the universe of objects by too many of them - with the well known disastrous result. If Frege had adhered in the *Grundgesetze* to his previous conception of numbers as second-order concepts - which, however, was thwarted by his idea that the category of names corresponds to the ontological category of objects, then we may presume that he would have been spared Russell's letter of June 16, 1902, since with respect to concepts Frege strictly observed the hierarchical system of types which he himself had discovered.

But nominalists do not have in mind the category of names when they accuse the realists of drawing ontological conclusions from mere linguistic facts; rather, they have in mind the category of predicates. (A predicate - in the sense of logical grammar - is obtained from a declarative sentence by removing one or more names from the latter and putting unbound variables in their places.) The realists, they say, naively assume that there exists an ontological category of *universals* (properties and relations)[*6] corresponding to the linguistic category of predicates; but in truth, there are no universals, and therefore no ontological category of them.

Nominalists, however, must then confront the following (standard) counter-argument. The sentence "red is a color" is undoubtedly true; hence the name "red" as it occurs in that sentence must refer to something; how else - assuming the correspondence theory of truth - could the sentence be true?[*7] But what could be its object of reference if not a universal? There is no good alternative to its being a universal. Hence universals exist.

The sentence "red is a color" might well have convinced Frege of the falsity of his conviction that whatever is designated by a name is an object in the specific sense intended by him. According to Frege, the color red - that what is designated by the name "red" - would have to be an object; but colors are not objects, they can be exemplified, and hence, unlike objects, they are unsaturated entities. Similarly, what is designated by the name "justice" as it occurs, for example, in the sentence "justice is a virtue": the virtue of justice, ought to be, according to Frege, an object; but virtues are not objects in Frege's sense. Note that the sentence "three is a number" has precisely the same character as "red is a color" and "justice is a virtue." If - to put it mildly - it is not obvious that red and justice are objects, why then should it be inescapable that numbers are objects? Frege, however, was not able to rid himself of his misconception. Wittgenstein once asked him whether he didn't ever find any difficulty in his theory that numbers are objects. Frege replied "Sometimes I seem to see a difficulty - but then again I don't see it." (Recounted in *Three Philosophers*, p. 130. Wittgenstein's reason for asking this question may, however, not have been the reason that is suggested by the remarks just made. Perhaps Wittgenstein intended to ask Frege whether he didn't ever see any difficulty in his theory that numbers are *entities*. The English word "object" as well as the German word "*Gegenstand*," which Wittgenstein presumably used, can also be interpreted in the very general sense of *entity*.)

The nominalists oppose the following strategy to the difficulty presented by the above argument. "Red is a color" is merely a rhetorical way of saying what is plainly expressed by "everything that is red is colored," where no singular term apparently referring to a universal occurs; and thus *mutatis mutandis* in all similar cases. But according to the rule of translation on which this strategy is based, the glaringly false sentence "being colored is a color" ought, on the contrary, to be true; for the sentence "everything that is colored is colored" is (trivially) true.[*8] Thus, rightly regarded, the nominalists' "strategy" is not a general strategy at all; it is an *ad hoc* construction without universal applicability.

Nominalists have so far not moved decisively beyond more or less implausible *ad hoc* constructions for surmounting the difficulties posed for their position by the fact that certain singular terms seem to refer to universals. (Quine's general elimination procedure for singular terms - replacing them by predicates that have at most one instance - is of no help: the elimination of singular terms apparently *referring to* universals merely results in predicates apparently *fulfilled by* universals.) It seems, the only way of avoiding these difficulties is to deny the correspondence theory of truth outright. But this, of course, would have philosophical consequences reaching far beyond ontology; it would be quite inappropriate for this step to be taken merely in order to uphold an ontological position. (For many nominalists, however, the denial of objective truth may well be the philosophical stance that motivates their nominalistic position in the first place.)

Here it is assumed that there are universals and that (most) predicates express universals (or rather "intend" universals if "to express" is to be understood in such a way that predicates express *meanings*; the meaning of a predicate is not exhausted by the universal that corresponds to it semantically). Hence to the linguistic category of predicates there corresponds the ontological category of universals (or of *attributes*, which means properties and relations).

A similar argument can be given for the numerical existence of states of affairs as we gave for the numerical existence of universals ("numerical existence" is a handy term for distinguishing existence that is expressed by a quantifier from existence that is expressed by a predicate). Consider the sentence "it is false that there are blue carnations". This sentence is true. Hence the name that occurs in it - "that there are blue carnations" - must refer to something (how else could the sentence be true?). But what could the object of reference be other than a state of affairs? There is no good alternative to its being a state of affairs. Hence there are states of affairs. (If it be objected that the expression "that there are blue carnations" is not a name, then the answer is that in the sense of logical grammar everything is a name which is not a quantifier and contains no free variable and occupies subject-position in a singular sentence of the form *a is F*. On "that"-expressions as names compare G. Bealer, *Quality and Concept*, p. 24f.[*9]) Here it is assumed that declarative sentences *intend* states of affairs. Hence the ontological category of states of affairs corresponds to the linguistic category of declarative sentences.[*10]

Individuals (*in a wide sense*; we will see that there are more specific senses of this word) are "ontologically immanent" entities that are neither states of affairs nor *functions* (including all universals). Besides ontologically immanent entities, to which belong precisely the states of affairs, functions and individuals, there may be "ontologically transcendent" entities, entities that are neither functions nor states of affairs nor individuals (see the *Epilogue*).

It can hardly be doubted that there are individuals; for the doubter would have to doubt that he himself is an individual - and this is not a very plausible doubt. Doubtless also, individuals constitute a fundamental kind of entity. But the ontological category of individuals is not mirrored in the core structures of language except in the following partial manner. No sentence and no predicate *intends* an individual, but there are names that designate individuals (designation, one might say, is the way in which names "intend"). These names may well be called "fundamental names." Specifying the concept of a fundamental name in a *purely syntactic manner* for a natural language poses a considerable problem. However this may be done, fundamental names always designate individuals, and hence they are the linguistic correlates of individuals; this is what can be salvaged from Frege's assertion that names (if they designate anything at all) always designate *Gegenstände*.

Within the very rich category of individuals (*in a wide sense*) only a few distinctions will be considered more closely in this book (see especially chapters 10 to 12 of part II, and chapters 11 to 13 of part III). Many other distinctions (for example, *abstract individual, individual accident*, perhaps *event*) certainly are also fundamental distinctions within that category, and thereby within the totality of being. But I do not aim at presenting a (conceptually) complete ontology here.

Universals will be further distinguished according to their *type*. The latter is determined by which kinds of entities in what order are needed to *saturate* the universal in such a way as to yield a state of affairs. Just as the saturation of a predicate by a name or names appropriate to that predicate is a statement, so the saturation of a universal by (non-linguistic) entities (in the manner prescribed by its type) is a state of affairs. And just as the result of extracting a name or names from a statement is a predicate, so the result of extracting entities from a state of affairs is a universal whose type is determined by the kinds of the entities extracted and by the manner of their extraction. This, roughly speaking, is the relationship between states of affairs and universals. Universals are, so to speak, shells of states of affairs, that which remains of a state of affair when the kernel or kernels inside it are taken away, and from which the state of affairs can be retrieved by putting back what has been taken out. All this, of course, is only metaphor. But the operational metaphors of taking out and putting back can be translated into precise ontological laws.

Consider monadic universals of individuals (for example, being a house at t_0), that is, *properties of individuals*. What are the most salient theoretical conceptions of these entities - the most familiar of all universals - in the ontological tradition? According to Plato, they are in fact special individuals - *individuo-properties* - that have a higher ontological status than ordinary individuals; the latter are merely more or less adequate copies of the former; moreover, individuo-properties and ordinary individuals form separate realms of being. According to Aristotle, on the other hand, properties of individuals are not individuals (in spite of this, it would be misleading to say that they form separate realms of being); also, the order of ontological precedence is reversed: individuals have ontologically higher status than their properties; the latter (considered as universals; Aristotle also conceives of properties as *individual accidents*) are merely humanly fabricated abstractions from the former and have no primary existence. (But Aristotle, like Plato, still adheres to the *epistemological* precedence of properties of individuals over individuals.) Frege's conception of functions, including properties of individuals, as *unsaturated* (hence incomplete) entities in contrast to objects, including individuals, as *saturated* (hence complete) entities also suggests a theory of the ontological precedence of individuals over their properties.

In this book, however, an almost perfect ontological parity of individuals and properties of individuals is assumed. The very role that individuals fulfill for properties of individuals (the latter ''result'' by the extraction of an individual from a state of affairs) is fulfilled by properties of individuals in turn for other - higher - universals. An ontological precedence may nevertheless still be accorded to individuals for the reason that they can merely be *objects of extraction* and not also *products of it* (in contrast, all universals can be both objects and products of extraction).

Whether extraction is always a creative act of the human mind, or at least sometimes merely highlights what is already objectively (mind-independently) given - this is a question that need not be answered here. (In any case, we have a cognitive grasp of extraction of the sort which makes it possible for us to theorize about it only via its *objectivation* in the structure of language. One might seek to find a more direct approach to extraction in perception; but perception is, as it were, too close to our eyes as to be able to provide a serviceable cognitive basis for ontological theory.) If the thesis of *weak realism* consists in the assertion that there are universals (we have seen an argument for this above), then an answer to the question formulated at the beginning of this paragraph is an answer to the question whether we should, in going beyond weak realism, assume *conceptualism* or *strong realism*. (Consider: If an objectively given individual is extracted from an objectively given state of affairs, then it appears that the result of this extraction - a property of individuals - is also objectively given. Hence, if there are at least some objectively given states of affairs that have objectively given individuals as their constituents, the conclusion seems unavoidable that there are also objectively given, mind-independent properties.)

States of affairs have in common with individuals that they are objects of (possible) extraction, but not also products of it. States of affairs can be extracted from states of affairs (and also from other entities); but no such extraction results in a state of affairs, the product is always a certain universal (a certain function). Moreover, both complex individuals and states of affairs are *absolute bases* for extraction (they are bases for extraction without being products of it), whereas universals (and other functions) can at most be *relative bases* for extraction. (Extraction in the *narrow sense* is from states of affairs and results in universals, its simplest case being the extraction of individuals; extraction in the *wide sense* is from any complex entity - an entity that has constituents - and results in functions.)

Abstraction is extraction. Hence abstract entities might well be defined as the entities that are the products of extraction. Those entities are precisely the functions; universals, in particular, are the functions that result via extraction from states of affairs. (If a function is the product of an extraction from another function, then the former function is in a clear sense more abstract than the latter.) States of affairs and individuals, on the other hand, are not abstract entities, since they are not products of extraction. But of course there are other meanings of "abstract" according to which certain states of affairs and individuals might be called "abstract," for example "abstract" in the sense of "non-concrete" (whatever this precisely means). However, the examples usually given for non-concrete individuals, numbers and pure sets, are far from being unproblematically clear cases of non-concrete individuality. For numbers could easily be certain universals (the fact that there are names for numbers is no reason whatever against this; see above); and the same holds true of sets.[*11] (For various attempts at a definititon of the concept of abstractness considered as non-concreteness and the difficulties thereby encountered see W. Künne, *Abstrakte Gegenstände*, chapter 2.)

Some entities are more important to us than others. This, too, is mirrored in language. For some entities there are *logically simple* expressions in the language (at a given time), for other entities only *logically complex* expressions, for others there are no expressions at all. Entities for which we have logically simple expressions certainly are epistemologically pre-eminent; but whether this epistemological pre-eminence is generally grounded in an ontological pre-eminence or is merely the result of our interests and cognitive organization is a rather controversial issue. (An ontological foundation for epistemological pre-eminence among properties and relations is propounded by G. Bealer in *Quality and Concept*, p. 177ff.) Surely, however, the logical simplicity of an expression is no sufficient basis for inferring the ontological simplicity of the entity that is invoked by it. In this book it will be made clear in what sense of "simple" (or "non-composed") there are simple states of affairs and simple universals; but no expressions, hence *a fortiori* no logically simple expressions of ordinary language, correspond to these entities.

The concept of *actuality* (or *actual existence*) is of much greater importance for ontology than the concept of simplicity. Like the latter concept, and like the concept of identity, it is not a categorial concept, but cuts across ontological categories; it is a *transcendental concept*, as the medievals would say - but not, as some ontologists hold, in the trivial sense that simply every entity, as a matter of analytical necessity, actually exists. In this book, a version of *possibilism* will be defended, according to which there are non-actual states of affairs, non-actual individuals and non-actual attributes of individuals. For entities differing widely in ontological category, the criteria for actual existence appear to be very different, and this may give rise to the idea that there is no common meaning attached to the concept. I sidestep this issue by simply defining actuality-concepts piecemeal for states of affairs, individuals, attributes of individuals, and functions in general. It then becomes clear that actual existence for states of affairs is in a sense (according to the natural order of definition) fundamental and can be regarded to be the core of actuality, whether there is *one* concept of actuality univocally applying to all actual entities, or merely the word "actual" applying equivocally - but analogously - to all actual entities, while representing a huge family of categorially restricted actuality-concepts.

Ontology is a *fundamental science* and hence a part of philosophy which we might regard as the sum total of all sciences concerned with fundamental questions. The nature of a fundamental science is different from that of a non-fundamental science such as the natural sciences of physics or biology (which of course may be "fundamental" in some other sense than is intended here, and whose practitioners may very well be led to fundamental questions in the course of their inquiries, which they then attempt to answer). The fundamental nature of the inquiries of philosophy yields a phenomenon that is often thought to be a very great evil: the extreme diversity of contrary opinions with respect to the very same subject matter, none of which ever gains unchallenged ascendency. It is quite pointless to ask "What does the *science of ethics* tell us about the foundations of morality?" in the same manner as one might ask "What does physics tell us about terrestrial mechanics?"; for there is no answer to the former question. There is only an answer to the question "What does this and that *moral philosopher* tell us about the foundations of morality?".

It is not otherwise with ontology. But it would be very wrong to draw the conclusion that there is no knowledge to be had about the subject matter of ontology, and that ontology is therefore an utterly useless undertaking. It can only be legitimately pointed out that it is very difficult, perhaps impossible, to reach a consensus in ontology (as is also true of other disciplines of philosophy). The fact that, in the fundamental sciences, there are today neither generally accepted methods for obtaining knowledge, nor generally accepted standards for evaluating knowledge claims (not even the canon of formal logic is generally accepted) may be more or less a historical accident. But it is in the nature of a fundamental science that it aims for knowledge which comes, as it were, "at the very beginning"; and how to begin, cannot be unequivocally made out, very likely not even if there were a methodological paradigm for the fundamental sciences (at present there is none). For this reason, the element of theoretical decision is incomparably more important in the fundamental sciences than in the other sciences, which accept much more than the fundamental sciences *without question*, although it is also not absent in them. Accordingly, one fundamental scientist may "freely" decide to take up this or that theoretical approach, another to take up a contrary approach: one ontologist claims that there are universals, another denies it; one moral philosopher claims that there are objective moral norms, another denies it. Both proponent and opponent have arguments for their several positions; but we may safely assume that these arguments will never suffice to determine irrevocably which of the two fundamental positions is correct - not even if the arguments conform to a common methodological basis. (On the other hand, in non-fundamental sciences, it can be determined - with a certain finality - whether, say, 2+2 equals 4, or whether the earth moves round the sun.) Thus, opponent and proponent, in answering a fundamental question, stick to the position which they have decided on (surely not arbitrarily). That they may continue to do so follows from the fact that within the framework of fundamental science distinct theoretical decisions cannot always be shown to be sufficiently unreasonable so as to make the repeal of one or the other of them unavoidable.

In much greater measure than other scientific theories, theories in fundamental sciences can be judged only *as a whole*. One may then arrive at the view that one fundamental theory is, on the whole, more satisfactory than another. But in this determination, purely aesthetic criteria and criteria merely relating to the economy of cognition will have had a much greater share than they are accorded in the judging of non-fundamental theories. (The weight of non-theoretical criteria for the evaluation of theories may of course easily be a moot point in scientific methodology.)

COMMENTS

[*1] By "language" I mean the idealized descriptive part of ordinary ("natural") language. It is idealized, since it is taken to be without occurrences of vagueness, ambiguity and pragmatic context-dependence.

[*2] There are two interpretations of the correspondence between the structure of language and the structure of reality (the totality of being): (1) The structure of reality is projected onto language. (2) The structure of language is projected onto reality. The first interpretation - the "realistic" one - is the one here adhered to. The second interpretation - the "relativistic" one - is implied by the thesis of linguistic relativity propounded by Sapir and Whorf: "the 'linguistic relativity principle,' which means, in informal terms, that users of markedly different grammars are pointed by their grammars toward different types of observations and different evaluations of externally similar acts of observation, and hence are not equivalent as observers but must arrive at somewhat different views of the world." (B. L. Whorf, cited in F. v. Kutschera, *Sprachphilosophie*, p. 301; the book contains on pp. 289-344 a thorough treatment of the subject *language and reality*.) The difference between the two interpretations is not so great as might appear at first sight. If the relativistic interpretation were correct, then we nevertheless would have to say that the structure which our (Indo-European) language projects onto reality is a structure which is such as to make us - doubtlessly - arrive at far-reaching insights about it. (According to the thesis of linguistic relativity, it ought to be the case that people with languages differing markedly from ours in grammatical structure do not arrive at such insights, and *cannot* arrive at them as long as they stick to their language. But are there really such people with such languages? Is it not rather the case that all languages, while doubtlessly having some disparate influence on the way in which we experience the world, are nevertheless grammatico-ontologically equivalent, and hence also essentially equivalent in their adequacy for cognitive purposes?) But how could the projected structur be so useful for cognition if it was not for the most part identical to the structure *objectively given* (which according to the realistic conception is projected onto language)? Thus, both interpretations lead to the same result (the one by accident, the other *eo ipso*): the structure of language mirrors the objectively given structure of reality. And this grounds the relevance of language for ontology.

[*3] Compare L. Borkowski, *Formale Logik*, p. 435ff (with bibliographical notes). The designation is Quine's; it need not be restricted to set-theoretical systems: a standard theory of types is any ontological theory in which differences of ontological type are not incorporated structurally into the syntax

of the language (because the latter is a simple first-order language), but are explicitly expressed by predicates.

[*4] Bealer's attack on set theory is substantial, but his verdict "while this new kind of sum [the set in the sense of set theory] is formally constructible, it has absolutely no place in nature or in logic, and there is no call to introduce it into mathematics or empirical science" ("Foundations without Sets," p. 353) is so immoderate as to be nonsensical.

[*5] D. M. Armstrong writes in *Universals and Scientific Realism*, vol. 1, p. 65: "There is a long but, I think, on the whole discreditable tradition which tries to settle ontological questions on the basis of semantic considerations." That there is such a tradition is hardly to be considered a historical accident. Ontological facts are mirrored in linguistic facts, albeit sometimes in a distorted manner. In spite of these distortions, why is the semantic tradition in ontology (that is, just about the entire tradition of ontology) "on the whole discreditable"? I fail to see this. It can, moreover, legitimately be doubted that natural science is a better guide in ontological matters than semantics, as Armstrong thinks it is (see *Universals and Scientific Realism*, vol. 1, p. xivf); the insights of natural science - quantum physics not excepted - seem to be already too specialized to be relevant for ontology (which, of course, should not *contradict* natural science). In particular, it is of no ontological relevance (for *ontologia generalis*) whether some universal or other is physical or not, or whether it is actually exemplified or not. If significant ontological insights can be gained from the natural sciences nevertheless, so much the better; but this, clearly, would be no reason to discard the semantic source of ontological insights. (I suspect that Armstrong does not so much oppose the semantic approach, but rather the semantic approach that starts from *natural language*, and not from the *language of physics*, which he - being a scientific realist and materialist - surely considers to be of greater ontological adequacy. In fact, Armstrong relies rather heavily on semantical considerations in both volumes of *Universals and Scientific Realism*.)

[*6] Bealer also calls *propositions* "universals" (see *Quality and Concept*, p. vii); this usage is, regarded from a historical point of view, a misnomer (I realize that it has become quite common).
D. Lewis distinguishes in ("New Work for a Theory of Universals," p. 344ff) (monadic and polyadic) *universals* on the one hand and *properties* on the other; the latter are for him classes of n-adic sequences (for n > 0) of possibilia (obviously, *relations* are also considered to be *properties* by Lewis; in view of this, I rather would prefer to say "attribute" where Lewis says "property"; it is a deeply entrenched assumption that properties, according to the meaning of the term, are not relations, something that does not hold for the vaguer term "attribute"); and *universals* are for Lewis the entities that D. M. Armstrong

calls "universals" in his book *Universals and Scientific Realism*; they, according to Lewis, correspond to *natural properties*.

The entities that are here called "universals" are with respect to instantiation very much like Armstrong's *universals*, but in abundance they are like Lewis's *properties*. (Lewis distinguishes between *universals* and *properties* mainly with respect to instantiation and abundance.)

[*7] Nominalists sometimes accuse realists of having the primitive semantic idea that every linguistic expression is a name (or functions just like a name). Realists, they say, consider predicates to be names; on the basis of this absurdity, they arrive at the equally absurd opinion that there are universals, since, for the realists, all names must refer *to something* (another primitive semantic idea nominalists accuse realists of having: the "Fido"-Fido-theory). The enlightened realist need only point out that no predicate is a name (of course), but that nevertheless *there are names for universals* (names intending to refer to universals); and if a names occurs together with a simple predicate in a true sentence, then we have good reason for supposing that it does indeed refer to something. It is then the task of the nominalist to show that - contrary to overwhelming appearance - this is in fact *not the case*, or at least could easily be not the case, *for every such name* (a feat, it seems, quite difficult to accomplish without presupposing at the very outset that there are no universals - that is, without begging the very question that is at issue).

If the truth of "red is a color" and "it is false that there are blue carnations" (see below) forces us, given the correspondence theory of truth, to conclude that the names "red" and "that there are blue carnations" refer to something (not to a *thing*, of course), are we then also forced to conclude from the truth of the sentence "the round square does not exist" that "the round square" refers to something, too (to one of Meinong's impossible objects)? The last example-sentence has a character different from that of the two preceding ones in virtue of the fact that the name occurring in it is a *definite description* whose presupposition (that there is precisely one round square) can very well be considered to be (necessarily) not fulfilled. Therefore, *it is possible*, given eliminative theory of definite descriptions (Russell's or Carnap's), to read the sentence as being true (even in classical logic) without needing to assume that the singular term "the round square" refers to anything that would correspond to its meaning. "Red" and "that there are blue carnations," on the other hand, are certainly not definite descriptions; nor can they be regarded as *truncated descriptions*, as Russell proposes for the treatment of "Romulus" in "Romulus did not exist" (see "The Philosophy of Logical Atomism," p. 213).

[*8] Compare W. Künne, *Abstrakte Gegenstände*, chapter 3, §6. See also D. Lewis, "New Work for a Theory of Universals," p. 348f. The problem that so-called *abstract singular terms* constitute for nominalists is thoroughly discussed

by M. J. Loux in "The Existence of Universals," p. 16ff; also by D. M. Armstrong in *Universals and Scientific Realism*, vol. I, p. 58ff.

[*9] In "The Philosophy of Logical Atomism," p. 167, Russell asserts (appealing to Wittgenstein) "propositions are not names for facts." *Propositions* are for Russell on the one hand independent declarative sentences (and here he is right about their not naming facts), and on the other hand "that"-sentences, dependent clauses (see *ibid.*, p. 165); these, however, in the eyes of logical grammar, *are* names for states of affairs and hence, indeed, sometimes names for facts. On p. 168 Russell says "You cannot properly name a fact." Russell does not give a satisfactory reason for this: "The only thing you can do is to assert it, or deny it, or desire it, or will it, or wish it, or question it, but all those are things involving the whole proposition. You can never put the sort of thing that makes a proposition to be true or false in the position of a logical subject. You can only have it there as something to be asserted or denied or something of that sort, but not something to be named." This piece of confused rhetoric at least shows that there is a pronoun ("it") for facts; why then not also names? On p. 178 Russell says "you cannot name anything you are not acquainted with." But if we are acquainted with anything at all, then we are also acquainted with facts; everything else we only know "directly" via the direct acquaintance with facts in which it occurs. Hence, according to Russells own theory of naming, facts are nameable *par excellence*. Russell says further (p. 179): "The only words one does use as names in the logical sense are words like 'this' or 'that'." But these words can be used as names for facts: we quite frequently say "this is a fact" and "that is a fact."

[*10] That predicates and statements are meaningful, or better *significant*, does not force one to conclude that there is *something* which they mean, hence that there are meanings; this is pointed out by Quine in "On what there is," p. 35. In this work it is assumed that (most) statements and (most) predicates *intend something* (as part of their total signification): statements intend states of affairs, predicates intend attributes. Intending and referring (which is the manner in which names, and singular terms in general, intend) are the ways in which language is connected to reality (the totality of being), and without sentences and predicates intending their respective ontological correlates, this connection becomes very precarious indeed.

There is moreover a very good reason for assuming that *meanings* exist (with *intensions* being normally parts of meanings). For this assumption makes it possible to ask how *the meaning of a sentence* results from *the meanings of the expressions* that are its constituents; in other words, through this assumption the way to a compositional semantics is opened up. A compositional conception of semantics allows us to do justice to the fact that language is not a list of autonomous signals, each being significant by and in itself, the occurrence of one signal within another having no semantic relevance whatever. Rather, it is an articulated system, in which the articulation of *meanings* more or less corresponds to the (syntactic) articulation of expressions. The development of a sophisticated compositional semantics for large parts of natural language has been one of the great success stories in logico-linguistic theory in recent years, and this success story has been written by *semantic realists* (by R. Montague and M. J. Cresswell, for example).

D. M. Armstrong does not seem to adequately appreciate this point, for he says in *Universals and Scientific Realism*, vol. 1, p. 64f: "This argument [from meaningful predicate to a universal as its meaning] takes meaning to be a dyadic relation holding between expressions and what is meant, and it is now widely appreciated that this is a crude and unsatisfactory theory of meaning. What is much more difficult is to provide a satisfactory substitute." Why, one wonders, is it so difficult to find a substitute for the semantic realist theory of meaning if the theory is as crude and unsatisfactory as Armstrong says it is?

The argument from meaningful predicate to the existence of a universal as its meaning is, however, problematic on other counts. The meaning of a predicate cannot be identified with a universal (conceived to be a language-independent entity). Normally, a universal is indeed in some sense part of that meaning; but it is likely enough that there are some meaningful predicates (predicates having a meaning) that *do not* even have a universal corresponding to them as part of their meaning (such predicates might be assigned a universal by courtesy; but they are of course useless for showing that there are universals). This being so, it seems difficult, if not impossible, to argue from the meaningfulness of a predicate to the existence of a universal as its intension without blatantly assuming from the very beginning that there is such a universal. (In fact, meaningful but intensionless predicates could very well be ontological predicates, as for example "is an entity," "is identical to," "is an element of." Talk of the *relation of elementhood*, or the *relation of identity* has thus to be taken *cum grano salis*.)

[*11] But let us assume that they *are* abstract individuals. Then they cannot be termed "universals"; for no individual is a universal. Nowadays, however, a usage of this word has become established according to which mere abstractness ("abstract" in a sense in which also individuals can be abstract, that is, in a sense that has nothing to do with extraction: "abstract in the sense of "non-concrete") is sufficient for calling an entity "a universal." On this account, numbers and sets are universals simply in virtue of being abstract, even though they are usually considered to be abstract individuals.

This usage is historically unjustifiable. (According to it, also propositions are called "universals" because they are usually considered to be abstract entities; compare above [*6].) D. Lewis calls it (in "New Work for a Theory of Universals," p. 343) "the modern terminology of Harvard", according to which "classes count as 'universals'." The remark is aimed at W. V. O. Quine who writes in "On what there is," p. 33: "Now let us turn to the ontological problem of universals: the question whether there are such entities as attributes, relations, classes, numbers, functions.'' Note that Quine may be quite correct in counting classes and numbers as universals, though not in the sense he intended: in case classes and numbers turn out to be indeed universals *in our sense* (but then they are not individuals).

I

THE ONTOLOGY OF STATES OF AFFAIRS

CHAPTER I.1

THE CENTRAL AXIOMS FOR THE PART-CONCEPT "P"

(a) For treating ontology, and first of all the ontology of states of affairs, in a precise framework, the (semi-formal) language L of classical first-order predicate logic with identity and definite descriptions (classical first-order logic being presupposed) is extended by the dyadic predicate "P" to form the language LP, such that for all names, variables and functional terms (all singular terms) t and t′ of LP, "(tPt′)" is a sentence-form of LP (let sentences, too, be counted as sentence-forms).[*1] In order to save brackets, it is stipulated that the strength of binding of the sentence-connectives "not", "and", "or" (non-exclusive), "iff" diminishes in this order, that outer brackets can be omitted, and that we can write "(A and B and C)" instead of "((A and B) and C)" and "(A and (B and C))," and "(A or B or C)" instead of "((A or B) or C)" and "(A or (B or C))." Also, we write "t=t′" and "tPt′" instead of "(t=t′)" and "(tPt′)," except in case these expressions form the scope of a quantifier or of a term-forming operator. Instead of "not t=t′" we write "t≠t."

(b) "if A, then B" is to be taken in the sense of "A materially implies B," that is, in the sense of "not A or B"; "A iff B" is to be taken in the sense of "A is materially equivalent to B," that is, in the sense of "(A and B) or (not A and not B)." "**all***x*" is short for "all *x* are such that" (for all variables *x* of LP); "**some***x*" is short for "some *x* is such that"; "**no***x*" is short for "no *x* is such that." "**one***x*" is an abbreviation for "precisely one *x* is such that"; "**the***x*" is an abbreviation for "the *x* which is such that."

(c) "tPt′" is to be read as "t is part of t′"; "part" is not to be taken in the sense of "proper part"; rather, every entity in the universe of discourse of LP, no matter how it is specified, is supposed to be part of itself.

We can define:

DP1 tP*t′ := tPt′ and t≠t′.
("t is a proper part of t′"; t, t′ always stand for singular terms of LP.)

As *central axioms* for the concept "P", we posit the following sentences:

AP1 **all***x***all***y***all***z*(if *x*P*y* and *y*P*z*, then *x*P*z*).

AP2 **all***x*(*x*P*x*).

AP3 **all***x***all***y*(if *x*P*y* and *y*P*x*, then *x*=*y*).

AP1 asserts the transitivity of the part concept ''P'', AP2 its reflexivity, and AP3 its antisymmetry. These three axioms are rightly called ''central axioms,'' for their validity is independent of the chosen universe of discourse of LP, just as in the case of the *logical* axioms for identity. Their validity is already determined by their syntactic structure and *that* meaning of the predicate ''P'' *which* it already has independent of the chosen universe of discourse, and by the meanings of the logical constants occurring in them; hence their validity is *logical* (in an *extended* sense that also admits the relevance of non-logical constants, for example ''P'').[*2]

(d) The universe of discourse of LP will now be specified. Since my first aim is to present the ontology of states of affairs as an axiomatized part-whole theory, I choose as constituting the universe of discourse of LP all states of affairs (and only states of affairs).[*3] We will see that by this step alone three further (true) axioms (or axiom-schemata) can be formulated in LP for ''P''. Those, however, are not logically valid; *at most* the correlates are logically valid that are obtainable from them if they are explicitly restricted to *states of affairs*.

We do not, however, wish to introduce the concept of a state of affairs into LP as yet. Rather, the axiom-system AP1 - AP6 is intended as a system that is capable of many interpretations, even though its *primary interpretation* is supposed to be that of stating *the fundamental ontology of states of affairs*. In accordance with the envisaged plurality of possible interpretations, we will frequently have occasion to use the heuristic assumption that the universe of discourse of LP is the set of the subsets of a set.

(e) From the central axioms we can deduce, using DP1:

TP1 **all***x***all***y***all***z*(if *x*P**y* and *y*P**z*, then *x*P**z*).
(Depending on DP1, AP1 and AP3.)

TP2 **all***x* not *x*P**x*.

TP3 **all***x***all***y*(*x*P**y* iff *x*P*y* and not *y*P*x*).
(Depending on DP1, AP3 and AP2.)

If we had chosen ''P*'' as primitive concept and defined

DP*1 tPt′ := tP*t′ or t=t′,

we would have obtained - by using TP1 and TP2 as central axioms - AP1, AP2 and AP3; AP1 would have depended on TP1 and DP*1, AP2 only on DP*1, and AP3 on DP*1, TP1 and TP2. Hence the systems {AP1,AP2,AP3,DP1} and {TP1,TP2,DP*1} are deductively equivalent; they can serve equivalently as basis of mereological systems (in a general sense), or in other words: parthood is always, however one may specify it, a *partial ordering*.

COMMENTS

[*1] Expressions of LP (and of its successor-languages, and other expressions, too) are put into quotation-marks in order to obtain meta-linguistic names of them (the quotation-marks are frequently omitted if the expression is properly isolated from the English text). Expressions can be considered *with* or *without* their intended meaning; this leads to a systematic ambiguity of names for expressions. In one important class of instances, the ambiguity is brought out by a difference in terminology: the (dyadic) *predicate* "=", for example, is "=" taken *with* or *without* a meaning; "predicate" applies to the expressions to which it applies on purely syntactic grounds. The (dyadic) *concept* "=", however, is "=" taken *with* a meaning (*its* meaning); for a predicate is a concept only if it is meaningful. (It is the same with "sentence" and "statement.") Sometimes several meanings are associated consecutively with one and the same predicate F; still, for the sake of simplicity, I will speak of "*the* concept F," which is made "narrower" or "wider," or modified in whatever manner, since one and only one concept F is what we finally want to arrive at. Note that in this book concepts are always meaningful linguistic expressions (usually meaningful predicates), except in case "concept" is used as a translation of "*Begriff*" in the Fregean sense: then concepts are certain language-independent entities.

Frequently, expressions of the object-language are used (not mentioned) in the meta-language. (The proofs, in particular, are strictly speaking in the meta-language; but they are formulated almost exclusively by using object-language expressions.) Letters t,t′,..., A,B,C,..., etc. are used as schematic place-holders for singular terms, sentences, etc.; but at times they are also bindable meta-linguistic variables for the intended object-language expressions (both these functions may be combined).

[*2] There may be doubts about the (extended) logical validity of AP3. To dispel these, consider that "tPt′" means no more than "t is either a proper part of t′ or is identical with t′."

"Is logically valid," "is logically true" are here used as predicates of sentences and, derivatively, as predicates of schemata of sentences. In their extended sense, which is the only one that will be from now on made use of, they are considered to be synonymous to "is true merely in virtue of the meaning it (the sentence) has *independent of the chosen universe of discourse*." Thus, the concept of logical truth is taken to imply analytically the concept of analytical truth ("is true merely in virtue of its meaning"), but not vice versa, since the meaning of a sentence is not necessarily identical with the meaning it has independent of the chosen universe of discourse of the language.

The concept of truth in all possible worlds, in turn, needs to be distinguished from the concept of analytical truth. Even if one does not believe in other possible worlds besides the actual world, one can surely use the concept of analytical truth without being committed to the view that every true sentence is analytically true. A sentence that is analytically true is true in all possible worlds; but a sentence may be true in all possible worlds without being analytically true. Consider, for example, "the world @ is actual" ("@" is taken to be a rigid designator for one special possible world: the actual world; "t is actual" is taken to express in all utterances the same completely specific property: the property of actuality which the actual world has).

In order to separate truth in all possible worlds more effectively from analytical truth, the expression "ontologically true" will be used synonymously with "true in all possible worlds." Indeed, many ontological principles are *ontologically true* without being analytically true. (Besides concepts of truth for statements, a concept of *truth for states of affairs* will be used and defined in this book.)

Later on, in applying terminology which has become very much associated with language also on the ontological level, I shall speak of *analytical implication* as a relation between states of affairs. Somewhat confusingly, analytical implication between states of affairs will be seen to correspond most closely to analytical implication as a relation between statements, if "statement S analytically implies statement S′" is taken to be synonymous to "there is no possible world in which S is true, but S′ is not," and not, if it is taken to be synonymous to "the statement 'if S, then S′' is analytically true."

[*3] As was indicated in the Introduction, the use of set-theoretical concepts in the meta-language will be avoided in this book - except for heuristic purposes (including discovery of models, considerations of cardinality). For this reason, I do not even say "the universe of discourse of LP is the *set* of all states of affairs." To say "the universe of discourse of LP is constituted by all states of affairs, and only by states of affairs" is, in deference to the customary way of speaking, just a way of saying that in LP all states of affairs, and no other entities, are being spoken about.

CHAPTER I.2

CONCEPTS BASED ON "P" AND ELEMENTARY THEOREMS

(a) The following important mereological concepts can be defined by using "P":

DP2 A(t) := **no***y*(*y*≠t and *y*Pt).
("t is an atom.")

According to DP2, an *atom* is something that has no proper part, that is (in view of AP2), something that has only itself as part.[*1]

DP3 C(t) := **no***y*(*y*≠t and tP*y*).
("t is a complete whole.")

According to DP3, a *complete whole* is something that is proper part of nothing, that is (in view of AP2), something that is only part of itself.
"Atom" and "complete whole" correspond to each other: we get from the definiens of the one concept to the definiens of the other simply by exchanging "*y*" and "t" in "*y*Pt." In the same manner, the two concepts defined next correspond to each other:

DP4 M(t) := **all***y*(tP*y*).
("t is a minimality," "t is minimal.")

According to DP4 a *minimality* is something that is part of everything.

DP5 T(t) := **all***y*(*y*Pt).
("t is a totality," "t is total.")

According to DP5 a *totality* is something of which everything is part.

(b) On the basis of the central axioms and these definitions we obtain:

TP4 **all***x***all***y*(if T(*x*) and T(*y*), then *x*=*y*).
("There is at most one totality." Depending on AP3 and DP5.)

TP5 **all***x***all***y*(if M(*x*) and M(*y*), then *x*=*y*).
("There is at most one minimality." Depending on AP3 and DP4.)

TP6 **all***x*(if T(*x*), then C(*x*)).

(“Every totality is a complete whole.” Depending on AP3, DP5 and DP3.)

TP7 **all***x*(if M(*x*), then A(*x*)).
(“Every minimality is an atom.” Depending on AP3, DP4 and DP2.)

TP8 if **some***x*T(*x*), then **one***x*C(*x*).
(“If there is a totality, then there is precisely one complete whole.” Depending on TP6, DP5 and DP3.)

TP9 if **some***x*M(*x*), then **one***x*A(*x*).
(“If there is a minimality, then there is precisely one atom.” Depending on TP7, DP4 und DP2.)

Given the further axioms (AP4 is sufficient), the converses of TP8 and TP9 become trivially provable; but they cannot be proved on the basis of the central axioms and the definitions alone.

TP10 if **some***x*T(*x*), then **the***x*T(*x*)=**the***x*C(*x*).
(“If there is a totality, then the only totality is the only complete whole.” Depending on TP8, TP4, DP3, DP5.)

TP11 if **some***x*M(*x*), then **the***x*M(*x*)=**the***x*A(*x*).
(“If there is a minimality, then the only minimality is the only atom.” Depending on TP9, TP5, DP2, DP4.)

TP12 **all***x*C(*x*) iff **all***x*A(*x*).
(“Everything is a complete whole iff everything is an atom.” Depending on DP2 and DP3.)

TP13 **all***y***all***x*(if **all***z*(*z*P*y* iff *z*P*x*), then *y*=*x*).
(“Whatever has the same parts is identical.” Depending on AP2 and AP3.)[*2]

According to TP13, everything is completely determined by its parts (and of course we can also prove: **all***y***all***x*(if **all***z*(*y*P*z* iff *x*P*z*), then *y*=*x*)). This consequence is not problematic, as one might be tempted to suppose; consider that “*x*P*y*” is taken to be synonymous to “*x* is proper part of *y*, or identical with *y*” (compare [*2] of chapter 1), and this makes the assertion that everything is completely determined by its parts trivially true. This assertion, however, could very well be denied if “P” is replaced by “P*”: for “**all***y***all***x*(if **all***z*(*z*P**y* iff *z*P**x*), then *y*=*x*)” cannot be proved on the basis of the central axioms. Even the additional axioms AP4-AP6, which we will obtain when we scrutinize the consequences of making the universe of discourse precisely comprise all states of affairs, will not make this provable (and nor will “**all***y***all***x*(if **all***z*(*y*P**z* iff *x*P**z*), then *y*=*x*)” be provable).[*3]

(c) The two concepts which are now to be defined are rather important for what follows:

DP6 QA(t) := **all**y(if yPt, then y=t or M(y)).
("t is a quasi-atom.")

A *quasi-atom* is defined by DP6 as something all of whose proper parts are minimal. Hence, by TP5, a quasi-atom has at most one proper part.[*4] Obviously, every atom is also a quasi-atom; hence, by TP7, every minimality is a quasi-atom.

DP7 QC(t) := **all**y(if tPy, then y=t or T(y)).
("t is a quasi-complete whole.")

A *quasi-complete whole* is defined by DP7 as something which is a proper part only of a totality. Hence, by TP4, a quasi-complete whole is a proper part of at most one whole.[*5] Obviously, every complete whole is also a quasi-complete whole; hence, according to TP6, every totality is a quasi-complete whole.

(d) Besides the monadic concepts already defined, we may, for example, define the following three dyadic ones:

DP8 OV(t,t′) := **some**z(zPt and zPt′).
("t and t′ have a common part, they overlap.")

DP9 EV(t,t′) := **some**z(tPz and t′Pz).
("t and t′ are in a common whole, they are enveloped.")

("**some**z(tPz and zPt′)," however, is logically equivalent to "tPt′", and "**some**z(zPt and t′Pz)" is logically equivalent to "t′Pt" by AP1 and AP2.)

DP10 CN(t,t′) := OV(t,t′) or EV(t,t′).
("t and t′ are mereologically connected.")[*6]

COMMENTS

[*1] The concept of an atom has to be distinguished from the concept of a *non-compositum*. A *compositum* is a whole that has at least two proper parts; hence a non-compositum is a whole that has at most one proper part. By definition all atoms are non-composita, but not all non-composita are by definition atoms. Non-composita might be called "atoms in a wider sense." We will see in what follows that the non-composita are precisely the quasi-atoms (see DP6 and [*4] below).

[*2] In the presence of AP1 and AP2, AP3 is equivalent to TP13.

[*3] However, it can be proved that composita that have the same proper parts are identical. Consider first P. Simons' *Proper Parts Principle* PPP (*Parts*, p. 28, p. 115 - p. 117). PPP, which is characteristic for *extensional mereology* (for a description of what is meant by the term "extensional mereology" see *Parts*, p. 6f), turns into "**all***x***all***y*[if **some***z*(*z*P**x*) and **all***z*(if *z*P**x*, then *z*P**y*), then *x*P*y*]," if it is transcribed into our notation. This is not provable in AP1 - AP6, and it should not be. What we can prove, however, is "**all***x***all***y*[if *compositum*(*x*) and **all***z*(if *z*P**x*, then *z*P**y*), then *x*P*y*]"; and, in view of AP3, we obtain from this that composita are identical if they have the same proper parts. In extensional mereology, the general principle for non-atoms that concludes identity from sameness of proper parts coincides with the corresponding principle which is limited to composita; for in extensional mereology every non-atom is a compositum (by Simons' *Weak Supplementation Principle*; see *Parts*, p. 28).

In "A World of Individuals" N. Goodman formulates a *principle of nominalism* that has the following content: "The nominalist denies that two different entities can be made up of the same entities [p. 158] ... In the nominalist's world, if we start from any two distinct entities and break each of them down as far as we like (by taking parts, parts of parts, and so on), we always arrive at some entity that is contained in one but not the other of our two original entities [p. 159]." According to this, Goodman's principle of nominalism can be formulated in LP in the following manner: (PN1) "**all***x***all***y*[if *x*≠*y*, then **some***z*(*z*P**x* and not *z*P**y*) or **some***z*(*z*P**y* and not *z*P**x*)]," or equivalently: "**all***x***all***y*[if **all***z*(*z*P**x* iff *z*P**y*), then *x*=*y*]." ("**all***x***all***y*[if *x*≠*y*, then **some***z*(*z*P*x* and not *z*P*y*) or **some***z*(*z*P*y* and not *z*P*x*)]" is of course not a nominalistic principle, but, on the contrary, provable on the basis of the central axioms; it it is logically equivalent to TP13.) According to PN1 there is at most one atom; but with at most one atom one cannot have a world of individuals, given Goodman's atomistic system. Goodman's own formalization of the principle "No distinction of entities without distinction of content" (p. 161) differs accordingly from PN1: (PN2) "**all**y**all**z[if **all**x(A(x,y) iff A(x,z)), then y=z]," where "A(x,y)" is defined by "A(x) and xPy" (p. 160); that is, Goodman interprets that principle as saying (p. 161): "For a nominalistic system, no two distinct things have the same atoms." Goodman does not mention that this interpretation of his principle of nominalism is not the original one, thus disguising the fact that he would be forced to give it up in the original interpretation (captured by PN1): atoms *are* distinct without having distinct content (in Goodman's sense).

The Platonist in Goodman's (slightly idiosyncratic) sense, if he sees two different entities *a* and *b*, where Goodman's nominalist sees only one (according to PN2), can cheerfully grant the nominalist PN2; he only needs to assert that *a* and *b* are atoms, and immediately PN2 has no force whatever against him. And why should he not be allowed to do this? Goodman himself says (p. 158, footnote): "An atomic element - or atom - of a system is simply an element of the system that contains no lesser elements for the system. Depending on the system, an electron or a molecule or a planet might be taken as an atom."

[*4] Every quasi-atom is a non-compositum; and every non-compositum is a quasi-atom if there is a minimality (which will subsequently become provable): Assume that z is a non-compositum, that is, **all**x**all**y'(if xPz and x≠z and y'Pz and y'≠z, then x=y'); assume that yPz and y≠z; hence **all**y'(if y'Pz and y'≠z, then y=y'); but **some**uM(u), that is, **some**u**all**x(uPx); hence uPz and u≠z (the latter holds, since from yPz and y≠z by AP3: not zPy; but uPy); hence y=u, hence M(y). Therefore: **all**y(if yPz, then y=z or M(y)), that is, QA(z).

[*5] Every entity, in virtue of having at least one part (itself), is a *relative whole*. On this basis I frequently use the word "whole" as a noun (without the adjective "complete"), when I refer non-discriminately to entities of the universe of discourse (see for example [*1] above).

[*6] The concepts defined in DP8 - DP10 are not used in what follows. The reason is: already in the system AP1-AP4 we can prove the existence of a minimality and a totality, and thus we can also prove: **all**x**all**yOV(x,y), **all**x**all**yEV(x,y). In other words, the concepts "OV" and "EV" become trivial: they apply to everything in the universe. In a system without minimality, however, "OV" can be chosen as primitive concept, and we can define: tPt′ := **all**x(if OV(x,t), then OV(x,t′)) (compare *Parts*, p. 53; LGD1, LGA3, LGD2).

CHAPTER I.3

THE CONCEPT OF STATE OF AFFAIRS

(a) *A state of affairs is the intension of a statement.*[*1] This is an *explicative definition* or *explication*; thus it is neither an analysis of established meaning, nor a purely conventional nominal definition. It is a weighty objection against this definition that it is too narrow; for one would certainly like to call some entities "states of affairs" which are not the intensions of statements (not the intensions of meaningful declarative sentences), although they could be. Moreover, it may be that the definition is also too wide. Do statements that are neither true nor false (let us not commit from the start to the thesis that there are no such statements) *intend* states of affairs (express states of affairs as their intensions), assuming that they do intend something?

If both these objections are acknowledged, then the definition which suggests itself next is: *a state of affairs is anything which can be the intension of a statement that is either true or false*. If only the first objection is taken account of, then the adaptation which would result is: *a state of affairs is anything which can be the intension of a statement*. If, however, only the second objection is accepted, then the adaptation which results is: *a state of affairs is the intension of a statement that is either true or false*. This last definition of the concept of state of affairs may well be regarded as the narrowest possible.

(b) The word "statement" in (a) was meant to apply only to sentences in the normal sense, that is, to sentences consisting of a finite number of letters. Now, for each of the four definitions under (a) there is an alternative version in which the word "statement" is taken in a wider sense, in a sense which is such that there are also statements consisting of a denumerable infinity of letters. Then the alternative version of the third definition is the widest definition of the concept of a state of affairs so far.

One corollary of this alternative version can be definitively accepted: that everything that can be the intension of a statement (be it finite or denumerably infinite) is a state of affairs. Hence also the intensions of statements that are neither true nor false are counted as states of affairs; if a statement that is neither true nor false intends anything at all (if it has an intension), then this entity can only be a state of affairs; this we may take to be part of the meaning of "to intend (semantically)" and of "statement." But it still seems that the concept of a state of affairs is too narrowly circumscribed by the third definition, even in its alternative version. Can every state of affairs be intended by a statement? Even if we admit statements consisting of a denumerable infinity of letters, it is not at all obvious that we have to give a positive answer. Presumably, sentences consisting of a non-denumerable infinity of letters have to be countenanced in order to make each and every state of affairs expressible by some statement. Countenancing such statements, however, would be such a departure from the normal conception of a linguistic statement that the essential linkage between states of affairs and statements loses its initial plausibility.

(c) Let us, therefore, look for a language-independent, non-semantic explicative definition of the concept of state of affairs. What comes to mind first is: *a state of affairs is such an intension which is either true or false*. Clearly, this non-semantic definition of the concept of state of affairs, notwithstanding its non-semantic nature, still relates states of affairs to statements. "True" and "false" can be used non-metaphorically as *semantic* concepts: such that only statements are true or false. But they can also be used non-metaphorically as *ontological* concepts: such that only entities that are states of affairs or *propositions* are true or false. (Those who hold that, in contrast to propositions, state of affairs are neither true nor false, may consider the following argument: that the moon is more than 100,000 miles away from the earth in 1995 is a state of affairs and a fact; that the moon is more than 100,000 miles away from the earth in 1995 is true; therefore: there is a state of affairs which is true. What good reason is there for objecting that the first occurrence of the "that"-clause refers to a state of affairs, but that the second occurrence refers only to a proposition, not to a state of affairs? To argue to this effect, seems a rather gratuitous move. Concerning the relationship between states of affairs and propositions, see section (e) below.)

The definition given above achieves a widening of the concept of a state of affairs if compared with the definition: *a state of affairs is anything which can be the intension of a - finite or infinite - statement*; for what cannot be the intension of a statement may yet be an intension that is either true or false. But on the other hand, it also effects a narrowing of that concept; what can be the intension of a statement may yet be an intension that is neither true nor false.

(d) Is there not another predicate with semantic and ontological uses which we might employ for a non-semantic, language-independent definition of the concept of state of affairs and which avoids the drawback of the proposal in (c)? There is such a predicate, namely the predicate "analytically implies" (and, of course, its converse "is analytically implied by"). In the semantic use, x analytically implies y, only if x and y are statements; but it can also be said, derivatively, that *concept* x analytically implies *concept* y. In the ontological use, x analytically implies y, only if x and y are states of affairs, (alternatively: propositions). But it can also be said, derivatively, that one *attribute* analytically implies another.

Using the predicate "analytically implies" in its primary (non-derivative) ontological sense, we can define: *a state of affairs is an intension that analytically implies something* (equally good would be: *a state of affairs is an intension that is analytically implied by something*). This definition is wider without being at the same time narrower than the definition: *a state of affairs is what can be the intension of a statement.* The world in the sense of Wittgenstein certainly is an intension that analytically implies something (it analytically implies everything that is the case); but it is highly doubtful whether it could be the intension of a statement. (The word "intension" may appear to be misapplied if something is called an "intension" that is not intended nor capable of being intended by some linguistic expression. But the whole group of entities - the intensions - is called after its most prominent members which *are intended* by linguistic expressions.[*2]) On the other hand, everything that can be the intension of a statement is necessarily an intension that analytically implies something (at least itself).

For an intension to analytically imply something, it is not conceptually necessary that it be true or false (but it is conceptually necessary for its being true or false that it analytically imply something). However, we shall see later on that it is a *contingent fact* that every intension which analytically implies something is either true or false. Therefore, given the new definition of "state of affair" in this section and what was said in (b), there are in fact no statements that have an intension, but whose intension is neither true nor false: if a statement has an intension, then it is a state of affairs, hence an intension that analytically implies something, and therefore, according to the contingent fact just mentioned, either true or false. And hence there are in fact no statements that have an intension but are themselves neither true nor false. Nevertheless, there still can be statements that are neither true nor false - and there are such, as long as we do not artificially assign an intension to every statement that does not naturally have one; "the king of France in the year 1995 is bald" is a case in point.

What matters here, however, is not contingent fact, but to choose a concept of state of affairs which in virtue of its conceptual content makes all possible intensions of statements states of affairs. In addition, it should *as far as its content goes* allow for states of affairs that cannot be intended by statements *and* for states of affairs that are neither true nor false. Such a concept of states of affairs has been introduced by the new definition in this section. Hence, let it be accepted definitively that *a state of affairs is an intension that analytically implies something.*

(e) A *proposition*, on the other hand, is what can be the intension of a *finite* statement. Therefore, every proposition is a state of affairs, but not every state of affairs is a proposition. However, the concept of proposition is also frequently distinguished from the concept of state of affairs by holding that, conceptually, no proposition is a state of affairs: propositions, being the meanings or intensions of statements, are supposed to be *abstract entities*, while states of affairs are something "out there in the world."[*3]

If propositions are defined as possible intensions of finite statements (this use of the word is surely legitimate), then there is no point in separating them from states of affairs (which then, of course, could not be defined as intensions that analytically imply something). There is no point in putting an intermediate level - the level of propositions - between the linguistic level and the level of truth-determination (the level of states of affairs and thus of facts). Why, in the course of answering the question what makes true statements true and false statements false, should we shoulder the considerable burden of elucidating how an intermediate level of abstract entities is related to the level of states of affairs? This needlessly generates difficulties that make the correspondence theory of truth seem much less plausible than it really is. In contrast, the answer which is here given to the question what makes true statements true and false ones false is rather simple: a true (finite) statement is true, because its intension (the state of affairs or proposition intended by it) is a fact (an obtaining state of affairs), is part of the world, part of the conjunction of all facts; and a false statement is false, because the intension of its negation (the negation of its intension) is a fact.

Many believe that all propositions are abstract (non-concrete) entities (for example W. Künne in *Abstrakte Gegenstände*, p. 11). If all propositions are states of affairs, this is untenable. The entity that is designated by the complex name "that Michael P. is smoking a cigarette at (time) t_0" is surely a proposition on any account. But if we disambiguate that complex name by having it refer not to the meaning [*4], but to the intension of the statement "Michael P. is smoking a cigarette at t_0" (hence to a state of affairs), then this entity is not abstract (it may be *non-actual*, or - in other words, because it is a state of affairs - *false*; but that is something distinct from being abstract). It is certainly possible that I *see* that Michael is smoking a cigarette at t_0.[*5] Can abstract entities be *seen* (where "to see" is to be taken in a non-metaphorical and non-analogical sense)?[*6] Surely not. Rather, the proposition is an excellent example for a *concrete* entity, at least as good an example as Michael himself; for how could I see Michael without seeing *that* ... *Michael* ..., that is, without seeing an obtaining proposition that involves Michael? Therefore, there are propositions that are not abstract entities.

(f) The universe of discourse of LP consists precisely of all states of affairs. Hence the predicate "*x*P*y*," interpreted relative to this universe of discourse, is to be read as "*x* is a state of affairs that is part of the state of affairs *y*." I interpret the part-concept "P" for states of affairs as being synonymous with the (primary) concept of analytical implication between intensions (or more precisely speaking with its converse).[*7] This can be done, since intensions are here taken to be *coarse-grained intensions* (see [*2]); for intensions thus conceived, AP3 does indeed hold true if "*x*P*y*" is interpreted as "intension *x* is analytically implied by intension *y*." "*x*P*y*" could not be interpreted in this manner if the concept of intension were not restricted to intensions which are coarse-grained. There are *fine-grained* intensions that analytically imply each other without being identical: *that all bachelors are unmarried* and *that all* *bachelors are men*, for example (*if* the names for intensions just used *are* taken to refer to fine-grained intensions); and ‘‘P’’ has already been interpreted in such a manner as to make AP3 hold true in every possible universe of discourse of LP (or in other words, so as to make being a *proper* or *asymmetrical* part of *y* logically equivalent to being a part of *y* and different from *y*).

Given the above interpretation of ‘‘P’’, it is fairly clear in what manner the axiom-system for the ontology of states of affairs is to be extended (for example, the axiomatized ontology of states of affairs will allow us to deduce the ontological equivalent of propositional logic).

We can define (within LP):

DP11 t′->t := tPt′.
(‘‘intension t′ analytically implies t’’; we may have to give up this reading if we change the universe of discourse.)

In complete harmony with our characterization of the universe of discourse as comprising all and only states of affairs which are precisely the intensions that analytically imply something (*something* that is an intension that analytically implies something, of course), we can then prove

TP14 **all***x***some***y*(*x*->*y*).
(‘‘Everything in the universe of discourse is an intension that analytically implies something.’’ Depending on DP11 und AP2.)

COMMENTS

[*1] The intension of a (meaningful) expression (that has an intension; but, if desired, expressions that do not have a "natural" intension might be assigned an artificial one) is part of the *total* (or *full*) *meaning* of the expression, and it is always a language-independent part of it, one that does not depend essentially on the expression. Clearly, as a rule, the intension of an expression will not be identical to its total meaning, to "its meaning," as one normally says. Nevertheless, there is no obstacle to saying that an expression *expresses* (or *intends*) its intension (as part of its meaning). The states of affairs envisaged here are fit to do the work only of statement-intensions, not of statement-meanings. This should not be held against them, since they will later on (in part IV) belong to the basic entities of an ontological theory in which statement-meanings can be specified to any desired degree of fulness.

[*2] The concept of intension (or *intensional entity*) is primitive here and will not be defined; but this book may well be characterized as being in good part a sustained clarification of it. Note that no individual is an intension, but that all states of affairs and attributes (properties and relations) are intensions. The distinction between intensions and non-intensions crosscuts the distinction between complete and incomplete entities (between states of affairs and individuals on the one hand, and functions, in particular attributes, on the other). Besides the distinction between complete and incomplete intensions, another fundamental distinction among intensions is that between *coarse-grained* and *fine-grained* intensions; the difference between the two is, roughly speaking, that coarse-grained intensions require much less than fine-grained ones in order to be the *same* intension. Attention in this book will be restricted to coarse-grained intensions, and therefore the very word "intension" is taken to mean *coarse-grained intension*. (Systems for coarse-grained and fine-grained intensions can be found in Bealer's *Quality and Concept*.)

[*3] For this distinction between states of affairs and propositions, compare K. Mulligan et al., "Truth-Makers," p. 287 and § 5. See also B. Smith, "Introduction to Adolf Reinach *On the Theory of the Negative Judgment*,", p. 293f.

[*4] We of course say such things as "the meaning of 'Michael is smoking a cigarette at t_0' is that Michael is smoking a cigarette at t_0." We do not ever say "the meaning of 'Michael is smoking a cigarette at time t_0' is true," though we may well say "that Michael is smoking a cigarette at t_0 is true." This quite clearly shows that the name "that Michael is smoking a cigarette at t_0" is ambiguous as to its referent, and the same holds for "that"-names generally.

On top of the referential ambiguity of ''that''-names between *meanings* and *intensions*, there is their referential ambiguity between *coarse-grained* and *fine-grained intensions*. Thus we say ''that triangles have three sides and that triangles have three angles are the same true proposition.'' But we can also say ''that triangles have three sides and that triangles have three angles are different true propositions.''

[*5] Barwise and Perry distinguish in *Situations and Attitudes*, p. 179f, between ''to see''+nounphrase (AcI) and ''to see''+dependent clause (constructed with ''that''); the former is said to express *epistemically neutral* seeing, the latter *epistemically positive* seeing. But it does not seem correct to assert that only the first kind of seeing is properly speaking seeing, such that *that Michael is smoking a cigarette at time* t_0 cannot, properly speaking, be seen, but only the concrete situation, the event to which that proposition corresponds. It does not seem correct, because it is unclear where the borderline between epistemically neutral seeing and epistemically positive seeing is to be drawn. Are there any pure cases of epistemically neutral seeing? Moreover, the semantic distinction pointed out by Barwise and Perry disappears if the present tense and the first person is used. I, for my part, am not able to notice any significant difference in meaning between ''I see Michael smoking a cigarette'' and ''I see that Michael is smoking a cigarette.'' This quite clearly shows that the semantic distinction is not grounded in an ontological, categorial distinction between the entities that are seen.

But setting all this aside. It is obviously possible that I empirically ascertain *that Michael is smoking a cigarette at* t_0. Can abstract (non-concrete) entities be empirically ascertained? Surely not. Indeed, I have just now empirically ascertained that Michael is smoking a cigarette at t_0. What is empirically ascertained are facts of the empirical world. And what could be concrete if those facts are not concrete?

[*6] But sentences - which considered as *types* (not *tokens*) surely are abstract entities - can be *seen*, can they not? Here ''to see'' is indeed not used metaphorically, but nevertheless *analogically*, that is, in a secondary meaning which is obviously definable in terms of the primary one: to see_2 sentence A is to see_1 a token of A.

[*7] P. Simons proposes in *Parts*, p. 170, an intensional part-whole-relation between propositions (which he takes to be abstract entities). According to his proposal (proposition) *p* is part of (proposition) *q* iff everything that makes *p* true also makes *q* true. In contrast to propositions, the entities which the quantifier ranges over, that is, all possible truth-makers, are supposed to be something ''out there in the world,'' for example, Wittgensteinian ''*Sachverhalte*''(see K. Mulligan *et al.*, ''Truth-Makers,'' paragraph 5). The part-relation between propositions introduced by Simons is intuitively obscure.

In what intuitive sense is *p* an (intensional) part of *q* if and only if everything that makes *p* true also makes *q* true? This seems uncontroversially true: *that George is a man* is an intensional part of *that George is a husband*; but clearly, some truth-makers that make the former proposition true do not make the latter proposition true, too. To get the desired result, we rather have to define: *p* is part of *q* iff everything that makes *q* true also makes *p* true. This is so clear that Simons' proposal is presumably no more than a misprint.

CHAPTER I.4

FUNCTIONAL TERMS DEFINABLE BY "P"

(a) In LP we have at our disposal the definite description operator "**the**." Therefore, we can define functional terms in LP, for example:

DP12 **conj**(t,t′) := **the***x*[tP*x* and t′P*x* and **all***y*(if tP*y* and t′P*y*, then *x*P*y*)].
("the conjunction of t and t′.")

By DP12 *the conjunction of t and t′* is defined as the smallest whole of which both t and t′ are part; the conjunction of the states of affairs t and t′ is the intensionally weakest state of affairs which analytically implies both t and t′.

DP13 **disj**(t,t′) := **the***x*[*x*Pt and *x*Pt′ and **all***y*(if *y*Pt and *y*Pt′, then *y*P*x*)].
("the disjunction of t and t′.")

By DP13 *the disjunction of t and t′* is defined as the greatest common part of t and t′; the disjunction of the states of affairs t and t′ is the intensionally strongest state of affairs that is analytically implied both by t and t′.

DP14 $\mathbf{neg}_1$(t) := **the***y*[**all***z*(if *z*Pt and *z*P*y*, then M(*z*)) and **all***k*(if **all***z*(if *z*Pt and *z*P*k*, then M(*z*)), then *k*P*y*)].
("the first negation of t.")

By DP14 *the first negation of t* is defined as the greatest whole that has at most a minimality in common with t; the first negation of the state of affairs t is the intensionally strongest state of affairs which is such that every state of affairs analytically implied both by it and by t is minimal.

DP15 $\mathbf{neg}_2$(t) := **the***y*[**all***z*(if tP*z* and *y*P*z*, then T(*z*)) and **all***k*(if **all***z*(if tP*z* and *k*P*z*, then T(*z*)), then *y*P*k*)].
("the second negation of t.")

By DP15 *the second negation of t* is defined as the smallest whole which is such that it and t are at most common parts of a totality; the second negation of the state of affairs t is the intensionally weakest state of affairs which is such that every state of affairs that analytically implies both it and t is a total state of affairs.

For all states of affairs *p* the first negation of *p* is identical with the second negation of *p*; thus, one can simply speak of "the negation of *p*."[*1] Hence, further axioms will have to be chosen in such a manner that "**all**x[**neg**$_1$(x)=**neg**$_2$(x)]" becomes provable; this theorem justifies the following definition:

DP16 **neg**(t) :=**the**y[y=**neg**$_1$(t) and y=**neg**$_2$(t)].
("the negation of t.")[*2]

(b) For the schemata of sentence-forms in the definientia of DP12 - DP16 we use the abbreviations A[x,t,t′], B[x,t,t′], C[y,t], D[y,t], E[y,t]. It is easy to prove:

TP15(a) **all**z**all**z'**all**x**all**y(if A[x,z,z'] and A[y,z,z'], then x=y);
(b) **all**z**all**z'**all**x**all**y(if B[x,z,z'] and B[y,z,z'], then x=y);
(c) **all**z'**all**x**all**y(if C[x,z] and C[y,z], then x=y);
(d) **all**z'**all**x**all**y(if D[x,z] and D[y,z], then x=y);
(e) **all**z**all**x**all**y(if E[x,z] and E[y,z], then x=y).
(Depending on AP3, except in the case of (e).)

Hence, for the justification of the definitions DP12 - DP16 it only remains to be shown: **all**z**all**z'**some**xA[x,z,z'], **all**z**all**z'**some**xB[x,z,z'], **all**z**some**yC[y,z], **all**z**some**yD[y,z], **all**z**some**yE[y,z]. For in the presence of TP15 we obtain from these statements: **all**z**all**z'**one**xA[x,z,z'], **all**z**all**z'**one**xB[x,z,z'], **all**z**one**yC[y,z], **all**z**one**yD[y,z], **all**z**one**yE[y,z]. But even though their truth is not to be denied if the intended universe of discourse (consisting of all and only states of affairs) is taken into consideration, they are not consequences of the central axioms. It is necessary, therefore, to extend the axiomatic system.

COMMENTS

[*1] It is a moot point in the literature whether there are negative facts or negative states of affairs. (See for example B. Smith, "Introduction to Adolf Reinach *On the Theory of the Negative Judgment*," p. 295f; B. Russell, "The Philosophy of Logical Atomism," p. 187ff.) Negative facts are negative states of affairs that obtain. Negative states of affairs are negations of states of affairs; the negation of a state of affairs *p* is (for example) identical with the (intensionally) greatest state of affairs that has at most a minimal state of affairs (intensionally) in common with *p*. This gives the expression "negative state of affairs" a clear mereological meaning. If there are states of affairs that have states of affairs as (intensional) parts, and which are parts of other states of affairs, then why should there not be negative states of affairs in the sense just stated? Moreover, the negative states of affairs are in fact all the states of affairs there are; for every state of affairs is a negative state of affairs in the sense defined above, because it is the negation of some state of affairs.

In "Negation and Generality," p. 296, H. Hochberg argues for the dispensability of conjunctive and disjunctive facts, but recognizes negative facts. Similarly, Russell: "on the whole I do incline to believe that there are negative facts and that there are no disjunctive facts." ("The Philosophy of Logical Atomism," p. 190.) Now, on the one hand, it is in a sense true that true sentences of the forms "AorB" and "AandB" do not need obtaining disjunctive or conjunctive states of affairs as truth-makers; but, on the other hand, this does not make conjunctive and disjunctive facts go away. What are the *primary* denotations (see [*4] of chapter 3) of singular terms of the forms "*that* AorB" and "*that* AandB," if they are not disjunctive or conjunctive states of affairs respectively (and which are facts if the sentences corresponding to the singular terms are true)? For a vindication of Hochberg's and Russell's position, "that"-clauses and equivalent means of expression (from the point of view of logical grammar they are singular terms) would have to be shown to be - contrary to appearances - non-denoting.

Correspondingly, any ontological theory that denies that there are negative facts must show convincingly that all expressions of the form "*that* notA" (and equivalent expressions) have in fact no denotations, that they are singular terms only syntactically, but not semantically. (Merely showing their eliminability as singular terms, if that were possible, is not enough; "the president of the United States in 1995" is an eliminable singular term; but this does not demonstrate that it does not have a denotation. Eliminability of a singular term only shows that we are *not forced* to assume a denotation for it merely by dint of its indispensable occurrence in true sentences. We may nevertheless have other good reasons for assuming a denotation in the given case.) The most plausible and natural view of these terms is, on the contrary, that (normally) they do in fact denote, and that their primary denotations are the negations of the states of affairs denoted by singular terms of the form "*that* A," hence certain *negative states of affairs*.

[*2] Given their definitions, "**conj**(t,t′)" corresponds to the union-symbol in Boolean Algebra, "**disj**(t,t′)" to the intersection-symbol, "**neg**(t)" to the symbol for complement. The new symbolism is intuitively advantageous for all *intensional* interpretations of Boolean Algebra, and particularly for the one based on states of affairs. But note: being accustomed to extensionalistic constructions of states of affairs as sets of possible worlds (the *smallest* sets representing the intensionally *strongest* states of affairs, the *biggest* sets the intensionally *weakest* ones), one tends to associate conjunction with intersection, and disjunction with union - contrary to the correspondence just established.

CHAPTER I.5

THE CONJUNCTION AXIOM

(a) The central axioms AP1 - AP3 are first of all extended by

AP4 **some***z*[**all***x*(if A[*x*], then *x*P*z*) and **all***y*(if **all***x*(if A[*x*], then *x*P*y*), then *z*P*y*)].

AP4 (properly speaking not an axiom, but an *axiom-schema* [*1]) asserts that for every LP-description A[*x*] some entity (in the universe of discourse) is such that all entities (in the universe of discourse) that satisfy A[*x*] are parts of it, while it is part of every entity of which all entities that satisfy A[*x*] are parts.
Let "[**all***x*(if A[*x*] ... *z*)]" be short for "**all***x*(if A[*x*], then *x*P*z*) and **all***y*(if **all***x*(if A[*x*], then *x*P*y*), then *z*P*y*)." It can easily be proved:

TP16 **all***z***all***z′*(if [**all***x*(if A[*x*] ... *z*)] and [**all***x*(if A[*x*] ... *z′*)], then *z*=*z′*).
(Depending on AP3.)

Hence we have

TP17 **one***z*[**all***x*(if A[*x*] ... *z*)].
(Depending on AP4 und TP16.)

This theorem justifies the following definition:

DP17 **conj***x*A[*x*] := **the***z*[**all***x*(if A[*x*], then *x*P*z*) and **all***y*(if **all***x*(if A[*x*], then *x*P*y*), then *z*P*y*)].
("the conjunction of all *x* such that A[*x*].")

By DP17 the conjunction of all *x* such that A[*x*] is defined as the smallest whole of which all entities satisfying A[*x*] are parts. Considering the chosen universe of discourse, the conjunction of all states of affairs satisfying A[*x*] is the intensionally weakest state of affairs that analytically implies all states of affairs that satisfy A[*x*].
It can be proved:

TP18 **all***x*(if A[*x*], then *x*P**conj***z*A[*z*]) and **all***y*(if **all***x*(if A[*x*], then *x*P*y*), then **conj***z*A[*z*]P*y*).
(Depending on TP17 und DP17.)

If we had chosen all expressions of the form "**conj**zA[z]" as basic functional terms, TP18 would have replaced AP4 (which is a direct logical consequence of TP18) as an axiom. For all practical purposes (that is, in proving theorems), TP18 is the principle to turn to, and not AP4. Note that the relation between TP18 and AP4 in view of AP3 is exactly analogous to the relation in set theory between the *axiom of comprehension* and the *principle of abstraction* (which determines the behavior of set-theoretical abstraction terms: {z:A[z]}) in view of the *principle of extensionality* - except for one very important point: the axiom of comprehension and the principle of abstraction need to be restricted with respect to the predicates they apply to in order to avoid the set-theoretical antinomies, whereas no such restriction is necessary for AP4 and TP18; taken by themselves, they are logically harmless.

(b) But the conjunction axiom is not true simply in virtue of the meaning it has even independent of the chosen universe of discourse of LP; the instances of AP4 are not logical truths. It is, however, surely (analytically) true (or rather: all its *instances* are true, even the instances where A[z] is a predicate that applies to nothing at all), if the universe of discourse consists precisely of all states of affairs (or in other words: coarse-grained intensions that analytically imply something) and if "xPy" for states of affairs is made synonymous with the (primary) concept of analytical implication for intensions. (AP4 would, for example, also hold true if the universe of discourse consisted of all the subsets of a certain set M and if "xPy" for subsets of M were made synonymous with the subset-concept for the subsets of M.) As an existence-principle the conjunction axiom is maximally weak, although it guarantees that infinitely many singular terms have their intended designatum. It is compatible with a universe of discourse comprising one entity only. (In the set-theoretical interpretation, let M be the empty set. Then the principles AP1 - AP4 are fulfilled, and so also are the further principles AP5 and AP6.)

(c) We have:

TP19 **all**z**all**z'**some**x(zPx and z'Px and **all**y(if zPy and z'Py, then xPy)).

TP19 justifies DP12 in view of TP15; and we can prove:

TP20 **all**z**all**z'(**conj**(z,z')=**conj**k(kPz or kPz')).
("The conjunction of z and z' is the conjunction of all k that are parts of z or z'." Depending on TP15, DP12, TP18, AP1 und AP2; consider the proof of TP19.)

Further we have

TP21 **all**z**all**z'**some**x(xPz and xPz' and **all**y(if yPz and yPz', then yPx)).

TP21 justifies DP13 in view of TP15; and we can prove:

TP22 **allzallz′(disj**(*z*,*z*′)=**conj***k*(*k*P*z* and *k*P*z*′)).
("The disjunction of *z* and *z*′ is the conjunction of all *k* that are parts *both of z and z*′." Depending on TP15, DP13, TP18; consider the proof of TP21.)

(d) With respect to "**conj**(t,t′)" and "**disj**(t,t′)," the following important theorems are provable on the basis of TP19 and TP21:

TP23 **allzallz′ally**(*y*P**disj**(*z*,*z*′) iff *y*P*z* and *y*P*z*′).
[**allzallz′ally**(**disj**(*z*,*z*′)->*y* iff *z*->*y* and *z*′->*y*).]

Analogous to TP23 we have

TP24 **allzallz′ally**(**conj**(*z*,*z*′)P*y* iff *z*P*y* and *z*′P*y*).
[**allzallz′ally**(*y*->**conj**(*z*,*z*′) iff *y*->*z* and *y*->*z*′).]

The proof of TP24, by applying AP1, also provides the proof for

TP25 **allzallz′ally**(if *y*P*z* or *y*P*z*′, then *y*P**conj**(*z*,*z*′)).

And the proof of TP23, by applying AP1, also provides the proof for

TP26 **allzallz′ally**(if *z*P*y* or *z*′P*y*, then **disj**(*z*,*z*′)P*y*).

The converses of the TP25 and TP26 cannot be proved, nor ought they to be provable, given the chosen universe of discourse of LP or any intuitive conception of parts.

(e) Of the definitions of functional terms introduced in chapter I.4, only those for $\mathbf{neg}_1$(t), $\mathbf{neg}_2$(t) and **neg**(t) remain to be justified. The existence-theorems are stated in chapter I.7 (and the proofs are given in the Appendix).
The conjunction axiom can also be used to obtain

TP27 **some***y*M(*y*) and **some***y*T(*y*).[*2]

Because of TP27, in view of TP4 and TP5, the following definitions are justified:

DP18 **t** := **the***y***all***x*(*y*P*x*).
("the minimality"; "the minimal - or *tautological* - state of affairs.")

DP19 **k** := **the***y***all***x*(*x*P*y*).

(''the totality''; ''the total - or *contradictory* - state of affairs.'')

(f) The following useful theorem is also obtainable from the axiomatic basis stated so far:

TP28 if **all***x*(if A[*x*], then B[*x*]), then **conj***z*A[*z*]P**conj***z*B[*z*].

Using TP28 and AP3, we have

TP29 if **all***x*(A[*x*] iff B[*x*]), then·**conj***z*A[*z*]=**conj***z*B[*z*].

It is easily seen that the converse of TP29 does not hold true. For it can already be proved:

TP30 **all***z*(*z*=**conj***z*′(*z*′P*z*)).[*3]
(''Every whole is the conjunction of its parts.'' ''Every state of affairs is the conjunction of all state of affairs analytically implied by it.'')

TP30 logically implies **t**=**conj***z*′(*z*′P**t**). But according to the proof of TP27, TP5 and DP18, we also have **t**=**conj***z*′(*z*′≠*z*′). Therefore, **conj***z*′(*z*′P**t**)=**conj***z*′(*z*′≠*z*′). However, not **all***x*(*x*P**t** iff *x*≠*x*). (From the foregoing it is apparent that the converse of TP28 is not valid either: **t**P**conj***z*′(*z*′≠*z*′), hence **conj***z*′(*z*′P**t**)P**conj***z*′(*z*′≠*z*′). However, not **all***x*(if *x*P**t**, then *x*≠*x*).)

COMMENTS

[*1] The schemata A[t], f[t] (B[t], f′[t] ...) are to be understood as follows: A[ ], f[ ] represent expressions (A[ ] sentence-forms, f[ ] singular terms) in which *one* name has been marked in some manner or other in at least one place of its occurrence, and in which the singular term t (name, variable or functional term) has been substituted for that name in all those places of its occurrence such that no occurrence of a variable in t has come to fall within the scope of the occurrence of a quantifier or term-forming operator in A[ ], f[ ] that is binding that variable.

Generalization: The schemata A[t_1,...,t_n], f[t_1,...,t_n] are to be understood as follows: A[,...,], f[,...,] represent sentence-forms or singular terms respectively in which *n* different names have each been marked in at least one place of their occurrence by "1," by "2" ..., by the respective cipher for *n*, and in which t_1 has been substituted for the name in the 1-places, t_2 for the name in the 2-places, ..., t_n for the name in the *n*-places, such that no occurrence of a variable in t_1,...,t_n has come to fall within the scope of the occurrence of a quantifier or term-forming operator in A[,...,], f[,...,] that is binding that variable.

Instead of meta-linguistic signs for variables of the object-language, the object-language variables themselves are used in an *exemplary* manner (as mere examples) in formulating schemata. Thus, in AP4 the object-language variables "*x*", "*y*", "*z*" are used as examples for the syntactically adequate variables corresponding to them in each instance of that axiom-schema. It is generally stipulated that variables in a schema represent variables in instances of the schema that occur only in the places corresponding to the places indicated by the variables in the schema. (Note that in every definition, too, the variables used are supposed to be merely *exemplary* variables; therefore one can, for example, substitute "**t**" for "**the***y′***all***x*(*y′*P*x*)" in "**the***y*(*y*P**the***y′***all***x*(*y′*P*x*))," even though "**t**" is defined - see DP18 - as "**the***y***all***x*(*y*P*x*).")

Lower-case indices attached to object-language variables are meta-linguistic indices; they turn the variables into meta-linguistic signs for appropriate object-language variables. (In forming further object-language variables from given ones, primes are used.)

Axioms and theorems with free variables (which may be obtained *immediately*, without any interposed logical step, from axiom- and theorem-schemata) are to be read as general statements (as if the free variables were all bound by "**all**"). This amounts to accepting the following inference-rule: If A[*z*] is an axiom or a theorem, then **all***z*A[*z*] is a theorem. (This rule cannot simply be obtained from the *rule of generalization* in predicate logic, since the axioms and theorems concerned are not always axioms and theorems of predicate logic, nor can they always be represented as being logically deduced from axioms in which the "generalized" variable - here represented by the variable *z* - does not occur *unbound*.)

[*2] Usually mereologists do not recognize a "null individual," an individual that is part of every individual (in the universe of discourse). Perhaps a null individual is indeed an "absurdity" (as P. Simons calls it; see *Parts*, p. 13, footnote 5) in the *mereologies of individuals* (see, however, II.11.(e) below), even though it seems not to be part of the meaning of the words "individual" and "part" that there cannot be any individual of kind X that is in some proper sense part of every individual of kind X. But a *null-element* is certainly not an absurdity, rather it is a necessity in the *mereology of states of affairs* (and also in the mereology of properties). Of course, one can be of the opinion that the ontology of states of affairs cannot properly be called a "mereology" (in spite of significant formal similarities to the mereologies of individuals), holding that a state of affairs can be *part* of another state of affairs at best in a metaphorical sense. (But the proviso needs to be added: *part* without being *constituent*; *that A* is surely non-metaphorically part of *that Jim believes at t that A* in the sense of being a *constituent* of that state of affairs.) But the word "part" as used in ordinary language is so vague that whether to agree or not to agree with this position seems no more than a matter of personal taste.

Nevertheless, in accordance with the received usage - not of the word "part," but of the word "mereology" - only a part-whole theory whose universe of discourse is constituted exclusively by *individuals* will here be called a "mereology." In contrast to the negative attitude towards the null individual, mereologists usually do not hesitate to assume a "universe" - an individual of which every individual (in the universe of discourse) is part (see *Parts*, p. 15f).

[*3] We also have: **all***z*(if not QA(*z*) or M(*z*), then *z*=**conj***z*′(*z*′P**z*)). To prove this additional axioms (AP5 and AP6) have to be used, which are to be introduced in the next two chapters. Yet, the proof is most fittingly presented right here:

Assume: not QA(*z*) or M(*z*).

(i) By definition **all***z*′(if *z*′P**z*, then *z*′P*z*); hence by TP28 **conj***z*′(*z*′P**z*) P**conj***z*′(*z*′P*z*), hence by TP30 **conj***z*′(*z*′P**z*)P*z*.

(ii) Assume for *reductio*: not *z*P**conj***z*′(*z*′P**z*); hence according to AP5 **some***y*(QA(*y*) and *y*P*z* and not *y*P**conj***z*′(*z*′P**z*)), hence **some***y*(QA(*y*) and *y*P*z* and not M(*y*) and not *y*P**conj***z*′(*z*′P**z*)) (according to DP4), hence by TP40 (which is proved on the basis of AP6) **all***k*(if *y*P*k*, then not *k*P**z*), hence by DP1 **all***k*(if *y*P*k*, then not *k*P*z* or *k*=*z*), consequently, since according to AP2 *y*P*y*, not *y*P*z* or *y*=*z*, consequently, because of *y*P*z*, *y*=*z*. Therefore, QA(*z*) and not M(*z*) - contradicting the first assumption for *z* above. Hence *z*P**conj***z*′(*z*′P**z*).

On the basis of **(i)** and **(ii)** and AP3: *z*=**conj***z*′(*z*′P**z*).

Moreover: **all**z(if z=**conj**z'(z'P*z), then not QA(z) or M(z)), and this can be proved without invoking additional axioms (hence it is a very elementary theorem):
Assume QA(z) and not M(z); hence by DP6 **all**y(if yPz and $y \neq z$, then M(y)), hence by TP28, DP1 **conj**z'(z'P*z)P**conj**z'M(z'). According to TP32, TP29, TP33 **conj**z'M(z')=**conj**z'(z'=**t**)=**t**. Hence **conj**z'(z'P*z)P**t**, hence by TP36 **conj**z'(z'P*z)=**t**, hence by TP32 M(**conj**z'(z'P*z)); therefore, since by assumption not M(z), $z \neq$**conj**z'(z'P*z). The desired result follows by contraposition.
According to DP20, *elements* are the quasi-atoms that are not minimal; hence we have proved: **all**z(z=**conj**z'(z'P*z) iff not EL(z)) - "the non-elements are precisely the wholes which are the sums of their proper parts"; hence by contraposition: "the elements are precisely the wholes that are *not* the sums of their proper parts."

CHAPTER I.6

THE EXHAUSTION AXIOM

(a) As a further axiom we have

AP5 **all**z**all**z'(if **all**x(if QA(x) and xPz, then xPz'), then zPz').

AP5 says that for z to be a part of z' it is in every case sufficient that all quasi-atoms which are part of z are also part of z'. If this is so, then every whole must be exhausted by its quasi-atoms; if they were all removed, nothing would remain of z; it is the sum of its quasi-atoms. Conversely, if z is exhausted by its quasi-atoms, AP5 must hold true. For this reason AP5 is called "the exhaustion axiom."[*1]

AP5 is valid if the universe of discourse of LP is taken to be constituted by the subsets of a certain set M and "tPt′" is accordingly interpreted as meaning the same as "t is a subset of M, and t′ is a subset of M, and t is a subset of t′." The quasi-atoms in this interpretation are the subsets of M that have at most one (set-theoretical) element.

AP5 is also valid if the universe of discourse consists precisely of all states of affairs and "tPt′" is taken to mean "t is a state of affairs, t′ is a state of affairs, and t is analytically implied by t′" (or in other words: "t is a - coarse-grained - intension that analytically implies something, t′ is an intension that analytically implies something, and t′ analytically implies t"). That this is so will become fairly clear later on, when the intuitively most satisfactory characterization of quasi-atomic state of affairs is made explicit (see I.10.(c) and (d)).[*2]

(b) On the basis of AP5, befitting its name, we can prove:

TP31 **all**z(z=**conj**z'(QA(z') and z'Pz)).

And conversely, AP5 can be gotten from TP31 (of course without using AP5): assume **all**x(if QA(x) and xPz, then xPz'); hence by TP28 **conj**y(QA(y) and yPz)P**conj**y(yPz'), hence by TP30 and TP31 zPz'.

We shall see that for all z **conj**z'(QA(z') and not z'Pz) is identical to the *negation of* z. But to prove this another axiom is needed.

(c) AP5 is independent of the axioms AP1 - AP4. Consider all the negative whole numbers, the number 0 and a singularity # that is not a whole number, but which is stipulated to be smaller than any whole number we have considered; call these entities the "N-entities," and let them constitute the universe of discourse of LP. Let "tPt′" be synonymous to "t is an N-entity, and t′ is an N-entity, and t is smaller than t′ or identical with t′." Then AP1 - AP4 turn out to be true. But AP5 turns out to be false, because there is precisely one quasi-atom (in the model), the singularity #, and this quasi-atom is part of every N-entity. Hence, if AP5 were correct, 0, for example, would be smaller than −1 or identical with −1 (since every quasi-atom in the model that is part of 0 is also part of −1).

COMMENTS

[*1] AP5 logically implies AP2, since **allzallx**(if QA(x) and xPz, then xPz) is a trivial logical truth. Nevertheless, I retain AP2 as an axiom, because many results depend only on AP2 and because AP2, but certainly not AP5, expresses a truth about every part concept that is not a concept of proper parthood.

[*2] It is obvious that AP5 is an *atomistic* principle, since the quasi-atoms are the *non-composita*, the *atoms in a wider sense* (see I.2.[*1] and I.2.[*4]). Relative to the chosen universe of discourse, AP5 implies that each state of affair is a conjunction of *non-composite* states of affairs.

CHAPTER I.7

THE CONNECTION AXIOM

(a) The connection axiom is an axiom-schema that has the following form:

AP6 **all**x[if x**Pconj**yA[y] and not M(x), then **some**k'(k'Px and not M(k') and **some**z(k'Pz and A[z]))].

If wholes that satisfy a certain description are "summed together" or conjunctively united, then neither the conjunction nor every one of its proper parts need satisfy that description. But there must certainly be a certain connection between the parts of the conjunction and the wholes that satisfy the description. AP6 describes the general form of that connection (and therefore it is called "the connection axiom"): *every non-minimal part of a conjunction of A-wholes has a non-minimal part in common with some A-whole*. (For *minimal* parts of the conjunction the connection is trivial.)

AP6 is a principle delicately poised between absurdity and triviality. This becomes apparent if we attempt to replace it by schemata more or less similar to it. The simplest one is

(i) **all**x(if x**Pconj**yA[y], then A[x]).

Because of TP18 we then have **all**x(x**Pconj**yA[y] iff A[x]), which recalls the abstraction-principle in set theory. But accepting **(i)** would lead to inconsistency, since the negation of one of its instances can already be proved: **t**=**t** and **tPconj**z'(z'≠z'), since

TP32 **all**x(M(x) iff x=**t**).
(Depending on TP27, TP5, DP4, DP18.)

We move on to the second proposal:

(ii) **all**x(if x**Pconj**yA[y] and not M(x), then A[x]).

This, too, is rather undesirable. For it has the consequence that the universe of discourse comprises only two wholes *at most*. If **(ii)**, then <u>**all**x(if x**Pconj**y(y=**k**) and non M(x), then x=**k**)</u>. But

TP33 **all**z(z=**conj**z'(z'=z)).

And

TP34 **all**x(T(x) iff x=**k**).
(Depending on TP27, TP4, DP5, DP19.)

Therefore, **all***x*(*x***Pk**) and **k**=**conj***y*(*y*=**k**), hence <u>**all***x*(*x***Pconj***y*(*y*=**k**))</u>. From the underlined results: **all***x*(M(*x*) or *x*=**k**), hence by TP32 **all***x*(*x*=**t** or *x*=**k**), which implies that there are at most two wholes in the universe of discourse.

The next proposal is

(iii) **all***x*(if *x***Pconj***y*A[*y*], then **some***k*′(*k*′P*x* and A[*k*′])).

This, again, leads to inconsistency; the negation of one of the instances of **(iii)** can already be proved: **tPconj***y*(*y*≠*y*), but not **some***k*′(*k*′**Pt** and *k*′≠*k*′).

Then

(iv) **all***x*(if *x***Pconj***y*A[*y*] and not M(*x*), then **some***k*′(*k*′P*x* and A[*k*′]))?

Proposal **(iv)** is undesirable, since one of its instances is: **all***x*(if *x***Pconj***y*(*y*=**k**) and not M(*x*), then **some***k*′(*k*′P*x* and *k*′=**k**)), from which one obtains **all***x*(if *x***Pconj***y*(*y*=**k**) and not M(*x*), then **kP***x*), hence because of **all***x*(*x***Pk**) [T(**k**)] and AP3: **all***x*(if *x***Pconj***y*(*y*=**k**) and not M(*x*), then *x*=**k**) - and for the consequences of this see above under **(ii)**.

What about

(v) **all***x*[if *x***Pconj***y*A[*y*], then **some***k*′(*k*′P*x* and **some***z*(*k*′P*z* and A[*z*]))]?

This is refuted by the provability of "**tPconj***y*(*y*≠*y*)" and of "not **some***k*′(*k*′**Pt** and **some***z*(*k*′P*z* and *z*≠*z*))." But the following schema may seem to be the right thing to be asserted as a new principle:

(vi) **all***x*[if *x***Pconj***y*A[*y*] and not M(*x*), then **some***k*′(*k*′P*x* and **some***z*(*k*′P*z* and A[*z*]))].

The objection using the predicate "*y*=**k**" cannot be raised against this proposal, since **some***k*′(*k*′P*x* and **some***z*(*k*′P*z* and *z*=**k**)) does not reduce to *x*=**k**, but is merely equivalent to **some***k*′(*k*′P*x*) - which is completely harmless, since it is already provable. However, proposal **(vi)** is quite *trivial*; for in case **some***z*A[*z*], then **all***x***some***k*′(*k*′P*x* and **some***z*(*k*′P*z* and A[*z*])) because of **all***x*(**tP***x* and **some***z*(**tP***z* and A[*z*])) (because of M(**t**)); and in case not **some***z*A[*z*], then not **some***x*(*x***Pconj***y*A[*y*] and not M(*x*)) because of TP32 and

TP35 if **no***z*A[*z*], then **conj***y*A[*y*]=**t**,

TP36 **no***x*(*x***Pt** and *x*≠**t**).

Proposal **(vi)** is trivial, since it is provable that in each instance of **(vi)** either the consequent of the instance applies to every entity in the universe of discourse, or its antecedent to none. However, the way to eliminate the triviality of **(vi)** is obvious; it consists precisely in going from **(vi)** to AP6 by inserting "and not M(*k*′)" into its consequent.

(b) AP6 is correct in every universe of discourse (of LP) that consists of all the subsets of a set M ("P" being interpreted accordingly): if *x* is a non-empty subset of the union (a subset of M) of all subsets of M that fulfill an arbitrary description, then (as is well known) there is a non-empty subset of *x* (and hence of M) that is a subset of a subset of M fulfilling the description. AP6 is also correct if the universe of discourse consists of all states of affairs (and nothing else). But in the case of states of affairs there are hardly any principles closer to satisfying our intuitions than AP6 from which it could be logically deduced (of course, only if we abstain from identifying states of affairs with *sets of possible worlds*). Rather, AP6 for states of affairs, in case it does not recommend itself to intuition, is justified "inductively" by the intuitive correctness of the many and diverse theorems that can be deduced by making essential use of it.

Note that AP6 is independent of the axioms AP1 - AP5. Consider the subsets of {1,2,3} *without* {1,2} as forming the universe of discourse of LP, and interpret "tPt′" as saying that t and t′ are each one of these sets and that t is a subset of t′. Then AP1 - AP5 are fulfilled, but we also have the truth of a counter-instance to AP6: {3}P**conj***y*(*y*={1} or *y*={2}) and not M({3}) and not **some***k′*(*k′*P{3} and not M(*k′*) and **some***z*(*k′*P*z* and (*z*={1} or *z*={2}))), since in the model **conj***y*(*y*={1} or *y*={2}) is not {1,2}, but {1,2,3}. (AP5, on the other hand, is independent of AP1 - AP4, AP6. The model for proving the independence of AP5 in I.6.(c) proves this, too, since not only AP1 - AP4, but also AP6 are verified by it.)

(c) The connection axiom makes it possible to prove *the principle of allotment*:

TP37 **all***z***all***z′***all***x*(if *x*P**conj**(*z*,*z′*) and not M(*x*), then **some***k′*(*k′*P*x* and not M(*k′*) and (*k′*P*z* or *k′*P*z′*))).

Assume that a non-tautological state of affairs *x* is analytically implied by the conjunction of states of affairs *z* and *z′*. One cannot conclude from this that *x* is analytically implied by *z* or by *z′*.But according to TP37 one can at least conclude that *some non-tautological state of affairs that is analytically implied by x* is also analytically implied by *z* or by *z′*. TP37 is called "principle of allotment," because it states that for every non-minimal part of a conjunction of wholes there is a non-minimal part of that part that is *allotted* either to the first or the second member or to both members of the conjunction. By using the principle of allotment we can prove a theorem which is a *restricted* converse of TP25:

TP38 **all***z***all***z′***all***x*(if QA(*x*) and *x*P**conj**(*z*,*z′*), then *x*P*z* or *x*P*z′*).

A quasi-atom that is part of a conjunction is invariably allotted to (at least) one of the members of the conjunction; it is small enough for this, so to speak.

(d) From TP38 one can deduce, using TP25 and TP20,

TP39 **all***x*(if QA(*x*), then **all***z***all***z′*(*x*P**conj***y*(*y*P*z* or *y*P*z′*) iff *x*P*z* or *x*P*z′*)).

One might surmise that this is a special case of a more general theorem:

(i) **all***x*(if QA(*x*), then (*x***Pconj***y*A[*y*] iff A[*x*])).
But in fact this cannot be proved, and indeed it is easily refuted: QA(**t**) and **tPconj***y*(*y*≠*y*), but **t**=**t**.
(ii) **all***x*(if QA(*x*) and not M(*x*), then (*x***Pconj***y*A[*y*] iff A[*x*])), on the other hand, has unbearable consequences: **k**=**conj***y*(*y*=**k**) [TP33] and **all***x*(*x***Pk**) [T(**k**)], hence **all***x*(if QA(*x*) and not M(*x*), then *x***Pconj***y*(*y*=**k**)), hence by (ii) **all***x*(if QA(*x*) and not M(*x*), then *x*=**k**), hence by TP32 **all***x*(if QA(*x*), then *x*=**t** or *x*=**k**). From this one obtains again that the universe of discourse comprises at most **t** and **k** (compare above section (a), **(ii)**): assume *z*≠**t**, hence, since **tP***z*, by AP3 not *z***Pt**, hence by AP5 **some***x*(QA(*x*) and *x*P*z* and not *x***Pt**); hence, by the underlined statement and AP2, **some***x*(QA(*x*) and *x*P*z* and *x*=**k**), hence **kP***z*, hence, since *z***Pk**, by AP3 *z*=**k**. ((ii), by the way, is a consequence of TP18 and proposal **(iv)** in (a), if "and not M(*k*′)" is inserted into its consequent.)
However, on the basis of the connection axiom we can prove:

TP40 **all***x*[if QA(*x*) and not M(*x*), then (*x***Pconj***y*A[*y*] iff **some***z*(*x*P*z* and A[*z*]))].

(In the presence of AP1 - AP5, AP6 is equivalent to "**all***x*[if QA(*x*) and not M(*x*) and *x***Pconj***y*A[*y*], then **some***z*(*x*P*z* and A[*z*])]," since "**all***x*[if not M(*x*), then **some***x*′(QA(*x*′) and not M(*x*′) and *x*′P*x*)]" is a theorem obtainable from AP1 - AP5: assume not M(*x*), and assume for *reductio* **all***x*′(if QA(*x*′) and *x*′P*x*, then M(*x*′)); hence by TP28 **conj***y*(QA(*y*) and *y*P*x*)**Pconj***y*M(*y*); **conj***y*M(*y*)=**t** [TP32, TP29, TP30], and **conj***y*(QA(*y*) and *y*P*x*)=*x* [TP31]; hence *x***Pt**, hence by TP36 and TP32: M(*x*) - contradiction.) From TP40 results

TP41 **all***x*(if QA(*x*) and not M(*x*), then (*x***Pconj***y*(QA(*y*) and A[*y*]) iff A[*x*])).

(Given QA(*x*) and not M(*x*), **some***z*(*x*P*z* and QA(*z*) and A[*z*]) is equivalent to A[*x*].)
Further we have:

TP42 **conj***y*(QA(*y*) and A[*y*])=**conj***y*(QA(*y*) and not M(*y*) and A[*y*]).

By the definition

DP20 EL(t) := QA(t) and not M(t)
("t is an element")[*1],

and the theorems TP41 and TP42 we obtain

TP43 **all***x*(if EL(*x*), then (*x***Pconj***y*(EL(*y*) and A[*y*]) iff A[*x*])).

TP43 is rather similar to the set-theoretical *principle of abstraction*. The similarity can be still further increased by using the definition

DP21 t∈t′ := EL(t) and tPt′.
("t is an element of t′.")

TP43 then amounts to

TP44 **all***x*(*x*∈ **conj***y*(EL(*y*) and A[*y*]) iff EL(*x*) and A[*x*]).[*2]

(e) Let us now consider the singular term "**conj***y*(QA(*y*) and not *y*P*x*)."
First we have:

TP45 **all***x*[**all***z*(if *z*P*x* and *z*P**conj***y*(QA(*y*) and not *y*P*x*), then M(*z*)) and **all***k*(if **all***z*(if *z*P*x* and *z*P*k*, then M(*z*)), then *k*P**conj***y*(QA(*y*) and not *y*P*x*))].

TP45 justifies DP14 in view of TP15, and we can easily deduce

TP46 **all***x*[**all***z*(if *z*P*x* and *z*P**neg**$_1$(*x*), then M(*z*)) and **all***k*(if **all***z*(*z*P*x* and *z*P*k*, then M(*z*)), then *k*P**neg**$_1$(*x*))]

and

TP47 **all***x*(**neg**$_1$(*x*)=**conj***y*(QA(*y*) and not *y*P*x*)).

Second we have

TP48 **all***x*[**all***z*(if *x*P*z* and **conj***y*(QA(*y*) and not *y*P*x*)P*z*, then T(*z*)) and **all***k*(if **all***z*(if *x*P*z* and *k*P*z*, then T(*z*)), then **conj***y*(QA(*y*) and not *y*P*x*)P*k*)].

TP48 justifies DP15 in view of TP15, and we can easily deduce

TP49 **all***x*[**all***z*(if *x*P*z* and **neg**$_2$(*x*)P*z*, then T(*z*)) and **all***k*(if **all***z*(if *x*P*z* and *k*P*z*, then T(*z*)), then **neg**$_2$(*x*)P*k*)]

and

TP50 **all***x*(**neg**$_2$(*x*)=**conj***y*(QA(*y*) and not *y*P*x*)).

Third we have

TP51 **all***x*(**neg**$_1$(*x*)=**neg**$_2$(*x*)).
(Depending on TP47 and TP50.)

TP51 justifies DP16 in view of TP15, and we can conclude

TP52 **all***x*(**neg**(*x*)=**neg**$_1$(*x*) and **neg**(*x*)=**neg**$_2$(*x*)).[*3]

COMMENTS

[*1] On p. 334 of his "On the Foundations of Boolean Algebra" Tarski presents five general equivalences for his concept of *atom*, which - as is clear from the definition he presents - amounts to our concept of *element*. All these equivalences are provable in the set-theoretically embedded system of *extended Boolean algebra* (see [*3]). Rewritten in the system used here, the first three of the mentioned five equivalences are
(i) **all***x*[EL(*x*) iff **all***y*(not *x*P*y* iff *x***Pneg**(*y*))],
(ii) **all***x*[EL(*x*) iff *x*≠**t** and **all***y***all***z*(if *x*=**conj**(*y*,*z*), then *x*=*y* or *x*=*z*)],
(iii) **all***x*[EL(*x*) iff *x*≠**t** and **all***y***all***z*(if *x***Pconj**(*y*,*z*), then *x*P*y* or *x*P*z*)].
The other two equivalences can only be represented in one direction of implication, since, unlike Tarski, we are not working in a set-theoretical framework:
(iv*) **all***x*(if EL(*x*), then (if *x*=**conj***y*A[*y*], then A[*x*])),
(v*) **all***x*[if EL(*x*), then (if *x***Pconj***y*A[*y*], then **some***y*(A[*y*] and *x*P*y*))].
(i) is TP83 (see I.10.(e)); (iii) from left to right is a consequence of TP38, applying DP20 and TP32; (v*) is a consequence of TP40, applying DP20. The rest can also be proved in AP1 - AP6:
Concerning (iv*): Assume EL(*x*) and *x*=**conj***y*A[*y*], hence by (v*) and AP2: **some***y*′(A[*y*′] and **conj***y*A[*y*]P*y*′); by TP18: *y*′**Pconj***y*A[*y*]; hence, by AP3, *y*′=**conj***y*A[*y*]; hence *y*′=*x*; therefore A[*x*], since A[*y*′].
Concerning (ii), *from left to right*: Assume EL(*x*); hence *x*≠**t** [DP20, TP32]; assume *x*=**conj**(*y*,*z*) (hence by AP2: *x***Pconj**(*y*,*z*)); hence *y*P*x* and *z*P*x* [TP25, AP2]; by (iii), from left to right: *x*P*y* or *x*P*z*; therefore by AP3: *x*=*y* or *x*=*z*.
Concerning (ii), *from right to left*: Assume *x*≠**t** and **all***y***all***z*(if *x*=**conj**(*y*,*z*), then *x*=*y* or *x*=*z*); hence not M(*x*) [TP32]; assume: *k*P*x* and not M(*k*); consider **f**(*x*,*k*) := **conj***y*(QA(*y*) and *y*P*x* and not *y*P*k*);
1) **conj**(*k*,**f**(*x*,*k*))P*x*: **all***y*(if QA(*y*) and *y*P*x* and not *y*P*k*, then QA(*y*) and *y*P*x*), hence by TP28 **f**(*x*,*k*)**Pconj***y*(QA(*y*) and *y*P*x*), hence by TP31 **f**(*x*,*k*)P*x*; therefore, since according to assumption *k*P*x*, **conj**(*k*,**f**(*x*,*k*))P*x* [by TP24].
2) *x***Pconj**(*k*,**f**(*x*,*k*)): assume QA(*y*) and *y*P*x* and not *y*Pk; hence by TP18: *y***Pf**(*x*,*k*); therefore: **all***y*(if QA(*y*) and *y*P*x*, then *y*P*k* or *y***Pf**(*x*,*k*)), hence by TP28 **conj***y*(QA(*y*) and *y*P*x*)**Pconj***y*(*y*P*k* or *y***Pf**(*x*,*k*)), hence by TP20 and TP31: *x***Pconj**(*k*, **f**(*x*,*k*)).
From 1) and 2) with AP3: *x*=**conj**(*k*,**f**(*x*,*k*)); hence on the basis of the assumption: *x*=*k* or *x*=**f**(*x*,*k*). But **f**(*x*,*k*)≠*x*: since not M(*k*), **some***z*(QA(*z*) and not M(*z*) and *z*P*k*) [see the proof in section (d), below TP40]; *z*P*x* with AP1 because of *k*P*x*, and not *z***Pf**(*k*,*x*) with TP41 because of *z*P*k*. Therefore *x*=*k*. We have now deduced from the assumption "*k*P*x* and not M(*k*)" *x*=*k* for arbitrary

k; therefore: **all***k*(if *k*P*x*, then *k*=*x* or M(*k*)), hence QA(*x*) by DP6. From the underlined results by DP20: EL(*x*).
Concerning (iii), *from right to left*: The proof is an adaptation of the one just given: we have *x***Pconj**(*k*,**f**(*x*,*k*)) and conclude on the basis of the assumption: *x*P*k* or *x*P**f**(*x*,*k*). But not *x*P**f**(*x*,*k*); else **f**(*x*,*k*)=*x* by AP3, since **f**(*x*,*k*)P*x* (see above); however, **f**(*x*,*k*)≠*x* (see above). Therefore *x*P*k*; hence *x*=*k* by AP3, since according to assumption *k*P*x*. The rest is clear.
Concerning the relationship between the concept of *element* and the concept of *atom* used *here* (which, while being the usual one, is like Tarski's concept not quite in accordance with the etymology of the word: according to etymology, the definiens of "atom" ought to be "is indivisible," that is "has not two proper parts [is a non-compositum]"), the following can be said: From "not **some***x*M(*x*)" we get, using the definitions: **all***x*(EL(*x*) iff A(*x*)); from **all***x*(EL(*x*) iff A(*x*)) we get "not **some***x*M(*x*)," using the definitions and TP7 (which is based on AP3). (The same is true of "**all***x*(EL(*x*) iff QA(*x*)).") If one assumes that at least two entities are in the universe of discourse, then "not **some***x*M(*x*)" is a consequence of extensional (Leśniewskian) mereology (see "On the Foundations of Boolean Algebra," p. 333, footnote; one finds there also some remarks by Tarski concerning the relationship between extended Boolean algebra and mereology), therefore in extensional mereology (with at least two entities): **all***x*(EL(*x*) iff A(*x*)) (and also: **all***x*(EL(*x*) iff QA(*x*)); the three concepts "A(*x*)", "EL(*x*)" and "QA(*x*)" are provably co-extensional in extensional mereology). This is so, because there we have the principle: **all***x***all***y*[if *x*P**y*, then **some***z*(*z*P**y* and not **some***k*(*k*P*z* and *k*P*x*))] (see Simons, *Parts*, p. 37: SA3; and p. 28: *Weak Supplementation Principle*).

[*2] The closest formal similarity, however, does not obtain between "∈" (as defined by DP21) and the "∈" of set theory, but between "∈" and the "ε" (*singular inclusion*) of *Leśniewski's Ontology*, in short: Ontology$_L$; this is not Leśniewski's First Philosophy, but a formal system with a certain favored interpretation: the theory of individual, empty and general (non-individual, non-empty) names (see G. Küng, *Ontologie und logistische Analyse der Sprache*, p. 92ff). In the principles T1, T5, T17, T18 - T27 in C. Lejewski, "Zu Leśniewskis Ontologie," pp. 59-62, we replace "ε" by "∈" and translate their logical notation into the logical notation used here. Then we read all these general equivalences as definitions; in this way the predicates of Ontology$_L$ - strong inclusion, weak inclusion, particular inclusion, singular exclusion, etc. - are defined merely by "∈" (and logical expressions). The original single axiom of Ontology$_L$ (see "Zu Leśniewskis Ontologie," p. 62: T34), reformulated with the logical notation used here (and with "∈" instead of "ε"), turns into the following statement: **all***x***all***y*(*x*∈*y* iff **some***z*(*z*∈*x*) and **all***z*(if *z*∈*x*, then *z*∈*y*) and **all***z***all***z*′(if *z*∈*x* and *z*′∈*x*, then *z*∈*z*′)). This becomes (according to DP21, after elimination of redundancies): **all***x***all***y*[EL(*x*) and *x*P*y* iff **some***z*(EL(*z*) and *z*P*x*)

and **all**z(if EL(z) and zPx, then zPy) and **all**z**all**z'(if EL(z) and zPx and EL(z') and z'Px, then zPz')] - a statement that can be proved in the system AP1, AP3, AP5 (plus definitions):
(i) Assume EL(x) and xPy; according to AP2 (a logical consequence of AP5): xPx, hence - by the assumption - **some**z(EL(z) and zPx); from xPy - by AP1 - **all**z(if EL(z) and zPx, then zPy); assume also EL(z) and zPx and EL(z') and z'Px; hence - because of EL(x) and according to DP20, DP6 - z=x and z'=x, hence z=z', hence by AP2 zPz'.
(ii) Assume: **some**z(EL(z) and zPx) and **all**z(if EL(z) and zPx, then zPy) and **all**z**all**z'(if EL(z) and zPx and EL(z') and z'Px, then zPz'); assume also: QA(z) and zPx; in case M(z), then zPy (according to DP4); in case not M(z), then EL(z) [according to DP20, since QA(z)], hence, according to assumption, zPy; therefore, from the first assumption, **all**z(if QA(z) and zPx, then zPy), hence by AP5 xPy. According to assumption: **some**z(EL(z) and zPx); if not xPz, then - by AP5 - **some**z'(QA(z') and z'Px and not z'Pz), hence, since not M(z'), according to DP20: **some**z'(EL(z') and z'Px and not z'Pz) - but this contradicts **all**z**all**z'(if EL(z) and zPx and EL(z') and z'Px, then zPz'); therefore: xPz, hence, since zPx, by AP3 x=z, hence, since EL(z), EL(x).

The proof shows that Ontology$_L$, as a formal system, is a deductive part of the system determined by AP1, AP3, AP5 (and definitions).

Ontology$_L$ can also be formulated by using the *predicate of weak inclusion* as its single non-logical primitive. This predicate corresponds to "P"; if we represent it by "P" (and continue to represent "ε" by "∈"), we obtain the following transliteration of Lejewski's definition of "ε":

t∈t′ := **some**y not tPy and tPt′ and **all**k**all**k'**all**k''(if kPt and k'Pt, then kPk' or k'Pk'').

And Sobociński's single axiom of Ontology$_L$ (with weak inclusion as its single non-logical primitive) turns into

(S) **all**x**all**y[xPy iff **all**z**all**z'(if not zPz' and zPx and **all**k**all**k'**all**k''(if kPz and k'Pz, then kPk' or k'Pk''), then zPy)].

(Compare "Zu Leśniewskis Ontologie," p. 64f: T54; T57.)

(S),AP3 is (given DP6, DP4) deductively equivalent to AP1,AP3,AP5; Lejewski's definition (or rather, the general principle corresponding to it) is a theorem of the latter system (using DP20 and DP21; the basic theorem is **all**x**all**y(QA(x) and not M(x) and xPy iff **some**z not xPz and xPy and **all**k**all**k'**all**k''(if kPx and k'Px, then kPk' or k'Pk''); DP21, on the other hand, is a theorem of the former system (using DP20 and Lejewski's definition; the basic theorem is the same).

It should not go unmentioned that adding AP3 to (S) is not in the spirit of the favored interpretation of Ontology$_L$ as a theory of names (see above): if all entities that are designated by name *a* are also designated by name *b*, and vice versa, this does not imply that *a* and *b* designate one and the same entity (consider general or empty names).

[*3] In "On the Foundations of Boolean Algebra," p. 321ff, Tarski formulates a set-theoretically embedded system of Boolean algebra (an "*extended* (or *complete*) *system of Boolean algebra*"). If the notation which is used in this book is set-theoretically enhanced, his postulate A_1 amounts to
(a) **all***x*(if *x*∈**B**, then *x*P*x*), (b) **all***x***all***y***all***z*(if *x*∈**B** and *y*∈**B** and *z*∈**B** and *x*P*y* and *y*P*z*, then *x*P*z*);
his postulate A_2 amounts to
all*x***all***y*(if *x*∈**B** and *y*∈**B**, then (*x*=*y* iff *x*P*y* and *y*P*x*));
and his postulate A_8 amounts to
all*x*[if *x*⊆**B**, then **conj***y*(*y*∈*x*)∈**B** and **all***z*(if *z*∈*x*, then *z*P**conj***y*(*y*∈*x*)) and **all***z*′(if *z*′∈**B** and **all***z*(if *z*∈*x*, then *z*P*z*′), then **conj***y*(*y*∈*x*)P*z*′)].

These postulates *correspond* in an obvious manner ("**B**" being taken to refer to the universe of discourse, "*y*∈*x*" being replaced by "A[*y*]") to AP1 - AP3 and TP18 (which because of AP3 and DP17 is equivalent to AP4). The principles corresponding in the manner indicated to the remaining postulates of Tarski's system A_1 - A_{10} can all be proved in the system AP1 - AP6 (plus definitions), as will become manifest in the next two chapters.

Tarski himself proves the deductive equivalence of A_1 - A_{10} (system A) with (system B) B_1 - B_4 (plus definitions; see p. 324ff), which can be formulated in the notation used in the present work, if this notation is set-theoretically enhanced, as follows:
B_1 **all***x***all***y*(if *x*∈**B** and *y*∈**B** and *x*P*y* and *y*P*x*, then *x*=*y*);
B_2 **all***x***all***y***all***z*(if *x*∈**B** and *y*∈**B** and *z*∈**B** and *x*P*y* and *y*P*z*, then *x*P*z*);
B_3 **all***x***all***y*[if *x*∈**B** and *y*∈**B** and not *x*P*y*, then **some***z*(*z*∈**B** and *z*P*x* and not *z*P*y* and **all***k*(if *k*∈**B** and *k*P*y* and *k*P*z*, then **all***v*(if *v*∈**B**, then *k*P*v*)))];
B_4 **all***x*[if *x*⊆**B**, then **some***x*′[*x*′∈**B** and **all***y*(if *y*∈*x*, then *y*P*x*′) and **all***z*(if *z*∈**B** and *z*P*x*′ and **all***y*(if *y*∈*x*, then **all***k*(if *k*∈**B** and *k*P*y* and *k*P*z*, then **all***v*(if *v*∈**B**, then *k*P*v*))), then **all***v*(if *v*∈**B**, then *z*P*v*))]]; *more perspicuously*: **all***x*[if *x*⊆**B**, then **some***x*′[*x*′∈**B** and **all***y*(if *y*∈*x*, then *y*P*x*′) and **all***z*(if *z*∈**B** and *z*P*x*′ and **all***y*(if *y*∈*x*, then **all***k*(if *k*∈**B** and *k*P*y* and *k*P*z*, then M_B(*k*))), then M_B(*z*))]].

The principle *without set-theoretical terms* "**some***x*′[**all***y*(if A[*y*], then *y*P*x*′) and **all***z*(if *z*P*x*′ and **all***y*(if A[*y*], then **all***k*(if *k*P*y* and *k*P*z*, then M(*k*))), then M(*z*))]" corresponds to B_4; it can be proved with the help of AP6:
all*y*(if A[*y*], then *y*P**conj***x*A[*x*]) [according to TP18]. Assume *z*P**conj***x*A[*x*]; assume also: not M(*z*); hence by AP6 **some***k*(*k*P*z* and not M(*k*) and **some***y*(*k*P*y* and A[*y*])), hence **some***y*(A[*y*] and **some***k*(*k*P*y* and *k*P*z* and not M(*k*))); this shows (by contraposition) that from *z*P**conj***x*A[*x*] and **all***y*(if A[*y*], then **all***k*(if *k*P*y* and *k*P*z*, then M(*k*))) we get M(*z*). The rest is clear.

The principle without set-theoretical terms corresponding to B_3 - **all***x***all***y*[if not *x*P*y*, then **some***z*(*z*P*x* and not *z*P*y* and **all***k*(if *k*P*y* and *k*P*z*, then M(*k*)))] - is also provable in AP1 - AP6 (B_1 and B_2 are, of course, represented by the axioms AP3 and AP1):

Assume: not *x*P*y*; hence by AP5: **some***z*(QA(*z*) and *z*P*x* and not *z*P*y*); assume *k*P*z* and *k*P*y*, and assume for *reductio*: not M(*k*); hence, since QA(*z*), *k*=*z* (according to DP6), and therefore *z*P*y* - contradicting not *z*P*y*.

In Tarski's proof of the equivalence of systems A and B the definitions used (see B_5, B_6) for +,·,0,1,′,Σ,Π correspond precisely to those here presented for **conj**,**disj**,**t**,**k**,**neg**,**conj***y*,**disj***y* - excepting the one for **neg** whose structure differs from Tarski's definition for ′. The precise translation of Tarski's definition - **Tneg**(t) := **the***y*[**all***z*(if *z*Pt and *z*P*y*, then M(*z*)) and **all***z*(if tP*z* and *y*P*z*, then T(*z*))] - is, however, provably equivalent to the definition of **neg** given here (DP16): according to TP45, TP48 and AP3 (and AP1) we have: **all***x*(**Tneg**(*x*)=**conj***y*(QA(*y*) and not *y*P*x*)), and consequently **all***x*(**Tneg**(*x*)= **neg**(*x*)) by TP50 and TP52.

On p. 334 Tarski defines "*x* is an atom" (in his notation "*x*∈At") just as we have here defined "*x* is an element" ("EL(*x*)"); therefore the principle "**all***x*(if *x*≠**t**, then **some***y*(EL(*y*) and *y*P*x*))" (which is provable with the help of AP5: the main part of the proof - the rest being obvious - has already been presented in section (d) of this chapter, below the presentation of TP40) corresponds to his *postulate of atomism* D on p. 335.

We can conclude that the deductive power of AP1 - AP6 (plus definitions) is at least as great as that of the representation in LP of Tarski's (set-theoretically formulated) *atomistic system of Boolean algebra*: A_1 - A_{10} (or B_1 - B_4), D (p. 335). Presumably it is not greater.

Note finally that the system obtained from AP1 - AP6 by replacing AP5 by D′, **all***x*(if not M(*x*), then **some***y*(EL(*y*) and *y*P*x*)), is weaker than AP1 - AP6. Take the natural numbers from 0 to 10 as constituting the universe of discourse of LP, and let "*x*P*y*" mean the same as "*x*∈{0, ..., 10} and *y*∈{0, ..., 10} and *x*≤*y*." Then AP1 - AP4 and AP6 turn out to be true, and so does D′, since "EL(1) and **all***x*(if not M(*x*), then 1P*x*)" is true in the model. AP5, however, is false in the model: "**all***z*(if QA(*z*) and *z*P5, then *z*P4)" is true in it, since 0 and 1 are its only quasi-atoms; but "5P4" is false in it. (D′, like AP5, is, however, independent of AP1 - AP4, AP6; the model in I.6.(c) demonstrates this, too.)

CHAPTER I.8

THEOREMS FOR NEGATION, CONJUNCTION AND DISJUNCTION

(a) Negation, conjunction and disjunction (as the defined expressions "**neg**", "**conj**" and "**disj**" are to be read, given that the universe of discourse consists precisely of all states of affairs) are Boolean functional terms; for we can prove:

TP53
(i) **all**_x_(**conj**(_x_,**t**)=_x_ and **disj**(_x_,**k**)=_x_);
(ii) **all**_x_(**conj**(_x_,**neg**(_x_))=**k** and **disj**(_x_,**neg**(_x_))=**t**);
(iii) **all**_x_**all**_y_(**conj**(_x_,_y_)=**conj**(_y_,_x_) and **disj**(_x_,_y_)=**disj**(_y_,_x_));
(iv) **all**_x_**all**_y_**all**_z_[**conj**(_x_,**disj**(_y_,_z_))=**disj**(**conj**(_x_,_y_),**conj**(_x_,_z_))];
(v) **all**_x_**all**_y_**all**_z_[**disj**(_x_,**conj**(_y_,_z_))=**conj**(**disj**(_x_,_y_), **disj**(_x_,_z_))].

(b) These "minor" principles, as is well known, suffice for proving the following "minor," but highly useful and familiar principles (for states of affairs as much as for other Boolean entities), since TP53 is a formulation of *ordinary Boolean algebra*. But their proofs solely on the basis of TP53 are mere exercises in logical acrobatics (see, as an example, the proof of TP55 in the Appendix); therefore, starting with TP56 I gladly revert to using "major" principles.

TP54 **neg**(**t**)=**k** and **neg**(**k**)=**t**.

TP55 **all**_x_[_x_=**neg**(**neg**(_x_))].

TP56 **all**_x_**all**_y_[**neg**(**disj**(_x_,_y_))=**conj**(**neg**(_x_),**neg**(_y_))].

TP57 **all**_x_**all**_y_[**disj**(_x_,_y_)=**neg**(**conj**(**neg**(_x_),**neg**(_y_)))].
(By TP56, TP55.)

(c) In the proof of TP61 we need

TP58 **all**_x_**all**_y_**all**_z_(if _x_P_y_, then **disj**(_x_,_z_)P**disj**(_y_,_z_)).

We also have the very useful *theorem of contraposition*:

TP59 **all**_x_**all**_y_(_x_P_y_ iff **neg**(_y_)P**neg**(_x_)).

From TP59 we easily obtain (by using TP55)

TP60 **allxally**(*x***Pneg**(*y*) iff *y***Pneg**(*x*)) and **allxally**(**neg**(*x*)P*y* iff **neg**(*y*)P*x*).

We define:

DP22 **impl**(t,t′) := **disj**(**neg**(t),t′).
("the implication from t to t′.")

By DP22 "the implication from t to t′" is defined in analogy to a frequently used definition of the sentence-connective of *material implication* in propositional logic. And we have the following theorem:

TP61 **allxally**[*x*->*y* iff M(**impl**(*x*,*y*))].

According to TP61, given the chosen universe of discourse of LP, a state of affairs *x* analytically implies a state of affairs *y*, precisely if the implication from *x* to *y* is a minimal ("tautological") state of affairs (in other words: if the implication from *x* to *y* is identical to **t**). This is the ontological correlate of the principle that a *statement* S analytically implies a *statement* S′, precisely if the *material implication* of S′ by S is *analytically true*. The correlation is closest when "S is analytically true" - not entirely true to its most commonly accepted meaning (see Introduction, comment [*2]) - is interpreted as "S is a statement that is true in every possible world," since a state of affairs is minimal precisely if it obtains in every possible world (considered as states of affairs); see TP86 and TP90 in chapter I.11.

CHAPTER I.9

THE BIG DISJUNCTION

(a) Just as there is a "big" conjunction that is a generalization of the "small" conjunction, so there is a "big" disjunction that is a generalization of the small one:

DP23 **disj***x*A[*x*] := **the***z*[**all***x*(if A[*x*], then *z*P*x*) and **all***y*(if **all***x*(if A[*x*], then *y*P*x*), then *y*P*z*)].
("the disjunction of all *x* such that A[*x*].")

By DP23 the disjunction of all *x* such that A[*x*] is defined as the greatest whole that is part of every whole that satisfies A[*x*]. In consideration of the chosen universe of discourse, the disjunction of all states of affairs that satisfy A[*x*] is the intensionally strongest state of affairs that is analytically implied by every state of affairs that satisfies A[*x*].

(b) According to AP3 there is *at most one z* for any given A[*x*] that fulfills the description in the definiens of DP23. That for any given A[*x*] there is also *some z* fulfilling the description in the definiens of DP23 need not be postulated, since it follows already from AP1 - AP4:

TP62 **all***x*[if A[*x*], then **conj***k***all***y*′(if A[*y*′], then *k*P*y*′)P*x*] and **all***y*[if **all***x*(if A[*x*], then *y*P*x*), then *y*P**conj***k***all***y*′(if A[*y*′], then *k*P*y*′)].

As a straightforward consequence of the results just mentioned, we have according to the logic of definite descriptions and DP23:

TP63 **disj***x*A[*x*]=**conj***y***all***x*(if A[*x*], then *y*P*x*).

According to TP57, the small disjunction can be expressed (in AP1 - AP6) by the small conjunction and negation. According to TP63, the big disjunction can be expressed merely by the big conjunction - without using negation. But in analogy to TP57 we also have the *generalized De Morgan theorem*

TP64 **disj***x*A[*x*]=**neg(conj***y***some***x*[A[*x*] and *y*=**neg**(*x*)]).[*1]

(c) The big disjunction is just as efficient in unifying Boolean functional terms as is the big conjunction. We can formulate an axiomatic system of the ontology of states of affairs that is appropriate for the big disjunction and which is deductively equivalent to AP1 - AP6 (on the basis of the definitions given) merely by replacing AP4 by AP4′: the existential generalization of TP62. (However, for reasons of symmetry it is aesthetically more satisfying to replace AP6 and AP5, too: AP5 by AP5′: **all***x***all***y*(if **all***z*(if QC(*z*) and *x*P*z*, then *y*P*z*), then *y*P*x*), and AP6 by AP6′: **all***x*[if **disj***y*A[*y*]P*x* and not T(*x*), then **some***k*′(*x*P*k*′ and not T(*k*′) and **some***z*(*z*P*k*′ and A[*z*]))].) Note that AP4 is deducible from the existential generalization of TP62 (AP4′) without using in the deduction AP1, AP5 or AP6, just as, conversely, TP62, and hence its existential generalization, is deducible from AP4 without applying AP1, AP5 or AP6 (check the proof of TP62 and the proofs of the theorems used in it); the deduction is merely a matter of AP2 and AP3. This is seen as follows. From the existential generalization of TP62 one obtains by AP3 and DP23

TP65 **all***x*(if A[*x*], then **disj***z*A[*z*]P*x*) and **all***y*(if **all***x*(if A[*x*], then *y*P*x*), then *y*P**disj***z*A[*z*]).

From TP65 we immediately get

TP66 if **all***x*(if A[*x*], then B[*x*]), then **disj***z*B[*z*]P**disj***z*A[*z*],

and, using AP2 and AP3, we obtain

TP67 **all***z*(*z*=**disj***z*′(*z*P*z*′)).

Consider now "**disj***k***all***y*′(if A[*y*′], then *y*′P*k*)." As a matter of predicate logic we have: **all***x*(if A[*x*], then **all***k*(if **all***y*′(if A[*y*′], then *y*′P*k*), then *x*P*k*)); hence by TP66 **all***x*(if A[*x*], then **disj***k*(*x*P*k*)P**disj***k***all***y*′(if A[*y*′], then *y*′P*k*)), hence by TP67 <u>**all***x*(if A[*x*], then *x*P**disj***k***all***y*′(if A[*y*′], then *y*′P*k*))</u>. Moreover we have according to TP65: <u>**all***x*(if **all***y*′(if A[*y*′], then *y*′P*x*), then **disj***k***all***y*′(if A[*y*′], then *y*′P*k*)P*x*)</u>. AP4 is an immediate consequence of the underlined results.

Because of TP16 and TP18 (which result from AP3, AP4 and DP17) we further have:

TP68 **conj***x*A[*x*]=**disj***y***all***x*(if A[*x*], then *x*P*y*).

TP68 shows that the big conjunction is definable by the big disjunction in an axiom-system that contains AP2 and AP3 and the existential generalization of TP62 instead of AP4. However, the big conjunction, it seems, is closer to our intuition than the big disjunction, since considering sums is easier for us than considering greatest common parts ("products," "nuclei"); moreover, considering a Boolean universe from the bottom (from the level of quasi-atoms), which fits the first approach, is easier for us than considering it from the top (from the level of quasi-complete wholes), which is appropriate for the second. For these epistemic reasons, the axiom system of the ontology of states of affairs has here been tailored *primarily* to the big conjunction, not to the big disjunction. Ontologically, the latter is completely on a par with the former.

COMMENTS

[*1] ‘‘**all**x(**conj**(x,**disj**yA[y])=**disj**y**some**z'[A[z'] and y=**conj**(x,z')])’’ is a generalization of TP53(iv), and it represents (non-set-theoretically) Tarski's axiom A_{10}(b) (see ‘‘On the Foundations of Boolean Algebra,’’ p. 323). Its proof reads as follows:
(**i**) Assume QA(z) and zP**conj**(x,**disj**yA[y]), hence by TP38: zPx or zP**disj**yA[y];
1) in case zPx: from this by TP25: **all**z'(zP**conj**(x,z')), hence **all**y'(if **some**z'[A[z'] and y'=**conj**(x,z')], then zPy'), hence by TP18 and TP63: zP**disj**y**some**z'[A[z'] and y=**conj**(x,z')];
2) in case zP**disj**yA[y]: from this by TP63 zP**conj**y(**all**y'(if A[y'], then yPy'); if M(z), then, trivially, **all**y'(if A[y'], then zPy'); if not M(z), then by TP40 and AP1: <u>**all**y'(if A[y'], then zPy')</u>; from the underlined result and TP25: **all**y'(if **some**z'[A[z'] and y'=**conj**(x,z')], then zPy'), hence by TP18 and TP63: zP**disj**y**some**z'[A[z'] and y=**conj**(x,z')].
(**ii**) Assume QA(z) and zP**disj**y**some**z'[A[z'] and y=**conj**(x,z')]. If M(z), then trivially zP**conj**(x,**disj**yA[y]). If not M(z), then by TP63, TP40 and AP1: **all**y'(if **some**z'[A[z'] and y'=**conj**(x,z')], then zPy'), hence <u>**all**z'[if A[z'], then zP**conj**(x,z')]</u>;
assume for *reductio*: not zPx and not zP**disj**yA[y]; hence by TP63, TP40: **all**k(if zPk, then **some**z'(A[z'] and not kPz')), hence by AP2 <u>**some**z'[A[z'] and not zPz']</u>; from the underlined results: **some**z'(A[z'] and zP**conj**(x,z') and not zPz'), hence by TP38 zPx - contradicting the assumption for *reductio*.
Therefore: zPx or zP**disj**yA[y], hence by TP25: zP**conj**(x,**disj**yA[y]).
From (**i**) and (**ii**) we obtain by AP5 and AP3 what was to be proved.
‘‘**all**x(**disj**(x,**conj**yA[y])=**conj**y**some**z'[A[z'] and y=**disj**(x,z')])’’ - the principle corresponding to Tarski's axiom A_{10}(a) - is of course also provable.

CHAPTER I.10

POSSIBLE WORLDS AND ELEMENTARY STATES OF AFFAIRS

(a) Analogues of the concepts defined by the following three definitions are highly important in logical semantics for the description of certain central deductive characteristics of sets of formulae. The corresponding ontological concepts are not less important in the ontology of states of affairs.

DP24 K(t) := not **some***x*(*x*Pt and **neg**(*x*)Pt).
("t is consistent.")

DP25 MX(t) := **all***x*(*x*Pt or **neg**(*x*)Pt).
("t is maximal.")[*1]

DP26 MK(t) := MX(t) and K(t).
("t is maximally consistent.")

The definitions immediately imply

TP69 **all***y*[MK(*y*) iff **all***x*(not *x*P*y* iff **neg**(*x*)P*y*)].

According to TP69, a whole *y* is maximally consistent if and only if every whole is such that *either* itself *or* its negation (less suggestive of a certain interpretation of LP: its *complement*) is part of *y*. Hence, in view of the chosen universe of discourse of LP, a maximally consistent state of affairs is a state of affairs that analytically implies either *x* or the negation of *x* (but not both), *x* being *any* state of affairs whatever. This justifies calling maximally consistent states of affairs "possible worlds." Accordingly, "MK(t)" may (and will) also be read as "t is a possible world" (as long as we do not change the universe of discourse, say, from states of affairs to properties of individuals).

The paradigm on which this reading is based - that *the world* (the actual world) is not an individual, but a certain state of affairs: the (maximally consistent) sum of all facts - is proposed by Wittgenstein in the *Tractatus* (see proposition 1.1). Conceiving of possible worlds as states of affairs does not at all force one to hold the modal anti-realist's view that possible worlds are in some way or other *our own constructions*; this view is largely due to the nominalistically inspired erroneous idea that only individuals (and not universals or states of affairs) can be entities that are, as entities, simply "given."

(b) We have the following three important theorems about the concepts just introduced which relate them to simpler concepts:

TP70 **all**x(K(x) iff x≠**k**).

TP71 **all**x(MX(x) iff QC(x)).

TP72 **all**x(MK(x) iff QC(x) and x≠**k**).
(Depending on TP70, TP71 and DP26.)

This means that the concepts of maximality, consistence and maximal-consistence can be expressed in AP1 - AP6 without using the functional expression "**neg**" - by concepts, in fact, that were already introduced in chapter I.2 (since "x≠**k**" can be replaced by "not T(x)" according to TP34).

(c) The following theorems reveal the connection between quasi-atoms and quasi-complete wholes and the connection between *possible worlds* and *elementary states of affairs* (states of affairs that are *elements* in the sense of DP20). The basic theorem is

TP73 **all**x(QA(**neg**(x)) iff QC(x)).

An immediate consequence of TP73 by TP55 is

TP74 **all**x(QA(x) iff QC(**neg**(x))).

Further we have:

TP75 **all**x[QA(x) iff **some**y(QC(y) and x=**neg**(y))].
("The quasi-atoms are precisely the negations of the quasi-complete wholes." Depending on TP74, TP55; TP73.)

TP76 **all**x[QA(x) iff x=**t** or **some**y(MK(y) and x=**neg**(y))].
(With reference to the chosen universe of discourse: "The quasi-atomic states of affairs are (1) the minimal state of affairs, and (2) the negations of the possible worlds.")

TP77 **all**x[EL(x) iff **some**y(MK(y) and x=**neg**(y))].
("The elementary states of affairs are precisely the negations of the possible worlds.")

TP78 **all**x(EL(**neg**(x)) iff MK(x)).

In view of the provability (by TP55) of "**all**x**all**y(if x≠y, then **neg**(x)≠**neg**(y))," TP73 and TP75 explicitly assert that "**neg**" induces a one-to-one-mapping of all quasi-complete wholes upon all quasi-atoms. In view also of the chosen universe of discourse, TP77 and TP78 explicitly assert that "**neg**" also induces a one-to-one-mapping of all possible worlds upon all elementary states of affairs. Thus, there must be just as many possible worlds as there are elementary states of affairs.

Given the intuitive reading of "MK(*x*)" (as "*x* is a possible world"), we can gather from TP76 and TP77 the intuitive reading of "QA(*x*)" and "EL(*x*)" (when these predicates are interpreted with respect to states of affairs). And given this reading, it is manifest that an elementary state of affairs (unlike a minimal one) is not easily expressed (made the intension of a sentence): for expressing an elementary state of affairs one would have to describe *completely* an entire possible world (that is, express a maximally consistent state of affairs), and then put a negation sign in front of the entire description (thus expressing the negation of a maximally consistent state of affairs: an elementary state of affairs). It is also manifest that the intensions of syntactically *elementary statements* are much higher up in the Boolean hierarchy than are elementary states of affairs; supposedly, those intensions are in some sense "elementary" (or "atomic"), but hardly in an ontological sense (they are certainly in a sense *elementary for us*; see also comment [*3] of this chapter).

(d) On the basis of the proved and intuitively satisfactory connection between "QA(*x*)" and "QC(*x*)" ("EL(*x*)" and "MK(*x*)"), we can now come to an intuitive understanding of the import of AP5 (which is definitionally - that is, provably via logic plus definitions - equivalent to "**all***x***all***y*(if **all***z*(if EL(*z*) and *z*P*x*, then *z*P*y*), then *x*P*y*)"). Consider the principle AP5′ (mentioned in I.9.(c)): **all***x***all***y*(if **all***z*(if QC(*z*) and *x*P*z*, then *y*P*z*), then *y*P*x*); it is definitionally equivalent to "**all***x***all***y*(if **all***z*(if QC(*z*) and not T(*z*) and *x*P*z*, then *y*P*z*), then *y*P*x*)," and hence by TP34 and TP72 equivalent to "**all***x***all***y*(if **all***z*(if MK(*z*) and *x*P*z*, then *y*P*z*), then *y*P*x*)," or, in other words, with "if state of affairs *y* obtains in every possible world in which state of affairs *x* obtains, then *y* is analytically implied [or entailed] by *x*." This latter principle is one of the very first principles of possible worlds ontology, call the principle "PWO." It is a consequence of AP5, since AP5′ is a consequence of AP5 (on the basis of the other axioms): assume **all***z*(if QC(*z*) and *x*P*z*, then *y*P*z*), hence **all***z*(if QC(**neg**(*z*)) and *x*P**neg**(*z*), then *y*P**neg**(*z*)), hence by TP74 and TP60 **all***z*(if QA(*z*) and *z*P**neg**(*x*), then *z*P**neg**(*y*)), hence by AP5 **neg**(*x*)P**neg**(*y*), hence by TP59: *y*P*x*. And in the system deductively equivalent to AP1 - AP6 where AP5 is replaced by AP5′, AP4 by AP4′, AP6 by AP6′ (see I.9.(c)) the *equivalence* of AP5 and PWO is a non-trivial theorem.[*2]

Thus AP5 inherits the plausibility of PWO (which is particularly high if possible worlds are considered to be maximally consistent states of affairs). Nevertheless, it must be remembered that, being an atomistic principle, AP5 is a rather far-reaching, and hence potentially controversial statement - much more so than AP4 and AP6 - about the universe of states of affairs. (Quite apart from the intended universe of discourse, AP5 is the principle which makes the system AP1 - AP6 properly *Boolean*; for AP1 - AP4, AP6 - taken by themselves, without AP5 - have some very *un-Boolean* interpretations. See I.6.(c).)

(e) The following theorem concerns how possible worlds are related to each other:

TP79 **all***x***all***y*(if MK(*x*) and MK(*y*) and *x*P*y*, then *y*=*x*).

According to TP79 there is no analytical implication between different possible worlds; they are independent of each other.[*3] Correlatively, there is no analytical implication between different elementary states of affairs; for we also have:

TP80 **all***x***all***y*(if EL(*x*) and EL(*y*) and *x*P*y*, then *x*=*y*).
(Depending on DP20, DP6.)

While "EL(*x*)" and "MK(*x*)" are correlative predicates (in a sense that has become clear), they are not correlatively defined (unlike the correlatives "QA(*x*)" and "QC(*x*)"). But we could very well have defined (in exact correlation to DP26): EL(t) := **all***x*(tP*x* or tP**neg**(*x*)) and not **some***x*(tP*x* and tP**neg**(*x*)), or more concisely: EL(t) := **all***x*(not tP*x* iff tP**neg**(*x*)), and then have obtained "**all***y*(EL(*y*) iff QA(*y*) and not M(*y*))" as a non-trivial theorem (in correspondence to TP72). Given DP20, however, the non-trivial theorem is

TP83 **all***y*[EL(*y*) iff **all***x*(not *y*P*x* iff *y*P**neg**(*x*))].

In both cases the respective theorem is straightforwardly obtainable from two theorems that are independent of the definition of "EL":

TP81 **all***y*[not M(*y*) iff not **some***x*(*y*P*x* and *y*P**neg**(*x*))],

and

TP82 **all***y*[QA(*y*) iff **all***x*(*y*P*x* or *y*P**neg**(*x*))].

Corresponding in an obvious manner to DP24 and DP25 (the "t" merely has switched its position relative to "P"), we can define

DP27 S(t) := not **some***x*(tP*x* and tP**neg**(*x*))
("t is substantial"),

DP28 MN(t) := **all***x*(tP*x* or tP**neg**(*x*))
("t is minute"),

and by TP83 we then have

TP84 **all**y(EL(y) iff MN(y) and S(y)).
("The elementary states of affairs are the minutely substantial states of affairs.")

COMMENTS

[*1] The definiens of DP25 is equivalent to ''**all***x*(if not *x*Pt, then **kPconj**(t,*x*))'' (''t cannot be enlarged without contradiction''):
(i) Assume **all***x*(*x*P*y* or **neg**(*x*)P*y*), not *x*P*y*; hence **neg**(*x*)P*y*; now *y***Pconj**(*y*,*x*) (by TP25); hence by AP1 **neg**(*x*)**Pconj**(*y*,*x*); moreover *x***Pconj**(*y*,*x*) [TP25]. Therefore by TP24: **conj**(*x*,**neg**(*x*))**Pconj**(*y*,*x*), hence by TP53(ii) **kPconj**(*y*,*x*).
(ii) Assume **all***x*(if not *x*P*y*, then **kPconj**(*y*,*x*)), not *x*P*y*; hence **kPconj**(*y*,*x*), hence by TP59 **neg**(**conj**(*y*,*x*))**Pneg**(**k**), hence by TP54 and TP55 **neg**(**conj**[**neg**(**neg**(*y*)),**neg**(**neg**(*x*))])**Pt**, hence by TP57 **disj**(**neg**(*y*),**neg**(*x*))**Pt**, hence by DP22 **impl**(*y*,**neg**(*x*))**Pt**, hence by TP36 and TP32 M(**impl**(*y*,**neg**(*x*))), hence by TP61 and DP11 **neg**(*x*)P*y*.
There is a close analogy between ''**all***x*(if not *x*Pt, then **kPconj**(t,*x*))'' and the definiens most frequently used for defining the maximality of sets of formulae in Henkin-style proofs of completeness.

[*2] Note that a set of possible worlds represents (''is'') the state of affairs which is the ''largest'' state of affairs that all its elements have in common (as obtaining in them). The idea that all states of affairs can be thus represented (i.e. represented in a one-to-one fashion) is mirrored by the principle ''**all***x*(*x*=**disj***y*(MK(*y*) and *x*P*y*),'' which is a consequence of T65, PWO and AP3; PWO, on the other hand, can be obtained from ''**all***x*(*x*=**disj***y*(MK(*y*) and *x*P*y*))'' by TP66 and TP67. This means that PWO and ''**all***x*(*x*=**disj***y*(MK(*y*) and *x*P*y*))'' are deductively equivalent on the basis of AP2, AP3, AP4′ and DP23 (consider I.9.(c)). Compare this with the equivalence result reached for AP5 and ''**all***x*(*x*=**conj***y*(QA(*y*) and *y*P*x*))'' in I.6.(b) (which is easily transformed into an equivalence result for ''**all***x***all***y*(if **all***z*(EL(*z*) and *z*P*x*, then *z*P*y*), then *x*P*y*)'' and ''**all***x*(*x*=**conj***y*(EL(*y*) and *y*P*x*)'').

[*3] We can distinguish the following concepts of independence:
(i) *x* and *y* are *weakly* independent of each other := not *x*P*y* and not *y*P*x*.
In this sense different possible worlds (as states of affairs) are independent of each other.
(ii) *x* and *y* are *strongly* independent of each other := not *x*P*y* and not **neg**(*x*)P*y* and not *y*P*x* and not **neg**(*y*)P*x*.
In the sense of (ii) different possible worlds are not independent of each other. But different elementary states of affairs, if there are more than two such states of affairs, *are* in this sense independent of each other.
(ii) still does not define the strongest concept of independence:

(iii) x and y are *absolutely* independent of each other := not M(x) and not M(y) and **allzallz**′(if not M(z) and not M(z') and zPx and z'Py, then z and z' are strongly independent of each other).

Only non-minimal states of affairs that have "nothing" in common with each other are in this sense independent of each other:

Assume x and y are absolutely independent of each other; hence both are non-minimal, according to (iii); since **disj**(x,y)Px and **disj**(x,y)Py, but **disj**(x,y) and **disj**(x,y) are, trivially, not strongly independent of each other, we have moreover according to (iii): M(**disj**(x,y)) - x and y merely have the tautological state of affairs in common with each other (consider the definition DP13 of "**disj**"), and this is as much as "nothing."

(Note that elementary states of affairs are absolutely independent of each other if and only if they are strongly independent of each other.)

With the atomicity of states of affairs there is frequently associated their "logical" independence (as we are speaking of ontological matters, "logical" is not quite the appropriate term here), for example by Wittgenstein; see E. Stenius, *Wittgenstein's Tractatus*, p. 33f. However, the states of affairs that are usually regarded as atomic states of affairs (Russell in "The Philosophy of Logical Atomism," p. 176: "The simplest imaginable facts are those which consist in the possession of a quality by some particular thing. Such facts, say, as 'This is white'.") are not at all atomic in the sense used here (not even, of course, if we let "atomic" be synonymous with "elementary" in our preferred sense of this term). In keeping with this, they are not strongly independent of each other: *that this is not entirely red* is analytically implied by *that this is entirely white*; hence *that this is entirely red* is not strongly independent of *that this is entirely white*.

Very frequently *epistemic simplicity* (as a comparative or absolute concept) is confused with *ontological simplicity* (as a comparative or absolute concept). For example, **disj**(x,y) is often regarded as being a state of affairs that is more complex than both state of affairs x and state of affairs y. But **disj**(x,y) is not in any way composed out of x and y; rather, being an intensional part of both, it is normally a *proper intensional part* of both, hence *ontologically simpler* than both. But suppose x and y are, for example, important basic objects of perception, so that we have simple sentences to express them. Then our primary epistemic interest in x and y may justify us in saying that they are *epistemically simpler* than **disj**(x,y), and perhaps even in saying that they are *epistemically simple tout court*. Ontological simplicity, however, is something else. (But is x not ontologically simpler than **disj**(x,y) in virtue of its having less *constituents*? If this were a good criterion, we would have to regard *that F(a)* as being ontologically simpler than *that F(a) and b=b* if a is different from b, although these states of affairs - we are talking of *coarse-grained* states of affairs - are identical. But nothing can be ontologically simpler than itself.)

CHAPTER I.11

POSSIBILITY AND NECESSITY

(a) States of affairs are the primary subjects of the predicates "possible" and "necessary," and a state of affairs is *analytically necessary* if and only if its negation is not *analytically possible*. In the philosophical tradition there are, however, two definitions of the concept of analytical possibility. According to the older definition, a state of affairs is analytically possible, precisely if it does not analytically imply a contradiction. According to the younger definition, which was advanced by Leibniz, a state of affairs is analytically possible, precisely if it obtains in some possible world.

The second definition is not circular in the ontology of states of affairs that we have been considering (call the formal system for it - so far consisting in AP1-AP6, DP1-DP28 - "system P"): we have identified possible worlds with maximally consistent states of affairs (an identification that is well motivated, given that the actual world is regarded as a maximally consistent fact), and for the definition of the concept of maximal-consistence (DP26) no concept of possibility is needed.[*1] The first definition is not circular either; the analysis of its definiens does not require the use of any concept of possibility; in the language LP it is simply represented by "not **k**Pt" ("not t->**k**"). The definiens of the second definition, on the other hand, is represented by "**some***y*(MK(*y*) and tP*y*)."

(b) It is not at all obvious that the two definitions are equivalent; their equivalence is least apparent, in particular, if neither the concept of (coarse-grained) states of affairs is reduced to the concept of possible world, nor the concept of possible world to the concept of states of affairs. Here, however, the concept of possible worlds is explicated on the basis of the concept of states of affairs, in accordance with the intensionalistic position adopted (and not in accordance with extensionalism that regards states of affairs as being sets of possible worlds). In the ontology of states of affairs, formally codified by system P, the two definitions do indeed turn out to be equivalent. But the proof requires some effort (and the force of the entire system). First we have

TP85 **all***x*(if **some***y*(MK(*y*) and *x*P*y*), then not **k**P*x*).

One easily proves (applying TP36, TP32, DP4)

TP86 **all***x*(if *x*P**t**, then **all***y*(if MK(*y*), then *x*P*y*)).

From *the converse of* TP86, however, one obtains *the converse of* TP85: Assume **all***x*(if **all***y*(if MK(*y*), then *x*P*y*), then *x***Pt**), hence: if **all***y*(if MK(*y*), then **neg**(*x*)P*y*), then **neg**(*x*)**Pt**, hence by contraposition: if not **neg**(*x*)**Pt**, then **some***y*(MK(*y*) and not **neg**(*x*)P*y*), hence by TP69: if not **neg**(*x*)**Pt**, then **some***y*(MK(*y*) and *x*P*y*), hence by TP60 and TP54: if not **kP***x*, then **some***y*(MK(*y*) and *x*P*y*). Thus the proof of the converse of TP86 will yield everything needed in order to establish the equivalence of the two definitions of possibility.

In proving the converse of TP86, we first prove

TP87 **all***x*[**all***y*(if MK(*y*), then *x*P*y*), then *x***Pt**] iff **disj***x*MK(*x*)=**t**,

TP88 **disj***x*MK(*x*)=**t** iff **conj***x*EL(*x*)=**k**,

TP89 **conj***x*EL(*x*)=**k**.

Then the converse of TP86,

TP90 **all***x*(if **all***y*(if MK(*y*), then *x*P*y*), then *x***Pt**),

is a straightforward consequence of TP89, TP88 and TP87. Hence, as has already been established, we also have the converse of TP85 as a theorem:

TP91 **all***x*(if not **kP***x*, then **some***y*(MK(*y*) and *x*P*y*)).

(c) Because of TP85 and TP91, we face a more or less arbitrary choice in defining the concept of analytical possibility. The following definition has at once the advantage of being more economical (in abbreviating the longer definiens) and more picturesque:

DP29 P(t) := **some***y*(MK(*y*) and tP*y*).
("t is analytically possible.")[*2]

The obvious follow-up is

DP30 N(t) := not P(**neg**(t)).
("t is analytically necessary.")[*3]

And it can be proved:

TP92 **all***x*(N(*x*) iff **all***y*(if MK(*y*), then *x*P*y*)).
("States of affairs are analytically necessary if and only if they obtain in every possible world.")[*4]

TP93
(i) **all**x(N(x) iff x=**t**);
(ii) **all**x**all**y(N(**conj**(x,y)) iff N(x) and N(y));
(iii) **all**x**all**y[if N(x) or N(y), then N(**disj**(x,y))].

TP94
(i) **all**x(P(x) iff x≠**k**);
(ii) **all**x**all**y(P(**disj**(x,y)) iff P(x) or P(y));
(iii) **all**x**all**y(P(**conj**(x,y)), then P(x) and P(y)).

But neither "**all**x[if N(x), then not N(**neg**(x))]" (in other words, because of DP30, TP55: "**all**x(if N(x), then P(x))"), " nor "**all**x[if not P(x), then P(**neg**(x))]" - principles that are surely true for the universe of states of affairs - can be proved; for both statements are equivalent on the basis of AP1 - AP6 to "**t**≠**k**," and the latter cannot be proved in AP1 - AP6: for "**t**≠**k**" implies that there are at least two wholes in the universe of discourse; but AP1 - AP6 can be interpreted in such a way as to be true for a universe of discourse that contains *precisely one* entity, for example the empty set. By the same token it is clear that neither "**some**x[P(x) and P(**neg**(x))]" nor "**some**x[not N(x) and not N(**neg**(x))]" - principles, too, that are certainly true for the universe of states of affairs - are provable in AP1 - AP6, for both principles are equivalent on the basis of AP1 - AP6 with "**some**x(x≠**k** and x≠**t**)." Last but not least, neither "**all**x(if N(x), then O(x))" - "analytically necessary states of affairs obtain" - nor "**all**x(if O(x), then P(x))" - "obtaining states of affairs are analytically possible" - can be proved in AP1 - AP6, although they are certainly true for states of affairs. In the present state of the development of system P, we can consistently add "**all**x not O(x)" to AP1 - AP6, and then we have "N(**t**) and not O(**t**)"; alternatively, we can consistently add "**all**xO(x)" to AP1 - AP6, and then we have "O(**k**) and not P(**k**)." (Both additions, by the way, are in accordance with the principle "**all**x**all**y(if O(x) and yPx, then O(y).")

These considerations reveal the serious incompleteness of AP1 - AP6 in codifying the ontology of states of affairs (note that certainly every one of the six principles just considered is of sufficient generality for having ontological status); those axioms and the accompanying definitions certainly do not constitute the entire system P. The next chapters concern the extensions to be made.

COMMENTS

[*1] The concept of possible world introduced by A. Plantinga in *The Nature of Necessity*, p. 44f, cannot be utilized for a definition of the concept of analytical possibility, since the former already presupposes the latter: "A possible world, then, is a possible state of affairs - one that is possible in the broadly logical sense. But not every possible state of affairs is a possible world. ... Let us say that a state of affairs S *includes* a state of affairs S′ if it is not possible (in the broadly logical sense) that S obtain and S′ fail to obtain ... Similarly, a state of affairs S *precludes* a state of affairs S′ if it is not possible that both obtain ... a state of affairs S is *complete* or *maximal* if for every state of affairs S′, S includes S′ or S precludes S′. And a possible world is simply a possible state of affairs that is maximal." Nevertheless, the close similarity of Plantinga's conception of possible worlds to the conception here advocated is quite obvious. (But other than making them serve as an ontological basis for possible worlds, Plantinga has not much use for states of affairs in *The Nature of Necessity*.)

N. Rescher's conception, however, is entirely different: it is not Wittgensteinian, but Leibnizian (for Leibniz's conception of possible worlds see B. Mates, "Leibniz über mögliche Welten," p. 317, and F. v. Kutschera, "Grundbegriffe der Metaphysik von Leibniz ...," p. 102, footnote): "possible worlds simply *are* collections of possible individuals duly combined with one another. ... A possible world is thus not just any set of possible individuals. Only a *compossible* set of possible individuals qualifies as a possible world, and any such world must, accordingly, meet not only the logical conditions of L-compossibility among its members, but also the conditions of metaphysical compossibility (M-compossibility) specified above - and perhaps ultimately those of nomic N-compossibility as well." (Rescher, *A Theory of Possibility*, p. 78 and p. 82.)

As has been said at the beginning of this chapter, states of affairs, and not individuals or sets of individuals, are the primary subjects of possibility ("it is possible *that* A" is the canonical form of possibility-statements). Thus, it is more natural to explain possibility - analytical, "metaphysical", "nomic" - first with respect to states of affairs (via possible worlds as maximally consistent states of affairs, or otherwise), and *then* to proceed on the basis of that explanation to explaining what *possible individuals* and *sets of compossible individuals* are. (Rescher, however, does not even consider states of affairs as subjects of possibility, not even as "conceptual artifacts," which is the view he advocates for possible individuals.)

For D. Lewis, in contrast to Plantinga and Rescher, possible worlds are neither states of affairs nor sets of (possible) individuals, but very comprehensive (possible) individuals: "The world we live in is a very inclusive thing. Every stick and every stone you have ever seen is part of it. And so are you and I. And so are the planet Earth, the solar system, the entire Milky Way, the remote galaxies we see through telescopes, and (if there are such things) all the bits of empty space between the stars and galaxies. ... Likewise the world is inclusive in time. ... There are countless other worlds, other very inclusive things. ... The other worlds are of a kind with this world of ours. ... The difference between this and the other worlds is not a categorial difference.'' (*On the Plurality of Worlds*, p. 1f.)

Lewis distinguishes between *worlds* and the *ways a world might be* (in short, *worldways*), including the way each world is, and then states a principle about the relation between worlds and worldways: ''The way things are, at its most inclusive, means the way this entire world is. But things might have been different, in ever so many ways. ... There are ever so many ways that a world might be; and one of these many ways is the way that this world is. Are there other worlds that are other ways? ... There are so many other worlds, in fact, that absolutely *every* way that a world could possibly be is a way that some world *is*.'' (*Ibid.*, p. 1f.) If this is more than rhetoric merely designed for making more palatable the otherwise unduly blunt declaration that there are very many (possible) worlds qua individuals, then Lewis is here using the indubitable *plurality of worldways* (that is, the plurality of maximally consistent states of affairs) as an argument for the plausibility of a *plurality of worlds* in his sense. It is at best an argument for plausibility. For does the fact that there are ever so many ways that an apple could possibly be make it plausible that there are as many possible apples that are in these ways? (The utter feebleness of the argument *does* make it rather probable that it is indeed not intended as an argument by Lewis; yet, there is also evidence to the contrary conclusion; see below in this comment.)

But why not straightforwardly identify possible worlds with worldways (as is done in this book, where worlds are identified with maximally consistent states of affairs)? The idea that possible worlds are individuals must of course then be given up. But the advantage gained would be that the argument just cited becomes superfluous: it is clear without argument, without a mediating principle, that there are many worlds, since there are many worldways. (Who would deny that ''this book of mine might have been finished on schedule. ... Or I might not have existed at all ... Or there might never have been any people. Or the physical constants might have had somewhat different values, incompatible with the emergence of life'' (*ibid.*, p. 1)?)

Lewis, however, is surely not ready to give up the idea that possible worlds - fundamental entities - are individuals, and adopt the idea that they are states of affairs. Like Quine, he is an extensionalist, but, unlike Quine, an extensionalist adhering to *possibilism*: the only basic entities he believes in are possible - actual *and* non-actual - individuals (possible worlds among them) and the sets that can be obtained by set theory from the set of them. (His position is neatly stated in the postscript to ''Counterpart Theory and Quantified Modal Logic,''

p. 40: "Provisionally, my ontology consists of iterative set theory with individuals; the only unorthodox part is my view about what individuals there are.") Therefore, he does not believe in states of affairs as basic entities; he only believes in states of affairs as sets of possible worlds *in his sense*: "Understand that I am *not* opposed to states of affairs, ways things might be, possibilities, propositions or structures. I believe in all those things. That is to say, I believe in entities that deserve the names because they are well suited to play the roles. The entities I put forward as candidates are the same in every case: sets of worlds. Worlds as *I* understand them: us and all our surroundings, and other things like that." (*Ibid.*, p. 185.)

According to this, worldways are - for Lewis - most naturally considered to be singleton sets of Lewis-worlds (the single element of the worldway is the world that is in this way). But then the argument from the plurality of worldways to the plurality of Lewis-worlds, which is stated at the very beginning of *On the Plurality of Worlds*, is blatantly circular, and the principle on which it is based - "absolutely every way that a world could possibly be is a way that some world is" - is, in fact, of no help at all for supporting any conclusion whatever about the number of possible worlds. (The problem is noticed by Lewis himself (*ibid.*, p. 87); he ends up by explicitly discarding the principle he started out with, and hence the argument in which it was employed, and moves on to a *principle of recombination*.)

[*2] D. M. Armstrong says in *A Theory of Universals*, vol. II, p. 14: "In general, a good philosophical methodology for an Empiricist seems to be this: be rather hospitable to claims about logical possibility, reserve one's scepticism for claims about what actually exists." This does not jibe well with Armstrong's general scepticism about *mere possibilia*, including possible worlds (see *ibid.*, vol. I, p. 22, p. 36, p. 128); after all, these entities are not claimed to be actually existent, but merely claimed to be (at least) analytically ("logically") possible.

Minor inconsistencies aside, it is clear that Armstrong has in mind an *actualistic* theory of possibility, that is, a theory of possibility without non-actual possibilia. Such a theory he attempts to formulate in his book *A Combinatorial Theory of Possibility*. But, actually, the theory there presented is not strictly actualistic, since it recognizes (on p. 46) *merely possible states of affairs*, or in other words: states of affairs that do not obtain. But Armstrong hastens to add: "A merely possible state of affairs does not exist, subsist or have any sort of being. It is no addition to our ontology." Well, presumably a merely possible states of affair is at least merely possible. If this were not so, what is the use of "merely possible" states of affairs for a theory of *possibility*? Hence: if there are merely possible states of affairs (that is, if the cardinal number of merely possible states of affairs is greater than 0), then, contrary to actualism, there are also non-actual possibilia (then the cardinal number of non-actual possibilia is greater than 0). But Armstrong cannot very well deny that there are (in the sense of numerical existence, which is expressed by a quantifier, not, of course, in the sense of actual existence, which is expressed by a predicate) merely possible states of affairs; he is constantly talking about them in a way that shows his ontological commitment. For example on p. 47: "So the possible atomic states of affairs are *all the combinations*. (The *merely* possible atomic states of affairs are the *re*combinations, the ones that do not exist.) ...The simplest way to specify a possible world would be to say that *any conjunction* of possible atomic states of affairs, including the unit conjunction, constitutes such a world. This is essentially correct ..."

The above discussion quite clearly shows that a theory of possibility that observes actualism *in the strict sense* (that allows no mere possibilia of any kind) is rather difficult to be had (some little progress is made in my "Propensity and Possibility"). It is a different matter, of course, with theories of possibility that observe restricted forms of actualism, for example, the fairly plausible actualism with respect to *individuals only*.

[*3] DP29 and DP30 introduce *modal predicates*, not term-forming *modal functors*. This comment is dedicated to modal functors.

For the modal functors "**p**" and "**n**" that are corresponding to the modal predicates "P" and "N" we must have:

(j) **all**y[if MK(y), then **all**x(**p**(x)Py iff **some**y'(MK(y') and xPy'))].
("The analytical possibility of x obtains in a possible world y if and only if x obtains in some possible world.")

(jj) **all**y[if MK(y), then **all**x(**n**(x)Py iff **all**y'(if MK(y'), then xPy'))].
("The analytical necessity of x obtains in a possible world y if and only if x obtains in every possible world.")

In other words, according to TP85, TP91, TP86 and TP90 we must have:

(j) **all**y(if MK(y), then **all**x(**p**(x)Py iff not **k**Px)),

(jj) **all**y(MK(y), then **all**x(**n**(x)Py iff xP**t**)).

In other words, if we assume "**some**yMK(y)," which on the basis of AP1 - AP6 (see the proof in I.16.(e)) is equivalent to "**t**≠**k**," then we must have:

all$x$(**n**(x)=**t** iff x=**t**), **all**x(**n**(x)=**k** iff x≠**t**), **all**x(**p**(x)=**t** iff x≠**k**), **all**x(**p**(x)=**k** iff x=**k**).

These four statements and (j) and (jj) are provable on the basis of AP1 - AP6 *plus* "**some**yMK(y)" (or "**t**≠**k**") if we use the following two definitions:

p(x) := **conj**y(x=**k** and y=**k**), **n**(x) := **conj**y(x≠**t** and y=**k**).

One need not restrict oneself to the modal functors corresponding to the predicates "P" and "N". For *arbitrary* modal functors "$\mathbf{p}_i$" and "$\mathbf{n}_i$" we must have:

(j′) **all**y[if MK(y), then **all**x($\mathbf{p}_i$(x)Py iff **some**y'(MK(y') and y'R$_i y$ and xPy'))];

(jj′) **all**y(if MK(y), then **all**x($\mathbf{n}_i$(x)Py iff **all**y'(if MK(y') and y'R$_i y$, then xPy'))].

And conversely: functors for which (j′) and (jj′) hold true are modal functors. Here "R$_i$" is the characteristic "accessibility-relation" for "$\mathbf{p}_i$" and "$\mathbf{n}_i$" which determines their content ("xR$_i y$": "x is i-accessible from y" might, for example, mean that in *x* the same natural laws obtain as in *y*); (j′) and (jj′) reflect the usual (Kripkean) way in intensional semantics of presenting the truth-conditions for sentences formed by possibility- or necessity-like modal operators ("nomic," "metaphysical," "epistemic," or whatever).

All modal functors can be defined as follows:

p$_i$(t) := **disj***y*′′(MK(*y*′′) and **some***y*′(MK(*y*′) and *y*′R$_i$*y*′′ and tP*y*′)).

n$_i$(t) := **neg**(**p**$_i$(**neg**(t)).

According to this, "**p**(t)" - that is, "**p**$_0$(t)" - is defined by the expression "**disj***y*′′(MK(*y*′′) and **some***y*′(MK(*y*′) and tP*y*′))" (the characteristic accessibility-relation for "**p**" - *y*′R$_0$*y*′′ := MK(*y*′) and MK(*y*′′) - is redundant and can be omitted from the definiens).

On the basis of the definition for "**p**$_i$" we prove (j′) ((jj′) can be easily obtained from (j′) on the basis of the definition of "**n**$_i$"):

Assume MK(*y*);

(**i**) assume **some***y*′(MK(*y*′) and *y*′R$_i$*y* and *x*P*y*′); hence by TP65 **disj***y*′′(MK(*y*′′) and **some***y*′(MK(*y*′) and *y*′R$_i$*y*′′ and *x*P*y*′))P*y*, hence: **p**$_i$(*x*)P*y*.

(**ii**) **p**$_i$(*x*)P*y*, hence - according to the theorem "**all***y*(if MK(*y*) and **disj***z*A[*z*]P*y*, then **some***z*(A[*z*] and *z*P*y*))" - **some***y*′′(MK(*y*′′) and **some***y*′(MK(*y*′) and *y*′R$_i$*y*′′ and *x*P*y*′) and *y*′′P*y*), hence, because of MK(*y*), by TP79: *y*=*y*′′, hence: **some***y*′(MK(*y*′) and *y*′R$_i$*y* and *x*P*y*′).

All that is left to do in the proof of (j′) is to prove the theorem used in (**ii**):

Assume MK(*y*) and **disj***z*A[*z*]P*y*; assume for *reductio*: not **some***z*(A[*z*] and *z*P*y*); from the first assumption by TP64: **neg**(**conj***x*′**some***z*[A[*z*] and *x*′=**neg**(*z*)])P*y*; from the second assumption and MK(*y*): **all***z*(if A[*z*], then **neg**(*z*)P*y*), hence **all***x*′(if **some***z*[A[*z*] and *x*′=**neg**(*z*)], then *x*′P*y*), hence by TP18: **conj***x*′**some***z*[A[*z*] and *x*′=**neg**(*z*)]P*y*. The underlined results contradict the assumption MK(*y*); therefore: **some***z*(A[*z*] and *z*P*y*).

[*4] B. Mates writes in *The Philosophy of Leibniz*, p. 73: "Insofar as I am aware, Leibniz never defines a necessary truth as a proposition true of all possible worlds; as definitions he gives, instead, various versions of 'a necessary truth is a proposition the opposite of which implies a contradiction'." In our system Leibniz' definition is represented by the theorem "**all***x*(N(*x*) iff **neg**(*x*)->**k**)," which is easily proved: N(*x*), that is (by DP30): not P(**neg**(*x*)), that is (by DP29, TP91, TP85): **kPneg**(*x*), that is (by DP11): **neg**(*x*)->**k**. However, there is a passage noted by Mates where Leibniz comes very close, if not to defining, so at least to characterizing necessity as truth in all possible worlds. See *The Philosophy of Leibniz*, p. 107.

CHAPTER I.12

THE WORLD AND THE TRUTH

(a) AP1 - AP6, while having other natural ontological interpretations, is an axiomatization of the *fundamental ontology of states of affairs* (compare I.1.(d)). The extension of the fundamental ontology of states of affairs to the *full ontology of states of affairs* consists, first, in adding the axioms AP7 - AP9, and, finally, in adding AP10 (the axiom-schema of infinity).

In order to formulate AP7 - AP9 (and not principles that, though equivalent to them, do not have their very brief form) the language LP needs to be extended by the singular term "**w**"("the (*actual*) world"). Given the chosen universe of discourse of LP, "**w**" must refer to a certain state of affairs. Much can be said about the world as a state of affairs; all sciences are concerned with (truly) describing it (that is, with stating states of affairs that are part of it, obtain in it); but AP7 - AP9 constitute its most fundamental, hence ontologically relevant description. The validity of these axioms is much more closely bound up with the universe of states of affairs than is the validity of AP4 - AP6 (the validity of AP1 - AP3, on the other hand, is not at all specifically related to that universe). And they have an altogether different character than all the preceding axioms: even if interpreted with respect to states of affairs, they *do not* appear to be *analytically true*. (In fact, one of them - AP8 - is slightly problematic. Thus, there is one slightly problematic axiom in each triadic group: AP3 in AP1 - AP3, AP5 in AP4 - AP6, AP8 in AP7 - AP9.)

(b) "Die Welt ist alles, was der Fall ist," says Wittgenstein in the *Tractatus*, and, substituting our understanding of "state of affairs" ("*Sachverhalt*" in German) for his, we take the inspiration from him of using the term "the world" (in German "*die Welt*") as a name for a rather special state of affairs, namely as a name for the conjunction of all *obtaining* (or *actually existing*) states of affairs (compare proposition 2.04 of the *Tractatus*), in other words, as a name for the sum of all *facts*. We need to add: "the world" (or "**w**" in LP) is supposed to be a *non-rigid* name of that whole: if there were other facts than there are (and this is surely possible), then "the world" would designate a state of affairs that is different from the state of affairs which it actually designates.

It has been noted above that "**all**x(A[x] iff x**Pconj**yA[y])" is not generally valid (see I.7.(a)). However, one of the instances of this schema *is* valid. Consider the predicate "O(x)", which, provisionally, we add as an undefined predicate to the language LP. With regard to the chosen universe of discourse we read it as "x obtains." "**all**x(O(x) iff x**Pconj**yO(y))" then says that a state of affairs obtains if and only if it is analytically implied by the conjunction of all obtaining states of affairs;[*1] that is, in the spirit of Wittgenstein: a state of affairs obtains, precisely if it is an intensional part of the world. Since "**all**x(O(x) iff x**Pconj**yO(y)/x**Pw**)" is analytically true with respect to the chosen universe of discourse, we are justified in choosing "**w**" as a basic expression of LP and in not leaving "O(x)" undefined:

DP31 O(t) := t**Pw**.
("t obtains"; "t is an actually existing state of affairs"; "t is a fact"; "t is the case.")

Alternatively, we could of course have chosen "O(x)" as a basic expression of LP and have defined: **w** := **conj**yO(y). Indeed, the second procedure is preferable on the grounds that it *exhibits* "**w**" as a non-rigid designator, which the first procedure does not. However, as we shall see, DP31 leads to a theory-construction that is much more elegant than the one its alternative requires.

The reading of "O(t)" is specific for the chosen universe of discourse. It will be inadequate if the universe of discourse is changed. This is even the case for the entirely unspecific reading "t is actual": not all entities are actual if and only if they are part of this or that special entity.

By DP31, TP29 and TP30 we immediately have Wittgenstein's famous dictum:

TP95 **w**=**conj**yO(y).

(c) There is a concept of *truth* that is not *semantical*, but *ontological* (and that, therefore, has nothing to do with correspondence, and certainly nothing to do with conventions or beliefs). This concept is synonymous with the concept of actual existence for states of affairs: *x is true* if and only if *x is an actually existing state of affairs*. For example: that Boris Yeltsin is the president of Russia in 1995 *is true*; hence: that Boris Yeltsin is the president of Russia in 1995 *is an actually existing state of affairs*. Conversely, that all human beings are born *is an actually existing state of affairs*; hence: that all human beings are born *is true*. Thus, if "*ens*" is restricted to actually existing states of affairs, the old *ontological* dictum "*ens et verum convertuntur*" is literally true. (It is not true if it is not thus restricted, even if we allow only actually existing entities that can be true in some sense to be meant by "*ens*." Take, for example, *statements*: there are all too many of them which actually exist without being true. And doubtless some of them, although true, will never come into actual existence.)

Since "t is an actually existing state of affairs" is one of the readings of "O(t)," we can define, true to the ontological use of "true,"

DP32 V(t) := O(t).
("t is true (*verum*)"; this reading has to be given up if the universe of discourse is changed.)

Corresponding to the ontological concept of truth there is the ontological concept of *falsity*. But in defining it, we have a choice. We can let "*x* is false" simply be synonymous with "*x* is a state of affair that is not true." But this does not make "false" a very interesting concept; it cannot be synonymous with "state of affair that is not true," if the question whether there are states of affairs that are neither true nor false is to be kept alive. Thus it is preferable to define

DP33 F(t) := V(**neg**(t)).
("t is false.")

(d) As a general principle for all predicates A[*z*] of LP we can prove (by merely applying TP18 and AP1) the generalization of TP24:

TP96 **all***x*(**conj***z*A[*z*]P*x* iff **all***y*(if A[*y*], then *y*P*x*)).

As an immediate consequence of TP96 (by substituting "**w**" for "*x*" - instantiation - and by applying DP31 and DP32) we then have

TP97 V(**conj***z*A[*z*]) iff **all***y*(if A[*y*], then V(*y*)).

TP97 is the central *law of truth* for states of affairs; it is, as it were, the ontological heart of propositional logic (whether truth-functional or modal). It implies (simply by instantiation) a truth-law (presenting a sufficient and necessary non-circular truth-condition) for every functor that is definable by the big conjunction "**conj***y*" by way of prefixing it to some predicate B[*y*]; hence, for example, a truth-law for "**conj**", "**disj**", "**neg**" and "**disj***y*" (and also for the modal functors "**p**" and "**n**" defined in [*3] of I.11). The truth-laws that result from TP97 for the mentioned functors (with the exception of the one for "**conj**") are, however, not those one would expect from the semantics of propositional logic. They are the truth-laws that are valid for those functors *independently* of how *the world* is ontologically characterized as a state of affairs by further principles. So far, as far as AP1 - AP6 are concerned, **w** might be any state of affairs whatever, TP95 notwithstanding (nevertheless we can alread prove "V(**w**)" and "V(**t**)"). Only after it has been characterized in such a manner that the ontological pendant of the *postulate of bivalence*, "**all***x*(not V(*x*) iff F(*x*))," becomes provable, does one obtain truth-laws for all the functors mentioned that are in precise analogy to the familiar semantic stipulations for the corresponding sentence-connectives.[*2] For "**conj**," however, we already have

TP98 **all***x***all***y*(V(**conj**(*x*,*y*)) iff V(*x*) and V(*y*)).

(e) One easily proves

TP99 **all***x*(F(*x*) iff **neg(w)**P*x*).
(Depending on DP33, DP32, DP31, TP60.)

And as a general principle for all predicates A[*z*] of LP we can prove (by merely applying TP65 and AP1) the generalization of TP23:

TP100 **all***x*(*x***Pdisj***z*A[*z*] iff **all***y*(if A[*y*], then *x*P*y*)).

From TP100 we get (by substituting "**neg(w)**" for "*x*"and applying TP99)

TP101 F(**disj***z*A[*z*]) iff **all***y*(if A[*y*], then F(*y*)).

TP101 is the central *law of falsity* for states of affairs. With respect to it the same obervations hold true *mutatis mutandis* as with respect to TP97. Now "**disj**" is the functor for which we can already prove the falsity-law that is to be expected for it from the semantics of propositional logic. For we have

TP102 **all***x***all***y*(**disj**(*x*,*y*)=**disj***z*(*z*=*x* or *z*=*y*)),

and with this and TP101 we obtain

TP103 **all***x***all***y*(F(**disj**(*x*,*y*)) iff F(*x*) and F(*y*)).

COMMENTS

[*1] The predicate "O" is *cumulative*: "if a sum exists, the predicate which applies to the parts applies to the whole" (P. Simons, *Parts*, p. 111); for we have (1): O(**conj***y*O(*y*)). And it is *homoeomerous*: "A property is homoeomerous if and only if for all particulars, *x*, which have that property, then for all *parts y* of *x*, *y* also has that property." (D. M. Armstrong, *A Theory of Universals*, vol. II, p. 68; replace "property" by "predicate," "particular" by "entity"); for we have (2): **all***x***all***y*(O(*x*) and *y*P*x*, then O(*y*)). Both (1) and (2) are consequences of (3): **all***x*(O(*x*) iff *x*P**conj***y*O(*y*)): From (3), by instantiating substitution of "**conj***y*O(*y*)" for "*x*" and AP2, we obtain: O(**conj***y*O(*y*)), that is, (1). And assume O(*x*) and *y*P*x*; hence by TP18 *x*P**conj***y*′O(*y*′); hence by AP1 *y*P**conj***y*′O(*y*′), hence by (3): O(*y*). Therefore (2). Conversely, (3) is a consequence of (1) and (2) (from left to right it is simply implied by TP18).

[*2] An infinitary sentence-connective that generates possibly infinite statements from sets of statements corresponds to the big disjunction for states of affairs. It is semantically defined as follows: *the disjunction of the statements in set M* is true if and only if at least one statement in M is true. *The conjunction of the statements in set M*, on the other hand, is true according to the semantics of infinitary languages if and only if every statement in M is true. This is the obvious analogue of TP97 (which is about the big conjunction for states of affairs). (Concerning infinitary sentence-connectives and languages see H. D. Ebbinghaus, J. Flum, W. Thomas, *Mathematical Logic*, p. 142ff.)

CHAPTER I.13

THE LAW OF NON-CONTRADICTION

(a) The world as a state of affairs is not the "*contradictory*" state of affairs (strictly speaking, of course, only statements and predicates can be contradictory). For if it were, then *every* state of affairs would be an obtaining state of affairs, according to DP31, since the contradictory state of affairs is **k**, the *total* state of affairs, of which all states of affairs are (intensional) parts. There is, however, no doubt that some states of affairs do not obtain.

Hence "**w≠k**" is true. But - speaking in LP of states of affairs - is "**w≠k**" a sentence that is *analytically true*? It does, indeed, not appear that the intension of "**w≠k**" (just as the intensions of all the statements provable on the basis of AP1 - AP6) could be any other state of affairs than **t**, the "tautological" state of affairs. And the thesis that the intension of "**w≠k**" is **t** (that its intension is *analytically necessary*) is equivalent to the truth of "**w≠k**" in every possible world (according to TP86, TP90, etc., and the obvious stipulation that a statement is true in a possible world, a maximally consistent state of affairs, if and only if its intension obtains in it, is part of it), or in short: to "**w≠k**" being *ontologically true*. However, all this does *not* imply (compare [*2] of I.1) that "**w≠k**" is also analytically true, that is, true merely in virtue of its meaning (more specifically, the meaning it has in consideration of the chosen universe of discourse of LP and the accompanying interpretation of the part-predicate "P"). We have no idea of the meaning of the expression "the world" - if it is used for designating a certain state of affairs - that goes beyond what is expressed by the analytically true principle "**all***x*(O(*x*) iff *x***Pw**)" (quantification is restricted to states of affairs, and, for the moment, "O(*x*)" is taken to be a primitive predicate), and perhaps our idea of the meaning of "the world" is even less than that: only what is expressed by the analytically true principle "**w=conj***y*O(*y*)." From this, by the (analytically valid) TP18, we easily obtain "**all***x*(if O(*x*), then *x***Pw**)"; but in order also to obtain the converse of this from "**w=conj***y*O(*y*)" via the analytically valid "**all***x***all***y*(if O(*x*) and *y*P*x*, then O(*y*))," we need "O(**conj***y*O(*y*))." Is this latter statement, too, analytically true beyond any reasonable doubt? See comment [*1] for some reason to doubt that it is. (Note that all statements mentioned after the last occurrence of "**all***x*(O(*x*) iff *x***Pw**)" can be deduced from it by using only analytically true principles. In fact, we have on the basis of AP1 - AP6, treating both "O" and "**w**" as primitive expressions, the following chain of non-trivial analytically valid equivalences: **all***x*(O(*x*) iff *x***Pw**) *iff* [**w=conj***y*O(*y*) and **all***x*(O(*x*) iff *x***Pconj***y*O(*y*))] *iff* [**w=conj***y*O(*y*) and **all***x***all***y*(if O(*x*) and *y*P*x*, then O(*y*)) and O(**conj***y*O(*y*))].)

On the basis of the analytically true ‘‘**all**x(O(x) iff x**P****w**)’’ (let us definitively accept it as such) and the axioms AP1 - AP6, which are analytically true for states of affairs, we have the analytically true ‘‘O(**k**) iff **w**=**k**.’’ Hence ‘‘**w**≠**k**’’ is analytically true precisely if ‘‘not O(**k**)’’ is. And we also have on the same basis the analytical truth of ‘‘O(**k**) iff **all**yO(y).’’ Hence ‘‘**w**≠**k**’’ is analytically true, precisely if ‘‘**all**yO(y)’’ is *analytically false*. But is it an analytical truth, i.e. merely a question of the meaning of the expressions involved (and their syntactical order), *that some state of affairs does not obtain*? It seems not to be an analytical truth *to me*, and it can at least be maintained that it is not at all clear which is the correct answer to the foregoing question. Then, given the vagueness of the expressions involved, one is surely allowed, in making them more precise, to decide that ‘‘**some**y not O(y),’’ and hence ‘‘not O(**k**)’’ and ‘‘**w**≠**k**’’ are *not* analytical truths.[*1]

Since ‘‘**w**≠**k**’’ is true, but not analytically true, it must be *synthetically true*. Is it also an *a priori* truth (a truth that can be known even without broadly verifying experiences)? In case it is, we have found a *synthetical a priori truth*. But no great importance attaches to this, since the Kantian tradition according to which (non-mathematical) *synthetical a priori truths* constitute *per definitionem* the sciences of metaphysics and ontology ought to be repudiated. Like other sciences, metaphysics and ontology are to be defined solely by their subject-matter; and this can be done without reference to any *epistemological* conception, without reference, therefore, to a certain problematical mode of cognition (*a priori*, but nevertheless synthetical). Thus, ‘‘**w**≠**k**’’ is a genuine, and apparently synthetical, *principle of ontology*, whether knowledge of its truth is to be had *a priori* or not.

(b) Besides ‘‘not O(**k**)’’ and ‘‘**some**y not O(y),’’ the following four statements are equivalent (on the basis of AP1 - AP6) to ‘‘**w**≠**k**’’: ‘‘K(**w**)’’ (by TP70), ‘‘not **some**x[O(x) and O(**neg**(x))]’’ (by TP70, DP24, DP31), ‘‘not **some**x(V(x) and F(x))’’ (by TP70, DP24, DP31, DP32, DP33), ‘‘**all**x not V(**conj**[x,**neg**(x)])’’ (*Proof*: Assume V(**conj**[x,**neg**(x)]), that is (by TP53): V(**k**), that is (by DP32, DP31): **kPw**, that is (by TP34, DP5, AP3; AP2) **w**=**k**.)

We choose as a further axiom the shortest one of the seven statements that are seven equivalent formulations of the *law of non-contradiction* for states of affairs:

AP7 **w**≠**k**.

All the other statements then appear as theorems. By AP7 we have moreover:

TP104 **t**≠**k**.

Given TP104, we can prove ``$\mathbf{all}x$[if N($x$), then not N($\mathbf{neg}(x)$)]'' and ``$\mathbf{all}x$[P(x) or P($\mathbf{neg}(x)$)],'' since these statements are equivalent to ``$\mathbf{t}\neq\mathbf{k}$'' (see I.11.(c)). (``$\mathbf{all}x$(if N(x), then O(x)),'' on the other hand, is an obvious consequence merely of TP93(i), ``M($\mathbf{t}$)'' and DP31; and, with regard to TP94(i) and DP31, ``$\mathbf{all}x$(if O(x), then P(x))'' is easily seen to be another statement that is equivalent to AP7.) Because of TP54 ``$\mathbf{t}\neq\mathbf{k}$'' is also equivalent to ``$\mathbf{t}\neq\mathbf{neg}(\mathbf{t})$,'' which, in turn, is only an instance of

TP105 $\mathbf{all}x(x\neq\mathbf{neg}(x))$,

``$\mathbf{all}x(x\neq\mathbf{neg}(x))$'' being implied by ``$\mathbf{t}\neq\mathbf{k}$'' on the basis of AP1 - AP6 (see the proof of TP105 in the Appendix).

COMMENTS

[*1] This, however, introduces a certain asymmetry. For ‘‘O(**t**)’’ and ‘‘**some***y*O(*y*),’’ in contrast to ‘‘not O(**k**)’’ and ‘‘**some***y* not O(*y*),’’ *are* analytical truths. But if we had chosen the weaker basis of analyticity for ‘‘O’’, namely ‘‘**all***x***all***y*(if O(*x*) and *y*P*x*, then O(*y*))’’ instead of the stronger basis ‘‘**all***x***all***y*(if O(*x*) and *y*P*x*, then O(*y*))’’ *plus* ‘‘O(**conj***y*O(*y*))’’ (equivalently: ‘‘**all***x*(O(*x*) iff *x*P**conj***y*O(*y*))’’; see [*1] of I.12), then, in addition to ‘‘not O(**k**)’’ and ‘‘**some***y* not O(*y*),’’ ‘‘O(**t**)’’ and ‘‘**some***y*O(*y*)’’ could not have been proved on the basis of the given analytical principles (including AP1 - AP6), although ‘‘O(**t**) iff **some***y*O(*y*)’’ and ‘‘O(**k**) iff **all***y*O(*y*)’’ would have remained provable. Hence we would then have had room for denying the analyticity of ‘‘O(**t**)’’ and ‘‘**some***y*O(*y*)’’ along with the analyticity of ‘‘O(**conj***y*O(*y*))’’ (while, of course, still accepting them and ‘‘O(**conj***y*O(*y*))’’ as *true*). Symmetry would have been preserved. But there seems to be no other theoretical advantage to be gained from the procedure just described.

CHAPTER I.14

THE LAW OF EXCLUDED MIDDLE

(a) ''QC(**w**)'' is according to TP71 equivalent to ''MX(**w**),'' this, in turn, according to DP25, is equivalent to ''**all***x*(*x*P**w** or **neg**(*x*)P**w**),'' this, in turn, according to DP31, to ''**all***x*[O(*x*) or O(**neg**(*x*))],'' and this, in turn, according to DP32 and DP33, equivalent to ''**all***x*(V(*x*) or F(*x*))'' - ''every state of affairs is true or false.'' All the mentioned equivalences hold true analytically with respect to states of affairs on the basis of the posited definitions, given that AP1 - AP6 are analytically true for states of affairs (''tPt′'' being synonymous with ''t is analytically implied by t′''). Consequently, we have in particular the analytical truth of ''QC(**w**) iff **all***x*[O(*x*) or O(**neg**(*x*))].''

(b) ''QC(**w**)/**all***x*[O(*x*) or O(**neg**(*x*))]'' are much more unequivocally non-analytic statements (neither analytically true nor analytically false) than ''**w≠k**/**all***x*[not O(*x*) or not O(**neg**(*x*))].''[*1] Moreover, it is even somewhat doubtful whether they are true at all. A semblance of analytical validity is produced for them by transferring the logical, hence analytical validity of ''**all***x*(O(*x*) or not O(*x*))'' to ''**all***x*[O(*x*) or O(**neg**(*x*))].'' But this transfer is unjustifiable, unless ''**all***x*[not O(*x*), then O(**neg**(*x*))]'' could be seen to be analytically true for states of affairs - which is precisely the issue in question. (More tempting than this is the semblance of analytical validity that is produced for ''**all***x*(V(*x*) or F(*x*))'' - and hence for ''QC(**w**)'' - by transferring to it the analytical validity of ''**all***x*(V(*x*) or not V(*x*))'' via the conflation of two different meanings of ''false.'' See I.12.(c).)

(c) The truth of ''QC(**w**)'' for states of affairs becomes very doubtful indeed if one adopts a *relativistic position* with respect to states of affairs and their actual existence (or truth). If even the ontological constitution of so-called ''external facts'' (facts about the external world) is supposed to depend largely *on us*,[*2] then, surely, also the ontological constitution of the sum of all facts - that is, of the (entire) actual world - must thus depend on us, and it is hardly to be believed that this sum is a quasi-complete whole. For it is certainly not to be supposed that with respect to each state of affairs (even though the relativist considers only states of affairs *for us* as states of affairs) the state of affairs itself or its negation is a fact (or truth) *for us* (a ''fact'' in the eyes of the relativist), even if we consider the whole course of human history.[*3] For the relativist, the presumable incompleteness of human knowledge turns into the incompleteness of the world itself. But even if one accepts that external facts are something objectively, mind-independently given, something that remains a fact whether somebody ever realizes it or not, describes it or not, is it certain that the sum of all facts is a quasi-complete whole?

(d) *Classical* ontology, however, the discipline that, like classical logic, was founded by Aristotle, accepts the *law of excluded middle* for states of affairs, and so do we in everyday life (as is testified to by our practice of moving from "it is not the case that A" to "it is the case that not A" and back without the slightest idea that there might be a problem in this). Its shortest formulation is

AP8 QC(**w**).

Even though we accept "QC(**w**)" as an axiom, it ought to be kept in mind that of all the axioms of the ontology of states of affairs AP8 is the most problematic. Nevertheless, it is deeply rooted in our ontological common sense, and it is not merely the unquestioned acceptance of ontological tradition which seems to be responsible for this. Rather, AP8 has the status of a *synthetical postulate* that expresses our firmly held assumption that, allowing for consistency, the world is as comprehensive as it can possibly be. (Note that, even though AP8 holds true, AP7 still requires that there are just as many states of affairs *that do not obtain* as there are obtaining ones.)

By AP8, AP7 and TP72 we immediately obtain

TP106 MK(**w**).
("The world is a maximally consistent state of affairs.")

TP106 justifies us in calling *precisely* the maximally consistent states of affairs "possible worlds." They are possible worlds, because the (actual) world is a maximally consistent state of affairs. In general, if the world is a consistent state of affairs, all and only consistent states of affairs are to be called "possible worlds" that have *at least* the degree of completeness the world itself enjoys. Thus, if the world were state of affairs that is not maximal (contrary to AP8), then not only maximally consistent states of affairs would be possible worlds, but other consistent states of affairs (including the world) as well (presupposing that the universe of states of affairs has more than two members). But according to TP106 and the mentioned rule to be observed in calling states of affairs "possible worlds," *precisely* the maximally consistent states of affairs are possible worlds.

From TP106 we obtain by TP69, DP31, DP32 and DP33:

TP107 **all***x*(not V(*x*) iff F(*x*)).
("State of affairs are false if and only if they are not true.")

TP107 is the *principle of ontological bivalence*. Both TP107 and TP106 could equivalently replace as a *single axiom* the pair of axioms "**w**≠**k**" and

"QC(**w**)." In comparison to other single equivalents for that pair, they have the advantage of being rather memorable formulations which connect ontological matters with logical and semantical ones.

(e) AP8 and its equivalent "**all***x*[V(*x*) or V(**neg**(*x*))]" are not deductively equivalent to the statement "**all***x*V(**disj**[*x*,**neg**(*x*)])." The latter is already provable on the basis of AP1 - AP6 and the definitions up to DP31 and DP32. Nor is "V(p) or V(¬p)" deductively equivalent to "V((p∨¬p))"; if appropriately interpreted (see below), the latter, and not the former, is already provable on the basis of AP1 - AP6 and the definitions up to DP31 and DP32.

Indeed, AP7 and AP8 are not needed for the proof of V(τ*) for any tautology τ of classical truth-functional propositional logic. τ* corresponds to τ in the following manner: let the propositional variables "p, p′, p″..." be names for states of affairs, and take each sentence-connective as being defined by the functional expression of LP that obviously corresponds to it: "∧" by "**conj**", "∨" by "**disj**", "¬" by "**neg**", "⊃" by "**impl**," and so on. V(τ*) is provable, no matter which classical truth-functional tautology τ is, *without* AP7 and AP8, i.e. merely on the basis of AP1 - AP6 and the definitions up to DP31 and DP32, since upon that basis we can prove τ*=**t** and V(**t**). (In order to show τ*=**t** for all tautologies τ of classical truth-functional propositional logic, take any complete axiomatization of them and demonstrate - using merely the indicated basis - α*=**t** for each axiom α; then demonstrate that each rule of the axiom system is such that if we can demonstrate π*=**t** - by using merely the indicated basis - for all premisses π of the rule, we can also demonstrate κ*=**t** for its conclusion κ.)

In fact, we can define *logical truth* for the formulae ϕ of the formal language PL of truth-functional propositional logic simply as follows: ϕ is logically true := ϕ*=**t** is provable in AP1 - AP6 together with the appropriate definitions (where ϕ* is the singular term of LP that corresponds as is indicated above to the formula ϕ of PL; the "appropriate definitions" are the definitions of the functors corresponding to the sentence-connectives of PL). Then, according to this definition and the result reached in the preceding paragraph, all tautologies of classical truth-functional propositional logic (as formulated in PL) are logically true formulae of PL (and presumably every logically true formula of PL is a tautology of classical truth-functional propositional logic; it would be very surprising indeed if this were not the case). Thus, the logical truth of *all* tautologies of classical truth-functional propositional logic, if they are interpreted ontologically, is seen to be independent of the assumption of bivalence for the formulae of PL, just as the provability of their ontological interpretations is independent of the principle of bivalence for states of affairs (or in other words: independent of the conjunction of AP7 and AP8).[*4]

These results (and the result in comment [*4]) can be extended *mutatis mutandis*, for example, to the tautologies of S5-modal propositional logic as formulated in the formal language MPL (PL + "*N*"). (Let "*N*" of MPL be defined by "**n**" of LP - see [*3] of I.11 - and the other sentence-connectives of MPL by functors of LP just as in the case of PL, and consider that already in AP1 - AP6 with definitions up to DP31 and DP32 we can prove "**all***x*(if *x*≠**t**, then **n**(*x*)=**k**)" and "**all***x*(if *x*=**t**, then **n**(*x*)=**t**)," defining "**n**(*x*)" by "**conj***y*(*x*≠**t** and *y*=**k**)."

COMMENTS

[*1] There is a tacit analytic assumption involved in declaring "QC(**w**)" to be non-analytic, to wit: that there are *more than two* states of affairs. Similarly, there is a tacit analytic assumption involved in declaring "**w**≠**k**" to be non-analytic, to wit: that there is *more than one* state of affairs. If the second assumption were false (hence analytically false), "QC(**w**)" would have to be analytically true (the universe of states of affairs being non-empty) and "**w**≠**k**" analytically false. If only the first assumption were false, "QC(**w**)" would still have to be analytically true.

[*2] The ontological constitution of facts is dependent on us if and only if their ontological constitution is not independent of our language and our doxastic attitudes. If it is asserted that the ontological constitution of facts depends on us, then there is still plenty of room for postulating different *degrees of dependence*. A relativistic attitude is adopted with respect to facts only if the degree of the dependence of facts on us is asserted to surpass a certain, not altogether low threshold. The border of *extreme ontological relativism* with respect to facts is certainly reached in the assertion: "Facts are the purely fictional correlates of the statements of our language that we, or our appropriate experts, accept by official common consent, and the purely fictional correlates of the statements analytically implied by the former statements." Starting with the Sophists (for example, Protagoras, for whom "man is the measure of all things, of those *that are* that/how they are, of those *that are not* that/how they are not"), radical and not so radical versions of ontological relativism (idealism, constructivism) can be found throughout the entire history of ideas, and in our own day, again, it is very influential.

[*3] M. Dummett has pointed out the connection between the denial of bivalence (albeit for statements, not for states of affairs; also, for Dummett the postulate of bivalence has an *undeniable* part: *no statement is both true and false*, or, alternatively, it merely consists in the postulate "every statement is true or false") and ontological relativism (or *anti-realism*). He writes: "the topic of bivalence raises very large issues ... they underlie the metaphysical disputes that arise in many different areas of philosophy between a realist and a positivist or idealist, or, in the colourless term I have preferred to use, an anti-realist, interpretation of some large class of statements." (*Truth and other Enigmas*, p. XXX.) But for Dummett it is not merely the case that anti-realism involves the denial of bivalence, but also vice versa: the denial of bivalence involves anti-realism, or at least: non-realism. I do not agree with the latter thesis: one may deny bivalence (more specifically, that part of the principle

which asserts that every statement/state of affairs is true or false), and yet still be a staunch realist, hence not an anti-realist. See the question at the end of section (c) of this chapter.

[*4] We can define, for all inferences $P_1,...,P_n \rightarrow C$ of PL:
$P_1,...,P_n \rightarrow C$ is logically valid := $(P_1 \wedge ... \wedge P_n \supset C)^*=$**t** is provable in AP1 - AP6 together with the appropriate definitions.
Then each valid inference $P_1,...,P_n \rightarrow C$ of classical truth-functional propositional logic (as formulated in PL) is seen to be a logically valid inference of PL (and presumably each logically valid inference of PL is a valid inference of classical truth-functional propositional logic). And, therefore, for each classically valid truth-functional propositional inference $P_1,...,P_n \rightarrow C$: "if $V(P_1^*)$ and ... and $V(P_n^*)$, then $V(C^*)$" is provable on the basis of AP1 - AP6 and the definitions up to DP31 and DP32. This is so, because if "$(P_1 \wedge ... \wedge P_n \supset C)^*=$**t**" is provable in AP1 - AP6 together with the appropriate definitions, then "if $V(P_1^*)$ and ... and $V(P_n^*)$, then $V(C^*)$" is provable on the basis of AP1 - AP6 and the definitions up to DP31 and DP32: Consider first that "**conj**$(t_1,...,t_n)$" is an obvious generalization of "**conj**(t,t')," and that the term $(P_1 \wedge ... \wedge P_n \supset C)^*$ is identical with the term "**impl**(**conj**$(P_1^*,...,P_n^*),C^*)$." From **impl**(**conj**$(P_1^*, ...,P_n^*),C^*)=$**t** we get by TP32, TP61 and DP11: C^***Pconj**$(P_1^*,...,P_n^*)$; hence by AP1, DP31 and DP32: if V(**conj**$(P_1^*,...,P_n^*)$), then $V(C^*)$. Therefore, by the generalization of TP98: if $V(P_1^*)$ and ... and $V(P_n^*)$, then $V(C^*)$.

CHAPTER I.15

LAWS OF TRUTH AND FALSITY

(a) The law of truth [*1] for "**conj**," TP98, has already been proved. The law of falsity for "**conj**" results from TP98 by TP107:

TP108 **all***x***all***y*(F(**conj**(*x*,*y*)) iff F(*x*) or F(*y*)).

The law of falsity for "**disj**," TP103, has already been proved. The law of truth for "**disj**" results from it by TP107:

TP109 **all***x***all***y*(V(**disj**(*x*,*y*)) iff V(*x*) or V(*y*)).

The law of truth for "**neg**" is simply the result of the definition of falsity:

TP110 **all***x*(V(**neg**(*x*)) iff F(*x*)).

If we had not defined falsity by means of truth, as we did in DP33, but had posited F(t) := **neg**(**w**)Pt (compare TP99), then TP110 would not have been the trivial consequence of a definition: V(**neg**(*x*)), that is (by DP32, DP31): **neg**(*x*)P**w**, that is (according to TP60): **neg**(**w**)P*x*, that is: F(*x*).
By DP33 and TP55 we obtain the law of falsity for "**neg**":

TP111 **all***x*(F(**neg**(*x*)) iff V(*x*)).

(b) The laws of truth and falsity for "**neg**" can already be obtained from AP1 - AP6 and the definitions. Also, we have seen that the law of falsity for "**disj**" results already from AP1 - AP6 and the definitions. This, however, is not the case for the law of truth for "**disj**." We can, indeed, prove on the basis of AP1 - AP6 and the definitions: **all***x***all***y*[if V(*x*) or V(*y*), then V(**disj**(*x*,*y*))] (apply TP26, AP1, AP2); but the converse of this is, on the basis of AP1 - AP6 and the definitions, equivalent to AP8, hence (because of the independence of AP8) not deducible from that basis:
(i) Assume **all***x***all***y*(if V(**disj**(*x*,*y*)), then V(*x*) or V(*y*)), hence **all***x*[if V(**disj**[*x*, **neg**(*x*)]), then V(*x*) or V(**neg**(*x*))].
Now: **all***x*V(**disj**[*x*,**neg**(*x*)]), for: **all***x*(**disj**[*x*,**neg**(*x*)]=**t**) by TP53(ii) and **tPw** (since M(**t**)), hence **all***x*(**disj**[*x*,**neg**(*x*)]**Pw**), hence by DP31 and DP32 the desired result.
Therefore: **all***x*[V(*x*) or V(**neg**(*x*))], that is: QC(**w**) (see I.14.(a)).
(ii) For the proof of the converse we need

TP112 **allxally**(if V(**neg**(*x*)) and V(**disj**(*x*,*y*)), then V(*y*)).

This is provable by using merely AP1 - AP6 and the definitions (see Appendix). Assume now: QC(**w**), hence **allx**(V(*x*) or V(**neg**(*x*)); assume also: V(**disj**(*x*,*y*)) and not V(*x*); from the two assumptions: V(**neg**(*x*)); from this and the second assumption by TP112: V(*y*).
Therefore: if QC(**w**), then **allxally**(if V(**disj**(*x*,*y*)), then V(*x*) or V(*y*)).
We have seen, too, that the law of truth for "**conj**" is already provable on the basis of AP1 - AP6 and the definitions. This is not the case for the law of falsity for "**conj**." We can, indeed, prove on the basis of AP1 - AP6 and the definitions: **allxally**[if F(*x*) or F(*y*), then F(**conj**(*x*,*y*))] (applying TP99, TP25, AP2, AP1); but the converse of this is, on the basis of AP1 - AP6 and the definitions, equivalent to AP8, and hence not deducible from that basis:
(**i**) Assume **allxally**(if F(**conj**(*x*,*y*)), then F(*x*) or F(*y*)), hence by DP33 **allxally**[if V(**neg**(**conj**(*x*,*y*))), then V(**neg**(*x*)) or V(**neg**(*y*))], hence **allx**[if V(**neg**(**conj**[*x*,**neg**(*x*)])), then V(**neg**(*x*)) or V(**neg**(**neg**(*x*)))].
Now: **allx**V(**neg**(**conj**[*x*,**neg**(*x*)])), for: V(**t**) and, by TP53(ii) and TP54, **allx**(**neg**(**conj**[*x*,**neg**(*x*)])=**t**).
Therefore: **allx**[V(**neg**(*x*)) or V(**neg**(**neg**(*x*)))], hence by TP55: **allx**[V(*x*) or V(**neg**(*x*))], that is: QC(**w**).
(**ii**) For the proof of the converse we need

TP113 **allxally**(if F(**neg**(*x*)) and F(**conj**(*x*,*y*)), then F(*y*)).

This is provable merely using AP1 - AP6 and the definitions. Assume now: QC(**w**), hence **allx**(V(*x*) or F(*x*)); assume also: F(**conj**(*x*,*y*)) and not F(*x*); by the first and second assumption V(*x*), hence by TP55 V(**neg**(**neg**(*x*))), hence by DP33 F(**neg**(*x*)); from this and the second assumption by TP113 F(*y*).
Therefore: if QC(**w**), then **allxally**(if F(**conj**(*x*,*y*)), then F(*x*) or F(*y*)).

(c) From TP97 and TP101 one obtains by TP107:

TP114 F(**conj***z*A[*z*]) iff **some***y*(A[*y*] and F(*y*));

TP115 V(**disj***z*A[*z*]) iff **some***y*(A[*y*] and V(*y*)).

We have seen that the law of truth for the big conjunction results already by AP1 - AP6 and the definitions (TP97). The same is true for "if **some***y*(A[*y*] and F(*y*)), then F(**conj***z*A[*z*])": assume **some***y*(A[*y*] and F(*y*)), hence by TP99 **some***y*(A[*y*] and **neg**(**w**)P*y*), hence by TP18 **some***y*(A[*y*] and **neg**(**w**)P*y* and *y***Pconj***z*A[*z*]), hence by AP1 **neg**(**w**)**Pconj***z*A[*z*], hence by TP99 F(**conj***z*A[*z*]). Its converse "if F(**conj***z*A[*z*]), then **some***y*(A[*y*] and F(*y*))," however, is on the basis of AP1 - AP6 and the definitions equivalent to "MK(**w**)," hence to *the conjunction of AP7 and AP8* (and not to "QC(**w**)" alone):

(i) Assume MK(**w**); assume F(**conj***z*A[*z*]), hence by TP99 **(1)** **neg(w)Pconj***z*A[*z*]. From MK(**w**) by DP26 and TP71: QC(**w**), hence by TP73 (**2**) QA(**neg(w)**). Also from MK(**w**) by DP26 and TP70: **w≠k**, hence by TP55 **neg(w)≠neg(k)**, hence by TP54 **neg(w)≠t**, hence by TP32 (**3**) not M(**neg(w)**). From (**1**), (**2**) and (**3**) by TP40: **some***y*(A[*y*] and **neg(w)P***y*), hence by TP99: **some***y*(A[*y*] and F(*y*)).

(**ii**) Assume: if F(**conj***z*A[*z*]), then **some***y*(A[*y*] and F(*y*)) (for all predicates A[*y*] of LP); assume for *reductio*: **w=k**, hence **neg(w)=neg(k)**, hence by TP54 **neg(w)=t**, hence **neg(w)Pconj***z*(*z≠z*) (M(**t**)), hence by TP99 F(**conj***z*(*z≠z*)); hence by the first assumption: **some***y*(*y≠y* and F(*y*)) - contradiction. Therefore: **w≠k**. By instantiation and TP99 from the first assumption: if **neg(w)P conj***z*QA(*z*), then **some***y*(QA(*y*) and **neg(w)P***y*). Now: **neg(w)Pconj***z*QA(*z*) by AP5, for according to TP18: **all***y*(if QA(*y*) and *y***Pneg(w)**, then *y***Pconj***z*QA(*z*)). Therefore: **some***y*(QA(*y*) and **neg(w)P***y*), hence by DP6 QA(**neg(w)**), hence by TP73 QC(**w**). From **w≠k** and QC(**w**) by TP70, TP71 and DP26: MK(**w**).

In contrast to "if F(**conj***z*A[*z*]), then **some***y*(A[*y*] and F(*y*))," "**all***x***all***y*(if F(**conj**(*x*,*y*)), then F(*x*) or F(*y*))" amounts only to AP8, not to the conjunction of AP8 and AP7, as we have seen. The same relationship obtains between "if V(**disj***z*A[*z*]), then **some***y*(A[*y*] and V(*y*))" and "**all***x***all***y*(V(**disj**(*x*,*y*)), then V(*x*) or V(*y*))." But "if **some***y*(A[*y*] and V(*y*)), then V(**disj***z*A[*z*])" results, just as the law of falsity for the big disjunction (TP101), already on the basis of AP1 - AP6 and the definitions: assume **some***y*(A[*y*] and V(*y*)), hence **some***y*(**disj***z*A[*z*]P*y* and *y***Pw**) by TP65, DP32, DP31; hence by AP1 **disj***z*A[*z*]**Pw**, hence V(**disj***z*A[*z*]) by DP31, DP32.

(d) To sum up: some of the ontological mirror-images of the general principles of truth and falsity that are familiar from the semantics of (finitary or infinitary) propositional logic are analytically true since they can be proved on the basis of the analytically true axioms AP1 - AP6 and the definitions (see also I.14.(e)); some, however, are synthetically true, since they are analytically equivalent (as is provable on the just indicated basis) to the synthetically true principle AP8, or even analytically equivalent to the synthetically true conjunction of AP7 and AP8.[*2] Thus, the semantics of propositional logic *can be regarded* (though it need not be so regarded) in such a manner that it has *synthetical content*: by defining in that semantics, which is about general principles of truth and falsity for statements (represented, as far as their relevant logical form is concerned, by the formulae of a formal language), truth and falsity for statements via the truth and falsity of the states of affairs those statements intend, *and* by interpreting sentence-connectives by the appropriate functors for states of affairs (all this being based on the system P of the ontology of states of affairs). However, even then there is *no synthetical content* in that part of the semantics of propositional logic in which it is stated categorically that, as a matter of semantic theory, this or that finite formula of the formal language (representing a certain class of statements having a common propositional form) *is true*, that is, there is no synthetical content in that part of the semantics of propositional logic that can be codified in a *sound* and *complete* standard calculus. *That part* (which incorporates standard propositional logic) is, even if based on the ontology of states of affairs, purely analytic (see I.14.(e) and comment [*4] of I.14).

COMMENTS

[*1] Frege defined *logic* as the *science of the laws of truth*. He is best understood as intending by "laws of truth" (in German: "*Gesetze des Wahrseins*") certain very *general truth-principles* (and not only laws of truth that present sufficient and necessary non-circular truth-conditions), and as counting among the "laws of truth" also the *general principles of falsity* (which are reducible to the general principles of truth by DP33, or its semantical analogue). Frege says literally (in order to separate logic from psychology): "Um jedes Mißverständnis auszuschließen und die Grenze zwischen Psychologie und Logik nicht verwischen zu lassen, weise ich der Logik die Aufgabe zu, die Gesetze des Wahrseins zu finden, nicht die des Fürwahrhaltens oder Denkens. In den Gesetzen des Wahrseins wird die Bedeutung des Wortes 'wahr' entwickelt." ("Logische Untersuchungen I: Der Gedanke," p. 343.) How does his conception of laws of truth compare with the conception of general principles of truth and falsity here employed?

It is clear from what he says before the quoted passage that "*Gesetz*" ("law") is not meant by him in a normative, but in a descriptive sense. Moreover, the subjects of the laws of truth, the truth-bearers, are for Frege primarily "thoughts" ("*Gedanken*"), only secondarily statements (see p. 344f; in contrast to other places in his works, he is not talking here about *an object* - "*Gegenstand*" - called "the true" - "*das Wahre*"). Fregean *thoughts* correspond naturally to finitely expressible states of affairs, or in other words to *propositions*.

They correspond to propositions, yet they cannot be identified with them. Certainly the subjective connotations of "*Gedanke*" are completely irrelevant for Frege. However, Frege also considers *thoughts* to be, without exception, abstract entities, and this is not the case for propositions as here conceived (see I.3.(e) above). Also, there seem to be *thoughts* for Frege that are neither true nor false (according to AP8 there are no propositions for which this is the case): "Der Satz 'Odysseus wurde tief schlafend in Ithaka ans Land gesetzt' hat offenbar einen Sinn. Da es aber zweifelhaft ist, ob der darin vorkommende Name 'Odysseus' eine Bedeutung [Bezug/*designatum*] habe, so ist es damit auch zweifelhaft, ob der ganze Satz eine [einen Wahrheitswert/truth value] habe. ... Käme es nur auf den Sinn des Satzes, den Gedanken, an, so wäre es unnötig, sich um die Bedeutung eines Satzteils zu kümmern; ... Der Gedanke bleibt derselbe, ob der Name 'Odysseus' eine Bedeutung hat oder nicht." ("Über Sinn und Bedeutung," p. 148f.)

Nevertheless, Fregean laws of truth *for thoughts* could still be considered to have by and large the same character as the general ontological principles of truth and falsity *for states of affairs* that have been stated and proved in this chapter and in the previous ones. However, the latter principles certainly cannot be obtained by a mere analysis of the meaning of the word "true," which Frege seems to claim for his "*Gesetze des Wahrseins*" (see the first quotation in this comment above); and not all of those general principles of truth and falsity are analytically true, which Frege certainly assumes for the laws of truth in his sense: non-analyticity is amply demonstrated in this chapter also for ontological laws of truth that, at first sight, are not suspected to be synthetical, for example "**all***x***all***y*(if V(**disj**(*x*,*y*), then V(*x*) or V(*y*))." Analogues to Frege's laws of truth can be found only among the general principles of truth and falsity that can be shown to be analytically true by being proved on the basis of the analytically true axioms AP1 - AP6 and the definitions.

On the basis of these clarifications concerning Fregean "laws of truth" Frege can certainly be said to have an *ontological conception* of logic, that is, he can be said to consider logic to be an *analytically valid part of ontology*.

[*2] What about the laws of truth for the functors of analytical possibility and necessity: (1) "**all***x*(V(**p**(*x*)) iff *x*≠**k**)" and (2) "**all***x*(V(**n**(*x*)) iff *x*=**t**)," and the corresponding laws of falsity (3) "**all***x*(F(**p**(*x*)) iff *x*=**k**)" and (4) "**all***x*(F(**n**(*x*)) iff *x*≠**t**)"? We can prove on the basis of AP1 - AP6 (and the definitions) alone: **all***x*(if *x*≠**k**, then **p**(*x*)=**t**), **all***x*(if *x*=**k**, then **p**(*x*)=**k**), **all***x*(if *x*=**t**, then **n**(*x*)=**t**), **all***x*(if *x*≠**t**, then **n**(*x*)=**k**), defining "**n**(*x*)" by "**conj***y*(*x*≠**t** and *y*=**k**)," "**p**(*x*)" by "**conj***y*(*x*=**k** and *y*=**k**)"; see comment [*3] of I.11. Call the latter four principles, for the sake of simple reference in the following proof, "the basic principles."

(1) is a consequence of AP7 (given AP1 - AP6): Assume V(**p**(*x*)), hence by AP7 (etc.) **p**(*x*)≠**k**, hence by the basic principles: *x*≠**k**. (The reverse is merely a matter of AP1 - AP6, which deductively include the basic principles, and the definitions.)

(2) is a consequence of AP7: Assume V(**n**(*x*)), hence by AP7 (etc.) **n**(*x*)≠**k**, hence by the basic principles: *x*=**t**. (The reverse is merely a matter of AP1 - AP6 and the definitions.)

(3) is a consequence of AP7: Assume F(**p**(*x*)), hence (by DP33, DP32, DP31) **neg**(**p**(*x*))**Pw**, hence by AP7 (etc.) **neg**(**p**(*x*))≠**k**, hence **p**(*x*)≠**t** (by TP54), hence by the basic principles: *x*=**k**. (The reverse is merely a matter of AP1 - AP6 and the definitions.)

(4) is a consequence of AP7: Assume F(**n**(*x*)), hence **neg**(**n**(*x*))**Pw**, hence by AP7 (etc.) **neg**(**n**(*x*))≠**k**, hence **n**(*x*)≠**t**, hence by the basic principles: *x*≠**t**. (The reverse is merely a matter of AP1 - AP6 and the definitions.)

Conversely, AP7 is a consequence both of (1) and of (4): By instantiation we have: V(**p**(**k**)) iff **k**≠**k** [F(**n**(**t**)) iff **t**≠**t**], hence: not V(**p**(**k**)) [not F(**n**(**t**)), that is, not V(**neg**(**n**(**t**)))], hence: not **p**(**k**)**Pw** [not **neg**(**n**(**t**))**Pw**], hence **w**≠**k**.

CHAPTER I.16

CONTINGENCY

(a) AP7 and AP8 do not exclude (on the basis of AP1 - AP6) "**w**=**t**." Nevertheless, the world is not the minimal state of affairs. Otherwise there would be only one obtaining state of affairs: the minimal state of affairs. For we have

TP116 **all**x(O(x) iff x=**t**) iff **w**=**t**.

But surely there are obtaining states of affairs other than the "tautological" one.

TP116 results by AP1 - AP6 and the definitions. If one draws AP8 into consideration, then the world is seen not to be the minimal state of affairs also for another reason. If it were the minimal state of affairs, then there would be at most two states of affairs: **t** and **k**; but surely there are also other states of affairs than these (it is very easy to adduce examples of states of affairs that neither analytically imply all states of affairs nor are analytically implied by all states of affairs): with the help of AP8 we can prove

TP117 if **w**=**t**, then **all**x(x=**t** or x=**k**).

And with the help of AP7 we also obtain (very easily) the converse of TP117:

TP118 if **all**x(x=**t** or x=**k**), then **w**=**t**.

(b) We posit as a further axiom:

AP9 **w**≠**t**.

AP9 (for states of affairs) cannot be regarded as being analytically true. It is not a matter of the present meaning of "**w**" (*the conjunction of all obtaining states of affairs*) and the present meaning of "**t**" (*the state of affairs that is intensional part of all states of affairs*) that **w** and **t** are different states of affairs.

By AP9 we have because of AP2, DP31 (yielding O(**w**)) and TP118:

TP119 **some**x(O(x) and x≠**t**) and **some**x(x≠**t** and x≠**k**).

AP9 is according to TP36 and AP2 equivalent to "not **wPt**," which is equivalent - because of TP59 and TP54 - to "not **kPneg(w)**," which is equivalent - because of TP91, TP85 and DP29 - to ‘‘P(**neg**(**w**)).’’ AP7, on the other hand, is equivalent to ‘‘not **kPw**,’’ which is - because of TP91, TP85 and DP29 - equivalent to ‘‘P(**w**).’’ We posit the definition

DP34 CT(t) := P(t) and P(**neg**(t))
(‘‘t is an analytically contingent state of affairs’’),

and obtain by AP7 and AP9 (according to DP34 and the remarks which immediately precede it):

TP120 CT(**w**).
(‘‘The world is an analytically contingent state of affairs.’’)

From TP120 we get immediately (applying DP34)

TP121 **some**x[P(x) and P(**neg**(x))].
(Version 1 of ‘‘there is an analytically contingent state of affairs.’’)

Thus, one can prove ‘‘**all**x[P(x) or P(**neg**(x))]’’ (see the remark below TP104 in I.13.(b)) *and* ‘‘**some**x[P(x) and P(**neg**(x))].’’ By TP94(i) and TP54 the latter amounts to ‘‘**some**x(x≠**k** and x≠**t**),’’ hence by TP117 and TP118 to ‘‘**w**≠**t**.’’

(c) ‘‘P(**w**) and P(**neg**(**w**))’’ is according to TP55 equivalent to ‘‘not [not P(**neg**(**neg**(**w**))) or not P(**neg**(**w**))],’’ hence, according to DP30, to ‘‘not [N(**neg**(**w**)) or N(**w**)],’’ hence to: ‘‘not N(**w**) and not N(**neg**(**w**)).’’ Therefore (applying DP34), TP120 is equivalent to

TP122 not N(**w**) and not N(**neg**(**w**)).

Note that ‘‘O(**w**)’’ is an analytical truth, TP122 (in particular its first conjunct) notwithstanding. There is nothing paradoxical in this. ‘‘O(**w**)’’ simply does not analytically imply ‘‘N(**w**)’’; otherwise, ‘‘O(**w**)’’ being an analytical truth, ‘‘N(**w**)’’ would be an analytical truth, and then ‘‘**w**’’ would not be a non-rigid designator (contrary to its semantics stated in I.12.(b)), since ‘‘N(**w**)’’ is analytically equivalent to ‘‘**w**=**t**’’ (TP93(i)), and ‘‘**t**’’ - although defined by a definite description - *is* a rigid designator: given the present interpretation of LP, it designates the same state of affairs under any circumstances.

TP122 immediately implies

TP123 **some**x[not N(x) and not N(**neg**(x))].
(Version 2 of ‘‘there is an analytically contingent state of affairs.’’)

Thus one can prove ‘‘not **some**x[N(x) and N(**neg**(x))]’’ (see the remark following TP104 in I.13.(b)) *and* ‘‘not **all**x[N(x) or N(**neg**(x))].’’ The latter is easily seen to be equivalent to "**some**x[P(x) and P(**neg**(x))]," and hence to "**w**≠**t**" (see the end of section (b) above).

Marshalling the relevant results, we obtain a table comparing the behavior of "V", "N" and "P" with respect to "**neg**":

N
not **some**x[(N(x) and N(**neg**(x))]
not **all**x[N(x) or N(**neg**(x))]
V
not **some**x[V(x) and V(**neg**(x))]
all$x$[V(x) or V(**neg**(x))]
P
some$x$[P(x) and P(**neg**(x))]
all$x$[(P(x) or P(**neg**(x))]

Moreover, because of TP121, we can prove the denial of the converse of TP94(iii): assume **all**x**all**y[if P(x) and P(y), then P(**conj**(x,y))], hence **all**x[if P(x) and P(**neg**(x)), then P(**conj**[x,**neg**(x)])]; but **all**x not P(**conj**[x,**neg**(x)]) [TP53(ii), TP94(i)]; therefore: **all**x[not P(x) or not P(**neg**(x))] - contradicting TP121. And because of TP123 we can prove the denial of the converse of TP93(iii): assume **all**x**all**y[if N(**disj**(x,y)), then N(x) or N(y)], hence **all**x[if N(**disj**[x,**neg**(x)]), then N(x) or N(**neg**(x))]; but **all**xN(**disj**[x,**neg**(x)]) [TP53(ii), TP93(i)]; therefore: **all**x[N(x) or N(**neg**(x))] - contradicting TP123. (The relevant results are easily arranged in a table comparing the behavior of "V", "N" and "P" with respect to "**disj**" and "**conj**.")

(d) Considering DP32 and the remarks following TP104 in I.13.(b) above, we already have the proof for

TP124 **all**x(if V(x), then P(x)) and **all**x(if N(x), then V(x)).

Given AP9, the converse of each of the two conjuncts of TP124 can be refuted, since in each case the negation is equivalent to "**w**≠**t**" (for the negation of the second conjunct, the equivalence holds on the basis of AP1 - AP6, for the negation of the first, on the basis of AP1 - AP8). Thus we have

TP125 **some**x(V(x) and not N(x)) and **some**x(P(x) and not V(x)).

Because of **all**x[if N(x), then not N(**neg**(x))] (which is equivalent to TP104) we have by DP30 and TP55: **all**x(if N(x), then P(x)), which, also, is an obvious logical consequence of TP124. The converse, however, can be shown not to obtain: **some**x(P(x) and not N(x)) is equivalent to TP121 according to DP30.

(e) According to TP106 there is a maximally consistent state of affairs, to wit, **w**, and both AP7 and AP8 are needed for proving this. But the mere assertion "**some***y*MK(*y*)" (without indication of an example) is on the basis of AP1 - AP6 (analytically) equivalent to TP104: "**t**≠**k**" (which is weaker than AP7):

(i) Assume **t**≠**k**, hence: not **kPt** (by TP36), hence by AP5 **some***x*(QA(*x*) and *x***Pk** and not *x***Pt**), hence **some***x*(QA(*x*) and *x*≠**t**) by AP2, hence by TP76: **some***y*MK(*y*).

(ii) Assume **t**=**k**, hence **neg(t)**=**neg(k)**, hence by TP54 **neg(t)**=**t**. **all***y*(**tP***y*), since M(**t**). Therefore: **all***y*(**tP***y* and **neg(t)P***y*), hence **all***y***some***x*(*x***P***y* and **neg**(*x*)**P***y*), hence **all***y* not K(*y*) by DP24, hence by DP26: not **some***y*MK(*y*).

AP9, in turn, is on the basis of AP1 - AP8 (synthetically) equivalent to the assertion "**some***x***some***y*(MK(*x*) and MK(*y*) and *x*≠*y*)" - "there are at least two maximal consistent states of affairs," or in other words: "there are at least two possible worlds":

(i) Assume **w**≠**t**, hence P(**neg(w)**) (see I.16.(b) above), hence by DP29 **some***y*(MK(*y*) and **neg(w)P***y*); *y*≠**w**, for otherwise **neg(w)Pw** - contradicting AP7 (**wPw** by AP2; hence, in case **neg(w)Pw**, by TP24, TP53(ii): **kPw**); hence by TP106: **some***x***some***y*MK(*x*) and MK(*y*) and *x*≠*y*).

(ii) Assume **some***x***some***y*(MK(*x*) and MK(*y*) and *x*≠*y*); assume for *reductio*: **w**=**t**, hence by TP117 (which is based on AP8) **all***x*(*x*=**t** or *x*=**k**); hence one of the possible worlds *x* and *y* must be **k** - contradicting TP72; therefore **w**≠**t**.

Thus, AP9 suffices (on the basis of AP1 - AP8) for establishing *possibilism with respect to possible worlds*: the assertion that there is a possible word that is not actual. For one will certainly accept the following principle (indeed, no matter which particular conception of possible worlds one has): *If there is more than one possible world, then not every possible world is actual.*[*1] And thus in the ontology of states of affairs the (numerical) existence of non-actual possible worlds is not a controversial issue: if **w** is not **t**, in other words: if not all states of affairs are either the contradictory or the tautological state of affairs (and this is as much as saying: if the ontology of states of affairs is not trivial), then there are non-actual possible worlds: maximally consistent states of affairs that do not obtain.

COMMENTS

[*1] Since possible worlds are maximally consistent states of affairs for which *to be actual* means *to obtain,* this principle can be expressed in LP (given the current interpretation of that language) as follows: if **some**x**some**y(MK(x) and MK(y) and $x \neq y$), then **some**x(MK(x) and not O(x)). For its proof neither AP8 nor AP9 is needed:
The proof is achieved by proving the contraposition of what is to be proved. Assume **all**x(if MK(x), then O(x)); assume also: MK(x) and MK(y); hence by the first assumption and DP31: xP**w** and yP**w**.
Therefore, in case MK(**w**), **w**=x and **w**=y (by TP79), hence x=y.
Assume now: not MK(**w**); hence by AP7 and TP72: not QC(**w**). Also by TP72: QC(y), since MK(y) (according to assumption); hence according to DP7, since yP**w** (according to assumption): **w**=y or T(**w**); the first member of the disjunction is contradicted by the conjunction of "QC(y)" and "not QC(**w**)"; the second member of the disjunction is contradicted by AP7 (in view of TP34).

CHAPTER I.17

A FURTHER EXAMINATION OF AXIOMS AP7 - AP9

(a) The general basis for examining AP7, AP8 and AP9 with respect to their deductive relations to each other and to other statements is the system AP1 - AP6 and the accompanying definitions (under the current interpretation of LP with respect to the universe of states of affairs).

First of all, the negation of AP7 is seen to imply AP8, since QC(**k**) is provable (on the basis of AP1 - AP6). Therefore: the negation of AP8 implies AP7. In other words: if the world were non-maximal, it would be *ipso facto* consistent.

Secondly, not only AP7, but also AP9 is sufficient, if added to AP1 - AP6, for proving "**t**≠**k**" (TP104). Assume for *reductio*: **t**=**k**, hence **all***x*(*x*P**t**), since T(**k**); therefore: **w**P**t**, hence, since **t**P**w** (M(**t**)), because of AP3: **w**=**t** - contradicting AP9. Thus, "**t**≠**k**" is seen to be (on the basis of AP1 - AP6) equivalent to "**w**≠**k** or **w**≠**t**," and although each member of this disjunction is a synthetic statement, the disjunction itself is not (since it is analytically equivalent to "**t**≠**k**" which is analytically true).

Thirdly, as another equivalent of "**t**≠**k**" with respect to AP1 - AP6 we have "**some***x***some***y*(*x*≠*y*)": for if **t**=**k**, then **all***x*(*x*P**t**) and **all***y*(**t**P*y*), hence by AP1 **all***x***all***y*(*x*P*y*), hence by AP3 **all***x***all***y*(*x*=*y*). Hence the disjunction of AP7 and AP9 amounts to stating that there are at least two states of affairs. In contrast to AP7 and AP9, AP8 makes no assertion whatever about the cardinality of the universe of discourse that goes beyond the merely logical assertion that it contains at least one entity.

Fourthly, we have seen that AP9 has equivalents (with respect to AP1 - AP8) in which the singular term "**w**" does not occur, not even hidden under the cover of an expression that is defined with its help. Hence, doubtless, those equivalents (for example, "**some***x*(*x*≠**t** and *x*≠**k**)" in I.16.(a), and "**some***x***some***y*(MK(*x*) and MK(*y*) and *x*≠*y*)" in I.16.(e)) are *analytic* statements. Therefore, it is clear that merely by appropriately strengthening the analytic foundations of system P (so far they merely comprise AP1 - AP6), AP9 would become superfluous as an axiom, since it could be proved on the basis of AP7, AP8 and the strengthened analytic foundations. This strengthening would be ideally achieved by the addition of axioms that state truthfully and as precisely as possible (in LP) *how many states of affairs there are* (surely a lot more than **t** and **k**),[*1] and to this purpose axiom-schema AP10 is introduced in I.20.

(b) For AP7 and AP8, in contrast to AP9, there are no equivalents (with respect to the remaining axioms) that do not contain "**w**." All their equivalents contain "**w**" overtly or hidden in a defined expression. But of course if we had chosen the predicate "O(*x*)" instead of the singular term "**w**" as *primitive expression* of LP, then, as for AP9, there would also be equivalents for AP7 and AP8 (with respect to AP1 - AP6) that do not contain "**w**." Choosing "O(*x*)" instead of "**w**" as primitive expression, the following system P′ is deductively equivalent to P:

P′

AP1 - AP6.
all*x***all***y*(if O(*x*) and *y*P*x*, then O(*y*)).
O(**conj***y*O(*y*)).
some*y* not O(*y*).
QC(**conj***y*O(*y*)).
some*y*(*y*≠**t** and O(*y*)).
w := **conj***y*O(*y*).
(All definitions of P, except DP31.)

The fourth, fifth and sixth item on this list are equivalents without "**w**" of (respectively) AP7, AP8 and AP9. System P has been preferred to system P′ on account of its greater economy in the number of its axioms: P needs no basic principles corresponding to the (analytically true) items holding second and third place on the list, since those principles can already be proved on the basis of AP1 - AP6 and the definition: O(t) := tP**w**. (Also, the axioms of P are syntactically simpler than the axioms of P′.)

(c) Finally, note that AP9 (unlike AP7 and AP8) is without exception irrelevant for the laws of truth and falsity for "**neg**" (TP110, TP111), "**conj**" (TP98, TP108), "**disj**"(TP109, TP103), "**conj***y*" (TP97, TP114), "**disj***y*" (TP115, TP101), "**p**" and "**n**" (see [*2] of I.15), irrelevant for the principle of (ontological) bivalence (TP107), and irrelevant (here indeed *like* AP7 and AP8) for the truth of "V(τ*)," where τ is any tautology of propositional (truth-functional or modal) logic (compare I.14.(e)). All these statements would also hold true if **t** and **k** were the only two states of affairs, **w** being identical with **t**. For the ontological foundations of propositional logic, indeed for those of logic as a whole,[*2] the existence of contingent states of affairs is of no importance at all.

COMMENTS

[*1] Not all statements of numerical existence (''for at least N *x*: A[*x*],'' ''for at most N *x*: A[*x*],'' for precisely N *x*: A[*x*],'' ''N'' designating a finite or infinite cardinal number) are synthetic. For example, all statements of numerical existence with respect to the predicate ''*x* is a natural number'' are analytic (analytically true or analytically false). (Another - very famous - example of a predicate having purely analytic statements of numerical existence is ''*x* is a divine being''.) Likewise, all statements of numerical existence with respect to the predicate ''*x* is a state of affairs'' are analytic. This does not make, for example, ''for at least one *x*: *x* is a state of affairs,'' ''for at least $\aleph_1$ *x*: *x* is a state of affairs'' trivially true, or trivially false, as if there were no room for ontological controversy with respect to these statements. But if they are false, they are analytically false; if they are true, they are analytically true. (If the first statement mentioned were false, we could not apply classical logic, which requires non-emptiness of the universe of discourse, in order to formulate a theory of states of affairs. We would then have to turn to *free logic*; but what would be the point of formulating a theory of states of affairs if there were no such entities?)

[*2] The idea that large and central parts of logic are founded upon the ontology of states of affairs is very clearly articulated by A Reinach in his ''Zur Theorie des negativen Urteils'' (which is certainly a milestone in the ontological investigation of states of affairs), p. 251 (a translation by B. Smith of the quotation can be found in *Parts and Moments*, p. 376; however, the translation seems not quite accurate to me: Smith translates ''*bestehen*'' by ''subsist'' instead of ''obtain'' which, however, is the better *terminus technicus* for what is meant, namely the actual existence of states of affairs): ''Ein Urteil ist richtig, wenn der zugehörige Sachverhalt besteht; und zwei kontradiktorische Urteile können nicht beide richtig sein, *weil* zwei kontradiktorische Sachverhalte nicht beide bestehen können. Das Urteilsgesetz findet also seine Begründung in dem Sachverhaltsgesetz. ... Zugleich haben wir hier ein Beispiel dafür, in welchem Sinne wir oben gemeint haben, daß große Teile der traditionellen Logik sich ihrem Fundamente nach als allgemeine Sachverhaltslehre herausstellen werden.'' Indeed, if the ontology of states of affairs is extended by the ontology of attributes and individuals, *logic in its totality* can be founded on *ontology* (this will be made plausible in parts III and IV of this book). (Logic *can* be so founded, and intensional ontological foundations for logic *are* rather natural; for modal predicate logic, this is argued in detail in my ''An Alternative Semantics for Modal Predicate-Logic.'' But, of course, it need not be so founded. See, for example, my ''Ontologically Minimal Logical Semantics''.)

If logic is founded upon ontology, we can either retain logic as a theory about *statements* and *inferences*, or, indeed, turn it into a part of ontology; and we have yet another choice: we can found logic either on *intensional ontology*, or on *extensional ontology*. Reinach, clearly, favors the first approach, and so do I. (Reinach also states the conception of the truth of a statement which is natural and proper for that approach: a statement (or "judgment") is true (or "correct") if and only if the corresponding state of affairs obtains.) Frege, on the contrary, is an advocate of the second approach; in his "Ausführungen über Sinn und Bedeutung" he writes on p. 31f: "Die Inhaltslogiker bleiben nur zu gerne beim Sinn stehen; denn, was sie Inhalt nennen, ist, wenn nicht gar Vorstellung, so doch Sinn. Sie bedenken nicht, daß es in der Logik nicht darauf ankommt, wie Gedanken aus Gedanken hervorgehen ohne Rücksicht auf den Wahrheitswert, daß der Schritt vom Gedanken zum Wahrheitswert, daß, allgemeiner, der Schritt vom Sinne zur Bedeutung [Bezug/*designatum*] getan werden muß; daß die logischen Gesetze zunächst Gesetze im Reich der Bedeutungen [Bezüge/*designata*] sind und sich erst mittelbar auf den Sinn beziehen." This does not agree very well with the passages that are referred to in comment [*1] of I.15, but that need not concern us here.

Frege is certainly right in arguing that the *mere* consideration of *sense* (in German: "*Sinn*") is not enough in logic. We would have remained on the level of the mere consideration of *sense* in the present work, if we had not introduced the axioms AP7 and AP8 (and had replaced AP9 by "**some**x(x≠**t** and x≠**k**)"), if, indeed, we had not introduced the singular term "**w**" or any other means of making an ontological truth-predicate available in LP, if, in other words, truth had been of no importance for us. Obviously, that we have left truth out of consideration is not a charge Frege could raise against us.

Frege is wrong in saying that logical laws are primarily laws in the realm of denotation (which, for Frege, leaving aside denotation in indirect contexts, comprises only extensional entities), and only indirectly refer to sense (or intensional entities). For sets, extensional functions, truth values - indeed, all extensional entities *other than* primary individuals (individuals not reducible to other entities) are reducible to intensional entities. Logic, therefore, can be constructed on any level without irreducible reference to extensions other than primary individuals. Indeed, is there any plausibility at all, for example, to the claim that truth-functional propositional logic is primarily about truth values and (extensional) truth-functions? This could only have been the idea of a mathematician (though its methodological usefulness is, of course, beyond question).

CHAPTER I.18

THE HIERARCHIES OF STATES OF AFFAIRS

(a) We inductively define an infinity of predicates of LP on the basis of "A(*x*)" ("*x* is an atom") and "C(*x*)" ("*x* is a complete whole"):

DP35 $A_0(t) := A(t)$;
$A_{n+1}(t) :=$ **all***y*(if *y*Pt, then *y*=t or $A_n(y)$).
("The lower degree of t *is at most* 0 [1,2,3,...].")

DP36 $C^0(t) := C(t)$;
$C^{n+1}(t) :=$ **all***y*(if tP*y*, then *y*=t or $C^n(y)$).
("The upper degree of t *is at most* 0 [1,2,3,...].")

DP37 $A_{=0}(t) := A_0(t)$;
$A_{=n+1}(t) := A_{n+1}(t)$ and not $A_n(t)$.
("The lower degree of t *is* 0 [1,2,3,...].")

DP38 $C^{=0}(t) := C^0(t)$;
$C^{=n+1}(t) := C^{n+1}(t)$ and not $C^n(t)$.
("The upper degree of t *is* 0 [1,2,3...].")

The defined predicates serve to describe the hierarchical structure of the universe of states of affairs (but they do this *completely* only in case the number of states of affairs is finite).

(b) We have:

TP126 **all***x*(M(*x*) iff $A_{=0}(x)$).
("A state of affairs is minimal if and only if its lower degree is 0.")

TP127 **all***x*(T(*x*) iff $C^{=0}(x)$).
("A state of affairs is total if and only if its upper degree is 0.")

TP128 **all***x*(QA(*x*) iff $A_1(x)$).
("A state of affairs is quasi-atomic if and only if its lower degree is at most 1.")

TP129 **all***x*(QC(*x*) iff $C^1(x)$).
("A state of affairs is quasi-complete if and only if its upper degree is at most 1.")

TP130 **all**x(EL(x) iff $A_{=1}(x)$).
("The elementary states of affairs - by TP84: the minutely substantial states of affairs - are precisely the states of affairs whose lower degree is 1." The proof depends on DP20, TP128, TP126, DP37.)

TP131 **all**x(MK(x) iff $C^{=1}(x)$).
(The possible worlds - the maximally consistent states of affairs - are precisely the states of affairs whose upper degree is 1." The proof depends on TP72, TP129, TP34, TP127, DP38.)

(c) Futher we have:

TP132 **all**x(if $A_n(x)$, then $A_{n+1}(x)$), **all**x(if $C^n(x)$, then $C^{n+1}(x)$).

This theorem implies

TP133 **all**x(if $A_n(x)$, then $A_m(x)$), **all**x(if $C^n(x)$, then $C^m(x)$)
(where m is an index higher than n).

By TP133 we obtain

TP134 **no**x($A_{=n}(x)$ and $A_{=m}(x)$), **no**x($C^{=n}(x)$ and $C^{=m}(x)$)
(where m is an index higher than n).
("No state of affairs has two lower or two upper degrees.")

(d) In the language LP we can express for any natural number n ($n \geq 0$) either that there are *at least*, or *at most*, or *precisely* n entities in the universe of discourse to which a certain predicates applies. The procedure according to which **≤N**xA[x] ("for at most N x: A[x]"), **≥N**xA[x] ("for at least N x: A[x]") is definable for any Arabic numeral N (starting with "1") can be gathered from the following examples:

≤1xA[x] := **all**x**all**x'(if A[x] and A[x'], then $x=x'$).
≥1xA[x] := **some**xA[x].
≤2xA[x] := **all**x**all**x'**all**x''(if A[x] and A[x'] and A[x''], then $x=x'$ or $x=x''$ or $x'=x''$).
≥2xA[x] := **some**x**some**x'(A[x] and A[x'] and $x \neq x'$).
≤3xA[x] := **all**x**all**x'**all**x''**all**x'''(if A[x] and A[x'] and A[x''] and A[x'''], then $x=x'$ or $x=x''$ or $x=x'''$ or $x'=x''$ or $x'=x'''$ or $x''=x'''$).
≥3xA[x] := **some**x**some**x'**some**x''(A[x] and A[x'] and A[x''] and $x \neq x'$ and $x \neq x''$ and $x' \neq x''$).

Then we define:

N*x*A[*x*] := **≥N***x*A[*x*] and **≤N***x*A[*x*].
(“For precisely N *x*: A[*x*].”)

Moreover we define:

<N*x*A[*x*] := not **≥N***x*A[*x*].
(“For less than N *x*: A[*x*].”)

>N*x*A[*x*] := not **≤N***x*A[*x*].
(“For more than N *x*: A[*x*].”)

For the sake of simplicity in formulating theorems we finally stipulate:

≤0*x*A[*x*] := not **some***x*A[*x*].

≥0*x*A[*x*] := **some***x*A[*x*] or not **some***x*A[*x*].

(The three definition-schemata above these two may also be applied to the numeral “0”.) One immediately obtains on the basis of these definitions: not **<0***x*A[*x*], **0***x*A[*x*] iff **no***x*A[*x*], **≥N+1***x*A[*x*] iff not **≤N***x*A[*x*]. (N+1 is, of course, the Arabic numeral following immediately upon N in the natural order of Arabic numerals. Likewise, *n*+1 is the Arabic index-numeral following immediately upon *n* in the natural order of Arabic indices.)

(e) After these definitional preparations, we are able to formulate in LP the following three perspicuous theorems:

TP135 **all***x*(if $A_n(x)$, then **≤N***y*($A_{=1}(y)$ and *y*P*x*)).
(“If the lower degree of *x* is at most *n*, then at most N states of affairs of lower degree 1 - by TP130: *elementary states of affairs* - are part of *x*.”)

TP136 **all***x*(if **≤N***y*($A_{=1}(y)$ and *y*P*x*), then $A_n(x)$).
(“If at most N states of affairs of lower degree 1 are part of *x*, then the lower degree of *x* is at most *n*.”)

TP137 **all***x*($A_{=n}(x)$ iff **N***y*($A_{=1}(y)$ and *y*P*x*)).
(“The lower degree of *x* is *n* if and only if N states of affairs of lower degree 1 are parts of *x*.”)

The three analogues of TP135 - TP137: "**all**x(if $C^n(x)$, then ≤**N**y($C^{=1}(y)$ and xPy))," "**all**x(if ≤**N**y($C^{=1}(y)$ and xPy), then $C^n(x)$)," "**all**x($C^{=n}(x)$ iff **N**y($C^{=1}(y)$ and xPy))" are of course also provable (in AP1 - AP6).

These results show that the lower and upper hierarchies of states of affairs described above are hierarchies of *intensional content*. The intensional content of a state of affairs x can be measured in two ways (*directly* and *indirectly*):

(1) It can be measured by the number of the elementary states of affairs that are intensional parts of x. The *greater* that number, *which in all finite cases can be shown to be precisely the lower degree of* x (TP137, TP130), the greater is the intensional content of x: the more states of affairs are analytically implied by that state of affairs. (If the number of elementary states of affairs is infinite, then there are states of affairs which consist of infinitely many elementary states of affairs. For example, if there is a denumerable infinity of them, then there are states of affairs which consist of $\aleph_0$ elementary states of affairs, *and* there are no states of affairs which consist of more than $\aleph_0$ states of affairs. Therefore in that case all *infinite* states of affairs have the same *transfinite lower degree*: $\aleph_0$. This is not the case if there are more than $\aleph_0$ elementary states of affairs.)

(2) The intensional content of a state of affairs x can also be measured by the number of the maximally consistent states of affairs of which x is an intensional part. The *smaller* that number, *which in all finite cases can be shown to be precisely the upper degree of* x (the pendant of TP137 for "$C^{=n}(x)$", TP131), the greater is the intensional content of x. (In case there are infinitely many maximally consistent states of affairs - this is precisely the case if there infinitely many elementary states of affairs - we have at least one *transfinite upper degree* which is held by certain states of affairs.)

Only in case the number of states of affairs is finite will the two ways of measuring their intensional content be equivalent in the sense that they will yield the same finite quasi-order of states of affairs from the state of affairs having least intensional content to the state of affairs having most intensional content. In the lower hierarchy this identical quasi-order is interpreted "from the bottom," in the upper hierarchy it is interpreted "from the top": *the upper degree of* x is equal to *the maximal lower degree* minus *the lower degree of* x; the *lower degree of* x is equal to the *maximal upper degree* minus the *upper degree of* x. But if the number of states of affairs is infinite, then, for example, the states of affairs which have the upper degrees 2 and 1 are assigned the *same* transfinite lower degree, and the indirect way of measuring the intensional content of states of affairs produces a quasi-order different from the one that is produced by the direct way.

(f) Where in the hierarchical structure of the universe of states of affairs is the position of states of affairs that are our daily "companions" as intensions of assertions and objects of perceptions and intentions? Take an ordinary state of affairs, for example the state of affairs p_0: that Michael is smoking a cigarette at t_0. It is most plausible that there are both infinitely many maximally consistent states of affairs of which p_0 is an intensional part, and infinitely many of which it is *not* an intensional part, therefore, infinitely many elementary states of affairs that are intensional parts of p_0. (Since there are infinitely many possible worlds of which p_0 is not part, there are infinitely many possible worlds of which its negation is part, hence - according to TP60 and **allxally**(if $x \neq y$, then **neg**(x)≠**neg**(y)) (a consequence of TP55) - there are infinitely many negations of possible worlds which are parts of p_0, hence - according to TP77 - there are infinitely many elementary states of affairs which are parts of p_0.) Therefore, both the upper and the lower degree of p_0 is transfinite.

In an infinite universe of states of affairs, states of affairs having finite lower degree are called "small," and states of affairs having finite upper degree "big," Thus, p_0 is neither big nor small, but of medium size. As with respect to other areas of the totality of being, so also with respect to the universe of states of affairs, human interest is directed primarily towards the *mesocosmos*.

CHAPTER I.19

THE DISCRETENESS OF "P*"

(a) The concept "smaller than" can be used in defining the concept "immediately smaller than": "*x* is immediately smaller than *y*" := "*x* is smaller than *y*, and there is no *z* such that *x* is smaller than *z*, and *z* smaller than *y*." In analogy to this, we can use the concept of proper part in defining the concept of *immediate proper part*. In LP:

DP39 tNP*t′ := tP*t′ and **no***z*(tP**z* and *z*P*t′).
("t is an immediate - or next - proper part of t′.")

The following theorem is provable:

TP138 **all***x***all***y*[*x*NP**y* iff **some***z*(EL(*z*) and not *z*P*x* and *y*=**conj**(*x*,*z*))].

"**some***z*(EL(*z*) and not *z*P*x* and *y*=**conj**(*x*,*z*))" can be equivalently replaced in TP138 by "**one***z*(EL(*z*) and not *z*P*x* and *y*=**conj**(*x*,*z*))" (Suppose EL(*z*) and not *z*P*x* and *y*=**conj**(*x*,*z*) and EL(*z*′) and not *z*′P*x* and *y*=**conj**(*x*,*z*′); hence, since *z*P**conj**(*x*,*z*), *z*P**conj**(*x*,*z*′), hence by TP38, DP20: *z*P*x* or *z*P*z*′; hence *z*P*z*′, hence, since EL(*z*) and EL(*z*′), by TP80: *z*=*z*′.) Another equivalent for "**some***z*(EL(*z*) and not *z*P*x* and *y*=**conj**(*x*,*z*))" is "**one***z*(EL(*z*) and not *z*P*x* and *z*P*y*)" (Suppose **some***z*(EL(*z*) and not *z*P*x* and *y*=**conj**(*x*,*z*)); hence, since *z*P**conj**(*x*,*z*), **some***z*(EL(*z*) and not *z*P*x* and *z*P*y*). Assume moreover: EL(*k*) and not *k*P*x* and *k*P*y* and EL(*k*′) and not *k*′P*x* and *k*′P*y*; therefore, since *y*=**conj**(*x*,*z*), by TP38, TP80: *k*=*z* and *k*′=*z*, hence *k*=*k*′. Suppose conversely: **one***z*(EL(*z*) and not *z*P*x* and *z*P*y*); in order to obtain **some***z*(EL(*z*) and not *z*P*x* and *y*=**conj**(*x*,*z*)) from this, consider (**i**) of the proof of TP138 in the Appendix (after (**3**)).) Thus, *x* is an immediate propert part of *y* if and only if there is precisely one element that is part of *y*, but not of *x*.

(b) Further we have

TP139 **all***x***all***y*(if *x*P**y*, then **some***z*′(*x*NP**z*′) and **some***z*′(*z*′NP**y*)).

(Note that in the proof of TP139 only "not *y*P*x*" in the antecedent "*x*P**y*" is actually used.) TP139 expresses the *discreteness* of "P*". With respect to the present interpretation of LP, TP139 says that for each state of affairs that analytically implies some *other* state of affairs, there is some state of affairs *closest to it* (in intensional content) that is analytically implied by it; and that for each state of affairs that is analytically implied by some *other* state of affairs, there is some state of affairs *closest to it* by which it is analytically implied.[*1] The discreteness of "P*" is independent of the cardinality of the universe of discourse since no non-logical assumption about its cardinality is used in the proof of TP139. Thus if, for example, the number of states of affairs were $\aleph_1$ - the cardinality of the set of real numbers - this would not falsify TP139.

(c) In accordance with the discreteness of "P*", every instance of proper analytical implication between states of affairs *y* and *x* can be divided into smallest steps of proper analytical implication, for we have:

TP140 **all***x***all***y*(*x*P**y* iff *x*NP**y* or **some***z*′(*z*′NP**y* and *x*P**z*′)).

Every such instance of proper analytical implication can be *divided* into smallest steps, but this does not mean that it can be *dissolved* into smallest steps such that *x* is reached from *y* after taking *finitely* many of them. However, even human logicians have no difficulty in covering infinite distances of analytical implication: the state of affairs that George is a male human being at t_0 is in fact inferred without difficulty from the state of affairs that George is a husband at t_0, although the former state of affairs, which is a proper intensional part of the latter, surely contains *infinitely fewer* elementary state of affairs (is contained in infinitely more maximally consistent states of affairs) than the latter (given that the number of states of affairs is infinite; that this is a correct assumption is argued in the next chapter). What is beyond the ken of human logicians are, indeed, not the large steps of analytical implication (at least not those between medium-sized, nevertheless infinite, ordinary states of affairs), but rather the tiny ones: we cannot distinguish, for example, from a given state of affairs - say, an ordinary one - a state of affairs that contains precisely one elementary state of affairs less than the given state of affairs of which it is intensional part, because it is quite impossible for us to grasp elementary states of affairs (negations of possible worlds) *in isolation*. Thus, we are actually acquainted (through language and through perception) only with *some* states of affairs from among those of medium size (other states of affairs are too big for our acquaintance, yet others are too small, or - though medium-sized - they are too elusive).

COMMENTS

[*1] If one assumed *density* for "P*", this would be expressed by "**allxally**(if xP*y, then **somez**(xP*z and zP*y))," which - in view of DP39 - is equivalent to (DN) "**allxally**(if xP*y, then not xNP*y)" (or to "**noxsomey**(xNP*y)"). (DN) is with respect to a universe of discourse that does not merely contain atoms (in the sense of DP2) inconsistent with (DC1) "**allx**(**somey**(xP*y), then **somez′**(xNP*z′))" (which is logically implied by TP139); for assume **somey**(xP*y), hence by (DC1) **somez′**(xNP*z′), hence by DP39 **somez′**(xP*z′ and xNP*z′), hence by (DN) **somez′**(xP*z′ and xNP*z′ and not xNP*z′) - which is a contradiction. Therefore: **allxnoy**(xP*y), that is (by DP1): **allxally**(if xPy, then x=y), that is (by DP2): **ally**A(y). (This deduction also shows that "**ally**A(y)" is definitionally equivalent to the conjunction of (DN) and (DC1).) Likewise, (DN) is with respect to a universe that does not merely contain atoms inconsistent with (DC2) "**ally**(**somex**(xP*y), then **somez′**(z′NP*y))" (which is also logically implied by TP139; the conjunction of (DC1) and (DC2) is logically equivalent to TP139).

CHAPTER I.20

THE CARDINALITY OF THE UNIVERSE OF STATES OF AFFAIRS

(a) There are infinitely many states of affairs. In fact, the cardinal number even of *obtaining* states of affairs is at least $\aleph_1$. This is shown by the following argument: Consider two material objects m_1 and m_2 moving continuously towards each other on a straight line in space until they collide. This process consists in the obtaining of non-denumerably many states of affairs: that the distance between m_1 and m_2 is *r* meters at **t**(*r*) is an obtaining state of affairs for every *r* in the appropriate continuous interval of real numbers IR, **t**(*r*) being *that* moment out of the appropriate time-interval IT in which the distance between m_1 and m_2 is *r*.

We *can* express in LP (fairly elegantly) that there are infinitely many states of affairs (see axiom-schema AP10 below); but any more precise description of the cardinality of the universe of states of affairs is impossible in LP if we do not turn it into a set-theoretical or a higher-order language or change it in some other fairly drastic way (for example, by introducing transfinite quantifiers).

(b) Also, the following result, *in the infinitary case*, cannot be expressed in LP, and hence not proved in an axiomatic system formulated in LP: The universe of states of affairs can be one-to-one mapped onto the power-set of the set of all elementary states of affairs. Therefore, its cardinality must be the cardinality of that power-set, that is, 2^C, where C is the cardinal number (finite or transfinite) of all elementary states of affairs.

The existence of a one-to-one mapping of all states of affairs onto all sets of elementary states of affairs is easily demonstrated. (1) To each state of affairs there correponds the set of all elementary states of affairs that are intensional parts of it. (2) Different states of affairs are such that different sets of elementary states of affairs correspond to them in the indicated manner (according to AP3, AP5). And (3): For each set of elementary states of affairs M there is a state of affairs *m*, to wit, the conjunction of all elements of M, such that M is the set of all elementary states of affairs which are intensional parts of *m*. This is so because for every set of elementary states of affairs M we have **all***x*(EL(*x*) and *x***P****conj***z*($z\in_S$M) iff $x\in_S$M). ("$\in_S$" is the relational concept of *set-theoretical* elementhood; remember that there is also a relational concept of elementhood *for states of affairs*; see DP21.) Assume M is a set of elementary states of affairs; hence **all***x*($x\in_S$M iff EL(*x*) and $x\in_S$M), hence by TP29 **conj***z*($z\in_S$M)=**conj***z*(EL(*z*) and $z\in_S$M), hence by TP44 and DP21 (remember **all***x*($x\in_S$M iff EL(*x*) and $x\in_S$M)): **all***x*(EL(*x*) and *x***P****conj***z*($z\in_S$M) iff $x\in_S$M).

It is obvious from this demonstration that we could prove its result also in AP1 - AP6 *as formulated in LP* if we only had in LP the concept "$\in_s$". But by turning LP into a set-theoretical language we would introduce set theory already into the very basis of ontology, namely into the theory of states of affairs. Given the intensionalistic approach defended here, this must be avoided. (The result of the demonstration could also be reached on the basis of AP1 - AP6 without using set-theoretical concepts if *any* set of elementary states of affairs could be picked out by some predicate of LP; this can be done in case the number of elementary states of affairs is finite; but in case there are infinitely many elementary states of affairs it is impossible; for then the sets of elementary states of affairs are *non-denumerable*, whereas the predicates of LP are *denumerable*.)

Thus, AP1 - AP6 *as formulated in LP* falls short of being a *power-set algebra* (which, interpreted with respect to states of affairs and analytical implication, would yield a more complete, true description of the universe of states of affairs than AP1 - AP6); AP1 - AP6 contains a power-set algebra only to the extent that such an algebra can be presented in a normal first-order language without the concept of set and set-theoretical elementhood. (But a power-set algebra of states of affairs can be had within the appropriate background theories by replacing "A[*x*]" in AP4 and AP6 by "$x \in_s m$" or, more generally, by "*f*(*x*)", and by putting "**all***m*(if SET OF STAT(*m*), then ..." or, more generally, "**all***f*(if PROP OF STAT(*f*), then ..." in front of those principles, all other things remaining equal.) The limitation is necessary at this stage of theoretical development; it is not a defect that could not be remedied later on (after one has introduced properties of states of affairs).

(c) For no cardinal number C is 2^C the cardinal number $\aleph_0$ of the natural numbers (the smallest transfinite cardinal). If C is a *finite* cardinal, then 2^C is also a finite cardinal, hence it is not $\aleph_0$. If C is a *transfinite* cardinal, then C either is identical with $\aleph_0$, or it is larger than $\aleph_0$; in the former case, 2^C is not identical with $\aleph_0$, since 2^C is larger than C (*Cantor's Principle*); in the latter case, 2^C is larger than $\aleph_0$, hence not identical with $\aleph_0$, since 2^C is larger than C which is larger than $\aleph_0$.

Given the result obtained in section (b), this implies that the cardinality of the universe of states of affairs *is not* $\aleph_0$. But according to the Löwenheim-Skolem Theorem this cannot be proved in any axiomatic theory formulated in LP in which the finiteness of the universe of discourse cannot be proved (for example, not in AP1 - AP6, and not in any extension of AP1 - AP6 that does not allow us to prove that there are at most *n* states of affairs for some natural number *n*). Thus, the limitations of LP are apparent also with respect to this purely negative result about the cardinal number of states of affairs.

(d) In AP1 - AP9 we can prove that there at least four states of affairs: **t**, **w**, **neg(w)**, and **k**. (By AP7, TP104 and AP9: **t**, **w** and **k** are different from each other; moreover: **neg(w)≠t**; otherwise **neg(neg(w))=neg(t)**, hence by TP54 and TP55 **w=k** - contradicting AP7; **neg(w)≠k**, otherwise **neg(neg(w)) =neg(k)**, hence by TP54 and TP55 **w=t** - contradicting AP9; **neg(w)≠w** by TP105.) That there are more than four states of affairs cannot be proved on the basis of AP1 - AP9: the four states of affairs **t**, **w**, **neg(w)** and **k** together with their appropriate relationships of parthood constitute a minimal model of AP1 - AP9 (a model in which the elementary states of affairs - **w** and **neg(w)** - coincide with the maximally consistent ones). But, in view of the argument in section (a), we are well advised to posit in addition to AP1 - AP9 also:

AP10 **some**xA$_{=n}(x)$.

AP10 is an axiom-schema; it is instantiated by an infinity of axioms: all statements of LP that can be obtained from AP10 by substituting the indices "0", "1" "2" ... for "n". Thus, AP10 asserts that each finite lower degree is held by some state of affairs. Because of TP134, this implies that *there are infinitely many states of affairs*.[*1] (AP10 makes AP9 redundant: on the basis of AP1 - AP6 and AP8, we can prove "if **some**x(x**≠t** and x**≠k**), then **w≠t**" (the contraposition of TP117); and "**some**x(x**≠t** and x**≠k**)" is a consequence of AP10 and AP1 - AP6.)

With the qualifications pointed out in this chapter, the ontology of states of affairs, in so far as it is merely a matter of the single category of states of affairs, can now be regarded as complete. No principle of a general and abstract nature involving merely the category of states of affairs needs to be added to system P (i.e. AP1 - AP10 plus the accompanying definitions). However, if we draw into consideration other categories besides the category of states of affairs - above all the category of individuals and the category of properties of individuals - if in other words we consider *the constituents* of states of affairs, then it becomes obvious that the end of the (true) ontological story of states of affairs has not been reached at all. The story is continued in part III and IV of this book.

COMMENTS

[*1] Let it be asserted without proof that an axiom of infinity which is a *statement*, not an *axiom-schema*, cannot be consistently added to AP1 - AP6 in LP. (''**allxsomey**(*y*P**x*)'' and ''**allxsomey**(*x*P**y*)'' will immediately lead to inconsistency.) It is known that there is no statement of infinity for the atomistic calculus of individuals - Goodman's mereology (see W. Hodges, D. Lewis, ''Finitude and Infinitude in the Atomic Calculus of Individuals''); the same method of proof should be applicable also to the ontology of states of affairs, which is, after all, an atomistic mereology of states of affairs (*with* a null-element).

II

ONTOLOGY OF PROPERTIES AND MEREOLOGY

CHAPTER II.1

INTENSIONAL PARTHOOD BETWEEN PROPERTIES

(a) The axioms AP1 - AP6 are the heart of the system P of the ontology of states of affairs. But this is not their only philosophically important interpretation. It is somewhat unusual to speak of one state of affairs *p* being part of another state of affairs *q* (that is, to conceive of the converse of analytical implication as a part-whole concept). In contrast, it is rather common in the onto-logical tradition to say that property *f* is part of property *g*. (Unmistakable instances of this usage can already be found in Plato's *Parmenides*.) And it is a commonplace of that tradition that there are two ways in which a property *f* can be a part of a property *g*, namely *extensionally* and *intensionally*: *being an animal* is an *intensional part* of *being human*, and not vice versa; but *being human* is an *extensional part* of *being an animal*, and not vice versa.

The two ways in which properties may be part of each other are not unconnected; they are interrelated by the following *inversion principle*:

(IP) For all properties *f* and *g*: *f* is an intensional part of *g* if and only if *g* is an extensional part of *f*.[*1]

If this is correct (and *it is* correct), then "*g* is an extensional part of *f*" cannot be simply made synonymous (for all properties *f* and *g*) with "all *g*s are *f*s."[*2] For if one used *that* definition, then, according to (IP), one would have to consider the property of being an animal with kidneys (at t_0) to be an intensional part of the property of being an animal with a heart (at t_0), because all animals with hearts are animals with kidneys. But being an animal with kidneys is surely *not* an intensional part of being an animal with a heart - at least not if intensional parthood between properties is analogous (and *it is* analogous) to intensional parthood between states of affairs, that is, analogous to the converse of analytical implication.

However, this argument against defining "*g* is an extensional part of *f*" as "all *g*s are *f*s," is based on a tacit presupposition which we are not at all forced to make: that "all *g*s are *f*s" is synonymous with "all *actually existing g*s are *f*s." The difficulty disappears if, instead, we make "all *g*s are *f*s" synonymous with "all *possible g*s are *f*s"; then, indeed, *all actually existing* animals with hearts are animals with kidneys; but this no longer means that *all* (*all possible*) animals with hearts are animals with kidneys. Therefore, given the requirement of preserving the validity of (IP), may we not define "*g* is an extensional part of *f*" as meaning the same as "all *g*s are *f*s" in the sense of "all possible *g*s are *f*s"?

(b) This definition may seem problematic because it leads unavoidably to the introduction of possible but not actually existing individuals. Being an animal with kidneys is surely not an intensional part of being an animal with a heart; hence by (IP) and the proposed definition (and the principle correlating the exemplification of the two properties with the application of the two predicates they are obviously intended by: "*x* is an animal with a heart," "*x* is an animal with kidneys"): some possible *x* is an animal - therefore, an individual - with a heart, but without kidneys. But, on the other hand, all *actually existing* animals with hearts are animals with kidneys. Therefore: some individual *x* does not actually exist, but is merely possible.

But let it pass that there are possible and not actually existing individuals. There is another problem with the proposed definition: According to it and (IP), it is necessary and *sufficient* for property *f* to be an intensional part of property *g* that every possible *x* that is *in fact* *g* is also *f*; but is this really sufficient? Should the correct sufficient and necessary condition not rather be: "for every possible *x* and *every possible world* *w*: if *x* is *g* in *w*, then *x* is *f* in *w*"? Note that this new proposal of a sufficient and necessary condition for property *f* being an intensional part of property *g* does not allow the reconstruction of the above argument for the numerical existence of individuals that do not actually exist. We have: (1) "every actually existing *x* that is an animal with a heart in **w** is an animal with kidneys in **w**" and (2) "some possible *x* and some possible world *w* is such that *x* is an animal with a heart in *w*, but without kidneys"; but we cannot deduce from this that the individual *x* does not actually exist. (We *can* deduce that either the possible world *w* or the individual *x* does not actually exist. Suppose *w* actually exists; hence *w* is identical with **w**, because **w** is the only actually existing possible world; hence contradiction ensues between (1) and (2) on the further assumption that *x* actually exists. But that possible world *w* or individual *x* does not actually exist is not enough for us to show that *some individual* does not actually exist: possible worlds need not be individuals; in fact, I have argued that they are best regarded as states of affairs.)

(c) We shall here not decide in favor of one or the other of the two proposed definitions of "property *g* is extensional part of property *f*" (definitions which, given the validity of (IP), immediately lead to two definitions of "property *f* is an intensional part of property *g*"). In part III, where intensional parthood between properties of individuals is defined directly, not via extensional parthood, we shall see that, given a certain conception of individuals (with good reason this conception can be called "the normal conception") and the corresponding conception of exemplification of a property by an individual, the second of our two definitions fits (in accordance with (IP)) intensional parthood between *properties of individuals*. A theorem to this effect will in fact be provable (see TPT207 in III.10.(c)). But there is a different conception of individuals, which views individuals as identical with or at least as one-to-one correlated with maximally consistent properties of individuals, and a corresponding conception of exemplification. According to this conception the first of our two definitions fits (in accordance with (IP)) intensional parthood between properties of individuals. A theorem to this effect can already be proved in this part (see TP22+ in II.6.(a), and the expositions that follow it).[*3]

Here, in part II of the book, we consider the concept of intensional parthood between properties of individuals as a *primitive concept* (though not defined, its meaning can nevertheless be illustrated to any extent by examples of its truthful predication or denial). Thus, in part II, this concept will not be definitionally reduced to the concept of exemplification (in various possible worlds or *simpliciter*) or to any other concept, for we certainly possess it even without having been presented with a definition of it. In the remainder of the book, however, we will provide a definition for it. In part II, also, (not in the remainder of the book) the category of properties of individuals will be considered in and of itself, though we note that individuals can be represented within that category by appeal to the second of the two conceptions of individuals referred to above.

(d) We now let the universe of discourse of LP consist of all and only properties of individuals, and we interpret ''P'' as the concept of intensional parthood for these entities. This interpretation of LP, we assume, makes the axioms AP1 - AP6 analytically true (if they are true at all in that interpretation, then they are analytically true in it). Hence all theorems logically deduced merely from AP1 - AP6 (plus definitions) are also analytically true in this interpretation.

No small ontological interest attaches to tracing the consequences of this new interpretation of LP. Which readings do the predicates and functional terms that were defined in part I now take on? Which further definitions are motivated by the new interpretation? Which axioms *in addition* to AP1 - AP6 are to be postulated? (It seems clear at the very outset that AP7 - AP9 ought to be omitted - not because they have become false, but because there is no ontologically interesting role for ''**w**'' in the new interpretation of LP. Thus we may as well omit ''**w**'' from LP, and make the very formulation of AP7 - AP9 impossible. On the other hand, it seems also clear at the very outset that AP10 ought to be retained as analytically true.) We shall see moreover that the new interpretation of LP opens up interesting perspectives on ontological themes from the history of philosophy.

COMMENTS

[*1] (IP) is - on one interpretation - closely related to the well known semantical *law of reciprocity* according to which the extensions and intensions of monadic concepts (or of meaningful monadic predicates) A and B are inversely proportional to each other. In the standard set-theoretical formulation: (LR) int(A)⊆int(B) if and only if ext(B)⊆ext(A). (IP) - in its *first* interpretation, which is determined by the *first* interpretation of "*g* is an extensional part of *f*" (in section (a) of this chapter) - can obviously be regarded as an ontological analogue of (LR) (although there is no mention of intensions and extensions in (IP)). However, (IP) can also be given an interpretation that does not make it an analogue of (LR): "*g* is an extensional part of *f*" does not necessarily mean "the extension of *g* is a subset of the extension of *f*"; see the *second* interpretation of (IP) which is determined by the *second* interpretation of "*g* is an extensional part of *f*" (in section (b) of this chapter).

[*2] But the following principle is surely correct (according to any adequate interpretation of "*g* is an extensional part of *f*"):
For all properties *f* and *g*: if *g* is an extensional part of *f*, then all *g*s are *f*s.
And hence by (IP):
For all properties *f* and *g*: if *f* is an intensional part of *g*, then all *g*s are *f*s.
D. M. Armstrong criticizes *this* principle (the differences in formulation are inessential) on p. 39 of vol. II of *Universals and Scientific Realism*. But the criticism is irrelevant, because from his remarks it is evident that *his* concept of intensional parthood for properties (he simply speaks of one property *being part* of another) is quite different from the concept one would normally think of as being the concept of intensional parthood for properties, and from the concept which is certainly intended by everyone asserting the principle (for example, by Frege; see Armstrong's quotation).

Curiously, Armstrong thinks that *his* concept is merely a special case of the global concept of parthood applying to subclass and class, province and country, conjunction-member and conjunction, etc. (*ibid.* p. 36f). If this were indeed the case, then there ought to be negative and disjunctive properties; for, in a normal homogeneous manifold of parts in the sense indicated by Armstrong's examples there are at least some *complements* and some *largest common parts*. But to the contrary: Armstrong argues against the existence of disjunctive and negative properties (*ibid.*, p. 19ff, p. 23ff). Armstrong uses the word "mereology" (*ibid.*, p. 38); it seems, however, that in *Universals and Scientific Realism* he had not taken notice of the contents of the science named by that word.

[*3] Instead of speaking of two different conceptions of the one category of individuals, we might, of course, speak of two different sorts of *individuals in a global sense*, with respect to each of which intensional parthood between properties of individuals is spelled out differently. This would turn conflict into peaceful co-existence, painful decision into careful distinction, and would epitomize a rather satisfactory way of resolving a good many ontological controversies. The indicated method should certainly be applied to the controversy about the nature of *events*. Yet we cannot always avoid making a decision: not if each side insists on claiming *the very same entities* as instances of the concept which it champions.

CHAPTER II.2

NEW READINGS OF PREDICATES AND FUNCTIONAL TERMS, AND INHERENCE

(a) Here and in the next chapters, I shall usually say "property" instead of "property of individuals" (the occasions when the word "property" is used in its wider sense will be clear).

"**conj**", "**disj**", "**neg**", "**conj***y*", and "**disj***y*" retain their definitions from part I, but they are now referred to properties: **conj**(*f*,*g*) is the conjunction, **disj**(*f*,*g*) the disjunction of properties *f* and *g*; **neg**(*f*) the negation of property *f*; **conj***f*A[*f*] is the conjunction of all properties *f* such that A[*f*]; **disj***f*A[*f*] is the disjunction of all properties *f* such that A[*f*]. "**conj**", "**disj**", "**neg**" applied to properties are already familiar,[*1] and "**conj***f*" and "**disj***f*" are obvious generalizations of "**conj**" and "**disj**."

"**t**" now designates the property which is an intensional part of every property (the "tautological" property), and "**k**" designates the property of which all properties are intensional parts (the "contradictory" property).

(b) In part I, *the maximally consistent states of affairs* were identified with *the possible worlds*. Does the present interpretation of LP provide the opportunity for an identification of *the maximally consistent properties* which is comparable in ontological significance? It does. The maximally consistent properties - the properties *g* such that for every property *f* either *f* or the negation of *f* is an intensional part of *g* - can be identified with *the (possible) individuals* (presupposing a certain conception of individuals - certainly not the only possible one), that is, precisely with the entities by which properties are exemplified (if at all). (Remember that "property" is here merely an abbreviation of "property of individuals"; we assume, moreover, the analytic co-extensionality of "individual" and "possible individual."). Ontologically, this move is more problematic than that of identifying possible worlds with maximally consistent states of affairs, and it will here not be made in complete ontological seriousness.[*2] Consider it rather as satisfying in the simplest possible manner the idea (which *is* an ontologically serious one) that individuals can be mapped in one-to-one fashion onto maximally consistent properties (in a natural and essential manner: each maximally consistent property being the sum of all the properties the corresponding individual *has* in a certain absolute sense which is not relative to worlds).

The identification of individuals with maximally consistent properties has several interesting consequences. First of all, it makes it possible to define *exemplification* (of a property by an individual) via intensional parthood for properties:

DP1+ t′<t> := MK(t) and t′Pt.
(“t exemplifies the property t′”; “t has the property t′”; “the property t′ applies to t.”)

The reading of “*f*<*x*>” as “*x* exemplifies the property *f*” is specific to the present interpretation of LP; it will change, when the interpretation is changed. This remark - made already on several occasions - can here be conveniently illustrated: according to the interpretation of LP underlying part I, “*f*<*x*>” must be read as “*x* is true/obtains in the possible world *f*.”

Note that, contrary to appearances, we do not have two different types of variables in LP; LP is not a two-sorted language. After the universe of discourse of LP has been newly determined, *all* variables of LP are variables *for properties*. But besides the variables “*x*”, “*y*”, “*z*”, etc. of LP, we now also use the variables “*f*”, “*g*”, “*h*”, etc. of LP. “*x*<*z*>” is as well-formed as “*f*<*g*>”, “*f*<*z*>” and “*x*<*g*>,” and “**some***x***some***z*(*x*<*z*>)” is synonymous with “**some***f***some***g*(*f*<*g*>)”, etc.; but it is surely most suggestive of the intended meaning to write “**some***f***some***z*(*f*<*z*>).”

(c) Leibniz says “*f* is in *g*” or “*g* contains *f*” (“*f inest g*” or “*g continet f*”; compare W. Lenzen, “Zur extensionalen und ‘intensionalen’ Interpretation der Leibnizschen Logik,” p. 131) where we say “property *f* is an intensional part of propery *g*,” or “*f*P*g*” according to the present interpretation of LP. Indeed, the Leibnizian readings of “*f*P*g*” are appropriate under any interpretation of LP, not only under the interpretation presently considered.

Traditionally the exemplification of (property) *f* by (individual) *z* is also expressed by “*f* is in *z*.” This of course manifests the historically very influential *inherence-theory of exemplification*, which in a rather radical form (which conceives inherence as a special case of intensional parthood between properties) is embodied by DP1+. We say - with Leibniz - “*f* is in *z*” or “*z* contains *f*” when we intend to express no more than “*f*P*z*” expresses according to the present interpretation of LP; and we say “*f inheres* in *z*” or “*z bears* the property *f*” (both well known idioms from the ontological tradition), when we intend to express what “*f*<*z*>” expresses according to DP1+ and the present interpretation of LP. Thus, “*f* inheres in *z*” and “*z* bears the property *f*” are further readings of “*f*<*z*>,” and they are the most characteristic readings of that predicate.

(d) As a first theorem we have:

TP1+ **all***x*(*x*<*x*> iff MK(*x*)).
(Depending on AP2, DP1+.)

On one historically rather interesting reading TP1+ says that *the (possible) substances* - the (possible) individuals - are precisely the self-inhering (or in other words, self-bearing) properties. This suggests that *accidents* are precisely the *non-self-inhering*, non-self-bearing properties. But according to the common philosophical meaning of the polysemous word "accident," *the accidents* simply are *the properties*,[*3] and according to the orthodox conception of properties, the modifier "non-self-inhering" is redundant because no property is self-inherent. These intuitions can, however, be accommodated simply by calling the entities in the universe of discourse of LP "first intensions" (the entities in the universe of discourse were the *first* intensions that came to ontological attention). Then the "individuals" (the *substances*) are the first intensions that are self-inherent (that is, maximally consistent), and the "properties" (the *accidents*) are the first intensions that are not self-inherent (that is, not maximally consistent); and we have a homogeneous realm of being - the realm of first intensions - which is divided among and exhausted by the substances ("individuals") and accidents ("properties").

There is, however, the intuition that not only properties (*accidents*), but also individuals (*substances*) do not self-inhere. If one wants to accommodate *this* intuition, then one needs to change the definition of inherence (the presently considered form of exemplification). Instead of DP1+ posit "t′<t>" := "MK(t) and t′P*t," that is, replace in DP1+ parthood by *proper* parthood. The new definition - with the help of TP3 - immediately yields the theorem "**all***f***all***x*(if *f*<*x*>, then not *x*<*f*>)," and hence the theorem "**all***x* not *x*<*x*>," and consequently one can only say that the "individuals" are those first intensions which are maximally consistent, "properties" those which are not: "self-inhering" can no longer be proved to be a precise description of substances (considered as first intensions), nor can "non-self-inhering" be proved to be a precise description of accidents.

But let us stick to DP1+ and allow that certain entities in the universe of discourse (which comprises precisely the first intensions, *alias* the properties of individuals) are self-inherent, self-exemplifying (for this, according to TP1+, we merely need to allow that there are maximally consistent properties). Self-inherence is certainly not a normal case of inherence. This is emphasized further by

TP2+ **all***x*(*x*<*x*> iff **all***y*(*x*<*y*> iff *x*=*y*)).

According to TP2+, an entity in the universe of discourse is self-inherent (an individual, according to TP1+) if and only if it inheres precisely in itself.[*4]

(e) Given the present interpretation of LP, DP29, in the presence of DP1+, says the following: a property (first intension) *f* is *analytically possible* if and only if it is exemplified by some possible individual. And according to TP94(i) a property f is analytically possible if and only if f is not identical with *the total property*. Hence every property except the total (or "contradictory") property is exemplified by some possible individual, that is, every property except the total one is *extensionally non-empty*. But that there are no extensionally empty properties other than **k** does not of course imply that the property of being a unicorn at t_0, for example, is exemplified in the stronger sense that some *actually existent* individual is a unicorn at t_0. That the property of being a unicorn at t_0 inheres in some possible individuals, that it is exemplified in this sense, does not imply that one of these individuals is actually existent, and thus it does not imply that it is exemplified in the mentioned stronger sense (see also II.3.(c)).

COMMENTS

[*1] In *Universals and Scientific Realism*, vol. II, pp. 19 - 29, D. M. Armstrong argues against disjunctive and negative universals, in particular, against disjunctive and negative properties. He *does* admit conjunctive properties (*ibid.* p. 30ff). Note that in our system all disjunctive and negative properties are conjunctive ones. The property-functors "**disj**" and "**neg**" can be expressed by the property-functor "**conj*f***" - the big conjunction of properties. Moreover, in our system, every property is a negative property since it is the negation of some property. In addition (given that there are at least four properties), every property, except **k** and maximally consistent properties, is a disjunctive property *in the strict sense* of being a disjunction of *two different* properties that are *both different from it*.

In defense of negative and disjunctive properties it has to be pointed out in the first place that the use of "not" and "or" as modifiers of properties is well entrenched in ordinary language. What is Jack trying at t_0 if the sentence "Jack is trying not to fall down the wall" is true at t_0? He is certainly trying to acquire certain properties. Which properties? For example, *the property of not falling down the wall at* t_1.(Similarly with respect to the sentence "Jack resolves not to lie to his mother.") What is the only thing that remains for them at t_0 if the sentence "the only thing that remains for them is to triumph or to die" is true at t_0? Certainly it is to have a certain property. Which property? *To triumph or to die at* t_1. Armstrong is confronted by an endless series of completely natural singular terms formed by "or" or "not" with infinitive expressions. Such singular terms do not only occur in natural language, about whose ontological significance Armstrong is rather skeptical, but also in the language of physics. If these singular terms designate anything at all, they designate *negative and disjunctive properties*. The onus is on Armstrong, and other opponents of negative and disjunctive properties, to show that, contrary to appearances, all of these singular terms do not designate anything at all; or alternatively, if it is admitted that some of them *do* designate something, that it is, contrary to appearances, in no case a negative or disjunctive property which they designate. Merely to assert that semantics is to be generally distrusted as a guide in ontological matters is certainly not enough.

In the second place, properties are remainders of states of affairs (after the extraction of individuals from them), and hence, as will be seen in part III, there are negative and disjunctive properties because there are negative and disjunctive states of affairs. That the numerical existence of negative and disjunctive states of affairs can hardly be denied has been argued in part I.

In the third place, in order to answer two arguments advanced by Armstrong:

(1) *Negation* is not to be confused with *privation*. Armstrong writes: "properties should be such that it at least makes sense to attribute causal

powers to objects in virtue of these properties. But how could a mere lack or absence endow anything with causal powers?'' (*Ibid.*, p. 25.) The negation of a property *f* is not ''a mere lack or absence,'' for otherwise the negation of the negation would have to be ''a mere lack or absence'' too (''Nothing will come of nothing,'' as Armstrong aptly remarks.) But, on the contrary, the negation of the negation of *f* is *f* - a property, and not ''a mere lack or absence.'' Whether we regard *f* or its negation (or neither) as a privation has nothing whatever to do with the fact that the one is the negation of the other; rather, it depends exclusively on our global human interests (practical, cognitive, emotional, etc.).
(2) Armstrong maintains that ''disjunctive properties offend against the principle that a genuine property is identical in its different particulars.'' (*Ibid.*, p. 20.) What have two individuals in common in virtue of **disj**(*f*,*g*) applying to them because the one has (''is'') *f* and not *g*, the other *g* and not *f*? This challenge presents no problem for our view: what they have in common is the intensionally largest property that is an intensional part both of *f* and *g* (which is surely a ''genuine'' property if both *f* and *g* are ''genuine'' properties). (Armstrong too allows himself to speak of parts of properties - without noticing what might be implied in this.) Which property is that? **disj**(*f*,*g*). (Further criticism of Armstrong's position along these lines can be found in my paper ''On Negative and Disjunctive Properties.'')
A final remark: If predicates P and Q express properties, then according to Armstrong ¬P, ¬Q and (¬P∨¬Q) do not express properties, but ¬(¬P∨¬Q) does (see *ibid.*, p. 42). But this is like saying that ''3:0'', ''2:0'' and ''(3:0)·(2:0)'' do not designate numbers, but ''((3:0)·(2:0)):0'' does.

[*2] Individuals - even if we use the word in accordance with the *second conception* of individuals that was indicated in II.1.(c) - are not to be ontologically reduced to maximally consistent properties. There is a *natural* one-to-one correlation of individuals and maximally consistent properties - a correlation that makes the identification of the former with the latter at all plausible - only if there are *relational properties* among the properties. If, on the contrary, all properties are *qualities* (non-relational properties), then surely some *two* (possible) individuals correspond to the *same* sum (or conjunction) of properties as the sum of *their* properties, because they have the very same qualities. (Thus, *if* all properties are qualities - as Leibniz apparently believed - then the *principle of the identity of indiscernibles* can be at all plausible only if it is restricted to individuals that actually exist. But even then it remains highly doubtful - *if* all properties are qualities.) Hence, if there are no relational properties, then the one natural candidate for a one-to-one mapping of individuals onto maximally consistent properties must fail.
It does not fail, and, therefore, some relational properties do indeed belong to our universe of discourse. But this means that individuals are presupposed from the very start; the ontological constitution of relational properties (of individuals), and hence of maximally consistent properties, requires them. No

entities, however, can be ontologically reduced to entities of which they are constituents. Hence individuals cannot be reduced to maximally consistent properties.

The maximally consistent properties cannot, in complete ontological seriousness, be assumed to *be* the individuals; but they can be identified with them (presupposing the appropriate conception of individuals) in the sense in which elements in a model are ''identified'' with elements in reality: they can represent them.

Did Leibniz *seriously* identify possible individuals and maximally consistent properties? B. Mates writes in *The Philosophy of Leibniz*, p. 73: ''Most of Leibniz's references to possible objects can be rephrased in terms of individual concepts [our maximally consistent properties] ... This is not to say that it would make sense, in Leibnizian terms, to assert that a possible object *is* an individual concept.'' According to H. Burkhardt, Leibniz distinguished *individuals* and *individual concepts* (see *Logik und Semiotik in der Philosophie von Leibniz*, p. 169). The contrary opinion is apparently held by F. von Kutschera in ''Grundbegriffe der Metaphysik von Leibniz im Vergleich zu Begriffsbildungen der heutigen Modallogik,'' p. 94: ''Nach Leibniz muß zunächst ein vollständiger Begriff (notio completa) [Mates' *individual concept*] einer Substanz alle Eigenschaften (praedicata) als Merkmale enthalten. Die Substanz ist also genau dann vollständig charakterisiert, wenn alle ihre Eigenschaften festliegen. Und darüber hinaus läßt sich über so etwas wie einen von ihnen verschiedenen Träger der Eigenschaften nichts aussagen. Danach kann man also die Substanz selbst mit der Menge ihrer Eigenschaften identifizieren.'' (It would doubtless be more in accordance with Leibnizian intentions not to identify the substance with *the set of its properties*, as von Kutschera suggests, but with *the conjunction of its properties*: the *notio completa*.)

[*3] According to the criteria of the *ontological square* of Aristotle, *accidents* in the common philosophical meaning of this word are *those entities which are in a subject and are predicated (''said'') of it*. (Compare I. Angelelli, *Studies on Gottlob Frege and Traditional Philosophy*, p. 12.) That is, the word ''accident'' in the common philosophical meaning is synonymous with ''universal accident.'' (According to the traditional interpretation of the ontological square, *universal accidents* are contrasted with *individual (particular) accidents*: entities ''in a subject, but never predicated of it,'' and with *universal* and *individual (particular) substances*: entities ''predicated of a subject, but never in it'' and entities ''never in a subject nor predicated of it.'') In the present context, ''accident'' will be used in this common philosophical sense: that of ''universal accident.'' (With one proviso: the contradictory property will be counted as an accident *by courtesy* - although it is never in a subject nor predicated of it.)

The word "substance" is commonly used as synonymous with "individual substance" (or "*first* substance"); here it is not used in that sense, but rather in the more general sense of "(possible) individual." Thus, we have two terminological equations for the words "substance" and "accident" used here: "accident" := "universal accident"; "substance" := "individual". According to the ontological square, these terminological equations are in fact supported by true assertions of co-extensionality *if* there are neither individual accidents (accidental individuals) nor universal substances (substantial universals); this is the case because according to the ontological square *substances* and *accidents* are either universal (predicated of a subject) or individual (never predicated of a subject), *individuals* and *universals* either substantial (never in a subject) or accidental (in a subject). That there are neither universal substances *nor* individual accidents has certainly been the drift of ontological opinion since the Renaissance (skepticism with respect to substantial universals *alone* is much older). The above terminological stipulations, although - in a way - supported by that tendency of ontological opinion, should not be taken to indicate support of it. (Widespread habitualized denial and/or neglect of individual accidents and universal substances is presumably the reason behind the modern terminological equation of "substance" with "individual substance," and of "accident" with "(monadic) universal" or "(universal) property" (we here leave aside the contrast between "accident" and "*essential* property" - another philosophically important use of the word "accident"). As is easily checked, on the basis of the ontological square the mentioned denials verify the assertions of co-extensionality that correspond to the terminological equations.)

[*4] In the ontological tradition there is a conception of individuals in this sense: an individual is an entity that inheres only in itself (is predicated only of itself); see the citation in J. J. E. Gracia, *Introduction to the Problem of Individuation in the Early Middle Ages*, p. 71, in Latin on p. 113f: (Boethius in the *Commentary on Porphyry's "Isagoge"*) "individua vero quoniam sub se nihil habent ubi secari distribuique possint, ad nihil aliud praedicantur nisi ad se ipsa, quae singula atque una sunt". However, see also *ibid.* the citation on p. 83, in Latin on p. 116f: (Boethius in the *Commentary on the "Categories"*) "Simpliciter autem quae sunt individua et numero singularia, de nullo subjecto dicuntur." This thesis can be expressed in LP by means of "**all***x*(if MK(*x*), then **no***y*(*x*<*y*>))"; this is provable if "*x*<*y*>" is defined by using "P*" instead of "P" in DP1+: Assume MK(*x*); and assume for *reductio*: *x*<*y*>; hence by the *alternative* DP1+: MK(*y*) and *x*P**y*, hence by DP1: MK(*y*) and *x*P*y* and *x*≠*y*; but this contradicts MK(*x*) in view of TP79. (In the interpretation of LP considered in this part of the book TP79 says that an individual *x* cannot be a proper *intensional* part of an individual *y*. But *x* may, of course, be a proper part of *y* in *another* sense, for example, *spatially*. However, we leave it to be clarified in what sense individuals that are taken to be maximally consistent properties can have individuals as proper spatial parts.)

CHAPTER II.3

ACTUAL EXISTENCE FOR ACCIDENTS AND SUBSTANCES

(a) The concept of actual existence for properties (of individuals), i.e. for first intensions, cannot be defined in the way actual existence has been defined for states of affairs in DP31. There is no special *one* among the properties such that *to be actually existent* is for properties the same as being an intensional part of *that special property*. But we can reasonably say that a property is actually existent if and only if it is an intensional part of some intension or other of a certain type of first intensions; let us call intensions of that type "primary actualities."

In order to express this idea in LP we introduce the predicate "PA(t)" as a new primitive predicate into LP. Given the present interpretation of LP, it is to be read as "t is a property which is a primary actuality." We can then define:

DP2+ AP(t) := **some***y*(PA(*y*) and tP*y*).
("t is an actually existent property.")

According to DP2+, *f* is an actually existent property if and only if *f* is an intensional part of a property that is a primary actuality.

(b) In DP2+ a more general concept is defined via a less general one. We could have done it the other way round; that is, we could have defined the less general concept by the more general one by choosing "AP" as primitive predicate of LP and positing: "PA(t)" := "AP(t) and MK(t)." ("t is a property which is a primary actuality if and only if t is a maximally consistent property that actually exists.") The *first way* has been chosen because the axioms for "PA" which need to accompany DP2+ are more economical than the axioms for "AP" which would need to accompany the alternative definition. (The axioms are such that, together with their respective accompanying definition, they are deductively equivalent on the basis of AP1 - AP6. See below at the end of section (c).) Given DP2+, we can simply postulate (in addition to AP1 - AP6):

AP7+ **all***x*(if PA(*x*), then MK(*x*)).
("Every first intension that is a primary actuality is an individual (a substance).")

AP7+ is an analogue of TP106, which is equivalent (on the basis of AP1 - AP6) to the conjunction of AP7 and AP8. But, in contrast to TP106, AP7+ can very well be assumed to be analytically true (with respect to the present interpretation of LP).

Some slight doubt can be raised about the *adequacy* of DP2+ (where there was none to be raised about the adequacy of DP31). If one took "AP" as primitive concept and defined "PA(t)" := "AP(t) and MK(t)," then would "**all***x*(AP(*x*) iff **some***y*(PA(*y*) and *x*P*y*))" (the general biconditional corresponding to DP2+) be *analytically true* (with respect to the present interpretation of LP)? (This is the central issue in the question whether DP2+ is an *adequate definition*. Analogously, in the question whether DP31 is an adequate definition, the central issue is whether "**all***x*(O(*x*) iff *x*P**w**)" (in our earlier interpretation of LP) is analytically true if one took "O" as primitive concept and defined "**w**" := "**conj***y*O(*y*).") "If a first intension *f* is an intensional part of a first intension that is a primary actuality, then *f* is actually existent," or in other words: "**all***f*(if **some***y*(PA(*y*) and *f*P*y*), then AP(*f*))" - *this* is analytically true, since both "**all***f*(if PA(*f*), then AP(*f*))" and "**all***f***all***g*(AP(*f*) and *g*P*f*, then AP(*g*))" are certainly analytically true, "AP(*f*)" being conceptually primitive, "PA(*f*)" being defined by "AP(*f*) and MK(*f*)." But does it really contradict the meaning of the terms involved to assume the truth of "some first intension *f* is actually existent, but *f* is not an intensional part of any first intension that is a primary actuality": "**some***f*(AP(*f*) and **no***y*(PA(*y*) and *f*P*y*))"? If this *were* true, then some *f* would be an *actually existing accident* that does not inhere *in any actually existing substance* ("**no***y*(PA(*y*) and *f*P*y*)" is definitionally equivalent to "**no***y*(MK(*y*) and AP(*y*) and *f*<*y*>)," "PA(*y*)" being defined by "AP(*y*) and MK(*y*)"; and given this definition, "AP(*f*) and **no***y*(PA(*y*) and *f*P*y*))" implies "not MK(*f*)" because of *f*P*f*). Does (ontologically refined) *language* really forbid there being, for example, an actually existent property of being beautiful at t_0 that does not inhere in any actually existing individual?[*1] Not in its present state of vagueness with respect to the meanings of the terms involved. But the very inconceivability of the described situation provides sufficient justification for our *stipulating* that language *does indeed* forbid it (and all other situations like it, too). (Note that language already did forbid there being an actually existent accident that does not inhere *in any (possible) individual*; this is so because "**all***x*(if AP(*x*), then *x*≠**k**)" and "**all***x*(if *x*≠**k**, then **some***y*(MK(*y*) and *x*P*y*))" are analytical truths. Compare II.2.(e).)

(c) DP1+ defines exemplification *simpliciter*. *Existential exemplification* is defined by

DP3+ t′<<t> := PA(t) and t′Pt.
("t existentially exemplifies t′"; "t′ existentially inheres in t.")

We can now prove the following theorems:

TP3+ **all***f***all***x*(if *f*<<*x*>, then *f*<*x*>).
(Depending on DP3+, AP7+, DP1+.)

TP4+ **all***x*(if PA(*x*), then AP(*x*)).
(Depending on DP2+, AP2.)

TP5+ **all***f***all***x*(if *f*<<*x*>, then AP(*x*) and AP(*f*)).
(Depending on DP3+, TP4+, DP2+.)

TP6+ **all***f***all***x*(*f*<*x*> and AP(*x*) iff *f*<<*x*>).

TP7+ **all***x*(PA(*x*) iff MK(*x*) and AP(*x*)).

If we had defined "PA(*x*)" by "MK(*x*) and AP(*x*)," instead of defining "AP(*x*)" by "**some***y*(PA(*y*) and *x*P*y*)," then how would we have obtained the principle corresponding to DP2+: **all***x*(AP(*x*) iff **some***y*(PA(*y*) and *x*P*y*))? As has been pointed out in section (b) above, one merely needs **(1)** "**all***f***all***g*(if AP(*f*) and *g*P*f*, then AP(*g*))" as a basic principle for obtaining "**all***x*(if **some***y*(PA(*y*) and *x*P*y*), then AP(*x*))." For the converse, one needs as a basic principle **(2)** "**all***x*(if AP(*x*), then **some***y*(MK(*y*) and AP(*y*) and *x*P*y*))," that is (according to DP1+): "**all***x*(if AP(*x*), then **some***y*(AP(*y*) and *x*<*y*>))" - "every actually existent first intension is exemplified by some actually existent first intension, that is: inheres in it." **(1)** and **(2)** and the definition "PA(*x*)" := "MK(*x*) and AP(*x*)" constitute a deductively equivalent alternative to AP7+ and DP2+ (on the basis of AP1 - AP6).

(d) Instead of "(individual) t exemplifies (property) t′," tradition - as was mentioned in II.2.(c) - has the simple expression "t′ is in t" - indicating the inherence-theory of exemplification. It occurs, for example, in Spinoza's first axiom of the *Ethica* : "All things *which are* are either in themselves or in another": "Omnia, quae sunt, vel in se, vel in alio sunt." That Spinoza's *in-being* is not simply parthood, but a form of *inherence* can be seen from the fact that most things *which are* are parts both of themselves and of other things; the "or" meant by the Latin "vel ... vel" is, however, *exclusive*.

But there are two concepts of inherence: inherence *simpliciter* (represented by "*f*<*y*>"), and existential inherence (represented by "*f*<<*y*>"). *Which one* is meant in Spinoza's axiom? A question which is perhaps difficult to answer; however, as far as concerns the truth of Spinoza's axiom for the universe of first intensions, it does not matter what is the correct answer to that question, as we shall presently see.

For both concepts of inherence the restriction "quae sunt" is necessary; without it the axiom would be incorrect; for if Spinoza's in-being is *existential inherence*, then there are many things (entities) that are neither "in themselves" nor "in another" (for example, the first intension *being a unicorn at* t_0); and if Spinoza's in-being is *inherence simpliciter*, then still one first intension, **k**, is neither "in itself" nor "in another." But the condition "quae sunt" in the meaning of "which are *actually existent*" excludes both **k** and being a unicorn at t_0, and together with them all first intensions that neither inhere (whether existentially or *simpliciter*) in themselves nor in another, from the scope of the axiom.

Moreover, no first intension inheres (whether existentially or *simpliciter*) both in itself and in another. Thus, if referred to first intensions, Spinoza's axiom is true for *both* concepts of inherence; it can be formulated in LP and proved in the two versions that correspond to the two concepts:

TP8+
(a) **all***x*[if AP(*x*), then (*x*<*x*> iff **no***y*(*x*≠*y* and *x*<*y*>))];
(b) **all***x*[if AP(*x*), then (*x*<<*x*> iff **no***y*(*x*≠*y* and *x*<<*y*>))].

The converse of TP8+(b) can also be proved:

TP9+ **all***x*[if (*x*<<*x*> iff **no***y*(*x*≠*y* and *x*<<*y*>)), then AP(*x*)].

From TP8+ and TP9+ we obtain:

TP10+ **all***x*[AP(*x*) iff (*x*<<*x*> iff **no***y*(*x*≠*y* and *x*<<*y*>))].
("A first intension is *actually existent* if and only if it *either* existentially exemplifies itself *or* is existentially exemplified by another first intension.")

The converse of TP8+(a) cannot be proved. But corresponding to TP10+ we have:

TP11+ **all***x*[P(*x*) iff (*x*<*x*> iff **no***y*(*x*≠*y* and *x*<*y*>))].
("A first intension is *analytically possible* if and only if it either exemplifies itself (*simpliciter*) or is exemplified by another first intension.")

COMMENTS

[*1] It is not at issue here whether language forbids the position of Plato. Rather, according to Plato, *actually existent beauty* is indeed *not* without an actually existing individual in which it inheres: because actually existent beauty is *itself* such an individual. Nor is it at issue whether language forbids there being an actually existent grin of a cat without there being any actually existing individual in which this grin inheres *in the manner* suggested by the scene in Lewis Carroll's *Alice's Adventures in Wonderland*: that particular grin of the Cheshire-cat is an individual accident (an *event*, most ontologists would nowadays say), and the concept of "inherence" that is relevant for it is not the one relevant in the present context, where we talk only of accidents that are universals. It *is*, however, at issue here whether language forbids the actual existence of, say, *being a grinning cat at* t_0 or of *being a cat-grin at* t_0 under the circumstance that these universal accidents do not inhere in any actually existent individual.

Thomas Aquinas, following Aristotle, can be interpreted as maintaining - as a matter of the conceptual framework - the position that will be presently adopted: "Illi enim proprie convenit *esse* [actual existence], quod habet *esse* [actual existence]; et hoc est *subsistens in suo esse* [substantial in its actual existence]. Formae autem et accidentia, et alia huiusmodi, non dicuntur *entia* [actual existents] *quasi ipsa sint* [as if they were actually existent in themselves], sed *quia eis aliquid est* [because by them something is actually such and such]; ut albedo ea ratione dicitur *ens* [an actual existent], *quia ea subiectum est album* [because by it the subject is actually white]. Unde, secundum Philosophum, accidens magis proprie dicitur *entis* [*of* an actual existent] quam *ens* [an actual existent]."(*Summa Theologiae*, I,45,4) Or more concisely: "*accidentis esse est inesse*." (Compare A. Kenny, *Aquinas*, p. 36; Kenny, as is clear from his examples, refers "accidens non est [proprie dictum] ens sed entis" and "accidentis esse est inesse" to *individual accidents*. This, surely, is Aquinas' prevailing intention. But notice that in the above quotation he is simply saying "albedo;" there is no indication that he means by this an *individual* whiteness. In any case, the Aristotelian slogans and the quotation from the *Summa Theologiae* make good sense for universal accidents, too.) That is: the actual existence of an accident is its *proper* inherence in something that actually exists. In LP: **all***x*(not MK(*x*) and AP(*x*) iff **some***y*(AP(*y*) and *x*<*y*> and *x*≠*y*). This is provable by using DP2+ and AP7+.

CHAPTER II.4

REAL SUBSISTENCE AS A PROPERTY?

(a) Our present universe of discourse of LP consists precisely of all properties of individuals, properties *simpliciter*. (Or, as has been pointed out, call those entities “first intensions,” and use the word “property” for *certain* properties of individuals only: precisely for those one would like to call “accidents”.) But is not *real subsistence*, the property of being an actually existent individual, a property of individuals, and hence should it not be in the universe of discourse?

Let us admit this for the moment, and let us designate the entity *real subsistence* which is supposed to be in the universe of discourse of LP by the new singular term “**rs**” of LP. What is the relationship between “**rs**” and “PA”? In view of TP7+ and the present readings of the predicates involved in that theorem, one would expect that “**rs**” can represent “PA” in its predicative function in LP via the concept of inherence. In other words, (RS) “**all***x*(PA(*x*) iff **rs**<*x*>)” appears to be (analytically) true in the present interpretation of LP. But (RS) seems also to yield consequences which some philosophers will find intolerable. A formally correct *ontological argument* for the numerical existence of an actually existent *divine individual* can be carried out on its basis:

Let “**d**”designate the property of *being divine* ; then “**conj(d,rs)**” designates the property of *being divine and really subsistent*; and we have:

(1) **conj(d,rs)≠k** (intuitively evident).

(2) **some***y*(MK(*y*) and **conj(d,rs)**P*y*) (from (1) by TP94(i) and DP29).

(3) **some***y*(MK(*y*) and **d**P*y* and **rs**P*y*) (from (2) by TP24).

(4) **some***y*(**d**<*y*> and **rs**<*y*>) (from (3) by DP1+).

(5) **some***y*(PA(*y*) and **d**<*y*>) (from (4) by (RS)).

(6) **some***y*(MK(*y*) and AP(*y*) and **d**<*y*>) (from (5) by TP7+).

Statement (6) asserts (under the present interpretation of LP) that there is an actually existent individual that exemplifies divinity - an astonishing result, though one unwelcome only for the atheist. However, in the same manner as statement (6) one can obviously derive statements asserting that there is an actually existent individual that exemplifies being a unicorn at t_0, being a witch at t_0, being a king of elves at t_0, etc. - results welcome at least to no philosopher.

Thus, *it seems* that (RS) is not tenable. But how, then, is the relationship between “**rs**” and “PA” to be otherwise described? The obvious alternative to (RS) is (RS′) “**all***x*(PA(*x*) iff **rs**<<*x*>).” Because of DP3+, (RS′) is equivalent to “**all***x*(if PA(*x*), then **rs**P*x*),” and this, because of AP7+ and DP1+, is equivalent to “**all***x*(if PA(*x*), then **rs**<*x*>).” (RS′), therefore, amounts to a weakening of (RS): merely its unproblematic half is retained, and then the above ontological argument can no longer be carried out. But we have to give up the idea that "**rs**" can represent "PA" in its predicative function in such a manner that the representation is based on *inherence simpliciter*: "**all***x*(if PA(*x*), then PA(*x*))" is a trivial logical truth, but "**all***x*(if **rs**<*x*>, then PA(*x*))" is false (or so it seems).

(b) Here it should be pointed out that a great many monadic predicates of LP cannot be represented in their predicative functions by LP-names for properties in the universe of discourse of LP, and that this is so whether the representation is based on inherence *simpliciter* or on existential inherence. The properties in the universe of discourse are the properties *of individuals*; modelling individuals by maximally consistent properties of individuals, we have in accordance with the description of the present universe of discourse of LP the easily provable truth: "**all***f***all***x*(if *f*<*x*> or *f*<<*x*>, then MK(*x*))" - "all properties of individuals apply, *simpliciter* or existentially, only to individuals." But many monadic predicates of LP *do not* merely apply to individuals (maximally consistent properties). (Even if the universe of discourse comprised only one entity, there still would be such predicates, for example, "*x*=**k**": this predicate applies to **k**, which must be in the universe of discourse given AP1 - AP6; but **k** is not a maximally consistent property.) Hence the properties (which are *not* properties *of individuals*) that may correspond to these predicates cannot be in the universe of discourse of LP, and hence there can be no LP-names for properties in the universe of discourse that represent those predicates in their predicative functions (via inherence *simpliciter* or existential inherence).

If one assumes, contrary to these insights, "**some***y***all***x*(A[*x*] iff *y*<*x*>)" as an axiom-schema, then - in steps that are familiar from the deduction of Russell's Antinomy - the system can be shown to have become incoherent: one obtains **some***y***all***x*(not *x*<*x*> iff *y*<*x*>), and hence **some***y*(not *y*<*y*> iff *y*<*y*>), which is a contradiction. But "**some***y***all***x*(A[*x*] iff *y*<*x*>)" can also be reduced to absurdity in the following more revealing manner: From **some***y***all***x*(A[*x*] iff *y*<*x*>) - applying DP1+ - **all***x*(if A[*x*], then MK(*x*)); this theorem-schema has the instance **all***x*(if not MK(*x*), then MK(*x*)), that is: **all***x*MK(*x*) (and conversely, from **all***x*MK(*x*) we get the schema **all***x*(if A[*x*], then MK(*x*))). Hence it is part of what is asserted by "**some***y***all***x*(A[*x*] iff *y*<*x*>)" that the universe of discourse of LP comprises *only* individuals, that is, that all predicates of LP apply *only* to individuals; but on the contrary we can already prove "not MK(**k**)." (It does not help, of course, to replace "*y*<*x*>" by "*y*<<*x*>.")

(c) On pain of inconsistency, we are not allowed to assume the truth of "**some***y***all***x*(A[*x*] iff *y*<*x*>)" for every predicate A[*x*] of LP. The next question is: according to which criterion are the predicates to be selected for which we *may* assume it? It seems it cannot even be assumed for all predicates A[*x*] of LP for which "**all**_x_(if A[_x_], then MK(_x_))" is true. "PA" is such a predicate, according to AP7+; but "**some**_y_**all**_x_(PA(_x_) iff _y_<_x_>)" is, of course, *also* sufficient for constructing "ontological arguments" (for whatever mythological property you like); the argument in (a) only needs to be slightly modified.[*1] *However*, faced with this, we cannot simply drop "**some**_y_**all**(PA(_x_) iff _y_<_x_>)"; because "if **all**_x_(if A[_x_], then MK(_x_)), then **some**_y_**all**_x_(A[_x_] iff _y_<_x_>)" is *already* provable on the basis of AP1 - AP6 (plus definitions). (See II.8.(a): TP29+.) Therefore, a different way out of the undesirable "ontological arguments" must be found than the rejection of "**some**_y_**all**_x_(PA(_x_) iff _y_<_x_>)." The latter is already provable, and dropping it would require modifications in the very basis of the system; such modifications, surely, should only be attempted as a last resort. (The matter is discussed further in chapter II.8.)

COMMENTS

[*1] In fact, the assumptions “**some*y*all*x***(PA(*x*) iff *y*<*x*>)” and “**all*x***(PA(*x*) iff **rs**<*x*>)” are equivalent: **all*x***(PA(*x*) iff **rs**<*x*>) results from **some*y*all*x***(PA(*x*) iff *y*<*x*>), because on the basis of AP1 - AP6 (plus definitions) we can prove **all*x*all*y***(**all*z***(*x*<*z*> iff *y*<*z*>), then *x*=*y*) (see TP19+ in chapter II.6), and we can define “**rs**” := “**the*y*all*x***(PA(*x*) iff *y*<*x*>).” Conversely, **some*y*all*x***(PA(*x*) iff *y*<*x*>) is a trivial consequence of **all*x***(PA(*x*) iff **rs**<*x*>).

This argument, obviously, is representative of a more general demonstration which shows that “**some*y*all*x***(A[*x*] iff *y*<*x*>)” and “**all*x***(A[*x*] iff **n**<*x*>)” are *generally* equivalent on the basis of AP1 - AP6 (plus definitions): for *all* predicates of LP A[*x*], and *all* names of LP **n** for which we have the following definition: **n** := **the*y*all*x***(A[*x*] iff *y*<*x*>).

CHAPTER II.5

LAWS OF ACTUAL EXISTENCE

(a) ''**somey**PA(*y*)'' (''there is a first intension that is a primary actuality'') is surely a correct statement. It is analytically equivalent, because of TP7+, to ''**somey**(MK(*y*) and AP(*y*))'' (''there is an actually existent individual'') and, because of TP4+ and DP2+, to ''**somey**AP(*y*)'' (''there is an actually existent first intension''; remember that AP1 - AP6 and AP7+ are analytically true in the present interpretation of LP). But it is not at all clear that ''**somey**PA(*y*)'' is *analytically* true, and hence it is not at all clear for ''**somey**AP(*y*)'' either. In the ontology of states of affairs, indeed, the statement that corresponds to ''**somey**AP(*y*)'': ''**somey**O(*y*)'' *is* analytically true, according to AP2 and DP31. This asymmetry between the ontology of states of affairs and the ontology of properties is due to the fact that the actual existence of *properties of individuals* is conceptually correlated with the actual existence of *individuals* (by DP2+ and TP7+); ''**somef**AP(*f*),'' in particular, is analytically equivalent to ''**somey**(MK(*y*) and AP(*y*)).'' Consider then that it is not at all clear that there being at least one actually existent individual is a purely conceptual matter.[*1]

(b) On the basis of **somey**PA(*y*), AP7+ and the definitions we can prove: **allf**[AP(*f*) or AP(**neg**(*f*))]. For assume: not AP(*f*), hence by DP2+: **noy**(PA(*y*) and *f*P*y*), hence **ally**(if PA(*y*), then not *f*P*y*), hence by applying **somey**PA(*y*): **somey**(PA(*y*) and not *f*P*y*), hence by AP7+ **somey**(PA(*y*) and MK(*y*) and not *f*P*y*), hence by DP26, DP25: **somey**(PA(*y*) and **neg**(*f*)P*y*), hence by DP2+: AP(**neg**(*f*)).

But we cannot prove on the basis of **somey**PA(*y*): **nof**[AP(*f*) and AP(**neg**(*f*))]; this - it is easily seen - does follow on the basis of AP1 - AP6, AP7+ and the definitions from **allxally**(if PA(*x*) and PA(*y*), then *x*=*y*), just as, conversely, the *latter* can be deduced on the same basis from **nof**(AP(*f*) and AP(**neg**(*f*)): Assume (1) **allf**[AP(*f*), then not AP(**neg**(*f*))], that is (according to DP2+): **allf**[if **somey**(PA(*y*) and *f*P*y*), then **ally**(if PA(*y*), then not **neg**(*f*)P*y*)]; assume now (2) PA(*x*) and PA(*y*), hence by AP2 **somey**′(PA(*y*′) and *x*P*y*′); hence by the first assumption: **ally**(if PA(*y*), then not **neg**(*x*)P*y*), hence, because of PA(*y*), not **neg**(*x*)P*y*, hence, because of PA(*y*), by AP7+, DP26, DP25: *x*P*y*, hence by TP79: *x*=*y* (since MK(*x*), MK(*y*): from the second assumption by AP7+).

(c) The statement ''**somexsomey**(PA(*x*) and PA(*y*) and *x*≠*y*)'' is just as correct as the statement ''**somey**PA(*y*),'' which is a logical consequence of it. We posit the former statement (its analyticity is, of course, just as doubtful as that of the latter) as a further axiom:

AP8+ **somexsomey**(PA(*x*) and PA(*y*) and *x*≠*y*).
("There are at least two first intensions that are primary actualities"; "there are at least two actually existent individuals.")

According to the considerations in section (b), we can immediately add:

TP12+ **allf**[AP(*f*) or AP(**neg**(*f*))].

TP13+ **somef**[AP(*f*) and AP(**neg**(*f*))].

Moreover we have:

TP14+ **allfallg**(AP(**disj**(*f*,*g*)) iff AP(*f*) or AP(*g*)).

TP15+ **allfallg**(if AP(**conj**(*f*,*g*)), then AP(*f*) and AP(*g*)).
(Depending on DP2+ and TP24.)

TP16+ **somefsomeg**[AP(*f*) and AP(*g*) and not AP(**conj**(*f*,*g*))].

As a generalization of TP14+ we have:

TP17+ AP(**disjf**A[*f*]) iff **someg**(A[*g*] and AP(*g*)).

And finally we add

TP18+ **allx**(if PA(*x*), then *x*≠**t**).

As AP7+ corresponds to the conjunction of AP7 and AP8, so TP18+ corresponds to AP9.[*2]

(d) As "N(*x*)" corresponds to "P(*x*)," so "GA(*x*)" corresponds to "AP(*x*)":

DP4+ GA(t) := not AP(**neg**(t)).
("t is general among primary actualities.")

Besides "**allx**(GA(*x*) iff **ally**(if PA(*y*), then *x*P*y*))," we can prove the following pendants of TP12+ - TP17+: **allf**[not GA(*f*) or not GA(**neg**(*f*))], **somef**[not GA(*f*) and not GA(**neg**(*f*))], **allfallg**(GA(**conj**(*f*,*g*)) iff GA(*f*) and GA(*g*)), **allfallg**(if GA(*f*) or GA(*g*), then GA(**disj**(*f*,*g*)), **somefsomeg**(GA(**disj**(*f*,*g*)) and not GA(*f*) and not GA(*g*)), GA(**conjf**A[*f*]) iff **allg**(if A[*g*], then GA(*g*)).

Although "N(x)" and "GA(x)" are related concepts (consider their definitions, the definitions of "P(x)" and "AP(x)," and AP7+), the contrast in their extensions is dramatic: there is just *one* property which is common to all possible individuals (one property which is "analytically necessary"): **t** (see TP93(i)); but surely there are many properties which are common to all *actually existing* individuals (many properties which are "general among primary actualities"). In saying this, we have a taken a stance on *actualism* with respect to individuals: it is *false*; for if it were correct, in other words, if "**all**x(if MK(x), then AP(x))" ("every individual is actually existent") were true, then, according to TP7+, "**all**x(MK(x) iff PA(x))" would be true, and consequently (considering the definitions involved) "GA(x)" would be co-extensional with "N(x)". Hence there would be only one property common to all actually existent individuals - contradicting *the plurality* of such properties.

(e) AP8+ could plausibly be replaced by an axiom-schema stating that there is an infinity of first intensions which are primary actualities (actually existent individuals, according to TP7+):

(PAI) (a) **≥1**xPA(x); (b) if **≥N**xPA(x), then **≥N**+1xPA(x) (for all Arabian numerals N).

AP10 would then become provable (on the basis of AP1 - AP6, AP7+ and the definitions), since (PAI) implies (because of AP7+) that there are infinitely many maximally consistent properties, hence infinitely many *elementary* properties: enough to have any finite lower degree of the universe of properties filled by some property (some conjunction of finitely many elementary properties). AP10 is certainly just as true (all its instances are just as true) for properties as it is for states of affairs (the argument in I.20.(a) is easily adapted to properties). But is the stronger (PAI) also true? There are infinitely many possible individuals; but are there infinitely many *actually existent* ones? This remains rather doubtful if we leave out of consideration (as we should) so-called "abstract individuals" (see comment [*1]). Therefore, AP8+ will not be replaced by (PAI) (or any statement of the form **≥N**xPA(x), N being an Arabian numeral after "2"; assuming some such statement, even if correct, as an *axiom* would be quite arbitrary from the ontological point of view); it will merely be be supplemented by AP10.

COMMENTS

[*1] The analytical truth of ''some individual is actually existent'' would be established by the analytical truth of ''D is actually existent,'' where D designates some individual. Prominent candidates for D such that the sentence ''individual D is actually existent'' turns out to be analytically true are, for example, ''God'' (Anselm's candidate), all names for natural numbers, ''∅'' (''the empty set''). However, in the first case not even believers are normally ready to turn the belief that God exists, which is the basis of any belief *in* God, into a matter of the understanding of concepts; and in the latter cases it can plausibly be argued that those names do not designate individuals at all (but, on the contrary, special properties). (I realize that it is quite common to call numbers and pure sets ''abstract individuals''; but very often nothing more is meant by this than is meant by ''abstract entity.'')

[*2] If one assumed in addition to AP1 - AP6 ''**one***y*PA(*y*)'' (instead of AP8+) as basic principle and defined ''**w**'' := ''**the***y*PA(*y*),'' then (applying DP31 and DP2+) ''**all***x*(AP(*x*) iff O(*x*))'' could be proved, and AP7+ could be shown to be equivalent to the conjunction of AP7 and AP8, TP18+ to be equivalent to AP9. This thought-experiment highlights at once the similarity and the contrast between the ontology of states of affairs and the ontology of properties.

CHAPTER II.6

LAWS OF INHERENCE, AND SUPERESSENTIALISM

(a) The schema "**some***y***all***x*(A[*x*] iff *y*<*x*>)" corresponds to the *naive* set-theoretical *principle of comprehension*. We have seen that it cannot be adopted. The twin of the set-theoretical *principle of extensionality* is, however, provable on the basis of AP1 - AP6 and the definitions:

TP19+ **all***f***all***g*(if **all***z*(*f*<*z*> iff *g*<*z*>), then *f*=*g*).

TP19+ asserts that properties are identical if they are exemplified by the same possible individuals (and only if: the converse of TP19+ is a pure matter of logic). This suggests the idea that properties are *their extensions*: sets of possible individuals, as is, for example, claimed by D. Lewis (*On the Plurality of Worlds*, p. 50ff). Extensionalistic prejudice in favor of sets aside, that idea *also* incorporates a certain conception of individuals and properties: individuals as identifiable (at least in terms of a model) with maximally consistent properties. (Note the following: if properties are sets of possible individuals, then maximally consistent properties are singleton sets of them; those sets can very well be identified with the individuals themselves.) This conception is being explored in this part of the book, but it is certainly not the only possible one (see II.1.(c)).
The proof of TP19+ contains the proof of

TP20+ **all***f***all***g*(if **all***z*(if *g*<*z*>, then *f*<*z*>), then *f*P*g*).

And it is easily seen that we also have:

TP21+ **all***f***all***g*(if *f*P*g*, then **all***z*(if *g*<*z*>, then *f*<*z*>)).
(Depending on DP1+, AP1.)

Hence we obtain

TP22+ **all***f***all***g*(**all***z*(if *g*<*z*>, then *f*<*z*>) iff *f*P*g*).

If we formulated the law (IP) in II.1.(a) about the connection between extensional and intensional parthood for properties as an analytical axiom in LP (introducing one more primitive predicate),

all*f***all***g*(*f*P*g* iff $g\mathrm{P}^{E}f$)

("property *f* is an intensional part of property *g* if and only if *g* is extensional part of *f*"),

then with the analytical principle TP22+ we would obtain the analytically true statement "**all***f***all***g*(*g*P^{E}*f* iff **all***z*(if *g*<*z*>, then *f*<*z*>))." Conversely, by the definition

DP5+ tP^{E}t′ := **all***z*(if t<*z*>, then t′<*z*>)
("property t is an extensional part of property t′.")

and the analytical TP22+ we obtain the *inversion principle* (IP) as an analytical theorem in LP:

TP23+ **all***f***all***g*(*f*P*g* iff *g*P^{E}*f*).

(b) Let us introduce for the moment the modal operator "*L*" into LP (in its present intepretation): for all sentence-forms A of LP "*L*A" is to be read as "it is conceptually necessary that A." For "*L*" we assume the modal logic S5 - with one restriction: the *rule of necessitation* ("if A is provable, then *L*A is provable") is only applicable to sentence-forms that are provable without recourse to AP8+ (which is itself of course a sentence-form that is *not* provable without recourse to AP8+); otherwise we could prove *L*A in cases where *L*A is presumably false (for example in the case of "**some***y*PA(*y*)"). (For a detailed description of S5 see Hughes/Cresswell, *An Introduction of Modal Logic*, chapter 3, especially p. 49ff, and chapter 8, especially p. 141ff, p. 145.)
The presence of "*L*" in LP makes it possible to express in LP that the concept of intensional parthood for properties is a concept which *applies essentially* (where it applies at all): it is *conceptually necessary* for all *f* and *g* that if property *f* is an intensional part of property *g*, then it is *conceptually necessary* that property *f* is an intensional part of property *g*" - in LP: *L***all***f***all***g*(if *f*P*g*, then *L*(*f*P*g*)). This (and "*L***all***f***all***g*(*f*P*g* iff *L*(*f*P*g*))" and "*L***all***f***all***g*(not *f*P*g* iff *L*not *f*P*g*)") becomes provable (the logic of LP having been strengthened by S5) if we add as an axiom (subject to the rule of necessitation)

<AP9+> **all***f***all***g*(if *f*P*g*, then *L*(*f*P*g*)).

"AP9+" is put in brackets, because "*L*" - and therefore <AP9+> - will soon be dropped from LP. LP, although interpreted as being about intensions, is, ultimately, to be kept free of modal sentence-connectives (which certainly are the main linguistic signals announcing intensions); for, if there are no modal contexts in LP, then *existential generalization* - B[t]; hence **some***y*B[*y*] - is guaranteed to be a logically valid inference-schema for *all* contexts of LP, and so is the substitution of identicals *salva veritate*.

(c) Using <AP9+>, we can prove that extensional parthood for properties is a concept which applies essentially:
(1) **all***f***all***g*(*f*P*g* iff *g*P^{E}*f*) (TP23+).
(2) *L***all***f***all***g*(*f*P*g* iff *g*P^{E}*f*) (rule of necessitation on (1)).
(3) **all***f***all***g*(*L*(*f*P*g*) iff *L*(*g*P^{E}*f*)) (purely logically from (2)).
(4) **all***f***all***g*(if *g*P^{E}*f*, then *L*(*g*P^{E}*f*)) (with (1) and (3) from <AP9+>).
(5) *L***all***f***all***g*(if *g*P^{E}*f*, then *L*(*g*P^{E}*f*)) (rule of necessitation on (4)).
That extensional parthood for properties is a concept which applies essentially is, of course, no more than one would expect given that *intensional parthood* for properties is a concept which applies essentially and given that (IP) is analytically true. However, instead of inherence *simpliciter*, *existential inherence* can be used as a basis for defining a concept of extensional parthood for which the corresponding version of (IP) is, in fact, *false*, and which is *not* a concept which applies essentially:

DP6+ tP^{EE}t′ := **all***z*(if t<<*z*>, then t′<<*z*>).
("property t is *existentially* extensional part of property t′.")

(Consider that "**all***z*(if *g*<<*z*>, then *f*<<*z*>)" is analytically equivalent to "**all***z*(if AP(*z*) and *g*<*z*>, then *f*<*z*>)," and compare II.1.(a).) Since intensional parthood of properties is a concept which applies essentially, there is prima facie a certain intuitive conflict with respect to extensional parthood of properties between the apparent analytic validity of (IP) for it on the one hand, and its apparently not being a concept which applies essentially on the other. The conflict is resolved by the distinction between extensional parthood *simpliciter* and *existential* extensional parthood (a distinction which is, in turn, based on the distinction between existential inherence and inherence *simpliciter*): the former concept applies essentially, and (IP) is analytically valid for it; the latter concept does not apply essentially, nor is (IP) valid for it.

(d) Using <AP9+>, we can also prove that inherence (*simpliciter*) is a concept which *applies essentially*: Assume *f*<*x*>, hence by DP1+: MK(*x*) and *f*P*x*; from *f*P*x* by <AP9+>: *Lf*P*x*; and from MK(*x*) by <AP9+> and its corollary (in S5) **all***f***all***g*(if not *f*P*g*, then *L*not *f*P*g*): *L*MK(*x*). This is seen as follows: By DP26, DP25 and DP24 from MK(*x*): **all***y*(not *y*P*x* or not **neg**(*y*)P*x*) and **all***y*(*y*P*x* or **neg**(*y*)P*x*), hence by <AP9+> and its corollary: **all***y*(*L*not *y*P*x* or *L*not **neg**(*y*)P*x*) and **all***y*(*L*(*y*P*x*) or *L*(**neg**(*y*)P*x*)), hence: **all***yL*(not *y*P*x* or not **neg**(*y*)P*x*) and **all***yL*(*y*P*x* or **neg**(*y*)P*x*), hence *L***all***y*(not *y*P*x* or not **neg**(*y*)P*x*) and *L***all***y*(*y*P*x* or **neg**(*y*)P*x*) (in S5-predicate-logic the Barcan-formula can be proved), hence *L*[**all***y*(not *y*P*x* or not **neg**(*y*)P*x*) and **all***y*(*y*P*x* or **neg**(*y*)P*x*)], hence by DP24, DP25, DP26: *L*MK(*x*).
From the two underlined results: *L*(MK(*x*) and *f*P*x*), hence by DP1+: *L*(*f*<*x*>). Therefore, **all***f***all***x*(if *f*<*x*>, then *L*(*f*<*x*>)), hence *L***all***f***all***x*(if *f*<*x*>, then *L*(*f*<*x*>)).

"*L***all***f***all***x*(*f*<*x*>, then *L*(*f*<*x*>))" and its corollary (in S5) "*L***all***f***all***x*(if not *f*<*x*>, then *L*not *f*<*x*>)" together assert as conceptually necessary a particularly strong version of *determinism*: determinism in the form of *superessentialism*, according to which *every* individual has *each* property it has as a matter of *conceptual necessity*, and as a matter of *conceptual necessity* does not have *each* property it does not have.[*1] Superessentialism appears to be bound up with an inherence-theory of exemplification together with the view that the individuals are correlated in one-to-one fashion with the maximally consistent properties (each having as intensional parts precisely the properties that inhere in the corresponding individual). But these ingredients do not suffice to produce superessentialism. The one-to-one correlation between individuals and maximally consistent properties must be thought of, in addition, as being a *necessary* one (see comment [*1] on Leibniz and Lewis) - a correlation which would be comparable in this respect to their identity, if they were identical. Moreover, inherence must be taken to be inherence *simpliciter*: superessentialism for *existential inherence*, even if it is defined - as in DP3+ - via intensional parthood of properties, is very probably false. In order to prove superessentialism for existential inherence, it would indeed be sufficient to postulate as an additional (analytical) axiom (subject to the rule of necessitation) "**all***y*(if PA(*y*), then *L*PA(*y*));" but this is not a plausible thesis.[*2] I, for example, am an actually existent individual; but my actual existence certainly does not appear to be conceptually necessary - even if individuals are considered to be maximally consistent properties.[*3] Therefore, according to TP7+, at least I am a primary actuality whose being a primary actuality is not conceptually necessary.

Superessentialism seems to be, initially, an entirely unacceptable position (though it has distinguished adherents). But it begins to appear more acceptable if it is compared with its alternatives. Shall we say that it is *conceptually possible* for each property an individual has that it does not have it, and that it is conceptually possible for each property it does not have that it does have it? If we do not want to accept this extreme position on the opposite end (which does not appear to be very reasonable) and yet do not want to become superessentialists, then we have the very difficult task before us of distinguishing between the properties an individual has as a matter of conceptual necessity, and those properties of it that it does not have as a matter of conceptual necessity (and of making the corresponding distinction for the properties it does not have).

COMMENTS

[*1] This is the kind of determinism Leibniz adhered to (see B. Mates, *The Philosophy of Leibniz*, p. 43). But Leibniz also believed in the *contingent* in-being of some first intensions in others, and certainly - rather as a special case of the former - in the occurrence of *contingent* inherence. His position can be described as follows:

Truth for Leibniz is the in-being of the predicate-concept in the subject-concept, and Leibnizian concepts can very well be identified with first intensions. Thus, everything that is true (every instance of one first intension being intensional part of another) is necessary *simpliciter*, i.e. conceptually necessary (cf. <AP9+>). But not everything that is true is necessary *for us*, where a truth is necessary for us precisely if it is necessary *simpliciter* and if it can be proved in finitely many steps: some truths cannot be proved in finitely many steps. Hence some truths are *contingent for us*: they are true, but not necessary for us (although they are necessary *simpliciter*, since they are matters of one first intension being an intensional part of another).

Leibniz then defines "contingent" by "contingent *for us*"; he thus "epistemizes" the concept of contingency (compare *The Philosophy of Leibniz*, p. 108f), and thus he can have instances of "contingent" inherence (where f inheres in x - as a matter of conceptual necessity - but cannot be finitely proved to inhere in x).

Another way of having instances of contingent inherence or exemplification (as is required by intuition), in spite of an underlying superessentialistic position, is championed by D. Lewis. Lewis has in effect the very same conception of individuals as Leibniz had (see *The Philosophy of Leibniz*, p. 139): an individual *cannot* (conceptually) have other properties than it has; for if it did have other properties, then it would not be (numerically) the same individual (this means that the individual is, as it were, *fused* with its "concept," i.e. with the maximally consistent property corresponding to it). Translating statements of possibility into statements about possible worlds, this becomes for Lewis: "So Humphrey, who is part of this world and here has five fingers on the left hand, is also part of some other world and there has six fingers on his left hand. *Qua* part of this world he has five fingers, *qua* part of that world he has six. He himself - one and the same and altogether self-identical - has five fingers on the left hand, and he has not five but six. How can this be?" (*On the Plurality of Worlds*, p. 199).

Lewis, however, sees no difficulty in his position for the occurrence of contingent exemplification, and he surely would not accept being called a "superessentialist." His way to contingency is the following (although it is not quite described by him in these words):

Every individual has as a matter of conceptual necessity (necessarily *simpliciter*) every property it has (without the property, it would not be *this* individual). But contingent exemplification is appropriately defined not via the concept of necessity *simpliciter*, but via the concept of *superapplication* (or *superexemplification* or *superinherence*). A property *superapplies* to an individual precisely if it applies to it and, in addition, to all of its *counterparts* which are different from it, that is, to all of its representatives in other possible worlds. (Lewis' *counterpart theory* is discussed in III.12.) Hence there are instances of contingent inherence, because surely not every property that applies to some individual also superapplies to it.

In Lewis' own words (*On the Plurality of Worlds*, p. 51f): "Consider the property of being a talking donkey, which I say is the set of all talking donkeys throughout the worlds. ... Take Brownie, an other-worldly talking donkey. Brownie himself is, once and for all [necessarily *simpliciter*], a member of the set; hence, once and for all, an instance of the property. But it is contingent whether Brownie talks; Brownie has counterparts who do and counterparts who don't. In just the same way, it is contingent whether Brownie belongs to the set: Brownie has counterparts who do and counterparts who don't. That is how it is contingent whether Brownie has the property."

Lewis is far from regarding his concept of contingent exemplification as an ad hoc construction that misses the very point of contingency, because the only concept of necessary exemplification he knows (or cares to recognize) is *superapplication*; and contingent exemplification is, after all, defined by him via necessity of exemplification in the usual way: as exemplification that is not necessary exemplification. (Concerning Lewis' understanding of contingency - in spite of his superessentialism - see also A. Plantinga in *The Nature of Necessity*, p. 103f.)

[*2] Leibniz denies "$\mathbf{all}y(\text{if } PA(y), \text{ then } LPA(y))$," or rather its analytical equivalent by TP7+: only God actually exists with (conceptual) necessity, all other actually existing substances actually exist contingently (in the normal sense: they actually exist, but not with conceptual necessity). (See *The Philosophy of Leibniz*, p. 36.) Hence for Leibniz there can be no property of individuals f corresponding to the concept of primary actuality (or of actual existence for individuals) such that $L\mathbf{all}y(f<y> \text{ iff } PA(y))$ [$L\mathbf{all}y(f<y> \text{ iff } MK(y) \text{ and } AP(y))$]. Otherwise Leibniz's superessentialism would be applicable to f, and therefore we could make the following deduction: assume $PA(y)$, hence $f<y>$, hence $L(f<y>)$, hence $LPA(y)$. B. Mates accordingly writes "actualized [individual] concepts are [according to Leibniz] not to be differentiated from the non-actualized ones by the presence of a simple or complex property called 'existence'." (*Ibid.*, p. 75).

We shall see, however, that one cannot well avoid having the *property of real subsistence* **rs** correspond to "$PA(y)$" in the manner just indicated. This circumstance - because (given AP1 - <AP9+>) we *do* have the theorem

*L***all***f***all***y*(if *f*<*y*>, then *L*(*f*<*y*>)) - leads to the semblance that the statement "**all***y*(if PA(*y*), then *L*PA(*y*))" is, after all, *provable* (without applying AP8+); on this, however, consider further the last comment of chapter II.8.

[*3] Indeed, neither "**some***xL*AP(*x*)" nor "*L***some***x*AP(*x*)" can be proved in AP1 - <AP9+>; applying AP8+ and DP2+, we *can* prove "AP(**t**)" and hence "**some***x*AP(*x*)," but the rule of necessitation must not be applied to these statements, since they are not provable without AP8+.
In contrast, "**some***xL*not AP(*x*)" (and hence "*L***some***x* not AP(*x*)") can be proved in AP1 - <AP9+>: assume for *reductio*: AP(**k**), that is (by DP2+): **some***y*(PA(*y*) and **k**P*y*), hence by AP7+ **some***y*(MK(*y*) and **k**P*y*), hence by DP26 **some***y*(K(*y*) and **k**P*y*), hence, because of **all***y*(*y*P**k**) and AP3, **some***y*(K(*y*) and *y*=**k**) - contradicting TP70. Since "not AP(**k**)" is provable without recourse to AP8+, we have by the rule of necessitation: *L*not AP(**k**), and hence **some***xL*not AP(*x*). (Note that "**k**" - although defined by a definite description - is a rigid designator: it would designate the same entity it does designate (given the present interpretation of LP) even if things (excepting, of course, the present interpretation of LP) were ever so much different from what they really are. Therefore, we can apply existential generalization without scruples to "not AP(**k**).")
Curiously, there is an affinity between **k** and the Neo-Platonic *One*. The latter, in one sense, is supposed to encompass everything, allowing all predications, and to be absolutely simple in another sense, allowing no predications (the second characterization is the dominant one). Moreover, the One is supposed to be *beyond being*. We can already prove "**all***f*(*f*P**k**)," "**no***f*(*f*<**k**>)" and "not AP(**k**)." And if - in view of DP1+ and DP26 - we split up the concept of inherence "*f*<*x*>"into "*f*<*x*>$_1$":= "K(*x*) and *f*P*x*," and "*f*<*x*>$_2$":= "MX(*x*) and *f*P*x*," then we can prove: "**no***f*(*f*<**k**>$_1$) and **all***x*(if **no***f*(*f*<*x*>$_1$), then *x*=**k**)" and "**all***f*(*f*<**k**>$_2$) and **all***x*(if **all***f*(*f*<*x*>$_2$), then *x*=**k**)." This fits the One in the first and second hypotheses in Plato's *Parmenides* (which was so important for the Neo-Platonists) just as much as it fits the much later characterization of God in medieval Platonism as both "*negatio negationis*" ("that where even the negation is to be denied") and "*coincidentia oppositorum*."
It would be interesting - but certainly very difficult - to find out whether this affinity is merely a superficial coincidence, or whether it is constituted by a metaphysical interpretation of relevant facts from the ontology of properties (or first intensions) that were already known - explicitly or implicitly - to philosophers in late antiquity.

CHAPTER II.7

LEIBNIZ'S *PRINCIPIUM*

(a) Let us now return again to the language LP without "*L*", dropping <AP9+> from our list of axioms.

The principle of the identity of indiscernibles - the *principium identitatis indiscernibilium* upheld by Leibniz - can be formulated in LP in a trivial and in a non-trivial version. The trivial version can be proved rather easily (on the basis of AP1 - AP6 and the definitions):

TP24+ **all***x***all***y*(if MK(*x*) and MK(*y*) and **all***f*(*f*<*x*> iff *f*<*y*>), then *x*=*y*).
("Substances which exemplify the same first intensions are identical.")

It can be gathered from the proof of TP24+ (see the Appendix) that we even have:

TP25+ **all***x***all***y*(if MK(*x*) and **all***f*(if *f*<*x*>, then *f*<*y*>), then *x*=*y*).

The non-trivial version of the *principium* (the version presumably intended by Leibniz) is, however, not quite so easily proved:

all*x***all***y*(if MK(*x*) and MK(*y*) and **all***f*(if not MK(*f*), then (*f*<*x*> iff *f*<*y*>)), then *x*=*y*).
("Substances in which the same accidents ('properties') inhere are identical.")

(b) On the basis of AP1 - AP6 and the definitions it can first of all be proved:

TP26+ **all***x***all***y*(if MK(*x*) and MK(*y*) and [not MK(**neg**(*x*)) or not MK(**neg**(*y*))] and **all***f*(if not MK(*f*), then (*f*<*x*> iff *f*<*y*>)), then *x*=*y*).

But the extra condition "[not MK(**neg**(*x*)) or not MK(**neg**(*y*))]" cannot be dropped from the antecedent of TP26+ as long as we do not go beyond AP1 - AP6. The statement resulting from TP26+ by replacing "[not MK(**neg**(*x*)) or not MK(**neg**(*y*))]" by the contradictorily opposed condition "MK(**neg**(*x*)) and MK(**neg**(*y*))" cannot be proved on the basis of AP1 - AP6 and the definitions. We *can* prove on that basis:

TP27+ **all***x*(if MK(*x*) and MK(**neg**(*x*)), then **all***z*(*z*=*x* or *z*=**neg**(*x*) or *z*=**t** or *z*=**k**)).

Consequently - assuming MK(*x*), MK(*y*), MK(**neg**(*x*)), MK(**neg**(*y*)) - we have: (*) *y*=*x* or *y*=**neg**(*x*) or *y*=**t** or *y*=**k**. Moreover, *y*≠**k** results by TP70 from K(*y*) (by DP26 from MK(*y*)). And we have: *y*≠**t**; for *otherwise*: from MK(*y*) by DP26 MX(*y*), hence by TP71 QC(*y*), that is (by DP7): **all***z*(if *y*P*z*, then *z*=*y* or T(*z*)); hence **all***z*(*z*=*y* or T(*z*)) (because of **all***z*(**t**P*z*): **all***z*(*y*P*z*) - given the *reductio*-assumption *y*=**t**), hence: *x*=*y* or T(*x*); not T(*x*), for otherwise by TP34 *x*=**k**, hence by TP70: not K(*x*) - contradicting MK(*x*); therefore: *x*=*y*; hence *x*=**t** (we are still proceeding on the *reductio*-assumption *y*=**t**), hence **neg**(*x*)=**neg**(**t**), hence by TP54 **neg**(*x*)=**k**, hence: not K(**neg**(*x*)) - contradicting MK(**neg**(*x*)).

But we cannot also show (on the basis of AP1 - AP6) *y*≠**neg**(*x*) (which, because of (*), would finally give us *x*=*y*). The assumption MK(**neg**(*y*)), which we have not so far used, and the *extra* assumption **all***f*(if not MK(*f*), then (*f*<*x*> iff *f*<*y*>)) are of no avail. This is demonstrated by the following set-theoretical model of AP1 - AP6: <the subsets of {1,2}, *x*P*y* := *x* and *y* are subsets of {1,2}, and *x* is a subset of *y*>. The "P"-hierarchy of the model looks like this:

{1,2}: T
{1},{2}: MK/EL
∅: M

It is easily checked on the basis of the definitions that we have as true in the model: MK({1}), MK(**neg**({1})), MK({2}), MK(**neg**({2})), **all***f*(if not MK(*f*), then (*f*<{1}> iff *f*<{2}>)) - that is, all statements corresponding to the above assumptions for *x* and *y*. But we also have as true in the model: {2}=**neg**({1}), {1}=**neg**({2}), {1}≠{2}.

(c) TP26+ is logically equivalent to "**all***x***all***y*[if MK(*x*) and MK(*y*) and not MK(**neg**(*x*)) and **all***f*(if not MK(*f*), then (*f*<*x*> iff *f*<*y*>)), then *x*=*y*] and **all***x***all***y*[MK(*x*) and MK(*y*) and not MK(**neg**(*y*)) and **all***f*(if not MK(*f*), then (*f*<*x*> iff *f*<*y*>)), then *x*=*y*]": to a conjunction whose conjuncts are logically equivalent to each other. TP26+ is, therefore, logically equivalent to each of the conjuncts. Let us consider TP26+ from now on in the logically equivalent version presented by the above *first conjunct*.

As a logical consequence of TP27+ we have: if **all***x***some***z*(*z*≠*x* and *z*≠**neg**(*x*) and *z*≠**t** and *z*≠**k**), then **all***x*[if MK(*x*), then not MK(**neg**(*x*))].[*1] Therefore, if we could prove "**all***x***some***z*(*z*≠*x* and *z*≠**neg**(*x*) and *z*≠**t** and *z*≠**k**)," then we could prove "**all***x*[if MK(*x*), then not MK(**neg**(*x*))]," and this would give us on the basis of TP26+ (since we can then eliminate "not MK(**neg**(*x*))" from its antecedent) the *principium identitatis indiscernibilium* in its non-trivial version.[*2] But "**all***x***some***z*(*z*≠*x* and *z*≠**neg**(*x*) and *z*≠**t** and *z*≠**k**)" is not a theorem of AP1 - AP6, nor even a theorem of AP1 - AP8+. It is, however, a theorem of AP1 - AP6 *plus* AP10: its negation implies that there are at most four entities in the universe of discourse - contradicting AP10. Indeed, "**all***x***some***z*(*z*≠*x* and *z*≠**neg**(*x*) and *z*≠**t** and *z*≠**k**)" amounts precisely (on the basis of AP1 - AP6) to a statement to the effect that there are *not* at most four entities in the universe of discourse, that is, that there are *at least* five entities in the universe of discourse.[*3]

(d) Given merely the truth of AP1 - AP6, Leibniz's *principium* (the non-trivial version) is trivially true if there is just one entity in the universe of discourse (because then we have **no***y*MK(*y*)); and it is trivially true if there are precisely two entities in the universe discourse (because then we have **one***y*MK(*y*)); it is also true, as we have seen, if there at least five entities in the universe of discourse. The case that there are precisely three entities in the universe of discourse is excluded, given the truth of AP1 - AP6. But there is *one* case of the cardinality of the universe of discourse in which, given merely the truth of AP1 - AP6, the *principium* would not be true: if there were precisely four entities in the universe of discourse - as is demonstrated by the model in section (b), which *falsifies* the *principium*. Thus, Leibniz's *principium* is (analytically) equivalent on the basis of AP1 - AP6 to an assumption that - although true - is not of an entirely elementary nature: that there are *not* precisely four first intensions.

COMMENTS

[*1] The converse of this statement cannot be proved in AP1 - AP6: "**all***x*[if MK(*x*), then not MK(**neg**(*x*))]" is a logical consequence of "**no***x*MK(*x*)," which is not excluded by AP1 - AP6; but "**no***x*MK(*x*)" also implies "**no***x*EL(*x*)" (by TP77), and hence that there is precisely one entity in the universe of discourse (see I.20.(b)); this falsifies "**all***x***some***z*(*z*≠*x* and *z*≠**neg**(*x*) and *z*≠**t** and *z*≠**k**)." Again, "**all***x*[if MK(*x*), then not MK(**neg**(*x*))]" is a consequence (on the basis of AP1 - AP6) of "**one***x*MK(*x*)"; but "**one***x*MK(*x*)" also implies "**one***x*EL(*x*)" (by TP77), and hence that there are precisely two entities in the universe of discourse (see I.20.(b)); this also falsifies "**all***x***some***z*(*z*≠*x* and *z*≠**neg**(*x*) and *z*≠**t** and *z*≠**k**)." "**all***x*[if MK(*x*), then not MK(**neg**(*x*))]" is however equivalent on the basis of AP1 - AP6 to "not **2***x*MK(*x*)," hence to "not **2***x*EL(*x*)" (because of the one-to-one correlation between the elementary first intensions and the maximally consistent ones; compare I.10.(c)), which means that there are *not* precisely four entities in the universe of discourse.

[*2] "**all***x*[if MK(*x*), then not MK(**neg**(*x*))]" would not only give us the non-trivial *principium*, but even "**all***x***all***y*(if MK(*x*) and MK(*y*) and **all***f*(if not MK(*f*) and *f*<*y*>, then *f*<*x*>), then *x*=*y*)," as can be seen from the proof of TP26+ in the Appendix: "**neg**(*x*)<*x*> iff **neg**(*x*)<*y*>" can be replaced in (**i**) by the weaker "if **neg**(*x*)<*y*>, then **neg**(*x*)<*x*>" without any damage to the proof at all.

[*3] Assume **all***x***some***z*(*z*≠*x* and *z*≠**neg**(*x*) and *z*≠**t** and *z*≠**k**), hence by substituting "**t**": **some***z*(*z*≠**t** and *z*≠**neg**(**t**) and *z*≠**t** and *z*≠**k**), hence by TP54 **some***z*(*z*≠**t** and *z*≠**k**), hence **some***z*(*z*≠**t** and *z*≠**k** and **t**≠**k**) (**t**=**k** is AP1-AP6-equivalent to **all***x***all***y*(*x*=*y*), which is already contradicted); hence by applying the assumption: **some***z***some***z*′(*z*′≠*z* and *z*′≠**neg**(*z*) and *z*′≠**t** and *z*′≠**k** and *z*≠**t** and *z*≠**k** and **t**≠**k**); in addition *z*≠**neg**(*z*) (*otherwise* **t**=**k**; see the proof of TP105), **neg**(*z*)≠**t** (*otherwise* *z*=**k** by TP55, TP54), **neg**(*z*)≠**k** (*otherwise* *z*=**t** by TP55, TP54). Therefore: there are at least five (distinct) entities in the universe of discourse: *z*′, *z*, **neg**(*z*), **t**, **k**. (If there at least five entities in the universe of discourse, we can conclude that there are at least eight, since there cannot be precisely five, six or seven; see I.20.(b).)

CHAPTER II.8

ONCE MORE: REAL SUBSISTENCE AS A PROPERTY?

(a) The following schema can be proved in AP1 - AP6:

TP28+ **all***x*(**disj***x*′(MK(*x*′) and A[*x*′])<*x*> iff MK(*x*) and A[*x*]).

We have seen in II.4.(b) that a representation of *all* monadic predicates of LP by properties in its universe of discourse is not possible. TP28+, however, shows that there is such a representation for *some* monadic predicates of LP, namely for those predicates A[*x*] of LP for which "**all***x*(if A[*x*], then MK(*x*))" is true:

TP29+ if **all***x*(if A[*x*], then MK(*x*)), then **all***x*(**disj***y*A[*y*]<*x*> iff A[*x*]).

But from TP29+, by applying AP7+, we immediately get

TP30+ **all***x*(**disj***y*PA(*y*)<*x*> iff PA(*x*)).

We can define

DP7+ **rs** := **disj***y*PA(*y*)
("the property of real subsistence is the intensionally greatest property all primary actualities (actually existent individuals) have in common"),

and hence we obtain

TP31+ **all***x*(**rs**<*x*> iff PA(*x*)),

and therefore (RS) - the thesis underlying the "proof" in II.4.(a) for the actual existence of a divine being - is a *theorem* (even in AP1 - AP6). Thus the ontological argument in II.4.(a) can no longer be defused by repudiating (RS) - if we do not want to shatter the very basis of the ontology of properties. Indeed, all that is left is the rejection (not the denial) of its premise: "**conj(d,rs)≠k**," which was considered to be "intuitively evident." But how could this premise be called into doubt? How could we withhold assent to it?

(b) Because (RS) is a theorem, the argument in II.4.(a) at least proves the following general principle:

TP32+ **all***f*(if **conj(***f***,rs)≠k**, then **some***y*(PA(*y*) and *f*<*y*>)).

("Every property that is consistent with *real subsistence* is exemplified by some actually existent individual.")

This seems to be utterly wrong. But appearances may be deceptive.

In the proof of TP32+ (see II.4.(a); but replace constant "**d**" with the variable "*f*") the theorem TP94(i) is used, which (by DP29) amounts to "**all**x(x≠**k** iff **some**y(MK(y) and xPy))." This theorem can be used in the ontology of states of affairs for proving a result that is analogous to TP32+:

TP141 **all**x(if **conj**(x,**w**)≠**k**, then V(x)).
("Every state of affairs that is consistent with *the world* is true.")

The analogy between TP141 and TP32+ is brought out particularly well if one considers that "**some**y(PA(y) and f<y>)" is - according to DP1+, AP7+, DP2+ - analytically equivalent (in virtue of the analytical truth of the corresponding general biconditional statement) to "AP(f)" - "*f* is an actually existent property"; and that "V(x)" is - according to DP32 - analytically equivalent to "O(x)" - "*f* is an actually existent (obtaining) state of affairs."[*1]

The analogy helps us to establish the correct point of view for judging TP32+. TP141 is *not* a counter-intuitive theorem; it *seems* counter-intuitive only if we confuse the world (a certain maximally consistent state of affairs) with our theories about the world. (Of course: not everything that is consistent with our theories about the world can be true; even in the *very* unlikely case that all of them are *true*, their sum would still be *incomplete*, i.e. such that some state of affairs *p* and its negation is consistent with that sum. But *p* and **neg**(*p*) are not both true.) Note that in very many cases it is rather difficult for us to find out whether a state of affairs is consistent with the world, although it may be an easy matter to determine whether it is consistent with this or that other state of affairs. The reason is: being consistent with the world amounts to *being true*; see comment [*1].

TP32+ seems counter-intuitive, because in many cases (being a unicorn at t_0, being a king of elves at t_0, etc.) it seems obvious that a property is consistent with real subsistence, and just as obvious that there is no actually existent individual that has this property. But the question whether a property is consistent with real subsistence is a question which is analogous to the question whether a state of affairs is consistent with the world. Deciding whether a state of affairs is consistent with the world is analytically equivalent to deciding whether it obtains (is true), and deciding whether a property is consistent with real subsistence is analytically equivalent to deciding whether it actually exists (is exemplified by an actually existing individual); see comment [*1]. Then how can we be so sure that *being divine*, for example, is consistent with real subsistence? We cannot, because consistence with the property of real subsistence amounts to *actual existence* for properties.

(c) It is just as easy to be wrong about the property of real subsistence as it is to be wrong about the state of affairs which is the world; that is, to be wrong about the very identity of those entities: to mistake some *other* state of affairs for the world, some *other* property for real subsistence. If we believe that a state of affairs obtains which in truth (say, as a matter of empirical fact) does not obtain, then we take **w** (=**conj***y*O(*y*)) *nolens volens* for a state of affairs which it really is not. And if we believe that an individual does not actually exist that in truth actually exists, then we take **rs** (=**disj***y*PA(*y*)) *nolens volens* for a property which it really is not.[*2] Surely some of our further judgments concerning consistency with **w** or **rs** might be adversely affected by these mistakes.

Thus, questions concerning consistency with **rs** or **w** are not generally questions that can be answered (if at all) *a priori* and with concomitant certainty. Normally, indeed, an answer to the question whether a statement of the form **conj**(t,t′)≠**k** is true does not depend on synthetic matters of which we have no *a priori* knowledge. This is always the case, if both t and t′ are *rigid* designators. But "**rs**" and "**w**" are not rigid designators; if other properties actually existed (as might very well have been the case), then "**rs**" would designate a property different from the one it designates in fact; and "**w**" would designate a different state of affairs if other states of affairs obtained. Which properties are actually existent, and which states of affairs obtain, hence which entities "**rs**" and "**w**" designate, are almost entirely synthetic matters (the obtaining of the "tautological" state of affairs is not), and thus they are infected with the uncertainty these matters normally have - an uncertainty that cannot but be transmitted to judgments concerning consistency with **rs** and **w**.

In view of the remarks in sections (b) and (c) "**conj(d,rs)≠k**" - the premise of our ontological argument - ceases to be intuitively evident and becomes a problematic statement, and hence the argument in II.4.(a) is *not conclusive*, the provable truth of TP32+ notwithstanding. And it is clear in view of those remarks that the consistency of real subsistence with being a unicorn at t_0, for example, is not so unproblematically certain that we cannot reasonably deny it.[*3] This, in fact, we should do on the basis of TP32+ and our firm conviction that there are no unicorns that actually exist.

COMMENTS

[*1] In fact we can prove in the respective ontologies (the ontology of properties, the ontology of states of affairs): **all***f*(**conj**(*f*,**rs**)≠**k** iff AP(*f*)), **all***x*(**conj**(*x*,**w**)≠**k** iff O(*x*)). All that remains to be shown are the left-to-right halves of these general biconditionals:
(1) AP(*f*), hence by DP2+ **some***y*(PA(*y*) and *f*P*y*), hence by TP31+ **some***y*(**rs**<*y*> and *f*P*y*), hence by DP1+ **some***y*(MK(*y*) and **rs**P*y* and *f*P*y*), hence by TP24 **some***y*(MK(*y*) and **conj**(*f*,**rs**)P*y*), hence by TP85: not **kPconj**(*f*,**rs**), hence by AP2: **conj**(*f*,**rs**)≠**k**.
(2) O(*x*), hence by DP31 *x***Pw**, hence, because of **wPw** (AP2), by TP24: **conj**(*x*,**w**)**Pw**; moreover by TP25: **wPconj**(*x*,**w**); hence by AP3 **conj**(*x*,**w**)=**w**, hence by AP7: **conj**(*x*,**w**)≠**k**.

In contrast to this perfect analogy, "**all***f*(AP(*f*) iff **rsP***f*)," which would correspond to the theorem "**all***x*(O(*x*) iff *x***Pw**)" in the ontology of states of affairs, is not a principle of ontology of properties: **rsPconj**(**rs**, **neg**(**rs**)), but not AP(**conj**(**rs**,**neg**(**rs**))); therefore: **some***f*(**rsP***f* and not AP(*f*)). And if one accepted at least the truth of "**all***f*(if AP(*f*), then **rsP***f*)," then one would also have to accept the truth of "**all***y*(PA(*y*) iff MK(*y*))" (the thesis of *actualism* for individuals): AP(**t**) (AP8+, **all***y*(**tP***y*), DP2+), hence on the basis of "**all***f*(if AP(*f*), then **rsP***f*)": **rsPt**, hence, because of **tPrs**, by AP3 **rs**=**t**, hence by TP31+ **all***y*(PA(*y*) iff **t**<*y*>), hence by DP1+ **all***y*(PA(*y*) iff MK(*y*) and **tP***y*), that is (because of **all***y*(**tP***y*)): **all***y*(PA(*y*) iff MK(*y*)). But one can very well assume that the latter statement is not true.

The deduction just made demonstrates the truth of "if **rs**=**t**, then **all***y*(PA(*y*) iff MK(*y*))." The converse of this is also provable: from **all***y*(PA(*y*) iff MK(*y*)) by TP66, AP3: **disj***y*PA(*y*)=**disj***y*MK(*y*); by TP89, TP88: **disj***y*MK(*y*)=**t**; hence by DP7+ **rs**=**t**. Thus, actualism for individuals can also be formulated by the thesis that real subsistence is the "tautological" property; we have (independently of AP8+):

TP33+ **rs**=**t** iff **all***y*(PA(*y*) iff MK(*y*)).

(Note that "**all***f*(AP(*f*), then **rsP***f*)" can now be seen to be provably equivalent to each side of TP33+.)

Moreover we have

TP34+ **rs**≠**k** iff **some***y*PA(*y*).

Not only the statement "**all***f*(AP(*f*) iff **rsP***f*)," but also the statement "**all***f*(AP(*f*) iff *f***Prs**)" can be refuted. From "**all***f*(AP(*f*), then *f***Prs**)" one obtains "**all***y*(if PA(*y*), then *y*=**rs**)" - contradicting AP8+. This is seen as follows: assume PA(*y*), hence by TP4+: AP(*y*), hence by **all***f*(if AP(*f*), then *f***Prs**): *y***Prs**; by TP65 from PA(*y*): **disj***z*PA(*z*)P*y*, that is (according to DP7+): **rs**P*y*; from the underlined results by AP3: *y*=**rs**.

But at least we have

TP35+ **all***f*(if *f***Prs**, then AP(*f*)).

[*2] Suppose we are in error about *x* in believing that it is *not* an actually existent individual, *not* a first intension which is a primary actuality (see TP7+), although it is in fact. Suppose we are correct about the actual existence of all other individuals. In that case we mistake **disj***y*(PA(*y*) and *y*≠*x*) for **rs**. The relationship between the two properties can be gathered from the following theorem:

TP36+ **all***x*[if PA(*x*), then **disj***y*PA(*y*)P***disj***y*(PA(*y*) and *y*≠*x*)].

And we can be in the same manner mistaken about any property which corresponds to a predicate "A[*x*]" for which "**all***x*(if A[*x*], then MK(*x*))" is analytically true; for, if this is analytically true, then, according to TP29+ and TP19+, the following is also analytically true: **the***f***all***y*(*f*<*y*> iff A[*y*])= **disj***y*A[*y*]; and in addition we have TP36+ as analytically true for all predicates "A[*x*]": **all***x*[if A[*x*], then **disj***y*A[*y*]P***disj***y*(A[*y*] and *y*≠*x*)].

However, it does not seem to be *generally* correct that in misapplying a monadic predicate of individuals in the way described in the first paragraph of this comment we are mistaken about the very identity of the property of individuals corresponding to it, as we certainly appear to be in the case of "PA(*x*)." What is to be said about this?

Suppose we accept the statement "not A[b]," while in fact "A[b]" is true. If we have a grasp of the property corresponding to "A[*x*]" which is *independent* of the descriptions "**the***f***all***y*(*f*<*y*> iff A[*y*])" and "**disj***y*A[*y*]," and any other description employing the predicate, then the misapplication does, of course, not imply that we are mistaken about the very identity of that property (even given the radical inherence-theory of exemplification we are currently exploring). But if, as in the case of "PA(*x*)" and "MK(*x*) and AP(*x*)," we have *no* grasp of the property corresponding to "A[*x*]" which is independent of descriptions employing the predicate, then the misapplication *does* imply that we are mistaken about the very identity of that property.

[*3] In a certain sense, however, unicornity-at-t_0 and real subsistence are consistent with each other. This sense, however, can only be expressed if the modal operator "*L*" ("it is conceptually necessary") is added to LP (see II.6.(b)). Let "**h**" designate (rigidly) the property unicornity-at-t_0. Then we have: **conj(h,rs)=k**; but we cannot conclude from this that *L*(**conj(h,rs)=k**),

because "**rs**" (and hence "**conj(h,rs)**") is *not* a rigid designator. On the contrary, it is to be assumed that *not* *L*(**conj(h,rs)=k**); in *this sense* unicornity-at-t_0 and real subsistence are consistent with each other. (For *rigid* property-designators t - "**h**" itself is one of them - we doubtless have *L*(**conj(h**,t)=**k** iff *L*(**conj(h**,t)=**k**)) and its logical equivalent *L*(**conj(h**,t)≠**k** iff *L*(**h**,t)≠**k**)).)

Is it possible to prove "**all***x*(PA(*x*), then *L*PA(*x*))" if one has "*L*" in LP and presupposes the concomitant logic (the modal system S5 with restricted rule of necessitation) *plus* <AP9+>? If it were possible, this would be a most unwelcome result. One migh propose the following deduction:

(1) **all***x*(**rs**<*x*> iff PA(*x*)) (TP31+).

(2) *L***all***x*(**rs**<*x*> iff PA(*x*)) (rule of necessitation on (1); AP8+ was not employed in the proof of TP31+).

(3) **all***x*(*L*(**rs**<*x*>) iff *L*PA(*x*)) (by modal logic from (2)).

(4) **all***x*(if **rs**<*x*>, then *L*(**rs**<*x*>)) (by the theorem in II.6.(d)).

(5) **all***x*(if PA(*x*), then *L*PA(*x*)) (logically from (1), (4) and (3)).

The *one* problematic step in this deduction is (4): (4) is inferred from "*L***all***f***all***x*(if *f*<*x*>, then *L*(*f*<*x*>))" (the theorem in II.6.(d)) by elimination of the initial "*L*" and by instantiating substitution of "**rs**." The former move is harmless, but the latter is not: because "**rs**" (:= "**disj***y*PA(*y*)") is not a rigid designator, but is nevertheless substituted into a *modal* context. As is very well known, instantiating substitution is frequently invalid under such circumstances. Therefore it cannot be relied on - especially in proving something which is as intuitively wrong as (5) is.

Consider, for reinforcement, an analogous case in the ontology of states of affairs. There we can deduce - in steps completely analogous to (1)-(5) above - the intuitively false statement "**all***x*(if O(*x*), then *L*O(*x*))" ("every obtaining state of affairs obtains as a matter of conceptual necessity") from the *correct* principles "**all***x*(O(*x*) iff *x*P**w**)" and "*L***all***y***all***x*(if *x*P*y*, then *L*(*x*P*y*))." In *that* deduction, (4′) "**all***x*(if *x*P**w**, then *L*(*x*P**w**))" must be considered problematic; it cannot be safely concluded from "*L***all***y***all***y*(if *x*P*y*, then *L*(*x*P*y*))," because in that inference "**w**" is substituted into a modal context, *although* it is not a rigid designator. (If one added "**some***x**L*(**w**=*x*)" and "**some***x**L*(**rs**=*x*)" - which express in LP that "**w**" and "**rs**" are rigid designators - as extra premises, the described deductions would be logically impeccable. But they still would not establish their conclusions; rather, each would be a *reductio ad absurdum* of its extra premise.)

CHAPTER II.9

THE PHILOSOPHY OF LEIBNIZ AND THE ONTOLOGY OF PROPERTIES

(a) In LP - given its current interpretation, which validates the axioms AP1 - AP6, AP7+, AP8+ and AP10 (and AP9+, if "*L*" is added to LP) - the ontological ideas of Leibniz can be represented in a most satisfactory manner. We have already considered: the intensional interpretation of Boolean algebra, individuals as quasi-identical with maximally consistent properties, exemplification as a special case of property-inclusion, Leibnizian determinism, Leibnizian "contingency" (which obviously requires that the universe of properties be infinite, as is asserted by AP10), the principle of the identity of indiscernibles. But this is not all. It was one of the most cherished ideas of Leibniz that every "concept" (first intension; in our terminology concepts are always *linguistic* entities; not so for Leibniz or Frege) is composed out of intensionally smallest atomic "concepts" in a purely "additive" or conjunctive manner. And Leibniz was right in this. On the basis of AP1 - AP6 we can prove: **all***x*(*x*=**conj***y*(EL(*y*) and *y*P*x*)) (by TP31, TP42 and DP20) - "every first intension is the sum of the elementary first intensions it contains."[*1]

(b) H. Burkhardt (*Logik und Semiotik in der Philosophie von Leibniz*, p. 170) describes "das Problem der ursprünglichen oder primitiven Begriffe" [the problem of the original or primitive concepts] as a fundamental problem of Leibnizian philosophy which divides into three distinct questions: the question of the existence of primitive concepts, the question of their cognizability, and the question of their number (primarily: whether this number is finite or infinite).

These three questions can be answered as follows. The primitive, original, simple concepts for Leibniz are the elementary first intensions. Since there are maximally consistent first intensions, there are elementary first intensions (according to TP77 and TP78, the latter are simply the negations of the former), and there are precisely as many elementary first intensions as there are maximally consistent ones. It is a direct consequence of AP10 that there are infinitely many elementary first intensions. To cognize an elementary first intension is to cognize the negation of a maximally consistent one, for example, to cognize **neg**(U.M.) (considering myself - in this context - as quasi-identical with a maximally consistent first intension). Although every first intension is conjunctively composed out of elementary first intensions, this does not mean that we are able to analyze *any* first intension into its separately cognized elements. If it consists of infinitely many elementary first intensions, then it is too large for this; if it consists of finitely many elementary first intensions (including the limit case of being itself elementary), then it is too small for this. Just as maximally consistent first intensions (substances) can be grasped only to a small extent in human cognition, so their negations - the minutely substantial first intensions (according to TP84) - can be grasped only to a small extent. (One may find out, for example, that *this or that* property *f* inheres in a substance *x*, hence the elementary property **neg**(*x*) is not an intensional part of *f*, hence it is an intensional part of **neg**(*f*). Or one may find out that this or that *f* does not inhere in *x*, hence **neg**(*f*) inheres in *x*, hence **neg**(*x*) is not an intensional part of **neg**(*f*), hence it is an intensional part of *f*.) H. Burkhardt (*Logik und Semiotik in der Philosophie von Leibniz*, p. 172f) correctly points out that neither the complete (that is: maximally consistent) nor the primitive (that is: elementary) Leibnizian concepts fall within the range of human cognition.

Thus, the *notiones absolutae primae* are not the *notiones secundum nos primae*; the latter, which are located somewhere "in the middle" of the universe of properties, but not the former, can be grasped to the maximal degree that is possible for us; of the former, not of the latter, it is true that every first intension is conjunctively composed of them. (For Leibnizian positions in these matters see *Logik und Semiotik in der Philosophie von Leibniz*, p. 170ff.)

(c) How can Leibniz's theory of possible worlds be represented in LP? We enhance LP by adding the dyadic predicate "$=^{w}$"; the interpretation of LP need not be changed. "t$=^{w}$t′" is to be read as "t and t′ are *compossible* [or *world-equal*] (individuals)." Characterizing the new predicate, the following axioms are added:

AC1 **all***x***all***y*(if $x=^{w}y$, then MK(x) and MK(y)).
(Restriction of world-equality to individuals ("individual concepts").)

AC2 **all***x*(if MK(x), then $x=^{w}x$).
(Reflexivity of world-equality among individuals.)

AC3 **all***x***all***y*(if $x=^{w}y$, then $y=^{w}x$).
(Symmetry of world-equality.)

AC4 **all***x***all***y***all***z*(if $x=^{w}y$ and $y=^{w}z$, then $x=^{w}z$).
(Transitivity of world-equality.)

AC5 **all***x***all***y*(if PA(x) and PA(y), then $x=^{w}y$).
(World-equality of actually existent individuals.)

AC6 **all***x***all***y*(if PA(x) and $y=^{w}x$, then PA(y)).
(Transmission of actual existence by world-equality.)

The first four axioms are analytically true (given the current interpretation of LP). This is not so clear for the last two. They are true; but is it conceptually impossible that some individuals are actually existent which are not world-equal, or that some individual is not actually existent, although it is world-equal with an actually existent individual? We may leave this undecided. (Note that AP7+ results from AC1 and AC5, and can be omitted from the list of the axioms.)

The following definitions are added to the axioms:

DC1 **w**(t) := **disj**$y(y={}^{w}\mathrm{t})$.
("the world of t.")

According to DC1, the world of t is the greatest common intensional part of all first intensions which are compossible with t.

DC2 WL(t) := **some**y'(MK(y') and t=**w**(y')).
("t is a possible world.")

According to DC2, t is a possible world if and only if t is the world of some possible individual.

Like the possible individuals, the possible worlds are represented in the ontology of properties by certain properties of individuals (or first intensions) which are taken to be basic entities. This is the *intensional* way of representing them. Leibniz himself chooses the *extensional* way: he represents the possible worlds by the maximal sets of compossible individuals, or, in other words, by the *equivalence classes* of the concept of compossibility (which according to AC1 - AC4 is an *equivalence relation* on individuals; compare B. Mates, *The Philosophy of Leibniz*, p. 77). If LP and its interpretation is set-theoretically extended, then the two ways can be formally proved to be equivalent: the entities u satisfying the predicate "**some**z(MK(z) and u=**disj**$y(y={}^{w}z)$)" and the entities v satisfying the predicate "**some**z(MK(z) and $v=\{y{:}y={}^{w}z\}$)" can be one-to-one mapped onto each other, and we have the theorem: **all**x**all**z(if MK(x) and MK(z), then (**disj**$y(y={}^{w}z)$Px iff $x\in_{s}\{y{:}y={}^{w}z\}$)). (Assume MK($x$) and MK($z$); by AC1 and TP29+: **disj**$y(y={}^{w}z)\langle x\rangle$ iff $x={}^{w}z$; hence, because of MK(x), by DP1+: **disj**$y(y={}^{w}z)$Px iff $x={}^{w}z$ iff $x\in_{s}\{y{:}y={}^{w}z\}$.)

According to both approaches, the world of an individual is a property of that individual (whether properties are basic entities or set-theoretical constructions, presupposing the current conception of individuals and exemplification), and according to the intensional approach, it is even an intensional part of it. Normally, indeed, one considers an individual to be part of or *in* its world and not vice versa. But reversing the relationship is not inappropriate, at least, for the philosophy of Leibniz. According to Leibniz, every substance mirrors its entire universe (in particular, every *actually existent* substance, every *monad*, mirrors *the* entire universe; see H. Burkhardt, *Logik und Semiotik in der Philosophie von Leibniz*, p. 168); thus, within the framework of Leibnizian metaphysics, *internalized* worlds are quite in order.[*2]

(d) The following Leibnizian principles can now be proved:

TC1 **all***x***all***y*[if MK(*x*) and MK(*y*), then (*x*$=^{w}$y iff **w**(*x*)=**w**(*y*))].
("Substances are compossible (or world-equal) if and only if their worlds are identical.")

TC2 **all***y***all***x*(if MK(*y*) and MK(*x*) and **w**(*y*)P*x*, then **w**(*y*)=**w**(*x*)).
("If a substance internalizes the world of another substance, then their worlds are identical.")

TC3 **all***x*(if MK(*x*), then **one***y*(WL(*y*) and *y*P*x*)).
("Every substance internalizes precisely one possible world.")

Given his extensional way of representing possible worlds, Leibniz's position can also be formulated in the following manner: every individual (or individual concept) belongs (as set-theoretical element) to precisely one possible world (see *The Philosophy of Leibniz*, p. 78 and p. 137). TC3 is the pendant of Lewis' position that every individual is part of precisely one possible world (see *On the Plurality of Worlds*, p. 213f).[*3]
Further we have:

TC4 **one***x***all***y*(if PA(*y*), then *x*=**w**(*y*)).
("Precisely one first intension is the world of every actually existent substance.")

Given TC4, *the (actual) world* may well be defined in the present context *as the common world of every actually existent substance*:

DC3 **w** := **the***x***all***y*(PA(*y*), then *x*=**w**(*y*)).
("the world.")

(We presuppose, of course, that "**w**" as an *undefined* expression has been dropped from LP.) Applying DC3 we can prove:

TC5 WL(**w**) and AP(**w**) and **all***y*(if WL(*y*) and AP(*y*), then *y*=**w**).
("The world is the only possible world that actually exists.")

TC6 **all***x*(if MK(*x*) and **w**P*x*, then AP(*x*)).
("Every substance that internalizes the world actually exists.")

TC7 **all**x(if MK(x) and AP(x), then **w**Px).
("Every substance that actually exists internalizes the world."

TC8 **w=disj**x(MK(x) and AP(x)).
("The world is the largest first intension that all actually existing substances have in common.")

The proof of TC8 uses the AP1-AP6-theorem

TP142 **all**y(y=**disj**x(MK(x) and yPx)).

TC9 **w=rs**.
("The world is the property of real subsistence.")

Since possible worlds are, in effect, properties in the Leibnizian metaphysics, it is only appropriate that the actual world is a property, too. Note, however, that its identity with real subsistence depends on truths that can very well be considered to be synthetic. If there were no actually existent individuals, or if actually existent individuals were scattered among several possible worlds, then "**w**" would not even be well-defined by DC3 (while there is no problem at all for "**rs**"); and if not all individuals compossible with an actually existent individual actually existed ("**w**" being indeed well-defined by DC3), then **w** would be a proper intensional part of **rs**.[*4]

COMMENTS

[*1] Kneale's critical comment "Leibniz's failure to produce a convincing example of his method [the combinatorial analysis of concepts] was due mainly to his obsession with the idea that all complexity must arise from the conjunction of attributes" (*The Development of Logic*, p. 326) is not entirely fair to Leibniz. In fact, if concepts are properties (as they are for Leibniz), then *all* conceptual complexity arises from the conjunction of *elementary* properties. But this is of no use for the combinatorial analysis of concepts (first intensions), since elementary concepts are outside the ken of human cognition. (We can, though, know that there are such concepts, and we can know other general truths about them.)

[*2] Moreover, according to Leibniz, only substances are actually existent *in the fundamental sense*; hence everything else that actually exists is actually existent in virtue of "being in some actually existent substance" ("inhering in it," "being carried by it"). (Compare *The Philosophy of Leibniz*, p. 47: "*Reality*, in the most fundamental sense of that term, is regarded as consisting exclusively of individual substances - the so-called monads.") This position is mirrored in DP2+.

But surely one can also say in accordance with Leibniz that only substances are possible *in the fundamental sense*; hence everything else that is possible - including possible worlds - is possible in virtue of being *in* a (possible) substance. This position is mirrored by DP29.

[*3] We may take it that Leibniz- and Lewis-worlds are correlated as follows: From every Lewis-world (a possible individual) we obtain precisely one Leibniz-world: the set of the individuals which are its parts; conversely, from every Leibniz-world we obtain precisely one Lewis-world: the mereological fusion of the individuals which are its elements.

[*4] TC7, which - like TC4 - does not depend on AC6, would remain true in the supposed situation, that is, we have: **all***x*(if MK(*x*) and AP(*x*), then MK(*x*) and **w**P*x*), hence by TP66 and TP7+: **disj***x*(MK(*x*) and **w**P*x*)P**disj***x*PA(*x*), hence by TP142 and DP7+: **w**P**rs**. But we also have **w≠rs** (hence by DP1 **w**P***rs**): **some***x***some***x′*(PA(*x*) and $x'=^{w}x$ and not AP(*x′*)) (as supposed); hence, because not PA(*x′*) (by TP4+ from not AP(*x′*)), (**1**) not **rs**<*x′*> (by TP31+); on the other hand (**2**) **w**<*x′*>: **w**=**w**(*x*) (TC4, DC3), **w**(*x*)=**w**(*x′*) (from $x'=^{w}x$ by AC1, TC1), **w**(*x′*)<*x′*> (because of MK(*x′*) by AC2: $x'=^{w}x'$; because of AC1: **all***y*(if $y=^{w}x'$, then MK(*y*)); hence by TP29+: **disj***y*($y=^{w}x'$)<*x′*>, hence by DC1 **w**(*x′*)<*x′*>). (**1**) and (**2**) establish **w≠rs**.

CHAPTER II.10

MEINONGIAN OBJECTS IN THE ONTOLOGY OF PROPERTIES

(a) In this part of the book individuals have been identified with maximally consistent properties - this merely a simple way of representing the only provisionally accepted idea that each individual is essentially connected - in a certain manner F - with precisely one maximally consistent property, each individual with a different one, exhausting all maximally consistent properties. Suppose now that individuals *in this sense* form a proper subcategory of a more general category: the category of *objects* (or *quasi-individuals*) which is such that each object is essentially connected - in the mentioned manner F - with precisely one property, a different one for each object, in such a way as to exhaust *all properties*. Suppose the correlating functor which expresses the manner F of essential one-to-one connection is "the conjunction of the properties of t," assuming in addition that not only no individual, but *no object* can have other properties than it has and stay the same object *numerically*. Then every property *f* is the conjunction of the properties of an object *x*, of precisely one object *x*, because the conjunctions of the properties of different objects are different properties. Then *x* also has - with conceptual necessity - precisely the properties that are intensional parts of *f*. (Since *f* is the conjunction of all the properties *x* has, *f* itself is a property *x* has, and hence *x* has every property contained in *f*; it has no property not contained in *f*, for every property *x* has is contained in the conjunction of all the properties *x* has: in *f*.)

What has just been described is a moderate version of *Meinongianism*; it will be explored in this chapter.

(b) Since objects are, in the described manner, essentially correlated one-to-one with properties (of individuals), we can represent objects by properties, that is, identify objects *representationally* with *first intensions*. As in chapter II.2, the neutral designation "first intensions" for the entities in the universe of discourse of property-based LP is advantageous - in case one wants to reserve the term "properties" for only some entities in that universe, or in case one balks at properties being termed "individuals" or "objects" (albeit they are merely called thus in virtue of the representational function accorded to them). And it has the following additional advantage:

If first intension *f* is an intensional part of first intension *g*, then their relationship can be interpreted *predicatively* (especially in view of the considerations in section (a), given that objects are identified with first intensions), with *g* as (non-linguistic) *subject* and *f* as (non-linguistic) *predicate*; it is clear that every first intension is in this sense both *subject* and *predicate*, because every first intension is at least an intensional part of itself. Then we can employ the term "object" for an entity in the universe of discourse, which we generally designate as a "first intension," when we think of it primarily as a *subject*, and use "property" for it when we think of it primarily as a *predicate*; although, of course, the first intensions are precisely the properties (of individuals), and the properties precisely the objects (the latter having been identified with the former).

If our reading of the singular term t′ is based on some general term G of ordinary language, and if in using "tPt′" we intend to speak *predicatively* in LP, then we read t′, the term that designates the first intension which is *subject*, not as "being G (at t_0)," "to be G," or "being a G," but as "*the* G." This kind of reading is *never* used for the singular term t which designates the first intension that is *predicate*. Thus, if our reading of t, too, is based on some general term of ordinary language H, then we read the entire expression "tPt′" - intending to speak predicatively - as "the (object which is) G (at t_0) has (the property of) being H (at t_0)," or simply as "the G is H."

(c) Certain defined predicates of LP and their definitions now take on a new - Meinongian - reading:

DP24 K(t) := not **some***f*(*f*Pt and **neg**(*f*)Pt).
("t is a consistent object": "an object that does not have both a property and its negation.")

DP25 MX(t) := **all***f*(*f*Pt or **neg**(*f*)Pt).
("t is a complete object": "an object that has any property or its negation.")

Note that Meinongian completeness coincides, according to the Meinongian reading of DP25 and TP71, with our quasi-completeness.

DP26 MK(t) := MX(t) and K(t).
("t is a possible object," "t is a (possible) individual": "an object that is complete and consistent.")

All three predicates and their negations are fulfilled (assuming AP1 - AP6, AP7+, AP8+, AP10). Thus there are complete objects and *incomplete* ones, possible objects and *impossible* ones, consistent objects and one *inconsistent* one. (That there is only one inconsistent object is one of the reasons why the present version of Meinongianism is called "moderate" above; for a less moderate version see comment [*2] of this chapter.)

Moreover, there are *existent* objects and *inexistent* ones. Existence for objects amounts to being an *actually existing individual*. Thus "PA(*x*)" (*not* "AP(*x*)," which cannot be read as "*x* is an actually existing individual") is to be read as "*x* is an existent object," and consequently AP7+ takes on the reading: "Only possible objects exist.'' And, therefore, *actualism for objects* is a completely absurd position: there are many incomplete objects (just as many of them as there are non-maximal properties), hence by DP26 there are many impossible objects, therefore by AP7+ *many inexistent objects*, all of them, in fact, objects that *cannot* exist. (Taking AP9+ and its logical background into account we can prove ''*L***all***x*(if not MK(*x*), then *L*not MK(*x*)),'' and AP7+ is subject to the rule of necessitation; hence we can prove ''*L***all***x*(if not MK(*x*), then *L*not PA(*x*))'' - ''as a matter of conceptual necessity, existence is conceptually impossible for every impossible object.'')

(d) Consider now some applications of Meinongian concepts. Suppose somebody imagines *the golden mountain*. He is imagining a consistent, but incomplete, therefore impossible and inexistent object. Suppose somebody thinks of *the round square*. She is thinking of a complete, but inconsistent, therefore impossible and inexistent object.[*1] Suppose somebody believes in *Bill Clinton*. He is believing in an existent, hence possible, and therefore consistent and complete object. Suppose somebody tries to describe *one of the versions of Bill Clinton, one that never became president*. She is trying to describe a possible, hence consistent and complete, but inexistent object (surely there is no *actually existent* counterpart of Bill Clinton that never became president).

As these examples illustrate, Meinongian objects allow a unified straightforward treatment of all situations of the following general form: person *x* is intentionally directed towards *y* (has *y* in mind), where the ontological role of *y* is very much like that of an individual. Also, Meinongian objects are of special importance for the ontology of fictional characters and mythological figures. If fictional characters are consistent objects (normally they are intended to be such by the authors who tell their tales), then there is good reason to assume that they are *incomplete objects*: if one regarded them as non-existent Leibniz-Lewis individuals, then it would be impossible to individuate them. The properties ascribed in a consistent novel to the hero of that novel can be consistently maximized in infinitely many different ways. To each of these ways there corresponds a different Leibniz-Lewis individual; which one of the infinitely many candidates is *the* hero of the novel? It is conceptually impossible to give an answer to this question that would not merely be a completely arbitrary decision. But if the hero is regarded as an incomplete object, then the chances of individuating him are much greater: the hero of the novel is the object corresponding to the conjunction of all properties (explicitly or inferentially) ascribed to him in the novel.[*2] The chances of individuation are much greater, but there is still a big problem: the extra-fictional basis of *inferential* property-ascription to the hero is, we may expect, not precisely determined. And we may expect that also for other reasons - for example, lack of temporal definiteness in the novel - it will not be entirely clear *which* (completely determined) properties are being ascribed to him. Nevertheless, treating the hero as an incomplete object at least induces a dramatic reduction in arbitrariness on the way to his individuation.

(e) Consider now the property of being an *actually existent golden mountain*: **conj(rs,g,m)** [:= **conj(rs,conj(g,m))**], or, in other words, *the object* which is *the actually existent golden mountain*. Obviously (by TP25, AP2): **rsP conj(rs,g,m)** and **gPconj(rs,g,m)** and **mPconj(rs,g,m)** - "the actually existent golden mountain is actually existent, golden and a mountain." Hence: **some***y*(**rsP***y* and **gP***y* and **mP***y*) - "there is an object which is actually existent, golden and a mountain." "But," some reader will surely protest, "there is no actually existent golden mountain." Well, it has not been asserted that there is an actually existent golden mountain *in the sense* that is intended in that protest. "There is an actually existent golden mountain" as intended in the protest is properly represented in LP by "**some***y*(**rs**<*y*> and **g**<*y*> and **m**<*y*>)," that is (according to DP1+, DP26), by "**some***y*(MX(*y*) and K(*y*) and **rsP***y* and **gP***y* and **mP***y*)" - "there is a *complete and consistent* object (a possible individual) that is actually existent, golden and a mountain" - which is a stronger assertion than "**some***y*(**rsP***y* and **gP***y* and **mP***y*)." (In order to obtain the former from the latter, one needs the truth of "**conj(rs,g,m)≠k**" - which is, however, not an unproblematic assertion at all; compare II.8.(b) and (c).)

Thus, the problem of the actually existent golden mountain is solved by distinguishing two concepts of (ontological) predication: "tPt′"and "t<t′>" (that is: "MK(t′) and tPt′"). "There is an actually existent golden mountain" in the sense of "**some***y*(**conj(rs,g,m)P***y*)" (or equivalently: "**some***y*(**rsP***y* and **gP***y* and **mP***y*)") is a true and provable assertion (if "**g**" and "**m**" are added to LP); but in the sense of "**some***y*(**conj(rs,g,m)**<*y*>)" (or equivalently: "**some***y*(**rs**<*y*> and **g**<*y*> and **m**<*y*>)," "**some***y*(**g**<<*y*>) and **m**<<*y*>)") it is a (probably) false and - as is very much to be desired - unprovable assertion.[*3] (Note, however, that one *can* prove "**conj(rs,g,m)=k** or **some***y*(**g**<<*y*> and **m**<<*y*>)." Consider TP32+, DP1+, DP3+, etc.)

(f) Should we resist the tempting idea that objects can not only be representationally identified with properties, but *are* properties (in full ontological seriousness); that is, should we resist the idea that objects can be *reduced* to properties? Why not say: objects *are* properties, but properties regarded in a certain manner: as *subjects* of predicatively interpreted intensional parthood (see above section (b))? Indeed, why not? This would give objects a respectable ontological home, and we would avoid inflating the receptacle of all dubious entities: the quarter of entities that are individuals only *in a wide (very wide) sense*. But this brings up again the question of the reducibility of Leibniz-Lewis-individuals to properties (maximally consistent ones); those individuals are, after all, merely special objects (objects which are both complete and consistent). In comment [*2] of chapter II.2 it was argued that individuals, including Leibniz-Lewis-individuals (individuals according to the second conception mentioned in II.1.(c)), are not ontologically reducible to properties. But perhaps Leibniz-Lewis individuals are ontologically reducible to properties *and normal individuals* (individuals according to the first conception mentioned in II.1.(c)). This question will be pursued in part III.

COMMENTS

[*1] For the two standard examples just mentioned compare J. N. Findlay, *Meinong's Theory of Objects and Values*, p. 11. Note that in our construction of inconsistent objects, inconsistent objects are *eo ipso* complete objects.

[*2] Compare T. Parsons, *Nonexistent Objects*, p. 54. Parsons' reconstruction of Meinong's ideas is different from the one presented here (but somewhat closer to the original Meinong); it leads to a much less moderate form of Meinongianism. He assumes a one-to-one mapping of objects onto *sets of nuclear properties* (a mapping which is also defined, as it is here, via the relational concept "*x* has property *f*"; however, he does not identify objects with these sets (not even representationally); see *ibid.*, p. 18, footnote):
"(1) No two objects (real *or* unreal) have exactly the same nuclear properties.
(2) For any set of nuclear properties, some object has all the properties in that set and no other nuclear properties."
(*Ibid.*, p. 19; why he speaks of "nuclear properties" instead of "properties" becomes clear in the next comment.) According to Parsons' approach there are objects which are not *analytically* (or "*logically*") *closed*: objects which, although they have all the properties in their set of (nuclear) properties, do not have all the properties (not even all the nuclear ones) that are intensional parts of the conjunction of all those properties. As a consequence of this, there are, according to Parsons, many, many objects that are both inconsistent and incomplete (even with respect to nuclear properties). For some applications the mentioned characteristics of Parsons' Meinongian theory are certainly advantageous (for example, for the ontology of inconsistent fiction); but his theory also has consequences that are rather absurd. The object *x* which corresponds to the set of nuclear properties {being golden, being a mountain} has, according to (2), the nuclear property of being golden, and the nuclear property of being a mountain; but it does not have, also according to (2), the nuclear property of being golden and a mountain. The object *y*, on the other hand, that corresponds to the set of nuclear properties {being golden and a mountain} has, according to (2), the nuclear property of being golden and a mountain; but, also according to (2), it neither has the nuclear property of being golden, nor the nuclear property of being a mountain. Therefore, according to (1), *x* and *y* are two different objects. But it is surely much more plausible that they are the very same object: *the golden mountain*.

It is easily appreciated that by allowing objects which are not analytically closed the universe of objects is gigantically inflated with redundant entities. In those cases where it is *conceivable* that they might be needed, why not use the corresponding sets of properties instead (without any talk of objects)? One should be careful in applying Ockham's Razor, but here it seems safe to apply it. (If the number of Leibniz-Lewis-individuals is at least $\aleph_0$, then the number of maximally consistent properties is at least $\aleph_0$, and hence the number of properties of individuals is at least $\aleph_1$ (compare I.20.(b), and transfer the results to the present case); this, then, is also the number of objects or quasi-individuals according to the version of Meinongianism presented in this chapter. According to Parsons' version of Meinongianism, however, there are then at least $\aleph_2$ objects: at least as many quasi-individuals as there are sets of nuclear properties (assuming, plausibly, that there just as many nuclear properties as there are properties). This certainly seems to be *more* than enough.)

[*3] Parsons solves the problem - or rather the analogue of it which occurs in his Meinongian theory - by holding that there is no object corresponding to the set {**rs**,**g**,**m**} (or any set of properties containing it) which has the properties in that set, and no other properties: **rs** (being an existent object, an actually existent individual: real subsistence) is not a *nuclear* property (compare *Nonexistent Objects*, p. 22ff; according to Parsons it is not even a property), and principle (2) (see comment [*2]) is restricted to sets consisting purely of *nuclear* properties. But Parsons gives no general and precise criterion for being a nuclear property. According to him, the recognition of nuclear properties is more or less a matter of intuition (*ibid.*, p. 24). Well, what if in somebody's intuition real subsistence *is* a nuclear property? Parsons owes us some other reason for the incorrectness of that intuition than that his version of Meinogianism would be rendered absurd if the intuition were correct.

Moreover, in other contexts the most plausible position is to recognize real subsistence as a nuclear property. Take a piece of fiction the beginning of which is "Ulysses is an actually existent individual. He was born ..." Take another piece of fiction which is just like the first, except that the beginning of it is "Ulysses is a possible individual. He was born ..." It seems undeniable that the two texts talk about *two different objects*, both named "Ulysses," both of which do not exist, since neither of them is an actually existent individual. But according to Parsons real subsistence and being a possible individual are not nuclear properties (see *ibid.*, p. 23f), and hence the very same nuclear properties are being ascribed to the Ulysses of story 1 and to the Ulysses of story 2; therefore, if they are objects at all (and it would be a major drawback to deny their being objects), then they have the same nuclear properties, and hence they are *identical* according to principle (1) (see comment [*2]).

A similar criticism is advanced by K. Fine in "Critical Review of Parsons' *Nonexistent Objects*," p. 103; Fine also critically examines Parsons' way out: that of assigning nuclear weakenings to extranuclear properties. On p. 97 Fine distinguishes between the *dual copula approach* and the *dual property approach* in Meinongian object-theory. Parsons' solution of the problem of the actually existent golden mountain belongs to the dual property approach (he does not only speak of extranuclear predicates, but also of extranuclear properties; see *Nonexistent Objects*, p. 25, footnote); our solution of that problem belongs to the dual copula approach - which, on the whole, appears to be preferable.

CHAPTER II.11

TIME-FREE AND MOMENTARY MATERIAL INDIVIDUALS

(a) According to the usual understanding of the term, a *mereology* is neither a theory of states of affairs nor a theory of properties, but a theory of *individuals*. Although it is not a matter of real importance, this usage will be respected (for historical reasons, and because it is good to have a term for distinguishing part-whole-theories for individuals from part-whole-theories for other kinds of entities; indeed, the former, as we shall see, can have a character quite different from the part-whole-theories considered so far).

Can the axiom-system AP1 - AP6 be conceived to be a mereology? Can we distinguish a universe of individuals and an interpretation of "P" as a part-concept for these individuals such that AP1 - AP6 turn out to be true? Obviously we can if we consider the subsets of a set - at least those of some set of individuals - to be *individuals*. But can we still do this if we leave out of consideration the somewhat dubious idea that (at least some) sets are individuals? Particularly interesting is the question whether AP1 - AP6 come out true, if we choose the universe of discourse of LP to be constituted precisely by the *material individuals* and interpret "P" as the concept of *spatial part* for these individuals.

(b) In considering material individuals one normally thinks of material *time-free individuals*, that is, material *individuals without temporal dimension* (individuals "not bound in time") and hence without *temporal parts*. The concept of spatial part for time-free material individuals is time-dependent: at some time t the time-free material individual x is a spatial part of the time-free material individual y, at time t' it is no longer (or not yet) a spatial part. Hence, if LP (without both "**w**" and "PA") is interpreted with respect to time-free material individuals and their spatial part-whole-relationships, then one must either expand "tPt′" by including an additional place for quantifiable temporal variables ("t","t'", "t''", ...), or interpret "P" as spatial parthood *at a certain moment of time* t_0. In the first case, one is confronted with the question whether one should also expand the identity-predicate by an additional place for temporal variables, in the second case by the question whether one should also interpret "=" as identity *at a certain moment of time* t_0. But in the first case the entire character of LP is changed to such an extent that one can hardly say that we still have the same language before us; since we want to conserve LP and merely want to interpret it in a new manner, the question connected to the first alternative need not be answered. However, we are now left with the second alternative and the question connected to it.

Time-dependent identity (*not* spatial coincidence or spatial indiscernibility, but *identity*) seems to be an incoherent notion. As R. Cartwright says (in "Scattered Objects," p. 165): "No object can be identical with something for a while and then become identical with something else. Once identical with one thing, never identical with another." Hence "at t_0" in "*x* is identical with *y* at t_0" is merely a redundant tag if this predicate is to be meaningful in the way an identity-predicate is normally intended to be meaningful: then "*x* is identical with *y* at t_0" is analytically equivalent to "*x* is *always* identical with *y*," and the latter analytically equivalent to "*x* is identical with *y*" as normally understood. (We might of course give up the normal reading of "*x* is identical with *y* at t_0" and make it synonymous with "*x* is spatially coincident with *y* at t_0"; then "at t_0" is *not* a redundant tag in a predicate that is nevertheless meaningful. But besides the fact that this would be a contribution to confusion, "$x=y$" of LP, if interpreted to be synonymous with "*x* is identical with *y* at t_0" *in this new sense*, would no longer be fit to do the work essential to an identity-predicate, as which "$x=y$" has so far been always employed; for example, to help formulate statements of finite number: **1***x*A[*x*], **2***x*A[*x*], etc.)

Therefore, "*x*P*y*" meaning the same as "time-free material individual *x* is a spatial part of time-free material individual *y* at t_0," we stick with "$x=y$" in the original *atemporal* (or *omnitemporal*) sense, which is merely relativized to time-free material individuals. However, there is an immediate problem with this: the central axiom AP3 cannot be retained. From the fact that the time-free material individuals *x* and *y* are spatial parts of each other at t_0 we *cannot* conclude that they are *identical* with each other, but only that they are *spatially coincident* at t_0.[*1]. If we want to keep AP3, we have to change the interpretation of LP. The change that comes to mind first is to retain the chosen universe of discourse and to reinterpret "*x*P*y*" as "time-free material individual *x* is *always* a spatial part of time-free material individual *y*." This, plausibly, saves AP3,[*2] and AP4 may perhaps not break down under this interpretation; but we shall nevertheless pursue a different way out of the above impasse.

(c) *Momentary* material individuals are material individuals *with* temporal dimension but *without* temporal extension.[*3] To each time-free material individual there corresponds at each moment of time *t* precisely one momentary material individual, at different moments of time always different such individuals. (Query: Is there for every momentary material individual *x* a time-free material individual *y* such *x* corresponds to *y* at some moment *t*?) It may however happen that the *same* momentary material individual corresponds at some moment *t* to two *different* time-free material individuals; in that case the latter are called "spatially indistinguishable at *t*"; nevertheless, those time-free material individuals are *different*, as is obviously the case if they have different momentary material individuals corresponding to them at *other* moments of time.

In contrast to the concept of spatial part for time-free material individuals, the corresponding concept for momentary material individuals is not time-dependent. It applies truthfully only to momentary material individuals which are *simultaneous*: Mont Blanc at moment t is not a spatial part of Mont Blanc at moment t', if t is different from t'. Thus, if one chooses the universe of discourse of LP to be constituted precisely by the momentary material individuals which are t_0-simultaneous (they are momentary with respect to the same moment t_0), and interprets "*xPy*" as meaning the same as "x and y are t_0-simultaneous momentary material individuals, and x is a spatial part of y," then AP3 - "=" having its normal meaning - apparently holds true (a doubt is raised in comment [*2]), and the other axioms out of AP1 - AP6 have the best chance of being true they can have in a classical mereological interpretation with spatial parthood.

(d) Does the last-mentioned interpretation of LP make those axioms come out true? In what follows, let a and b be *arbitrary* t_0-simultaneous momentary material individuals. Every momentary material individual has a certain spatially localized *spatial configuration*, the spatial region occupied by it: a certain sum of points in space.[*4] (Instead of "spatial configuration" we also say simply "configuration.") The following two principles hold true:

(SI) a is a spatial part of b if and only if the configuration of a is part of the configuration of b.

(SII) a ist identical with b if and only if the configuration of a is identical with the configuration of b.[*5]

It is essential for the truth of these two principles that a and b are *simultaneous* momentary material individuals. If they were not simultaneous, then they would be non-identical, and neither one would be a spatial part of the other, although the configuration of a might well be a part of the configuration of b or identical with it.

Against (SII) the following objection might be raised:

To time-free individuals there correspond t_0-simultaneous momentary individuals. Persons are time-free *material* individuals; therefore, t_0-simultaneous momentary *material* individuals correspond to them, for example, a and b. But a and b may easily differ from each other, although the configuration of a is identical with the configuration of b: suppose a and b are t_0-persons that arise from a classical case of multiple personality.

The answer to this objection is as follows: Let us not dispute whether there can be *two* persons at t_0 in one body, giving rise to *two* t_0-persons with the same spatial configuration. But in allowing that a and b are different, although their configurations are identical, one denies the central presupposition of the objection, namely, that persons are time-free *material* individuals. Thus, *either* persons are time-free *material* individuals, and then - in virtue of (SII) - the *material* t_0-persons *a* and *b* are identical, given that their configurations are identical; *or* the t_0-persons *a* and *b* are not identical, although their configurations are identical, hence they are not momentary material individuals, and hence the persons (in one body at t_0) that they correspond to are not time-free material individuals.

(e) Given the two bridging principles (SI) and (SII), the axioms AP1 - AP3 in the current interpretation of LP - call it ''interpretation **1**'' - are easily justified on the basis of *another* interpretation of LP - call it ''interpretation **2**'': Let the universe of discourse of LP consist precisely of *all parts of space* (among them all the configurations of the material t_0-individuals); let ''*x*P*y*'' mean that part of space *x* is part of (contained in) part of space *y*. AP1 - AP6 will turn out to be true in that interpretation *if* we postulate in addition to all the *real* parts of (real) space, none of which is part of every part of space, one *unreal* part that *is* part of every part of space; this postulate can be justified as introducing a useful fiction (see comment [*7]). (All definitions in part I, provided they do not involve ''**w**,'' have, of course, been carried along; it is easily seen that the one unreal part of space is designated by ''**t**'' of LP, according to DP18, space itself by ''**k**,'' according to DP19, and that the entities the predicate ''EL(*x*)'' of LP truthfully applies to (according to DP20) are precisely the *points* in space.)

The bridging principles (SI) and (SII) provide the means of obtaining well-founded LP-statements in interpretation **1** from well-founded LP-statements in interpretation **2**. But, unfortunately, the method does not reach very far: already AP4 for material t_0-individuals cannot be justified by that method. Can it be justified independently? There are several difficulties connected with AP4:

(1) AP4 implies according to interpretation **1** that there is a momentary material individual, more precisely: a material t_0-individual of which, for example, both the moon at t_0 and my left hand at t_0 are spatial parts.[*6] Is there such a t_0-individual? Only if the configuration of a momentary material individual need not be *connected*. Let us allow this. (Compare R. Cartwright, ''Scattered Objects,'' p. 157: ''That there are scattered material objects seems to me beyond reasonable doubt. If natural scientists are to be taken at their word, all the familiar objects of everyday life are scattered.'')

(2) Suppose the predicate ''A[*x*]'' of LP in interpretation **1** applies truthfully to infinitely many material t_0-individuals that do not overlap (in the sense that they do not occupy common points in space). According to AP4 there is a material t_0-individual of which they are all spatial parts. This individual will have infinite size (since the infinitely many material t_0-individuals that go into its composition all have *positive* volume). Can there be a material individual of infinite size? Considering that we do not exclude material t_0-individuals which are scattered (see (1)), there *is* such an individual if ''A[*x*]'' applies truthfully - as we have supposed - to infinitely many material t_0-individuals that do not overlap.

(3) According to AP4 and AP3 (in interpretation **1**) there is precisely one material t_0-individual which is a spatial part of every material t_0-individual (compare TP27 and TP5). How can there be such an individual? Note that it is no great matter to assume that are many time-free material individuals that *do not exist* at t_0. (Let t_0 be the present moment, and everyone can make his own choice of examples. That *x* is a time-free individual does of course not imply that *x* always exists.) Which are the material t_0-individuals corresponding to the time-free material individuals that do not exist at t_0? There is in fact precisely one such material t_0-individual: the material t_0-individual which is a spatial part of every material t_0-individual.[*7] This means: all time-free material individuals that do not exist at t_0 are spatially indistinguishable (coincident) at t_0 - which is as it ought to be. (Although my first car and my first watch are rather different time-free material individuals, (my first car)-at-t_0 and (my first watch)-at-t_0 are identical. The reason for this is easily guessed.)
"**t**" (:= "**thexally**(*x*P*y*)"), according to interpretation **1**, designates the one *unreal* material t_0-individual. Hence we can define:

DP1# R(t) := t≠**t**.
("t is a real material t_0-individual.")

As the above considerations show, the material t_0-individual that is a spatial part of every material t_0-individual can be put to good use. And we need not be scandalized about its being a spatial part of every material t_0-individual; after all, it is *unreal* (and this as a matter of conceptual necessity); every *real* material t_0-individual is, of course, *not* a spatial part of every material t_0-individual. (But why is there just one unreal material t_0-individual? Because occupying a *real* part of real space is certainly analytically sufficient for reality, and because all material t_0-individuals different from **t** occupy such a part, or else they would not be *material*; **t**, and **t** only, is a material individual *by courtesy*.)
(4) On the basis of AP1 - AP6 (applying AP4) we can prove a statement that in interpretation **1** of LP asserts that each non-elementary material t_0-individual is the sum of the material t_0-individuals which are its proper spatial parts: **all***z*(if not EL(*z*), then **conj***x*(*x*P**z*)=*z*) (see comment [*3] of chapter I.5; apply DP20). But is it not correct to say that at least some non-elementary momentary material individuals are not simply the sums of their proper parts, that for their constitution the organisation of these parts matters as well? Summing up the proper parts of a momentary material individual - say, of a t_0-flower - does not consist in dividing the individual into pieces (in thought) and calling the heap of its pieces (which is obviously different from it) "the sum of its proper parts." That it *does* consist in this is the *false* idea that generates the difficulty. On the contrary, the proper parts of a momentary material individual are summed up right where they are in space, that is, in such a manner that their spatial organisation is not destroyed, but kept entirely intact. Thus, non-elementary

momentary material individuals are the sums of their proper parts, *and*, nevertheless, the (spatial) organisation of these parts matters (very much) for their constitution.

(f) AP4 can be assumed for material t_0-individuals, yet only with considerable effort. What about AP5 and AP6, which were already touched by difficulty (4) for AP4?

In the current interpretation of LP AP6 asserts the following: For each real material t_0-individual x which is a spatial part of the sum of material t_0-individuals satisfying description "A[y]" there is a real material t_0-individual that is a spatial part of x and of a material t_0-individual satisfying "A[y]." This is, indeed, correct, which is seen as follows. Let a be a *real* material t_0-individual. The spatial configuration of a - and of each *real* material t_0-individual - is called a "receptacle"; a *receptacle* is a spatially localized three-dimensional form that satisfies several additional topological conditions (compare R. Cartwright, "Scattered Objects," p. 153ff). Let a be a spatial part of the sum of all material t_0-individuals satisfying "A[y]." Then the configuration (that is, the receptacle) of a is, according to (SI), part of the configuration (that is, the receptacle) of that sum (which must be a *real* material t_0-individual because a, which is real, is a spatial part of it). And then, doubtless, some receptacle z is both part of the configuration of a and part of the configuration of some material t_0-individual u satisfying "A[y]." Thus far for the time being.

We assume now (b being an arbitrary material t_0-individual):

(SIII) For all z: if z is a receptacle and part of the configuration of b, then there is a material t_0-individual y such that z is the configuration of y.

(SIV) If b is not real, then the configuration of b is the unreal part of space (the sum of all points in space that are not self-identical). (If b is real, then the configuration of b is a receptacle.)

(SV) The unreal part of space is not a receptacle.

These principles imply:

(SVI) For all z: if z is a receptacle and part of the configuration of b, then there is a *real* material t_0-individual y such that z is the configuration of y.

And in continuation of the above argument we have on the basis of (SVI): there is a *real* material t_0-individual y such that z is the configuration of y; hence the configuration of y is both part of the configuration of a and of the configuration of u, hence by (SI): y is both a spatial part of a and a spatial part of u. This demonstrates AP6.

(g) The most problematic axiom is AP5. According to DP4, it is analytically equivalent to "**all**y**all**z(if **all**x(if QA(x) and not M(x) and xPy, then xPz), then yPz)." Hence, according to DP6, TP32 and DP1#, it is analytically equivalent to "**all**y**all**z(if **all**x(if **all**k(if kPx and R(k), then k=x) and R(x) and xPy, then xPz), then yPz)." A real material t_0-individual which is such that every real material t_0-individual which is a spatial part of it is identical with it is called a "*normal* material t_0-atom." (Note that x is a material t_0-element if and only if it is a *normal* material t_0-atom. The one *non-normal* material t_0-atom is **t**, which, however, is also the only atom in the strict sense of DP2.) Then AP5, in the current interpretation of LP, asserts the following: if every normal material t_0-atom which is a spatial part of the material t_0-individual y is also a spatial part of the material t_0-individual z, then y is a spatial part of z. But the big question is: Are there normal material t_0-atoms? This question has not been answered by modern physics: t_0-atoms *in the sense of physics* are real material t_0-individuals which have real material t_0-individuals as spatial parts that are *not* identical with them (for example t_0-neutrons). If there are no normal material t_0-atoms, then AP5 implies: **all**x**all**y(xPy), hence by AP3 **all**y(y=**t**), hence by DP1# **no**yR(y) - "there is no real material t_0-individual," which is absurd. Thus, in effect, AP5 forces us to accept that there are normal material t_0-atoms, even though that assumption is far from being unproblematic. This is a reason for rejecting AP5. However, we need not yet assume its negation.

But that there are indeed *no* normal material t_0-atoms, although there obviously are real material t_0-individuals - put together these two assertions refute AP5 - is demonstrated by the following argument. The following is a highly plausible principle:

(SVII) For all x: if x is a receptacle (a part of space satisfying certain topological conditions), then some receptacle z is a proper part of x (a part of x that is not identical with x).[*8]

Now assume: *a* is a real material t_0-individual; the spatial configuration of *a* is a receptacle, hence we have according to (SVII): some receptacle z is a proper part of the configuration of *a*. But this implies according to (SVI) that there is a real material t_0-individual y which is such that z is the configuration of y; hence the configuration of y is a proper part of the configuration of *a*, hence by (SI) and (SII): y is a proper spatial part of *a*. Thus every real material t_0-individual has a real material t_0-individual as proper spatial part, or in other words: there are no normal t_0-atoms. If one wants to block that conclusion, then (SVI) could be drawn into doubt, and hence (SIII) (since (SIV) and (SV) rest secure). But this would deprive AP6 of its support.

(h) Without AP5, the remaining system AP6, AP1 - AP4 is a mere torso (given the current interpretation of LP). But it can be made *the mereology* of material

t_0-individuals (albeit, of course, not the *classical* one: the latter would require having *no* null-element if the universe of discourse has at least two members; see comment [*1] of chapter I.7) by adding to it the supplementation-axiom

AP5# **all**x**all**y[if xP*y, then **some**z(zP*y and not M(z) and **no**u(not M(u) and uPx and uPz))].

This is an adaptation of Simons' *Weak Supplementation Principle* (see *Parts*, p. 28) to the presence of a null individual (**t**). AP5# is independent of AP1 - AP4, AP6. If it were provable in that system, then we could also prove in AP1 - AP4, AP6: **no**yEL(y) - which, of course, we *cannot* prove in that system. (Assume EL(y), hence by DP20: QA(y) and not M(y), hence by TP32, DP4: **t**Py and y≠**t**, hence by DP1 **t**P*y, hence by AP5# **some**z(zP*y and not M(z)), hence because of QA(y) (according to DP1, DP6): z=y - contradicting zP*y. Therefore: **no**yEL(y).) Moreover, AP6 rather seems to be independent of AP1 - AP4, AP5#.

But we can prove (as has just been shown) "**no**yEL(y)" (or in other words "there are no normal material t_0-atoms") in AP1 - AP4, AP5# (TP32, which is used in the proof, is already provable in AP1 -AP4). Thus, AP5# turns out to be an anti-atomism principle. (Add AP5, and the whole system *does not* become inconsistent, but it does collapse into triviality because of the provability of "**all**x**all**y(xPy).") The utter plausibility of AP5# for material t_0-individuals is additional evidence against the (numerical) existence of *normal* material t_0-atoms.

AP5# is incompatible with AP10 (in view of TP130, which is provable already on the basis of AP1 - AP4 plus definitions); but with its help we can also derive the thesis that there are infinitely many material t_0-individuals. We have

TP1# **all**y(if not M(y), then **some**z(zP*y and not M(z)).

(A provably equivalent version of TP1# is "**all**y(if not A(y), then **some**z(zP*y and not A(z))"; use TP7, TP27, TP5, TP9 and TP11 to obtain "**all**y(A(y) iff M(y).") To this we need only add the axiom

AP7# not M(**k**),

and TP1# generates an infinite regress of real material t_0-individuals which is such that the next member in the regress is always a proper spatial part of the prior one (and hence of *all* previous ones). (In view of TP32, DP1# and the present interpretation of LP, AP7# amounts to stating that the material t_0-universe is a *real* material t_0-individual. Notice that we could prove AP9, AP8 and the negation of AP7 if we took *the world* to be the material t_0-universe and defined "**w**" := "**k**.")

Compare finally Simons' axiomatization of Classical Extensional Mereology (on p. 37 of *Parts*) with TP1, TP2, AP5# and

TP2# **all***y*[**some***k*(not M(*k*) and *k*P*y* and *k*P**conj***x*A[*x*]) iff **some***z*(A[*z*] and **some***k*(not M(*k*) and *k*P*y* and *k*P*z*))].

Clearly, the four just-mentioned principles are an adaptation of Simons' SA1, SA2, SA3 and SA24 (in view of SD2, SD3, SD9) to the presence of a null individual. But the adaptation has some side-effects (which are not unwelcome in the present interpretation of LP): the numerical non-existence of elementary material t_0-individuals, and (given AP7#) the infinite number of material t_0-individuals.

COMMENTS

[*1] Here an example of time-free material individuals which are different, but coincide spatially at a moment *t* (are spatial parts of each other at *t*): Consider the cat Tibbles, its tail: Tail, and the rest: Tib. Obviously Tib is not Tibbles, since *now* they are not spatially coincident: Tib is now a proper spatial part of Tibbles. But one day Tibbles will have an accident and lose its tail, but fortunately survive. After the accident (for example at *t*) Tibbles is spatially coincident with Tib.

On the other hand, Tib+Tail - the group consisting precisely of the members Tib and Tail (for more information about groups see the next chapter) - is, we may assume, at *t* no longer spatially coincident with Tibbles; this group - a time-free material individual - is scattered at *t*: Tib is where Tibbles is, but Tail is preserved in alcohol. Therefore, Tib+Tail is not Tibbles, although *now* they are spatially coincident.

The misinterpretation of Tibbles' fate accorded by the so-called *Flux Argument* is described in *Parts*, p. 118f. In view of the many different attempts at resolving this paradoxical argument (see *Parts*, p. 119ff), it is obvious that the correct description of Tibbles' fate is connected with considerable conceptual difficulties. But the Flux Argument (see also [*6] below) is simply based on not distinguishing time-free material individuals (and their identity) from *momentary* material individuals (and their identity). (For momentary material individuals see section (c).) The very same non-distinction of what is in fact different is the main source of the plausibility of the venerable principle that *two* material individuals cannot fill exactly the same space at exactly the same time. (See for this [*2] and [*5] below).

[*2] But *are* time-free material individuals that are spatially coincident at all times (always spatial parts of each other) *identical*? Assume Tibbles never loses its tail; is Tib+Tail therefore identical with Tibbles? Simons writes (*Parts*, p. 115): "Even if Tibbles fortunately never parts company with Tail, the essential possibility that she could do so is enough to distinguish her from the sum [Tib+Tail]. ... Two distinct material objects can then coincide spatially for their whole lives, yet not be identical." Two comments:
(1) Might not Tib+Tail also lose Tail? Yes, but only if Tail ceases to exist. But, then, does not Tib+Tail also cease to exist (as Simons thinks it does)? Perhaps. But another possibility would be that Tib+Tail becomes spatially coincident with Tib.
(2) If, like Simons, we draw into consideration modal properties (being *possibly* F), then it even becomes uncertain whether momentary material individuals which we will consider to be identical *really* are identical. Is Tib-at-*t*′ (*t*′ after the accident in which Tibbles loses its Tail) able to do something that

Tibbles-at-*t′* cannot do, or vice versa? If so, then Tib-at-*t′* and Tibbles-at-*t′* are not identical.

In what follows we will, however, accept an identity-principle for momentary material individuals which implies that Tib-at-*t′* *is* identical with Tibbles-at-*t′*; it is a *reconstruction* of the principle that two bodies cannot be in the same place at the same time. To deny that Tib-at-*t′* is identical with Tibbles-at-*t′* is to deny that identity-principle. But yet it would be necessary to deny it if we did *not* understand "*x*-at-*t*" as we do understand it here: in the sense of "*x-in the actual world*-at *t*." If Tib-at-*t′* and Tibbles-at-*t′* were not *actuality*-determined in the manner just indicated (that is, if they were not intrinsically bound to a certain privileged point-like "modal position": the actual world), then they would be different, although they occupy the very same part of space; for in another world in which Tibbles has still its tail at *t′* (not actuality-determined) Tibbles-at-*t′* and (not actuality-determined) Tib-at-*t′* would *not* occupy the same part of space, and this would be enough to distinguish them.

[*3] Individuals *with* temporal dimension and individuals *without* temporal dimension ought both to find a place in our ontology. The main aim of ontology is not *reduction* (denying that there are - properly speaking - entities of a certain category, and having entities of another - more favored - category take over their functions), but *distinction*. This needs to be said, on the one hand, in view of the intentions of not a few ontologists (Quine, for example) to "abolish" material time-free individuals, and, on the other hand, in view of the intransigent denial of temporally dimensioned individuals by contrary-minded ontologists (Geach, for example). The science of ontology would be well served in many questions if one followed the maxim "distinction, not reduction" instead of having Ockham's Razor ready in one's hand on every occasion. Only after *distinction* has been sufficiently pursued (it usually is not) may one consider *reduction* (but often, I suspect, it will have become plain by then that both kinds of entities considered ought to be retained as exemplified and separate categories).

Individuals can be rather satisfactorily classified according to distribution of *dimension* (or *intrinsic locality*). (Note for the following (1) that being temporally/spatially extended implies having temporal/spatial dimension, but not vice versa; (2) that being spatially extended is understood in such a way as to be already implied by being longitudinally or superficially extended; (3) that being temporally extended implies having a duration, but not vice versa: some individuals have a duration without having temporal dimension, and hence without having a temporal extension; (4) that in order to avoid further complications the classification below is restricted to individuals that are understood to be *actuality-determined* individuals: to individuals which, being intrinsically located in the actual world, have a certain non-extended "modal position" and, therefore, "modal dimension"; see the previous comment, and further III.11.(e).)

(1) *Individuals without spatial and without temporal dimension*: ''abstract'' individuals.
Example: Beethoven's Fifth Symphony.

(2) *Individuals with spatial but without temporal dimension*: time-free individuals with spatial dimension.
Examples: (i) *fully* spatially extended time-free individuals (''three-dimensional things''), in particular: material time-free individuals or *continuants* (as time-free individuals are usually called; material continuants are the prime paradigms of Aristotelian substances); (ii) time-free individuals that have spatial dimension, but are not spatially extended (''zero-dimensional things''), in particular: ends of edges; (iii) only longitudinally extended time-free individuals (''one-dimensional things''), in particular: edges; (iv) only superficially extended time-free individuals (''two-dimensional things''), in particular: shadows on the wall, mirror-images. (All the most specific examples adduced are *mutabilia*; we could also have adduced the corresponding time-free individuals with spatial dimension which are *immutabilia*: receptacles in (real) space, points in space, lines in space, surfaces in space - in general: *spatial configurations*.)

(3) *Individuals with spatial and temporal dimension*.
Examples: individuals with spatial and temporal dimension, but without temporal extension, in particular: momentary material individuals (which are fully spatially extended), the mirror-image *c*-at-t_0 (which is only superficially extended), etc. (Note that the mirror-image *c*-at-t_0 is, properly speaking, not a surface; only its spatial configuration is. This spatial configuration is an immutable two-dimensional thing and, in contrast to *c*-at-t_0, without temporal dimension, hence a time-free individual.)

(4) *Individuals without spatial but with temporal dimension*.
Examples: a performance of Beethoven's Fifth Symphony, its first sound, the beginning of its first sound (an individual with temporal dimension, but without temporal extension), the *temporal configuration* of that beginning: the temporal region it occupies: a point in time. (Note that just as something may have a duration without having temporal dimension, so something may have a *spatial location* without having spatial dimension: every performance of Beethoven's Fifth Symphony takes place somewhere, although no such performance has spatial dimension.)

Events and processes - if they are individuals - belong to category (3) or to category (4) (depending on whether they are conceived as ''4-dimensional things,'' or not; one certainly must not jump to the conclusion that they have spatial dimension - and sometimes spatial extension - from the fact that they have a more or less comprehensive spatial location, just as one must not jump to the conclusion that something has temporal dimension from the fact that it has a duration.)

This fourfold classification corresponds in several points to the distinction of four alternative ontologies in E. Zemach's paper "Four Ontologies": "An ontology carves its entities as either bound or continuous in time and space. Hence, four kinds of ontology: an ontology whose entities are bound in space and in time [corresponding to (3)], an ontology whose entities are bound in space and continuous in time [corresponding to (2)], an ontology whose entities are bound in time and continuous in space [corresponding to (4)], and an ontology whose entities are continuous in space and in time [corresponding to (1)]." (*Ibid.*, p. 233.)

Zemach claims "that each one of these ontologies is complete and self-sufficient and that it *need* not be used in conjunction with any other." (*Ibid.*, p. 231.) Given a non-nominalistic point of view, this is obviously false; for it is intended by Zemach that each one of the mentioned ontologies implies that there are *only individuals*, and this is false for non-nominalism. (Zemach even professes nominalism in the sense of "Everything is a non-abstract individual" (*ibid.*, p. 231); but the entities in Zemach's fourth ontology - "types" - presumably must be regarded as being in some appropriate sense *abstract* individuals. Zemach's assertion that they are "material objects" (*ibid.*, p. 241) is absurd.) If there are universals and states of affairs (and not merely individuals that *act* as universals or states of affairs), then none of Zemach's four ontologies is complete and self-sufficient. And even if one conceived of them more modestly as being mere ontologies *of individuals*, it is still rather implausible that *each* one of them should be complete and self-sufficient - even if it is thus restricted in its intended scope of application. (It might *perhaps* be true of Zemach's first and second ontology (corresponding to (3) and (2) in the above classification). Zemach tries to show that the ontology of types is sufficient by itself (*ibid.*, p. 244ff); but in the attempt he is constantly talking about *places*, *spatial locations* at which types occur; *spatial locations*, however, are not types, but time-free individuals with spatial dimension (moreover *immutabilia*); in his classification they belong to ontology 2. This effectively destroys the intended demonstration of self-sufficiency. For the same reason his attempt to demonstrate the self-sufficiency of the third of his ontologies (*ibid.*, p. 239) is unsuccessful.

[*4] Here the expression "spatial configuration" is always to be understood in the sense of "*localized* spatial configuration." This is a slight departure from ordinary usage: two "totally similar" billiard balls lying next to each other on the billiard table are normally said to have the very same "spatial form" or "spatial configuration"; here however their spatial configurations are different, since they do not have the same *localized* spatial configuration because the one is lying in *this* place and the other one in *that*.

Do we understand what we mean when we say that a material individual *occupies* or *fills* a certain spatial region? It is intuitively clear what is meant, and perhaps we had better rest content with this. Any attempt at analyzing that concept might well generate more questions than are answered by it. R. Cartwright, too, does not explain it in "Scattered Objects." (He - like Hobbes - speaks of the *coincidence* or *co-extension* of a material individual with a spatial region (*ibid.*, p. 153); spatial regions (we also say "spatial configurations," "parts of space") are for him arbitrary *sets* - not *sums* - of points in space.)

The central difficulty in explaining spatial occupation is the following. On the one hand, if a material individual occupies a certain spatial region only if it occupies every part of it, then most material individuals do not occupy the spatial region we think they occupy, and it is hard to say which spatial region they *do* occupy. On the other hand, in what sense does a material individual occupy a certain region of space if it does not occupy every part of it?

[*5] (SII) from the right to the left - letting *a* and *b* be arbitrary *simultaneous* momentary material individuals - is a reconstruction of the classical ontological principle *that there cannot be two bodies in the same place at the same time*: "Nam locus cuiuslibet corporis est alius a loco alterius corporis: nec est possibile, secundum naturam, duo corpora esse simul in eodem loco, qualiacumque corpora sint" (Thomas Aquinas, *Summa Theologiae*, I,67,2). "Being in a certain place at a certain time" needs to be understood in the sense of "occupying a certain spatial region at a certain moment of time" (otherwise there might very well be two bodies in the same place at the same time). Then the precise formulation of the principle is: "*Two* bodies cannot occupy the same spatial region at the same moment of time," in other words, "*Two* bodies cannot have the same (localized) spatial configuration at the same moment of time."

But since time-free material individuals are bodies, and this is a conceptual necessity, the principle is *false*: it can be that two time-free material individuals have the same (spatial) configuration at the same moment *t* (see Tib and Tibbles); then, indeed, they coincide spatially at *t*, but that does not make them identical.

Therefore, if the principle is to be correct, it has to be restricted: "Two *simultaneous momentary* bodies cannot have the same configuration at the same moment of time," or in other words: "It cannot be that two *simultaneous momentary* material individuals have the same configuration" (assuming for any momentary material individual (*momentary body*) *a* and moment *t*: the configuration of *a* at *t* := the configuration of *a*), or in other words: "It is conceptually necessary that simultaneous momentary material individuals with the same configuration are identical." This is (SII), from right to left, letting *a* and *b* be arbitrary simultaneous momentary material individuals (and considering in addition that (SII) is analytically equivalent to its necessitation).

[*6] By attaching "at t_0" to it one transforms a singular term designating a time-free material individual into a singular term that designates the momentary material individual which corresponds to the time-free one at t_0. But P. T. Geach asks in *Logic Matters*, p. 308: "What *is* (say) the England of 1984? Is there really such an object *in rerum natura*, distinct from the England of 1965?" These questions concern individuals with temporal dimension in general, and hence also momentary material individuals, which are special temporally dimensioned individuals (those which are material and whose temporal extension is zero). Geach offers the following answer to them: "I conclude that temporal slices are merely 'dreams of our language'. It is no less a mistake to treat 'McTaggart in 1901' and 'McTaggart in 1921' as designating individuals than it would be so to treat 'nobody' or 'somebody'." (*Ibid.*, p. 311.) His reason for this is the alleged absurdity of singular statements like "Tabby-at-t_n is eating mice": "for a cat can eat mice at time *t*, but a temporal slice of a cat, Tabby-at-*t*, cannot eat mice anyhow." (*Ibid.*, p. 310.)

But what Geach attacks is not the theory of temporally dimensioned individuals *itself*, but only its expression with the aid of terms like "temporal slice", "space-time worm", etc. At least for basic predications with respect to momentary individuals *a*, there are no problems which are not founded in the grotesquery of mere images; for we simply have for all moments of time *t*: *a*-at-*t* is F if and only if *a* is F-at-*t* (for instance, Jack-at-t_0 is tall if and only if Jack is tall-at-t_0). If one uses an atemporal copula (hence an atemporal concept of predication), then the temporal index can be attached to the predicate-term, and, alternatively, it can also be attached to the subject-term (if a temporal index is *at all* appropriate for both terms, which is not always the case: thus, for example, it is not the case if the predicate-term is derived from the identity-predicate in its normal sense, and it is not the case if the subject-term is a name for a number). Both manners of speaking occur, and both are on a par. Why declare the less usual one to be absurd?

With regard to ordinary language, attaching the temporal index to the predicate-term is not in the least privileged; it, too, can be made to look absurd: "An SA [Strawsono-Aristotelian] object thus does not have purely three-dimensional properties such as being spherical or ellipsoidal: it has more complex properties, such as being *spherical at such and such a time*. (For if it had the simpler properties, it would have incompatible ones, such as being both spherical and ellipsoidal.) On the Minkowskian view objects (such as temporal parts or 'time-slices' of oranges) can have the simpler properties, such as being spherical." (J. J. C. Smart, "Space-Time and Individuals," p. 4.) And as Geach correctly says: "Predicates of this sort, in which dates are mentioned, are a long way above the most fundamental level of temporal discourse." (*Logic Matters*, p. 311.) *Any* attaching of temporal indices - whether to subject- or to predicate-terms - is "a long way above the most fundamental level of temporal discourse" (but one can hardly dispense with attaching such indices).

Therefore, as far as ordinary language is concerned, one is free to decide which manner of speaking is to be preferred, and one is free to switch between the two. An expansion of our ontology cannot be avoided in either case: we either have to reckon with additional individuals, or with additional universals. It could only be avoided if we attached the temporal index to the copula (to the "is" in "a is F"), instead of attaching it to the subject- or the predicate-term.

R. Cartwright - a champion of temporally dimensioned material individuals - constructs another example of non-identical time-free material individuals which are spatially coincident at a certain moment of time in "Scattered Objects," p. 164ff; the main character is not Tibbles the cat, but a matchbook called "Charlie." Concerning Charlie, Cartwright presents a variant of the *Flux Argument* (see [*1] above), which can be simply formulated as follows:

Charlie = (the Charliematches + the package). (This sum is also called "Harry.")

Now a Charliematch *a* is taken out and laid down beside Charlie.

Therefore: Charlie = (the Charliematches without *a* + the package). (This sum is also called "Sam.")

But obviously: (the Charliematches + the package) ≠ (the Charliematches without *a* + the package).

One might think that the identity-statements only need to be relativized by attaching temporal indices to their predicates ("at t_0," "at t_1"), and then the paradox will disappear. But as Cartwright correctly says: once identical, always identical. The correct analysis is: neither one of the two identity-statements is true; that they *seem* to be true is the consequence of not distinguishing what is in fact different: time-free material individuals and momentary material individuals (and their identities). For indeed we have: Charlie-at-t_0 = (the Charliematches + the package)-at-t_0, Charlie-at-t_1 = (the Charliematches without *a* + the package)-at-t_1 (in other words: Charlie is at t_0 spatially coincident with Harry, and at t_1 spatially coincident with Sam); *however*, Charlie ≠ (the Charliematches + the package), for Charlie-at-t_1 ≠ (the Charliematches + the package)-at-t_1 (the latter individual is obviously *scattered*, Charlie-at-t_1 is not); and Charlie ≠ (the Charliematches without *a* + the package), for (the Charliematches without *a* + the package)-at-t_0 is a proper spatial part of Charlie-at-t_0.

Cartwright's resolution of the argument is, in effect, the one here given (see "Scattered Objects," p. 169). But he goes one step further: "Charlie, Harry and Sam thus come to be conceived as distinct four-dimensional objects, which happen on occasion to share a common temporal part." This additional step is not necessary. We may continue to think of Charlie, Harry and Sam in the manner we naturally think of them: as being time-free material individuals (material continuants), hence individuals without temporal dimension. Nothing forces us to accept that, say, Charlie-at-t_0 is a *temporal part* of Charlie. However, there is an individual of which Charlie-at-t_0 *is* a temporal part: the four-dimensional material Charlie-"worm" (a certain "space-time-worm").

But this individual is - contrary to the opinion of the advocates (Whitehead, McTaggart, Russell, Carnap, Quine, Smart and others; for criticism see *Parts*, p. 123ff) of the four-dimensionality of ordinary things (of tables, chairs, stones, trees, etc.) - obviously not Charlie. Or is it?

[*7] Why is this so? All time-free material individuals that do not exist at t_0 have the same spatial configuration at t_0, since at t_0 they are *nowhere*: the sum of all points in space that are not self-identical, or in other words, *the unreal part of space*, that is, the part of space which is part of every part of space. We have, therefore, according to (SII) (the configuration of *x* at *t* being the configuration of *x*-at-*t*) that the t_0-individuals that correspond to the time-free material individuals that do not exist at t_0 are all identical with each other, and according to (SI) that they are part of every material t_0-individual. Consequently, since some time-free material individual does not exist at t_0, there is precisely one material t_0-individual that corresponds to all time-free material individuals that do not exist at t_0; it is a spatial part of every material t_0-individual, and because of the validity of AP3 for material t_0-individuals (by (SI) and (SII)) there is also at most one such t_0-individual.

[*8] In Tarski's paper "Foundations of the Geometry of Solids" the word "solid" is used in the sense of "receptacle." (Solids, according to Tarski, are intuitively the correlates of (non-null) open regular point-sets - or non-null "open domains"; concerning receptacles, compare "Scattered Objects," p. 156f.) Tarski writes: "The specific character of such a geometry of solids [a geometry whose universe of discourse is constituted by solids or receptacles] - in contrast to all point geometries - is shown in particular in the law according to which each figure [i.e. each solid or receptacle, since a geometry of solids is destitute of figures which are not solids] contains another figure as a proper part." (*Ibid.*, p. 24.) Hence in point geometry, since the geometry of receptacles can be modelled in it (*ibid.*, p. 29), we have at least the truth of "every receptacle has a receptacle as proper part," although we do not have the truth of "every part of space has a part of space as proper part" (the counter-example is the unreal part of space), and although, more significantly, we do not have the truth of "every real part of space has a real part of space as proper part" (the counter-examples are the points in space).

CHAPTER II.12

THE MEREOLOGY OF GROUPS

(a) An interpretation of LP (without "**w**" and "PA") can be formulated which verifies the axioms AP1 - AP6 (*including* AP5) and in which all entities in the universe of discourse - with the exception of a single one - are *time-free material individuals*. The concept of parthood "P" on this interpretation is not time-dependent (and, therefore, it cannot be spatial parthood between time-free material individuals). In order to state this interpretation we select *appropriate* time-free material individuals (we cannot choose arbitrary ones; see for this section (e) below) - the Xs - as *elements* (they are precisely the entities to which the predicate "EL" as defined by DP20 - and further by DP5, DP6 - can be truthfully applied in our interpretation) and declare that the entities that are spoken about in LP are all *groups* of Xs, all Xs, and *Nothing*. (The choice of the word "group" for what is meant is not entirely arbitrary; nevertheless, its appropriateness will be felt to vary with the choice of the Xs - depending on whether they are rather heterogeneous or have a natural affinity; the specific meaning in which "group" is used here is further described below. Concerning "Nothing," we will see below what this notoriously dark metaphysical notion is good for; see, in particular, comment [*5].)

The groups of Xs together with the Xs and Nothing, and all relationships of parthood between them, are in the obvious natural manner isomorphic to the subsets of the set of all Xs and all relationships of parthood between those sets (Nothing corresponds to the empty set, every X corresponds to the set of which it is sole element, every group of Xs corresponds to the set of the members of the group). Since the subsets of the set of all Xs together with the subset-concept for these entities make AP1 - AP6 come out true when they are taken to constitute an interpretation of LP, it is clear that also all groups of Xs together with the Xs, Nothing and the corresponding part-concept for them fulfill AP1 - AP6 when taken to constitute an interpretation of LP.

(b) The groups of Xs are - in contrast to the subsets of the set of all Xs - time-free *material* individuals. Since Tib and Tail (which we can assume to belong to the Xs) are time-free material individuals, the group consisting of Tib and of Tail: Tib+Tail (which is a two-membered group of Xs if Tib and Tail belong to the Xs) is also a time-free material individual: like Tib and like Tail, and in the same manner as they do, Tib+Tail has at any moment of time a certain localized spatial configuration, a certain mass, etc. But Tib+Tail is not, as we have seen, the cat Tibbles, although Tib+Tail is at a certain moment of time spatially coincident with Tibbles (in fact, spatially coincident with Tibbles as long as Tibbles does not lose its tail); indeed, it seems that groups of spatial parts of cats *never* are cats, even if they spatially coincide with a cat at all moments of time.

(c) The concept of a group is a useful concept. In ordinary language we have besides (designative, non-predicative) *singular terms* (for example, "Fido") - and besides (predicative, non-designative) *general terms in the singular* (for example, "dog") and (predicative, non-designative) *general terms in the plural* (for example, "dogs") - also (designative, non-predicative) *plural terms*: "the Benelux-countries", "the fishermen of England", "these books", "we", "Tom, Dick and Harry", "Jason and the Argonauts." (These examples - except the fourth - are mentioned in P. Simons, "Number and Manifolds," p. 165.) At first sight, it seems obvious that not every occurrence of a plural term can be eliminated by providing an analytically equivalent paraphrase which uses singular terms only. Providing such a paraphrase is easy in the case of a statement like "Tom, Dick and Harry are ill": "Tom is ill, Dick is ill, and Harry is ill"; but the statement "Tom, Dick and Harry are lifting a log which weighs a quarter of a ton" cannot be treated in like manner. Nevertheless in this case too the plural terms can be eliminated: "*The group* of which Tom is a member, Dick is a member, and Harry is a member, and which has no other member, is lifting the log."

But there are other difficulties. There are predicates that form grammatically correct sentences only with plural terms, for example "fight with each other", "love each other," "are together 100 years old." (Singular and plural are here considered to be merely two grammatical forms of one and the same predicate, which in itself is neither singular nor plural. The adduced examples, however, do not have a singular; therefore they may be called "plural predicates.") The analytically equivalent paraphrases containing only singular terms of statements that contain *these* predicates are, indeed, easily found: "Jack and Fred fight with each other": "Jack is fighting with Fred"; "Jack and Jill love each other": "Jack loves Jill, and Jill loves Jack"; "George and Jim are together 100 years old": "George is 0 years old and Jim 100, or George is 1 year old and Jim 99, or ..., or George is 100 years old and Jim 0." (Note that "years" in the last example is a (predicative) *general term in the plural*, not a (designative) plural term; we are not required to eliminate it.) But whether there is an analytically equivalent paraphrase that contains only singular terms for *every* statement containing a *plural predicate* must remain an open question.

Simons writes ("Number and Manifolds," p. 174): "It may be that plural reference is eliminable in these cases. In the case of number-properties I am not so sure."[*1] But precisely in the case of number-properties plural terms are quite easily eliminated. Simons is thinking of examples like "the men in the car are four"; this statement is analytically equivalent to "*the group* of which each man in the car is a member, and that has no other member, has four members (is four-membered)." (Note again that "members" in the last-mentioned sentence is not a plural term, but a general term in the plural; we are not required to eliminate it.) The general procedure of elimination can be easily derived from this example.[*2]

Whatever is the answer to the question of the general eliminability of plural terms, we can surely conclude: if plural terms can always be "paraphrased away" - and this may well be possible - then only with the aid of the *concept of a group*.

(d) A group is not a *plural entity* (there are no plural entities), but it can be said to be *several* entities which are of the *same* ontological category taken as *one* entity of that same ontological category (for example, *several time-free material individuals* as *one time-free material individual*); they are, if we disregard the ingredient of sameness of ontological category, Simons' *manifolds* (and if we disregard, in addition, his untenable characterization of the latter as plural entities).[*3] A group is, therefore, not a set (in the technical sense of the term): it cannot be completely heterogeneous, and it cannot be abstract if its *elements* (or members) are concrete. (Because of the demand of sameness of ontological category, a group of numbers would have to be a number; this indicates that there are no groups of numbers, though there are arbitrary sets of them. Note that a group of human beings need not be a human being; for *being a human being* is not a categorial ontological distinction, but a very *specific* subcategorial one.)

The relationship between element and group is fundamentally different from that between element and set; an element of a group is always a part of a group, but an element of a set is not normally a part (subset) of the set. Each part of a set of Ys is again a set of Ys, but not every part of a group of Ys is also a group of Ys: each human being is a part of the group of all human beings (the group of which precisely the human beings are members); but no human being is a group of human beings. Groups are always the sums of their proper parts; but there are sets - singleton sets - which are not the sums of their proper parts. There is an empty set, but there is no empty group.

(e) Moreover, groups are, in contrast to sets, *ontologically relative* entities. The specification of a group, like that of a set, always depends on the specification of its elements: by simply listing them, or by the description of *certain elements* from which by an additional description *the elements of the group* are selected. (In the latter case, the two descriptions frequently coincide; the group is then characterized as the *maximal* group with respect to certain elements.) But one and the same entity can figure relative to different *bases of elements* both as group and as non-group; this has no analogue in the case of sets. If Tib and Tail, as has been assumed in (b), are among the appropriate time-free material individuals that are considered to be elements in the current interpretation of LP - i.e. the Xs - then there is relative to that basis of elements an entity - a time-free material individual - which is the group consisting precisely of both of them: *Tibtail*, which is identical to Tib+Tail (or **conj**(Tib,Tail) in LP under its current interpretation, if LP is expanded by the names "Tib" and "Tail"). But Tibtail and *other* entities can of course also be considered to be elements, and then, relative to that new basis of elements, Tibtail is *not* a group.

But what happens if we consider Tibtail to be an element *besides* Tib and Tail? This we cannot do if AP1 - AP6 are to be valid (relative to the basis of elements under consideration). Let us describe the situation in LP: EL(Tib), EL(Tail), EL(Tibtail); since Tib≠Tail, it follows by AP1 - AP6: not EL(**conj**(Tib,Tail)); but Tibtail = **conj**(Tib,Tail); therefore: not EL(Tibtail) - contradicting our assumptions. This shows that we have to be careful - in choosing a basis of elements - that one and the same entity does not figure both as a group relative to that basis *and* as an element. Retaining AP1 - AP6, it is for example impossible to consider *all* (and only) time-free material individuals as elements for LP; for then Tib, Tail and Tibtail would be among the elements - with the consequences just described. (*Safe* bases of elements are, for example, the now-existing human beings, the *pairs* (two-membered groups) of now-existing human beings, and so on.)

One might be tempted to block the above *reductio ad absurdum* by denying "Tibtail = **conj**(Tib,Tail)." But if "Tibtail = **conj**(Tib,Tail)" was correct before Tibtail was considered to be an additional element, why has this become incorrect after it is considered to be an additional element? The only thing that remains is that "Tibtail = **conj**(Tib,Tail)" was false from the start. But then one has to conclude that **conj**(Tib,Tail) (or Tib+Tail) is not a time-free material individual; for if it were one, which time-free material individual could it be other than Tibtail (*that* time-free material individual which is at first for a long time spatially coincident with Tibbles, and then, when Tibbles has this accident, becomes scattered beyond any hope of reunification)? But if **conj**(Tib,Tail) is not a time-free material individual, then it is not a group either; for if it were a group, then it would have to be of the same ontological category as Tib and Tail, which are time-free material individuals. Thus, the final result of denying the truth of "Tibtail = **conj**(Tib,Tail)" is that Tib+Tail can hardly be said to be different from the set {Tib, Tail}.

(f) Let us now consider in detail a specific interpretation of LP which is appropriate for a *mereology of groups*. Let the universe of discourse of LP consist of: all human beings existing now (we take them to be time-free material individuals), all groups of them, and Nothing. Then we can read "EL(x)" as "x is a human being existing now," "**t**" as "Nothing," "not EL(x) and not M(x)" as "x is a group of human beings that now exist," "**k**" as "the group of all human beings that now exist." (Note that in any group-interpretation of LP and AP1 - AP6 the relational concept of (mereological) elementhood "∈" is actually more basic than "P" - something which does not hold in the ontology of states of affairs; in such an interpretation, instead of defining the former in terms of the latter (DP21, DP20, DP6, DP4), the latter ought rather to be defined in terms of the former: tPt′ := **all***x*(if *x*∈t, then *x*∈t′), adding the definition of the monadic correlate "EL" of "∈": EL(t) := t∈t. But when "∈" is taken as primitive, the system of axioms requires reformulation; we stick with the old system and the old order of definitions, which gives us on the basis of AP1 - AP6 the theorems: **all***x***all***y*(*x*P*y* iff **all***z*(if *z*∈*x*, then *z*∈*y*)), **all***x*(EL(*x*) iff *x*∈*x*).)

One of the groups we now consider is Yeltsin+Clinton (**conj**(Yeltsin,Clinton)), another Yeltsin+Kohl. Both groups are today (on the 4th of July, 1996) *scattered* time-free material individuals (Clinton is in the United States, Yeltsin in Russia, Kohl in Germany). Each of them has, qua having now-existing human beings as elements (qua consisting of such elements), precisely two proper parts which are different from Nothing, in short: precisely two *non-trivial* parts; and they both have, qua having now-existing human beings as elements, precisely one non-trivial common part: Yeltsin. (Yeltsin+Clinton+Kohl is a time-free material individual that, qua having now-existing human beings as elements, has precisely six non-trivial parts; the number of its non-trivial *spatial* parts - the number of time-free material individuals that are proper spatial parts of it at this moment, and which are at this moment not spatially coincident with Nothing: which exist at this moment - is beyond reckoning.)

Consider in particular Yeltsin+Clinton: Y+C. Each spatial part of Y at a moment of time, and each spatial part of C at that moment of time is at the same time also a spatial part of Y+C; but Y+C also has spatial parts at that time that are *never* spatial parts of Y or of C (for example, the sum of Y's and C's respective heads). Like Y and C, Y+C can lose spatial parts without detriment to its existence; if C or Y loses a spatial part (as they constantly do), then so does Y+C. If a time-free material individual loses a spatial part, then the lost part need not have ceased to exist; it may only have become separated from the rest. But in *this manner* Y+C cannot lose its spatial part C (though it can very well lose other spatial parts in this manner); let C travel to the moon or to a place even further away, Y+C only becomes more scattered in virtue of this, but continues to include C as a spatial part.

But what if C has ceased to exist at some future time *t*, while Y still remains in existence?[*4] Then the place of C at *t* is nowhere, his spatial configuration at *t* is the sum of all points in space which are not self-identical: the unreal part of space. This is also the spatial configuration of *Nothing* at *any* moment of time. Therefore, C and Nothing have the same spatial configuration at *t*, they are spatially coincident at *t*.[*5] But what has become of Y+C at *t*? If we make the highly plausible assumption that the (spatial) configuration that Y+C has at *t* is the conjunction (or sum) of the configuration of Y at *t* and of the configuration of C at *t*, then the configuration of Y+C at *t* is identical with the configuration of Y at *t*: Y and Y+C have become spatially coincident at *t*. (That *does not* make them identical, as by now everybody ought to be convinced; Y-at-*t* and

Y+C-at-*t*, however, *are* identical; see the preceding chapter.) Nevertheless, C is at *t* still a spatial part of Y+C, but only because it is a spatial part at *t* of *any* time-free material individual (its spatial configuration at *t* being part of every part of space), including even the ones that are non-existent at *t* (with those C is spatially coincident at *t*); C is at *t* a spatial part of Y+C, but only a *trivial* spatial part; and therefore one can say that Y+C has *lost* (its former spatial part) C at *t*. Nevertheless, C is *atemporally* a part and member of Y+C qua group with now-existing human beings as elements.

(g) Prima facie the actual existence of a group at a time can be defined in various ways. Let *g* be a group (with respect to some appropriate basis of elements) and *t′* a moment of time:
(i) *g* is a group that exists at *t′* if and only if every element of *g* exists at *t′*.
(ii) *g* is a group that exists at *t′* if and only if some element of *g* exists at *t′*.
(iii) *g* is a group that exists at *t′* if and only if at least two of *g*'s elements exist at *t′*.
According to (ii) Y+C is a group that exists at *t* (because Y still exists at *t*); this is rather counter-intuitive. In contrast, both according to (i) and according to (iii) Y+C is not a group that exists at *t*. But (iii) is a better definiens than (i), as can easily be seen by considering the totality of all currently existing human beings (in LP: **k**, according to our most recent interpretation of LP). (The reference of "currently" is kept *rigid* in what follows.) This totality is a currently existing group. But at a later time some of the currently existing human beings have ceased to exist. Has the totality of all currently existing human beings as a result become a non-existent group (as is required by (i))? No, this totality then surely is still an existent group; it has only shrunk spatially (but it still has the very same elements and hence the very same parts in the atemporal, non-spatial sense). And it will remain an existent group as long as at least two of the currently existing human beings continue to exist. But when only one of them is left, then, indeed, the totality of the currently existing human beings has ceased to be an *existing group*, although in so far as it is spatially coincident with a single time-free material individual (the sole survivor), it still exists - until even the last one of our contemporaries dies, and the totality of all currently existing human beings (not however, we may be sure, the totality of the currently existing flesh and bones of all currently existing human beings) becomes spatially indistinguishable from Nothing.

(h) In concluding this chapter and this part of the book, let me remark that, in contrast to the ontology of states of affairs and properties, the most adequate language for the treatment of the mereology of material individuals is not LP (whether in the interpretation of chapter II.11 or in a group-interpretation), but a much richer language where we have *at least*: (1) TIM(*x*) ("*x* is a time-free material individual (in the chosen universe of discourse)"), (2) MIM(*x*) ("*x* is a momentary material individual"), (3) MOM(*t*), $t < t'$ ("*t* is a moment of time,"

"t is before t'"), (4) $\mathbf{m}(x,t)$ ("the momentary material individual corresponding to x at t"), (5) $\mathbf{t}(y)$ ("the moment of y"), (6) $x\mathrm{P_S}y$ ("the momentary material individual x is spatial part of the simultaneous momentary material individual y"), (7) $x\mathrm{P_{EL}}y$ ("the time-free material individual x is - with respect to a chosen basis of elements - part of the time-free material individual y"). Let the universe of discourse of this richer language consist of a basis of elements (certain appropriate time-free material individuals), the groups of those elements, all moments of time, all momentary material individuals, and Nothing. Assume the appropriate axioms (this and the preceding chapter will be helpful for this). Finally, assume, for example, these definitions (for time-dependent spatial parthood, existence and spatial coincidence for time-free material individuals): xTIMP$_S y$ at t := TIM(x) and TIM(y) and MOM(t) and $\mathbf{m}(x,t)$ P$_S\mathbf{m}(y,t)$; EXTIM(x,t) := TIM(x) and **some**y(MIM(y) and $\mathbf{t}(y)=t$ and not $\mathbf{m}(x,t)$P$_S y$); xTIMCOINy at t := TIM(x) and TIM(y) and MOM(t) and $\mathbf{m}(x,t)=\mathbf{m}(y,t)$.

COMMENTS

[*1] P. Simons defends the following difficult position: ''I take number to be a property of manifolds, and manifolds to stand to plural terms as individuals stand to singular ... For an expression to designate a manifold is simply for it to designate each of a number of individuals. There is no difference between the manifold, and the several individuals, despite the fact that we can talk about *a* manifold, and indeed can count manifolds to some extent as though they were individuals.'' (''Number and Manifolds,'' p. 165f.) According to Simons, each plural term, if it is not empty, designates a manifold. But Simons then treats reference to manifolds as a mere *compendium loquendi*: reference to *a manifold* (by a plural term) is according to him nothing but reference to *each of several individuals*; for manifolds are nothing but several individuals. But how, then, can *a manifold* have certain properties, for example a number-property? Modifying Quine's dictum, we may declare: *no entity without unity* - an ontological principle that has a very long tradition. Thomas Aquinas, for example, says ''unum enim nihil aliud significat quam ens indivisum. Et ex hoc ipso apparet quod unum convertitur cum ente. Nam omne ens aut est simplex, aut compositum. Quod autem est simplex, est indivisum et actu et potentia. Quod autem est compositum, non habet esse quandiu partes eius sunt divisae, sed postquam constituunt et componunt ipsum compositum. Unde manifestum est quod esse cuiuslibet rei consistit in indivisione.'' (*Summa Theologiae*, I,11,1.) Simons' manifolds - *such as they are characterized by him* - are not unities, therefore not entities, and hence not bearers of properties. Since everything is an entity, and since manifolds in Simons' sense are not entities, there simply are no such things as manifolds in Simons' sense.

This verdict is not reversed by the following remark of Simons: ''This is an aspect of the prejudice in favour of the singular: it is deemed that whatever has a property must be *one* thing, so whatever has number-properties must also, in some sense, be one thing. It seems to me, on the contrary, that some properties of their very nature are borne by more than one thing.'' (''Number and Manifolds,'' p. 173). It is unclear what is meant here by ''[properties] borne by more than one thing.'' (By ''thing'' Simons apparently means *entity*, and in what follows ''thing'' is to be understood in that way.) *Properties that apply to more than one thing*? That there are *such* properties cannot be questioned (if there are universals at all); but they are properties of *one thing* in each case of application. *Properties that are polyadic*? There are no polyadic properties; polyadic universals (or polyadic attributes) are relations. But let it be true in some relevant sense that ''some properties of their very nature are [if at all] borne by more than one thing.'' *Irreducible* (monadic) predicates that form a meaningful sentence with no singular term, that is, *irreducible* plural predicates presumably must be considered to be predicates that intend such properties; let us call them "plural properties." If there are exemplified plural properties, then, indeed, in some cases that which has a property is not one thing. But if it is not *one thing*, then it is not a thing at all, but *several things*; thus, from the premise that there are exemplified plural properties one cannot infer the conclusion that there are *plural things* - Simons' manifolds - that exemplify them.

In *Parts*, p. 144, Simons says "a more difficult question is whether there are plural *objects*, objects that are essentially not one thing but many things." The answer to this question is: "There is not one thing that is many things."

[*2] In *Parts*, p. 147, Simons asserts the following: " 'if there are 10 *a*s, there are 1023 classes [= manifolds ≡ groups] of *a*s' ... Such examples strongly suggest the ineliminability of plural reference." Do they? What about the following paraphrase: "if the group of which every *a* is a member, and which has no other member, is ten-membered, then there are 1023 [this is the correct number only if the *a*s themselves absurdly count as groups or classes of *a*s; otherwise it is 1013] groups such that every member of each group is an *a*." ("groups" in that sentence is a predicative general term in the plural, not a plural term.)

[*3] Compare comment [*1]. Simons himself distinguishes *groups* and *manifolds*. In "Plural Reference and Set Theory," p. 211, he writes: "we may regard manifolds as limiting cases of groups: those whose identity is exhausted by that of their members. In such circumstances the 'foundation relation' [between the members] is the purely formal one of being just these several individuals and no others." What is meant by Simons is appropriately illustrated by his examples: "in the days of the Empire, three of the orchestras of Vienna had the same personnel: when they played in the Court Chapel they were the Orchestra of the Court Chapel, when they played in the pit at the opera they were the Court Opera Orchestra, and when they played symphony concerts in the Musikverein they were the Vienna Philharmonic. Similarly two committees may have exactly the same members, yet not be one committee." (*Ibid.*, p. 210.) The adduced "wholes" are groups in Simons' sense which are not manifolds in Simons' sense (and hence they are *not* groups in our sense).

[*4] When a time-free material individual has ceased to exist depends on which are the spatial parts of it which are *essential to its existence*. (These parts can be small compared with the whole; for example, in persons they might be a specific portion of the brain; if one of these parts has been destroyed, then the person has ceased to exist, even if everything else in her is intact, even alive. Note: if persons do not have spatial parts essential to their existence, then persons are not time-free material individuals.) We can define (confining ourselves to time-free material individuals and expressing time-dependent

spatial parthood and proper parthood between them by "xP(t)y" and "xP*(t)y", using special variables for moments of time: t, t', t''...):

x is at t an existence-essential spatial part of y := xP(t)y and E(t)(y) and E(t)(x) and *L***all**t'(if E(t')(y), then E(t')(x) and xP(t')y).
x is at t an existence-essential proper spatial part of y := xP*(t)y and E(t)(y) and E(t)(x) and *L***all**t'(if E(t')(y), then E(t')(x) and xP*(t')y).

R. Chisholm's *mereological essentialism* consists in the following assertion: **all**x**all**y(if **some**t(E(t)(x) and E(t)(y) and xP*(t)y), then *L***all**t'(if E(t')(y), then E(t')(x) and xP*(t')y)). (Compare "Mereological Essentialism," p. 149. "x is part of y at t" is taken by Chisholm in the sense of "the time-free material individual x which exists at t is at t proper spatial part of the time-free material individual y which exists at t." The just-mentioned predicate - when Chisholm goes about defending mereological essentialism - acquires a meaning that is totally different from its normal one, which Chisholm calls "the loose and popular sense" (*ibid.*, p. 154f).) The assertion is definitionally equivalent to "**all**x**all**y**all**t(if E(t)(x) and E(t)(y) and xP*(t)y, then x is at t an existence-essential proper spatial part of y)" - a grotesquely false statement; my body, for example, now exists, and also a certain hair that is now a proper spatial part of it; but surely it is conceptually, nomologically, or in whatever sense, possible that my body exists at a certain time t' without the hair existing at that time, or without its being a proper spatial part of my body at that time. (I just removed it, and my body still exists - an experiment that falsifies mereological essentialism. Chisholm would of course reply that now a body of mine is existing that is *numerically different* from the old one, although very similar to it.)

The designation "mereological essentialism" is not quite fitting for Chisholm's position; it should rather be called "mereological *super*essentialism." There are other mereological essentialisms. One mereological essentialism that recommends itself much more to intuition than Chisholm's is represented by the following statement: **all**y**all**t(if E(t)(y), then **some**x(x is at t an existence-essential proper spatial part of y)). But even the truth of this is doubtful: consider the Ship y of Theseus. If y still exists at a time t at which every original part of it (down to the last nail) has been replaced by a new one (gradually, in the course of intermittent repairs), then we obviously have: **no**x(xP(t)*y and E(t)(y) and E(t)(x) and *L***all**t'(if E(t')(y), then E(t')(x) and xP*(t')y)), that is, **no**x(x is at t an existence-essential proper spatial part of y), for we then have: **all**x(if xP*(t)y and E(t)(x), then **some**t'(E(t')(y) and E(t')(x) and not xP*(t')y)). Confronted with this, but wanting to retain *moderate* mereological essentialism, one can react in one of two ways:

(1) One denies that the Ship of Theseus is a time-free material individual: every individual that can completely exchange all its original spatial parts and still exist is not a time-free material individual but a "material" *ens successivum* (to

use Chisholm's term); one could also say: a *materially incarnated abstract individual*. Non-mythological examples for "material" *entia successiva* are the Old Town of Warsaw, the Semper Opera House of Dresden, and, perhaps, persons. (But the latter are definitely not *entia successiva* for Chisholm; see *Person and Object*, p. 104. Concerning Chisholm on *entia successiva*, see *Person and Object*, p. 98ff. According to him, *entia successiva* are logical constructions on the basis of genuine time-free individuals, that is: they are *abstract individuals*; Chisholm calls them "*entia per alio* [*sic*]" (*ibid*., p. 104). According to him (*ibid*. p. 103), familiar things like ships, trees and houses, which we naively consider to be time-free material individuals, are in fact - like the Ship of Theseus - *entia successiva*.)
(2) Alternatively one can deny that the Ship of Theseus (or the Old Town of Warsaw, or the Semper Opera House of Dresden) exists at *t* (or: now). With the designation "the Ship of Theseus" one refers to the *original* ship, and that ship has surely ceased to exist at the very latest at *t*. (But assume that somebody has preserved all the replaced parts of the original ship and fits them together again according to the original plan; then the original ship - resurrected, as it were - exists *again* at *t*; but then the ship does not provide a counter-example to moderate mereological essentialism.) Although one is quite positive that the (original) Ship of Theseus no longer exists at *t*, one may still be uncertain as to the precise time at which the Ship of Theseus ceased to exist; this is so because its planks, masts, etc. were replaced gradually, and because it is not clear for every original proper spatial part of the ship whether it is an (at some time) existence-essential proper spatial part of it or not. (In the case of the Old Town of Warsaw and the Semper Opera House - that is, the *original* Old Town of Warsaw and the *original* Semper Opera House - there is no such uncertainty as to the time when they ceased to exist, although in their cases, too, it is not clear for every original proper spatial part of them whether it is an existence-essential proper spatial part of them or not.)

[*5] Then C-at-*t* (the momentary material individual corresponding to C at *t*) is identical with the unreal material *t*-individual; but the latter is not also identical with Nothing-at-*t*, although C and Nothing are spatially coincident at *t*). The momentary individual corresponding to Nothing at *t* (if, indeed, there is such an entity) must not be considered to be a momentary *material* individual, not even one by courtesy (compare the remarks about **t** in II.11.(e)), because Nothing is surely not a time-free *material* individual.

Although every time-free material individual (even if it never exists) and every momentary material individual is different from Nothing, there are time-free material individuals and momentary material individuals which are spatially coincident with it (at certain times only, or always). Consider Socrates (letting "Socrates" - as previously "Clinton" and "Yeltsin" - designate a certain time-free material individual); he is *now* spatially coincident with Nothing, and *the present Socrates* is always spatially coincident with Nothing; but there is an earlier momentary Socrates that is *at his time* not spatially coincident with Nothing (at all other times he is indeed coincident with it), and Socrates himself was also not always spatially coincident with Nothing (for example not at the time of the just-mentioned momentary Socrates). It is clear that existence at time t for time-free material individuals and for momentary material individuals can be defined by spatial *non*-coincidence at t with Nothing; this, besides completing the mereology of groups to a power-set algebra, is the principal use of *Nothing*.

At no time t one is at a loss to say which particular individual fills the definition of the unreal material t-individual (the material t-individual that is spatial part of every material t-individual): it is the momentary t-individual that corresponds to a certain time-free material individual that does not exist at t (there always are such time-free material individuals). But which individual is *Nothing*? There is a *natural* candidate for this in moderate Meinongian object-theory: the inconsistent object (see chapter II.10). If one does not believe in such an object (one surely cannot rationally believe that such an object is actually existent), then stipulation is all that remains: Nothing is some freely chosen abstract individual (but it should be one to which assigning a *real* spatial configuration is not only "far-fetched," "artificial" and "contrived," but utter nonsense).

III

FULL ONTOLOGY
LIMITED TO PROPERTIES OF INDIVIDUALS

CHAPTER III.1

CATEGORIAL PREDICATES, LANGUAGE LPT1, SYSTEM PT1

(a) The language LP in the state it ultimately reached in its application to states of affairs (hence including the singular term "**w**") will now be transformed to such an extent that it becomes a (numerically) different language bearing a different name:
(1) (*i*) The numerals "0" and "1" are *types*.
(*ii*) If $T_1,...,T_n$ are types, then $<T_1,...,T_n>$ is also a type.
(*iii*) Only expressions according to (*i*) and (*ii*) are types.
(2) If T is a type, then $T(x)$ is a *categorial predicate* (the variable "x" represents any variable of LP).
(3) The language LPT1 is (syntactically) the language LP (a language of first-order predicate logic plus identity and definite description together with "P" and "**w**") extended by the categorial predicates "0(x)", "1(x)" and "<0>(x)" (other additions will follow soon).

(b) "0(t)" is synonymous with "t is an individual," "1(t)" is synonymous with "t is a state of affairs," "<0>(t)" is synonymous with "t is a property of individuals." (These meanings of the three categorial predicates of LPT1 are to be kept constant in all its interpretations.) The chosen universe of discourse of LPT1 consists of all individuals, all states of affairs, and all properties of individuals (as long as no other properties are drawn into consideration, we will simply call them "properties"), and nothing else. Note that *the individuals* in the present conception presumably are *only some* of the individuals *in a wider sense*; they are the "normal" individuals, in contradistinction to Leibniz/Lewis-individuals and Meinongian objects; they will not be categorially subdivided, but time-free material individuals (now taken to be without modal dimension; compare comment [*3] of chapter II.11) are surely among them.

One might be tempted to interpret "P" as the *global* part-concept for all entities in the universe of discourse. But this is not advisable; for states of affairs are parts of states of affairs in a sense that is totally different from the sense in which individuals are parts of individuals, and the same is true for properties and individuals (and, to a lesser degree, also for states of affairs and properties). And again, in a totally different sense from the sense in which an individual is part of an individual, an individual is part of a state of affairs, and so on. Therefore: the global part-concept for all entities in the universe of discourse of LPT1 cannot be simply and concisely specified. Indeed, in the beginning it cannot be specified at all; extensive investigations are necessary until it is sufficiently clear what is meant by the unwieldy disjunction "(x and y are states of affairs, and x is part of y) or (x is an individual, y a state of affairs, and x is part of y) or (x is an individual, y a property, and x is part of y) or ...". We may expect that the axiomatic system for "P" *in this sense* is as inelegant as is the description of that sense.

(c) Instead, "P" is interpreted as the (intensional) part-concept for states of affairs; it is understood in LPT1 (in all interpretations of it) precisely in the sense we took it in the first interpretation of LP of part I. Thus, for a start, we accept the appropriate *adaptations* of axioms AP1 - AP9 (no formal use will be made of the LPT1-correlate of AP10, so we leave it out of the picture); some of the principles AP1 - AP9 have to be reformulated in view of the presence of three categories of entities in the universe of discourse of LPT1. The *repostulations* of AP1 - AP9 are preceded by the new axiom

APT0 **all**x**all**y(if xPy, then 1(x) and 1(y)).

APT0 states that "P" is the part-concept for states of affairs - the interpretation of "P" we have decided on. While "P" in LP was used in such a way independently of any particular universe of discourse of LP that "**all**x(xPx)" was a logical truth of LP, this is not the case for LPT1. Instead, APT0 is a logical truth of it (a statement that is true in virtue of the meaning it has independently of any chosen universe of discourse of LPT1), and hence "**all**x(xPx)" cannot also be a logical truth of LPT1; or else "**all**x1(x)" would be a logical truth of it, too - which it is not.

AP1 can be repostulated without reformulation:

APT1 **all**x**all**y**all**z(if xPy and yPz, then xPz).

But AP2 turns into

APT2 **all**x(if 1(x), then xPx).

AP3 need not be changed:

APT3 **all**x**all**y(if xPy and yPx, then x=y).

But the axiom (-schema) AP4 turns into

APT4 **some**z[1(z) and **all**x(if 1(x) and A[x], then xPz) and **all**y(if 1(y) and **all**x(if 1(x) and A[x], then xPy), then zPy)].

In the axioms AP5 and AP6 defined expressions occur; the definitions for these expressions, and all definitions DP1 - DP39, are to be reformulated in LPT1 according to the following general procedure (which yields DPT1 - DPT39):

(*i*) "**some***x*" in the definiens turns into "**some***x*(1(*x*) and ...)"; "**all***x*" in the definiens turns into "**all***x*(if 1(*x*), then ...)"; "**the***x*" in the definiens turns into "**the***x*(1(*x*) and ...)." (The variable "*x*" is used in representative function. Before applying (*i*), replace "**no***x*" by "not **some***x*.")
(*ii*) For the symbols for singular terms "t", "t′", ... in the definiens of the definition of a predicate "and 1(t) and 1(t′) and ..." is appended to the definiens.
(Frequently the resulting definitions can be simplified by applying predicate logic and the analytically true axiom APT0.)
The original definition for "M": DP4 was

M(t) := **all***y*(tP*y*).

But DPT4 (according to the reformulation-procedure just described) is

M(t) := **all***y*(if 1(*y*), then tP*y*) and 1(t).

The original definition of "QA": DP6 is

QA(t) := **all***y*(if *y*Pt, then *y*=t or M(*y*)).

But DPT6 is

QA(t) := **all***y*(if 1(*y*), then (if *y*Pt, then *y*=t or M(*y*))) and 1(t),

and this can be simplified because of APT0:

QA(t) := **all***y*(if *y*Pt, then *y*=t or M(*y*)) and 1(t).

The original definition of "**conj***x*": DP17 is

conj*x*A[*x*] := **the***z*[**all***x*(if A[*x*], then *x*P*z*) and **all***y*(if **all***x*(if A[*x*], then *x*P*y*), then *z*P*y*)].

But DPT17 (logically simplified) is

conj*x*A[*x*] := **the***z*[1(*z*) and **all***x*(if 1(*x*) and A[*x*], then *x*P*z*) and **all***y*(if 1(*y*) and **all***x*(if 1(*x*) and A[*x*], then *x*P*y*), then *z*P*y*)].

Then the axiom AP5 - when repostulated in LPT1 - turns into

APT5 **all***z***all***z*′(if 1(*z*) and 1(*z*′) and **all***x*(if QA(*x*) and *x*P*z*, then *x*P*z*′), then *z*P*z*′), and AP6 need not be changed:

APT6 **all***x*[if *x*P**conj***y*A[*y*] and not M(*x*), then **some***k′*(*k′*P*x* and not M(*k′*) and **some***z*(*k′*P*z* and A[*z*]))].

AP7 is repostulated without change:

APT7 **w**≠**k**.

(The reformulated definition of "**k**" is DPT19: **k** := **the***y*(1(*y*) and **all***x*(if 1(*x*), then *x*P*y*)).) AP8, too, is repostulated without change:

APT8 QC(**w**).

(The reformulated definition of "QC" is DPT7: QC(t) := **all***y*(if tP*y*, then *y*=t or T(*y*)) and 1(t). The truth of "1(**w**)" is, therefore, a definitional consequence of the truth of "QC(**w**)".) AP9, finally, remains also unchanged:

APT9 **w**≠**t**.

(The reformulated definition of "**t**" is DPT18: **t** := **the***y*(1(*y*) and **all***x*(if 1(*x*), then *y*P*x*)).)

The reformulation of the theorems TP1 - TP142 of system P, according to the reformulation-procedure described above, yields the theorems TPT1 - TPT142 of system PT1. (The proofs of TP1 - TP142 on the basis of AP1 - AP9, DP1 - DP39 can of course be rewritten as proofs of TPT1 - TPT142 on the basis of APT0 - APT9, DPT1 - DPT39. Note that none of the proofs of TP1 - TP142 depends on AP10.) The reformulation of TP18: TPT18, for example, looks like this: **all***x*(if 1(*x*) and A[*x*], then *x*P**conj***z*A[*z*]) and **all***y*(if 1(*y*) and **all***x*(if 1(*x*) and A[*x*], then *x*P*y*), then **conj***z*A[*z*]P*y*). Often it is possible to restate theorems in TP1 - TP142 without change, or to simplify greatly their immediate reformulations.

(d) To the axioms APT0 - APT9 the following *intercategorial* axioms, which separate the categories in the universe of discourse, are added first:

APT10 **all***x*(if 1(*x*), then not 0(*x*)).
("States of affairs are not individuals.")

APT11 **all***x*(if 1(*x*), then not <0>(*x*)).
("States of affairs are not properties.")

APT12 **all***x*(if 0(*x*), then not <0>(*x*)).
("Individuals are not properties.")

APT13 **some**_x_0(_x_).
("There are individuals.")

APT0 - APT13 constitute part of the axiom-system PT1. Other axioms will follow - axioms that will enable us to prove, among other things, "**some**_x_<0>(_x_)"; therefore, this true statement is not added as a companion-axiom to APT13 ("**some**_x_1(_x_)" is already a consequence both of APT4 and of APT8). However, the further axioms will not enable us to prove "**all**_x_(0(_x_) or 1(_x_) or <0>(_x_))," nor will we add this as an axiom, although it is true, given the chosen universe of discourse of LPT1, and would complete the categorial description of that universe; but the truth of "**all**_x_(0(_x_) or 1(_x_) or <0>(_x_))" is altogether "transitory": the statement is verified merely by our current limitation of interest to individuals, states of affairs and properties of individuals. (This limitation notwithstanding, we will see that the intercategorial ontology of "the three most familiar categories" is surprisingly rich; the entire third part of this book is devoted to it.) In contrast, not one of the axioms APT0 - APT13 needs to be given up on the way to universal intensional ontology (see part IV), which is infinitely richer in categories than PT1.

SATURATION AND EXTRACTION

(a) The language LPT1 contains also the dyadic *saturation functor* "**(**t,t′**)**". For all singular terms (names, variables, functional expressions) t and t′ of LPT1, "**(**t,t′**)**" is to be read as "the saturation of t by t′". (Let the word "saturation" connote in this context not the *process* of saturation, but its *result*. The same remark applies to the less suggestive word that could here be used instead of "saturation": "concatenation": "the concatenation of t with t′." It is less suggestive because it does not by itself connote an asymmetry between concatenated entities, whereas there are standard applications of the intended functional concept for which commutativity fails.) Note that the saturation functor of LPT1 cannot be defined by the ordered-pair-functor: sometimes the saturation of *x* by *y* is identical with the saturation of *x* by *z*, although *y* and *z* are non-identical.

The basic characterization of the saturation functor of LPT1 is provided by the following two axioms that connect all three categorial predicates of LPT1. Note that the first of these axioms is logically true (true in virtue of the meaning it has independent of the chosen universe of discourse of LPT1) - like the axioms APT0 - APT6 and APT10 - APT13, but unlike the axioms APT7 - APT9; whereas the second axiom is not logically true, but only analytically true with respect to the chosen universe of discourse:

APT14 **allxally**[if <0>(x) and 0(y), then 1(**(**x,y**)**)].
("The saturation of a property by an individual is a state of affairs.")

APT15 **allxally**(if not <0>(x) or not 0(y), then **(**x,y**)**=**k**).

Taking our inspiration from Frege, properties (of individuals) are here conceived of as (monadically) *unsaturated entities.*[*1] The result of saturating a property - a certain unsaturated entity - by an individual is a state of affairs; this is the rather natural assertion made by APT14. APT15, on the other hand, has a purely stipulative character; it guarantees - in the most convenient manner - a value to the saturation functor of LPT1 even for those arguments for which, without stipulation, it would not have a value (given the chosen universe of discourse of LPT1; APT15 has to be given up, for example, if the universe of discourse is extended by a property of properties of individuals such that the saturation of that property by a property of individuals is obviously not **k**).

(b) LPT1 also comprises certain special *extraction-variables*: *o*, *o*′, *o*″... . Extraction-variables occur in well-formed expressions of LPT1 only if they are bound by its *extraction-operator* "**ex**". (Thus, extraction variables are not singular terms; they are not also symbolized by "t", "t′", etc.) The extraction-operator forms singular *extraction-terms* according to the following syntactical rule:

(*i*) If f[y] is a functional expression of LPT1 in which the (normal) variable y of LPT1 occurs unbound in certain places (in the places indicated by "[ ]"), then **ex***o*f[*o*] is an *extraction-term* of LPT1, where *o* is an extraction-variable of LPT1 not yet occurring in f[y] (it replaces y in the places indicated by "[ ]").
(*ii*) Only expressions that can be generated according to (*i*) are extraction-terms of LPT1.

The extraction-operator is characterized in LPT1 by the following analytically valid axioms. (We use the extraction-variable "*o*" as representative for whichever the appropriate extraction-variable might be, just like we have used and are using, for example, "*x*" as representative for the appropriate normal variable.)

APT16 **all***x*(if 0(*x*) and 1(f[*x*]), then **(ex***o*f[*o*],*x***)**=f[*x*]).

APT17 **all***x*(if not 1(f[*x*]), then **(ex***o*f[*o*],*x***)**=**k**).

APT18 if **no***x*(0(*x*) and 1(f[*x*]) and f[*x*]≠**k**), then <0>(**ex***o*f[*o*]).

APT16 asserts that the saturation by an individual *x* of the *residue* **ex***o*f[*o*] that results by extracting *x* from a state of affairs f[*x*] is the state of affairs f[*x*] itself. (According to our conventions in stating axiom-schemata, "*x*" represents a variable that does not occur in **ex***o*f[*o*].)
To what category does the residue **ex***o*f[*o*] belong? Using APT16 and APT15 we can prove:

TPT143 if **some***x*(0(*x*) and 1(f[*x*]) and f[*x*]≠**k**), then <0>(**ex***o*f[*o*]).
("If there is an individual *x* such that f[*x*] is a non-contradictory state of affairs, then the residue obtained by extracting *x* from f[*x*] is a property.")

And TPT143 and APT18 together give us

TPT144 <0>(**ex***o*f[*o*]).
("The residue obtained by extracting *x* from f[*x*] is a property.")

The truth of APT18 is in part the result of mere stipulation (occasioned by the chosen universe of discourse of LPT1, and limited to that universe). For example, consider "**no***x*(0(*x*) and 1(f[*x*]))" (which logically implies the antecedent of APT18); if this is true, then the residue obtained by extracting *x* from f[x] is *stipulated* to be a property. It is, however, not a property by mere stipulation in case "**some**x(0(x) and 1(f[x])) and **no**x(f[x]≠**k**)" is true (which also logically implies the antecedent of APT18); in *that case* it is simply natural to say that **ex**of[o] is "a contradictory property." APT17, in contrast, has a purely stipulative character.

For every case subsumable under "**no**x(0(x) and 1(f[x]) and f[x]≠**k**)" it is found on the basis of APT15, APT16 and APT17 that the saturation of **ex**of[o] by any entity in the universe of discourse is *the contradictory state of affairs*:

TPT145 if **no**x(0(x) and 1(f[x]) and f[x]≠**k**), then **all**x((**ex**of[o],x)=**k**).

Thus, given the antecedent of APT18, the residue which is obtained by extracting x from f[x] is on the basis of APT18 and TPT145 seen to be a property (of individuals) whose saturation by any individual in the universe of discourse is the contradictory (or total) state of affairs. (Note that according to APT15 "**all**x(if 0(x), then (**ex**of[o],x)=**k**)" is equivalent to "**all**x((**ex**of[o],x) =**k**).") Such a property is called a "contradictory property":

DPT40 <0>$_{CD}$(t) := <0>(t) and **all**x(if 0(x), then (t,x)=**k**).
("t is a contradictory property.")

We shall see later on that there is precisely one contradictory property.

(c) Corresponding to TPT144 we have

TPT146 **all**x**all**y1((x,y)).
(Depending on APT14, APT15, and the theorem "1(**k**).")

A theorem useful for simplification is

TPT147 **all**x**all**y[if **all**z(if 0(z), then (x,z)P(y,z)), then **all**z((x,z)P(y,z))] and **all**x**all**y[if **all**z(if 0(z), then (x,z)=(y,z)), then **all**z((x,z)=(y,z))].

Moreover we have:

TPT148 **all**x((**ex**of[o],x)=f[x] or (**ex**of[o],x)=**k**).

TPT149 **all**x**all**y((x,y)=(**ex**o(x,o),y)).

TPT150 **all**x**all**y((**ex**o(o,y),x)=**k**).

TPT151 **all**x((**ex**o'**ex**of[o,o'],x)=**k**).

According to TPT151 and TPT144 an (immediately) iterated extraction yields a contradictory property. According to TPT150 and TPT144 the same is true if extraction is applied to the *first* argument of a saturation. These results - like all results in this section - are due to the restricted character of the universe of discourse of LPT1 and of the language LPT1 itself. They cannot be retained in *universal* intensional ontology (nor can, indeed, APT16; see IV.2.(d)).

COMMENTS

[*1] The Fregean conception of universals as monadically or polyadically "unsaturated" entities (saturation by individuals being only a special case) has more in its favor than the *traditional* conception, even if one restricts the range of the word "universals" to properties of individuals. In "New Work for a Theory of Universals" D. Lewis writes on p. 343 (footnote): "In this paper, I follow Armstrong's traditional terminology: 'universals' are repeatable entities, wholly present wherever a particular instantiates them"; and in *On the Plurality of Worlds*, p. 2: "Nor do they [possible worlds] overlap; they have no parts in common, with the exception, perhaps, of immanent universals exercising their characteristic privilege of repeated occurrence."

In fact, however, it is not true that universals enjoy the exclusive privilege of repeated occurrence. Lewis refers to the unspectacular phenomenon that several individuals a_1, a_2, ... exemplify one and the same universal F; this may be described by saying that *universal F occurs repeatedly*: at individual a_1, at individual a_2, ... But, of course, there is also the commonplace phenomenon that several universals F_1, F_2, ... are exemplified by one and the same individual a; there is no reason why we should not describe this by saying that *individual a occurs repeatedly* (unusual as this may sound): at universal F_1, at universal F_2, and so on. Thus, the traditional criterion of (the ability of) repeated occurrence is not adequate to distinguish individuals from universals.

Though the idea of saturated and unsaturated entities originates with Frege, the present ontological theory differs essentially from that of Frege: the saturations of universals (for the time being: merely properties of individuals) are (coarse-grained) states of affairs, and not truth values (or, alternatively, "thoughts") as for Frege. (It should be kept in mind that talking of "saturated" and "unsaturated" entities is a *metaphorical* way of speaking: unlike unsaturated chemical compounds, an ontologically unsaturated entity can, although there is already one saturation of it, be saturated over and over again, yielding ever new saturations. The general non-metaphorical designation for unsaturated entities is "functions"; Frege - generalizing a mathematical designation into an ontological one - was the first to call them by that name. Unsaturated entities or functions are in a manner *incomplete*; but this does not mean that they are in any way ontologically deficient; rather, they have a capability saturated entities do not have: to yield an entity through saturation by an entity.)

The present theory also exhibits connections to Wittgensteinian conceptions, as will become particularly evident later on when for every number of places n ($n \geq 2$) we consider an n-adic saturation- or *concatenation*-functor "$(t_1,...,t_n)$"; compare this nomenclature and the syntactic appearance of the expressions with what Wittgenstein says in the *Tractatus* at 2.01: "Der Sachverhalt ist eine Verbindung von Gegenständen (Sachen, Dingen)." And especially *ibid.*, 2.03: "Im Sachverhalt hängen die Gegenstände ineinander, wie die Glieder einer Kette." To accord well with the present conception of universals and individuals in states of affairs, these quotes have to be read in the light of the conclusion E. Stenius arrives at in *Wittgenstein's Tractatus*, p. 63: "Wittgenstein counts as 'things' [*Gegenstände*, *Dinge*] not only individual objects but also predicates with different numbers of places." (For Stenius, the term "predicate" does not designate a linguistic, but an ontological category: the category of properties and relations of individuals; see *ibid.*, p. 21f.)

PARTHOOD AND IDENTITY FOR PROPERTIES

(a) The part-concept for properties of individuals can be defined on the basis of the part-concept for states of affairs:

DPT41 t$\mathrm{P}_{<0>}$t′ := <0>(t) and <0>(t′) and **all***x*(if 0(*x*), then **(**t,*x***)P(**t′,*x***)**).
("property t is an intensional part of property t′.")

According to this definition, the property (of individuals) *being married at* t_0 is intensional part of the property *being a husband at* t_0 for the conceptual reason that for every individual *x* the state of affairs *that x is married at* t_0 (the saturation of *being married at* t_0 by *x*) is an intensional part of the state of affairs *that x is a husband at* t_0 (the saturation of *being a husband at* t_0 by *x*). (In view of TPT147, "**all***x*(if 0(*x*), then **(**t,*x***)P(**t′,*x***)**)" can be replaced in the definiens of DPT41 by the simpler "**all***x*(**(**t,*x***)P(**t′,*x***)**).")
Applying DPT41 it is easy to prove three theorems that correspond to APT0 - APT2:

TPT152 **all***f***all***g*(if *f*$\mathrm{P}_{<0>}$*g*, then <0>(*f*) and <0>(*g*)).
(Depending on DPT41.)

TPT153 **all***f***all***g***all***h*(if *f*$\mathrm{P}_{<0>}$*g* and *g*$\mathrm{P}_{<0>}$*h*, then *f*$\mathrm{P}_{<0>}$*h*).
(Depending on DPT41, APT1.)

TPT154 **all***f*(if <0>(*f*), then *f*$\mathrm{P}_{<0>}$*f*).

(b) The principle for properties corresponding to APT3 can be proved on the basis of DPT41 if we assume as a further axiom the following (analytically true) *principle of the identity of properties*:

APT19 **all***f***all***g*(if <0>(*f*) and <0>(*g*) and **all***x*(if 0(*x*), then **(***f*,*x***)=(***g*,*x***)**), then *f*=*g*).

According to APT19, properties *f* and *g* are identical if (and only if) they always yield the same state of affairs if saturated by the same individual.[*1] Since states of affairs are here conceived to be *coarsely individuated* intensions, properties, too, according to APT19, turn out to be coarsely individuated intensions; they inherit their coarse individuation from the coarse individuation of states of affairs.
The principle for properties corresponding to APT3,

TPT155 **all***f***all***g*(if *f*P$_{<0>}$*g* and *g*P$_{<0>}$*f*, then *f*=*g*),

is an easily derivable consequence of APT3 and APT19, employing DPT41. Conversely, APT19 can be deduced from TPT155 (on the basis of the remaining axioms): Assume: <0>(*f*) and <0>(*g*) and **all***x*(if 0(*x*), then **(***f*,*x***)**=**(***g*,*x***)**); hence because of APT14 and APT2: **all***x*(if 0(*x*), then **(***f*,*x***)**P**(***g*,*x***)**) and **all***x*(if 0(*x*), then **(***g*,*x***)**P**(***f*,*x***)**), hence by DPT41: *f*P$_{<0>}$*g* and *g*P$_{<0>}$*f*, hence by TPT155: *f*=*g*.

(c) The principle for properties corresponding to APT4 can also be proved on the basis of the axioms introduced so far (see the Appendix):

TPT156 **some***h*[<0>(*h*) and **all***f*(if <0>(*f*) and A[*f*], then *f*P$_{<0>}$*h*) and **all***g*(if <0>(*g*) and **all***f*(if <0>(*f*) and A[*f*], then *f*P$_{<0>}$*g*), then *h*P$_{<0>}$*g*)].

From TPT156 and TPT155 there results the strengthening of TP156 from "**some***h*[...]" to "**one***h*[...]"; this justifies the following definition that corresponding to DPT17:

DPT42 **conj**$_{<0>}$*f*A[*f*] := **the***h*[<0>(*h*) and **all***f*(if <0>(*f*) and A[*f*], then *f*P$_{<0>}$*h*) and **all***g*(if <0>(*g*) and **all***f*(if <0>(*f*) and A[*f*], then *f*P$_{<0>}$*g*), then *h*P$_{<0>}$*g*)].

And from the proof of TPT156 we can then gather the proof of

TPT157 **conj**$_{<0>}$*f*A[*f*]=**ex***o***conj***y***some***k*(<0>(*k*) and A[*k*] and *y*=**(***k*,*o***)**).

The conjunction of the properties *f* that satisfy A[*f*] - in short: the conjunction of the A-properties - is identical with the property obtained by extracting in the appropriate manner an individual *x* from the conjunction of all states of affairs which are saturations of A-properties by *x*. And therefore:

TPT158 **all***z*[if 0(*z*), then **(conj**$_{<0>}$*f*A[*f*],*z***)**=**conj***y***some***k*(<0>(*k*) and A[*k*] and *y*=**(***k*,*z***)**)].
(Depending on TPT157, APT16.)

(In case not 0(*z*), then according to APT15 **(conj**$_{<0>}$*f*A[*f*],*z***)**=**k**; but one cannot prove that in that case one also has **conj***y***some***k*(<0>(*k*) and A[*k*] and *y*=**(***k*,*z***)**) =**k**; for this one needs the extra assumption **some***k*(<0>(*k*) and A[*k*]).)

COMMENTS

[*1] D. M. Armstrong writes in *Universals and Scientific Realism*, vol. I, p. 29: "Quine says the identity-conditions for classes are 'crystal-clear' while the identity-conditions for properties are 'obscure'." One wonders why the set-theoretical principle of extensionality should be called "crystal-clear," and why APT19, for example, "obscure"? Both principles are formulated in a logically precise manner with concepts that are precisely known in so far (and only in so far) as there are logically precise principles involving them; hence, with respect to logical perspicuity, the latter principle is as crystal-clear (or obscure) as the former. Note also that the clarity with which classes can be distinguished from each other depends on the clarity with which their elements are distinguishable, and that the clarity of the distinction of properties (not only for properties of individuals) depends on the clarity of the distinction of states of affairs; thus, according to their very identity-principles, neither in the case of classes nor in the case of properties can absolute clarity be had about identity and non-identity purely on the basis of the mentioned identity-principles. We can conclude that there simply is no clear contrast in clarity between classes and properties with respect to identity which could make the latter entities ontologically suspect. (Interestingly, nominalists are blind with respect to the faults of their own favorite entities: individuals; the identity-conditions for individuals are surely far from being generally "crystal-clear" if they have to be formulated without recourse to properties. If this is not a good reason for impugning individuals, why then should the purported lack of clarity in the identity-conditions for properties be a good reason for impugning properties?)

CHAPTER III.4

IMPORTANT SINGULAR TERMS FOR PROPERTIES

(a) In the realm of properties the deductive power of TPT152 - TPT156 is equal to the deductive power of APT0 - APT4 in the realm of states of affairs. In the next chapter we will see that the principles for properties corresponding to APT5 and APT6 can also be proved; this chapter, first of all, prepares the way for their proofs.

The definitions DP1 - DP39, if neither "**w**" nor expressions defined with the help of "**w**" occur in their definientia, can be systematically reformulated *explicitly for properties* according to the following procedure:

(*i*) For "P" put everywhere "$\mathrm{P}_{<0>}$".

(*ii*) Mark the definienda by "$_{<0>}$" in the case of predicates, and by "$_{\mathbf{<0>}}$" in the case of singular terms (including functional terms).

(*iii*) For "**some**x", "**all**x", "**the**x" in the definientia put "**some**x(<0>(x) and ...)", "**all**x(if <0>(x), then ...)", **the**x(<0>(x) and ...)" (first replacing "**no**x" by "not **some**x").

(*iv*) Where designator-symbols "t", "t′" ... occur in the definientia of predicate-definitions, add "and <0>(t) and <0>(t′) ..." to the definiens concerned.

(Variables and designator-symbols other than those used in the original definitions may be chosen, and, after rewriting, the definitions may be simplified as far as possible.)

This reformulation-procedure has, in effect, already been used in the case of DPT42, which can be obtained, in the way described, from DP17; and if we apply it to DP19, we get:

DPT43 $\mathbf{k}_{<0>}$:= **the**y(<0>(y) and **all**x(if <0>(x), then $x\mathrm{P}_{<0>}y$)).

Completely analogous to the proof of "1(**k**) and **k**=**conj**x(x=x)" (applying APT4, APT3, DPT19, DPT17) we can show "<0>($\mathbf{k}_{<0>}$) and $\mathbf{k}_{<0>}$= $\mathbf{conj}_{<0>}f(f{=}f)$" - "The total property is the conjunction of all properties" (applying TPT156, TPT155, DPT42, DPT43). We have moreover

TPT159 $<0>_{\mathrm{CD}}(\mathbf{k}_{<0>})$.
("The total property is a contradictory property.")

This can be seen in several steps. First of all, a new functional term is introduced:

DPT44 **b**(t) := **exoconj**x(x=t and o=o).

("the *property-image* of t"; "**b**" from German "*Bild*" - "image.")

It can be proved (see the Appendix):

TPT160 **all***x*(if 1(*x*), then **all***z*(if 0(*z*), then **(b(***x***),***z***)=***x*)).
("The saturation of the property-image of a state of affairs by an individual is the state of affairs itself.")[*1]

Since **k** is (provably) a state of affairs, **all***z*(if 0(*z*), then **(b(k),***z***)=k**) is a straightforward consequence of TPT160. By TPT144 and DPT44 we have moreover: <0>(**b(k)**). Therefore by DPT40:

TPT161 $<0>_{CD}$(**b(k)**).
("The property-image of the contradictory state of affairs is a contradictory property.")

And further we have

TPT162 **b(k)=**$\mathbf{k}_{<0>}$.

TPT161 and TPT162 together give us TPT159.
There is, moreover, at most one contradictory property:

TPT163 **all***f***all***g*(if $<0>_{CD}(f)$ and $<0>_{CD}(g)$, then $f=g$).

TPT159 and TPT163 together assert that there is *precisely one* contradictory property, and that that property is the total property: the property of which all properties are intensional parts (= the conjunction of all properties), which in its turn is identical with the property-image of the total (or contradictory) state of affairs (see TPT162).

(b) The pendant of DPT40 is

DPT45 $<0>_{TL}$(t) := <0>(t) and **all***z*(if 0(*z*), then **(**t**,***z***)=t**).
("t is a tautological property.")

According to DPT45, a tautological property is a property whose saturation by an individual is always the tautological (or minimal) state of affairs. Because of the provability of 1(**t**) and <0>(**b(t)**) we obtain via TPT160 (applying DPT45)

TPT164 $<0>_{TL}$(b(**t**)).
("The property-image of the tautological state of affairs is a tautological property.")

Moreover we have

TPT165 $\mathbf{b(t)=t}_{<0>}$,

which is proved *mutatis mutandis* as is TPT162, ``$\mathbf{t}_{<0>}$'' being defined as follows (by transforming DP18):

DPT46 $\mathbf{t}_{<0>}$:= **the**y(<0>(y) and **all**x(if <0>(x), then $y\mathrm{P}_{<0>}x$)).

(Completely analogous to the proof of ``1(**t**) and **t**=**conj**$x$($x$≠$x$)'' one easily proves ``<0>($\mathbf{t}_{<0>}$) and $\mathbf{t}_{<0>}=\mathbf{conj}_{<0>}f(f\neq f)$.'') TPT164 and TPT165 together immediately imply

TPT166 $<0>_{\mathrm{TL}}(\mathbf{t}_{<0>})$.

And corresponding to TPT163 (adapting its proof) we obtain

TPT167 **all**f**all**g(if $<0>_{\mathrm{TL}}(f)$ and $<0>_{\mathrm{TL}}(g)$, then f=g).

TPT166 and TPT167 together assert that there is precisely one tautological property, and that that property is the minimal property: the property which is an intensional part of all properties, which in its turn is identical with the property-image of the tautological (or minimal) state of affairs (see TPT165).

(c) It can be proved (see the Appendix)

TPT168
(i) **all**x**all**x'(if x=x', then **conj**y(x=x' and y=**k**)=**k**).
(i′) **all**x**all**x'(if x≠x', then **conj**y(x=x' and y=**k**)=**t**).
(ii) **all**x**all**x'(if **conj**y(x=x' and y=**k**)=**k**, then x=x').
(ii′) **all**x**all**x'(if **conj**y(x=x' and y=**k**)=**t**, then x≠x').

Inspecting the proof of TPT168, it is seen that TPT168 can be generalized by omitting the initial quantifiers and replacing ``$x$=$x'$'' by a symbol for sentence-forms, say, ``B'' (hence ``$x$≠$x'$'' by ``not B''). The following results, therefore, are examples of far more general results. We define:

DPT47 **d**(t) := **ex**o**conj**y(o=t and y=**k**).
(``the property of differing from t.'')

Using TPT168 and DPT47, one obtains

TPT169

(i) **allxallz**′[if O(z′), then ((**d**(x),z′)=**t** iff z′≠x)].
(ii) **allxallz**′[if O(z′), then ((**d**(x),z′)=**k** iff z′=x)].

This theorem obviously justifies the reading of "**d**(x)" as "the property of differing from x."
Corresponding to TPT168, DPT47 and TPT169 we finally have:

TPT170
(i) **allxallx**′(if x=x′, then·**conjy**(x≠x′ and y=**k**)=**t**).
(i′) **allxallx**′(if x≠x′, then·**conjy**(x≠x′ and y=**k**)=**k**).
(ii) **allxallx**′(if **conjy**(x≠x′ and y=**k**)=**t**, then x=x′).
(ii′) **allxallx**′(if **conjy**(x≠x′ and y=**k**)=**k**, then x≠x′).

DPT48 **i**(t) := **exoconjy**(o≠t and y=**k**).
("the property of being identical with t.")

TPT171
(i) **allxallz**′[if O(z′), then ((**i**(x),z′)=**t** iff z′=x)].
(ii) **allxallz**′[if O(z′), then ((**i**(x),z′)=**k** iff z′≠x)].

The proofs of TPT170 and TPT171 are routine modifications of the proofs of TPT168 and TPT169. Like TPT168, TPT170 is an instance of a much more general theorem.

COMMENTS

[*1] If states of affairs differ, then their property-images differ, too. For assume: 1(x), 1(y), $x \neq y$ and **b**(x)=**b**(y); hence **all**z(if 0(z), then (**b**(x),z)= (**b**(y),z)). But according to TPT160 we also have: **all**z(if 0(z), then (**b**(x),z)=x) and **all**z(if 0(z), then (**b**(y),z)=y); and according to APT13: **some**z0(z). Therefore x=y - contradicting the assumption. Consequently, there are precisely as many property-images of states of affairs as there are states of affairs, and since property-images of states of affairs are properties of individuals, it is clear that there are at least as many properties of individuals as there are states of affairs.

CHAPTER III.5

THE PRINCIPLE OF PROPERTY-QUANTA AND THE EXHAUSTION- AND CONNECTION-PRINCIPLE FOR PROPERTIES

(a) The axioms of PT1 given so far are sufficient for the proof of the *exhaustion-principle for properties* (compare APT5, and the discussion of the exhaustion axiom in I.6), the *connection-principle for properties* (compare APT6, and the discussion of the connection axiom in I.7) and the *principle of property-quanta*:

PPQ $\mathbf{all}f[\text{if } QA_{<0>}(f), \text{ then not } \mathbf{some}z\mathbf{some}z'(0(z) \text{ and } 0(z') \text{ and } (f,z)\neq\mathbf{t} \text{ and } (f,z')\neq\mathbf{t} \text{ and } z\neq z')]$.

But at first sight this statement seems to be independent of those axioms. Provisionally (and only provisionally), we postulate it as a further axiom.

According to it, *f* is a quasi-atomic property or *property-quantum* only if for *at most one* individual *x* the saturation of *f* by *x* differs from the tautological state of affairs. And according to PPQ, a property-quantum is totally or almost totally devoid of substantial intensional content, its intensional content being measured by the intensional content of its saturations; this, precisely, is stated in the following theorem which is provable on the basis of PPQ:

TPT174 $\mathbf{all}f[\text{if } QA_{<0>}(f), \text{ then } \mathbf{all}z(\text{if } 0(z), \text{ then } (f,z)=\mathbf{t}) \text{ or } \mathbf{some}z(0(z) \text{ and } (f,z)\neq\mathbf{t} \text{ and } QA((f,z)) \text{ and } \mathbf{all}z'(\text{if } 0(z') \text{ and } z'\neq z, \text{ then } (f,z')=\mathbf{t}))]$

("*Either* the saturations of a property-quantum by individuals are all identical with the minimal state of affairs, *or* its saturation by some individual *z* is not the minimal state of affairs, but nevertheless a quasi-atomic one, all its saturations by other individuals than *z* remaining identical with the minimal one.")

Before proving TPT174, we state two other theorems (their proofs, which do not rest upon PPQ, can be found in the Appendix):

TPT172 $\mathbf{all}f\mathbf{all}z\mathbf{all}y[\text{if } <0>(f) \text{ and } 0(z) \text{ and } yP(f,z), \text{ then } \mathbf{some}h(hP_{<0>}f \text{ and } y=(h,z))]$.

("If state of affairs *y* is an intensional part of the saturation of property *f* by individual *z*, then there is a property which is an intensional part of *f* such that the saturation of it by *z* is identical with *y*.")

TPT173 $\mathbf{all}f(\text{if } QA_{<0>}(f), \text{ then } \mathbf{all}z[\text{if } 0(z), \text{ then } QA((f,z))])$.

("The saturation of a quasi-atomic property by an individual is always a quasi-atomic state of affairs.")

TPT174, then, is a consequence of PPQ and TPT173: Assume $QA_{<0>}(f)$, hence by PPQ: **all***z*(if 0(*z*), then **(***f*,*z***)=t**) or **some***z*(0(*z*) and **(***f*,*z***)≠t** and **all***z′*(if 0(*z′*) and *z′*≠*z*, then **(***f*,*z′***)=t**)), hence by TPT173: **all***z*(if 0(*z*), then **(***f*,*z***)=t**) or **some***z*(0(*z*) and **(***f*,*z***)≠t** and QA(**(***f*,*z***)**) and **all***z′*(if 0(*z′*) and *z′*≠*z*, then, **(***f*,*z′***)=t**)). Conversely, PPQ is logically implied by TPT174.

(b) The truth of PPQ in the present interpretation of LPT1 is demonstrable if we accept the presupposition that for every given property (of individuals) there is a property that is just like it in all saturations involving other individuals than a given individual *z*, whose saturation by *z*, however, is the given states of affairs *y*. Assume for *reductio*: $QA_{<0>}(f)$ and **some***z***some***z′*(0(*z*) and 0(*z′*) and **(***f*,*z***)≠t** and **(***f*,*z′***)≠t** and *z*≠*z′*). Consider *g*, for which we have (applying the just-mentioned presupposition to *f*, *z* and **t**): <0>(*g*) and **all***x*(if 0(*x*) and *x*≠*z*, then **(***g*,*x***)=(***f*,*x***)**) and **(***g*,*z***)=t**. Hence:
(1) $gP_{<0>}f$, according to DPT41; for: <0>(*f*) and <0>(*g*) and **all***x*(if 0(*x*), then **(***g*,*x***)P(***f*,*x***)**): Assume 0(*x*). In case *x*≠*z*, then (by the description of *g*) **(***g*,*x***)=(***f*,*x***)**, hence **(***g*,*x***)P(***f*,*x***)** because of 1(**(***f*,*x***)**) (APT14, <0>(*f*), 0(*x*)) and APT2. In case *x*=*z*, then **(***g*,*x***)=t** (by the description of *g*), hence **(***g*,*x***)P(***f*,*x***)** because of 1(**(***f*,*x***)**) and M(**t**) (TPT32, 1(**t**)), according to DPT4.
(2) *g*≠*f*, for **(***g*,*z***)≠(***f*,*z***)**.
(3) not $M_{<0>}(g)$. For *otherwise* by the theorem for properties that is parallel to TPT32: $g=\mathbf{t}_{<0>}$, hence by TPT166 $<0>_{TL}(g)$, hence, according to DPT45, for the *z′* mentioned in the assumption for *reductio*: **(***g*,*z′***)=t**; but since 0(*z′*) and *z′*≠*z*, according to the description of *g*: **(***g*,*z′***)=(***f*,*z′***)**; therefore: **(***f*,*z′***)=t** - contradicting the assumption.
According to the definition for properties that is parallel to DPT6, (1), (2) and (3) together imply: not $QA_{<0>}(f)$ - contradicting the assumption.

In other words: if we posit the *principle of singular variation* "**all***f***all***z***all***y*(if <0>(*f*) and 0(*z*) and 1(*y*), then **some***g*(<0>(*g*) and **all***x*(if 0(*x*) and *x*≠*z*, then **(***g*,*x***)=(***f*,*x***)**) and **(***g*,*z***)=***y*))" as an axiom, then PPQ need not be counted as an axiom of PT1. But the *principle of singular variation* may not appear to be sufficiently plausible to merit being made an axiom, because it easily yields the existence of properties many people would regard as "monstrous." Also sufficient, however, for obtaining a proof of PPQ (see the deduction just presented above) would be the postulation of a single instance of the principle of singular variation: **all***f***all***z*(if <0>(*f*) and 0(*z*), then **some***g*(<0>(*g*) and **all***x*(if 0(*x*) and *x*≠*z*, then **(***g*,*x***)=(***f*,*x***)**) and **(***g*,*z***)=t**)). And, in fact, we need not postulate this, for it (and therefore PPQ) is already provable without any new axiom: Assume: <0>(*f*) and 0(*z*). Consider $g := \mathbf{disj}_{<0>}(\mathbf{conj}_{<0>}(\mathbf{d}(z),f),\mathbf{i}(z))$. Assume: 0(*x*) and *x*≠*z*; then **(***g*,*x***)=disj(conj((d(***z***),***x***),(***f*,*x***)),(i(***z***),***x***))** (for the theorems justifying this, see the next chapter), and by TPT169 **(d(***z***),***x***)=t**, by TPT171 **(i(***z***),***x***)=k**; hence **(***g*,*x***)=disj(conj(t,(***f*,*x***)),k)**, hence **(***g*,*x***)=(***f*,*x***)** by TPT53.

Moreover: **(***g*,*z***)=disj(conj((d(***z***),***z***),(***f*,*z***)),(i(***z***),***z***))**, and by TPT171 **(i(***z***),***z***)=t**; hence **(***g*,*z***)=t** ("**all***y*(if 1(*y*), then **disj(***y***,t)=t)**" is easily proved applying APT2, TPT26, TPT32, APT3).

This proof, in turn, provides us with the idea needed for proving the general principle of singular variation itself: Assume <0>(*f*), 0(*z*), 1(*y*), and consider *g* := $\mathbf{disj}_{<0>}(\mathbf{conj}_{<0>}(\mathbf{d}(z),f),\mathbf{conj}_{<0>}(\mathbf{i}(z),\mathbf{b}(y)))$; one obtains **(***g*,*x***)=(***f*,*x***)**, if 0(*x*) and *x*≠*z*, and **(***g*,*z***)=***y* - *mutatis mutandis* as in the previous paragraph. The only additional theorem that has to be used is TPT160, which gives us: **(b(***y***),***x***)=***y* and **(b(***y***),***z***)=***y*. Thus, anyone who thinks the principle of singular variation problematic will have to tamper with the axioms given so far, in particular with APT16 (which, however, seems impeccable); for the principle of singular variation is not independent of these axioms.

(c) The proof of the converse of TPT174 (restricted, of course, to properties) makes crucial use of APT19 (see the Appendix):

TPT175 **all***f*(<0>(*f*) and [**all***z*(if 0(*z*), then **(***f*,*z***)=t**) or **some***z*(0(*z*) and **(***f*,*z***)≠t** and QA(**(***f*,*z***)**) and **all***z*′(if 0(*z*′) and *z*′≠*z*, then **(***f*,*z*′**)=t**))], then $QA_{<0>}(f)$).

TPT174 and TPT175 together offer a sufficient and necessary description of quasi-atomic properties by way of their saturations (which are at most two different states of affairs). Clearly, atomic, quasi-atomic, elementary properties (according to the adaptations for properties of DPT2, DPT6 and DPT20) are "atomic" in an entirely different sense from that in which quite other properties are often described as being "atomic" by other ontologists (for example, basic qualities of perception, basic properties in quantum mechanics); but this latter sense, really, has more to do with epistemology than with ontology.

Using TPT175, the exhaustion-principle for properties,

TPT176 **all***f***all***g*(if <0>(*f*) and <0>(*g*) and **all***h*(if $QA_{<0>}(h)$ and $hP_{<0>}f$, then $hP_{<0>}g$), then $fP_{<0>}g$),

can be proved (see the Appendix), according to which every property is the sum or conjunction of the quasi-atomic properties which are its intensional parts (compare TPT31).

In the proof of the connection-principle for properties,

TPT177 **all***f*[if $fP_{<0>}\mathbf{conj}_{<0>}gA[g]$ and not $M_{<0>}(f)$, then **some***h*($hP_{<0>}f$ and not $M_{<0>}(h)$ and **some***k*′($hP_{<0>}k'$ and A[*k*′]))],

we can use the central idea of the proof of TPT176 - the introduction of a certain complex functional term - once more.

(d) TPT152 - TPT156, TPT176, TPT177 are principles for properties which are, in an obvious sense, *parallel* to APT0 - APT6. This means that every theorem (concerning states of affairs) that is a consequence merely of APT0 - APT6 (for example, TPT1 - TPT94) has a theorem concerning properties *parallel* to it. We have already referred to one of these parallel theorems by using an expressions of the form "the theorem for properties that is parallel to TPTn.n."; from now on this will be abbreviated by "ParTPTn.n." (The construction of the theorem for properties that is parallel to a given theorem for states of affairs (parallel in virtue of the parallelism of TPT152 - TPT156, TPT176, TPT177 to APT0 - APT6) is easily effected: Put "<0>" in place of "1", "$P_{<0>}$" in place of "P"; attach the index "$_{<0>}$" or "$_{<0>}$" to defined expressions at the appropriate places.) Moreover, the reformulation *for properties* of those definitions out of DP1 - DP39 that do not explicitly or implicitly involve "**w**" (the procedure of reformulation is described in III.4.(a)) can be carried out completely parallel to the reformulation of DP1 - DP39 which yields DPT1 - DPT39; this makes it possible to speak of "the definition for properties that is parallel to DPTn.n." - from now on abbreviated by "ParDPTn.n."

In part II it was assumed that the part-whole structure of the universe of properties (of individuals), *in so far as it is describable by* AP1 - AP6, is the same as the part-whole structure of the universe of states of affairs. In this chapter of part III that assumption has been proved by showing that the part-whole structure of the universe of states of affairs, in so far as it is describable by AP1 - AP6, induces the very same structure in the universe of properties, given entirely natural axioms and definitions that connect properties with states of affairs.

CHAPTER III.6

PROPERTIES BY CONJUNCTION AND PROPERTIES BY EXTRACTION

(a) This short chapter treats the relationship between **neg**$_{<0>}$(*f*) and **ex***o***neg**((*f*,*o*)), **conj**$_{<0>}$(*f*,*g*) and **ex***o***conj**((*f*,*o*),(*g*,*o*)), **disj**$_{<0>}$(*f*,*g*) and **ex***o***disj** ((*f*,*o*),(*g*,*o*)). The first member of each of these three pairs is a *property by conjunction*; employing an operational metaphor, it is the result of the conjugating or summing up of properties; or speaking non-metaphorically: it could be defined in a straightforward intuitively satisfactory manner by employing **conj**$_{<0>}$*f* (compare TPT50, TPT51, TPT52, TPT20, TPT22). The second member of each of the three pairs is a *property by extraction* (it is the result of extracting an individual, in a certain manner, from a certain state of affairs). Intuitively, one expects that the first member of each pair will be identical with the second one (given that *f* and *g* are properties). And, indeed, this can be proved in each case. Here are the respective theorems, together with important corollaries, which in the case of conjunction and disjunction have already been used in the previous chapter (proofs in the Appendix):

TPT178
all*f***all***g*[if <0>(*f*) and <0>(*g*), then **conj**$_{<0>}$(*f*,*g*)=**ex***o***conj**((*f*,*o*),(*g*,*o*))].
all*f***all***g***all***z*[if <0>(*f*) and <0>(*g*) and 0(*z*), then **(conj**$_{<0>}$(*f*,*g*),*z*)=**conj**((*f*,*z*),(*g*,*z*))].
("The saturation of the conjunction of properties *f* and *g* by individual *z* is the conjunction of their saturations by *z*.")

TPT179 **all***f***all***g*[if <0>(*f*) and <0>(*g*), then **disj**$_{<0>}$(*f*,*g*)=**ex***o***disj**((*f*,*o*),(*g*,*o*))].
all*f***all***g***all***z*[if <0>(*f*) and <0>(*g*) and 0(*z*), then **(disj**$_{<0>}$(*f*,*g*),*z*)=**disj**((*f*,*z*),(*g*,*z*))].
("The saturation of the disjunction of properties *f* and *g* by individual *z* is the disjunction of their saturations by *z*.")

TPT180 **all***f*[if <0>(*f*), then **neg**$_{<0>}$(*f*)=**ex***o***neg**((*f*,*o*))].
all*f***all***z*[if <0>(*f*) and 0(*z*), then **(neg**$_{<0>}$(*f*),*z*)=**neg**((*f*,*z*))].
("The saturation of the negation of property *f* by individual *z* is the negation of its saturation by *z*.")

(b) Note that every property is both a property by conjunction and a property by extraction. We can prove both "**all***f*(if <0>(*f*), then *f*=**conj**$_{<0>}$*g*(QA$_{<0>}$(*g*) and *g*P$_{<0>}$*f*)" (ParTPT31) and "**all***f*(if <0>(*f*), then *f*=**ex***o*(*f*,*o*))": assume <0>(*f*), and assume 0(*z*), hence by APT14 1((*f*,*z*)), hence by APT16 (**ex***o*(*f*,*o*),*z*)=(*f*,*z*); hence from the first assumption alone: **all***z*(if 0(*z*), then (**ex***o*(*f*,*o*),*z*)=(*f*,*z*)), hence, since <0>(**ex***o*(*f*,*o*)) by TPT144, by APT19: *f*=**ex***o*(*f*,*o*). (As a pendant to this, every state of affairs is both a state of affairs by conjunction and a *state of affairs by saturation*; we can prove both "**all***x*(if 1(*x*), then *x*=**conj***y*(QA(*y*) and *y*P*x*))" (TPT31) and "**all***x*[if 1(*x*), then **some***z*(0(*z*) and *x*=(**b**(*x*),*z*))]" (by APT13 and TPT160).) Note finally that the conjunctive "production" of properties stays within their realm, whereas the extractive production of them intercategorially relates the realm of properties both to the universe of states of affairs and the universe of individuals.

CHAPTER III.7

ESSENTIAL AND ACCIDENTAL PROPERTIES

(a) *Simpliciter* essential and accidental properties are defined as follows:

DPT49 <0>$_{\mathrm{ES}}$(t) := <0>(t) and **all***z*(if 0(*z*), then **(**t,*z***)=t** or **(**t,*z***)=k**).
(“t is an (*simpliciter*) essential property.”)

DPT50 <0>$_{\mathrm{AC}}$(t) := <0>(t) and **all***z*(if 0(*z*), then **(**t,*z***)≠t** and **(**t,*z***)≠k**).
(“t is an (*simpliciter*) accidental property.”)

According to DPT49, an essential property is a property whose saturation by any individual is either the contradictory or the tautological state of affairs. In view of APT14, TPT93, TPT94, “<0>(t) and **all***z*(if 0(*z*), then **(**t,*z***)=t** or **(**t,*z***)=k**)” is analytically equivalent to “<0>(t) and **all***z*(if 0(*z*), then N(**(**t,*z***)**) or not P(**(**t,*z***)**))”; thus, an essential property is a property whose saturation by any individual is either an analytically necessary or an analytically impossible state of affairs. In this sense **t**$_{<0>}$, **k**$_{<0>}$, **d**(*x*) and **i**(*x*) (*x* being an arbitrary individual) are essential properties.

According to DPT50, an accidental property is a property whose saturation by any individual is neither the contradictory nor the tautological state of affairs (or in other words: whose saturation by any individual is an analytically possible, but not an analytically necessary, state of affairs). There is an accidental property if and only if there is an analytically contingent state of affairs:

TPT181 **some***f*<0>$_{\mathrm{AC}}$(*f*) iff **some***y*(1(*y*) and *y*≠**t** and *y*≠**k**).

The proof of TPT181 utilizes the fact that, if there are analytically contingent states of affairs, then the property-images of them are accidental properties. Therefore, since 1(**w**) and **w≠t** and **w≠k** (by APT8, APT9, APT7), or in other words (according to TPT94, TPT54, TPT55): since P(**w**) and P(**neg**(**w**)), it is apparent from the proof of TPT181 that the following statement is also true:

TPT182 <0>$_{\mathrm{AC}}$(**b**(**w**)).
(“The property-image of the world is an accidental property.”)

(b) Further we have

TPT183 **all***f*(if <0>(*f*), then <0>$_{\mathrm{ES}}$(*f*)) iff **all***y*(if 1(*y*), then *y*=**t** or *y*=**k**) and

TPT184 **all***f*(if <0>(*f*), then <0>$_{ES}$(*f*)) iff **no***f*<0>$_{AC}$(*f*).
(Depending on TPT181, TPT183.)

According to TPT184, *either* all properties are essential, *or* some property is accidental. This does not of course logically imply the stronger thesis that all properties are *either* essential *or* accidental, which is, in fact, false. This is seen as follows. We can prove:

TPT185 **all***f***all***g*[if <0>$_{ES}$(*f*) and not <0>$_{CD}$(*f*) and not <0>$_{TL}$(*f*) and <0>$_{AC}$(*g*), then not <0>$_{ES}$(**conj**$_{<0>}$(*f*,*g*)) and not <0>$_{AC}$(**conj**$_{<0>}$(*f*,*g*))].
("The conjunction of an essential property that is neither tautological nor contradictory with an accidental property is neither an essential nor an accidental property.")

If one strengthens APT13 and assumes what surely is also true: **some***z***some***z*′(0(*z*) and 0(*z*′) and *z*′≠*z*) ("There are at least two individuals"), then it becomes demonstrable that there is an essential property that is neither contradictory nor tautological; by TPT182 and TPT185 one then obtains *that there is a property that is neither essential nor accidental*.[*1] For we can prove:

TPT186 **all***z*[if 0(*z*) and **some***z*′(0(*z*′) and *z*≠*z*′), then <0>$_{ES}$(**i**(*z*)) and not <0>$_{CD}$(**i**(*z*)) and not <0>$_{TL}$(**i**(*z*))].
("If besides an individual *z* there is *another* individual, then the property of being identical with *z* is an essential property that is neither contradictory nor tautological.")

(c) Although not every property is either essential or accidental *simpliciter*, every property is either essential or accidental *with respect to any given individual*:

DPT51 <0>$_{ES}$(t,t′) := <0>(t) and 0(t′) and (**(**t,t′**)=t** or **(**t,t′**)=k**).
("t is an essential property *with respect to individual* t′.")

DPT52 <0>$_{AC}$(t,t′) := <0>(t) and 0(t′) and **(**t,t′**)≠t** and **(**t,t′**)≠k**.
("t is an accidental property *with respect to individual* t′.")

It is natural to relativize the concepts "<0>$_{CD}$(*f*)" and "<0>$_{TL}$(*f*)" in the same manner:

DPT53 <0>$_{CD}$(t,t′) := <0>(t) and 0(t) and **(**t,t′**)=k**.
("t is a contradictory property with respect to individual t′.")

DPT54 <0>$_{TL}$(t,t′) := <0>(t) and O(t′) and **(t,t′)=t**.
(“t is a tautological property with respect to individual t′.”)

Instead of “*f* is a tautological property with respect to individual *x*” one normally says “*f* is an essential property *of* individual *x*.” For “**(***f***,***x***)=t**” in the definiens of “<0>$_{TL}$(*f*,*x*)” analytically implies “O((*f*,*x*))” (“the saturation of *f* by *x* is an obtaining state of affairs”), and the latter means that *f applies* to *x*, that *x has*, *exemplifies*, “is” *f* (see the chapter after the next one); in addition, the definiens of “<0>$_{TL}$(*f*,*x*)” logically implies the definiens of “<0>$_{ES}$(*f*,*x*).” Conversely, “<0>$_{ES}$(*f*,*x*) and O((*f*,*x*))” implies “<0>$_{TL}$(*f*,*x*)” (applying APT7). (Accordingly, “*f* is an accidental property *of x*” is a reading of “<0>$_{AC}$(*f*,*x*) and O((*f*,*x*)).”)

(d) The *essence of x*, **ess**(*x*), is the conjunction of all essential properties *of x*: **conj**$_{<0>}$*h*(<0>$_{ES}$(*h*,*x*) and O((*f*,*x*)), which is identical with **conj**$_{<0>}$*h*<0>$_{TL}$(*h*,*x*), which, in its turn, is identical with **conj**$_{<0>}$*h*((*h*,*x*)**=t**) (because of DPT54, APT15, TPT104, ParTPT29). The essential truths with respect to essences are expressed by the following three provable principles:

all*z*[if O(*z*), then **all***f*(*f*P$_{<0>}$**ess**(*z*) iff <0>$_{TL}$(*f*,*z*))].
(“The intensional parts of the essence of individual *z* are precisely the essential properties of *z*.”)

all*y*′**all***z*[if MK(*y*′) and O(*z*), then **(ess(***z***),***z***)P***y*′ and **all***z*′(if O(*z*′) and **(ess(***z***),***z*′**)P***y*′, then *z*′=*z*)].
(“The essence of an individual applies to it, and to no other individual, in every possible world.” Since “O((*f*,*x*)),” that is: “**(***f***,***x***)Pw**,” means *f* applies to *x*, “**(***f***,***x***)P***y*′ and MK(*y*′)” means *f* applies *in world y*′ to *x*; compare DPT56 in III.10.)

all*z*(if O(*z*), then **ess**(*z*)=**i**(*z*)).
(“The essence of an individual is the property of being identical with it.”)

Proof: We use the shortest of the above three equivalent descriptions of the essence of an individual *z*: **ess**(*z*)=**conj**$_{<0>}$*h*((*h*,*z*)**=t**).
Assume: O(*z*), MK(*y*′).
(11) Assume *f*P$_{<0>}$**ess**(*z*), hence *f*P$_{<0>}$**conj**$_{<0>}$*h*((*h*,*z*)**=t**), hence by DPT41 **(***f***,***z***)P(conj**$_{<0>}$*h*((*h*,*z*)**=t**),*z*), hence by TPT158 **(***f***,***z***)Pconj***y***some***k*(<0>(*k*) and **(***k***,***z***)=t** and *y*=**(***k***,***z***)**), hence **(***f***,***z***)Pt** (**all***y*(if **some***k*(<0>(*k*) and **(***k***,***z***)=t** and *y*=**(***k***,***z***)**), then *y*=**t**), TPT28, TPT33, APT1), hence by TPT36 **(***f***,***z***)=t**, hence by DPT54 <0>$_{TL}$(*f*,*z*).
(12) Assume <0>$_{TL}$(*f*,*z*), hence by DPT54: <0>(*f*) and **(***f***,***z***)=t**, hence by ParTPT18 *f*P$_{<0>}$**conj**$_{<0>}$*h*((*h*,*z*)**=t**), hence *f*P$_{<0>}$**ess**(*z*).

(**2**) **(ess(*z*),*z*)=(conj**$_{<0>}$*h*((*h*,*z*)=**t**),*z*)=**t** (compare (**11**)); **t**P*y*′; hence **(ess(*z*),*z*)**P*y*′. Assume: 0(*z*′) and *z*′≠*z*; **(ess(*z*),*z*′)=conj***y***some***k*(<0>(*k*) and **(*k*,*z*)=t** and *y*=**(*k*,*z*′)**) (compare (**11**)); **(i(*z*),*z*′)Pconj***y***some***k*(<0>(*k*) and **(*k*,*z*)=t** and *y*=**(*k*,*z*′)**) by TPT18, because: <0>(**i**(*z*)) and **(i(*z*),*z*)=t** (by TPT171) and **(i(*z*),*z*′)=(i(*z*),*z*′)** and 1(**(i(*z*),*z*′)**) (APT14). But according to assumption and TPT171(b): **(i(*z*),*z*′)=k**. Therefore: **kP(ess(*z*),*z*′)**, and hence **(ess(*z*),*z*′)=k** (by APT3, since **(ess(*z*),*z*′)Pk**). Hence: not **(ess(*z*),*z*′)**P*y*′, since not **k**P*y*′ because MK(*y*′) (compare TPT72).
(**3**) We have seen: **(ess(*z*),*z*)=t** and **all***z*′(if 0(*z*′) and *z*′≠*z*, then **(ess(*z*),*z*′)=k**); hence by TPT171: **all***z*′(if 0(*z*′), then **(ess(*z*),*z*′)=(i(*z*),*z*′)**), hence by APT19 **ess(*z*)=i(*z*)**.

Thus the essence of an individual turns out to be its *haecceity*: the property of being identical with it, or in other words: the property of being *this individual*. Its haecceity (its essence) is *the only* property that *individuates* an individual under all possible circumstances, that is, applies to it, and only to it, in all possible worlds (maximally consistent states of affairs). For suppose that for individual *z* there is besides **i**(*z*) a property *f* such that: **all***y*′(if MK(*y*′), then (*f*,*z*)P*y*′ and **all***z*′(0(*z*′) and (*f*,*z*′)P*y*′, then *z*′=*z*)). Hence: (1) **all***y*′(if MK(*y*′), then (*f*,*z*)P*y*′), and hence **(*f*,*z*)=t=(i(*z*),*z*)** (see mainly TPT86, TPT90); (2) **all***z*′(if 0(*z*′) and *z*′≠*z*, then **no***y*′(MK(*y*′) and (*f*,*z*′)P*y*′)), and hence **all***z*′(if 0(*z*′) and *z*′≠*z*, then **(*f*,*z*′)=k=(i(*z*),*z*′)**) (see mainly TPT85, TPT91). Therefore: **all***z*′(if 0(*z*′), then **(*f*,*z*′)=(i(*z*),*z*′)**), and hence by APT19 *f*=**i**(*z*).[*2]

The considerations in this section demonstrate that there need not be anything mysterious or unclear in the notions of essence and hacceity. From the present vantage point the suspicion with which some philosophers treat these notions seems misguided.

COMMENTS

[*1] G. H. von Wright writes in *An Essay in Modal Logic*, p. 27: ''If a property can be significantly predicated of the individuals of a certain Universe of Discourse, then either the property is necessarily present in some or all individuals and necessarily absent in the rest, or else the property is possibly but not necessarily (i.e. contingently) present in some or all individuals and possibly but not necessarily (i.e. contingently) absent in the rest.'' G. H. von Wright's ''Principle of Predication'' can be represented in LPT1 as follows:
P1 **all***h*{if <0>(*h*), then **all***z*[if 0(*z*), then N((*h*,*z*)) or N((**neg**$_{<0>}$(*h*),*z*))] or **all***z*[if 0(*z*), then P((*h*,*z*)) and not N((*h*,*z*)) or P((**neg**$_{<0>}$(*h*),*z*)) and not N((**neg**$_{<0>}$(*h*),*z*))]}.
This statement is equivalent to
P2 **all***h*[if <0>(*h*), then **all***z*(if 0(*z*), then (*h*,*z*)=**t** or (**neg**$_{<0>}$(*h*),*z*)=**t**) or **all***z*(if 0(*z*), then (*h*,*z*)≠**k** and (*h*,*z*)≠**t** or (**neg**$_{<0>}$(*h*),*z*)≠**k** and (**neg**$_{<0>}$(*h*),*z*)≠**t**)],
for: **all***y*(if 1(*y*), then (N(*y*) iff *y*=**t**)) and **all***y*(if 1(*y*), then (P(*y*) iff *y*≠**k**)) (see TPT93, TPT94). And P2, in turn, is equivalent to
P3 **all***h*[if <0>(*h*), then **all***z*(if 0(*z*), then (*h*,*z*)=**t** or (*h*,*z*)=**k**) or **all***z*(if 0(*z*), then (*h*,*z*)≠**k** and (*h*,*z*)≠**t**)],
for: **all***h***all***z*(if <0>(*h*) and 0(*z*), then [(*h*,*z*)=**k** iff (**neg**$_{<0>}$(*h*),*z*)=**t**] and [(*h*,*z*)=**t** iff (**neg**$_{<0>}$(*h*),*z*)=**k**]) ((**neg**$_{<0>}$(*h*),*z*)=**neg**((*h*,*z*)) by the corollary of TPT180, and apply TPT54 and TPT55). P3, however, is in its turn, according to DPT49 and DPT50, equivalent to
P4 **all***h*(if <0>(*h*), then <0>$_{ES}$(*h*) or <0>$_{AC}$(*h*)).
(''Every property is either essential or accidental.'')
We have seen that P4 is false; hence von Wright's ''Principle of Predication'' is also false. (It is also criticized by A. Plantinga in *The Nature of Necessity*, p. 68, and by F. von Kutschera in *Einführung in die intensionale Semantik*, p. 37 (footnote).)

[*2] Compare A. Plantinga on essence and essentialism in *A Companion to Metaphysics*, p. 139: ''A special case of a property essential to an object is its *essence* (or essences): an essence *E* of an object *x* is a property it has essentially which is furthermore such that it is not possible that there be something distinct from *x* that has *E*. ... Haecceities are a special kind of individual essence; the HAECCEITY of an object is the property of being that very object. (Clearly an object *x* has essentially the property of being that very object; and clearly nothing else could have had the property of being *x*.)'' This chimes, in part, with what has been said here; but we have also seen that there is *just one* essence, even in Plantinga's sense, of each individual (and not essences, as he says in parenthesis), and that this essence is precisely the individual's haecceity

(therefore, haecceities are not a *special* kind of individual essence, as Plantinga says; they are *precisely* the individual essences). It must, however, be kept in mind that we are here presupposing a *coarse-grained* conception of properties; this presumably leads us to *one* (coarse-grained) property (the essence of x, in Plantinga's sense), whereas the adherent of a *fine-grained* conception is led to several (fine-grained) properties (the essences of x).

CHAPTER III.8

MAXIMALLY CONSISTENT PROPERTIES AND THE PROPERTY SPECIFIC TO AN INDIVIDUAL

(a) According to TPT174 and TPT175, a property-quantum is a property that is non-tautological with respect to one individual z at most, but whose saturation by z is nevertheless *merely* (in consideration of intensional content) a quasi-atomic states of affairs. Are there other property-quanta than the, as it were, trivial property-quantum $\mathbf{t}_{<0>}$?
Yes, as can be seen from the following. We have:

TPT187 **all**z[if 0(z), then QC$_{<0>}$(**conj**$_{<0>}$(**b**(**w**),**i**(z)))].
(''The conjunction of the property-image of the world with the haecceity of an individual is a quasi-complete property.'')

And moreover:

TPT188 **all**z(if 0(z), then **conj**$_{<0>}$(**b**(**w**),**i**(z))≠$\mathbf{k}_{<0>}$).

From TPT187 and TPT188, by ParTPT72, one obtains

TPT189 **all**z[if 0(z), then MK$_{<0>}$(**conj**$_{<0>}$(**b**(**w**),**i**(z)))].
(''The conjunction of the property-image of the world with the haecceity of an individual is a maximally consistent property.'')

From TPT189, by ParTPT78, one obtains

TPT190 **all**z[if 0(z), then EL$_{<0>}$(**neg**$_{<0>}$(**conj**$_{<0>}$(**b**(**w**),**i**(z))))].

Thus, using APT13, ParDPT20, ParTPT32 we get

TPT191 **some**z[0(z) and QA$_{<0>}$(**neg**$_{<0>}$(**conj**$_{<0>}$(**b**(**w**),**i**(z)))) and **neg**$_{<0>}$(**conj**$_{<0>}$(**b**(**w**),**i**(z)))≠$\mathbf{t}_{<0>}$].

TPT91 implies that there is at least one property-quantum that is not the tautological property. We will see shortly that there are at least as many property-quanta differing from $\mathbf{t}_{<0>}$ as there are individuals.

(b) If z is an individual, then **conj**$_{<0>}$(**b**(**w**),**i**(z)) is called ''the property specific to z''. The property specific to z is, as it were, the result of the individual's haecceity or essence meeting the actual world; quite in accordance with this description, we will see in the next chapter that the property specific to *z* is the sum of all properties that *z* (actually) has (or exemplifies).

As their name suggests, the properties *specific* to different individuals are different:

TPT192 **allzallz**′[if $0(z)$ and $0(z')$ and $z \neq z'$, then $\mathbf{conj}_{<0>}(\mathbf{b}(\mathbf{w}),\mathbf{i}(z)) \neq \mathbf{conj}_{<0>}(\mathbf{b}(\mathbf{w}),\mathbf{i}(z'))$].

Thus, in view of TPT189, there is a different maximally consistent property corresponding to each individual as the property specific to it, and therefore there are at least as many maximally consistent properties as there are individuals. Hence there are also at least as many *elementary* properties (or non-tautological property-quanta) as there are individuals (because in virtue of ParTPT77 and ParTPT78 there are precisely as many elementary properties as there are maximally consistent ones).

Is every maximally consistent property the property specific to some individual? If this were the case, then in view of TPT189 and TPT192 we would have a complete one-to-one natural correspondence between maximally consistent properties and individuals, and in fact precisely the correspondence that was assumed in part II, according to which each maximally consistent property corresponded to an individual as the sum (or conjunction) of all the properties that individual has; for the property specific to an individual is no other property than the sum of all its properties. However, we shall see that the present conception of individuals and of their *having* of properties - conceptions rather different from the ones presupposed in part II - preclude that every maximally consistent property is the property specific to some individual (remembering APT9).

CHAPTER III.9

<0>-EXEMPLIFICATION

(a) The concept of exemplification for individuals and their properties - in short: the concept of <0>-exemplification - is introduced by the following definition:

DPT55 t(t′) := O((t,t′)).
(“individual t′ exemplifies (has) property t,” “property t applies to individual t′.”)

According to DPT55, individual *x* exemplifies property *f* if and only if the saturation of *f* by *x* is an obtaining state of affairs. On the basis of DPT55 we have:

TPT193 **all***x***all***f*(if *f*(*x*), then <0>(*f*) and 0(*x*)).

This theorem is specific to <0>-exemplification. The *general* concept of *property-exemplification* does of course truly apply also to other entities than individuals and properties *of individuals* (for example, also to states of affairs and properties *of states of affairs*; remember that “property” is in part III merely short for “property of individuals”). Thus, if “*f*(*x*)” is understood as expressing that general concept, then TPT193 will be falsified.

TPT194 **all***f***all***x*(if *f*(*x*), then not *x*(*f*)).
(“<0>-exemplification is asymmetrical.”)

A corollary of TPT194 is the irreflexivity of <0>-exemplification. Since the categories of individuals and properties of individuals have - as a matter of analytical truth - no common member, there can be no doubt about the truth of this - Platonic *ideas* notwithstanding. It is, however, doubtful whether property-exemplication *in general* - not merely <0>-exemplification - is irreflexive. The property of self-identity, for example, which is a *transcendental* property in the medieval sense (that is, a property that is not bound as a *property of* Ks to a particular category K), is apparently self-exemplifying (whereas the property of the self-identity *of individuals* surely is not). We will come back to these issues in the much more general framework of part IV.

(b) We can prove the following central theorem:

TPT195 **all***z*(if 0(*z*), then [**conj**$_{<0>}$*g*A[*g*](*z*) iff **all***f*(if <0>(*f*) and A[*f*], then *f*(*z*))]).
("An individual exemplifies the conjunction of the A-properties if and only if it exemplifies every A-property.")

Equally important is

TPT196 **all***z***all***f***all***g*{if 0(*z*) and <0>(*f*) and <0>(*g*), then [**neg**$_{<0>}$(*f*)(*z*) iff not *f*(*z*)] and [**conj**$_{<0>}$(*f*,*g*)(*z*) iff *f*(*z*) and *g*(*z*)] and [**disj**$_{<0>}$(*f*,*g*)(*z*) iff *f*(*z*) or *g*(*z*)]}.

Connecting this chapter with the previous one, we can prove a theorem that together with TPT189 implies that the conjunction of all properties of an individual is always a maximally consistent property:

TPT197 **all***z*[if 0(*z*), then **conj**$_{<0>}$*h*[*h*(*z*)]=**conj**$_{<0>}$(**b**(**w**),**i**(*z*))].
("The conjunction of all properties of an individual is the property that is specific to it.")

From TPT197 results

TPT198 **all***z***all***z*′[if 0(*z*) and 0(*z*′), then (if *z*′=*z*, then (**conj**$_{<0>}$*h*[*h*(*z*)],*z*′)=**w** and **conj**$_{<0>}$*h*[*h*(*z*)](*z*′)) and (if *z*′≠*z*, then (**conj**$_{<0>}$*h*[*h*(*z*)],*z*′)=**k** and not **conj**$_{<0>}$*h*[*h*(*z*)](*z*′))],

following (by now) familiar steps of deduction. According to TPT198, the conjunction of all properties of an individual - or in other words: the property specific to it - is exemplified by that individual alone, and its saturation by that individual is, indeed, the world (thus, knowing *all* the properties of *one* individual means knowing the world), while its saturation by every other individual is the contradictory state of affairs. The property specific to an individual - or in other words: the conjunction of all of its properties - is easily seen not to be identical with its haecceity, or in other words: its essence, the conjunction of all of its *essential* properties. For individuals *z*′ that are different from individual *z* the saturations by *z*′ of the property specific to *z* and of the haecceity of *z* (that is, of **i**(*z*)) do, indeed, coincide: for those individuals those saturations are always **k**. However, the saturation of the haecceity of *z* by *z* is **t**, and the saturation by *z* of the property specific to *z* is **w** - and **w**≠**t** by APT9; hence, according to APT19, the haecceity of *z* and the property specific to *z* are non-identical for every individual *z*. (Consequently, every individual has a property that is not an essential property of it; *otherwise* the conjunction of its properties would be identical with the conjunction of its essential properties and, therefore, its haecceity identical with the property specific to it - contradicting the result just reached.)

CHAPTER III.10

THE RELATIONSHIP BETWEEN MAXIMALLY CONSISTENT PROPERTIES, INDIVIDUALS AND POSSIBLE WORLDS

(a) As a consequence of TPT175 one obtains (see the Appendix) its counterpart concerning the other extreme of the Boolean universe of properties:

TPT199 **all***f*(if <0>(*f*) and [**all***z*(if 0(*z*), then **(***f*,*z***)=k**) or **some***z*(if 0(*z*) and **(***f*,*z***)≠k** and QC((*f*,*z*)) and **all***z*′(if 0(*z*′) and *z*′≠*z*, then **(***f*,*z*′**)=k**))], then $QC_{<0>}$(*f*)),

and *mutatis mutandis* from TPT174 its counterpart:

TPT200 **all***f*[if $QC_{<0>}$(*f*), then **all***z*(if 0(*z*), then **(***f*,*z***)=k**) or **some***z*(0(*z*) and **(***f*,*z***)≠k** and QC((*f*,*z*)) and **all***z*′(if 0(*z*′) and *z*′≠*z*, then **(***f*,*z*′**)=k**))].

TPT199 and TPT200 tell us how maximally consistent properties are to be described *in terms of their saturations* (their description *in terms of their intensional parts* is their definition: ParDPT26, building on ParDPT25 and ParDPT24):

TPT201 **all***f*[$MK_{<0>}$(*f*) iff <0>(*f*) and **some***z*(0(*z*) and MK((*f*,*z*)) and **all***z*′(if 0(*z*′) and *z*′≠*z*, then **(***f*,*z*′**)=k**))].
("A maximally consistent property is a property whose saturation by *one* individual is a maximally consistent state of affairs, whose saturations by all other individuals are identical with the contradictory state of affairs.")

(b) At the end of the last but one chapter the question was raised whether every maximally consistent property is the property specific to some individual. This question has to be answered in the negative, as can be seen as follows:

According to TPT121 (which depends on APT9) and DPT29: **some***x***some***y***some***y*′(1(*x*) and MK(*y*) and *x*P*y* and MK(*y*′) and **neg**(*x*)P*y*′); hence *y* and *y*′ have to be different possible worlds (according to DPT26, DPT24); hence there are at least two possible worlds, and hence there is a possible world *y* different from **w**. Consider then $\mathbf{conj}_{<0>}$**(b(***y***),i(***z***))** for some individual *z* (there is such an individual according to APT13); this property can be shown to be like $\mathbf{conj}_{<0>}$**(b(w),i(***z***))** maximally consistent, because MK(*y*), that is (by TPT72): QC(*y*) and *y*≠**k**, and because in the proofs leading up to TPT189 - the proofs of TPT187 and TPT188 - only "QC(**w**)" and "**w**≠**k**" are employed as truths about **w**. But the property is not identical with any property that is specific to some individual *z*′: Suppose: 0(*z*′) and $\mathbf{conj}_{<0>}$**(b(***y***),i(***z***))**=

conj$_{<0>}$(**b**(**w**),**i**(*z*′)); hence *z*=*z*′ (if *z*≠*z*′, then the assumption just made would be contradicted, for then: **(conj**$_{<0>}$**(b(***y***),i(***z***)),***z*′**)=k** and **(conj**$_{<0>}$**(b(w),i(***z*′**)),***z*′**)=w**, and we have **w≠k** by APT7), and hence: *y*=**w** (because *y*=**(conj**$_{<0>}$**(b(***y***),i(***z***)),***z***)** =**(conj**$_{<0>}$**(b(w),i(***z*′**)),***z*′**)=w**). This, however, contradicts the result already obtained about the possible worlds *y* and **w**.

Thus there can be no complete one-to-one correspondence between individuals *z* and maximally consistent properties in virtue of the functional expression "**conj**$_{<0>}$(**b**(**w**),**i**(*z*))" (or - what amounts to the same thing according to TPT197 - in virtue of "**conj**$_{<0>}$*h*[*h*(*z*)]").

(c) But it can be shown that *the pairs of individuals and possible worlds* can be mapped one-to-one onto the maximally consistent properties (without explicitly mentioning such pairs). For this, one employs "**conj**$_{<0>}$(**b**(*y*),**i**(*z*))" - "the property specific to *z in y*" - (instead of "**conj**$_{<0>}$(**b**(**w**),**i**(*z*))"), and one obtains

TPT202 **allzall***y*[if 0(*z*) and MK(*y*), then MK$_{<0>}$(**conj**$_{<0>}$(**b**(*y*),**i**(*z*)))]

(the proof has already been explained in section (b)),

TPT203 **allzall***z*′**all***y***all***y*′[if 0(*z*) and 0(*z*′) and MK(*y*) and MK(*y*′) and (*z*′≠*z* or *y*′≠*y*), then **conj**$_{<0>}$(**b**(*y*),**i**(*z*))≠**conj**$_{<0>}$(**b**(*y*′),**i**(*z*′))]

and *also*

TPT204 **all***f*[if MK$_{<0>}$(*f*), then **some***z***some***y*(0(*z*) and MK(*y*) and *f*= **conj**$_{<0>}$(**b**(*y*),**i**(*z*)))].

The same mapping-result is obtainable by using "**conj**$_{<0>}$*h*[*h*/in *y*/(*z*)]" instead of "**conj**$_{<0>}$(**b**(*y*),**i**(*z*))," the predicate in the first functional expression being defined as follows:

DPT56 t/in t′/(t′′) := (t,t′′)Pt′ and MK(t′).
("(individual) t′′ exemplifies (property) t in (possible world) t′; t′′ has t in t′; t applies in t′to t′′." Note that "t(t′′)" is by DPT55, DPT31 and TPT106 equivalent to "(t,t′′)P**w** and MK(**w**)," and hence by DPT56 to "t/in **w**/(t′′).")

For, as a generalization of TPT197, we have:

TPT205 **allzall***y*[if 0(*z*) and MK(*y*), then **conj**$_{<0>}$*h*[*h*/in *y*/(*z*)]=**conj**$_{<0>}$(**b**(*y*), **i**(*z*))].
("The conjunction of the properties that individual *z* exemplifies in possible world *y* is the property specific to *z* in *y*.")

(The proof of TPT205 is *mutatis mutandis* as that of TPT197.)

For the predicate of <0>-exemplification *relative to possible worlds* (the predicate introduced by DPT56), we have, moreover, the following two further rather significant theorems:

TPT206 **all***f*[<0>(*f*) and $f \neq \mathbf{k}_{<0>}$ iff <0>(*f*) and **somezsomey**(0(*z*) and MK(*y*) and *f*/in *y*/(*z*))].
("The non-contradictory properties are precisely the properties that are exemplified by some individual in some possible world.")

TPT207 **all***f***all***g*(if <0>(*f*) and <0>(*g*), then [$f\mathrm{P}_{<0>}g$ iff **all***y***all***z*(if MK(*y*) and 0(*z*) and *g*/in *y*/(*z*), then *f*/in *y*/(*z*))]).
("Property *f* is an intensional part of property *g* if and only if *f* applies in every possible world *y* to every individual to which *g* applies in *y*.")

On the basis of TPT155 and TPT207 it is easily seen that properties of individuals are identical if and only if they apply to the same individuals in every possible world.

(d) In part II the (possible) individuals were regarded as being precisely mirrored by the maximally consistent properties, each one considered to be essentially correlated with some single individual as the sum of the properties *simpliciter had* by that individual. (Consider what this implied for the notions of <0>-exemplification and intensional parthood in comparison to the results reached in this part: compare the intended readings of DP1+ and TP22+ with those of TPT207, DPT56 and DPT55; see also II.1.(c).) But according to the present conception of individuals it is doubtful whether there is any natural or even describable one-to-one mapping of individuals *onto* maximally consistent properties at all. (Because of TPT202, TPT203 and TPT204 there would certainly be no such mapping if there were several, but finitely many, possible worlds and finitely many individuals.) It can, however, be shown that there is a natural one-to-one mapping of all individuals onto certain *special* maximally consistent properties:

DPT57 MK$\mathbf{w}_{<0>}$(t) := MK$_{<0>}$(t) and **b**(**w**)P$_{<0>}$t.
("t is a **w**-maximally-consistent property.")

According to DPT57, a **w**-maximally-consistent property is a maximally consistent property of which the property-image of the world is an intensional part. Since (provably) **b**(**w**)P$_{<0>}$$\mathbf{conj}_{<0>}$(**b**(**w**),**i**(*z*)) for all individuals *z*, one obtains from TPT189:

TPT208 **all***z*[if 0(*z*), then MK$\mathbf{w}_{<0>}$($\mathbf{conj}_{<0>}$(**b**(**w**),**i**(*z*)))].

In view of TPT208 and TPT192, the desired mapping is secured by

TPT209 **all**f[if MK**w**$_{<0>}$(f), then **some**z(0(z) and f=**conj**$_{<0>}$(**b**(**w**),**i**(z)))].

And on the basis of TPT208, TPT209 and TPT197 we have:

TPT210 **all**f[MK**w**$_{<0>}$(f) iff **some**z(0(z) and f=**conj**$_{<0>}h$[h(z)])].
("The **w**-maximally-consistent properties are precisely the properties which are each the conjunction of the properties (actually) had by some individual.")

On the basis of of TPT202, TPT204 and TPT205, on the other hand, we have:

TPT211 **all**f[MK$_{<0>}$(f) iff **some**z**some**y(0(z) and MK(y) and f=**conj**$_{<0>}h$[h/in y/(z)])].
("The maximally consistent properties are precisely the properties which are each the conjunction of the properties had by some individual in some possible world.")

"MK**w**$_{<0>}$(f)" as defined by DPT57 is equivalent (in virtue of TPT106) to the particularization by "**w**" of the dyadic predicate "MK$y_{<0>}$(f)," which is defined by "MK$_{<0>}$(f) and MK(y) and **b**(y)P$_{<0>}f$". It is easily seen that for this latter predicate the following two statements hold true: **all**f[if MK$_{<0>}$(f), then **some**y(MK(y) and MK$y_{<0>}$(f))] (apply TPT204), **all**y**all**y'**all**f(if MK$y_{<0>}$(f) and MK$y'_{<0>}$(f), then y=y'): assume MK$y_{<0>}$(f) and MK$y'_{<0>}$(f), hence by definition: MK$_{<0>}$(f) and MK(y) and MK(y') and **b**(y)P$_{<0>}f$ and **b**(y')P$_{<0>}f$, hence by TPT201, DPT41: **some**z(0(z) and MK((f,z)) and (**b**(y),z)P(f,z) and (**b**(y'),z)P(f,z)), hence by TPT160: yP(f,z) and y'P(f,z), hence by TPT79: (f,z)=y and (f,z)=y', hence y=y'.

Thus, every maximally consistent property f is a y-maximally-consistent-property with respect to *precisely one* possible world y: *the world of f*. The predicate "x=$^w y$" of world-equality for maximally consistent properties (the latter representing Leibniz-individuals), which was introduced in II.9.(c), can therefore be defined in LPT1 by "**some**k(MK$k_{<0>}$(x) and MK$k_{<0>}$(y))." *The f-world qua property* (see II.9.(c)) for a maximally consistent property (Leibniz-individual) f, **disj**$_{<0>}h$(h=$^w f$), then turns out to be the property-image of the world of f: *the f-world qua state of affairs*.

CHAPTER III.11

INDIVIDUALS AND LEIBNIZ-INDIVIDUALS

(a) The two conceptions of individuals, the "normal" and the Leibnizian, can be illuminated by contrasting their applications in the ontological analysis of an example-sentence: "John did not study biology in 1995, but he could have." The ontological analysis of what is stated by this sentence (choosing the weakest construal of "could") is - according to the presently adopted "normal" conception of individuals - the following:
(1) The property of *studying biology in 1995* is not **1**-exemplified by **1**-individual **1**-John (that is: it is not **1**-exemplified by **1**-John *in the actual world* **w**); but in some possible world *w′* the property of *studying biology in 1995* is **1**-exemplified by **1**-John.
According to the Leibnizian conception adopted in part II, the ontological analysis of the example-sentence looks, however, like this:
(2) The property of *studying biology in 1995* is not **2**-exemplified by **2**-individual **2**-John; but there is a **2**-individual *x* which is a *counterpart* of **2**-John and which **2**-exemplifies the property *of studying biology in 1995*.
Clearly, different conceptions of <0>-exemplification correspond to the two different conceptions, **1** and **2**, of individuals; the conception of properties, however, is the same for both of them. It is also clear that according to conception **1** we are dealing, in the ontological analysis of the example-sentence, with *one* **1**-individual and *two* possible worlds: **1**-John, **w** and *w′*; according to conception **2**, we are simply dealing with *two* individuals: **2**-John and *x*.

(b) The two analyses **(1)** and **(2)** can be shown to be equivalent in the framework of PT1 if we adopt the following definitions of **1**- and **2**-concepts by concepts available in PT1:
(i1) *x* is a **1**-individual := 0(*x*).
(i2) *x* is a **2**-individual := $MK_{<0>}(x)$.[*1]
(ii1a) *x* **1**-exemplifies *f* := *f*(*x*).
(ii1b) *x* **1**-exemplifies *f* in *w* := *f*/in *w*/(*x*).
(ii2) *x* **2**-exemplifies *f* := *x* is a **2**-individual and $fP_{<0>}x$.
(iii) *y* is a possible world := MK(*y*).
(iv) *x* is a counterpart of *y* := *x* and *y* are **2**-individuals and **some***z*(0(*z*) and $\mathbf{i}(z)P_{<0>}x$ and $\mathbf{i}(z)P_{<0>}y$).
(v) 2-John := $\mathbf{conj}_{<0>}h$[*h*/in **w**/(**1**-John)].
Let **f** be the property of studying biology (at some time) in 1995, and let "**1J**" be short for "**1**-John", "**2J**" short for "**2**-John." Then the following statements are the transcriptions of **(1)** and **(2)** into LPT1 (employing - with the

exception of (**v**) - the definitions given above, and eliminating logical redundancies):
(**1′**) 0(**1J**) and not **f**(**1J**) and **some***w′*(MK(*w′*) and **f**/in *w′*/(**1J**)).
(**2′**) MK$_{<0>}$(**2J**) and not **f**P$_{<0>}$**2J** and **some***x*(MK$_{<0>}$(*x*) and **some***z*(0(*z*) and **i**(*z*)P$_{<0>}$**2J** and **i**(*z*)P$_{<0>}$*x*) and **f**P$_{<0>}$*x*).
<u>Assume (1′)</u>.
Because of 0(**1J**) and MK(**w**) (TPT106) by TPT205, TPT202: MK$_{<0>}$(**conj**$_{<0>}$*h*[*h*/in **w**/(**1J**)]), hence by (**v**): MK$_{<0>}$(**2J**).
According to assumption: not **f**(**1J**), hence: not (**f**,**1J**)P**w** (DPT55, DPT31), hence **neg**((**f**,**1J**))P**w** (MK(**w**); 1((**f**,**1J**)) by APT14), hence by the corollary of TPT180 (**neg**$_{<0>}$(**f**),**1J**)P**w**, hence because of MK(**w**) and DPT56: **neg**$_{<0>}$(**f**)/in **w**/(**1J**), hence by ParTPT18 and (**v**): **neg**$_{<0>}$(**f**)P$_{<0>}$**2J**, hence because of MK$_{<0>}$(**2J**): not **f**P$_{<0>}$**2J**.
According to assumption: 0(**1J**) and **some***w′*(MK(*w′*) and **f**/in *w′*/(**1J**)). Hence by TPT205, TPT202: MK$_{<0>}$(**conj**$_{<0>}$*h*[*h*/in *w′*/(**1J**)]). Hence by ParTPT18 **f**P$_{<0>}$**conj**$_{<0>}$*h*[*h*/in *w′*/(**1J**)]. **i**(**1J**)/in *w′*/(**1J**) (TPT171, M(**t**), DPT56), hence by ParTPT18 **i**(**1J**)P$_{<0>}$**conj**$_{<0>}$*h*[*h*/in *w′*/(**1J**)]. **i**(**1J**)/in **w**/(**1J**), hence by ParTPT18 and (**v**): **i**(**1J**)P$_{<0>}$**2J**. Therefore: **some***x*(MK$_{<0>}$(*x*) and **some***z*(0(*z*) and **i**(*z*)P$_{<0>}$**2J** and **i**(*z*)P$_{<0>}$*x*) and **f**P$_{<0>}$*x*).
Thus the deduction of (**2′**) from (**1′**) is complete.
<u>Assume now (2′)</u>.
Because of MK$_{<0>}$(**2J**) by (**v**): MK$_{<0>}$(**conj**$_{<0>}$*h*[*h*/in **w**/(**1J**)]), hence <u>0(**1J**)</u>; for *otherwise* by APT15, APT7, DPT56, etc.: **no***h*[*h*/in **w**/(**1J**)], and hence by ParTPT35 **conj**$_{<0>}$*h*[*h*/in **w**/(**1J**)]=**t**$_{<0>}$, therefore: MK$_{<0>}$(**t**$_{<0>}$) - but, contradicting this, neither **b**(**w**) nor **neg**$_{<0>}$(**b**(**w**)) are intensional parts of **t**$_{<0>}$ (because of APT9, APT7, etc.).
<u>not **f**(**1J**)</u>; for *otherwise* by DPT56, TPT106 **f**/in **w**/(**1J**), hence by ParTPT18 and (**v**): **f**P$_{<0>}$**2J** - contradicting the assumption.
According to assumption: **some***x***some***z*(MK$_{<0>}$(*x*) and 0(*z*) and **i**(*z*)P$_{<0>}$*x* and **i**(*z*)P$_{<0>}$**2J** and **f**P$_{<0>}$*x*). *z*=**1J**; for suppose *z*≠**1J**, then by TPT171 (given 0(**1J**)) (**i**(*z*),**1J**)=**k**, but also (**2J**,**1J**)=**w** - because **2J**=**conj**$_{<0>}$(**b**(**w**),**i**(**1J**)) by (**v**) and TPT205, and (**conj**$_{<0>}$(**b**(**w**),**i**(**1J**)),**1J**)=**w** - and not **k**P**w** (APT7, etc.) - contradicting, according to DPT41, **i**(*z*)P$_{<0>}$**2J**. Therefore: **i**(**1J**)P$_{<0>}$*x*. Consider (*x*,**1J**). Since **f**P$_{<0>}$*x*, by DPT41: (**f**,**1J**)P(*x*,**1J**). Because of MK$_{<0>}$(*x*) by TPT201 **some***z′*[0(*z′*) and MK((*x*,*z′*))]; suppose *z′*≠**1J**, hence by TPT171 (**i**(**1J**),*z′*)=**k**, hence, because of **i**(**1J**)P$_{<0>}$*x*, by DPT41: **k**P(*x*,*z′*), and hence (*x*,*z′*)=**k** - contradicting MK((*x*,*z′*)) in virtue of TPT72. Therefore: MK((*x*,**1J**)) and (**f**,**1J**)P(*x*,**1J**), hence by DPT56: <u>**some***w′*(MK(*w′*) and **f**/in *w′*/(**1J**))</u>.
Thus the deduction of (**1′**) from (**2′**) is complete.

(c) Both approaches to *modal realism*, which are exemplified respectively by the ontological analyses (**1**) and (**2**) of the example-sentence, have been advanced in recent times (the (**2**)-approach most forcefully, but in an interpretation different from the one employed here, by D. Lewis; see the next chapter). We have seen that they are the outcome of two different conceptions of what it is to be an individual, and how, in the framework of PT1, they can be regarded as being interrelated in such a manner so as to enable us to move from one to the other in applying them in the ontological analyses of modal statements. (Note, however, that the two approaches are not on a par in PT1: Leibniz-individuals (or **2**-individuals), in contrast to "normal" individuals (or **1**-individuals), are strictly speaking not *themselves* present in that theory, only their models are, namely the maximally consistent properties.) In general: reading "**lb**(*x*,*y*)" as "the Leibnizian representative of *x* in *y*," and defining it by "**conj**$_{<0>}$*h*[*h*/in *y*/(*x*)]" or, equivalently (*y* being a possible world), by **conj**$_{<0>}$(**b**(*y*),**i**(*x*))," one can prove in PT1 the transcriptions (based on the above definitions **(i1)** - **(iv)**) of the following statements (applying only principles and definitions already given):

(t1) For all **1**-individuals *x* and possible worlds *y*: **lb**(*x*,*y*) is a **2**-individual.
(t2) For all **1**-individuals *x* and *z*, possible worlds *y* and *w*: if *x*≠*z* or *y*≠*w*, then **lb**(*x*,*y*)≠**lb**(*z*,*w*).
(t3) For every **2**-individual *u*: *u*=**lb**(*x*,*y*), for some **1**-individual *x* and possible world *y*.
(t4) For all **1**-individuals *x*, possible worlds *y*, and properties *f*: **lb**(*x*,*y*) **2**-exemplifies *f* iff *x* **1**-exemplifies *f* in *y*.
(t5) For all **1**-individuals *x* and properties *f*: **lb**(*x*,**w**) **2**-exemplifies *f* iff *x* **1**-exemplifies *f*.
(t6) For all *u* and *v*: *u* is a counterpart of *v* iff for some **1**-individual *x* and possible worlds *y* and *y*′: *u*=**lb**(*x*,*y*) and *v*=**lb**(*x*,*y*′).

(The relationships between **1**-individuals and **2**-individuals in the framework of PT1 are further explored in the next two chapters.)

(d) Speaking in PT1 of **2**-individuals side by side with **1**-individuals, interrelating them with the help of the functional term "**lb**(*x*,*y*)," as if they were two *kinds* of individuals ("individuals" taken in a wide sense), must not make one forget that **2**-individuals - as has been pointed out in the previous section - are present in the currently considered theory only vicariously: via their models; strictly speaking, we are talking about maximally consistent properties, not about Leibniz-individuals themselves.

And these models of Leibniz-individuals might, after all, model nothing at all; they might not be, properly speaking, *models*: models *of something*. People who think otherwise may simply be reifying (or individualizing) maximally consistent properties. We can, of course, be sure that there is John and other things like him; but the question is: is John a **2**-individual (if so, then he is identical with **2**-John), or is he a **1**-individual (if so, then he is identical with **1**-John)? If John is a **1**-individual, then it seems absurd to assume that there is, besides John, also the **2**-individual **2**-John (the Leibniz-individual itself, not merely its model). And conversely: if John is a **2**-individual, then it seems absurd to assume that there is also the **1**-individual **1**-John (the "normal" individual itself, not some model of it). The two conceptions of individuals are applied by their proponents to the very same field of entities: John, tables, stars, etc., to the exclusion of other fields of application (in the, perhaps, very extensive realm of individuals in a global sense). Considered thus, the two conceptions cannot well coexist as *exemplified* conceptions, and there can be no interesting theory interrelating them. In PT1, however, one is really merely speaking about the models of Leibniz-individuals, and they *do* have interesting relations to normal individuals, as we have seen.

(e) In a classification of individuals *in a global sense*, one can, however, allot separate places to the instances of both conceptions (no matter whether the places are filled or not). "Individuals" in comment [*3] of chapter II.11 meant *actuality-determined individuals*; in fact, it applied precisely to the Leibnizian representatives of **1**-individuals in the actual world **w**, that is, to *special* Leibniz- or **2**-individuals: those that are representable by **w**-maximally-consistent properties (or, alternatively, by <**1**-individual, possible world>-pairs the second member of which is **w**). Individuals in that sense were exhaustively categorized (in comment [*3] of II.11) according to the presence or absence of temporal and spatial dimensions in them. But, besides the temporal and spatial dimensions, there is another ontological dimension: the *modal dimension* (at least for the modal realist). Individuals (globally conceived) that do not have a modal dimension are *modal continuants* (as they may be called in obvious analogy to continuants *tout court*, that is, temporal continuants): they are not intrinsically, in their very constitution, bound to any possible world; those individuals are the "normal" individuals, the **1**-individuals, the entities the concept "0(*x*)" of LPT1 is applied to. (Note that we can prove in PT1: **all***z*[if 0(*z*), then **all***y*(if MK(*y*), then $<0>_{AC}$(**b**(*y*),*z*))] - "The property image of every world is an accidental property with respect to every individual.")

Leibniz-individuals, on the other hand, are individuals (globally conceived) that *have a modal dimension, but no modal extension*; positioned in *modal space*, they are *point-like*: they are intrinsically located in *one* possible world and in no other. (Note that we can prove in PT1: **all***f*(MK$_{<0>}$(*f*), then **one***y*(MK(*y*) and **b**(*y*)P$_{<0>}$*f*)) - "For every maximally consistent property *f* there is precisely one world such that its property-image is intensionally included in *f*.")

Individuals, in turn, having a modal extension (and hence *a fortiori* a modal dimension) are so-called "trans-world individuals." Such entities are discussed by D. Lewis in *On the Plurality of Worlds*, pp. 210 - 220. He cannot find much use for them in the ontological theory of ordinary things, and in this I am inclined to suppose that he is right; nevertheless, they have a place in a classification of individuals (globally conceived) according to the dimensions (and, collaterally, extensions) present or absent in their constitution.

Now, what is the place of *this table*, for example, in that classification? In my opinion, it is a spatially (in all three spatial dimensions) extended (hence spatially dimensioned) individual without either a temporal or a modal dimension (and hence without either temporal or modal extension). (For further explanations, see [*3] of II.11.) According to Lewis, however, it is a spatially and temporally extended (hence spatially and temporally dimensioned) individual, having in addition a modal dimension, but no modal extension. The two classifications are incompatible. This, however, does not of course preclude the possibility that there are two internally consistent equally powerful ontological theories one of which applies the first classification, the other the second, not only to this table, but also to all the ordinary material things around us - without us ever being able to say which one of the two theories is correct, or even which of them is to be preferred. It seems that the first classification is the more natural; but perhaps that means only that it is the more familiar. Perhaps it is also in some way simpler than the second; but the second may counter this by being simpler in other ways. Surely there can be no decisions in these theoretical matters via single decisive arguments. At best, only the comparison of entire ontological theories, which relate to a range of other matters as well (mainly in the ontology of possibility and time), can tell us how we can best conceive ontologically of *this table*.

COMMENTS

[*1] Leibniz-individuals could also be modelled by pairs of "normal" individuals (the entities fulfilling "0(x)" as interpreted in LPT1) and possible worlds (the entities fulfilling "MK(x)" as interpreted in LPT1): such pairs are, as we have seen, one-to-one correlated with the *natural* models of Leibniz-individuals: the maximally consistent properties - each of the pairs $<x,w>$ determining "its own" maximally consistent property as the sum of the properties had by individual x in world w, each maximally consistent property being the sum of the properties had by some individual x in some possible world w. But introducing such pairs as objects of explicit reference means leaving the framework of the language LPT1, and hence going beyond theory PT1.

CHAPTER III.12

COUNTERPART THEORY

(a) Lewis' *Counterpart Theory* can be modelled in PT1 (or ''reduced'' to PT1). We assume that the Lewis-individuals are the Leibniz-individuals, and therefore we represent the former like the latter by maximally consistent properties (which correspond one-to-one, as we have seen, to pairs of ''normal'' individuals and possible worlds) and use the functional term ''**lb**(*z*,*w*)'' (''the Leibnizian representative of *z* in *w*''), defined as in III.11.(c). We make use of some of the principles (**t1**) - (**t6**) in III.11.(c), which, transcribed into PT1 (according to (**i1**) - (**iv**) in III.11.(b)), are theorems of PT1. The primitive predicates of Counterpart Theory (to be defined in PT1) and its postulates (to be proved in PT1) can be found in Lewis' ''Counterpart Theory and Quantified Modal Logic'' on p. 27 of *Philosophical Papers*, vol. I. These, then, are the definitions of the primitives of Counterpart Theory:

DL1 *x* is a possible world := MK(*x*).
(Lewis has: *Wx*.)
DL2 *x* is in (possible world) *y* := $MK_{<0>}$(*x*) and MK(*y*) and **some***z*[0(*z*) and *x*=**lb**(*z*,*y*)].
(Lewis has: *Ixy*.)
DL3 *x* is actual := *x* is in **w**.
(Lewis has: *Ax*.)
DL4 *x* is a counterpart of *y* := **some***z*[0(*z*) and **some***w*(MK(*w*) and *x*=**lb**(*z*,*w*)) and **some***w′*(MK(*w′*) and *y*=**lb**(*z*,*w′*))].
(Lewis has: *Cxy*.)

(DL4 is equivalent to definition (**iv**) in III.11.(b); this is what (**t6**) in III.11.(c) amounts to.) The postulates of Counterpart Theory together with the proofs that, on the basis of DL1 - DL4, turn them into theorems of PT1 can now be given as follows:

PL1 **all***x***all***y*(if *x* is in *y*, then *y* is a possible world).
(Lewis' informal reading of *his* formal postulate is: ''Nothing is in anything except a world.'')
Proof: By DL2, DL1.

PL2 **all***x***all***y***all***z*(if *x* is in *y* and *x* is in *z*, then *y*=*z*).
(Lewis has: ''Nothing is in two worlds.'')

Proof: Assume: *x* is in *y* and *x* is in *z*, hence by DL2: $\text{MK}_{<0>}$(*x*) and MK(*y*) and MK(*z*) and **some***u*(0(*u*) and *x*=**lb**(*u*,*y*)) and **some***u*′(0(*u*′) and *x*=**lb**(*u*′,*z*)), hence **lb**(*u*,*y*)=**lb**(*u*′,*z*), hence by **(t2)** in III.11.(c): *u*=*u*′ and *y*=*z*.

PL3 **all***x***all***y*(if *x* is a counterpart of *y*, then **some***z*(*x* is in *z*)).
(Lewis has: "Whatever is a counterpart is in a world.")
Proof: Assume *x* is a counterpart of *y*, hence by DL4: **some***u*[0(*u*) and **some***z*(MK(*z*) and *x*=**lb**(*u*,*z*))]; hence by **(t1)** in III.11.(c): **some***z*[$\text{MK}_{<0>}$(*x*) MK(*z*) and **some***u*(0(*u*) and *x*=**lb**(*u*,*z*))], hence by DL2 **some***z*(*x* is in *z*).

PL4 **all***x***all***y*(if *x* is a counterpart of *y*, then **some***z*(*y* is in *z*)).
(Lewis has: "Whatever has a counterpart is in a world.")
Proof: Assume *x* is a counterpart of *y*, hence by DL4: **some***u*[0(*u*) and **some***z*(MK(*z*) and *y*=**lb**(*u*,*z*))], and further as in the proof of PL3.

PL5 **all***x***all***y***all***z*(if *x* is in *y* and *z* is in *y* and *x* is a counterpart of *z*, then *x*=*z*).
(Lewis has: "Nothing is a counterpart of anything else in its world.")
Proof: Assume the antecedent of PL5, hence by DL2, DL4: $\text{MK}_{<0>}$(*x*) and MK(*y*) and **some***u*[0(*u*) and *x*=**lb**(*u*,*y*)] and $\text{MK}_{<0>}$(*z*) and **some***u*′[0(*u*′) and *z*=**lb**(*u*′,*y*)] and **some***v*[0(*v*) and **some***w*(MK(*w*) and *x*=**lb**(*v*,*w*)) and **some***w*′(MK(*w*′) and *z*=**lb**(*v*,*w*′))]. Hence **lb**(*u*,*y*)=**lb**(*v*,*w*), hence by **(t2)**: *y*=*w*. Hence also: **lb**(*u*′,*y*)=**lb**(*v*,*w*′), hence by **(t2)**: *y*=*w*′. Therefore: *w*=*w*′, and hence *x*=*z* (because *x*=**lb**(*v*,*w*) and *z*=**lb**(*v*,*w*′)).

PL6 **all***x***all***y*(if *x* is in *y*, then *x* is a counterpart of *x*).
(Lewis has: "Anything in a world is a counterpart of itself.")
Proof: Assume *x* is in *y*, hence by DL2: $\text{MK}_{<0>}$(*x*) and MK(*y*) and **some***u*(0(*u*) and *x*=**lb**(*u*,*y*)), hence logically: **some***u*[0(*u*) and **some***w*(MK(*w*) and *x*=**lb**(*u*,*w*)) and **some***w*′(MK(*w*′) and *x*=**lb**(*u*,*w*′))], hence by DL4: *x* is a counterpart of *x*.

PL7 **some***x*(*x* is a possible world and **all***y*(*y* is in *x* iff *y* is actual)).
(Lewis has: "Some world contains all and only actual things.")
Proof: According to TPT106: MK(**w**), hence by DL1: **w** is a possible world; **all***y*(*y* is in **w** iff *y* is actual) simply by DL3.

PL8 **some***x*(*x* is actual).
(Lewis has: "Something is actual.")
Proof: According to APT13: **some***u*0(*u*). According to TPT106: MK(**w**). Hence by **(t1)** $\text{MK}_{<0>}$(**lb**(*z*,**w**)). Therefore by DL2: **lb**(*z*,**w**) is in **w**, and hence by DL3: **lb**(*z*,**w**) is actual.

(b) Thus, all the postulates of Lewis' Counterpart Theory can be deductively incorporated into PT1. However, there are principles that can be proved in PT1 for "*x* is a counterpart of *y*" which Lewis does not assume, considering them to be implausible on this or that particular interpretation of the counterpart-predicate *as a similarity-relation* (which is Lewis' preferred general reading of the counter-part predicate). It is, for example, immediately seen from DL4 that the counterpart-predicate as here defined is *symmetric*. Moreover, it is *transitive*: Assume: x is a counterpart of y, y a counterpart of z; then according to DL4: $\mathbf{some}u[0(u)$ and $\mathbf{some}w(\mathrm{MK}(w)$ and $x{=}\mathbf{lb}(u,w))$ and $\mathbf{some}w'(\mathrm{MK}(w')$ and $y{=}\mathbf{lb}(u,w'))]$ and $\mathbf{some}v[0(v)$ and $\mathbf{some}m(\mathrm{MK}(m)$ and $y{=}\mathbf{lb}(v,m))$ and $\mathbf{some}m'(\mathrm{MK}(m')$ and $z{=}\mathbf{lb}(v,m'))]$, hence $\mathbf{lb}(u,w'){=}\mathbf{lb}(v,m)$, hence by **(t2)** $u{=}v$, hence $z{=}\mathbf{lb}(u,m')$, and therefore by DL4: x is a counterpart of z. Hence the counterpart-concept turns out to be *an equivalence-relation* - directly for maximally consistent properties, indirectly for the inviduals that are, if anything, represented by them: Leibniz-individuals.

Both symmetry and transitivity and other formal principles that can here be proved for the counterpart-predicate are rejected by Lewis in "Counterpart Theory and Quantified Modal Logic" (*Philosophical Papers* I, p. 28f). (However, in *On the Plurality of Worlds*, p. 214, he assumes symmetry; he also expresses doubts about PL5.) He anticipates the idea on which the present interpretation of the "x is a counterpart of y" is based (since the Leibnizian representative of z in w - for $0(z)$ and $\mathrm{MK}(w)$ - could just as well be taken to be <z,w> instead of $\mathbf{conj}_{<0>}h[h/\mathrm{in}\ w/(z)]$) when he says in "Counterpart Theory and Quantified Modal Logic" (*Philosophical Papers* I, p. 28): "Carnap, Kanger, Hintikka, Kripke, Montague, and others have proposed interpretations of quantified modal logic on which one thing is allowed to be in several worlds. A reader of this persuasion might suspect that he and I differ only verbally: that what I call a thing in a world is just what he would call a <thing,world> pair, and that what he calls the same thing in several worlds is just what I would call a class of mutual counterparts. But beware. Our difference is not just verbal, for I enjoy a generality he cannot match. The counterpart relation will not, in general, be an equivalence relation. So it will not hold just between those of his <thing,world> pairs with the same first term, no matter how he may choose to identify things between worlds."[*1]

(c) The counterpart-predicate will certainly not in general be an equivalence-relation if it is interpreted as it is invariably interpreted by Lewis, namely as some similarity-relation. But why, indeed, should I-in-w' (another world) be similar to me-in-actuality (that is, for Lewis, *to me*), or rather, more similar to me-in-actuality than any other Leibniz-individual of w'? (*Ibid.* p. 28: "Your counterparts resemble you closely in content and context in important respects. They resemble you more closely than do the other things in their worlds.") In the possible world w' the counterpart of I-in-actuality might well be, say, a heinous mad scientist striving for world-domination - and *not* the fairly reasonable human being that - in character and looks just like me - leads in w' *precisely* the same life I lead here. (Plantinga is doubtless correct when he considers the sentence "Socrates and Xenophon could have been such that the latter should have resembled Socrates as he was in the actual world more than the former'' to be true (*The Nature of Necessity*, p. 110). Lewis' Counterpart Theory, however, - with the counterpart-concept being a similarity-relation - falsifies that sentence about Socrates - and therefore that theory is itself falsified.)

That in another world w' the counterpart of me-in-actuality does not need to be more similar to me-in-actuality than other things in w', or even similar to me-in-actuality at all, does not mean that I-in-w' might just be anything: a stone, an electron, a teapot, or what not. What I can or cannot be - I as a ``normal'' individual, I as an entity to which ``$0(x)$'' (as interpreted in LPT1) applies - depends on which properties f are essential with respect to me (see DPT51). If f is a property that is not essential with respect to me, if *neither* $(f,$U.M$)=$**t** *nor* $(f,$U.M$)=$**k**, then in some possible world w I am f (f/in w/(U.M.)), in some other world w'' I am not f. Hence some of the Leibniz-individuals corresponding to me - the counterparts of I-in-actuality - have f, and some do not. If f is a tautological property with respect to me (an essential property of me), if $(f,$U.M$)=$**t** (see DPT54), then I am f in every possible world, and hence all the counterparts of I-in-actuality have f. If, however, f is a contradictory property with respect to me, if $(f,$U.M$)=$**k** (see DPT53), then I am f in no world, and hence none of the counterparts of me-in-actuality has f. Therefore: since, for example, *being sometimes a teapot* is surely a contradictory property with respect to me, U.M.-in-w', like all other counterparts of me-in-actuality, does not have that property.

(d) Lewis is very well aware of the initial vagueness of the counterpart-concept if considered to be a similarity-relation (for him, however, that vagueness is a virtue): ``Like any relation of comparative overall similarity, it is subject to a great deal of indeterminacy (1) as to which respects of similarity and difference are to count at all, (2) as to the relative weights of the respects that do count, (3) as to the minimum standard of similarity that is required, and (4) as to the extent to which we eliminate candidates that are similar enough when they are beaten by competitors with stronger claims.'' (*Ibid.*, p. 42.) And further: ``the vagueness of the counterpart relation ... may be subject to pragmatic pressures, and differently resolved in different contexts.'' Clearly, Lewis' counterpart-concept can hardly be considered to be an *objective* ontological concept at all; it has, if made precise, at least as much to do with *us* as with the objective nature of Leibniz-individuals. But whereas we may not always know what can and what cannot be, and certainly have often rather differing opinions in these matters, what can and cannot be surely does not depend *conceptually* on us. The counterpart-predicate as defined by DL4 is, in contrast, a precise and totally objective ontological concept, and the counterpart-relation that is induced by it among Leibniz-individuals - via their pairwise ``symbioses'' with maximally consistent properties - is just as objective and precise, and, I submit, the best concept ``x is a counterpart of y'' could be explicated by. Lewis, however, is quite unable to see it that way, because the specification of that concept (compare DL4, or (**iv**) in III.11.(b)) depends on the concept of **1**-individuals (individuals in the sense of "0(z)"), and because the adequacy of the specification depends on there being such individuals. Lewis, however, believes only in Leibniz-individuals (or **2**-individuals), in any case: only in Leibniz-individuals as *basic* individuals; **1**-individuals are available to him, if at all, only as the outcome of constructions which already presuppose a counterpart-relation - a counterpart-relation specified without referring to **1**-individuals. And what could it then be but some relation of similarity?

COMMENTS

[*1] How may an ontologist like Carnap, Kanger, Hintikka, etc. who believes in things "being in several possible worlds" (if things are for him *modal continuants*, this is a somewhat *misleading* description of his position; indeed, Lewis seems primarily to have in mind *modally extended* individuals as the things favored by those other ontologists, not modal continuants) *choose* to identify things between worlds? If we are speaking of modal continuants, then, for conceptual reasons, there is nothing to choose, there is only one way this can be done: Suppose the following situation: $0(x)$ and $0(z)$; x is being considered with respect to possible world w, z is being considered with respect to possible world w'; w and w' are different worlds, and x does not exemplify the same properties in w as z exemplifies in w'. Under what sufficient and necessary condition involving w and w' are x and z nonetheless identical? They are identical if and only if the essence of x applies in w' to z, or the essence of z applies in w to x.

It is a *different* question how, using which *pragmatic* criteria, we may find out whether the criterion just stated is fulfilled by x and z (w and w'), and in this matter the criterion is not very helpful; for in III.7.(d) we have seen that the essence of an individual is precisely the property of being identical with that individual. Luckily we are never confronted *in experience* with a situation like the one described, i.e. a *trans-world* situation that requires of us to find out whether x and z are identical. (We are, however, confronted in experience - including *experience as remembered* - with situations structurally completely analogous to the one described, namely situations in which we are called upon to distinguish and identify persons and objects with respect to different *times*.)

CHAPTER III.13

ACTUAL EXISTENCE FOR INDIVIDUALS AND LEIBNIZ-INDIVIDUALS

(a) In what follows I shall return to my previous practice of saying simply "individuals" when (and only when) "normal" individuals, **1**-individuals, the entities "0(*x*)" applies to are meant. Whether we have been talking in this book about individuals or about Leibniz-individuals, in both cases *possible* entities were intended. Of these some are actually existent, others *are not*. (There is no inherent absurdity in this thesis, but the thesis will not be formally adopted - at least not for *individuals*; it is a different matter for Leibniz-individuals; see comment [*3].)[*1]

With respect to individuals and Leibniz-individuals, the concept of actual existence is synonymous to the concept of *real subsistence*. The *property* of real subsistence *for individuals* is designated by "**sr**," which is meant to be a rigid designator. We will have to consider the relationship of **sr** to **rs**, which is the property of real subsistence *for Leibniz-individuals* (see II.4. and II.8), but which is nevertheless, like **sr**, a property *of individuals*: an entity satisfying the type-predicate "<0>(*x*)."

sr is not a time-relative property. (*None* of the properties we have been considering in this book is time-relative, that is: such that it applies to an individual at some time, and not at another. If temporal specifications that abolish relativity to time are missing in the designation of a property, the reader is asked to assume them.) Thus, Socrates, though not alive today, (atemporally) exemplifies **sr**, just as George Bush and Julius Caesar do.

Hence the following is a true statement, and is assumed as an axiom:

APT20 **somezsomez**′(**sr**(*z*) and **sr**(*z*′) and $z \neq z'$).

APT20 would in fact be analytically true (since what it says would be conceptually necessary) if there were at least *two* individuals *z* and *z*′ with respect to which **sr** is a tautological property; for then we have as conceptual necessities besides $z \neq z'$: (**sr**,*z*)=**t**, (**sr**,*z*′)=**t**, and hence as conceptual necessities: O((**sr**,*z*)), O((**sr**,*z*′)), and hence by DPT55 also: **sr**(*z*), **sr**(*z*′). But is there *any* individual with respect to which **sr** is a tautological property, hence *of which* **sr** is an essential property? We leave the question unanswered.[*2]

Two definitions follow:

DPT58 0_{AE}(t) := **sr(t)**.

("t is an actually existent individual.")

DPT59 $<0>_{AE}$(t) := **some***z*(0_{AE}(*z*) and t(*z*)).
("t is an actually existent property.")

According to DPT58, an actually existent individual is an individual that exemplifies the property of real subsistence; according to DPT59, an actually existent property is a property exemplified by an actually existent individual. Hence: being an actually existent property definitionally implies being an exemplified property; and conversely, real subsistence even is, as a matter of definition, an actually existent property if it is exemplified. But the latter need not be true for all properties: some properties might be exemplified, though not actually existent.

(b) As instances of the principles (**t4**) and (**t5**) in III.11.(c) (which are provable in PT1, as also are (**t1**), (**t2**), (**t3**) and (**t6**)), we obtain:

(**t4**′) For all [**1**-] individuals *z* [0(*z*)], possible worlds *y* [MK(*y*)]: **lb**(*z*,*y*) **2**-exemplifies **sr** iff *z* **1**-exemplifies **sr** in *y* [**sr**/in *y*/(*z*)].
(**t5**′) For all [**1**-] individuals *z*: **lb**(*z*,**w**) **2**-exemplifies **sr** iff *z* **1**-exemplifies **sr** [**sr**(*z*)].

What, then, is the relationship of "**sr**" to the predicate "PA(*x*)" and the term "**rs**" in part II? The principles that govern the use of the latter two expressions and the translations of those principles into LPT1 are as follows:

AP7+ **all***x*(if PA(*x*), then MK(*x*)) : APT7+ **all***f*(if PA(*f*), then $MK_{<0>}$(*f*)).
DP7+ **rs** := **disj***y*PA(*y*) : DPT7+ **rs** :=$\mathbf{disj}_{<0>}$*f*PA(*f*).
TP31+ **all***x*(**rs**<*x*> iff PA(*x*)) : TPT31+.
AP8+ **some***x***some***y*(PA(*x*) and PA(*y*) and *x*≠*y*) : APT8+.

Leibniz-individuals (or **2**-individuals) are again represented by maximally consistent properties, with **lb**(*z*,*y*) := $\mathbf{conj}_{<0>}$*h*[*h*/in *y*/(*z*)]. And moreover: *f*<*x*>:= *x* **2**-exemplifies *f* := $MK_{<0>}$(*x*) and *f*$P_{<0>}$*x* (see (**i2**), (**ii2**) in III.11.(b), and compare DP1+).
"PA(*x*)" - representing the concept of actual existence for Leibniz-individuals (compare chapter II.3) - can be defined in terms of "0_{AE}(*z*)" - expressing the concept of actual existence for individuals - in such a manner that the extensions of the two predicates can be mapped one-to-one onto each other:

(D) PA(t) := **some***z*(0_{AE}(*z*) and t=**lb**(*z*,**w**)).[*3]

According to (D), an actually existent Leibniz-individual is the Leibnizian representative *in the actual world* of an *actually existent individual*. It is easily seen that APT7+ and APT8+ are deducible on the basis of (D) (apply (**t1**), (**t2**), APT20 and the definitions), and thus TPT31+ is a theorem of PT1 (since the proof of TP31+ can be completely reconstructed in PT1). We have moreover: **all***f*(if PA(*f*), then **sr**<*f*>): assume PA(*f*), hence by (D) and DPT58 **some***z*(**sr**(*z*) and *f*=**lb**(*z*,**w**)), hence in view of TPT193 by (**t5**′): *f* **2**-exemplifies **sr**, hence **sr**<*f*>.

But the converse of the underlined general implication cannot be proved. On the contrary, we can prove its negation, "**some***f*(**sr**<*f*> and not PA(*f*))," if we make the plausible assumption that "some actually existent individual could have been actually existent even without possessing some property which it (actually) exemplifies": **some***z***some***g*[**sr**(*z*) and *g*(*z*) and **some***y*(MK(*y*) and **sr**/in *y*/(*z*) and not *g*/in *y*/(*z*))], hence by (**t4**′) **some***z***some***g***some***y*(**sr**(*z*) and *g*(*z*) and MK(*y*) and **sr**<**lb**(*z*,*y*)> and not *g*<**lb**(*z*,*y*)>). Assume now: PA(**lb**(*z*,*y*)), hence by (D) **some***z*′(0_{AE}(*z*′) and **lb**(*z*,*y*)=**lb**(*z*′,**w**)), hence by (**t2**) (since MK(**w**), MK(*y*), 0(*z*), 0(*z*′)): *y*=**w**. Therefore: not *g*<**lb**(*z*,**w**)>, hence by (**t5**′): not *g*(*z*) - contradicting the assumption. Therefore: not PA(**lb**(*z*,*y*)). Thus (from the two underlined results): **some***f*(**sr**<*f*> and not PA(*f*)).

And thus the property **sr** is seen to be not identical with the property **rs**, (=$\mathbf{disj}_{<0>}$*f*PA(*f*)), for which, after all, we have TPT31+.

(c) Note that "**rs**" is a *non-rigid* designator which is definitionally depending on the synthetic predicate "PA(*f*)," whereas "**sr**" is a *rigid* designator on which the synthetic predicate "0_{AE}(*x*)" definitionally depends. This is the reason why it can be uncertain, with respect to certain properties *f*, whether $\mathbf{conj}_{<0>}$(**rs**,*f*) is different from or identical with $\mathbf{k}_{<0>}$ (as was pointed out in II.8.(c)), and why, on the contrary, there is never any uncertainty at all about the identity or non-identity of $\mathbf{conj}_{<0>}$(**sr**,*f*) with $\mathbf{k}_{<0>}$. For example, **sr** is undoubtedly consistent with **d** ("**d**" being a rigid designator for the property of being divine): we have $\mathbf{conj}_{<0>}$(**sr**,**d**)≠$\mathbf{k}_{<0>}$, and hence: not $\mathbf{k}_{<0>}P_{<0>}\mathbf{conj}_{<0>}$(**sr**,**d**), hence by ParTPT91 **some***y*($MK_{<0>}$(*y*) and $\mathbf{conj}_{<0>}$(**sr**,**d**)$P_{<0>}$*y*) - "Some Leibniz-individual **2**-exemplifies the property of real subistence *for individuals* together with divinity." But this is a result the atheist can very well accept; for - according to (**t3**), (**t1**), (**t4**′) - this amounts precisely to: **some***x***some***y*′(0(*x*) and MK(*y*′) and $\mathbf{conj}_{<0>}$(**sr**,**d**)/in *y*′/(*x*)) - i.e. "Some individual **1**-exemplifies in some possible world the property of real subsistence *for individuals* together with divinity."

Things are not so harmless if we proceed on the supposition that not only **sr**, but also **rs** (real subsistence *for Leibniz-indivduals*) is consistent with **d**: We get **some***y*(**rs**<*y*> and **d**<*y*>), and hence by TPT31+ **some***y*(PA(*y*) and **d**<*y*>) - "There is an actually existent Leibniz-individual that **2**-exemplifies **d**." This is surprising enough (compare chapters II.4 and II.8); but now we can even go further: for by (D) it follows that **some***y*(**some***z*(0_{AE}(*z*) and *y*=**lb**(*z*,**w**)) and **d**<*y*>), hence **lb**(*z*,**w**) **2**-exemplifies **d**, hence by (**t5**′): **some***z*(0_{AE}(*z*) and **d**(*z*)) - "There is an actually existent individual that **1**-exemplifies divinity," or in other words (according to DPT59): "Being divine is an actually existent property."

I surmise that the perennial lure of the Ontological Argument is in part also due to the confusion of **sr** (a property to which we can refer directly and rigidly) with **rs** (a property to which we can only refer indirectly and non-rigidly: via the predicate "PA(*x*)," whose extension, and hence the reference of "**rs**" := "**disj**$_{<0>}$*f*PA(*f*)," varies according to factual circumstance). The immediate effect of this confusion is the confusion of the uncontroversial premise **conj**$_{<0>}$**(sr,d)≠k**$_{<0>}$ with the problematic premise **conj**$_{<0>}$**(rs,d)≠k**$_{<0>}$. The first leads to a metaphysically harmless conclusion, the second does not.

(d) How **rs** and **sr** are related to each other is stated in the following provable principles:

(A) **all***z*(**rs**(*z*) iff **sr**(*z*)).
("**rs** and **sr** are **1**-exemplified by the same individuals.")
Proof: (i) Assume **rs**(*z*), hence by DPT7+ **disj**$_{<0>}$*f*PA(*f*)(*z*), hence by ParTPT63 **conj**$_{<0>}$*f***all***g*(if <0>(*g*) and PA(*g*), then *f*P$_{<0>}$*g*)(*z*), hence by TPT195 ((0(*z*) from **rs**(*z*) by TPT193): **(1) all***f*(<0>(*f*) and **all***g*(if <0>(*g*) and PA(*g*), then *f*P$_{<0>}$*g*), then *f*(*z*)). And we also have **(2)** <0>(**sr**) (by APT20, TPT193), and **(3) all***g*(if <0>(*g*) and PA(*g*), then **sr**P$_{<0>}$*g*): assume PA(*g*), hence by (D) **some***z*′(0$_{AE}$(*z*′) and *g*=**lb**(*z*′,**w**)), hence by DPT58, DPT55, DPT31, TPT106: **some***z*′((**sr**,*z*′)**Pw** and MK(**w**) and *g*=**conj**$_{<0>}$*h*[*h*/in **w**/(*z*′)]), hence by DPT56 **some***z*′(**sr**/in **w**/(*z*′) and *g*=**conj**$_{<0>}$*h*[*h*/in **w**/(*z*′)]), hence by ParTPT18 **sr**P$_{<0>}$*g*. By **(1)**, **(2)** and **(3)**: **sr**(*z*).
(ii) Assume **sr**(*z*).
Assume: <0>(*f*) and **all***g*(if <0>(*g*) and PA(*g*), then *f*P$_{<0>}$*g*). It is to be deduced: *f*(*z*). Because of **sr**(*z*), according to DPT58, (D), **(t1)** (0(*z*), MK(**w**)): MK$_{<0>}$(**lb**(*z*,**w**)) and PA(**lb**(*z*,**w**)), and hence by the assumptions: *f*P$_{<0>}$**lb**(*z*,**w**); hence also **lb**(*z*,**w**) **2**-exemplifies *f*, hence by **(t4)** *f*/in **w**/(*z*), hence by DPT56, DPT55: *f*(*z*).
We have now deduced: **all***f*(if <0>(*f*) and **all***g*(if <0>(*g*) and PA(*g*), then *f*P$_{<0>}$*g*), then *f*(*z*)); hence by TPT195 **conj**$_{<0>}$*f***all***g*(if <0>(*g*) and PA(*g*), then *f*P$_{<0>}$*g*)(*z*), hence by ParTPT63 **disj**$_{<0>}$*f*PA(*f*)(*z*), hence by DPT7+: **rs**(*z*).

On the other hand, "**all***x*(**rs**<*x*> iff **sr**<*x*>)" - "**rs** and **sr** are **2**-exemplified by the same Leibniz-individuals" - cannot be proved; one can only prove "**all***x*(if **rs**<*x*>, then **sr**<*x*>)." In section (b) we have already shown "**all***x*(if PA(*x*), then **sr**<*x*>)," from which "**all***x*(if **rs**<*x*>, then **sr**<*x*>)" results by TPT31+; and, making a plausible additional assumption, which is certainly consistent with PT1, we have *refuted* in section (b) "**all***x*(if **sr**<*x*>, then PA(*x*))," hence by TPT31+ also "**all***x*(if **sr**<*x*>, then **rs**<*x*>)."
It can, however, be shown:

(B) **all***x*(**rs**<*x*> iff **some***z*(0(*z*) and *x*=**lb**(*z*,**w**)) and **sr**<*x*>).

(‘‘A Leibniz-individual **2**-exemplifies **rs** if and only if it **2**-exemplifies **sr** *and* is the Leibnizian representative in the actual world of some individual.’’)
Proof: (i) **all***x*(if **rs**<*x*>, then PA(*x*) and **sr**<*x*>) by TPT31+ and the theorem **all***x*(if PA(*x*), then **sr**<*x*>); hence by (D), DPT58, TPT193: **all***x*(if **rs**<*x*>, then **some***z*(0(*z*) and *x*=**lb**(*z*,**w**)) and **sr**<*x*>).
(ii) Assume: **some***z*(0(*z*) and *x*=**lb**(*z*,**w**)) and **sr**<*x*>, hence *x* **2**-exemplifies **sr**, hence (because of *x*=**lb**(*z*,**w**)) **lb**(*z*,**w**) **2**-exemplifies **sr**, hence by **(t5′)** **sr(***z***)**, hence by DPT58 0_{AE}(*z*). Therefore, according to (D): PA(*x*), hence by TPT31+: **rs**<*x*>.

Moreover:

(C1) **all***z*[if 0(*z*), then (**rs**<**lb**(*z*,**w**)> iff **sr(***z***)**)].
(‘‘An individual **1**-exemplifies **sr** if and only if its Leibnizian representative in the actual world **2**-exemplifies **rs**.’’)
Proof: (i) Assume 0(*z*), **rs**<**lb**(*z*,**w**)>; hence by (B) **sr**<**lb**(*z*,**w**)>, hence by **(t5′)** **sr(***z***)**.
(ii) Assume **sr(***z***)**, hence by (A) **rs(***z***)**, hence by **(t5′)** **rs**<**lb**(*z*,**w**)>.

(C2) **all***z*[if 0(*z*), then (**sr**<**lb**(*z*,**w**)> iff **rs(***z***)**)].
Proof: (i) Assume 0(*z*), **sr**<**lb**(*z*,**w**)>; hence by **(t5′)** **sr(***z***)**, hence by (A) **rs(***z***)**.
(ii) Assume **rs(***z***)**, hence by (A) **sr(***z***)**, hence by **(t5′)** **sr**<**lb**(*z*,**w**)>.

As an easy corollary of (C1) and (C2) via (A) we have:

(C3) **all***z*[if 0(*z*), then (**rs**<**lb**(*z*,**w**)> iff **sr**<**lb**(*z*,**w**)>)]
(‘‘The Leibnizian representative in the actual world of an individual *z* **2**-exemplifies **rs** if and only if it **2**-exemplifies **sr**.’’ ‘‘(D)’’ is already the designation of the definition in section (b).)

One may wonder what is the rationale of these somewhat puzzling results that interrelate **rs** and **sr** while distinguishing them. Why can they nevertheless be so easily confused? The explanation is this: **rs**=$\mathbf{conj}_{<0>}$(**sr**,**b**(**w**)) - real subsistence for Leibniz-individuals is the conjunction of real subsistence for individuals with the property-image of the world.[*4] **rs** is, as it were, **sr** *bound to the actual world*; it is not **sr** itself. But since one normally does not take much notice of properties which are property-images of states of affairs (and even less if the latter are possible worlds), one may easily overlook what makes the difference between **sr** itself and **sr** *bound to the actual world*.

(e) The Leibnizian representative of an individual *z* in a possible world *y that is different from* **w** is not an actually existent Leibniz-individual; thus all the counterparts of **2**-John (see III.11.(a)) that, in contrast to **2**-John, study biology at some time in 1995 are not actually existent (or really subsistent) Leibniz-individuals:

(E) **all**x(if **some**z**some**y(0(z) and MK(y) and y≠**w** and x=**lb**(z,y)), then not PA(x)).

Proof: Assume **some**z**some**y(0(z) and MK(y) and y≠**w** and x=**lb**(z,y)). Hence not **some**z'(0(z') and x=**lb**(z',**w**)), for otherwise by **(t2)** y=**w**. Hence by (B) not **rs**<x>, hence by TPT31+: not PA(x).

The Leibnizian representative in **w** of a *not actually existent individual* z is not an actually existent Leibniz-individual:

(F) **all**x(if **some**z(0(z) and not 0_{AE}(z) and x=**lb**(z,**w**)), then not PA(x)).

Proof: Assume **some**z(0(z) and not 0_{AE}(z) and x=**lb**(z,**w**)), hence by DPT58: not **sr**(z), hence by (C1): not **rs**<**lb**(z,**w**)>, hence: not **rs**<x>, and hence by TPT31+: not PA(x).

From (E) and (F) and APT7+ one easily gets *the converse* of the following also provable principle:

(G) **all**x[if $MK_{<0>}$(x) and not **some**z**some**y(0(z) and MK(y) and y≠**w** and x=**lb**(z,y)) and not **some**z(0(z) and not 0_{AE}(z) and x=**lb**(z,**w**)), then PA(x)].

("A Leibniz-individual that is neither the Leibnizian representative in a world different from **w** of some individual nor the Leibnizian representative in **w** of some not actually existent individual is an actually existent Leibniz-individual.")

Proof: Assume $MK_{<0>}$(x), hence by **(t3)** **some**z**some**y(0(z) and MK(y) and x=**lb**(z,y)). Assume also: not **some**z**some**y(0(z) and MK(y) and y≠**w** and x=**lb**(z,y)). Hence: **some**z(0(z) and x=**lb**(z,**w**)). Assume also: not **some**z(0(z) and not 0_{AE}(z) and x=**lb**(z,**w**)). Hence: **some**z(0_{AE}(z) and x=**lb**(z,**w**)), hence by (D) PA(x).

COMMENTS

[*1] In *The Nature of Necessity* Plantinga argues strenuously and at great length (pp. 121 - 152) against purported good reason for there being possible but *nonexistent* individuals (or ‘‘objects’’). With respect to states of affairs, he makes a conceptual distinction between ‘‘nonexistent’’ and ‘‘unactual’’: ‘‘So a possible but unactual state of affairs is not a *nonexistent* state of affairs; it exists just as serenely as your most solidly actual state of affairs.’’ (*Ibid.*, p. 132). Strangely, Plantinga fails to make the analogous distinction *for individuals*. Rather he assumes from the start, without offering one single reason for this, that for individuals ‘‘nonexistent’’ and ‘‘unactual’’ mean the same (this assumption is apparent on p. 121, and also on p. 136 and p. 153). Therefore for Plantinga the status of the proposition that there are unactual individuals is equal to the status of the proposition that there are nonexistent individuals - because for him they are the very same proposition. In contrast, he upholds that there are unactual (or non-obtaining) states of affairs, while denying that there are nonexistent ones.

Surely it is more reasonable to distinguish ‘‘nonexistent’’ also with respect to individuals *conceptually* from ‘‘unactual’’ (or ‘‘not actually existent’’). Then one can firmly believe that there are no nonexistent individuals (after all, in a perfectly legitimate sense of ‘‘exist,’’ *everything exists*), while allowing that there may be possible but unactual individuals. One may, indeed, come to believe that there are no unactual individuals; but this is not simply an analytical consequence of the belief that there are no nonexistent individuals.

[*2] APT20 implies APT13 (because of TPT193). Nevertheless, we retain the latter as an axiom because for many results only APT13 is necessary.

APT20 need not remain the only axiom characterizing **sr**. Another, very plausible one, would be ‘‘**all***z*(if 0(*z*), then **some***y*[**sr**/in *y*/(*z*)])’’ - ‘‘Every individual **1**-exemplifies **sr** in some possible world (*is an individual actually existent in some possible world*).’’ (Generalizing DPT58, one might define: 0_{AE}(t,t′) := **sr**/in t′/(t).) Some plausibility can also be accorded to ‘‘**all***y*(if MK(*y*), then **some***x*[**sr**/in *y*/(*x*)])’’ - ‘‘In every possible world at least one individual is actually existent.’’ *Actualists* with respect to individuals would accept ‘‘**all***x*(if 0(*x*), then **sr**(*x*))’’ as an axiom, which - in contrast to the entirely implausible ‘‘**all***x***all***y*(if MK(*y*) and 0(*x*), then **sr**/in *y*/(*x*))’’ - is not without credentials. But being a *possibilist* with respect to individuals, I would prefer to postulate ‘‘**some***x*(0(*x*) and not **sr**(*x*)),’’ and certainly we can feel entirely safe about ‘‘**some***y*(MK(*y*) and **some***x*(0(*x*) and not **sr**/in *y*/(*x*)))’’ - ‘‘In some possible world some individual is not actually existent’’ (but not about ‘‘**all***y*(if MK(*y*), then **some***x*(0(*x*) and not **sr**/in *y*/(*x*)))’’).

[*3] That is (according to DPT58): **some**z(**sr**(z) and t=**lb**(z,**w**)). Given this, it is immediately clear how to generalize the concept of actual existence for Leibniz-individuals:

(D′) PA(t,t′) := **some**z(**sr**/in t′/(z) and t=**lb**(z,t′)).
("t is a Leibniz-individual actually existent in world t′.")

On the basis of (D) and (D′), "**all**x(PA(x) iff PA(x,**w**))" is easily proved.

For D. Lewis (and already for Leibniz), "(Leibniz-individual) x is in **w** (the actual world)" and "(Leibniz-individual) x is actual" are co-extensional (and, indeed, synonymous). This result can be obtained in the framework of PT1 by choosing as definiens of "PA(x)" "**some**z(0(z) and x=**lb**(z,**w**))" instead of "**some**z(0_{AE}(z) and x=**lb**(z,**w**))"; the former is provably equivalent to "x is in **w**" as defined by DL2 in III.12.(a). Making "x is actual" for Leibniz-individuals synonymous with "x is in **w**" can, however, hardly recommend itself to an ontologist who is in the fortunate situation Lewis is not in: to have at his or her disposal independently of the concept of Leibniz-individual (which Lewis can indeed have independently of the concept of individual) not only the concept of *individual*, but in addition, distinct from the latter, the concept of *actually existent individual*.

If, however, we retain (D) in its present form, still using "x is in **w**" as defined by DL2, then "**all**x(PA(x) iff x is in **w**)" can be derived as a theorem *if* we assume as an axiom "**all**z(if 0(z), then 0_{AE}(z))" - *actualism for individuals*; and conversely (given (D)): "**all**z(if 0(z), then 0_{AE}(z))" can be derived as a theorem *if* we assume "**all**x(PA(x) iff x is in **w**)" as an axiom: Assume 0(z), hence **lb**(z,**w**) is in **w** (DL2, MK(**w**), **(t1)**), hence by the axiomatically assumed thesis: PA(**lb**(z,**w**)), hence by (D) **some**z'(0_{AE}(z') and **lb**(z,**w**)=**lb**(z',**w**)), hence by **(t2)** z=z', hence 0_{AE}(z).

Actualism *for individuals* is not an absurd position; but actualism *for Leibniz-individuals* certainly is: even if all individuals (and there are individuals according to APT20) are actually existent, the Leibniz-individuals corresponding to them in possible worlds *other than* **w** are not actually existent. Thus, actualism for Leibniz-individuals can only be maintained if there is no possible world that is different from **w** - contradicting what is provable with the help of APT9.

"**all**z(if 0(z), then 0_{AE}(z))" *may* be synthetically true (it certainly does not appear to be analytically true); but this is not sufficient to allow us to assume it as a further axiom. And thus the possibility remains open of distinguishing, even extensionally, between "(Leibniz-individual) x is in **w**" and "(Leibniz-individual) x is actual." Even given Lewis' own interpretation of the counterpart-predicate, this possibility serves to ward off an objection that Lewis raises against the principle: **all**x**all**y[if Wx and Wy and $x \neq y$, then **all**z(if Izx, then **some**k(Iky and Czk))]: "It would not have been plausible to postulate that, for any two worlds, anything in one was a counterpart of something in the other. Suppose there is something x_5 in world w_5 - say, Batman -which does not much resemble anything actual. If so, x_5 is not a counterpart of anything in the actual world.'' (''Counterpart Theory and Quantified Modal Logic,'' *Philosophical Papers* I, p. 29.) But Batman (as a Leibniz-individual) not being similar to any *actually existent Leibniz-individual* does not imply *for us* that he is not similar to any *Leibniz-individual in the actual world*, since, for us, there may be Leibniz-individuals in the actual world that are not actual. Thus, even on Lewis' own interpretation of the counterpart-predicate, Lewis' otherwordly Batman has not been shown for us to be the counterpart of nothing in the actual world.

[*4] To obtain this result, start from (B) and apply ParTPT66 and TPT155. Consider then: **disj**$_{<0>}$*x*[**rs**<*x*>]=**rs**; **disj**$_{<0>}$*x***some***z*(0(*z*) and *x*=**lb**(*z*,**w**))=**b**(**w**); **disj**$_{<0>}$*x*[**sr**<*x*>]=**sr**. And moreover: **disj**$_{<0>}$*x*(**some***z*(0(*z*) and *x*=**lb**(*z*,**w**)) and **sr**<*x*>)=**conj**$_{<0>}$(**disj**$_{<0>}$*x***some***z*(0(*z*) and *x*=**lb**(*z*,**w**)),**disj**$_{<0>}$*x*[**sr**<*x*>]), since the predicates in the disjunction-terms imply ''MK$_{<0>}$(*x*).'' This is a theorem:
if **all***x*(if A[*x*] or B[*x*], then MK$_{<0>}$(*x*)), then **disj**$_{<0>}$*x*(A[*x*] and B[*x*])= **conj**$_{<0>}$(**disj**$_{<0>}$*x*A[*x*],**disj**$_{<0>}$*x*B[*x*]).

Instead of DPT7+ we could have chosen ''**rs**'' := ''**conj**$_{<0>}$(**sr**,**b**(**w**))'' as definition of ''**rs**.'' But note that this would not have eliminated the non-rigidity of ''**rs**'' because ''**w**'' - although syntactically simple and a primitive term - is a non-rigid designator.

CHAPTER III.14

THE MODELLING OF SETS AND EXTENSIONS

(a) There is a relationship between properties and (*simpliciter*) essential properties that enables the latter to serve as sets (of individuals). First of all:

TPT212 **all***f*[if $<0>(f)$, then **some***g*($<0>_{ES}(g)$ and **all***z*(*g*(*z*) iff *f*(*z*)))].
("For every property *f* there is an essential property that applies to exactly the same individuals *f* applies to.")

TPT212 immediately brings to mind the set-theoretical *axiom of comprehension*. (Note that in the proof of TPT212 - see the Appendix - the assumption "$<0>(f)$" is not employed; thus the condition "$<0>(f)$" in TPT212 can be omitted.)

Furthermore we can prove a theorem which will bring to mind the set-theoretical *axiom of extensionality*:

TPT213 **all***g***all***g′*(if $<0>_{ES}(g)$ and $<0>_{ES}(g')$ and **all***z*(*g*(*z*) iff *g′*(*z*)), then *g*=*g′*).
("Essential properties that apply to exactly the same individuals are identical.")

From TPT212 (without the omittable condition "$<0>(f)$") and TPT213 one easily obtains

TPT214 **all***f***one***g*($<0>_{ES}(g)$ and **all***z*(*g*(*z*) iff *f*(*z*))).
("For every *f* there is *precisely one* essential property that applies to exactly the same individuals *f* applies to.")

Therefore, we are justified in defining:

DPT60 **rep**(t) := **the***g*($<0>_{ES}(g)$ and **all***z*(*g*(*z*) iff t(*z*))).
("the essential representative of t.")

Consider now that "*g*(*z*)" in DPT60, TPT212 - TPT214 can be equivalently replaced by "$<0>_{TL}(g,z)$" (and in TPT213, in addition, "*g′*(*z*)" by "$<0>_{TL}(g',z)$") because (as is easily proved) an essential property applies to *z* if and only if it is a tautological property with respect to *z* (or essential property *of z*; compare III.7.(c)). Then "$<0>_{ES}(f)$", "$<0>_{ES}(f)$ and $<0>_{TL}(f,x)$" and "**rep**(*f*)" have the *primary readings* already indicated; but given the also provable variants of TPT212 - TPT214 and DPT60 that have just been pointed out, they have *secondary readings* as well: "$<0>_{ES}(f)$": "*f* is a set of individuals"; "$<0>_{ES}(f)$ and $<0>_{TL}(f,x)$": "individual *x* is element of the set of individuals *f*'; "**rep(***f***)**": "the set of the individuals that are *f*' (or "the extension of *f*'). Thus the variant of TPT212 can also be read as the axiom of comprehension for sets of individuals (if A[*z*] is a predicate that applies only if *z* is an individual, then "*f*(*z*)" in TPT212 can be replaced by A[*z*]; see the next chapter); the variant of TPT213 can also be read as the axiom of extensionality for those sets, and it is apparent that the theory of *sets of individuals* is *formally* reducible to PT1. (Note that the basic idea of this reduction is closely related to that given in §23 of Carnap's *Meaning and Necessity*.) Moreover, being an intensionalist, I suggest that sets of individuals can be identified in all ontological seriousness with (*simpliciter*) essential properties (of individuals): such sets *are* such properties; they are not only modelled by them.

The theory of sets of individuals is, of course, only a small part of general set theory. Most sets have sets as elements; but no set that has sets as elements is a set of individuals as individuals are here conceived; thus it cannot be identified with a property of individuals. How general set theory - even axiomatic set theory - is reducible to general intensional ontology will be shown in part IV. But the central idea of the reduction is clear even now: sets are essential properties (not only of individuals).[*1]

(b) TPT212 and TPT213 can be strengthened. Going beyond TPT213, we can prove:

TPT215 **all***g***all***g*′(if <0>$_{ES}$(*g*) and <0>$_{ES}$(*g*′) and **some***y*(MK(*y*) and **all***z*[*g*/in *y*/(*z*) iff *g*′/in *y*/(*z*)]), then *g*=*g*′).
("Essential properties that apply in some possible world to the same individuals are identical.")

Surpassing TPT212, we have

TPT216 **all***f***all***y*[if <0>(*f*) and MK(*y*), then **some***g*(<0>$_{ES}$(*g*) and **all***z*[*g*/in *y*/(*z*) iff *f*/in *y*/(*z*)])].
("For every property *f* and every possible world *y* there is an essential property that applies in *y* to the same individuals *f* applies to in *y*.")

From TPT216 (without the omittable condition "<0>(*f*)") and TPT215 we obtain

TPT217 **all***f***all***y*[if MK(*y*), then **one***g*(<0>$_{ES}$(*g*) and **all***z*[*g*/in *y*/(*z*) iff *f*/in *y*/(*z*)])].

Thus, generalizing DPT60, we can define:

DPT61 **rep**(t,t′) := **the***g*(<0>$_{ES}$(*g*) and **all***z*[*g*/in t′/(*z*) iff t/in t′/(*z*)]).
("the essential representative of t in t′.")

The essential representative of *f* in a world *y* can be regarded to be the set of individuals to which *f* applies in *y*. Therefore, "the extension of *f in y*" is a secondary reading of "**rep**(*f*,*y*)" (a reading besides the primary one that is indicated below DPT61).

It is a widely accepted tenet of intensional ontology that (coarse-grained) properties are identical if they have the same extensions in every possible world. And indeed we can prove (employing TPT207):

TPT218 **all***f***all***g*(if <0>(*f*) and <0>(*g*) and **all***y*(if MK(*y*), then **rep**(*f*,*y*)= **rep**(*g*,*y*)), then *f*=*g*).

"**all***f***all***g*(if <0>(*f*) and <0>(*g*) and **rep**(*f*)=**rep**(*g*), then *f*=*g*)," on the other hand, is a false statement. If it were true, then the clearly false statement "**all***f***all***g*(if <0>(*f*) and <0>(*g*) and **all***z*(*f*(*z*) iff *g*(*z*)), then *f*=*g*)" would have to be true also. Both statements are, however, true (and provable) if they are restricted to essential properties.

COMMENTS

[*1] In "Towards a Generalized Mereology of Lesniewski" J. Słupecki proposes on p. 152f to treat sets as properties that are the conjunctions of all properties that are equal in extension to a given property. In other words (speaking of properties and sets *of individuals*):

ST$_S$(*f*) := **some***g*[<0>(*g*) and *f*=**conj**$_{<0>}$*h***all***x*(*h*(*x*) iff *g*(*x*))].

For Słupecki-sets, we have as analogue to TPT212:

all*f*[if <0>(*f*), then **some***g*(ST$_S$(*g*) and **all***z*′(*g*(*z*′) iff *f*(*z*′)))].

And as analogue to TPT213:

all*g***all***g*′(ST$_S$(*g*) and ST$_S$(*g*′) and **all***z*′(*g*(*z*′) iff *g*′(*z*′)), then *g*=*g*′).

Proof of both theorems:
(1) Assume <0>(*f*), and consider **conj**$_{<0>}$*h***all***z*(*h*(*z*) iff *f*(*z*)). Obviously ST$_S$(**conj**$_{<0>}$*h***all***z*(*h*(*z*) iff *f*(*z*))); and moreover: **all***z*′(**conj**$_{<0>}$*h***all***z*(*h*(*z*) iff *f*(*z*))(*z*′) iff *f*(*z*′)): **(i)** Assume *f*(*z*′), hence: 0(*z*′) and **all***h*(<0>(*h*) and **all***z*(*h*(*z*) iff *f*(*z*)), then *h*(*z*′)); hence by TPT195: **conj**$_{<0>}$*h***all***z*(*h*(*z*) iff *f*(*z*))(*z*′). **(ii)** Assume **conj**$_{<0>}$*h***all***z*(*h*(*z*) iff *f*(*z*))(*z*′), hence 0(*z*′) (by TPT193). Because of <0>(*f*) and **all***z*(*f*(*z*) iff *f*(*z*)) by ParTPT18: *f*P$_{<0>}$**conj**$_{<0>}$*h***all***z*(*h*(*z*) iff *f*(*z*)). Therefore from the assumption (by DPT55, DPT31, DPT41): *f*(*z*′).
(2) Assume: ST$_S$(*g*) and ST$_S$(*g*′) and **all***z*′(*g*(*z*′) iff *g*′(*z*′)); hence **some***f*[<0>(*f*) and *g*=**conj**$_{<0>}$*h***all***z*(*h*(*z*) iff *f*(*z*))] and **some***k*[<0>(*k*) and *g*′=**conj**$_{<0>}$*h***all***z*(*h*(*z*) iff *k*(*z*))]. As has been shown in (1): **all***z*′(**conj**$_{<0>}$*h***all***z*(*h*(*z*) iff *f*(*z*))(*z*′) iff *f*(*z*′)). Hence **all***z*′(*g*(*z*′) iff *f*(*z*′)), hence by assumption: **all***z*′(*g*′(*z*′) iff *f*(*z*′)), hence by ParTPT18 (we also have <0>(*g*′)), *g*′P$_{<0>}$**conj**$_{<0>}$*h***all***z*(*h*(*z*) iff *f*(*z*)), and hence *g*′P$_{<0>}$*g*. Analogously one obtains *g*P$_{<0>}$*g*′. Therefore by TPT155: *g*=*g*′.

There is, therefore, more than one way of modelling sets of individuals by properties. It is also possible to define

ST$_T$(*f*) := **some***g*[<0>(*g*) and *f*=**disj**$_{<0>}$*h***all***z*(*h*(*z*) iff *g*(*z*))].

Again the (appropriate) analogues of TPT212 and TPT213 can be proved. (Consider **disj**$_{<0>}$*h*(*h*(*z*) iff *f*(*z*)), and use the theorem for property-disjunction that corresponds to TPT195: **all***z*(if 0(*z*), then [**disj**$_{<0>}$*h*A[*h*](*z*) iff **some***h*(<0>(*h*) and A[*h*] and *h*(*z*))]).)

A particularly elegant way of obtaining set-like properties is the following:

ST_L(*f*) := **some***g*(<0>(*g*) and *f*=**conj**$_{<0>}$(*g*,**b**(**w**)).

According to this definition, sets are the **w**-limitations of properties. (In the previous chapter **rs** was seen to be the **w**-limitation of **sr**.) It is easily seen that the **w**-limitation of a property applies to the same individuals to which the property applies. And **w**-limitations of properties *h* and *h′* are identical if they apply to the same individuals: Assume **all***z*[**conj**$_{<0>}$(*h*,**b**(**w**))(*z*) iff **conj**$_{<0>}$(*h′*, **b**(**w**))(*z*)], assume 0(*z*). Now: [(**conj**$_{<0>}$(*h*,**b**(**w**)),*z*)=**w** or (**conj**$_{<0>}$(*h*, **b**(**w**)),*z*) =**k**], according to (*h*,*z*)**Pw** or not (*h*,*z*)**Pw** (consider the corollary of TPT178, and TPT160, TPT106). And the same can be shown to hold for *h′*. Hence by the first assumption: (**conj**$_{<0>}$(*h*,**b**(**w**)),*z*)=**w** and (**conj**$_{<0>}$(*h′*,**b**(**w**)), *z*)=**w**, or (**conj**$_{<0>}$(*h*,**b**(**w**)),*z*)=**k** and (**conj**$_{<0>}$(*h′*,**b**(**w**)),*z*)=**k** (considering the definitions, APT7, APT2, etc.), and hence: (**conj**$_{<0>}$(*h*,**b**(**w**)),*z*)=(**conj**$_{<0>}$(*h′*, **b**(**w**)),*z*). The rest is clear in the light of APT19.

But in fact this last method of modelling sets by properties is equivalent to the Słupecki-method, for we have: **all***g*[if <0>(*g*), then **conj**$_{<0>}$*h***all***x*(*h*(*x*) iff *g*(*x*)) =**conj**$_{<0>}$(*g*,**b**(**w**))]. **conj**$_{<0>}$(*g*,**b**(**w**)) is the *strongest* property (with respect to intensional content) that is co-extensional with the given property *g*, that is, it is the property whose saturation by an individual *z* is **w** in case *g*(*z*), and **k** in case not *g*(*z*); it is easily seen to be identical with **conj**$_{<0>}$*h***all***x*(*h*(*x*) iff *g*(*x*)). Consider also the *intensionally weakest* property that is co-extensional with *g*, that is, the property whose saturation by an individual *z* is **t** in case *g*(*z*), and **neg**(**w**) in case not *g*(*z*), in other words: **disj**$_{<0>}$(*g*,**b**(**neg**(**w**))). This latter property, in turn, can be seen to be identical with **disj**$_{<0>}$*h***all***z*(*h*(*z*) iff *g*(*z*)). Therefore, the Słupecki- or conjunction-method of representing sets of individuals by properties of individuals takes such sets to be **w**,**k**-properties (that is: properties of which all saturations are either **w** or **k**); the disjunction-method, in contrast, takes them to be **t**,**neg**(**w**)-properties. We have neither followed the one nor the other method, but have taken sets to be **t**,**k**-properties, in other words: essential properties.

CHAPTER III.15

PREDICATES AND PROPERTIES

(a) To each predicate A[*z*] of LPT1 which applies to *z* only if *z* is an individual there corresponds an essential property **ex*o*conj*y***(not A[*o*] and *y*=**k**) in the following manner:

TPT219 if **all***z*(if A[*z*], then 0(*z*)), then **all***z*(**ex*o*conj*y***(not A[*o*] and *y*=**k**)(*z*) iff A[*z*]).

TPT219 is only a special case of a stronger theorem whose proof is analogous to that of TPT219:

TPT220 if **all***z*(if A[*z*], then 0(*z*)), then **all***x*(if MK(*x*), then **all***z*[**ex*o*conj*y***(not A[*o*] and *y*=**k**)/in *x*/(*z*) iff A[*z*]]).

TPT212 can now be recognized to be a corollary of TPT219, since "**all*f*all***z*(if *f*(*z*), then 0(*z*))" is a theorem, as is also

TPT221 $<0>_{ES}$(**ex*o*conj*y***(not A[*o*] and *y*=**k**)).

TPT216, moreover, can be seen to be a corollary of TPT220, since "**all*f*all*y*all***z*(if *f*/in *y*/(*z*), then 0(*z*))" is a theorem (and hence we have according to TPT220: **all***x*(if MK(*x*), then **all***z*[**ex*o*conj*y***(not *f*/in *y*′/(*o*) and *y*=**k**)/in *x*/(*z*) iff *f*/in *y*′/(*z*)]); therefore if MK(*y*′): **all***z*[**ex*o*conj*y***(not *f*/in *y*′/(*o*) and *y*=**k**)/in *y*′/(*z*) iff *f*/in *y*′/(*z*)] (and note that the latter is trivially the case if not MK(*y*′), hence the condition "MK(*y*)" in TPT216 is not needed).

In view of TPT219, TPT221 and TPT213 and what has been said in section (a) of the previous chapter, "**ex*o*conj*y***(not A[*o*] and *y*=**k**)" for predicates of individuals A[*z*] can be read as "the set of individuals *z* such that A[*z*]."

(b) If A[*z*] is a monadic predicate of LPT1 that applies exclusively to individuals, which property of individuals is *intended* by it? (In other words: which intension is expressed by it?) One cannot generally assume that it is **ex*o*conj*y***(not A[*o*] and *y*=**k**) - certainly not if one considers *non-ontological predicates* F(*x*), F′(*x*), ... of LPT1, which are taken to be synonymous to non-ontological predicates of ordinary language, as for example "*x* is a bachelor at t_0."[*1]

"0_{AE}(*x*)" even seems to be an ontological predicate which is yet such that **ex*o*conj*y***(not 0_{AE}(*o*) and *y*=**k**) is not the property intended by it. According to DPT58 it is synonymous with "**sr**(*x*)." Is, therefore, **sr** the property intended by "$0_{AE}(x)$"? If this were the case, then, according to DPT55 and DPT31, **sr** is also the property intended by "**(sr**,*x***)Pw**." But which property is then intended by "**(sr**,*x***)Pm**" (where "**m**" is the name of a possible world that is not **w**)? Clearly, either **sr** is intended by both or by neither of the two predicates. Since the former does not appear to be a reasonable position, we must conclude that the latter is the case.

So which property is intended by "$0_{AE}(x)$" (that is, by "**(sr**,*x***)Pw**")? Can there be a better candidate than **sr**? Indeed, there is a better one: **rs**, that is, $\mathbf{disj}_{<0>}$*f*PA(*f*), that is (according to definition (D) in III.13.(b)): $\mathbf{disj}_{<0>}$*f***some***z*($0_{AE}(z)$ and *f*=**lb**(*z*,**w**)). (Note that according to (A) in III.13.(d) and DPT58 we can prove: **all***z*($0_{AE}(z)$ iff **rs**(*z*)).) Fittingly, if **rs** is intended by "**(sr**,*x***)Pw**," the property that is intended by "**(sr**,*x***)Pm**" is $\mathbf{disj}_{<0>}$*f***some***z*(**(sr**,*z***)Pm** and *f*=**lb**(*z*,**m**)).

Which properties are intended by monadic predicates A[*z*] that are restricted to individuals cannot be said *in a general way* as long as we stick to the present means of expression of LPT1. But if we added to it the functor "**that**" which applied to sentence-forms yields singular terms for states of affairs, then we *could* say in a general way which properties such predicates intend: The property intended by A[*z*] is **exo***o***that**A[*o*]; sometimes **exo***o***that**A[*o*] is **exo***o***conj***y*(not A[*o*] and *y*=**k**), but not always. "**that**," however, creates intensional contexts; it is, therefore, a functor reserved for the maximal system treated in part IV.

COMMENTS

[*1] We can also prove: O(**conj***y*(not A and *y*=**k**)) iff A. Thus for each sentence A of LPT1 there is a state of affairs that obtains if and only if the sentence is true: for every true sentence that state of affairs is **t**, for every false sentence it is **k**. In view of this, we can very well say that **t** and **k** are the two *truth values*, and that **conj***y*(not A and *y*=**k**) is *the truth value of* A. However we cannot say in general that **conj***y*(not A and *y*=**k**) is the state of affairs *intended* by sentence A. This is certainly not the case if A is a non-ontological sentence (a sentence synonymous to a non-ontological sentence of ordinary language, as for example "George is a bachelor at t_0").

CHAPTER III.16

MODALIZERS AND QUANTIFIERS

(a) LPT1 is a rather elementary language, but its expressive powers (on the basis of PT1) are not at all exhausted by the definitions given so far. In this chapter I will briefly consider two groups of functional expressions that are definable in LPT1, the first generating *modal properties* from properties (hence they are called "modalizers"), the second generating *quantificational states of affairs* from properties (hence they are called "quantifiers").

Modal properties of individuals are, for example, the properties: being necessarily a bachelor at t_0, being possibly a bachelor at t_0, and so on.[*1] How does one obtain a modal property corresponding to a given property *f*? If we already have the property of being necessarily non-*f*, then the property of being possibly *f* is already determined, since we can define:

DPT63 $\mathbf{pos}_{<0>}(\mathrm{t}) := \mathbf{neg}_{<0>}(\mathbf{nec}_{<0>}(\mathbf{neg}_{<0>}(\mathrm{t})))$.
("being possibly t.")

According to DPT63 (DPT62 is reserved for "$\mathbf{nec}_{<0>}$"), being possibly *f* is the negation of the property of being necessarily non-*f*. But what kind of property is being necessarily *f*? Given a certain conception of "necessary," the following statement is certainly true:

all*f*all*z*[if <0>(*f*) and 0(*z*), then [$\mathbf{nec}_{<0>}$(*f*)(*z*) iff **all*y***(if MK(*y*), then *f*/in *y*/(*z*))]].

Or more generally:

TPT222 **all*f*all*z*all*x***[if <0>(*f*) and 0(*z*) and MK(*x*), then [$\mathbf{nec}_{<0>}$(*f*)/in *x*/(*z*) iff **all*y***(if MK(*y*), then *f*/in *y*/(*z*))]].
("The property of being necessarily *f* is exemplified by individual *z* in world *x* if and only if property *f* is exemplified by *z* in all possible worlds.")

Because of DPT56, TPT86, TPT90, TPT36, etc.: "**all*y***(if MK(*y*), then *f*/in *y*/(*z*))" in TPT222 simply amounts to "(*f*,*z*)=**t**." And hence we get from TPT222 (which remains to be proved):

TPT223 **all*f*all*z*all*x***(if <0>(*f*) and 0(*z*) and MK(*x*), then [$\mathbf{nec}_{<0>}$(*f*)/in *x*/(*z*) iff (*f*,*z*)=**t**]).

Now, let *f* be any arbitrary property, *z* an individual:
(i) Assume ($\mathbf{nec}_{<0>}$(*f*),*z*)=**t**, hence $\mathbf{nec}_{<0>}$(*f*)/in **w**/(*z*), hence by TPT223 (*f*,*z*)=**t**.

(ii) Assume **(***f*,*z***)=t**, hence by TPT223 **all***x*(if MK(*x*), then **nec**$_{<0>}$(*f*)/in *x*/(*z*)), hence according to the argumentation leading from TPT222 to TPT223: **(nec**$_{<0>}$(*f*),*z***)=t**.
(iii) **(nec**$_{<0>}$(*f*),*z***)=k**, hence not **nec**$_{<0>}$(*f*)/in **w**/(*z*), hence by TPT223 **(***f*,*z***)≠t**.
(iv) (*f*,*z*)**≠t**, hence by TPT223 **all***x*(if MK(*x*), then not **nec**$_{<0>}$(*f*)/in *x*/(*z*)), hence by DPT56 **all***x*(if MK(*x*), then not **(nec**$_{<0>}$(*f*),*z***)P***x*), hence by TPT91 **kP(nec**$_{<0>}$(*f*),*z***)**, hence **(nec**$_{<0>}$(*f*),*z***)=k**.
Thus we have proved:

TPT224 **all***f***all***z*[if <0>(*f*) and 0(*z*), then ((**nec**$_{<0>}$(*f*),*z***)=t** iff **(***f*,*z***)=t**) and ((**nec**$_{<0>}$(*f*),*z***)=k** iff **(***f*,*z***)≠t**)].

And it is immediately seen from this (according to DPT49, the necessitation of a property being certainly a property) that the necessitation of every property *f* is an essential property. (The essential properties are moreover, as can also be seen from TPT224, precisely those properties that are identical with their necessitations.)
All these results are made good by the following definition, which is suggested by TPT224:

DPT62 **nec**$_{<0>}$(t) := **ex***o***conj***y*((t,*o*)**≠t** and *y*=**k**).[*2]
("being necessarily t.")

According to DPT62 and what has been said in the previous chapter, being necessarily *f* is the *set* of all individuals *z* such that the saturation of *f* by *z* is the tautological state of affairs, or in other words: it is the set of all individuals *z* such that *f* is an essential property *of z*. On the basis of this definition TPT222 can be proved in PT1 (see the Appendix), and this vindicates TPT223 and TPT224 as well.
Given **pos**$_{<0>}$ and **nec**$_{<0>}$, more complex modalizers are easily defined, for example "being contingently *f*": **conj**$_{<0>}$(*f*,**neg**$_{<0>}$(**nec**$_{<0>}$(*f*))).

(b) The definitions of "quantifiers" in PT1 are straightforward. Here is the *universal* quantifier:

DPT64 ∀(t) := **conj***x***some***z*(0(*z*) and *x*P(t,*z*)).
("the universal state of affairs for t.")

According to DPT64, the universal state of affairs for a property *f* is the conjunction of all states of affairs each of which is an intensional part of some saturation of *f* by an individual. Alternatively, but equivalently, one could have defined: ∀(t) := **conj***x***some***z*(0(*z*) and *x*=(t,*z*)). The two definitions are equivalent (remember TPT146), since we have:

TPT225 **conj***x***some***z*(A[*z*] and *x*Pp[*z*])=**conj***x***some***z*(A[*z*] and 1(p[*z*]) and *x*=p[*z*]).

For the universal quantifier we have the following law of truth:

TPT226 **all***f*[V(∀(*f*)) iff **all***z*(if 0(*z*), then *f*(*z*))].
("The universal state of affairs for *f* is true if and only if *f* is exemplified by all individuals." Note that "*f*(*z*)" in TPT226 can be replaced by the definitionally equivalent expression "V((*f*,*z*))."")

The proof of TPT226 (which, incidentally, contains the proof of "**all***f***all***z*(if 0(*z*), then (*f*,*z*)P∀(*f*))") can be generalized, since only the truth of "1(**w**)" is used in it concerning **w**, so as to become a proof of

TPT227 **all***y*[if 1(*y*), then **all***f*(∀(*f*)P*y* iff **all***z*(if 0(*z*), then (*f*,*z*)P*y*))].

Because of APT0 and APT13 - which allow us to deduce "1(*y*)" from "**all***z*(if 0(*z*), then (*f*,*z*)P*y*)" - the condition "1(*y*)" can also be omitted from TPT227.

(c) The (weak) *existential* quantifier is defined as follows:

DPT65 ∃(t) := **conj***x***all***z*(if 0(*z*), then *x*P(t,*z*)).
("the (weak) existential state of affairs for t.")

(The *strong* existential quantifier "∃*(t)" is defined by "**conj***x***all***z*(if 0_{AE}(*z*), then *x*P(t,*z*))"; it yields the *strong* existential state of affairs for *f*: the state of affairs that there is at least one *actually existent* individual which is *f*.) According to DPT65, the existential state of affairs for a property *f* is the conjunction of all states of affairs which are intensional parts of *all* saturations of *f* by an individual. Alternatively, but equivalently, one could also have defined: ∃(t) := **disj***x***some***z*(0(*z*) and *x*=(t,*z*)). The definitions are equivalent because we have:

TPT228 **all***f*[**conj***x***all***z*(if 0(*z*), then *x*P(*f*,*z*))=**disj***x***some***z*(0(*z*) and *x*=(*f*,*z*))].

For the existential quantifier we have in general:

TPT229 **all***y***all***f*(if **some***z*(0(*z*) and (*f*,*z*)P*y*), then ∃(*f*)P*y*).

An easy consequence of TPT229 (applying DPT31, DPT32, DPT55) is the theorem

TPT230 **all***f*[if **some***z*(0(*z*) and *f*(*z*)), then V(∃(*f*))].

("If property *f* is exemplified by some individual, then the existential state of affairs for *f* is true.")

The converse of TPT229 cannot be proved. This is as it should be: it frequently happens (compare TPT233 below) that the existential state of affairs for *f* is analytically implied by a state of affairs *y*, although *y* does not analytically imply the saturation of *f* by *z* for *any* individual *z*. There is an analogue to this in the fact that (using standard logic) one is frequently able to deduce an existential statement (statement of *numerical existence*) ∃*x*F(*x*) from certain axioms via *reductio ad absurdum* of the contrary assumption, without being able to give a *direct* proof of it, that is, without being able to prove an instance F(t) of the existential statement. It may very well be that there is no direct proof of ∃*x*F(*x*) because the conjunction of the intensions (states of affairs) expressed (*intended*) by the invoked axioms, while analytically implying the existential state of affairs for the property which is *the intension of* F (the intension expressed by F), does not analytically imply the saturation of that property by any individual.

The converse of TPT229 *restricted to maximally consistent states of affairs* is, however, provable:

TPT231 **all***y*[if MK(*y*), then **all***f*(if ∃(*f*)P*y*, then **some***z*(0(*z*) and (*f*,*z*)P*y*))].

From TPT231 one obtains, because of MK(**w**), etc., the converse of TPT230:

TPT232 **all***f*[if V(∃(*f*)), then **some***z*(0(*z*) and *f*(*z*))].
("If the existential state of affairs for *f* is true, then property *f* is exemplified by some individual.")

(d) Consider now the converse (restricted to states of affairs) of TPT231. If this statement were true, then for every state of affairs *y* that is not maximally consistent there would be a property *f* such that the existential state of affairs for *f* is analytically implied by *y*, but *not* the saturation of *f* by *z* for *any* individual *z*. However, the converse of TPT231 is not true: 1(**k**) and **all***f*(if ∃(*f*)P**k**, then **some***z*(0(*z*) and (*f*,*z*)P**k**)) (a consequence of APT13, TPT146 and **all***y*(if 1(*y*), then *y*P**k**)); but not MK(**k**) (according to TPT72).

But **k** is the *only* counter-instance to the converse (restricted to states of affairs) of TPT231: for all states of affairs that are different from **k** are consistent (see TPT70), and we can indeed prove

TPT233 **all***y*[if K(*y*) and **all***f*(if ∃(*f*)P*y*, then **some***z*(0(*z*) and (*f*,*z*)P*y*)), then MK(*y*)].[*3]

In view of TPT233, the rejection of *non-constructive* (or *non-effective*, or *unavoidably indirect*) existence-proofs by the intuitionists [*4] appears to be particularly misguided. That some indirect classical existence-proofs cannot be replaced by direct ones - if there really is anything reprehensible in this situation - is not the fault of classical logic and the means of proof afforded by it; according to TPT233, the occurrence of such existence-proofs is to be expected already in consistent theories of individuals simply because such theories do not express maximally consistent states of affairs: none of them is a complete description of some possible world. Thus, weakening the means of proof to such an extent as to make unavoidably indirect existence-proofs impossible, is like healing the hand by cutting it off.

But suppose - forgetting for the moment about APT9 - that there are only two states of affairs, **t** and **k**; and suppose that the conjunction ***c*** of the states of affairs expressed by the axioms of a logically consistent theory ***C*** about individuals is a consistent state of affairs. Hence ***c*** (the intension of ***C***) is a maximally consistent state of affairs (because, under the supposition that **t** and **k** are the only states of affairs, any consistent state of affairs is a maximally consistent one), and hence we have according to TPT231: **all***f*(if ∃(*f*)P***c***, then **some***z*(0(*z*) and **(***f*,*z***)**P***c***)). Suppose now ∃*x*F(*x*) is an existential statement that is logically deducible from ***C***; then the intension of that existential statement is ∃(int(F)), where int(F) is the intension of F. Then we can certainly conclude: ∃(int(F))P***c***, and hence: **some***z*(0(*z*) and **(**int(F),*z***)**P***c***)**. But this by no means implies that, for some singular term t, F(t) is logically deducible from ***C***. We cannot even conclude this if **(**int(F),d(t)**)**P***c***, where d(t) is the individual that t refers to. If F(t) is logically deducible from ***C***, then we certainly have **(**int(F),d(t)**)**P***c***, but not vice versa - unless each instance of the intensional parthood of states of affairs is matched by a logical deducibility of statements corresponding to the states of affairs. But this ideal is not to be had, even if there are only two states of affairs: for then the intension of every true sentence is **t**, and the intension of every false one **k**; thus we have: int(A)Pint(B), for all true sentences A and B. But, of course, on no reasonable conception of logical deducibility can every true sentence be logically deduced from every true sentence.

Therefore, even in the supposed (counterfactual) situation, even under ideal conditions, there might be no direct proof of "∃*x*F(*x*)" via one of its instances. But note that this is still not the fault of classical logic.

(e) Concluding this chapter let me add that *numerically specific* quantifiers can also be defined on the basis of PT1:

DPT66 For every Arabic numeral k (starting with "1"):
(i) $\exists^{\geq k}$(t) := **disj***y***some***z_1*...**some***z_k*[0(z_1) and ... and 0(z_k) and D(z_1,...,z_k) and *y*=**conj((**t,z_1**)**,...,**(**t,z_k**))**].

(If k follows upon "1": "D(z_1,...,z_k)" := "z_1,...,z_k are pairwise different from each other." If k is "1": omit "D(z_1)," and replace "**conj**((t,z_1))" by "(t,z_1)." **conj**(t_1,...,t_k) := **conj**(**conj**(t_1,...,t_{k-1}),t_k), for $k \geq 3$.)
(ii) $\exists^{\leq k}$(t) := **neg**($\exists^{\geq k+1}$(t)).
(iii) $\exists^{=k}$(t) := **conj**($\exists^{\geq k}$(t),$\exists^{\leq k}$(t)).

Applying this definition-schema, it is a matter of routine to prove the following truth-laws: **all**f[V($\exists^{\geq k}$(f)) iff **≥K**z(0(z) and f(z))], **all**f[V($\exists^{\leq k}$(f)) iff **≤K**z(0(z) and f(z))], **all**f[V($\exists^{=k}$(f)) iff **K**z(0(z) and f(z))]. (**K** is "**1**", "**2**"..., and k is "1", "2"... .) This by itself shows that, as far as quantifiers are concerned, the theoretical possibilities of PT1 reach far beyond merely mirroring the principles of monadic (first-order) predicate logic - not to mention PT1-provable truths about quantifiers that have no analogue even among the principles of *full* predicate logic (with identity), like for example "**all**f[if $QA_{<0>}$(f), then QA($\forall$(f))]." Nevertheless, if we want to consider the ontological pendants of all the principles of full first-order predicate logic, then the present theoretical framework has to be abandoned: for then *relations of individuals* must become a matter of ontological investigation, and they are not capable of being treated in the present framework.

COMMENTS

[*1] Considered ontologically, the dispute (see A. Plantinga, *The Nature of Necessity*, pp. 222 - 251) whether besides modalities *de dicto* (for example M**some***x*F(*x*)) modalities *de re* (generated by quantification into modal contexts, for example **some***x*MF(*x*)) are meaningful ways of modal discourse reduces to the question whether there are modal properties. Anyone who rejects negative and disjunctive properties (like Armstrong, for example; see comment [*1] of chapter II.2) may be expected to reject modal properties as well. But given the generally acknowledged indispensability of dispositional predicates for science, the latter repudiation seems even more unreasonable than the first: There is something that is *soluble*; hence there is something such that it is possible that it (at some time) dissolves (this is a modality *de re*), and hence there is an individual that has *the property of possibly dissolving*, and that does not have *the property of necessarily not dissolving*. What, indeed, could be reprehensible about this?

In contrast, given the theoretical framework of PT1, which is defined by axioms that are very likely true and definitions that are intuitively adequate, modal properties - like disjunctive and negative ones - are not even *new* properties that need to be postulated besides the properties already there; rather, they are from the start among all the properties there are, quite independently of *how many* properties there are. Only the functional expressions "$\mathbf{disj}_{<0>}$", "$\mathbf{neg}_{<0>}$", "$\mathbf{pos}_{<0>}$", "$\mathbf{nec}_{<0>}$" are new when, on the occasion of their definition, they are introduced into the theory.

[*2] "$\mathbf{nec}_{<0>}$" as defined by DPT62 is *only one* among many necessitation-functors for properties. In comment [*3] of chapter I.11 we have seen how, in P, various necessitation-functors can be defined for states of affairs; and, of course, this can also be done *mutatis mutandis* in PT1. Thus we have for states of affairs a plethora of functors $\mathbf{n}_i$(t) (R_i being the "accessibility-relation" entering into the definition of $\mathbf{n}_i$). And in order to obtain just as many necessitation-functors (and in consequence also possibility-functors) for properties, we can simply define: $\mathbf{nec}_{i<0>}$(t) := **exo***n*$_i$((t,*o*)).

[*3] The proof of TPT233 also shows: **all***y*[if 1(*y*) and **all***f*(if ∃(*f*)P*y*, then **some***z*(0(*z*) and (*f*,*z*)P*y*)), then MX(*y*)]. And conversely we have: **all***y*[if MX(*y*), then 1(*y*) and **all***f*(if ∃(*f*)P*y*, then **some***z*(0(*z*) and (*f*,*z*)P*y*))], because in TPT231 "MK(*y*)" can be replaced by "MX(*y*) and *y*≠**k**" (according to TPT72, TPT71), and because: 1(**k**) and **all***f*(if ∃(*f*)P**k**, then **some***z*(0(*z*) and (*f*,*z*)P**k**)). Thus we have found yet another way of describing the maximality of a state of affairs.

[*4] See E. W. Beth, *Mathematical Thought*, p. 82f, and L. Borkowski, *Formale Logik*, p. 372ff. The intuitionists also reject *non-constructive disjunction-proofs*. A non-constructive disjunction-proof is a proof of a disjunctive statement in which *none* of the disjuncts is proved, and which cannot be replaced by a proof in which *one* of the disjuncts is proved. The rejection of non-constructive disjunction-proofs leads, like the rejection of non-constructive existence-proofs (both rejections are of course internally connected, but the former makes itself felt already on the level of propositional logic), to the repudiation of classical logical principles, the most prominent example being the *tertium non datur*. From the ontological point of view, this repudiation seems misguided. Axiomatic systems do not express (*intend*) maximally consistent states of affairs; but then the occurrence of non-constructive disjunction-proofs is to be expected: because for every non-maximal state of affairs *x* there are two states of affairs *y* and *z* such that *x* analytically implies **disj**(*y*,*z*), and such that *x* analytically implies neither *y* nor *z*. Hence an axiomatic system that expresses the state of affairs *x* (whose intension is *x*) and from which the sentence "(A or B)" can be logically deduced will not also be one from which sentence A or sentence B can be logically deduced *if* the intension of A is *y* and the intension of B *z*.

I fail to see anything problematic in non-constructive disjunction-proofs; after all, what is proved in them (or, for that matter, in non-constructive existence-proofs) *is certainly true if the axiomatic basis is true*. But if one does not like such proofs, then one should at least recognize that it is really not the fault of classical logic that they do occur, and that classical logic should not be decapitated for this (although, admittedly, this radical measure does prevent their occurrence).

CHAPTER III.17

CONCEPTIONS OF PROPERTIES, AND THEIR NUMBER

(a) Let **W** be the cardinal number of the possible worlds (or maximally consistent states of affairs), **S** the cardinal number of the states of affairs, **I** the cardinal number of the individuals, **M** the cardinal number of the maximally consistent properties (representing Leibniz-individuals), **F** the cardinal number of the properties (of individuals). We have seen in part I that (1) $\mathbf{S}=2^{\mathbf{W}}$. The universe of properties has precisely the same structure as the universe of states of affairs (compare APT0 - APT6 with TPT152 - TPT156, TPT176, TPT177); therefore: (2) $\mathbf{F}=2^{\mathbf{M}}$. Because of TPT202, TPT203, TPT204 we have moreover (3) $\mathbf{M}=(\mathbf{I}\mathrm{x}\mathbf{W})$. Hence by (2) and (3): (4) $\mathbf{F}=2^{(\mathbf{I}\mathrm{x}\mathbf{W})}$. If, for example, there are only *two* individuals and *two* possible worlds - the smallest values for **I** and **W** that are compatible with the axioms of PT1 - then according to (4) there are 16 properties (according to (3): 4 maximally consistent properties, according to (1): 4 states of affairs).

(b) Every property is a *function* (in a primitive and intuitive, not in a set-theoretical sense) *that maps individuals into states of affairs*, for short: an IS-function. Such functions are identical if they always take the same state of affairs as value for each individual as argument; thus, since all properties are IS-functions, we have the truth of APT19. Moreover, if every IS-function is a property, then we have (5) $\mathbf{F}=\mathbf{S}^{\mathbf{I}}$, since the cardinal number of the IS-functions is $\mathbf{S}^{\mathbf{I}}$. But are all IS-functions properties? The following shows that this is indeed the case: Let φ be an arbitrary IS-function, hence we have: **all***z*(if 0(*z*), then 1(φ[*z*])). Consider **ex***o*φ[*o*], which, being a property (by TPT144), is also an IS-function. φ must be identical with **ex***o*φ[*o*], since we have as an immediate consequence of APT16 and **all***z*(if 0(*z*), then 1(φ[*z*])): **all***z*(if 0(*z*), then **(ex***o*φ[*o*],*z*)=φ[*z*]), and since IS-functions are identical if they take the same state of affairs as value for each individual as argument (and of course **ex***o*φ[*o*][*z*] - the value of **ex***o*φ[*o*] for argument *z* - is **(ex***o*φ[*o*],*z*)). Therefore: φ is a property (because **ex***o*φ[*o*] is a property).

By (4) and (5) we obtain: $\mathbf{S}^{\mathbf{I}}=2^{(\mathbf{I}\mathrm{x}\mathbf{W})}$; this can also be had more directly as follows: $\mathbf{S}^{\mathbf{I}}=(2^{\mathbf{W}})^{\mathbf{I}}$ (according to (1)) $=2^{(\mathbf{W}\mathrm{x}\mathbf{I})}=2^{(\mathbf{I}\mathrm{x}\mathbf{W})}$.

(c) The cardinal number **F** of the properties can be determined in various equivalent ways (we have just seen two of them). To each there corresponds a certain conception of (coarse-grained) properties that has been put forward in the literature:

(i) $\mathbf{F}=2^{(\mathrm{I}\times\mathrm{W})}$: "Properties are functions assigning a truth value to each individual in each possible word." (Alternatively: "Properties are sets of ordered individual-world pairs.")
(ii) $\mathbf{F}=(2^{\mathrm{I}})^{\mathrm{W}}$: "Properties are functions assigning a set of individuals to each possible world." (Alternatively: "Properties are functions assigning to each possible world a function from individuals into truth values.")
(iii) $\mathbf{F}=(2^{\mathrm{W}})^{\mathrm{I}}$: "Properties are functions assigning to each individual a set of possible worlds." (Alternatively: "Properties are functions that assign to each individual a function from possible worlds into truth-values.")
(iv) $\mathbf{F}=\mathbf{S}^{\mathrm{I}}$: "Properties are functions assigning to each individual a state of affairs."
(v) $\mathbf{F}=2^{\mathrm{M}}$: "Properties are sets of Lewis-individuals." (Alternatively: "Properties are functions from Leibniz-individuals into truth values.")

Each of the equations in (i) - (v) can be seen to be true in the framework of PT1 (consider (2), (4) and (5), which have been shown to be true in sections (a) and (b); the equations in (ii) and (iii) are arithmetical variants of the equation in (i)). And the statement beside each equation can also be seen to be true in that framework *if and only if* "are" is replaced in it by "are isomorphically represented by." The literal truth, however, is only expressed by the "are"-statement in (iv). (Carnap seems to have been the first philosopher to formulate it; see *Meaning and Necessity*, p. 182.) For Lewis, in contrast, only the "are"-statement in (v) expresses a literal truth (see *On the Plurality of Worlds*, p. 50ff); he does of course not talk of Lewis- or Leibniz-individuals, because from his point of view the Leibniz-individuals are the possible individuals *par excellence*. In turn, the "are"-statements in (i), (ii) and (iii) express variants of the *usual extensionalistic* conception of properties (a conception which can also be traced back to Carnap's *Meaning and Necessity*): like Lewis' conception, it is embedded in an *extensional* ontological framework (standardly a set-theoretical one) where no *basic* intensional entities are assumed (where all the non-sets are individuals, the latter including, for the Fregean-minded, truth values - which, however, can also be regarded as sets). Note that an extensionalistic ontologist will not be able to distinguish between (iii) and (iv), since for him states of affairs simply are "nothing but" sets of possible worlds (that is, sets of certain individuals), or extensional, usually set-theoretical functions assigning truth values to possible worlds.

IV

UNIVERSAL INTENSIONAL ONTOLOGY

CHAPTER IV.1

THE SYSTEM IOU: FIRST STAGE

(a) The language LPT1 in the previous part can be extended in various more or less restricted ways, leading to various more or less restricted extensions of the system PT1, that is, to various more less restricted versions of a *full ontology* (an ontology that treats states of affairs, individuals and functions). It could, for example, be extended *infinitely, but purely vertically* by adding to "0(*z*)", "1(*z*)", "<0>(*z*)" the infinite hierarchy of categorial predicates that progresses from "<0>(*z*)" in a strictly upward direction: <<0>>(*z*), <<<0>>>(*z*), <<<<0>>>>(*z*), and so on. This means that besides individuals, states of affairs and properties of individuals also properties of properties of individuals, properties of properties of properties of individuals, and so on, are drawn into consideration. The described expansion in categorial predicates would require appropriate modifications in the interpretation of the saturation-functor "**(***x*,*y***)**" and in the interpretation of the extraction-operator "**ex**"; but we would still need only a dyadic saturation-functor, and extraction would still be always monadic (we would, however, need to attach type-indices to the extraction-variables for all types of the form <n>). The resulting system is quite powerful: set theory in the form of a "standard theory of types" (see comment [*3] of the Introduction) can be incorporated into it. (How to do this should be quite clear after chapters III.14 and III.15. Extending PT1 in the described manner obviously involves giving up axioms APT15 and APT18, which were based solely on the limitations of the universe of discourse of LPT1: not because they have become unnecessary as axioms, but because they are likely to be false in the intended interpretation of the new system; an "extension" of PT1 is, therefore, not simply an "additive" extension.)

Or LPT1 could be extended *infinitely, but purely horizontally* by adding to its categorial predicates the infinite sequence of such predicates that progresses from "<0>(*z*)" in a strictly lateral direction: <0,0>(*z*), <0,0,0>(*z*), <0,0,0,0>(*z*), and so on. This means that besides individuals, states of affairs and properties of individuals, *n*-adic relations between individuals are drawn into consideration ($n \geq 2$). In that case we will need an *n*-adic saturation-functor for every $n \geq 2$, and, correspondingly, extraction will not always be monadic.

Finally, LPT1 could be extended *infinitely in all type-theoretical directions* by simply adding to it all the categorial predicates that where syntactically specified in III.1.(a). The required modifications of PT1 would result in the system PT. PT would carry the idea of an *intensional* standard theory of types very far. But we will not explore the possibilities of PT; rather we shall consider an even more general and powerful system, one in which no categorial predicates besides "0(*z*)" and "1(*z*)" are primitives because they can all be defined in it, a system in which the conception of types (as defined in III.1.(a)) can itself be generalized, the categorial predicates based on *generalized types* (except, of course, "0(*z*)" and '1(*z*)") remaining all definable. In this system even such cross-type categorial predicates as "*x* is a property (*of arbitrary entities*)" can be defined. The envisaged system is fittingly called IOU - "intensional ontology universalized." The universal nature of IOU is, last but not least, shown in the fact that it is able to swallow up axiomatic set theory within itself (as we will see).

(b) The language LIOU of IOU is an extension of LPT1 minus the predicate "<0>(*z*)" (as primitive predicate). Instead of having only the dyadic saturation-functor **(t,t′)**, LIOU has infinitely many saturation-functors **(t_1,...,t_k)** - one for every $k \geq 2$. Corresponding to this, LIOU has terms of *k*-adic extraction (for every $k \geq 1$): **ex**$o_1 \ldots o_k$f[$o_1, \ldots, o_k$]. Moreover, besides "**w**" and "**sr**" there is another primitive singular term in LIOU: "**o**" - "Nothing." Finally, LIOU comprises infinitely many non-ontological predicates (having the same role as the ordinary predicates - with low level of generality - of ordinary language): "F(*x*)," "F′(*x*,*y*)," and so on. (Such predicates belonged to LP and LPT1, too; but so far there was not much reason to take notice of them.)

The new singular term "**o**" is first of all characterized by the following additional *logical* axiom:

AX-L0 if not **one***x*A[*x*], then **the***x*A[*x*]=**o**.

In all systems considered so far it was left unspecified what is the designation of a definite description whose presupposition is not fulfilled. In IOU this is taken care of, in a quite natural manner, by AX-L0.

The universe of discourse of LIOU, howsoever it is determined, is supposed to comprise only *genuine* entities *and* the entity that is designated by "**o**"; *that* entity is supposed to be not a genuine one. Thus we can very well define:

DEF0 E*(t) := t≠**o**.
("t is a genuine entity (in the universe of discourse).")

(One could identify the genuine entities with the *non-linguistic entities*, and then it would be natural to let "**o**" designate some *linguistic entity*, for example *itself*.)

(c) The definitions DEF1 - DEF39 of IOU are the definitions DPT1 - DPT39 of PT1 *verbatim*. The axioms AX-P0 - AX-P9 of IOU are the axioms APT0 - APT9 of PT1 *verbatim*. AX-C0 is APT13, and AX-C1 is APT10. But APT11 and APT12 are replaced in IOU by the following two axioms:

AX-C2 **all***x*(if 1(*x*), then E*(*x*)).

("Every state of affairs is a genuine entity.")

AX-C3 **all**x(if 0(x), then E*(x)).
("Every individual is a genuine entity.")

To the L-axioms (logical axioms), P-axioms (axioms concerning solely states of affairs and intensional parthood between them) and C-axioms (axioms concerning solely categorial predicates), the S-axioms (axioms prominently concerning saturation-functors) are added. Consider first the following axiom-schema:

AX-S0 **all**x[if 0(x) or 1(x) or not E*(x), then not E*((x,t_1,...,t_n))], for all natural numbers $n \geq 1$.
("If x is an individual or a state of affairs or not a genuine entity, then the saturation of x by any n entities is not a genuine entity.")

AX-S0 states that individuals, states of affairs and Nothing are *complete* or *saturated entities*. Saturated entities are, properly speaking, the entities which *have* no saturations (they may, however, very well *be* the saturation of some entity); but since the saturation-functors are defined for all entities, this becomes: saturated entities are the entities of which all saturations are Nothing. The *functions*, on the other hand, are precisely the *incomplete* or *unsaturated entities*, the entities that have a saturation, or in other words: the entities at least one saturation of which is not Nothing. While it is not possible to define in LIOU the general concept of a function, we can define in it the concept of a k-place function for every natural number $k \geq 1$:

DEF40 k-FUNC(t) := **some**x_1...**some**x_kE*((t,x_1,...,x_k)).
("t is a k-adic function." In every instance of the schema, "k" is replaced by the Arabic numeral that designates k.)

Every k-adic function is a genuine entity that is neither a state of affairs nor an individual; this is an immediate consequence of AX-S0 and DEF40, and we can put down:

THE1 **all**x(if k-FUNC(x), then E*(x) and not 1(x) and not 0(x)), for all Arabic numerals k, starting with "1".

Moreover, no k-adic function is an n-adic function, where n and k are *different* natural numbers ≥ 1. But to prove this in IOU we need another axiom-schema:

AX-S1 if E*((t,t_1,...,t_n)), then not E*((t,t'_1,...,t'_k)), for all natural numbers k and n such that $n \geq 1$, and $k > n$ or $1 \leq k < n$.

("If the saturation of t by n entities is a genuine entity, then the saturation of t by more or less than n entities is not a genuine entity.")

On the basis of AX-S1 and DEF40 one easily obtains:

THE2 **all**x(if k-FUNC(x), then not n-FUNC(x)), for all Arabic numerals k and n - starting with "1" - that are different from each other.

(d) Relations, properly speaking, are n-place functions *with* $n>1$ which have a saturation that is a state of affairs. For the sake of conceptual unification it is, however, convenient to stretch the concept of relation a bit, making it comprise also 1-place functions which have a saturation that is a state of affairs. Such functions are normally called "properties."

As with respect to the general concept of function, it is not possible to define in LIOU the general concept of relation (we might, of course, add both concepts as further primitives); but we can define in LIOU the concept of a k-adic relation for every natural number $k \geq 1$ (k being designated by the Arabic numeral k):

DEF41 k-RELT(t) := **some**x_1...**some**x_k1((t,x_1,...,x_k)).

And it is important to append:

DEF42 PROP(t) := 1-RELT(t).
("t is a property.")

By AX-C2, DEF41 and DEF40 we obtain:

THE3 **all**x(if k-RELT(x), then k-FUNC(x)), for all Arabic numerals k, starting with "1".

On the basis of this theorem, the analogues of THE1 and THE2 for k-and n-adic relations are easily proved. Note that functions in general, and properties and relations in particular, need not be type-restricted *in their arguments*; the definitions do not require this, and there is no further postulate concerning this. If, for example, f is a k-adic relation, then the x_1,...,x_k such that 1((f,x_1,...,x_k)) could belong to any categories whatever. Nor do the definitions require that f be type-restricted *in its values*: as far as the definitions are concerned, we may have, for example, 0((f,y_1,...,y_k)) for some y_1,...,y_k. In section (f), however, another axiom-schema is added that states that all functions are indeed type-restricted *in their values*.

(e) *Generalized types* are syntactically defined as follows:

(1) “0” and “1” are generalized types.
(2) If $T_1,\ldots,T_k,T_{k+1}$ are generalized types, then $<T_1,\ldots,T_k>T_{k+1}$ is a generalized type.
(3) Only expressions according to (1) and (2) are generalized types.

Types as defined at the beginning of chapter III.1 - from now on they will be called “ordinary types” - either are also generalized types (in the case of “0” and “1”), or, if complex, they are abbreviations of certain generalized types: *the* 1-*types*:

(1′) “0” and “1” are 1-types.
(2′) If $T_1,\ldots,T_k$ are 1-types, then $<T_1,\ldots,T_k>1$ is a 1-type.
(3′) Only expressions according to (1′) and (2′) are 1-types.

Omitting in a 1-type every occurrence of “1” that stands *immediately after* an occurrence of “>” yields an ordinary type, and every ordinary type that is not “0” or“1” can be obtained in this way. Consider, for example, the ordinary type “<0>”; it is the abbreviation of the 1-type “<0>1”; or the ordinary type “<<0>,0>”; it is the abbreviation of the 1-type “<<0>1,0>1.”

Why can complex ordinary types be regarded as abbreviations of 1-types? Consider again “<<0>,0>.” Dyadic relations between properties of individuals and individuals are dyadic functions assigning states of affairs to the following arguments in the following order: (1) monadic functions that assign states of affairs to individuals, and (2) individuals. In other words: the entities of ordinary type <<0>,0> are precisely the entities of 1-type (hence of generalized type) <<0>1,0>1. What has just been demonstrated for one particular ordinary type could quite obviously have been demonstrated for any complex ordinary type whatever. The reason is: entities of ordinary type, if they are not states of affairs or individuals, are properties or relations (*attributes*) - in other words: *functions whose values are states of affairs* - and they involve at most individuals, states of affairs, and properties or relations (of lower type) in their type-structure.

(f) We need not encumber the language LIOU with an infinity of categorial predicates that are based on generalized types because all such predicates other than “$0(x)$” and “$1(x)$” - and hence also all categorial predicates other than “$0(x)$” and “$1(x)$”that are based on *ordinary types* - are definable in LIOU:

DEF43 $<T_1,\ldots,T_k>T_{k+1}(t)$:= **all**x_1...**all**x_k[$T_{k+1}((t,x_1,\ldots,x_k))$ iff $T_1(x_1)$ and ... and $T_k(x_k)$] and **some**x_1...**some**$x_k T_{k+1}((t,x_1,\ldots,x_k))$.

In this definition-schema $<T_1,\ldots,T_k>T_{k+1}$ is any complex generalized type ($k\geq 1$), T_{k+1} being its single component type outside its main bracket, $T_1,\ldots,T_k$ its component types immediately within its main bracket. (The component types of

$<T_1,...,T_k>T_{k+1}$ are of course themselves generalized types, and if they are complex, then the predicates corresponding to them - they are less complex then the one corresponding to $<T_1,...,T_k>T_{k+1}$ - are themselves defined according to schema DEF43.) "$<T_1,...,T_k>T_{k+1}(x)$" is read as: "*x* is a *k*-adic function whose arguments are entities of type $T_1,...,T_k$ (in that order), and whose values are entities of type T_{k+1}."

The categorial predicate "<0>(*y*)" ("*y* is a property of individuals"), for example, is defined by "<0>1(*y*)," which in turn, according to DEF43, is defined by "**all***x*(1((*y*,*x*)) iff 0(*x*)) and **some***x*1((*y*,*x*))." It is, therefore, clear that axiom APT14 of PT1 is a trivial, purely definitional theorem of IOU. (The statement which is APT15 in PT1, however, needs to be unprovable in IOU: in the *universal* framework of the latter system it obviously should not be provable that (*x*,*y*) is the contradictory state of affairs if *x* is not a property of individuals or *y* not an individual.) APT11 and APT12, too, are easily derived in it: By DEF43, DEF41 and THE3: **all***x*(if <0>(*x*), then 1-FUNC(*x*)), hence by THE1: **all***x*(if <0>(*x*), then not 1(*x*) and not 0(*x*)).

Note that the first occurrence of "T_{k+1}"in the definiens of DEF43 (the one which is within the scope of "**all**x_1") can be equivalently replaced by "E*" because the *principle of the type-uniformity of saturations* is a further S-axiom:

AX-S2 if **some**x_1...**some**$x_k$$T$((t,$x_1$,...,$x_k$)), then **all**$x_1$...**all**$x_k$[if E*((t,$x_1$,...,$x_k$)), then T((t,x_1,...,x_k))], *T* being any generalized type.
("If some saturation of t by *k* entities belongs to type *T*, then every saturation of t by *k* entities belongs to type *T*, *if* that saturation is a genuine entity.")

"**all**x_1...**all**x_k[if T((t,x_1,...,x_k)), then E*((t,x_1,...,x_k))]" is already provable on the basis of the rest of the axioms (see below THE5). An immediate consequence of AX-S2 and DEF41 is

THE4 if k-RELT(t), then **all**x_1...**all**x_k[if E*((t,x_1,...,x_k)), then 1((t,x_1,...,x_k))].

Thus, all saturations of a relation which are genuine entities have a certain type, and it is the same type for all of them: type 1, they are states of affairs. In contrast, it would not have been plausible to demand that every relation *itself* have a certain generalized type. Consider, for example, number-properties *f*: *being twice instantiated*, *being thrice instantiated*, etc.; they are monadic relations, all their genuinely existing saturations are states of affairs; but the entities for which, if saturated by them, they yield genuinely existing saturations can certainly not all be subsumed under one and the same type. If *f* is a number-property, then "**all***x*(if E*((*f*,*x*)), then *T*(*x*))" is *false* for every generalized type *T*; in other words - in view of the truth of "**some***x*1((*f*,*x*))" and because of DEF41, THE4 and AX-C2 - "**all***x*(if 1((*f*,*x*)), then *T*(*x*))" is false for every such type, and hence number-properties *f* cannot be assigned a generalized type of the form $<T>1$. Hence they cannot be assigned any generalized type at all;[*1] they are therefore *typeless* or *type-transcendent* properties.

(g) Consider, finally, the following very general theorems about generalized and ordinary types (the proofs are in the Appendix):

THE5 **all**x(if $T(x)$, then E*(x)), for all *generalized types* T.
(The ultimate generalization of AX-C2 and AX-C3.)

THE6 **all**x(if $<T_1,...,T_k>(x)$, then k-RELT(x)), for all *ordinary types* $T_1,...,T_k$.

THE7 **all**x(if $T(x)$, then not $T'(x)$), T and T' being *distinct ordinary types*.
(A far-reaching generalization of AX-C1.)

THE8 **all**x(if $<T_1,...,T_k>T_{k+1}(x)$, then k-FUNC(x)), for all *generalized types* $T_1,...,T_k,T_{k+1}$.

THE9 **all**x(if $T(x)$, then not $T'(x)$), for *distinct generalized types* T and T'.
(The ultimate generalization of AX-C1.)

COMMENTS

[*1] Let f be a number property. If is has any type at all, f can only have a generalized type of the form $<T>1$:
Since f is a property, f is a monadic relation by DEF42, and hence f is a monadic function (by THE3); but if it had a generalized type of the form $<T_1,\ldots,T_k>T_{k+1}$, with $k \geq 2$, then f would not be a monadic function: according to DEF43 we would get **some**y_1...**some**$y_k T_{k+1}((f,y_1,\ldots,y_k))$, hence according to THE5 (in section (g)): **some**y_1...**some**y_kE*$((f,y_1,\ldots,y_k))$, hence by DEF40: k-FUNC(f), and hence by THE2: not 1-FUNC(f) (since $k \geq 2$). Moreover, being a monadic function, f cannot have the types "1" or "0" (according to THE1). Thus a generalized type of f can only have the form $<T>T'$. Suppose now: $<T>T'(f)$, T' *being different from* "1"; then according to DEF43: **some**$y T'((f,y))$, hence by AX-S2: **all**y[if E*$((f,y))$, then $T'((f,y))$]. Since f is a property, by DEF42, DEF41: **some**$y 1((f,y))$. Therefore, applying AX-C2: **some**x($1(x)$ and $T'(x)$). But the negation of this is already provable: by AX-C1, if T' is "0"; by DEF43, THE5, DEF40 and THE1, if T' is some complex generalized type.
Therefore: since, as we have seen, f does not have a generalized type of the form $<T>1$, it does not have *any* type, whether generalized or ordinary.

Another typeless property is the property of being self-identical **id** (not the property of being a self-identical individual, state of affairs, etc., but simply the property of being self-identical). Take any individual z (there is at least one such entity according to AX-C0); we have $1((\mathbf{id},z))$. Take any state of affairs p (there is at least one such entity according to AX-P4); we have $1((\mathbf{id},p))$. Hence we have because of AX-C1: **some**x($1((\mathbf{id},x))$ and not $0(x)$), **some**x($1((\mathbf{id},x))$and not $1(x)$); hence we also have for every *complex* generalized type T: **some**x($1((\mathbf{id},x))$ and not $T(x)$) (because $1(p)$, $1((\mathbf{id},p))$, **no**x($1(x)$ and $T(x)$), for every complex generalized type T). Since **id** is a property, a generalized type for **id** would have to be of the form $<T>1$ (see above); but we have just seen that **id** has no generalized type of that form. Hence it has no type at all.

CHAPTER IV.2

THE SYSTEM IOU: SECOND STAGE

(a) Relations are special functions, properties are special relations, sets are special properties:

DEF44 SET(t) := PROP(t) and **all**y(if E*((t,y)), then **(t,y)=t** or **(t,y)=k**).

In chapter III.14 sets of individuals were modelled by (*simpliciter*) essential properties of individuals, and DEF44 is merely a generalization of that idea. However, sets are now to be identified with properties *in all ontological seriousness*. (Note that we can easily derive "**all**x(if $<0>_{ES}(x)$, then SET(x))": assume $<0>_{ES}(x)$, hence by DPT49: $<0>(x)$ and **all**y(if 0(y), then **(x,y)=t** or **(x,y)=k**). From $<0>(x)$ by DEF43 (since $<0>$:= $<0>1$): **some**y1((x,y)) and **all**y[if 1((x,y)), then 0(y)], hence by AX-S2 **all**y[if E*((x,y)), then 0(y)]. Therefore: PROP(x) and **all**y(if E*((x,y)), then **(x,y)=t** or **(x,y)=k**) (the first conjunct is obtained by applying THE6, DEF42 to $<0>(x)$), hence SET(x) by DEF44.)

Set-theoretical elementhood is closely related to monadic exemplification, which is a special case of general (monadic or polyadic) exemplification:

DEF45 $\mathrm{t}(\mathrm{t}_1,\ldots,\mathrm{t}_k)$:= $\mathrm{O}((\mathrm{t},\mathrm{t}_1,\ldots,\mathrm{t}_k))$.
("$\mathrm{t}_1,\ldots,\mathrm{t}_k$ (in that order) exemplifies t; t applies to $\mathrm{t}_1,\ldots,\mathrm{t}_k$ (in that order).")

DEF46 $\mathrm{t}' \in_S \mathrm{t}$:= SET(t) and **(t,t′)=t**.

By DEF45, DEF31 (=DPT31=DP31), AX-P0 (=APT0) and DEF41, we easily obtain "**all**x(if **some**y_1...**some**y_k[$x(y_1,\ldots,y_k)$], then k-RELT(x))"; the converse is neither provable nor true (contrary to the opinion of some ontologists, for example Armstrong). Also, we can easily prove "**all**x**all**y_1...**all**y_k(if $<T_1,\ldots,T_k>(x)$ and $x(y_1,\ldots,y_k)$, then $T_1(y_1)$ and ... and $T_k(y_k)$)," for all ordinary types $T_1,\ldots,T_k$. Connecting set-theoretical elementhood and monadic exemplification we have: "**all**x(if SET(x), then **all**y($x(y)$ iff $y \in_S x$))."

(b) In order to prove the set-theoretical *principle of extensionality* we need one more saturation-axiom, which states the sufficient condition under which k-adic functions (for any natural number $k \geq 1$) are identical:

AX-S3 **all**f**all**g(if k-FUNC(f) and k-FUNC(g) and **all**y_1...**all**y_k((f,$y_1,\ldots,y_k$)= (g,$y_1,\ldots,y_k$)), then f=g).

("k-adic functions are identical if they always yield the same values for the same arguments.")

Given AX-S3, the axiom APT19 of PT1 becomes a theorem of IOU. Assume: <0>(*f*) and <0>(*g*) and **all***y*(if 0(*y*), then (*f*,*y*)=(*g*,*y*)); hence by THE6, THE3: 1-FUNC(*f*) and 1-FUNC(*g*). Assume now: not 0(*y*); hence from "<0>1(*f*) and <0>1(*g*)" (see the first assumption) by DEF43, AX-S2: not E*((*f*,*y*)) and not E*((*g*,*y*)), hence by DEF0: (*f*,*y*)=**o** and (*g*,*y*)=**o**, hence (*f*,*y*)=(*g*,*y*). Therefore: **all***y*((*f*,*y*)=(*g*,*y*)). From the underlined results by AX-S3: *f*=*g*.

And given AX-S3, the *weak principle of extensionality* becomes a theorem of IOU:

THE10 **all***x***all***y*(if SET(*x*) and SET(*y*) and **all***z*[E*((*x*,*z*)) iff E*((*y*,*z*))] and **all***z*($z \in_S x$ iff $z \in_S y$), then *x*=*y*).

The weak principle of extensionality is not *the* principle of extensionality. But the condition "**all***z*[E*((*x*,*z*)) iff E*((*y*,*z*))]" can be omitted for all sets *x* and *y* that have a common generalized type. And it can be omitted for all sets *x* and *y* which are *supersets*:

DEF47 SSET(t) := SET(t) and **all***y*E*((t,*y*)).

Supersets - sets with a universal domain - are actually what set-theoreticians that work with axiomatic set theory have in mind when they talk about "sets." Type-theoreticians, on the other hand, work with sets that *are not* supersets. The following theorem, which is an easy consequence of THE10 and DEF47, thus expresses what the theoreticians working with axiomatic set theory - have in mind when they talk about the "principle of extensionality":

THE11 **all***x***all***y*(if SSET(*x*) and SSET(*y*) and **all***z*($z \in_S x$ iff $z \in_S y$), then *x*=*y*).

(c) In order to derive the *principle of abstraction* for supersets in IOU - in a version, of course, that is not "naive" (i.e. that does not fall prey to antinomies) - we have to add the *axiom* (-schema) *of extraction* to the list of the basic principles of IOU:

AX-E0 if **all**x_1...**all**x_k(if E*(f[x_1,...,x_k]), then *T*(f[x_1,...,x_k])) and E*(**ex**o_1...o_kf[o_1,...,o_k]), then **all**x_1...**all**x_k(f[x_1,...,x_k]=(**ex**o_1...o_kf[o_1,...,o_k],x_1,...,x_k)), *T* being any generalized type.

Consider then the already familiar functional terms of the form **conj***y*(not A[*x*] and *y*=**k**) and the already familiar extraction-terms of the form **exoconj***y*(not

A[*o*] and *y*=**k**)) (compare chapter III.15), for which we now introduce standard abbreviations by the following definition-schema:

DEF48 λ*x*A[*x*] := **ex***o***conj***y*(not A[*o*] and *y*=**k**).
("the class of all *x* such that A[*x*]"; "*x*" represents a variable that does not occur in the definiens.)

We can easily prove "**all***x*1(**conj***y*(not A[*x*] and *y*=**k**))," and therefore we have by AX-E0 and DEF48:

THE12 if E*(λ*x*A[*x*]), then **all***z*(**conj***y*(not A[*z*] and *y*=**k**)=(λ*x*A[*x*],*z*)).

On the basis of the ontology of states of affairs, THE12 has the following corollaries: if E*(λ*x*A[*x*]), then (1) **all***z*(A[*z*] iff (λ*x*A[*x*],*z*)=**t**), (2) **all***z*(not A[*z*] iff (λ*x*A[*x*],*z*)=**k**), (3) **all***z*((λ*x*A[*x*],*z*)=**t** or (λ*x*A[*x*],*z*)=**k**), (4) PROP(λ*x*A[*x*]) (applying DEF41, DEF42), (5) **all***z*E*((λ*x*A[*x*],*z*)) (applying AX-C2). From this we obtain according to DEF44, DEF46, DEF47: if E*(λ*x*A[*x*]), then SSET(λ*x*A[*x*]) and **all***z*($z \in_S$ λ*x*A[*x*] iff A[*z*]). Since we can also prove "if SSET(λ*x*A[*x*]), then E*(λ*x*A[*x*])" (supersets are by definition properties, and properties, being monadic functions according to their definition and THE3, are genuine entities according to THE1), we therefore obtain the principle of abstraction for supersets:

THE13 if SSET(λ*x*A[*x*]), then **all***z*($z \in_S$ λ*x*A[*x*] iff A[*z*]).

If we want to have a workable set theory, then the all-important question is, of course, for which predicates "A[*x*]" we can assume the truth of "SSET(λ*x*A[*x*])"; so far, nothing whatever has been determined in this respect. But, as everyone knows, we certainly cannot assume the truth of "SSET(λ*x*A[*x*])" for *every* predicate "A[*x*]" (remember "$x \notin_S x$"). The question will be discussed further in the next chapter.

(d) The second of the two restricting conditions of AX-E0 - "E*(**ex**$o_1 \ldots o_k$f[$o_1, \ldots, o_k$])" - is absolutely necessary: without it, we would not only be able to prove THE13, but also "**all***z*($z \in_S$ λ*x*A[*x*] iff A[*z*])," and hence "$\lambda x(x \notin_S x) \in_S \lambda x(x \notin_S x)$ iff $\lambda x(x \notin_S x) \notin_S \lambda x(x \notin_S x)$" - Russell's Antinomy. As it is, we merely obtain "not E*($\lambda x(x \notin_S x)$)."

There is only a certain degree of plausibility to the first restricting condition of AX-E0. Consider the following functional term: ι(*x*) := **the***y*(*y*=*x*). For no generalized type *T* do we have: **all***x*(if E*(ι(*x*)), then *T*(ι(*x*)) (consider an individual *z* and a state of affairs *p*: ι(*z*) is an individual, and ι(*p*) a state of affairs; both are genuine entities, but there is no generalized type they both have); nevertheless, plausibly, E*(**ex***o*ι(*o*)). Hence, if the first restricting condition of AX-E0 were omitted, we would obtain: (*) **all***x*(ι(*x*)=(**ex***o*ι(*o*),*x*)). But we also have **some***z*0(ι(*z*)) (by AX-C0); therefore by (*): **some***z*0((**ex***o*ι(*o*),*z*)), and hence by AX-S2: **all***z*[if E*((**ex***o*ι(*o*),*z*)), then 0((**ex***o*ι(*o*),*z*))]. Moreover, by AX-P4 we also have **some***p*1(ι(*p*)), therefore by (*): **some***p*1((**ex***o*ι(*o*),*p*)), hence by AX-C2 E*((**ex***o*ι(*o*),*p*)), and hence according to the final result in the previous sentence: 0((**ex***o*ι(*o*),*p*)) - contradicting 1((**ex***o*ι(*o*),*p*)) in virtue of AX-C1.

We might simply react to this by concluding: not E*(**ex***o*ι(*o*)). Another, much more drastic reaction would be to reject AX-S2. (The other principles involved are too basic to be tampered with.) On the whole, it seems best to stick with AX-S2 and the truth of "E*(**ex***o*ι(*o*))," and to accept AX-E0 in its already given, doubly conditioned form. (But what kind of genuine entity is **ex***o*ι(*o*), if it is a genuine entity? It is a monadic function, since we can safely and plausibly assume: (**ex***o*ι(*o*),**ex***o*ι(*o*))=**ex***o*ι(*o*), and hence conclude **some***x*E*((**ex***o*ι(*o*),*x*)) from E*(**ex***o*ι(*o*)). Or, alternatively, we can even consider **ex***o*ι(*o*) a function of the type <0>0 (or of the type <1>1); then we do have **all***x*(if E*((**ex***o*ι(*o*),*x*)), then 0(*x*)), although we do not have **all***x*(if E*(ι(*x*)), then 0(*x*)).)

Note, finally, that it is not safe to assume the truth of APT16 in IOU. We can prove in IOU "**some***z*[0(*z*) and 1(**conj***y*(not A[*z*] and *y*=**k**))]"; hence by applying APT16 and DEF48 we could conclude: **some***z*1((λ*x*A[*x*],*z*)), and therefore (by AX-C2 and AX-S0): E*(λ*x*A[*x*]). But this can already be refuted in IOU (see above). Thus, APT16 itself can be refuted in IOU. (Clearly APT17 and APT18, too, cannot be retained in the universal framework of that system.) In the restricted environment of PT1, however, APT16 is completely harmless.

CHAPTER IV.3

THE SYSTEM IOU: THIRD STAGE

(a) The formidable definitional power of IOU may have produced the impression that the ontological commitments incurred by it are likewise formidable, both as to the number and categorial diversity of entities. This impression is false. In its present state, IOU is utterly weak in its assumptions of numerical existence. Of all the categorial predicates that correspond to generalized types, only "0(*x*)" and "1(*x*)" are provably non-empty. IOU allows us to build an imposing categorial structure, a huge mansion with countless rooms - but, as far as IOU is concerned, almost all of the rooms may be empty.

In fact, a nominalist - who presumably likes empty mansions as much as desert landscapes - can easily feel at home in the IOU-mansion. Let him replace AX-P9 (=APT9) by its negation, that is, by "**w**=**t**"; then it becomes provable that there are only two states of affairs: **t** and **k** - the two truth values, for which a harmless ontological interpretation can surely be found (along the lines of the ontological interpretation of **o**). Without incurring contradiction, he can add to the given list of basic principles of IOU the *principle of nominalism*: **all***x*(if E*(*x*) and not 1(*x*), then 0(*x*)). According to his more or less austere ontological tastes, he is, moreover, free to decide (as far as IOU is concerned) which (and how many) individuals ought to be admitted alongside the merely "formal" entities **o**, **k** and **t**.

Nominalism is a comparatively rare position among ontologists. Much more common is *set-theoretical extensionalism* (sometimes also called "nominalism" because sets are thought to be "abstract individuals"), i.e. the view that, basically, there are only individuals and sets. A set-theoretical extensionalist, too, can easily feel at home in the IOU-mansion. Like the nominalist, he only needs to replace AX-P9 by "**w**=**t**." Without incurring contradiction, he can add to the given list of basic principles of IOU the *principle of set-theoretical extensionalism*: **some***x*SET(*x*) and **all***x*(if E*(*x*) and not 0(*x*) and not 1(*x*), then SET(*x*)). (This implies: **all***x*(PROP(*x*) iff SET(*x*)).) IOU leaves him completely free to decide both which individuals he wants, and also which sets. Most set-theoretical extensionalists agree in the *pure* sets they accept (the whole hierarchy of axiomatic set theory); much more controversial among them is the question which individuals there are. For example, both Quine and Lewis are set-theoretical extensionalists; they would not find much to disagree about in pure set theory, but Quine rejects *merely possible* individuals, while Lewis accepts them.

Note that if **w**=**t**, then there is only one possible world *as state of affairs*: **w**; but this does not preclude that there are infinitely many possible worlds *as* *individuals*, and hence infinitely many states of affairs *as sets* of such possible worlds - as is in fact assumed by Lewis. Note, moreover, that the distinction between "normal" individuals and Leibniz-individuals can no longer be significantly drawn (with respect to possible worlds that are states of affairs) if we have in IOU: **w**=**t**. This may be one of the reasons why for a set-theoretical extensionalist like Lewis the conception of Leibniz-individuals - individuals welded, as it were, to their properties - appears to be the normal and basic conception of individuals. In any case, assuming "**w**=**t**" to be true, the set-theoretical extensionalist who works within the framework of IOU can very well let "<0>(*x*)" apply to Leibniz-individuals, since they have become indistinguishable from "normal" individuals.

(b) Axiomatic set theory can be incorporated into IOU, but only at a price. Existence-principles for properties have to be added to IOU from which the existence-principles of axiomatic set theory - for example, the power-set axiom - can then be deduced on the basis of the definitions of the fundamental set-theoretical expressions. In its present state, IOU does not tell us which properties there are, and hence it does not tell us either which sets or which supersets there are.

This can of course be easily changed. But notice that it can be quite unclear whether an entity is a superset or not, even when it is clear that it is a property and even a set. Concerning supersets, our intuitions are by no means well-established. Consider, for example, the property **id** - being self-identical - which was discussed in comment [*1] of chapter IV.1. **id** appears to be a clearcut example of a superset because we apparently have: **all***x*((**id**,*x*)=**t**). However, applying the definitions, we obtain from this: **all***x*(*x*∈$_S$**id**), **id**∈$_S$**id**; most set-theoreticians consider these two statements to be false (since they conflict with standard set-theoretical principles). If they are false, then "**some***x*((**id**,*x*)≠**t**))" must be correct, and hence, since we certainly have the truths "SET(**id**)" and "**no***x*((**id**,*x*)=**k**)," we obtain by DEF44: **some***x* not E*((**id**,*x*)), which means that, contrary to first appearances, **id** is *not* a superset. But then, which entities should be among those entities *x* for which "(**id**,*x*)=**o**" holds true? Every choice we make seems entirely arbitrary; for example, "(**id**,**id**)=**t**" seems just as correct as "(**id**,*z*)=**t**," where *z* is some individual. (**id** is a *typeless* property. In contrast, for no *typed* property *f* can "(*f*,*f*)=**t**" or "O((*f*,*f*))" be true, since for every typed property "1((*f*,*f*))" is false: Suppose *f* is a typed property, hence its type has the form <*T*>1, *T* being some generalized type; suppose now 1((*f*,*f*)), hence, because of <*T*>1(*f*), by DEF43: *T*(*f*) - contradicting <*T*>1(*f*) in virtue of THE9.)

While **id** is a doubtful case, *the empty set* λ*x*(*x*≠*x*) (or in other words: **ex***o***conj***y*(not *o*≠*o* and *y*=**k**)) is an entirely uncontroversial example of a superset. It is the foundation of the universe of pure supersets (usually they are simply called "pure *sets*"), the basis of the hierarchy that is generated by the existence-axioms of axiomatic set theory (in IOU they concern certain properties). To get set theory really going, albeit not in a pure form, we may plausibly postulate that there are infinitely many *possible* individuals (by the axiom-schema: ≥Nx0(x), for all Arabic numerals N), and then assume as another starting point besides "SSET(λx(x≠x))": SSET(λx0(x)).

(c) Sets and individuals (besides the merely "formal" entities **t**, **k** and **o**) are not enough. The minimal ration of realism with respect to universals is constituted (1) by properties of individuals ("first intensions"): entities of the type <0>1, (2) relations *between* up to *four* individuals (compare E. Tegtmeier, *Grundzüge einer kategorialen Ontologie*, p. 44): entities of the types <0,0>1, <0,0,0>1, <0,0,0,0>1, and (3) by dyadic relations between individuals and states of affairs: entities of the type <0,1>1 (to which belong the very important so-called "propositional attitudes," for example, *believing at* t_0 that Vienna is the capital of Austria, *seeing at* t_0 that Michael is smoking a cigarette). Postulating that the categorial predicates corresponding to the mentioned "natural" types of universals are non-empty will already by itself guarantee that there are universals that are not sets: dyadic relations between individuals, for example, (each ordered pair of individuals, by the way, is such a relation) are not sets, because they are not properties. (They are not sets, yet they may well be modelled by sets.) And certainly not all properties are sets. But in order to show this in IOU, we need AX-P9 - the *principle of intensionalism*. This principle establishes - on the basis of the other axioms - that there are more states of affairs than just **t** and **k**, and this is the *conditio sine qua non* of there being properties that are not sets. It is, moreover, the *conditio sine qua non* of the numerical existence of *non-extensional relations* (of relations at least one saturation of which is a state of affairs that is neither **t** nor **k**). The broadest basis for intensionalism is reached if it is postulated that there are infinitely many states of affairs. (This can be done by an adaptation of AP10 in part I, or - more simply - by the axiom-schema: ≥Nx1(x), for all Arabic numerals N.) Consider, then, that the entire universe of pure supersets and also of supersets ultimately based on individuals has infinitely many copies in the universe of discourse of LIOU (however grandiose that universe of sets may be): Take any arbitrary state of affairs p that is different from **t** and **k**, and replace "**k**" in all given definitions of IOU for set-theoretical terms by a standard name of p, indexing the terms in an appropriate manner (for example: $\lambda_p x$A[x] := **ex**o**conj**y(not A[o] and y=**p**)). So far we have been considering only the **k**-supersets (the supersets *tout court*); consider now also the p-supersets. Whatever is true of the **k**-supersets, is *mutatis mutandis* also true of the p-supersets - including the existence-principles. There is no reason at all to accord, with respect to numerical existence, a privileged status to **k**-supersets.

(d) We have seen how to obtain for any monadic predicate an extraction-term that refers to a superset, if what the term refers to is a genuine entity. Given this, it is fairly obvious how to obtain - more generally - for any k-adic predicate (for any natural number $k \geq 1$) an extraction-term that refers to a *globally defined* k-adic extensional relation (a Fregean k-adic *Begriff* with universal domain), if what the term refers to is a genuine entity:

DEF49 $\lambda x_1 \ldots x_k R[x_1,\ldots,x_k]$:= **exo**$o_1 \ldots o_k$**conj**y(not R$[o_1,\ldots,o_k]$ and y=**k**).

And in particular we can define:

DEF50 $<t_1,\ldots,t_k>$:= $\lambda x_1 \ldots x_k(x_1=t_1$ and ... and $x_k=t_k)$.
("the ordered sequence consisting of $t_1,\ldots,t_k$.")

If a λ-extraction-term, as defined by DEF49, refers to a genuine entity, then this entity is a relation whose saturations are either **k** or **t** - **t** for precisely the entities in the very same order that, in a certain order, fulfill the corresponding predicate. It is, moreover, easily verified that DEF50 yields an adequate conception of ordered sequences. Assume, for example, E*(<t,t′>) and E*(<t″,t‴>) and <t,t′>=<t″,t‴>; hence by DEF50, DEF49: **(exo**oo'**conj**y(not (o=t and o'=t′) and y=**k**),t,t′)=**(exo**oo'**conj**y(not (o=t″ and o'=t‴),t,t′), and hence by AX-E0: **t=conj**y(not (t=t and t′=t′) and y=**k**)= **conj**y(not (t=t″ and t′=t‴) and y=**k**), hence t=t″ and t′=t‴ (by the ontology of states of affairs). Thus we can prove, as is required for the adequacy of DEF50, that ordered pairs (y is a ordered pair := E*(y) and **some**x**some**z(y=<x,z>)) are identical if and only if their first and second components are pairwise identical - and *mutatis mutandis* we can prove the corresponding results for all k-adic sequences.

(e) But how do we get extraction-terms that are based on predicates but refer to relations (including properties) that are *restricted* in their domains, or *non-extensional*, or both restricted in their domains and non-extensional? In part this depends of course on the predicates that are available. In IOU we have, for example, the non-ontological predicate "F(x)." Let it be a predicate that applies to individuals only. Then it is very plausible to assume: E*(λxF(x)). Hence we have: SSET(λxF(x)). Consider now the following functional term: $\mu(z)$:= **the**y'(0(z) and y'=(λxF(x),z)). It is easily proved: **all**z(if 0(z), then $\mu(z)$=(λxF(x),z)), **all**z[if not 0(z), then not E*($\mu(z)$)] (by applying AX-L0, DEF0). Then it is highly plausible to assume E*(**exo**$o'\mu(o')$), and in consequence we have - because **all**z[if E*($\mu(z)$), then 1($\mu(z)$)], too, easily follows - by AX-E0: **all**z((**exo**$o'\mu(o')$,z)=$\mu(z)$). On the basis of this and the above, one easily obtains: **some**z1((**exo**$o'\mu(o')$,z)) and **all**z(1((**exo**$o'\mu(o')$,z)) iff 0(z)), that is (according to DEF43): <0>1(**exo**$o'\mu(o')$) - **exo**$o'\mu(o')$) is a relation restricted in its domain: a *property of individuals*.

But it is also a set (albeit not a superset, although it has precisely the same elements λxF(x) has), and therefore we still do not have an extraction-term that is based on a predicate and refers to a non-extensional relation. The intension of "F(*x*)" is such a relation (let us assume): a non-extensional monadic relation (or property); but so far we lack the means of systematically referring to the intensions of predicates (if they have one) by extraction-terms that are based on them.[*1]

To rectify this, add to LIOU the term-forming operator "**that**": if A is a sentence-form of LIOU, then **that**A is a singular term of LIOU. (To increase readability in case A is a long expression, brackets should be used for marking the scope of "**that**" even where they are not required.) The newly introduced operator is characterized in the most general fashion by the following two axiom-schemata:

AX-I0 if E*(**that**A), then 1(**that**A).[*2]
("If **that**A is a genuine entity, then it is a state of affairs.")

AX-I1 if 1(**that**A), then (O(**that**A) iff A).
("If **that**A is a state of affairs, then it is an obtaining state of affairs precisely if A.")

These two axiom-schemata do not suffice to distinguish **that**A from **conj***y*(not A and *y*=**k**). As far as AX-I0 and AX-I1 are concerned, we may assume **that**A=**conj***y*(not A and *y*=**k**) for all sentence-forms A of LIOU; both axiom-schemata become provable if we define: **that**A := **conj***y*(not A and *y*=**k**). But we merely need to add: **(1)** **some***x*(0(*x*) and **that**F(*x*)≠**t** and **that**F(*x*)≠**k**), and that definition is blocked.

Consider now the functional term "**that**F(*x*)." By AX-I0 we have: **all***x*[if E*(**that**F(*x*)), then 1(**that**F(*x*))]. Hence, assuming **(2)** E*(**ex***o***that**F(*o*)), we obtain by AX-E0: **(3)** **all***x*((**ex***o***that**F(*o*),*x*)=**that**F(*x*)). Because of **(2)**, the predicate "F(*x*)" has an intension, and **ex***o***that**F(*o*) is *its intension*. (In general: the predicate "R[$x_1,\ldots,x_k$]" has an intension if and only if E*(**ex**$o_1\ldots o_k$**that**R[$o_1,\ldots,o_k$]); and if "R[$x_1,\ldots,x_k$]" has an intension, then **ex**$o_1\ldots o_k$**that**R[$o_1,\ldots,o_k$] is *its intension*. Concerning extensions of predicates, see comment [*1] of this chapter.)

What kind of a genuine entity is **ex***o***that**F(*o*)? This depends on which kinds of values the functional term "**that**F(*x*)" yields for which kinds of arguments; and this, again, depends on the meaning of the predicate "F(*x*)." It may, for example, be plausible to assume: **(4)** **all***x*(E*(**that**F(*x*)) iff 0(*x*)). In that case, by AX-I0 and AX-C2: **all***x*(1(**that**F(*x*)) iff 0(*x*)), and hence by AX-C0 **some***x*1(**that**F(*x*)). Therefore, by **(3)** and DEF43: <0>1(**ex***o***that**F(*o*)) - the intension of "F(*x*)" is a *property of individuals*. Moreover, because of **(3)**, **(1)**, **(4)** and DEF44, it is not a set (therefore it is distinct both from **ex***o*′μ(*o*′) and λ*x*F(*x*)).

It may, on the contrary, be plausible on the basis of the meaning of "F(*x*)" not to assume **(4)**, but rather: **(4′)** **all***x*[if 0(*x*), then E*(**that**F(*x*))] and **all***x*(if not

0(x), then **thatF(x)=k**. In that case (holding on to **(2)**), **ex**o**that**F(o) is not of the type <0>1, it is, rather, a *typeless* property. **(1)** still guarantees that it is not a set, and *a fortiori* not a superset.

Whether we take **ex**o**that**F(o) together with **(4)**, or together with **(4′)**, in both cases we obtain: (*) **all**x(**ex**o**that**F(o)(x) iff F(x)) (read metalinguistically: the intension of "F(x)" applies [as a property] exactly to those entities that "F(x)" [as a predicate] applies to). In case we take **ex**o**that**F(o) together with **(4′)**, (*) follows by applying the following much more general theorem:

THE14 if E*(**ex**o_1...o_k**that**R[o_1,...,o_k]) and **all**x_1...**all**x_kE*(**that**R[x_1,...,x_k]), then **all**x_1...**all**x_k(**ex**o_1...o_k**that**R[o_1,...,o_k](x_1,...,x_k) iff R[x_1,...,x_k]).

In case we take **ex**o**that**F(o) together with **(4)**, then we have to remember that "F(x)" was supposed to apply only to individuals, and (*) follows by applying the more general theorem

THE15 if <0>1(**ex**o**that**A[o]) and **all**x(if A[x], then 0(x)), then **all**x(**ex**o**that**A[o](x) iff A[x]).

(f) Although the axiomatic systems of this book were about intensional entities (primarily properties and states of affairs), none of them - so far - was an *intensional system*: a system that contains *intensional contexts*. The reason is that the expressions that generate intensional contexts were avoided (except for an interlude in part II, in which the modal operator "L" was temporarily introduced into LP). IOU *with* "**that**" is, however, an intensional system: "**that**" generates intensional contexts in IOU (supposing that for some sentence-forms A of LIOU we have: 1(**that**A) and **that**A≠**t** and **that**A≠**k**; given this, "**that**" is called "the intensionalizer"). This is most easily seen by considering that "**that**" can be used to define a possibility-operator (such operators are typical generators of intensional contexts):

DEF51 ◊A := 1(**that**A) and **that**A≠**k**.

According to DEF51, it is possible that A if and only if **that**A is a state of affairs that is not the contradictory one.

Intensional contexts are notorious for the fact that the substitutivity of identicals *salva veritate* frequently fails in such contexts. That was good reason for avoiding them: substitutivity of identicals *salva veritate* is a powerful instrument of proof, and without intensional contexts we need not worry at all whether we can apply it safely.

In IOU with "**that**" we *have* to worry, and this is a drawback to the introduction of "**that**," the increase in expressive power notwithstanding. Bill Clinton is the president of the United States in 1995; asserting this in LIOU, we have: **(x)** **bc=pusa95**. Moreover, we very plausibly have: **(xx)**

1(**that(bc≠pusa95)**) and **that(bc≠pusa95)≠k**. Therefore by DEF51: **◊(bc≠pusa95)**, and hence on the basis of **(x)** - *naively* applying substitutivity of identicals *salva veritate* - **◊(bc≠bc)**, hence (according to DEF51): **that(bc≠bc) ≠k** - contradicting **(xxx) that(bc≠bc)=k**. Instead of denying at least one of the assumptions **(x)**, **(xx)** and **(xxx)** (the denial of **(x)** and **(xxx)** really is out of the question)[*3], it seems best to locate the trouble in the fact that ''**pusa95**'' is a *non-rigid designator* occurring in an intensional context; a substitution of identicals that involves non-rigid designators and takes place in an intensional context is bound to produce a *non sequitur* (remember Quine's examples). In the present case, therefore, **◊(bc≠bc)** simply does not follow from **◊(bc≠pusa95)** and **(x)**.

COMMENTS

[*1] We *do* already have the means of systematically referring to their *unrestricted extensions* (if they have one), and sometimes - for example, in the case of ''0(x)'' - intension, extension *simpliciter* and unrestricted extension coincide: The predicate ''R[x_1,...,x_k]'' has an unrestricted extension if and only if E*($\lambda x_1 \ldots x_k$R[x_1,...,x_k]); if ''R[x_1,...,x_k]'' has an unrestricted extension, then $\lambda x_1 \ldots x_k$R[x_1,...,x_k]) is its unrestricted extension. ''0(x)'' has an unrestricted extension, and λx0(x), its unrestricted extension, is also its extension *simpliciter* and its intension. (In the case of ''F(x),'' which also has an unrestricted extension, we have to decide whether its extension *simpliciter* is its unrestricted extension λxF(x), or rather the restricted extension **ex**$o'\mu(o')$ of it. The decision depends on whether, for a non-individual *a* that is designated by the name ''**a**,'' it is more natural - in view of the meaning of ''F'' - to say of ''F(**a**)'' that it is neither true nor false, or rather that it is false. Given bivalence for LIOU, ''F(**a**)'' *is* true or false; but this may not be the most natural option, although it is surely the most convenient one for theoretical purposes.)

[*2] Why not be so audacious as to assert the following axiom-schema: 1(**that**A)? We may take LIOU to be similar to a natural language in its non-ontological predicates; ''F(x),'' for example, might mean the same as ''x has a toothache at t_0.'' Should we say that **that**(New York has a toothache at t_0) is a state of affairs? While we might say that it is a state of affairs because it is **k**, it is at least as correct to say that *it is not a genuine entity*. This suffices for preferring the schema ''if E*(**that**A), then 1(**that**A)'' to the unconditioned schema ''1(**that**A).''

[*3] One may think it possible to deny (**xx**) by denying its second conjunct. Suppose it is denied, that is, suppose: **that(bc≠pusa95)=k**; hence (by the ontology of states of affairs) **neg(that(bc≠pusa95))=t**, hence - by the correct schema ''if 1(**that**(not A)), then **neg(that**(not A))=**that**A'' - **that(bc=pusa95) =t**. But this is obviously false, because **that(bc=pusa95)** - which is identical with **that**[PUSA95(**bc**) and **all**x(if PUSA95(x), then x=**bc**)] - is not a state of affairs that obtains in every possible world. Replace, however, ''**pusa95**'' by any rigid designator δ of Bill Clinton (by ''**bc**'' foremost); invariably we have: **that(bc=**δ**)=t**, and hence - applying the correct schema ''if 1(**that**A), then **neg(that**A)=**that**(not A)'' - also **that(bc≠**δ**)=k**.

CHAPTER IV.4

ACTUAL EXISTENCE, IDENTITY, AND THE FUNDAMENTAL STATUS OF STATES OF AFFAIRS

(a) A lot of work remains to be done in the codification of the logic of "**that**"; the axioms AX-I0 and AX-I1 are certainly not enough. For example, the correct schemata mentioned in comment [*3] of the last chapter, and *all* principles concerning the **that**-connection between functors for states of affairs and sentence-connectives have to be incorporated into IOU (as theorems or axioms). (Another example of such a principle is: if 1(**that**A) and 1(**that**B), then **that**(A and B)=**conj**(**that**A,**that**B).) Also, we would certainly like to have the following theorem in IOU: if **all***x*(0(*x*), then 1(**that**A[*x*])), then **thatall***x*(if 0(*x*), then A[*x*]))=**conj***y***some***z*(0(*z*) and *y*=**that**A[*z*]). However, these further developments will not be treated here; the final chapter of this book is dedicated to other subjects.

(b) The general concept of actual existence (like the general concept of relation and function) cannot be defined in IOU. We might add to LIOU a primitive predicate "AE(*x*)" - "*x* is actually existent" - and then simply define for every generalized type *T*: AE*T*(*x*) := AE(*x*) and *T*(*x*). But this way of defining "*x* is an actually existent entity of type *T*" is, taken by itself, not very illuminating. Whether "AE(*x*)" is introduced as another primitive predicate or not, it seems best to proceed in the following manner.

LIOU also comprises the singular term "**sr**," interpreted just as in PT1 (as designating the property of real subsistence for entities of type 0). In IOU we have the following axioms for this expression: AX-R1, which is APT20, and

AX-R0 <0>1(**sr**).

We then define:

DEF52
(i) AE0(t) := **sr**(t); AE1(t) := O(t).
(ii) $AE\langle T_1,\ldots,T_k\rangle T_{k+1}(t)$:= $\langle T_1,\ldots,T_k\rangle T_{k+1}(t)$ and **some**x_1...**some**x_k[AE$T_1(x_1)$ and ... and AE$T_k(x_k)$ and AET_{k+1}((t,$x_1,\ldots,x_k$))].

DEF52 tells us that an actually existent state of affairs is an obtaining state of affairs (O(t) implies 1(t): consider DEF31, AX-P0); that an actually existent individual is an individual that exemplifies real subsistence (compare DPT58; **sr(t)** implies 0(t): from **sr(t)** by DEF45, DEF31, AX-P0: 1((**sr**,t)), hence, because of AX-R0 and DEF43, 0(t)); that an actually existent function of type

$<T_1,\ldots,T_k>T_{k+1}$ is a function of type $<T_1,\ldots,T_k>T_{k+1}$ that yields for some actually existent appropriately typed arguments an actually existent appropriately typed value. In particular, we have (according to DEF52, DEF45): $AE<0>1(y) := <0>1(y)$ and **some**x[AE0(x) and AE1((y,x))] := $<0>1(y)$ and **some**x(AE0(x) and $y(x)$) - an actually existent property of individuals is a property of individuals that is exemplified by some actually existent individual. Nothing else is said by DPT59 of PT1.

Let now "AE(x)" be added to LIOU. Then we have as further axiom-schemata:

AX-A0 **all**x[if $T(x)$, then (AE(x) iff AE$T(x)$)], for every generalized type T.

AX-A1 not AE(**o**).

AX-A2 if k-FUNC(t), then [AE(t) iff **some**x_1...**some**x_k(AE(x_1) and AE(x_k) and AE((t,x_1,...,x_k)))].

In view of DEF52, AX-A0 gives substantial content to the concept of actual existence. (If we had followed the procedure suggested first in this section, AX-A0 would have been an empty triviality.) For typed k-adic functions, AX-A2 is already a consequence of AX-A0 and AX-A1 (AX-A2, therefore, does not conflict with AX-A0):

Assume: (1) $<T_1,\ldots,T_k>T_{k+1}$(t), where $<T_1,\ldots,T_k>T_{k+1}$ is a generalized type.

(**i**) Assume AE(t); hence by AX-A0 and (1): AE$<T_1,\ldots,T_k>T_{k+1}$(t), hence by DEF52: **some**x_1...**some**x_k[AET_1(x_1) and ... and AET_k(x_k) and AET_{k+1}((t,x_1,...,x_k))], hence by AX-A0 (by DEF52, etc.: **all**x(if AE$T(x)$, then $T(x)$), for every generalized type T): **some**x_1...**some**x_k[AE(x_1) and ... and AE(x_k) and AE((t,x_1,...,x_k))].

(**ii**) Assume **some**x_1...**some**x_k[AE(x_1) and ... and AE(x_k) and AE((t,x_1,...,x_k))], hence by AX-A1, DEF0: E*((t,x_1,...,x_k)), hence, because of (1) (in view of DEF43, AX-S2), T_{k+1}((t,x_1,...,x_k)), and hence (according to DEF43): $T_1(x_1)$ and ... and $T_k(x_k)$. Consequently by AX-A0: **some**x_1...**some**x_k[AET_1(x_1) and ... and AET_k(x_k) and AET_{k+1}((t,x_1,...,x_k))], hence, since we also have (1), by DEF52: AE$<T_1,\ldots,T_k>T_{k+1}$(t), hence by AX-A0: AE(t).

(c) According to DEF52, the actual existence of entities of higher types depends conceptually on the actual existence of entities of lower types. Ultimately, the actual existence of all entities having complex types depends on the actual existence of individuals and states of affairs. There is, therefore, a clear sense in which these entities are *fundamental entities*.

Moreover, the actual existence of individuals can be conceptually reduced to the actual existence of states of affairs: According to DEF52 and DEF45, "x is an actually existent individual" is defined by "the saturation of **sr** by x is an *obtaining* state of affairs," which, according to DEF52, is definitionally equivalent to "the saturation of **sr** by x is an *actually existent* state of affairs." Thus, we might as well have defined "x is an actually existent individual" by "the saturation of **sr** by x is an actually existent state of affairs."

States of affairs, therefore, turn out to be, in a certain sense, the most fundamental entities: their actual existence makes everything else that actually exists in the hierarchy of typed entities *actually exist*. A similar point can be made with respect to identity: According to AX-S3, etc., functions f and g of type $<T_1,...,T_k>T_{k+1}$ are identical if (and only if) all their saturations (by the same k entities in the same order) of type T_{k+1} are identical:
Assume $<T_1,...,T_k>T_{k+1}(f)$, $<T_1,...,T_k>T_{k+1}(g)$, **all**x_1...**all**x_k(if $T_{k+1}((f,x_1,...,x_k))$ and $T_{k+1}((g,x_1,...,x_k))$, then $(f,x_1,...,x_k)=(g,x_1,...,x_k))$. Assume now: not $T_{k+1}((f,x_1,...,x_k))$, hence, because of the first assumptions, by DEF43, AX-S2, DEF0: $(f,x_1,...,x_k)=\mathbf{o}$, and (not $T_1(x_1)$ or ... or not $T_k(x_k)$), hence, because of the first assumptions, not $T_{k+1}((g,x_1,...,x_k))$, and therefore (as for f): $(g,x_1,...,x_k)=\mathbf{o}$. Thus finally: $(f,x_1,...,x_k)=(g,x_1,...,x_k)$. The same result is obtained from the first assumptions in the same way under the assumption: not $T_{k+1}((g,x_1,...,x_k))$. Therefore from the first assumptions: **all**x_1...**all**x_k($(f,x_1,...,x_k)=(g,x_1,...,x_k)$), and by THE8 also: k-FUNC(f), k-FUNC(g). Hence by AX-S3: $f=g$.
This means that the identity of entities of all complex types ultimately depends on the identity of individuals and states of affairs. But the identity of individuals depends, in turn, on the identity of states of affairs, in virtue of the following principle: **all**x**all**z(if $0(x)$ and $0(z)$ and **all**f(if $<0>1(f)$, then $(f,x)=(f,z)$), then $x=z$) - individuals are identical if (and only if) they yield identical saturations (certain states of affairs) for all properties of individuals.

Whether with regard to actual existence or to identity, states of affairs are *the* fundamental entities; to them - not to individuals (as has normally been supposed since Aristotle) - one should accord the status of *ontological priority*. This result depends, of course, on the chosen theoretical framework; but the choice of that framework is by no means arbitrary: it is a framework that combines universal range and unifying systematic power (regarding both principles and concepts) with intuitive well-foundedness.

EPILOGUE

The last chapter has made it clear that the *obtaining* of states of affairs is fundamental for the actual existence of all typed entities. Given which states of affairs obtain and which do not, it is a matter of conceptual necessity which typed entities are actually existent, and which are not. But which states of affairs obtain and which do not, does not itself appear to be a matter of conceptual necessity. As a matter of conceptual possibility, other states of affairs might have obtained than those which do; "**w**" might have designated a different state of affairs than it actually does; indeed, it might have designated **t**. ("**w**" is a non-rigid designator: if things had been otherwise, it would have designated something else. But it is not an indexical: in every utterance in which it occurs "**w**" has the same designatum.) It is, therefore, not unreasonable to ask: what is the reason for the obtaining of states of affairs other than **t**, and for the obtaining of precisely *these* states of affairs? ("O(**w**)" is, indeed, provable and an analytical truth; but this does not mean that it is pointless to search for an explanation of why **w** - *this particular state of affair* - obtains. In contrast, there is indeed no point in looking for an explanation for the obtaining of **t**; it is self-explanatory because "O(**t**)" is a provable, analytical truth. This contrast between "**w**" and "**t**" results from the latter being a rigid designator, the former a non-rigid one.)

Of course, some states of affairs obtain or do not obtain, *because* (in some appropriate sense of "because") other states of affairs obtain. It is an essential part of the business of science to establish such because-connections between states of affairs. But ultimately the pursuit of such connections does not yield a satisfactory answer to the above question: if it does not lead into an infinite regress or a vicious circle, then, ideally, it reaches the point where all non-obtaining states of affairs *do not obtain, because* certain states of affairs - call them "the primary states of affairs" - obtain; and where all obtaining states of affairs other than the primary ones *do obtain*, again *because* the primary ones obtain. But why do the primary states of affairs obtain? Their obtaining is not self-explanatory, since the conjunction of them will certainly not amount to **t**.

Perhaps the obtaining and non-obtaining of states of affairs, as we find it, is simply a brute ontological fact that does not have an ultimate explanation because there is no ultimate reason for it; it is perhaps itself the ultimate ontological "circumstance." Alternatively, and somewhat more satisfactorily, given our hunger for explanation, there might be an entity, and only one such, that is the active *source* of the obtaining of those states of affairs that do obtain (**t** being excepted), and of the non-obtaining of all others. This entity would have to be actually existent in some form (but in a form different from the forms of actual existence captured by DEF52, and from any form conceptually connected to them), for it is quite incomprehensible how an entity that is not actually existent can *make* anything (for example, states of affairs) be actually existent. But it could not be a state of affairs, function or individual - all these entities are, with conceptual necessity, (actual or potential) *recipients* of actual existence, not (actual or potential) *sources* of it. We might say that it is an individual *in a wide sense*, in a sense wider than the one in which the predicate "0(x)" was understood in IOU and PT1. But all the individuals in a wide sense other than 0-individuals which have been considered by us (mainly Leibniz-individuals and Meinongian objects) are, like "normal" individuals, not sources of actual existence but, with conceptual necessity, mere recipients thereof (and some of them are not even this, not even potentially). Since we have considered the representative kinds of individuals in a wide sense, it seems adequate to adopt a notion of individual according to which also individuals in a wide sense (they should, in significant ways, be similar to "normal" individuals) cannot have a source of actual existence among them.

Thus it appears that the active source of the obtaining and non-obtaining of states of affairs, if there is such a source, is best taken to be an *ontologically transcendent* entity, an entity beyond all categories, even if widely conceived; and this entity we could, indeed, call "God." But it would certainly not be a bearer of the *property of individuals* **d** - *being a divine individual* - which is considered in chapters II.4, II.8 and III.13, since it is not an individual; nor could it be Nothing (that is: **o**; see IV.1.(b)) which, if not taken to be an individual in a wide sense, is also an entity beyond all categories - but in no manner an actually existent one. (Compare the axioms and definitions of IOU that involve "**o**.") Rather, it is similar to the Neo-Platonic One, something that is "beyond being (or beings)" and "the source (or cause) of all beings" - and something which is the former because it is the latter. It is in no category of beings and actually existent in a sense entirely different from that in which categorized beings actually exist, because via the actual existence of states of affairs it is the active source of the actual existence of all actually existent beings that have a generalized type (compare IV.4.(c)) - which are per se not capable of being such a source. We may assume further that it is the active source of the actual existence *of all actually existent entities* (except those whose actual existence is grounded merely in the actual existence of **t** - for example {**t**}). Or in the words of Thomas Aquinas (*Summa contra Gentiles*, III,1): "Unum [est] primum entium, totius esse perfectionem plenam possidens, quod Deum dicimus, ... qui ex sui perfectionis abundantia omnibus existentibus esse largitur, ut non solum primum entium, sed et principium omnium esse comprobetur." And Thomas continues (and we may agree): "Esse autem aliis tribuit non necessitate naturae, sed secundum suae arbitrium voluntatis."

APPENDIX

PRINCIPLES, PROOFS AND DEFINITIONS

SYSTEM P

•AP1 **all**x**all**y**all**z(if xPy and yPz, then xPz).
•AP2 **all**x(xPx).
•AP3 **all**x**all**y(if xPy and yPx, then x=y).
•AP4 **some**z[**all**x(if A[x], then xPz) and **all**y(if **all**x(if A[x], then xPy), then zPy)].
•AP5 **all**z**all**z′(if **all**x(if QA(x) and xPz, then xPz′), then zPz′).
•AP6 **all**x[if xP**conj**yA[y] and not M(x), then **some**k′(k′Px and not M(k′) and **some**z(k′Pz and A[z]))].
•AP7 **w**≠**k**.
•AP8 QC(**w**).
•AP9 **w**≠**t**.
•AP10 **some**x$A_{=n}(x)$.

•DP1 tP*t′ := tPt′ and t≠t′.
•DP2 A(t) := **no**y(y≠t and yPt).
•DP3 C(t) := **no**y(y≠t and tPy).
•DP4 M(t) := **all**y(tPy).
•DP5 T(t) := **all**y(yPt).
•DP6 QA(t) := **all**y(if yPt, then y=t or M(y)).
•DP7 QC(t) := **all**y(if tPy, then y=t or T(y)).
•DP8 OV(t,t′) := **some**z(zPt and zPt′).
•DP9 EV(t,t′) := **some**z(tPz and t′Pz).
•DP10 CN(t,t′) := OV(t,t′) or EV(t,t′).
•DP11 t′->t := tPt′.
•DP12 **conj**(t,t′) := **the**x(tPx and t′Px and **all**y(if tPy and t′Py, then xPy)).
•DP13 **disj**(t,t′) := **the**x(xPt and xPt′ and **all**y(if yPt and yPt′, then yPx)).
•DP14 **neg**$_1$(t) := **the**y[**all**z(if zPt and zPy, then M(z)) and **all**k(if **all**z(if zPt and zPk, then M(z)), then kPy)].
•DP15 **neg**$_2$(t) := **the**y[**all**z(if tPz and yPz, then T(z)) and **all**k(if **all**z(if tPz and kPz, then T(z)), then yPk)].
•DP16 **neg**(t) :=**the**y[y=**neg**$_1$(t) and y=**neg**$_2$(t)].

•DP17 **conj***x*A[*x*] := **the***z*[**all***x*(if A[*x*], then *x*P*z*) and **all***y*(if **all***x*(if A[*x*], then *x*P*y*), then *z*P*y*)].
•DP18 **t** := **the***y***all***x*(*y*P*x*).
•DP19 **k** := **the***y***all***x*(*x*P*y*).
•DP20 EL(t) := QA(t) and not M(t).
•DP21 t∈t′ := EL(t) and tPt′.
•DP22 **impl**(t,t′) := **disj**(**neg**(t),t′).
•DP23 **disj***x*A[*x*] := **the***z*[**all***x*(if A[*x*], then *z*P*x*) and **all***y*(if **all***x*(if A[*x*], then *y*P*x*), then *y*P*z*)].
•DP24 K(t) := not **some***x*(*x*Pt and **neg**(*x*)Pt).
•DP25 MX(t) := **all***x*(*x*Pt or **neg**(*x*)Pt).
•DP26 MK(t) := MX(t) and K(t).
•DP27 S(t) := not **some***x*(tP*x* and tP**neg**(*x*)).
•DP28 MN(t) := **all***x*(tP*x* or tP**neg**(*x*)).
•DP29 P(t) := **some***y*(MK(*y*) and tP*y*).
•DP30 N(t) := not P(**neg**(t)).
•DP31 O(t) := tP**w.**
•DP32 V(t) := O(t).
•DP33 F(t) := V(**neg**(t)).
•DP34 CT(t) := P(t) and P(**neg**(t)).
•DP35 A_0(t) := A(t);
A_{n+1}(t) := **all***y*(if *y*Pt, then *y*=t or A_n(*y*)).
•DP36 C^0(t) := C(t);
C^{n+1}(t) := **all***y*(if tP*y*, then *y*=t or C^n(*y*)).
•DP37 $A_{=0}$(t) := A_0(t);
$A_{=n+1}$(t) := A_{n+1}(t) and not A_n(t).
•DP38 $C^{=0}$(t) := C^0(t);
$C^{=n+1}$(t) := C^{n+1}(t) and not C^n(t).
•DP39 tNP*t′ := tP*t′ and **no***z*(tP**z* and *z*P*t′).

•TP1 **all***x***all***y***all***z*(if *x*P**y* and *y*P**z*, then *x*P**z*).
•TP2 **all***x* not *x*P**x*.
•TP3 **all***x***all***y*(*x*P**y* iff *x*P*y* and not *y*P*x*).
•TP4 **all***x***all***y*(if T(*x*) and T(*y*), then *x*=*y*).
•TP5 **all***x***all***y*(if M(*x*) and M(*y*), then *x*=*y*).
•TP6 **all***x*(if T(*x*), then C(*x*)).
•TP7 **all***x*(if M(*x*), then A(*x*)).
•TP8 if **some***x*T(*x*), then **one***x*C(*x*).
•TP9 if **some***x*M(*x*), then **one***x*A(*x*).
•TP10 if **some***x*T(*x*), then **the***x*T(*x*)=**the***x*C(*x*).

•TP11 if **some***x*M(*x*), then **the***x*M(*x*)=**the***x*A(*x*).

•TP12 **all***x*C(*x*) iff **all***x*A(*x*).

•TP13 **all***y***all***x*(if **all***z*(*z*P*y* iff *z*P*x*), then *y*=*x*).

•TP14 **all***x***some***y*(*x*->*y*).

•TP15 [the "at most one"-principles for DP12 - DP16].

•TP16 [the "at most one"-principle for DP17].

•TP17 [the "precisely one"-principle for DP17].

•TP18 **all***x*(if A[*x*], then *x*P**conj***z*A[*z*]) and **all***y*(if **all***x*(if A[*x*], then *x*P*y*), then **conj***z*A[*z*]P*y*).

•TP19 **all***z***all***z*′**some***x*(*z*P*x* and *z*′P*x* and **all***y*(if *z*P*y* and *z*′P*y*, then *x*P*y*)).

Proof: According to TP18 we have: **all***x*(if *x*P*z* or *x*P*z*′, then *x*P**conj***k*(*k*P*z* or *k*P*z*′)) and **all***y*(if **all***x*(if *x*P*z* or *x*P*z*′, then *x*P*y*), then **conj***k*(*k*P*z* or *k*P*z*′)P*y*). But according to AP2: *z*P*z* and *z*′P*z*′. Hence: *z*P**conj***k*(*k*P*z* or *k*P*z*′) and *z*′P**conj***k*(*k*P*z* or *k*P*z*′). Assume: *z*P*y* and *z*′P*y*, hence, according to AP1, **all***x*(if *x*P*z* or *x*P*z*′, then *x*P*y*), hence, according to TP18, **conj***k*(*k*P*z* or *k*P*z*′)P*y*. Therefore: **all***y*(if *z*P*y* and *z*′P*y*, then **conj***k*(*k*P*z* or *k*P*z*′)P*y*). TP19 is an immediate consequence of the underlined results.

•TP20 **all***z***all***z*′(**conj**(*z*,*z*′)=**conj***k*(*k*P*z* or *k*P*z*′)).

•TP21 **all***z***all***z*′**some***x*(*x*P*z* and *x*P*z*′ and **all***y*(if *y*P*z* and *y*P*z*′, then *y*P*x*)).

Proof: According to TP18 we have: **all***y*(if *y*P*z* and *y*P*z*′, then *y*P**conj***k*(*k*P*z* and *k*P*z*′)) and **all***y*(if **all***x*(if *x*P*z* and *x*P*z*′, then *x*P*y*), then **conj***k*(*k*P*z* and *k*P*z*′)P*y*). Moreover, trivially, **all***x*(if *x*P*z* and *x*P*z*′, then *x*P*z*) and **all***x*(if *x*P*z* and *x*P*z*′, then *x*P*z*′). Hence: **conj***k*(*k*P*z* and *k*P*z*′)P*z* and **conj***k*(*k*P*z* and *k*P*z*′)P*z*′. TP21 is an immediate consequence of the underlined results.

•TP22 **all***z***all***z*′(**disj**(*z*,*z*′)=**conj***k*(*k*P*z* and *k*P*z*′)).

•TP23 **all***z***all***z*′**all***y*(*y*P**disj**(*z*,*z*′) iff *y*P*z* and *y*P*z*′).

[**all***z***all***z*′**all***y*(**disj**(*z*,*z*′)->*y* iff *z*->*y* and *z*′->*y*).]

Proof: According to TP21, TP15 and DP13 we have: **disj**(*z*,*z*′)P*z* and **disj**(*z*,*z*′)P*z*′ and **all***y*(if *y*P*z* and *y*P*z*′, then *y*P**disj**(*z*,*z*′)). Hence because of AP1: **all***y*(if *y*P**disj**(*z*,*z*′), then *y*P*z* and *y*P*z*′).

•TP24 **all***z***all***z*′**all***y*(**conj**(*z*,*z*′)P*y* iff *z*P*y* and *z*′P*y*).

[**all***z***all***z*′**all***y*(*y*->**conj**(*z*,*z*′) iff *y*->*z* and *y*->*z*′).]

Proof: According to TP19, TP15 und DP12 we have: *z*P**conj**(*z*,*z*′) and *z*′P**conj**(*z*,*z*′) and **all***y*(if *z*P*y* and *z*′P*y*, then **conj**(*z*,*z*′)P*y*). Hence because of AP1: **all***y*(if **conj**(*z*,*z*′)P*y*, then *z*P*y* and *z*′P*y*).

•TP25 **all***z***all***z*′**all***y*(if *y*P*z* or *y*P*z*′, then *y*P**conj**(*z*,*z*′)).

•TP26 **all***z***all***z*′**all***y*(if *z*P*y* or *z*′P*y*, then **disj**(*z*,*z*′)P*y*).

•TP27 **some***y*M(*y*) and **some***y*T(*y*).

Proof: **(i)** According to TP18 we have: **all***x*(if *x*≠*x*, then *x*P**conj***z*(*z*≠*z*)) and **all***y*(if **all***x*(if *x*≠*x*, then *x*P*y*), then **conj***z*(*z*≠*z*)P*y*); hence, because of **all***y***all***x*(if *x*≠*x*, then *x*P*y*), **all***y*′(**conj***z*(*z*≠*z*)P*y*′), hence by DP4: **some***y*M(*y*).

(**ii**) According to TP18 we have: **all***x*(if *x*=*x*, then *x*P**conj***z*(*z*=*z*)) and **all***y*(if **all***x*(if *x*=*x*, then *x*P*y*), then **conj***z*(*z*=*z*)P*y*); hence, because of **all***x*(*x*=*x*), **all***x*(*x*P**conj***z*(*z*=*z*)), hence by DP5: **some***y*T(*y*).

•TP28 if **all***x*(if A[*x*], then B[*x*]), then **conj***z*A[*z*]P**conj***z*B[*z*].

Proof: Assume **all***x*(if A[*x*], then B[*x*]); according to TP18, **all***x*(if B[*x*], then *x*P**conj***z*B[*z*]); hence: **all***x*(if A[*x*], then *x*P**conj***z*B[*z*]). According to TP18, **all***y*(if **all***x*(if A[*x*], then *x*P*y*), then **conj***z*A[*z*]P*y*). Therefore: **conj***z*A[*z*]P**conj***z*B[*z*].

•TP29 if **all***x*(A[*x*] iff B[*x*]), then **conj***z*A[*z*]=**conj***z*B[*z*].

•TP30 **all***z*(*z*=**conj***z*′(*z*′P*z*)).

Proof: According to AP2, *z*P*z*; hence by TP18 *z*P**conj***z*′(*z*′P*z*). According to TP18, **all***y*(if **all***z*′(if *z*′P*z*, then *z*′P*y*), then **conj***z*′(*z*′P*z*)P*y*); hence, because of **all***z*′(if *z*′P*z*, then *z*′P*z*), **conj***z*′(*z*′P*z*)P*z*. The underlined results entail *z*=**conj***z*′(*z*′P*z*), according to AP3.

•TP31 **all***z*(*z*=**conj***z*′(QA(*z*′) and *z*′P*z*)).

Proof: According to TP18 we have **all***x*(if QA(*x*) and *x*P*z*, then *x*P**conj***z*′(QA(*z*′) and *z*′P*z*)), hence by AP5 *z*P**conj***z*′(QA(*z*′) and *z*′P*z*). Trivially, **all***x*(if QA(*x*) and *x*P*z*, then *x*P*z*); according to TP18, **all***y*(if **all***x*(if QA(*x*) and *x*P*z*, then *x*P*y*), then **conj***z*′(QA(*z*′) and *z*′P*z*)P*y*); hence: **conj***z*′(QA(*z*′) and *z*′P*z*)P*z*. The underlined results entail *z*=**conj***z*′(QA(*z*′) and *z*′P*z*) on the basis of AP3.

•TP32 **all***x*(M(*x*) iff *x*=**t**).

•TP33 **all***z*(*z*=**conj***z*′(*z*′=*z*)).

Proof: According to TP18: *z*P**conj***z*′(*z*′=*z*). Also according to TP18: **all***y*(if **all***z*′(if *z*′=*z*, then *z*′P*y*), then **conj***z*′(*z*′=*z*)P*y*), and according to AP2: **all***z*′(if *z*′=*z*, then *z*′P*z*); hence: **conj***z*′(*z*′=*z*)P*z*. From the underlined results *z*=**conj***z*′(*z*′=*z*) follows by AP3.

•TP34 **all***x*(T(*x*) iff *x*=**k**.)

•TP35 if **no***z*A[*z*], then **conj***y*A[*y*]=**t**.

Proof: Assume: not **some***z*A[*z*], hence **all***z*(A[*z*] iff *z*≠*z*), hence by TP29: **conj***y*A[*y*]=**conj***y*(*y*≠*y*); but **conj***y*(*y*≠*y*) is **t** (compare the proof of TP27).

•TP36 **no***x*(*x*P**t** and *x*≠**t**).

Proof: Assume *x*P**t**; because of M(**t**): **t**P*x*; hence by AP3: *x*=**t**.

•TP37 **all***z***all***z*′**all***x*(if *x*P**conj**(*z*,*z*′) and not M(*x*), then **some***k*′(*k*′P*x* and not M(*k*′) and (*k*′P*z* or *k*′P*z*′))).

Proof: As an instance of AP6 we have: **all***x*[if *x*P**conj***y*(*y*P*z* or *y*P*z*′) and not M(*x*), then **some***k*′(*k*′P*x* and not M(*k*′) and **some***m*(*k*′P*m* and (*m*P*z* or *m*P*z*′)))]. Moreover, **conj***y*(*y*P*z* or *y*P*z*′)=**conj**(*z*,*z*′) according to TP20, and from **some***m*(*k*′P*m* and (*m*P*z* or *m*P*z*′)) one obtains by AP1: *k*′P*z* or *k*′P*z*′.

•TP38 **all***z***all***z*′**all***x*(if QA(*x*) and *x*P**conj**(*z*,*z*′), then *x*P*z* or *x*P*z*′).

Proof: Assume: QA(*x*) and *x*P**conj**(*z*,*z*′). In case M(*x*), then *x*P*z* [because of **all***y*(*x*P*y*)], hence: *x*P*z* or *x*P*z*′. In case not M(*x*), then by TP37: **some***k*′(*k*′P*x* and not M(k′) and (k′Pz or k′Pz′)); but, according to assumption, QA(x); hence according to DP6: k′=x or M(k′); therefore [because not M(k′)] k′=x, and hence: xPz or xPz′.

•TP39 **all**x(if QA(x), then **all**z**all**z′(xP**conj**y(yPz or yPz′) iff xPz or xPz′)).

•TP40 **all**x[if QA(x) and not M(x), then (xP**conj**yA[y] iff **some**z(xPz and A[z]))].

Proof: Assume: QA(x) and not M(x). Assume - besides the first assumption - **some**z(xPz and A[z]); hence by TP18: **some**z(xPz and zP**conj**yA[y]), hence by AP1: xP**conj**yA[y]. Assume conversely - besides the first assumption - xP**conj**yA[y]; hence by AP6: **some**k′(k′Px and not M(k′) and **some**z(k′Pz and A[z])), hence by DP6 because of QA(x), k′Px, not M(k′): k′=x, hence **some**z(xPz and A[z]).

•TP41 **all**x(if QA(x) and not M(x), then (xP**conj**y(QA(y) and A[y]) iff A[x])).

•TP42 **conj**y(QA(y) and A[y])=**conj**y(QA(y) and not M(y) and A[y]).

Proof: Because of **all**y(if QA(y) and not M(y) and A[y], then QA(y) and A[y]) we have according to TP28: **conj**y(QA(y) and not M(y) and A[y])P**conj**y(QA(y) and A[y]). And we also have **conj**y(QA(y) and A[y])P**conj**y(QA(y) and not M(y) and A[y]): from TP41 one obtains by TP18: **all**x(if QA(x) and not M(x) and xP**conj**y(QA(y) and A[y]), then xP**conj**y(QA(y) and not M(y) and A[y])); "not M(x)" can be omitted from the antecedent of this, since the restriction it expresses is inessential; therefore, one obtains the desired result by AP5. TP42 follows from the underlined results by AP3.

•TP43 **all**x(if EL(x), then (xP**conj**y(EL(y) and A[y]) iff A[x])).

•TP44 **all**x(x∈ **conj**y(EL(y) and A[y]) iff EL(x) and A[x]).

•TP45 **all**x[**all**z(if zPx and zP**conj**y(QA(y) and not yPx), then M(z)) and **all**k(if **all**z(if zPx and zPk, then M(z)), then kP**conj**y(QA(y) and not yPx))].

Proof: (**i**) Assume zPx and zP**conj**y(QA(y) and not yPx); assume for *reductio*: not M(z); hence by TP32: z≠**t**, hence by TP36: not zP**t**, hence by AP5: **some**m(QA(m) and mPz and not mP**t**), hence because of AP2 and TP32: **some**m(QA(m) and not M(m) and mPz), hence: **some**m(QA(m) and not M(m) and mPx and mP**conj**y(QA(y) and not yPx)), by AP1 and the first assumption; hence by TP41: mPx and not mPx - contradiction. Therefore from the first assumption: M(z).

(**ii**) Assume **all**z(if zPx and zPk, then M(z)); assume: QA(y′) and y′Pk; (**x**) y′Px; hence by the first assumption: M(y′), hence: y′P**conj**y(QA(y) and not yPx); (**xx**) not y′Px; hence by TP18: y′P**conj**y(QA(y) and not yPx). Therefore: **all**y′(if QA(y′) and y′Pk, then y′P**conj**y(QA(y) and not yPx)), hence by AP5: kP**conj**y(QA(y) and not yPx).

•TP46 **all**x[**all**z(if zPx and zP$\textbf{neg}_1$(x), then M(z)) and **all**k(if **all**z(zPx and zPk, then M(z)), then kP$\textbf{neg}_1$(x))].

•TP47 **all**x($\textbf{neg}_1$(x)=**conj**y(QA(y) and not yPx)).

•TP48 **all**x[**all**z(if xPz and **conj**y(QA(y) and not yPx)Pz, then T(z)) and **all**k(if **all**z(if xPz and kPz, then T(z)), then **conj**y(QA(y) and not yPx)Pk)].

Proof: **(i)** Assume: *x*P*z* and **conj***y*(QA(*y*) and not *y*P*x*)P*z*; assume for *reductio*: not T(*z*); hence by TP34 *z*≠**k**, hence, because of *z*P**k** and AP3, not **k**P*z*, hence by AP5: **some***m*(QA(*m*) and not *m*P*z*). But, because of *x*P*z* and AP1, **all***m*(if QA(*m*) and *m*P*x*, then *m*P*z*), and - because of **conj***y*(QA(*y*) and not *y*P*x*)P*z*, TP18 und AP1 - **all***m*(if QA(*m*) and not *m*P*x*, then *m*P*z*); hence: **all***m*(if QA(*m*), then *m*P*z*) - and we have a contradiction between the underlined results. Therefore from the first assumption: T(*z*).
(ii) Assume **all***z*(if *x*P*z* and *k*P*z*, then T(*z*)); assume: QA(*y*′) and *y*′P**conj***y*(QA(*y*) and not *y*P*x*); **(x)** M(*y*′); hence *y*′P*k*; **(xx)** not M(*y*′); hence by TP41: not *y*′P*x*. Now: *x*P**conj**(*x*,*k*) and *k*P**conj**(*x*,*k*) (TP19, TP15, DP12), hence by the first assumption: T(**conj**(*x*,*k*)), hence: *y*′P**conj**(*x*,*k*), hence, because of QA(*y*′) and TP38, *y*′P*x* or *y*′P*k*, hence, because not *y*′P*x*, *y*′P*k*. We have now shown: **all***y*′(if QA(*y*′) and *y*′P**conj***y*(QA(*y*) and not *y*P*x*), then *y*′P*k*), hence by AP5: **conj***y*(QA(*y*) and not *y*P*x*)T*k*.

•TP49 **all***x*[**all***z*(if *x*P*z* and $\mathbf{neg}_2$(*x*)P*z*, then T(*z*)) and **all***k*(if **all***z*(if *x*P*z* and *k*P*z*, then T(*z*)), then $\mathbf{neg}_2$(*x*)P*k*)].

•TP50 **all***x*($\mathbf{neg}_2$(*x*)=**conj***y*(QA(*y*) and not *y*P*x*)).

•TP51 **all***x*($\mathbf{neg}_1$(*x*)=$\mathbf{neg}_2$(*x*)).

•TP52 **all***x*(**neg**(*x*)=$\mathbf{neg}_1$(*x*) and **neg**(*x*)=$\mathbf{neg}_2$(*x*)).

•TP53
(i) **all***x*(**conj**(*x*,**t**)=*x* and **disj**(*x*,**k**)=*x*);
(ii) **all***x*(**conj**(*x*,**neg**(*x*))=**k** and **disj**(*x*,**neg**(*x*))=**t**);
(iii) **all***x***all***y*(**conj**(*x*,*y*)=**conj**(*y*,*x*) and **disj**(*x*,*y*)=**disj**(*y*,*x*));
(iv) **all***x***all***y***all***z*[**conj**(*x*,**disj**(*y*,*z*))=**disj**(**conj**(*x*,*y*),**conj**(*x*,*z*))];
(v) **all***x***all***y***all***z*[**disj**(*x*,**conj**(*y*,*z*))=**conj**(**disj**(*x*,*y*), **disj**(*x*,*z*))].

Proof: **(i)** *x*P**conj**(*x*,**t**) and **t**P**conj**(*x*,**t**) and **all***y*(if *x*P*y* and **t**P*y*, then **conj**(*x*,**t**)P*y*) [TP19, TP15, DP12]; because of AP2: *x*P*x*; because of M(**t**) [TP32]: **t**P*x*; hence: **conj**(*x*,**t**)P*x*; therefore, by AP3, **conj**(*x*,**t**)=*x*.
disj(*x*,**k**)P*x* and **disj**(*x*,**k**)P**k** and **all***y*(if *y*P*x* and *y*P**k**, then *y*P**disj**(*x*,**k**)) [TP21, TP15, DP13]; because of AP2: *x*P*x*; because of T(**k**) [TP34]: *x*P**k**; hence *x*P**disj**(*x*,**k**); therefore, by AP3, **disj**(*x*,**k**)=*x*.
(ii) **all***z*(if *x*P*z* and **neg**(*x*)P*z*, then T(*z*)) [TP49, TP52]; *x*P**conj**(*x*,**neg**(*x*)) and **neg**(*x*)P**conj**(*x*,**neg**(*x*)) [TP25, AP2]; hence: T(**conj**(*x*,**neg**(*x*))), hence by TP34: **conj**(*x*,**neg**(*x*))=**k**.
all*z*(if *z*P*x* and *z*P**neg**(*x*), then M(*z*)) [TP46, TP52]; **disj**(*x*,**neg**(*x*))P*x* and **disj**(*x*,**neg**(*x*))P**neg**(*x*) [TP26, AP2]; hence: M(**disj**(*x*,**neg**(*x*))), hence by TP32: **disj**(*x*,**neg**(*x*))=**t**.
(iii) **all***k*(*k*P*x* or *k*P*y* iff *k*P*y* or *k*P*x*), hence by TP29: **conj***k*(*k*P*x* or *k*P*y*)=**conj***k*(*k*P*y* or *k*P*x*), hence by TP20: **conj**(*x*,*y*)=**conj**(*y*,*x*).
all*k*(*k*P*x* and *k*P*y* iff *k*P*y* and *k*P*x*), hence by TP29: **conj***k*(*k*P*x* and *k*P*y*)=**conj***k*(*k*P*y* and *k*P*x*), hence by TP22: **disj**(*x*,*y*)=**disj**(*y*,*x*).
(iv) *x*P**conj**(*x*,*y*) and *x*P**conj**(*x*,*z*) [TP25, AP2]; hence by TP23: *x*P**disj**(**conj**(*x*,*y*),**conj**(*x*,*z*));

disj(*y*,*z*)P*y* [TP26, AP2]; *y***Pconj**(*x*,*y*) [TP25, AP2]; hence by AP1 **disj(*y*,*z*)Pconj(*x*,*y*)**;
disj(*y*,*z*)P*z*; *z***Pconj**(*x*,*z*); hence by AP1 **disj(*y*,*z*)Pconj(*x*,*z*)**;
from the last two underlined results by TP23: **disj**(*y*,*z*)P **disj(conj**(*x*,*y*),**conj**(*x*,*z*)), hence by the first underlined result and TP24: **conj**(*x*,**disj**(*y*,*z*))**Pdisj(conj**(*x*,*y*), **conj**(*x*,*z*)); this is the *first part*.
Assume now: QA(*z*′) and *z*′**Pdisj(conj**(*x*,*y*),**conj**(*x*,*z*)); hence by TP23: *z*′**Pconj**(*x*,*y*) and *z*′**Pconj**(*x*,*z*), hence by TP38: (*z*′P*x* or *z*′P*y*) and (*z*′P*x* or *z*′P*z*), that is: *z*′P*x* or (*z*′P*y* and *z*′P*z*), hence by TP23: *z*′P*x* or *z*′**Pdisj**(*y*,*z*), hence by TP25: *z*′**Pconj**(*x*,**disj**(*y*,*z*)). Therefore: **all***z*′[if QA(*z*′) and *z*′**Pdisj(conj**(*x*,*y*), **conj**(*x*,*z*)), then *z*′**Pconj**(*x*,**disj**(*y*,*z*))], hence by AP5: **disj(conj**(*x*,*y*),**conj**(*x*,*z*)) **Pconj**(*x*,**disj**(*y*,*z*)); this is the *second part*.
From the first and second part by AP3: **conj**(*x*,**disj**(*y*,*z*))=**disj(conj**(*x*,*y*), **conj**(*x*,*z*)).
(**v**) **disj**(*x*,*y*)P*x* and **disj**(*x*,*z*)P*x* [TP26, AP2]; hence by TP24:
conj(disj(*x*,*y*),disj(*x*,*z*))P*x*;
disj(*x*,*y*)P*y* [TP26, AP2]; *y***Pconj**(*y*,*z*) [TP25, AP2]; hence by AP1: **disj(*x*,*y*)Pconj(*y*,*z*)**;
disj(*x*,*z*)P*z*; *z***Pconj**(*y*,*z*); hence by AP1 **disj(*x*,*z*)Pconj(*y*,*z*)**;
from the last two underlined results by TP24: **conj(disj**(*x*,*y*),**disj**(*x*,*z*))P **conj**(*y*,*z*), hence by the first underlined result and TP23: **conj(disj**(*x*,*y*), **disj**(*x*,*z*))**Pdisj**(*x*,**conj**(*y*,*z*)); this is the *first part*.
Assume now: QA(*z*′) and *z*′**Pdisj**(*x*,**conj**(*y*,*z*)); hence by TP23: *z*′P*x* and *z*′**Pconj**(*y*,*z*), hence by TP38: *z*′P*x* and (*z*′P*y* or *z*′P*z*), that is: (*z*′P*x* and *z*′P*y*) or (*z*′P*x* and *z*′P*z*), hence by TP23: *z*′**Pdisj**(*x*,*y*) or *z*′**Pdisj**(*x*,*z*), hence by TP25: *z*′**Pconj(disj**(*x*,*y*),**disj**(*x*,*z*)). Therefore: **all***z*′[if QA(*z*′) and *z*′**Pdisj**(*x*,**conj**(*y*,*z*)), then *z*′**Pconj(disj**(*x*,*y*),**disj**(*x*,*z*))], hence by AP5: **disj**(*x*,**conj**(*y*,*z*))P **conj(disj**(*x*,*y*),**disj**(*x*,*z*)); this is the *second part*.
From the first and second part by AP3: **disj**(*x*,**conj**(*y*,*z*))=**conj(disj**(*x*,*y*), **disj**(*x*,*z*)).

•TP54 **neg(t)=k** and **neg(k)=t**.

Proof: According to TP53(ii): **conj(t,neg(t))=k**; according to TP53(i): **conj(neg(t),t)=neg(t)**, hence by TP53(iii): **conj(t,neg(t))=neg(t)**; therefore: **neg(t)=k**. According to TP53(ii): **disj(k,neg(k))=t**; according to TP53(i): **disj(neg(k),k)=neg(k)**, hence by TP53(iii): **disj(k,neg(k))=neg(k)**; therefore: **neg(k)=t**.

•TP55 **all***x*(*x*=**neg(neg**(*x*))).

Proof: *x*=**conj**(*x*,**t**), according to TP53(i);
disj[neg(*x*),**neg(neg**(*x*))]=**t**, according to TP53(ii);
hence: *x*=**conj**[*x*,**disj[neg**(*x*),**neg(neg**(*x*))]], hence:
x=**disj[conj**[*x*,**neg**(*x*)],**conj**[*x*,**neg(neg**(*x*))]], according to TP53(iv);
hence by TP53(ii): *x*=**disj[k,conj**[*x*,**neg(neg**(*x*))]],
hence by TP53(iii) und TP53(i): *x*=**conj**[*x*,**neg(neg**(*x*))] This is the *first result*.

neg(neg(*x***))=conj[neg(neg(***x***)),t]**, according to TP53(i);
disj[neg(*x***),***x***]=t**, according to TP53(ii) and TP53(iii);
hence: **neg(neg(***x***))=conj[neg(neg(***x***)),disj[neg(***x***),***x***]]**, hence:
neg(neg(*x***))=disj[conj[neg(neg(***x***)),neg(***x***)],conj[neg(neg(***x***)),***x***]]**, according to TP53(iv);
hence: **neg(neg(***x***))=disj[k,conj[neg(neg(***x***)),***x***]]**
[for **conj[neg(neg(***x***)),neg(***x***)]=k**, according to TP53(ii) and TP53(iii)]; hence by TP53(i) and TP53(iii): **neg(neg(***x***))=conj[***x***,neg(neg(***x***))]**. This is the *second result*.
x=**neg(neg(***x***))** is a logical consequence of the two results.

•TP56 **all***x***all***y***[neg(disj(***x,y***))=conj(neg(***x***),neg(***y***))]**.

Proof: **(i)** Assume: QA(*z*) and *z***Pneg(disj(***x,y***))**; in case M(*z*), then, trivially, *z***Pconj(neg(***x***),neg(***y***))**; in case not M(*z*), then by TP41, TP52, TP47: not *z***Pdisj(***x,y***)**, hence by TP23: not *z*P*x* or not *z*P*y*, hence, because of QA(*z*), by TP18: *z***Pconj***k*(QA(*k*) and not *k*P*x*) or *z***Pconj***k*(QA(*k*) and not *k*P*y*), hence by TP47, TP52: *z***Pneg(***x***)** or *z***Pneg(***y***)**, hence by TP25 *z***Pconj(neg(***x***),neg(***y***))**.
(ii) Assume: QA(*z*) and *z***Pconj(neg(***x***),neg(***y***))**, hence by TP38: *z***Pneg(***x***)** or *z***Pneg(***y***)**; if M(*z*), then, trivially, *z***Pneg(disj(***x,y***))**; if not M(*z*), then by TP41, TP52, TP47: not *z*P*x* or not *z*P*y*, hence by TP23: not *z***Pdisj(***x,y***)**, hence, because of QA(*z*), by TP18: *z***Pconj***k*(QA(*k*) and not *k***Pdisj(***x,y***)**), hence by TP47, TP52: *z***Pneg(disj(***x,y***))**.
On the basis of **(i)**, **(ii)**, AP5 and AP3, we have: **neg(disj(***x,y***))= conj(neg(***x***),neg(***y***))**.

•TP57 **all***x***all***y***[disj(***x,y***)=neg(conj(neg(***x***),neg(***y***)))]**.

•TP58 **all***x***all***y***all***z*(if *x*P*y*, then **disj(***x,z***)Pdisj(***y,z***)**).

Proof: Assume *x*P*y*; by TP26: **disj(***x,z***)**P*x* and **disj(***x,z***)**P*z*; hence by AP1: **disj(***x,z***)**P*y* and **disj(***x,z***)**P*z*, hence by TP23: **disj(***x,z***)Pdisj(***y,z***)**.

•TP59 **all***x***all***y*(*x*P*y* iff **neg(***y***)Pneg(***x***)**).

Proof: **(i)** Assume *x*P*y*. We deduce: **all***z*(if QA(*z*) and *z***Pneg(***y***)**, then *z***Pneg(***x***)**), from which we get by AP5: **neg(***y***)Pneg(***x***)**. Assume QA(*z*) and *z***Pneg(***y***)**; 1) M(*z*), hence: *z***Pneg(***x***)**; 2) not M(*z*), hence by TP41, TP52 and TP47: not *z*P*y*, hence, because of *x*P*y* and AP1, not *z*P*x*; hence by TP18: *z***Pconj***k*(QA(*k*) and not *k*P*x*), hence by TP52 and TP47: *z***Pneg(***x***)**.
(ii) According to what has just been proved, **neg(neg(***x***))Pneg(neg(***y***))** is a consequence of **neg(***y***)Pneg(***x***)**, hence also *x*P*y* (because of TP55).

•TP60 **all***x***all***y*(*x***Pneg(***y***)** iff *y***Pneg(***x***)**) and **all***x***all***y*(**neg(***x***)**P*y* iff **neg(***y***)**P*x*).

•TP61 **all***x***all***y*[*x*->*y* iff M(**impl(***x,y***)**)].

Proof: **(i)** Assume *x*->*y*; hence according to DP11: *y*P*x*, hence by TP58: **disj(***y***,neg(***x***))Pdisj(***x***,neg(***x***))**, hence by TP53(ii) and TT53(iii): **disj(neg(***x***),***y***)** P**t**; **tPdisj(neg(***x***),***y***)**, since M(**t**); hence by AP3: **disj(neg(***x***),***y***)=t**, hence by TP32 and DP22: M(**impl(***x,y***)**).

(ii) Assume M(**impl**(x,y)), hence: **disj**(y,**neg**(x))**P****disj**(x,**neg**(x)) [tracing backwards the proof under **(i)**], hence by TP23: **disj**(y,**neg**(x))Px. Assume QA(z) and zPy;
1) assume: not z**P****disj**(y,**neg**(x)), hence: not zPy or not z**P****neg**(x), according to TP23; hence, according to assumption, not z**P****neg**(x), hence: not M(z) and not z**P****conj**k(QA(k) and not kPx) [by TP52, TP47], hence, since QA(z), by TP41: not not zPx, hence zPx;
2) assume z**P****disj**(y,**neg**(x)); hence, because of the underlined result, by AP1: zPx.
Therefore: **all**z(if QA(z) and zPy, then zPx), hence by AP5: yPx, that is, x->y, according to DP11.

•TP62 **all**x[if A[x], then **conj**k**all**y′(if A[y′], then kPy′)Px] and **all**y[if **all**x(if A[x], then yPx), then y**P****conj**k**all**y′(if A[y′], then kPy′)].

Proof: As a theorem of predicate logic: **all**x[if A[x], then **all**k(if **all**y′(if A[y′], then kPy′), then kPx)]; hence by TP28: **all**x[if A[x], then **conj**k**all**y′(if A[y′], then kPy′)**P****conj**k(kPx)], hence by TP30 **all**x[if A[x], then **conj**k**all**y′(if A[y′], then kPy′)Px] - the first part of TP62. According to TP18 we have: **all**y[if **all**x(if A[x], then yPx), then y**P****conj**k**all**y′(if A[y′], then kPy′)] - the second part of TP62.

•TP63 **disj**xA[x]=**conj**y**all**x(if A[x], then yPx).

•TP64 **disj**xA[x]=**neg**(**conj**y**some**x[A[x] and y=**neg**(x)]).

Proof: **(i)** Assume: QA(z) and z**P****neg**(**conj**y**some**x[A[x] and y=**neg**(x)]); for M(z), z**P****disj**xA[x] is a trivial consequence; for not M(z), we have according to TP52, TP47 and TP41: not z**P****conj**y**some**x[A[x] and y=**neg**(x)], hence according to TP40: not **some**k(zPk and **some**x[A[x] and k=**neg**(x)]).
Assume, too, **some**x(A[x] and not zPx); hence by TP18, because of QA(z), z**P****conj**k(QA(k) and not kPx); moreover by TP52 and TP47: **conj**k(QA(k) and not kPx)=**neg**(x); hence we obtain from the second assumption: **some**x[A[x] and **some**k(zPk and k=**neg**(x))] - contradicting the underlined result.
Therefore, **all**x(if A[x], then zPx), hence by TP18: z**P****conj**y**all**x(if A[x], then yPx), hence by TP63: z**P****disj**xA[x].
(ii) Assume: QA(z) and z**P****disj**xA[x], hence by TP63: z**P****conj**y**all**x(if A[x], then yPx); for M(z), z**P****neg**(**conj**y**some**x[A[x] and y=**neg**(x)]) is a trivial consequence; for not M(z), we have according to TP40: **some**k(zPk and **all**x(if A[x], then kPx)), hence by AP1: **all**x(if A[x], then zPx).
Assume, too, z**P****conj**y**some**x[A[x] and y=**neg**(x)]; hence by TP40: **some**k(zPk and **some**x[A[x] and k=**neg**(x)]), hence: **some**x(A[x] and z**P****neg**(x)), hence by TP52, TP47 and TP41 (because of QA(z) and not M(z)): **some**x(A[x] and not zPx) - contradicting the underlined result.
Therefore, not z**P****conj**y**some**x[A[x] and y=**neg**(x)], hence, because of QA(z), by TP18, TP47, TP52: z**P****neg**(**conj**y**some**x[A[x] and y=**neg**(x)]).
From **(i)** and **(ii)** we obtain by AP5 and AP3:
disjxA[x]=**neg**(**conj**y**some**x[A[x] and y=**neg**(x)]).

•TP65 **all***x*(if A[*x*], then **disj***z*A[*z*]P*x*) and **all***y*(if **all***x*(if A[*x*], then *y*P*x*), then *y*P**disj***z*A[*z*]).

•TP66 if **all***x*(if A[*x*], then B[*x*]), then **disj***z*B[*z*]P**disj***z*A[*z*].

Proof: Assume **all***x*(if A[*x*], then B[*x*]), hence by TP65 [first conjunct, applied to B[*x*]]: **all***x*(if A[*x*], then **disj***z*B[*z*]P*x*), hence by TP65 [second conjunct, applied to A[*x*]]: **disj***z*B[*z*]P**disj***z*A[*z*].

•TP67 **all***z*(*z*=**disj***z*′(*z*P*z*′)).

Proof: *z*P*z* by AP2, hence by TP65: **disj***z*′(*z*P*z*′)P*z*; **all***x*(if *z*P*x*, then *z*P*x*), hence by TP65: *z*P**disj***z*′(*z*P*z*′); therefore, by AP3, *z*=**disj***z*′(*z*P*z*′).

•TP68 **conj***x*A[*x*]=**disj***y***all***x*(if A[*x*], then *x*P*y*).

•TP69 **all***y*[MK(*y*) iff **all***x*(not *x*P*y* iff **neg**(*x*)P*y*)].

•TP70 **all***x*(K(*x*) iff *x*≠**k**).

Proof: (**i**) Assume K(*x*), that is [by DP24], **all***y*(not *y*P*x* or not **neg**(*y*)P*x*); but **kPk** and **neg**(**k**)**Pk** [for **all***y*(*y***Pk**), since T(**k**) by TP34]; hence *x*≠**k**.

(**ii**) Assume *x*≠**k**; assume for *reductio*: **some***y*(*y*P*x* and **neg**(*y*)P*x*); hence, because of TP49 and TT52, T(*x*), hence by TP34: *x*=**k** - contradicting the assumption. Therefore [applying DP24]: K(*x*).

•TP71 **all***x*(MX(*x*) iff QC(*x*)).

Proof: (**i**) Assume MX(*x*), and assume: *x*P*y* and not T(*y*). For QC(*x*) [according to DP7] we have to deduce from these assumptions: *y*=*x*. But according to assumption: *x*P*y*; hence, because of AP3, only *y*P*x* remains to be shown. Assume for *reductio*: not *y*P*x*; hence by DP25, because of MX(*x*), **neg**(*y*)P*x*, hence, because of *x*P*y*, by AP1: **neg**(*y*)P*y*; by AP2: *y*P*y*; therefore, by TP49 and TP52, T(*y*) - contradicting the assumption.

(**ii**) Assume QC(*x*), that is, **all***y*(if *x*P*y*, then *y*=*x* or T(*y*)); assume for *reductio*: not *y*P*x* and not **neg**(*y*)P*x*. By TP25, AP2: *x*P**conj**(*x*,*y*) and *x*P**conj**(*x*,**neg**(*y*)); hence (because of QC(*x*)): [**conj**(*x*,*y*)=*x* or T(**conj**(*x*,*y*))] and [**conj**(*x*,**neg**(*y*))=*x* or T(**conj**(*x*,**neg**(*y*)))]. **conj**(*x*,*y*)≠*x*, for otherwise because of *y***Pconj**(*x*,*y*): *y*P*x* - contradicting the assumption; **conj**(*x*,**neg**(*y*))≠*x*, for otherwise because of **neg**(*y*)**Pconj**(*x*,**neg**(*y*)): **neg**(*y*)P*x* - contradicting the assumption. From the three underlined results: T(**conj**(*x*,*y*)) and T(**conj**(*x*,**neg**(*y*))); hence by DP5: **kPconj**(*x*,*y*) and **kPconj**(*x*,**neg**(*y*)), hence by TP23: **kPdisj**[**conj**(*x*,*y*), **conj**(*x*,**neg**(*y*))], hence by TP53(iv): **kPconj**(*x*,**disj**(*y*,**neg**(*y*))), hence by TP53(ii): **kPconj**(*x*,**t**), hence by TP53(i): **kP***x*, hence by AP3: *x*=**k**, because we also have *x***Pk** [T(**k**) by TP34]; consequently: T(*x*), and hence by DP5: *y*P*x* - contradicting the assumption. Therefore: **all***y*(*y*P*x* or **neg**(*y*)P*x*), and hence MX(*x*), according to DP25.

•TP72 **all***x*(MK(*x*) iff QC(*x*) and *x*≠**k**).

•TP73 **all***x*(QA(**neg**(*x*)) iff QC(*x*)).

Proof: (**i**) Assume QC(*x*), that is, **all***y*(if *x*P*y*, then *y*=*x* or T(*y*)); assume: *y***Pneg**(*x*) and *y*≠**neg**(*x*); for QA(**neg**(*x*)) we have to deduce: M(*y*). From *y***Pneg**(*x*) by TP60: *x***Pneg**(*y*); hence: **neg**(*y*)=*x* or T(**neg**(*y*)). **neg**(*y*)≠*x*, for *oth-*

erwise **neg(neg**(y))=**neg**(x), hence by TP55: y=**neg**(x) - contradicting the assumption y≠**neg**(x). Therefore: T(**neg**(y)), hence by TP34: **neg**(y)=**k**, hence **neg(neg**(y))=**neg(k)**, hence by TP55 and TP54: y=**t**, hence by TP32: M(y).

(**ii**) Assume QA(**neg**(x)), that is, **all**y(if yP**neg**(x), then y=**neg**(x) or M(y)); assume xPy and y≠x; for QC(x) we have to deduce T(y). From xPy by TP59 **neg**(y)P**neg**(x); hence: **neg**(y)=**neg**(x) or M(**neg**(y)). **neg**(y)≠**neg**(x), for *otherwise* **neg(neg**(y))=**neg(neg**(x)), hence by TP55 y=x - contradicting the assumption y≠x. Therefore: M(**neg**(y)), hence by TP32: **neg**(y)=**t**, hence **neg(neg**(y))=**neg(t)**, hence by TP55 and TP54: y=**k**, hence by TP34: T(y).

•TP74 **all**x(QA(x) iff QC(**neg**(x))).

•TP75 **all**x[QA(x) iff **some**y(QC(y) and x=**neg**(y))].

•TP76 **all**x[QA(x) iff x=**t** or **some**y(MK(y) and x=**neg**(y))].

Proof: (**i**) Assume: QA(x) and x≠**t**; hence by TP75: **some**y(QC(y) and x=**neg**(y)); hence y≠**k** (for *otherwise* x=**neg(k)**, hence by TP54: x=**t** - contradicting the assumption); hence by TP72: **some**y(MK(y) and x=**neg**(y)).

(**ii**) Assume: x=**t** or **some**y(MK(y) and x=**neg**(y)); in the first case QA(x) by TP36, DP6; in the second case QA(x) by TP72 and TP73.

•TP77 **all**x[EL(x) iff **some**y(MK(y) and x=**neg**(y))].

Proof: (**i**) Assume EL(x), that is, QA(x) and not M(x) [by DP20]; hence by TP76, TP32: **some**y(MK(y) and x=**neg**(y)).

(**ii**) Assume **some**y(MK(y) and x=**neg**(y)); hence by TP72, TP73: <u>QA(x)</u>; and hence: <u>not M(x)</u> [*otherwise* x=**t** by TP32; hence: **neg**(y)=**t**, hence: **neg(neg**(y))=**neg(t)**, hence by TP55, TP54: y=**k**; but from MK(y) by TP72: y≠**k**]. From the underlined results by DP20: EL(x).

•TP78 **all**x(EL(**neg**(x)) iff MK(x)).

Proof: (**i**) Assume EL(**neg**(x)), hence by DP20: QA(**neg**(x)) and not M(**neg**(x)); hence by TP73: <u>QC(x)</u>; hence by TP32: **neg**(x)≠**t**, hence **neg(neg**(x))≠**neg(t)** [*otherwise* from **neg(neg(neg**(x)))=**neg(neg(t))** by TP55: **neg**(x)=**t** - contradicting the previous result], hence by TP55, TP54: <u>x≠**k**</u>; from the underlined results by TP72: MK(x).

(**ii**) Assume MK(x), hence by TP72: QC(x) and x≠**k**, hence by TP73, TP55, TP54: QA(**neg**(x)) and **neg**(x)≠**t**, hence by TP32, DP20: EL(**neg**(x)).

•TP79 **all**x**all**y(if MK(x) and MK(y) and xPy, then y=x).

Proof: Assume: MK(x) and MK(y) and xPy, hence by TP72: QC(x) and QC(y) and y≠**k**; hence by DP7: y=x or T(y); but according to TP34: not T(y) (since y≠**k**); therefore: y=x.

•TP80 **all**x**all**y(if EL(x) and EL(y) and xPy, then x=y).

•TP81 **all**y[not M(y) iff not **some**x(yPx and yP**neg**(x))].

Proof: (**i**) If y is a minimal state of affairs, then - by definition - it is (intensional) part of every state of affairs; hence it is both part of itself and of

its negation, hence there is some state of affairs such that *y* is part of it and of its negation.
(ii) From **some***x*(*y*P*x* and *y***Pneg**(*x*)) we obtain, by TP46 and TP52, M(*y*).
•TP82 **all***y*[QA(*y*) iff **all***x*(*y*P*x* or *y***Pneg**(*x*))].
Proof: (i) Assume: QA(*y*) and not *y*P*x*, hence by TP18: *y***Pconj***z*(QA(*z*) and not *z*P*x*), hence by TP50, TP52: *y***Pneg**(*x*). Therefore: if QA(*y*), then **all***x*(*y*P*x* or *y***Pneg**(*x*)).
(ii) Assume **all***x*(*y*P*x* or *y***Pneg**(*x*)); assume: *z*P*y* and not M(*z*); for QA(*y*) it is to be shown: *z*=*y*. According to the first assumption: *y*P*z* or *y***Pneg**(*z*). If *y*P*z*, then by AP3 because of *z*P*y*: *z*=*y*. If *y***Pneg**(*z*), then by AP1 because of *z*P*y*: *z***Pneg**(*z*), hence (because of *z*P*z* [AP2], TP46, TP52): M(*z*) - contradicting the assumption. Therefore: *z*=*y* follows from the assumptions.
•TP83 **all***y*[EL(*y*) iff **all***x*(not *y*P*x* iff *y***Pneg**(*x*))].
•TP84 **all***y*(EL(*y*) iff MN(*y*) and S(*y*)).
•TP85 **all***x*(if **some***y*(MK(*y*) and *x*P*y*), then not **k**P*x*).
Proof: Assume **some***y*(MK(*y*) and *x*P*y*); assume for *reductio*: **k**P*x*; by TP34 T(**k**), hence by DP5: *x*P**k**; hence by AP3: *x*=**k**; and hence: **some***y*(MK(*y*) and **k**P*y*), hence, since *y*P**k**, by AP3: *y*=**k** - contradicting TP72. Therefore: not **k**P*x*.
•TP86 **all***x*(if *x*P**t**, then **all***y*(if MK(*y*), then *x*P*y*)).
•TP87 **all***x*[if **all***y*(if MK(*y*), then *x*P*y*), then *x*P**t**] iff **disj***x*MK(*x*)=**t**.
Proof: (i) Assume **disj***x*MK(*x*)=**t**; assume **all***y*(if MK(*y*), then *x*′P*y*), hence by TP65: *x*′P**disj***x*MK(*x*); hence *x*′P**t**.
(ii) Assume **all***x*[if **all***y*(if MK(*y*), then *x*P*y*), then *x*P**t**]; **all***y*(if MK(*y*), then **disj***x*MK(*x*)P*y*), according to TP65; hence: **disj***x*MK(*x*)P**t**, hence (because of **tPdisj***x*MK(*x*) and AP3): **disj***x*MK(*x*)=**t**.
•TP88 **disj***x*MK(*x*)=**t** iff **conj***x*EL(*x*)=**k**.
Proof: **disj***x*MK(*x*)=**neg**(**conj***x***some***y*[MK(*y*) and *x*=**neg**(*y*)]), according to TP64; hence by TP77 and TP29: **disj***x*MK(*x*)=**neg**(**conj***x*EL(*x*)). Therefore according to TP55 and TP54: **disj***x*MK(*x*)=**t** iff **neg**(**conj***x*EL(*x*))=**t** iff **neg**(**neg**(**conj***x*EL(*x*)))=**neg**(**t**), hence: **disj***x*MK(*x*)=**t** iff **conj***x*EL(*x*)=**k**.
•TP89 **conj***x*EL(*x*)=**k**.
Proof: Since T(**k**), **conj***x*EL(*x*)P**k**. **all***y*(if QA(*y*), then *y***Pconj***x*EL(*x*)), for according to TP18, DP20: **all***y*(if QA(*y*) and not M(*y*), then *y***Pconj***x*EL(*x*)), and of course: **all***y*(if M(*y*), then *y***Pconj***x*EL(*x*)); therefore: **all***y*(if QA(*y*) and *y*P**k**, then *y***Pconj***x*EL(*x*)), hence by AP5: **kPconj***x*EL(*x*). From the underlined results by AP3: **conj***x*EL(*x*)=**k**.
•TP90 **all***x*(if **all***y*(if MK(*y*), then *x*P*y*), then *x*P**t**).
•TP91 **all***x*(if not **k**P*x*, then **some***y*(MK(*y*) and *x*P*y*)).
•TP92 **all***x*(N(*x*) iff **all***y*(if MK(*y*), then *x*P*y*)).
Proof: Assume N(*x*), that is [''hence equivalently''] by DP30: not P(**neg**(*x*)), that is [by DP29]: not **some***y*(MK(*y*) and **neg**(*x*)P*y*), that is [by TP85, TP91]:

kPneg(*x*), that is [by TP60, TP54]: *x*P**t**, that is [by TP86, TP90]: **all***y*(if MK(*y*), then *x*P*y*).

•TP93

(i) **all***x*(N(*x*) iff *x*=**t**);

(ii) **all***x***all***y*(N(**conj**(*x*,*y*)) iff N(*x*) and N(*y*));

(iii) **all***x***all***y*[if N(*x*) or N(*y*), then N(**disj**(*x*,*y*))].

Proof: (**i**)Assume N(*x*), that is [by TP92]: **all***y*(if MK(*y*), then *x*P*y*), that is [by TP90, TP86]: *x*P**t**, that is [by TP36, AP2]: *x*=**t**.

(**ii**) Assume N(**conj**(*x*,*y*)), that is: **conj**(*x*,*y*)P**t** [by TP92, TP90 and TP86], that is: *x*P**t** and *y*P**t** [by TP24], that is: N(*x*) and N(*y*) [by TP92, TP90 and TP86].

(**iii**) Assume: N(*x*) or N(*y*), that is [by TP92, TP90 and TP86]: *x*P**t** or *y*P**t**, hence [*not* ''that is''] by TP26: **disj**(*x*,*y*)P**t**, that is: N(**disj**(*x*,*y*)).

•TP94

(i) **all***x*(P(*x*) iff *x*≠**k**);

(ii) **all***x***all***y*(P(**disj**(*x*,*y*)) iff P(*x*) or P(*y*));

(iii) **all***x***all***y*(P(**conj**(*x*,*y*)), then P(*x*) and P(*y*)).

Proof: (**i**) Assume P(*x*), that is [by DP29]: **some***y*(MK(*y*) and *x*P*y*), that is [by TP85, TP91]: not **k**P*x*, that is [by AP2, AP3, T(**k**), DP5]: *x*≠**k**.

(**ii**) P(**disj**(*x*,*y*)), that is: not **kPdisj**(*x*,*y*) [by DP29, TP91 and TP85], that is [by TP23]: not **k**P*x* or not **k**P*y*, that is: P(*x*) or P(*y*) [by DP29, TP91 and TP85].

(**iii**) Assume P(**conj**(*x*,*y*)), that is [by DP29, TP91 and TP85]: not **kPconj**(*x*,*y*), hence [*not* ''that is''] by TP25: not **k**P*x* and not **k**P*y*, that is: P(*x*) and P(*y*).

•TP95 **w**=**conj***y*O(*y*).

•TP96 **all***x*(**conj***z*A[*z*]P*x* iff **all***y*(if A[*y*], then *y*P*x*)).

Proof: (**i**) Assume **conj***z*A[*z*]P*x*; assume A[*y*], hence by TP18: *y*P**conj***z*A[*z*]; hence by AP1: *y*P*x*. Therefore: **all***y*(if A[*y*], then *y*P*x*).

(**ii**) Assume **all***y*(if A[*y*], then *y*P*x*), hence by TP18: **conj***z*A[*z*]P*x*.

•TP97 V(**conj***z*A[*z*]) iff **all***y*(if A[*y*], then V(*y*)).

•TP98 **all***x***all***y*(V(**conj**(*x*,*y*)) iff V(*x*) and V(*y*)).

Proof: By TP97 and TP20 one obtains: **all***x***all***y*[V(**conj**(*x*,*y*)) iff **all***k*(if *k*P*x* or *k*P*y*, then V(*k*))]; moreover, by AP1, AP2 and DP31, DP32: **all***x***all***y*(**all***k*(if *k*P*x* or *k*P*y*, then V(*k*)) iff V(*x*) and V(*y*)). Combine the two biconditionals.

•TP99 **all***x*(F(*x*) iff **neg**(**w**)P*x*).

•TP100 **all***x*(*x*P**disj***z*A[*z*] iff **all***y*(if A[*y*], then *x*P*y*)).

Proof: (**i**) Assume *x*P**disj***z*A[*z*]; assume A[*y*], hence by TP65: **disj***z*A[*z*]P*y*; hence by AP1: *x*P*y*. Therefore: **all***y*(if A[*y*], then *x*P*y*).

(ii) Assume **all***y*(if A[*y*], then *x*P*y*), hence by TP65: *x*P**disj***z*A[*z*].

•TP101 F(**disj***z*A[*z*]) iff **all***y*(if A[*y*], then F(*y*)).

•TP102 **all***x***all***y*(**disj**(*x*,*y*)=**disj***z*(*z*=*x* or *z*=*y*)).

Proof: According to TP65: **all***z*′(if *z*′=*x* or *z*′=*y*, then **disj***z*(*z*=*x* or *z*=*y*)P*z*′) and **all***k*(if **all***z*′(if *z*′=*x* or *z*′=*y*, then *k*P*z*′), then *k*P**disj***z*(*z*=*x* or *z*=*y*)); hence: **disj***z*(*z*=*x* or *z*=*y*)P*x* and **disj***z*(*z*=*x* or *z*=*y*)P*y* and **all***k*(if *k*P*x* and *k*P*y*, then *k***Pdisj***z*(*z*=*x* or *z*=*y*)); hence we have because of TP21, TP15 and DP13: **disj**(*x*,*y*)=**disj***z*(*z*=*x* or *z*=*y*).

•TP103 **all***x***all***y*(F(**disj**(*x*,*y*)) iff F(*x*) and F(*y*)).

Proofs: According to TP102 and TP101: **all***x***all***y*[F(**disj**(*x*,*y*)) iff **all***z*(if *z*=*x* or *z*=*y*, then F(*z*))]; moreover, by pure logic: **all***x***all***y*(**all***z*(if *z*=*x* or *z*=*y*, then F(*z*)) iff F(*x*) and F(*y*)). Combine the two biconditionals.

•TP104 **t**≠**k**.

Proof: By DP4: **tPw**, since M(**t**) [TP32]. Therefore: from **t**=**k** we would obtain **kPw**, hence, because of **wPk** [TP34, DP5], by AP3: **w**=**k** - contradicting AP7.

•TP105 **all***x*(*x*≠**neg**(*x*)).

Proof: Assume for *reductio*: *x*=**neg**(*x*); hence according to TP53(ii): **conj**(*x*,*x*)=**k** and **disj**(*x*,*x*)=**t**. Therefore: *x*=**k** and *x*=**t** [*x*=**conj**(*x*,*x*), according to TP24, AP2, TP25 and AP3; *x*=**disj**(*x*,*x*), according to TP23, AP2, TP26 and AP3], hence: **t**=**k** - contradicting TP104.

•TP106 MK(**w**).

•TP107 **all***x*(not V(*x*) iff F(*x*)).

•TP108 **all***x***all***y*(F(**conj**(*x*,*y*)) iff F(*x*) or F(*y*)).

•TP109 **all***x***all***y*(V(**disj**(*x*,*y*)) iff V(*x*) or V(*y*)).

•TP110 **all***x*(V(**neg**(*x*)) iff F(*x*)).

•TP111 **all***x*(F(**neg**(*x*)) iff V(*x*)).

Proof: According to TP55: V(**neg**(**neg**(*x*))) iff V(*x*), hence by DP33: F(**neg**(*x*)) iff V(*x*).

•TP112 **all***x***all***y*(if V(**neg**(*x*)) and V(**disj**(*x*,*y*)), then V(*y*)).

Proof: Assume: V(**neg**(*x*)) and V(**disj**(*x*,*y*)),
hence by TP98: V(**conj**[**neg**(*x*),**disj**(*x*,*y*)]),
hence by TP53(iv): V(**disj**[**conj**(**neg**(*x*),*x*),**conj**(**neg**(*x*),*y*)]),
hence by TP53(iii),(ii): V(**disj**[**k**,**conj**(**neg**(*x*),*y*)]),
hence by TP53(iii),(i): V(**conj**(**neg**(*x*),*y*)),
hence by TP98: V(*y*).

•TP113 **all***x***all***y*(if F(**neg**(*x*)) and F(**conj**(*x*,*y*)), then F(*y*)).

Proof: Assume F(**neg**(*x*)) and F(**conj**(*x*,*y*)),
hence by TP103: F(**disj**[**neg**(*x*),**conj**(*x*,*y*)]),
hence by TP53(v): F(**conj**[**disj**(**neg**(*x*),*x*),**disj**(**neg**(*x*),*y*)]),
hence by TP53(iii),(ii): F(**conj**[**t**,**disj**(**neg**(*x*),*y*)]),
hence by TP53(iii),(i): F(**disj**(**neg**(*x*),*y*)),
hence by TP103: F(*y*).

•TP114 F(**conj***z*A[*z*]) iff **some***y*(A[*y*] and F(*y*)).

•TP115 V(**disj***z*A[*z*]) iff **some***y*(A[*y*] and V(*y*)).

•TP116 **all***x*(O(*x*) iff *x*=**t**) iff **w**=**t**.

Proof: (i) Assume **all***x*(O(*x*) iff *x*=**t**); by AP2: **wPw**, hence by DP31: O(**w**); hence **w**=**t**.

(ii) Assume **w**=**t**; (1) assume O(*x*), hence by DP31: *x***Pw**; hence *x***Pt**, hence by TP36: *x*=**t**; (2) by DP31: O(**t**), since **tPw** [M(**t**) by TP32]; therefore: **all***x*(if *x*=**t**, then O(*x*)); from (1) and (2): **all***x*(O(*x*) iff *x*=**t**).

•TP117 if **w**=**t**, then **all***x*(*x*=**t** or *x*=**k**).

Proof: Assume **w**=**t**; QC(**w**) [AP8]; hence: QC(**t**), that is [by DP7]: **all***y*(if **tP***y*, then *y*=**t** or T(*y*)); but **all***y*(**tP***y*), for M(**t**) by TP32; hence: **all***x*(*x*=**t** or T(*x*)), hence by TP34: **all***x*(*x*=**t** or *x*=**k**). (Conversely, QC(**t**) is obtained from **all***x*(*x*=**t** or *x*=**k**) by DP7 and TP34.)

•TP118 if **all***x*(*x*=**t** or *x*=**k**), then **w**=**t**.

•TP119 **some***x*(O(*x*) and *x*≠**t**) and **some***x*(*x*≠**t** and *x*≠**k**).

•TP120 CT(**w**).

•TP121 **some***x*[P(*x*) and P(**neg**(*x*))].

•TP122 not N(**w**) and not N(**neg**(**w**)).

•TP123 **some***x*[not N(*x*) and not N(**neg**(*x*))].

•TP124 **all***x*(if V(*x*), then P(*x*)) and **all***x*(if N(*x*), then V(*x*)).

•TP125 **some***x*(V(*x*) and not N(*x*)) and **some***x*(P(*x*) and not V(*x*)).

Proof: The conjuncts are equivalent to AP9:

(i) Assume **w**≠**t**; because of AP2: **wPw**, hence by DP31, DP32: <u>V(**w**)</u>; from **w**≠**t** [see I.16.(b)] P(**neg**(**w**)), hence by DP30: <u>not N(**w**)</u>; therefore, **some***x*(V(*x*) and not N(*x*)).

(ii) Assume **some***x*(V(*x*) and not N(*x*)), hence **some***x*(*x***Pw** and not **kPneg**(*x*)) (DP32, DP31, DP30, DP29, TP85), hence by TP60, TP54: **some***x*(*x***Pw** and not *x***Pt**), hence **w**≠**t**.

(i') Assume **w**≠**t**, hence: P(**neg**(**w**)); not **neg**(**w**)**Pw**, for *otherwise*, because of **wPw**, **conj**(**w**,**neg**(**w**))**Pw** [by TP24], hence by TP53(ii): **kPw**, hence: **w**=**k** [because of T(**k**), AP3] - contradicting AP7; hence by DP31, DP32: not V(**neg**(**w**)). Therefore: **some***x*(P(*x*) and not V(*x*)).

(ii') Assume **some***x*(P(*x*) and not V(*x*)), hence: **some***x*(not **kP***x* and not *x***Pw**) (DP29, TP85, DP32, DP31), hence by AP8 [one of its equivalents]: **some***x*(not **kP***x* and **neg**(*x*)**Pw**), hence by TP59, TP54: **some***x*(not **neg**(*x*)**Pt** and **neg**(*x*)**Pw**), hence **w**≠**t**.

•TP126 **all***x*(M(*x*) iff $A_{=0}$(*x*)).

Proof: **all***x*(if M(*x*), then $A_{=0}$(*x*)), according to TP7, DP35, DP37. Assume $A_{=0}$(*x*), hence by DP37, DP35, DP2: **all***y*(if *y***P***x*, then *y*=*x*); **tP***x*, since M(**t**) by TP32; therefore: **t**=*x*, hence by TP32: M(*x*).

•TP127 **all***x*(T(*x*) iff $C^{=0}$(*x*)).

Proof: **all***x*(if T(*x*), then $C^{=0}$(*x*)), according to TP6, DP36, DP38. Assume $C^{=0}$(*x*), hence by DP38, DP36, DP3: **all***y*(if *x***P***y*, then *y*=*x*); *x***Pk**, since T(**k**) by TP34; therefore: **k**=*x*, hence by TP34: T(*x*).

•TP128 **all***x*(QA(*x*) iff A_1(*x*)).

Proof: **all**x[QA(x) iff **all**y(if yPx, then y=x or M(y))] by DP6, hence by TP126, DP37: **all**x[QA(x) iff **all**y(if yPx, then y=x or A_0(x))], hence by DP35: **all**x(QA(x) iff A_1(x)).

•TP129 **all**x(QC(x) iff C^1(x)).

Proof: By applying DP7, TP127, DP38 and DP36 in complete analogy to the proof of TP128.

•TP130 **all**x(EL(x) iff $A_{=1}$(x)).

•TP131 **all**x(MK(x) iff $C^{=1}$(x)).

•TP132 **all**x(if A_n(x), then A_{n+1}(x)), **all**x(if C^n(x), then C^{n+1}(x)).

Proof: By complete syntactical induction with respect to the indices n ["0", "1", "2"...]:

(1) For n="0": Assume A_0(x), hence by DP35, DP2: **all**y(if yPx, then y=x), hence **all**y(if yPx, then y=x or A_0(y)), hence by DP35: A_1(x). Assume C^0(x), hence by DP36, DP3: **all**y(if xPy, then y=x), hence **all**y(if xPy, then y=x or C^0(y)), hence by DP36: C^1(x).

(2) Assume the assertion to hold true for all indices up to and including n. Then it also holds true for index n+1: Assume for *reductio*: A_{n+1}(x) and not $A_{(n+1)+1}$(x); hence: **all**y(if yPx, then y=x or A_n(y)) and **some**y(yPx and y≠x and not A_{n+1}(y)), hence: **some**y(A_n(y) and not A_{n+1}(y)); but according to induction-assumption: **all**x(if A_n(x), then A_{n+1}(x)). Therefore: **all**x(if A_{n+1}(x), then $A_{(n+1)+1}$(x)).

Completely analogous is the proof that the induction-assumption implies **all**x(if C^{n+1}(x), then $C^{(n+1)+1}$(x)).

(1) and (2) establish the theorem.

•TP133 **all**x(if A_n(x), then A_m(x)), **all**x(if C^n(x), then C^m(x)) (where m is a higher index than n).

•TP134 **no**x($A_{=n}$(x) and $A_{=m}$(x)), **no**x($C^{=n}$(x) and $C^{=m}$(x)) (where m is a higher index than n).

Proof: Assume for *reductio*: $A_{=n}$(x) and $A_{=m}$(x), m being a higher index than n; hence by DP37: A_n(x) and A_m(x) and not A_{m-1}(x); since m is a higher index than n, m−1 is n, or m−1 is a higher index than n; in the first case we have: A_n(x) and not A_n(x) - contradiction; in the second case we have according to TP133: A_n(x) and A_{m-1}(x) - contradicting: not A_{m-1}(x). Completely analogous is the proof of **no**x($C^{=n}$(x) and $C^{=m}$(x)), m being a higher index than n.

•TP135 **all**x(if A_n(x), then **≤N**y($A_{=1}$(y) and yPx)).

Proof: By complete syntactical induction with respect to the indices n and numerals N.

(1) For n,N="0": Assume A_0(x), hence by TP126: M(x), hence: not **some**y(EL(y) and yPx). For *otherwise* by TP32: yP**t**, hence by TP36: y=**t**, hence by TP32: M(y) - contradicting EL(y) according to DP20. Hence by TP130: not **some**y($A_{=1}$(y) and yPx), that is: **≤0**y($A_{=1}$(y) and yPx).

(2) Assume that the assertion holds true for all indices and numerals up to and including n,N. Assume A_{n+1}(x), hence by DP35: **all**y(if yPx, then y=x or A_n(y)),

hence by induction-assumption: **all**y(if yPx, then y=x or **≤N**z($A_{=1}(z)$ and zPy)). Assume for *reductio*: not **≤N**+1z($A_{=1}(z)$ and zPx), that is, **>N**+1z($A_{=1}(z)$ and zPx), hence: **some**y(yPx and y≠x and **N**+1z($A_{=1}(z)$ and zPy)).
For connect conjunctively N+1 of the more than N+1 z for which we have: $A_{=1}(z)$ and zPx; this conjunction, k, is according to TP24 [generalized for all small conjunctions of any finite length] part of x. k is, moreover, different from x, for k has *precisely* N+1 z such that $A_{=1}(z)$ as parts: *at least* N+1 z such that $A_{=1}(z)$ are parts of k according to TP25 [generalized for all small conjunctions of any finite length], AP2; *at most* N+1 z such that $A_{=1}(z)$ are parts of k: every z' for which we have $A_{=1}(z')$ and which is part of k is identical with one of the N+1 conjuncts of k, since from $A_{=1}(z')$ by TP130: EL(z'), hence QA(z'), hence by TP38 [generalized for all small conjunctions of any finite lenght]: z' is part of a conjunct of k, hence by TP80 (because the conjunct is an elementary state of affairs, according to the construction of k and TP130): z' is identical with a conjunct of k.
Hence one obtains: **some**y[**≤N**z($A_{=1}(z)$ and zPy) and **N**+1z($A_{=1}(z)$ and zPy)], which is a contradiction. Therefore: **all**x(if $A_{n+1}(x)$, then **≤N**+1y($A_{=1}(y)$ and yPx)).
(1) and (2) establish the theorem.
•TP136 **all**x(if **≤N**y($A_{=1}(y)$ and yPx), then $A_n(x)$).
Proof: By complete syntactical induction with respect to the indices n and numerals N:
(1) For N,n="0": Assume **≤0**y($A_{=1}(y)$ and yPx), that is [by TP130]: not **some**y(EL(y) and yPx); assume for *reductio*: not xPz, hence by AP5: **some**y(QA(y) and yPx and not yPz), hence by DP4: **some**y(QA(y) and not M(y) and yPx), hence by DP20: **some**y(EL(y) and yPx)- contradicting the underlined result. Therefore: **all**z(xPz), hence by DP4: M(x), hence by TP126: $A_0(x)$.
(2) Assume that the assertion holds true for all indices and numerals up to and including n,N. Assume (*) **≤N**+1y($A_{=1}(y)$ and yPx); assume: yPx and y≠x. For $A_{n+1}(x)$, it remains to be shown (according to DP35): $A_n(y)$; we deduce **≤N**z($A_{=1}(z)$ and zPy); then by induction-assumption: $A_n(y)$.
Assume for *reductio*: not **≤N**z($A_{=1}(z)$ and zPy), hence: **≥N**+1z($A_{=1}(z)$ and zPy), hence by AP1 because of yPx: **≥N**+1z($A_{=1}(z)$ and zPy and zPx).
Since yPx and y≠x, by AP3: not xPy, hence by AP5: **some**z(QA(z) and zPx and not zPy), hence: **some**z(EL(z) and zPx and not zPy) [by DP20 because of not M(z)], hence by TP130: **some**z'($A_{=1}(z')$ and z'Px and not z'Py). This z', because not z'Py, must be different from the at least N+1 z which are parts of y and parts of x; hence: **≥**(**N**+1)+1z($A_{=1}(z)$ and zPx), hence: not **≤N**+1z($A_{=1}(z)$ and zPx) - contradicting the assumption (*).
Hence: **≤N**z($A_{=1}(z)$ and zPy) - what was to be shown.
Therefore (as has already been explained): **all**x(if **≤N**+1y($A_{=1}(y)$ and yPx), then $A_{n+1}(x)$).

(1) and (2) establish the theorem.

•TP137 **all**x($A_{=n}(x)$ iff **N**y($A_{=1}(y)$ and yPx)).

Proof: (1) For n,N="0":

(i) Assume $A_{=0}(x)$, hence by DP37: $A_0(x)$, hence by TP135: **≤0**y($A_{=1}(y)$ and yPx), that is: **0**y($A_{=1}(y)$ and yPx). **(ii)** Assume **0**y($A_{=1}(y)$ and yPx), that is: **≤0**y($A_{=1}(y)$ and yPx), hence by TP136: $A_0(x)$, hence by DP37: $A_{=0}(x)$.

(2) For every index and numeral after "0":

(i) Assume $A_{=n}(x)$, hence by DP37: $A_n(x)$ and not $A_{n-1}(x)$, hence by TP135: **≤N**y($A_{=1}(y)$ and yPx), and by TP136: not **≤N−1**y($A_{=1}(y)$ and yPx), that is, **≥N**y($A_{=1}(y)$ and yPx); hence: **N**y($A_{=1}(y)$ and yPx). **(ii)** Assume **N**y($A_{=1}(y)$ and yPx), that is: **≤N**y($A_{=1}(y)$ and yPx) and **≥N**y($A_{=1}(y)$ and yPx), hence: **≤N**y($A_{=1}(y)$ and yPx) and not **≤N−1**y($A_{=1}(y)$ and yPx), hence by TP136 and TP135: $A_n(x)$ and not $A_{n-1}(x)$, hence by DP37: $A_{=n}(x)$.

•TP138 **all**x**all**y[xNP*y iff **some**z(EL(z) and not zPx and y=**conj**(x,z))].

Proof: **(i)** Assume xNP*y, hence by DP39: xP*y and **no**k(xP*k and kP*y), hence by TP3: not yPx, hence by AP5: **some**z(QA(z) and zPy and not zPx), hence: **(1)** **some**z(EL(z) and zPy and not zPx), according to DP20, since not M(z) because not zPx.

Assume for *reductio*: EL(z) and zPy and not zPx and EL(z') and z'Py and not z'Px and z≠z';

hence: xP**conj**(x,z) and not **conj**(x,z)Px, because of TP25 and AP2, not zPx and TP24;

by DP1: xPy, since xP*y [first assumption]; hence, because of zPy, according to TP24: conj(x,z)Py;

not z'P**conj**(x,z), for in case z'P**conj**(x,z), then by TP38 [from EL(z') by DP20 QA(z')]: z'Px or z'Pz; but according to assumption: not z'Px; hence: z'Pz, hence by TP80, since EL(z) and EL(z'): z=z' - contradicting assumption z≠z';

from not z'P**conj**(x,z) and z'Py by AP1: not yP**conj**(x,z);

from the underlined results by TP3: xP***conj**(x,z) and **conj**(x,z)P*y, hence: **some**k(xP*k and kP*y) - contradicting the first assumption. Hence from the first assumption: **(2)** **all**z**all**z'(if EL(z) and zPy and not zPx and EL(z') and z'Py and not z'Px, then z=z').

From **(1)** and **(2)** we get: **(3)** **one**z(EL(z) and zPy and not zPx); μ := **the**z(EL(z) and zPy and non zPx); hence by **(3)**: **(4)** EL(μ) and μPy and not μPx.

Moreover: **(5)** y=**conj**(x,μ):

(x) xPy and μPy, hence by TP24: **conj**(x,μ)Py;

(xx) assume for *reductio*: not yP**conj**(x,μ), hence by AP5: **some**z(QA(z) and zPy and not zP**conj**(x,μ)), hence by TP25: **some**z(QA(z) and zPy and not zPx and not zPμ), hence by AP2 [etc.]: **some**z(EL(z) and zPy and not zPx and z≠μ) - contradicting the conjunction of **(3)** and **(4)**; therefore: yP**conj**(x,μ).

For obtaining **(5)**, apply AP3 to the results of **(x)** and **(xx)**.

By **(4)** and **(5)**: **some**z(EL(z) and not zPx and y=**conj**(x,z)).

(ii) Assume **some***z*(EL(*z*) and not *z*P*x* and *y*=**conj**(*x*,*z*)); hence by DP1: **(1)** *x*P**y*; for on the one hand: *x*P*y*, since *x***Pconj**(*x*,*z*) [AP2, TP25] and *y*=**conj**(*x*,*z*); and on the other hand: *x*≠*y*, because not *z*P*x* and *z*P*y* [*y*=**conj**(*x*,*z*) and *z***Pconj**(*x*,*z*)].
Assume: *x*P**k* and *k*P**y*, hence: *x*P*k* and not *k*P*x* and *k*P*y* and not *y*P*k* [TP3]; assume: EL(*z*) and not *z*P*x*. We deduce: (*) *y*≠**conj**(*x*,*z*):
some*m*(QA(*m*) and *m*P*k* and not *m*P*x*) and **some***m*′(QA(*m*′) and *m*′P*y* and not *m*′P*k*) [by AP5 from: not *k*P*x* and not *y*P*k*], hence **some***m***some***m*′(QA(*m*) and QA(*m*′) and *m*P*k* and not *m*P*x* and *m*′P*y* and not *m*′P*k*); now: not *m*′P*x* [because of *x*P*k*, from *m*′P*x* according to AP1: *m*′P*k*; but on the contrary: not *m*′P*k*], *m*P*y* [according to AP1, for: *m*P*k* and *k*P*y*]; hence: *m*P*y* and not *m*P*x*, *m*′P*y* and not *m*′P*x*; moreover: *m*≠*m*′ [because *m*P*k* and not *m*′P*k*]. From the underlined results: **(x)** not *y***Pconj**(*x*,*z*), since AP1 and **some***h*(*h*P*y* and not *h***Pconj**(*x*,*z*)), for: *m*P*y* and not *m***Pconj**(*x*,*z*), or *m*′P*y* and not *m*′**Pconj**(*x*,*z*); *otherwise* [in the contrary case], because of *m*P*y* and *m*′P*y*: *m***Pconj**(*x*,*z*) and *m*′**Pconj**(*x*,*z*), hence, because of QA(*m*) and QA(*m*′), by TP38: (*m*P*x* or *m*P*z*) and (*m*′P*x* or *m*′P*z*), hence, since not *m*P*x* and not *m*′P*x*, *m*P*z* and *m*′P*z*; hence, since EL(*m*) [QA(*m*) and not M(*m*)] and EL(*z*) [assumption], by TP80: *m*=*z*; and hence, since EL(*m*′) [QA(*m*′) and not M(*m*′)] and EL(*z*), by TP80: *m*′=*z*; therefore: *m*=*m*′ - contradicting *m*≠*m*′. From **(x)** by AP2: *y*≠**conj**(*x*,*z*), that is: (*).
We have now proved: if **some***k*(*x*P**k* and *k*P**y*), then **all***z*(if EL(*z*) and not *z*P*x*, then *y*≠**conj**(*x*,*z*)); therefore, because of **some***z*(EL(*z*) and not *z*P*x* and *y*=**conj**(*x*,*z*)) [first assumption]: **(2)** **no***k*(*x*P**k* and *k*P**y*).
From **(1)** and **(2)** by DP39: *x*NP**y*.
•TP139 **all***x***all***y*(if *x*P**y*, then **some***z*′(*x*NP**z*′) and **some***z*′(*z*′NP**y*)).
Proof: Assume *x*P**y*, hence by TP3: *x*P*y* and not *y*P*x*, hence by AP5 **some***z*(QA(*z*) and *z*P*y* and not *z*P*x*).
Consider **conj**(*x*,*z*); *x***Pconj**(*x*,*z*) and not **conj**(*x*,*z*)P*x* [the latter by AP1, since: *z***Pconj**(*x*,*z*) and not *z*P*x*], hence by TP3: *x*P***conj**(*x*,*z*).
Assume for *reductio*: **some***k*(*x*P**k* and *k*P***conj**(*x*,*z*)), hence by TP3: **some***k*(*x*P*k* and not *k*P*x* and *k***Pconj**(*x*,*z*) and not **conj**(*x*,*z*)P*k*); by AP5 from not *k*P*x*: **some***r*(QA(*r*) and *r*P*k* and not *r*P*x*), hence: *r***Pconj**(*x*,*z*) [by AP1, since: *r*P*k* and *k***Pconj**(*x*,*z*)], hence by TP38 [because of QA(*r*)]: *r*P*x* or *r*P*z*, hence [since not *r*P*x*]: *r*P*z*, hence, because not M(*r*) [not *r*P*x*] and QA(*z*), according to DP6: *r*=*z*, hence: *z*P*k* [*r*P*k*], hence, because of *x*P*k*, by TP24: **conj**(*x*,*z*)P*k* - contradiction. Therefore from the first assumption: **no***k*(*x*P**k* and *k*P***conj**(*x*,*z*)).
From the underlined results according to DP39: *x*NP***conj**(*x*,*z*), hence: **some***z*′(*x*NP**z*′).
For proving the second conjunct of the succedent of TP139, consider **conj***k*(QA(*k*) and *k*P*y* and *k*≠*z*).

conj$k$(QA(k) and kPy and $k \neq z$)Py: assume: QA(k') and k'P**conj**k(QA(k) and kPy and $k \neq z$); if M(k'), then trivially k'Py; if not M(k'), then k'Py according to TP41. Therefore: **all**k'(if QA(k') and k'P**conj**k(QA(k) and kPy and $k \neq z$), then k'Py), hence by AP5 what was to be deduced.

not yP**conj**k(QA(k) and kPy and $k \neq z$) by AP1; for zPy, but not zP**conj**k(QA(k) and kPy and $k \neq z$), according to TP41, since not M(z) [not zPx], QA(z), not (zPy and $z \neq z$).

no$r$(**conj**k(QA(k) and kPy and $k \neq z$)P*r and rP*y): assume the contrary, hence by TP3: **some**r(**conj**k(QA(k) and kPy and $k \neq z$)Pr and not rP**conj**k(QA(k) and kPy and $k \neq z$) and rPy and not yPr), hence by AP5 [since not rP**conj**k(QA(k) and kPy and $k \neq z$)]: **some**m(QA(m) and mPr and not mP**conj**k(QA(k) and kPy and $k \neq z$)), hence, since not M(m), by TP41: not mPy or m=z; but mPy by AP1, since: mPr and rPy; hence: m=z; hence: zPr [for mPr]. Consequently yPr, in contradiction to: not yPr: assume QA(r') and r'Py; if r'=z, then r'Pr because of zPr; if $r' \neq z$, then by TP18: r'P**conj**k(QA(k) and kPy and $k \neq z$), hence, because of **conj**k(QA(k) and kPy and $k \neq z$)Pr, by AP1: r'Pr. Therefore by AP5: yPr.

From the underlined results after application of TP3 and DP39: **some**z'(z'NP*y).

•TP140 **all**x**all**y(xP*y iff xNP*y or **some**z'(z'NP*y and xP*z')).

Proof: (**i**) From right to left, TP140 is a trivial consequence of the definition of "NP*" and the transitivity of "P*".

(**ii**) Assume: xP*y and not xNP*y; hence by TP3: not yPx, hence by AP5: **some**z(QA(z) and zPy and not zPx). Consider **conj**k(QA(k) and kPy and $k \neq z$). According to the proof of TP139: **conj**k(QA(k) and kPy and $k \neq z$)NP*y. Moreover: xP**conj**k(QA(k) and kPy and $k \neq z$); for assume: QA(r) and rPx, hence: rPy (because of xPy [xP*y] and AP1); $r \neq z$, since rPx and not zPx; hence by TP18: rP**conj**k(QA(k) and kPy and $k \neq z$); therefore, according to AP5, what was to be deduced. Finally: **conj**k(QA(k) and kPy and $k \neq z$)$\neq x$; for *otherwise*: xNP*y (because **conj**k(QA(k) and kPy and $k \neq z$)NP*y); but according to assumption: not xNP*y.

From the underlined results: **some**z'(z'NP*y and xP*z').

•TP141 **all**x(if **conj**(x,**w**)$\neq$**k**, then V(x)).

Proof: Assume **conj**(x,**w**)$\neq$**k**, hence by TP94(i), DP29: **some**y(MK(y) and **conj**(x,**w**)Py), hence by TP24: **some**y(MK(y) and xPy and **w**Py); MK(**w**) [TP106]; hence by TP79: **w**=y, and therefore from xPy: xP**w**, hence by DP31 and DP32: V(x).

•TP142 **all**y(y=**disj**x(MK(x) and yPx)).

Proof: (**i**) Assume: not yP**disj**x(MK(x) and yPx), hence by TP100: **some**x(MK(x) and yPx and not yPx) - contradiction.

(ii) Assume: not **disj***x*(MK(*x*) and *y*P*x*)P*y*; **disj***x*(MK(*x*) and *y*P*x*)=**conj***k***all***x*(if MK(*x*) and *y*P*x*, then *k*P*x*), according to TP63; hence: not **conj***k***all***x*(if MK(*x*) and *y*P*x*, then *k*P*x*)P*y*, hence by TP96:
some*k*(**all***x*(if MK(*x*) and *y*P*x*, then *k*P*x*) and not *k*P*y*), hence by AP5: **some***z*(QA(*z*) and *z*P*k* and not *z*P*y*), hence by DP20 [because not M(*z*)]: **some***z*(EL(*z*) and *z*P*k* and not *z*P*y*), hence by TP78, TP55, TP59: **some***z*(MK(**neg**(*z*)) and **neg**(*k*)P**neg**(*z*) and not **neg**(*y*)P**neg**(*z*)), hence by DP26, DP25, DP24: **some***z*(MK(**neg**(*z*)) and not *k*P**neg**(*z*) and *y*P**neg**(*z*)), hence: **some***x*(MK(*x*) and *y*P*x* and not *k*P*x*) - contradicting what is true of *k* according to the underlined result.

A VARIANT OF SYSTEM P

•AP1 - AP6.
•AP7+ **all***x*(if PA(*x*), then MK(*x*)).
•AP8+ **some***x***some***y*(PA(*x*) and PA(*y*) and *x*≠*y*).
•<AP9+> **all***f***all***g*(if *f*P*g*, then *L*(*f*P*g*)).
•AP10.

•All definitions of P which do not involve "**w**".
•DP1+ t′<t> := MK(t) and tPt′.
•DP2+ AP(t) := **some***y*(PA(*y*) and tP*y*).
•DP3+ t′<<t> := PA(t) and t′Pt.
•DP4+ GA(t) := not AP(**neg**(t)).
•DP5+ $tP^{E}t'$:= **all***z*(if t<*z*>, then t′<*z*>).
•DP6+ $tP^{EE}t'$:= **all***z*(if t<<*z*>, then t′<<*z*>).
•DP7+ **rs** := **disj***y*PA(*y*).

•TP1+ **all***x*(*x*<*x*> iff MK(*x*)).
•TP2+ **all***x*(*x*<*x*> iff **all***y*(*x*<*y*> iff *x*=*y*)).
Proof: (**i**) Assume **all***y*(*x*<*y*> iff *x*=*y*); hence *x*<*x*> iff *x*=*x*, hence *x*<*x*>. (**ii**) Assume *x*<*x*>, that is [by TP1+]: MK(*x*); (**x**) assume *x*=*y*; hence: *x*<*y*>; (**xx**) assume *x*<*y*>, hence by DP1+: MK(*y*) and *x*P*y*, hence, because of MK(*x*), by TP79: *x*=*y*.
•TP3+ **all***f***all***x*(if *f*<<*x*>, then *f*<*x*>).
•TP4+ **all***x*(if PA(*x*), then AP(*x*)).
•TP5+ **all***f***all***x*(if *f*<<*x*>, then AP(*x*) and AP(*f*)).
•TP6+ **all***f***all***x*(*f*<*x*> and AP(*x*) iff *f*<<*x*>).
Proof: (**i**) Assume: *f*<*x*> and AP(*x*), hence by DP1+, DP2+: MK(*x*) and *f*P*x* and **some***y*(PA(*y*) and *x*P*y*), hence by AP7+: MK(*x*) and *f*P*x* and **some***y*(PA(*y*) and MK(*y*) and *x*P*y*), hence by TP79: *x*=*y*, hence: PA(*x*) and *f*P*x*, hence by DP3+: *f*<<*x*>. (**ii**) Assume *f*<<*x*>, hence by TP3+ and TP5+: *f*<*x*> and AP(*x*).
•TP7+ **all***x*(PA(*x*) iff MK(*x*) and AP(*x*)).
Proof: (**i**) **all***x*(if PA(*x*), then MK(*x*) and AP(*x*)), according to AP7+ and TP4+. (**ii**) This part of the proof is contained in the proof of TP6+.
•TP8+
(a) **all***x*[if AP(*x*), then (*x*<*x*> iff **no***y*(*x*≠*y* and *x*<*y*>))];
(b) **all***x*[if AP(*x*), then (*x*<<*x*> iff **no***y*(*x*≠*y* and *x*<<*y*>))].
Proof: (**ia**) Assume AP(*x*), *x*<*x*>; hence by TP2+: **no***y*(*x*≠*y* and *x*<*y*>).

(**iia**) Assume AP(*x*), **no***y*(*x*≠*y* and *x*<*y*>); from the first assumption by DP2+: **some***y*(PA(*y*) and *x*P*y*), hence by AP7+: **some***y*(MK(*y*) and *x*P*y*), hence by DP1+: **some***y*(*x*<*y*>); hence by applying the second assumption: *x*<*x*>.
(**ib**) Assume AP(*x*), *x*<<*x*>; hence by TP3+ and TP2+: **no***y*(*x*≠*y* and *x*<*y*>), hence by TP3+: **no***y*(*x*≠*y* and *x*<<*y*>).
(**iib**) Assume AP(*x*), **no***y*(*x*≠*y* and *x*<<*y*>); from the first assumption by DP2+: **some***y*(PA(*y*) and *x*P*y*), that is [by DP3+]: **some***y*(*x*<<*y*>); hence by applying the second assumption: *x*<<*x*>.
•TP9+ **all***x*[if (*x*<<*x*> iff **no***y*(*x*≠*y* and *x*<<*y*>)), then AP(*x*)].
Proof: Assume: *x*<<*x*> iff **no***y*(*x*≠*y* and *x*<<*y*>); (**x**) *x*<<*x*>, hence by TP5+: AP(*x*); (**xx**) not *x*<<*x*>; hence by the first assumption: **some***y*(*x*≠*y* and *x*<<*y*>), hence by TP5+: AP(*x*).
•TP10+ **all***x*[AP(*x*) iff (*x*<<*x*> iff **no***y*(*x*≠*y* and *x*<<*y*>))].
•TP11+ **all***x*[P(*x*) iff (*x*<*x*> iff **no***y*(*x*≠*y* and *x*<*y*>))].
Proof: (**i**) Assume P(*x*), *x*<*x*>; hence by TP2+: **no***y*(*x*≠*y* and *x*<*y*>).
(**ii**) Assume P(*x*), **no***y*(*x*≠*y* and *x*<*y*>); from P(*x*) by DP29: **some***y*(MK(*y*) and *x*P*y*), hence by DP1+: **some***y*(*x*<*y*>); hence by applying the second assumption: *x*<*x*>.
(**iii**) Assume: *x*<*x*> iff **no***y*(*x*≠*y* and *x*<*y*>); (**x**) *x*<*x*>, hence: MK(*x*) and *x*P*x* [by DP1+], hence: **some***y*(MK(*y*) and *x*P*y*), hence by DP29: P(*x*); (**xx**) not *x*<*x*>, hence by the first assumption: **some***y*(*x*≠*y* and *x*<*y*>), hence by DP1+: **some***y*(MK(*y*) and *x*P*y*), hence by DP29: P(*x*).
•TP12+ **all***f*[AP(*f*) or AP(**neg**(*f*))].
•TP13+ **some***f*[AP(*f*) and AP(**neg**(*f*))].
•TP14+ **all***f***all***g*(AP(**disj**(*f*,*g*)) iff AP(*f*) or AP(*g*)).
Proof: (**i**) Assume: AP(*f*) or AP(*g*), hence by DP2+: **some***y*(PA(*y*) and *f*P*y*) or **some***y*(PA(*y*) and *g*P*y*); according to TP26, AP2: **disj**(*f*,*g*)P*f*, **disj**(*f*,*g*)P*g*; from the underlined results we obtain by applying AP1: **some***y*(PA(*y*) and **disj**(*f*,*g*)P*y*), hence by DP2+: AP(**disj**(*f*,*g*)).
(**ii**) Assume AP(**disj**(*f*,*g*)), hence by DP2+: **some***y*(PA(*y*) and **disj**(*f*,*g*)P*y*), hence by AP7+: **some***y*(PA(*y*) and MK(*y*) and **disj**(*f*,*g*)P*y*). Hence we can conclude: (**1**) **some***y*(PA(*y*) and (*f*P*y* or *g*P*y*)).
This is seen as follows: Assume for *reductio* on the basis of the underlined result: not *f*P*y* and not *g*P*y*,
hence: **neg**(*f*)P*y* and **neg**(*g*)P*y* [because of MK(*y*), in particular: MX(*y*)],
hence: **conj**(**neg**(*f*),**neg**(*g*))P*y* [by TP24],
hence: not **neg**(**conj**[**neg**(*f*),**neg**(*g*)])P*y* [because of MK(*y*), in particular: K(*y*)].
But **neg**(**conj**[**neg**(*f*),**neg**(*g*)]) is, according to TP57, identical with **disj**(*f*,*g*), and we already have **disj**(*f*,*g*)P*y*, hence a contradiction to the underlined result.
From (**1**) by DP2+: AP(*f*) or AP(*g*).
•TP15+ **all***f***all***g*(if AP(**conj**(*f*,*g*)), then AP(*f*) and AP(*g*)).
•TP16+ **some***f***some***g*[AP(*f*) and AP(*g*) and not AP(**conj**(*f*,*g*))].

Proof: According to TP13+: **some***f*[AP(*f*) and AP(**neg**(*f*))]; but: not AP(**conj**[*f*,**neg**(*f*)]); for *otherwise* by DP2+: **some***y*(PA(*y*) and **conj**[*f*,**neg**(*f*)]P*y*), hence by AP7+: **some***y*(MK(*y*) and **conj**[*f*,**neg**(*f*)]P*y*), hence by TP53(ii): **some***y*(MK(*y*) and **k**P*y*) - but the contrary is provable according to TP72, etc.

•TP17+ AP(**disj***f*A[*f*]) iff **some***g*(A[*g*] and AP(*g*)).

Proof: (**i**) Assume AP(**disj***f*A[*f*]), hence by DP2+: **some***y*(PA(*y*) and **disj***f*A[*f*]P*y*), hence by TP64: **some***y*(PA(*y*) and **neg**(**conj***f***some***g*[A[*g*] and *f*=**neg**(*g*)])P*y*), hence, because of PA(*y*), by AP7+, DP26, DP24: not **conj***f***some***g*[A[*g*] and *f*=**neg**(*g*)]P*y*, hence by TP96: **some***f*(**some***g*[A[*g*] and *f*=**neg**(*g*)] and not *f*P*y*), hence: **some***g*(A[*g*] and not **neg**(*g*)P*y*), hence, because of PA(*y*), by AP7+, DP26, DP25: **some***g*(A[*g*] and *g*P*y*), hence, because of PA(*y*), by DP2+: **some***g*(A[*g*] and AP(*g*)).

(**ii**) Assume **some***g*(A[*g*] and AP(*g*)); according to TP65: **all***g*(if A[*g*], then **disj***f*A[*f*]P*g*); from the assumption by DP2+: **some***g*(A[*g*] and **some***y*(PA(*y*) and *g*P*y*)); hence by AP1 and the underlined result: **some***y*(PA(*y*) and **disj***f*A[*f*]P*y*), hence by DP2+: AP(**disj***f*A[*f*]).

•TP18+ **all***x*(if PA(*x*), then *x*≠**t**).

Proof: Assume PA(*x*), hence by AP7+: MK(*x*); assume for *reductio*: *x*=**t**; hence QC(**t**) from MK(*x*) by DP26, TP71; hence because of **all***y*(**t**T*y*) [TP32]: **all***y*(*y*=**t** or *y*=**k**) [according to DP7, TP34]; but in contradiction to this there are at least three first intensions: two primary actualities (according to AP8+), and *moreover* **k**, which is not a primary actuality (*otherwise* we would have MK(**k**) by AP7+, hence by DP26: K(**k**) - contradicting TP70).

•TP19+ **all***f***all***g*(if **all***z*(*f*<*z*> iff *g*<*z*>), then *f*=*g*).

Proof: Assume **all***z*(*f*<*z*> iff *g*<*z*>), hence by DP1+: **all***z*(if MK(*z*), then (*f*P*z* iff *g*P*z*)); assume for *reductio*: *f*≠*g*, hence by AP3: not *f*P*g* or not *g*P*f*. This is reduced *ad absurdum* by reducing both disjuncts *ad absurdum*:

(**x**) Assume: not *f*P*g*, hence by AP5: **some***m*(QA(*m*) and *m*P*f* and not *m*P*g*), hence, because not *m*P*g*, by DP20, DP4: **some***m*(EL(*m*) and *m*P*f* and not *m*P*g*), hence by TP78, TP55: **some***m*(MK(**neg**(*m*)) and *m*P*f* and not *m*P*g*), hence according to the above underlined result: if *g*P**neg**(*m*), then *f*P**neg**(*m*). Not *f*P**neg**(*m*), for *otherwise* because of *m*P*f* by AP1: *m*P**neg**(*m*) - which contradicts: **neg**(*m*)P**neg**(*m*) [AP2] and K(**neg**(*m*)) [from MK(**neg**(*m*)) by DP26]. Therefore: not *g*P**neg**(*m*). Moreover, because not *m*P*g*, by TP59: not **neg**(*g*)P**neg**(*m*). But the latter two underlined results contradict MX(**neg**(*m*)) [from MK(**neg**(*m*)) by DP26].

(**xx**) Assume: not *g*P*f*; the *reductio* is *mutatis mutandis* as in (**x**).

•TP20+ **all***f***all***g*(if **all***z*(if *g*<*z*>, then *f*<*z*>), then *f*P*g*).

Proof: Assume **all***z*(if *g*<*z*>, then *f*<*z*>), hence by DP1+: **all***z*(if MK(*z*), then (if *g*P*z*, then *f*P*z*)); assume: not *f*P*g*; this is reduced *ad absurdum* as in (**x**) of the proof of TP19+.

•TP21+ **all***f***all***g*(if *f*P*g*, then **all***z*(if *g*<*z*>, then *f*<*z*>)).

•TP22+ **all***f***all***g*(**all***z*(if *g*<*z*>, then *f*<*z*>) iff *f*P*g*).

•TP23+ **all***f***all***g*(*f*P*g* iff *g*P^{E}*f*).

•TP24+ **all***x***all***y*(if MK(*x*) and MK(*y*) and **all***f*(*f*<*x*> iff *f*<*y*>), then *x*=*y*).

Proof: Assume: MK(*x*) and MK(*y*) and **all***f*(*f*<*x*> iff *f*<*y*>); hence: *x*<*x*> iff *x*<*y*>; because of MK(*x*) according to TP1+: *x*<*x*>; hence: *x*<*y*>; and according to TP2+ and *x*<*x*>: **all***y*(*x*<*y*> iff *x*=*y*). From the underlined results: *x*=*y*.

•TP25+ **all***x***all***y*(if MK(*x*) and **all***f*(if *f*<*x*>, then *f*<*y*>), then *x*=*y*).

•TP26+ **all***x***all***y*(if MK(*x*) and MK(*y*) and [not MK(**neg**(*x*)) or not MK(**neg**(*y*))] and **all***f*(if not MK(*f*), then (*f*<*x*> iff *f*<*y*>)), then *x*=*y*).

Proof: Assume: MK(*x*) and MK(*y*) and **all***f*(if not MK(*f*), then (*f*<*x*> iff *f*<*y*>)).

(**i**) Assume in addition: not MK(**neg**(*x*)); hence by the first assumption: **neg**(*x*)<*x*> iff **neg**(*x*)<*y*>, hence by DP1+: MK(*x*) and **neg**(*x*)P*x* iff MK(*y*) and **neg**(*x*)P*y*. Not (MK(*x*) and **neg**(*x*)P*x*), for *otherwise* because of AP2: **some***y*(*y*P*x* and **neg**(*y*)P*x*), hence by DP24: not K(*x*) - contradicting MK(*x*), according to DP26. Therefore: not (MK(*y*) and **neg**(*x*)P*y*). Hence [because of MK(*y*)]: not **neg**(*x*)P*y*, hence [because of MX(*y*): by DP26 from MK(*y*)]: *x*P*y* (by DP25), and hence [because of MK(*x*), MK(*y*) and TP79]: *x*=*y*.

(**ii**) Assume in addition to the first assumption: not MK(**neg**(*y*)); one obtains *x*=*y* as in (**i**) (*mutatis mutandis*).

•TP27+ **all***x*(if MK(*x*) and MK(**neg**(*x*)), then **all***z*(*z*=*x* or *z*=**neg**(*x*) or *z*=**t** or *z*=**k**)).

Proof: Assume: MK(*x*) and MK(**neg**(*x*)).

Because of MX(*x*) [from MK(*x*) by DP26]: *z*P*x* or **neg**(*z*)P*x* (DP25). Because of MX(**neg**(*x*)): *z*P**neg**(*x*) or **neg**(*z*)P**neg**(*x*). Therefore: *z*P*x* and *z*P**neg**(*x*), or *z*P*x* and **neg**(*z*)P**neg**(*x*), or **neg**(*z*)P*x* and *z*P**neg**(*x*), or **neg**(*z*)P*x* and **neg**(*z*)P**neg**(*x*).

(1) From *z*P*x* and *z*P**neg**(*x*) by TP23: *z*P**disj**(*x*,**neg**(*x*)), hence by TP53(ii): *z*P**t**, hence by TP36: *z*=**t**;

(2) from *z*P*x* and **neg**(*z*)P**neg**(*x*) by TP59: *z*P*x* and *x*P*z*, hence by AP3: *z*=*x*;

(3) from **neg**(*z*)P*x* and *z*P**neg**(*x*) by TP60: **neg**(*x*)P*z* and *z*P**neg**(*x*), hence by AP3: *z*=**neg**(*x*);

(4) from **neg**(*z*)P*x* and **neg**(*z*)P**neg**(*x*) by TP23: **neg**(*z*)P**disj**(*x*,**neg**(*x*)), hence [see (1)]: **neg**(*z*)=**t**, hence: **neg**(**neg**(*z*))=**neg**(**t**), hence by TP54, TP55: *z*=**k**.

•TP28+ **all***x*(**disj***x*′(MK(*x*′) and A[*x*′])<*x*> iff MK(*x*) and A[*x*]).

Proof: From TP44 we obtain by DP21: **all***x*(EL(*x*) and *x*P**conj***y*(EL(*y*) and A[*y*]) iff EL(*x*) and A[*x*]). Hence as a specification of that schema: **all***x*(EL(*x*) and *x*P**conj***y*(EL(*y*) and A[**neg**(*y*)]) iff EL(*x*) and A[**neg**(*x*)]), hence: **all***x*(EL(**neg**(*x*)) and **neg**(*x*)P**conj***y*(EL(*y*) and A[**neg**(*y*)]) iff EL(**neg**(*x*)) and A[**neg**(**neg**(*x*))]). Hence by TP55, TP78 and TP60: **all***x*(MK(*x*) and **neg**(**conj***y*(EL(*y*) and A[**neg**(*y*)]))P*x* iff MK(*x*) and A[*x*]).

According to TP78, TP55: **all***y*(EL(*y*) and A[**neg**(*y*)] iff MK(**neg**(*y*)) and A[**neg**(*y*)]), that is: **all***y*(EL(*y*) and A[**neg**(*y*)] iff **some***x*′(MK(*x*′) and A[*x*′] and **neg**(*y*)=*x*′)), and hence by TP55: **all***y*(EL(*y*) and A[**neg**(*y*)] iff **some***x*′(MK(*x*′)

and A[x′] and y=**neg**(x′))), hence by TP29: **neg**(**conj**y(EL(y) and A[**neg**(y)]))=**neg**(**conj**y**some**x′(MK(x′) and A[x′] and y=**neg**(x′))), hence by TP64: **neg**(**conj**y(EL(y) and A[**neg**(y)]))=**disj**x′(MK(x′) and A[x′]).
From the two underlined results: **all**x(MK(x) and **disj**x′(MK(x′) and A[x′])Px iff MK(x) and A[x]), and hence by DP1+ what was to be proved.

•TP29+ if **all**x(if A[x], then MK(x)), then **all**x(**disj**yA[y]<x> iff A[x]).

Proof: Assume **all**x(if A[x], then MK(x)), hence: **all**x(MK(x) and A[x] iff A[x]), hence by TP66, AP3: **disj**y(MK(y) and A[y])=**disj**yA[y]. Therefore by TP28+: **all**x(**disj**yA[y]<x> iff A[x]).

•TP30+ **all**x(**disj**yPA(y)<x> iff PA(x)).

•TP31+ **all**x(**rs**<x> iff PA(x)).

•TP32+ **all**f(if **conj**(f,**rs**)≠**k**, then **some**y(PA(y) and f<y>)).

•TP33+ **rs**=**t** iff **all**y(PA(y) iff MK(y)).

•TP34+ **rs**≠**k** iff **some**yPA(y).

Proof: **some**yPA(y), that is [by TP31+]: **some**y(**rs**<y>), that is [by DP1+]: **some**y(MK(y) and **rs**Py), that is [by DP29]: P(**rs**), that is [by TP94(i)]: **rs**≠**k**.

•TP35+ **all**f(if f**Prs**, then AP(f)).

Proof: Assume f**Prs**; by AP8+: **some**yPA(y), hence by TP31+, DP1+: **some**y(PA(y) and **rs**Py); hence, because of f**Prs**, by AP1: **some**y(PA(y) and fPy), hence by DP2+: AP(f).

•TP36+ **all**x[if PA(x), then **disj**yPA(y)P***disj**y(PA(y) and y≠x)].

Proof: Assume PA(x); **all**y(if PA(y) and y≠x, then PA(y)), hence by TP66: **(1)** **disj**yPA(y)P**disj**y(PA(y) and y≠x). Moreover:
(2) **disj**yPA(y)≠**disj**y(PA(y) and y≠x): from PA(x) by TP65: **disj**yPA(y)Px; but not **disj**y(PA(y) and y≠x)Px:
Otherwise by TP63: **conj**z**all**y(if PA(y) and y≠x, then zPy)Px, hence by TP96: **all**z(if **all**y(if PA(y) and y≠x, then zPy), then zPx). Now: **all**y(if PA(y) and y≠x, then **neg**(x)Py); *otherwise* **some**y(PA(y) and y≠x and not **neg**(x)Py), hence by AP7+: **some**y(MK(y) and y≠x and not **neg**(x)Py), hence because of MX(y) [by DP26 from MK(y)] and DP25: **some**y(MK(y) and y≠x and xPy), hence, because of MK(x) [from PA(x) by AP7+], by TP79: x=y - contradiction. From the two underlined sentence-forms: **neg**(x)Px - contradicting MK(x) [in view of DP26, DP24, AP2].
From **(1)** and **(2)** according to DP1: **disj**yPA(y)P***disj**y(PA(y) and y≠x).

THE LEIBNIZIAN SYSTEM

•All the axioms of the previous system (with optional AP9+).
•AC1 **all***x***all***y*(if $x=^{w}y$, then MK(*x*) and MK(*y*)).
•AC2 **all***x*(if MK(*x*), then $x=^{w}x$).
•AC3 **all***x***all***y*(if $x=^{w}y$, then $y=^{w}x$).
•AC4 **all***x***all***y***all***z*(if $x=^{w}y$ and $y=^{w}z$, then $x=^{w}z$).
•AC5 **all***x***all***y*(if PA(*x*) and PA(*y*), then $x=^{w}y$).
•AC6 **all***x***all***y*(PA(*x*) and $y=^{w}x$, then PA(*y*)).

•All the definitions of the previous system.

•DC1 **w**(t) := **disj***y*($y=^{w}$t).
•DC2 WL(t) := **some***y*′(MK(*y*′) and t=**w**(*y*′)).
•DC3 **w** := **the***x***all***y*(PA(*y*), then *x*=**w**(*y*)).

•TC1 **all***x***all***y*[if MK(*x*) and MK(*y*), then ($x=^{w}y$ iff **w**(*x*)=**w**(*y*))].
Proof: **(i)** Assume $x=^{w}y$; hence, because of AC3 and AC4, **all***z*($z=^{w}x$ iff $z=^{w}y$), hence by TP66 and AP3: **disj***z*($z=^{w}x$)=**disj***z*($z=^{w}y$), hence by DC1: **w**(*x*)=**w**(*y*).
(ii) Assume: MK(*x*), MK(*y*), **w**(*x*)=**w**(*y*); hence by DC1 **disj***z*($z=^{w}x$)= **disj***z*($z=^{w}y$); because of MK(*x*) by AC2 and TP65: **disj***z*($z=^{w}x$)P*x*; hence: **disj***z*($z=^{w}y$)P*x*, hence, because of MK(*x*), by DP1+: **disj***z*($z=^{w}y$)<*x*>, hence, because of AC1, by TP29+: $x=^{w}y$.
•TC2 **all***y***all***x*(if MK(*y*) and MK(*x*) and **w**(*y*)P*x*, then **w**(*y*)=**w**(*x*)).
Proof: Assume: MK(*y*), MK(*x*), **w**(*y*)P*x*; hence by DC1: **disj***z*($z=^{w}y$)P*x*; from this as in **(ii)** of the proof of TC1: $x=^{w}y$, hence by TC1: **w**(*y*)=**w**(*x*).
•TC3 **all***x*(if MK(*x*), then **one***y*(WL(*y*) and *y*P*x*)).
Proof: Assume MK(*x*); hence by AC2, TP65, DC1 and DC2: WL(**w**(*x*)) and **w**(*x*)P*x*, hence: <u>**some***y*(WL(*y*) and *y*P*x*)</u>. Assume: WL(*z*) and WL(*z*′) and *z*P*x* and *z*′P*x*; hence by DC2: **some***y*(MK(*y*) and *z*=**w**(*y*)) and **some***y*′(MK(*y*′) and *z*′=**w**(*y*′)) and *z*P*x* and *z*′P*x*, hence: **some***y***some***y*′(MK(*y*) and MK(*y*′) and *z*=**w**(*y*) and *z*′=**w**(*y*′) and **w**(*y*)P*x* and **w**(*y*′)P*x*), hence by TC2: **w**(*y*)=**w**(*x*) and **w**(*y*′)=**w**(*x*), hence: **w**(*y*)=**w**(*y*′), hence: *z*=*z*′. This, in view of the underlined result, gives us: **one***y*(WL(*y*) and *y*P*x*).
•TC4 **one***x***all***y*(if PA(*y*), then *x*=**w**(*y*)).
Proof: By AP8+: **some***z*PA(*z*); hence according to AC5: **all***y*(if PA(*y*), then $z=^{w}y$), hence by TC1 and AP7+: **all***y*(if PA(*y*), then **w**(*z*)=**w**(*y*)). Therefore: **some***x***all***y*(if PA(*y*), then *x*=**w**(*y*)).

Assume now: **all***y*(if PA(*y*), then *x*=**w**(*y*)), **all***y*(if PA(*y*), then *x′*=**w**(*y*)); hence because of **some***z*PA(*z*): *x*=**w**(*z*) and *x′*=**w**(*z*), hence: *x*=*x′*.

•TC5 WL(**w**) and AP(**w**) and **all***y*(if WL(*y*) and AP(*y*), then *y*=**w**).

Proof: By TC4, DC3: **all***y*(if PA(*y*), then **w**=**w**(*y*)); by AP8+: **some***y*PA(*y*); hence: **some***y*(PA(*y*) and **w**=**w**(*y*)), hence by AP7+: **some***y*(MK(*y*) and **w**=**w**(*y*)), hence by DC2: WL(**w**). From **some***y*(PA(*y*) and **w**=**w**(*y*)) by DC1: **some***y*(PA(*y*) and **w**=**disj***y′*(*y′*$=^{w}$*y*)); by AP7+, AC2, TP65: **disj***y′*(*y′*$=^{w}$*y*)P*y*; hence: **some***y*(PA(*y*) and **w**P*y*), hence by DP2+: AP(**w**). Assume: WL(*y*) and AP(*y*), hence by DC2 and DP2+: **some***x′*(MK(*x′*) and *y*=**w**(*x′*)) and **some***x*(PA(*x*) and *y*P*x*); hence: **w**(*x′*)P*x*, hence by DC1: **disj***y′*(*y′*$=^{w}$*x′*)P*x*, hence by AC1, TP29+, AP7+: *x*$=^{w}$*x′*, hence by TC1: **w**(*x*)=**w**(*x′*); by TC4, DC3: **all***x*(if PA(*x*), then **w**=**w**(*x*)); hence, because of PA(*x*), **w**(*x′*)=**w**, and therefore: *y*=**w** (because of *y*=**w**(*x′*)).

•TC6 **all***x*(if MK(*x*) and **w**P*x*, then AP(*x*)).

Proof: According to TC4 and DC3: **all***y*(if PA(*y*), then **w**=**w**(*y*)); according to AP8+: **some***y*PA(*y*); assume: MK(*x*) and **w**P*x*; hence: **some***y*(PA(*y*) and MK(*x*) and **w**(*y*)P*x*), hence by TC2, AP7+: **w**(*y*)=**w**(*x*), hence by TC1: *x*$=^{w}$*y*, hence by AC6: PA(*x*), hence by TP4+: AP(*x*).

•TC7 **all***x*(if MK(*x*) and AP(*x*), then **w**P*x*).

Proof: Assume: MK(*x*) and AP(*x*), hence by TP7+: PA(*x*); according to TC4, DC3: **all***y*(if PA(*y*), then **w**=**w**(*y*)); hence: **w**=**w**(*x*); according to MK(*x*), AC2, TP65, DC1: **w**(*x*)P*x*; hence: **w**P*x*.

•TC8 **w**=**disj***x*(MK(*x*) and AP(*x*)).

Proof: According to TC6, TC7: **all***x*(MK(*x*) and AP(*x*) iff MK(*x*) and **w**P*x*), hence by TP66, AP3: **disj***x*(MK(*x*) and AP(*x*))=**disj***x*(MK(*x*) and **w**P*x*). According to TP142: **disj***x*(MK(*x*) and **w**P*x*)=**w**. Hence we obtain what was to be proved.

•TC9 **w**=**rs**.

Proof: By TP7+: **all***x*(MK(*x*) and AP(*x*) iff PA(*x*)), hence by TP66, AP3: **disj***x*(MK(*x*) and AP(*x*))=**disj***x*PA(*x*); hence by TC8 and DP7+: **w**=**rs**.

THE MEREOLOGY OF MOMENTARY MATERIAL INDIVIDUALS

•AP1 - AP4.
•AP5# **all**x**all**y[if xP*y, then **some**z(zP*y and not M(z) and **no**u(not M(u) and uPx and uPz))].
•AP6.
•AP7# not M(**k**).

•All definitions of P that do not involve "**w**".
•DP1# R(t) := t≠**t**.

•TP1# **all**y(if not M(y), then **some**z(zP*y and not M(z)).
Proof: Assume: not M(y); hence: **some**x(xP*y) [for *otherwise* because of DP1: **all**x(if xPy, then x=y), hence because of **t**Py: **t**=y, hence by TP32: M(y) - contradicting the assumption]; hence by AP5#: **some**z(zP*y and not M(z)).
•TP2# **all**y[**some**k(not M(k) and kPy and kP**conj**xA[x]) iff **some**z(A[z] and **some**k(not M(k) and kPy and kPz))].
Proof: (**i**) Assume **some**k(not M(k) and kPy and kP**conj**xA[x]); hence by AP6: **some**u(uPk and not M(u) and **some**z(A[z] and uPz)), hence by AP1: **some**u(uPy and not M(u) and **some**z(A[z] and uPz)), hence: **some**z(A[z] and **some**k(not M(k) and kPy and kPz)) [using "k" instead of "u"].
(**ii**) Assume **some**z(A[z] and **some**k(not M(k) and kPy and kPz)), hence by TP18: **some**z(zP**conj**xA[x] and **some**k(not M(k) and kPy and kPz)), hence by AP1: **some**k(not M(k) and kPy and kP**conj**xA[x]).

SYSTEM PT1

•APT0 **allxally**(if *x*P*y*, then 1(*x*) and 1(*y*)).
•APT1 **allxallyallz**(if *x*P*y* and *y*P*z*, then *x*P*z*).
•APT2 **allx**(if 1(*x*), then *x*P*x*).
•APT3 **allxally**(if *x*P*y* and *y*P*x*, then *x*=*y*).
•APT4 **somez**[1(*z*) and **allx**(if 1(*x*) and A[*x*], then *x*P*z*) and **ally**(if 1(*y*) and **allx**(if 1(*x*) and A[*x*], then *x*P*y*), then *z*P*y*)].
•APT5 **allzallz′**(if 1(*z*) and 1(*z*′) and **allx**(if QA(*x*) and *x*P*z*, then *x*P*z*′), then *z*P*z*′).
•APT6 **allx**[if *x***Pconjy**A[*y*] and not M(*x*), then **somek′**(*k*′P*x* and not M(*k*′) and **somez**(*k*′P*z* and A[*z*]))].
•APT7 **w**≠**k**.
•APT8 QC(**w**).
•APT9 **w**≠**t**.
•APT10 **allx**(if 1(*x*), then not 0(*x*)).
•APT11 **allx**(if 1(*x*), then not <0>(*x*)).
•APT12 **allx**(if 0(*x*), then not <0>(*x*)).
•APT13 **somex**0(*x*).
•APT14 **allxally**[if <0>(*x*) and 0(*y*), then 1(**(***x*,*y***)**)].
•APT15 **allxally**(if not <0>(*x*) or not 0(*y*), then **(***x*,*y***)**=**k**).
•APT16 **allx**(if 0(*x*) and 1(f[*x*]), then **(exo**f[*o*],*x***)**=f[*x*]).
•APT17 **allx**(if not 1(f[*x*]), then **(exo**f[*o*],*x***)**=**k**).
•APT18 if **nox**(0(*x*) and 1(f[*x*]) and f[*x*]≠**k**), then <0>(**exo**f[*o*]).
•APT19 **allfallg**(if <0>(*f*) and <0>(*g*) and **allx**(if 0(*x*), then **(***f*,*x***)**=**(***g*,*x***)**), then *f*=*g*).
•APT20 **somezsomez′**(**sr(***z***)** and **sr(***z*′**)** and *z*≠*z*′).

•DPT1 - DPT39: the reformulations in LPT1 of DP1 - DP39.
•DPT40 $<0>_{CD}$(t) := <0>(t) and **allx**(if 0(*x*), then **(**t,*x***)**=**k**).
•DPT41 $tP_{<0>}t'$:= <0>(t) and <0>(t′) and **allx**(if 0(*x*), then **(**t,*x***)**P**(**t′,*x***)**).
•DPT42 $\mathbf{conj}_{<0>}$*f*A[*f*] := **the***h*[<0>(*h*) and **allf**(if <0>(*f*) and A[*f*], then $fP_{<0>}h$) and **allg**(if <0>(*g*) and **allf**(if <0>(*f*) and A[*f*], then $fP_{<0>}g$), then $hP_{<0>}g$)].
•DPT43 $\mathbf{k}_{<0>}$:= **they**(<0>(*y*) and **allx**(if <0>(*x*), then $xP_{<0>}y$)).
•DPT44 **b**(t) := **exoconjx**(*x*=t and *o*=*o*).
•DPT45 $<0>_{TL}$(t) := <0>(t) and **allz**(if 0(*z*), then **(**t,*z***)**=**t**).
•DPT46 $\mathbf{t}_{<0>}$:= **they**(<0>(*y*) and **allx**(if <0>(*x*), then $yP_{<0>}x$)).

•DPT47 **d**(t) := **ex***o***conj***y*(*o*=t and *y*=**k**).
•DPT48 **i**(t) := **ex***o***conj***y*(*o*≠t and *y*=**k**).
•DPT49 <0>$_{ES}$(t) := <0>(t) and **all***z*(if 0(*z*), then **(t,*z*)=t** or **(t,*z*)=k**).
•DPT50 <0>$_{AC}$(t) := <0>(t) and **all***z*(if 0(*z*), then **(t,*z*)≠t** and **(t,*z*)≠k**).
•DPT51 <0>$_{ES}$(t,t′) := <0>(t) and 0(t′) and (**(t,t′)=t** or **(t,t′)=k**).
•DPT52 <0>$_{AC}$(t,t′) := <0>(t) and 0(t′) and **(t,t′)≠t** and **(t,t′)≠k**.
•DPT53 <0>$_{CD}$(t,t′) := <0>(t) and 0(t) and **(t,t′)=k**.
•DPT54 <0>$_{TL}$(t,t′) := <0>(t) and 0(t′) and **(t,t′)=t**.
•DPT55 t(t′) := O((t,t′)).
•DPT56 t/in t′/(t′′) := (t,t′′)Pt′ and MK(t′).
•DPT57 MK**w**$_{<0>}$(t) := MK$_{<0>}$(t) and **b(w)**P$_{<0>}$t.
•DPT58 0$_{AE}$(t) := **sr(t)**.
•DPT59 <0>$_{AE}$(t) := **some***z*(0$_{AE}$(*z*) and t(*z*)).
•DPT60 **rep**(t) := **the***g*(<0>$_{ES}$(*g*) and **all***z*(*g*(*z*) iff t(*z*))).
•DPT61 **rep**(t,t′) := **the***g*(<0>$_{ES}$(*g*) and **all***z*[*g*/in t′/(*z*) iff t/in t′/(*z*)]).
•DPT62 **nec**$_{<0>}$(t) := **ex***o***conj***y*((t,*o*)≠t and *y*=**k**).
•DPT63 **pos**$_{<0>}$(t) := **neg**$_{<0>}$(**nec**$_{<0>}$(**neg**$_{<0>}$(t))).
•DPT64 ∀(t) := **conj***x***some***z*(0(*z*) and *x*P(t,*z*)).
•DPT65 ∃(t) := **conj***x***all***z*(if 0(*z*), then *x*P(t,*z*)).
•DPT66 For every Arabic numeral k that is ''1'' or greater than ''1'':
(i) $\exists^{\geq k}$(t) := **disj***y***some***z*$_1$...**some***z*$_k$[0(z_1) and ... and 0(z_k) and D(z_1,...,z_k) and *y*=**conj**((t,z_1),...,(t,z_k))]. [If k is greater than ''1'': D(z_1,...,z_k) := z_1,...,z_k are pairwise different from each other; this can be expressed by means of ''=''. If k is ''1'': omit ''D(z_1)''.]
(ii) $\exists^{\leq k}$(t) := **neg**($\exists^{\geq k+1}$(t)).
(iii) $\exists^{=k}$(t) := **conj**($\exists^{\geq k}$(t),$\exists^{\leq k}$(t)).

•TPT1 - TPT142: the reformulations in LPT1 of TP1 - TP142.
•TPT143 if **some***x*(0(*x*) and 1(f[*x*]) and f[*x*]≠**k**), then <0>(**ex***o*f[*o*]).
Proof: Assume **some***x*(0(*x*) and 1(f[*x*]) and f[*x*]≠**k**), hence by APT16: (**ex***o*f[*o*],*x*)=f[*x*], hence: (**ex***o*f[*o*],*x*)≠**k**, hence by APT15: <0>(**ex***o*f[*o*]).
•TPT144 <0>(**ex***o*f[*o*]).
•TPT145 if **no***x*(0(*x*) and 1(f[*x*]) and f[*x*]≠**k**), then **all***x*((**ex***o*f[*o*],*x*)=**k**).
Proof: **all***x*(if not 1(f[*x*]), then (**ex***o*f[*o*],*x*)=**k**), according to APT17. **all***x*(if not 0(*x*), then (**ex***o*f[*o*],*x*)=**k**), according to APT15. Assume f[*x*]=**k**, hence: 1(f[*x*]), because of 1(**k**) [TPT27, TPT4, DPT5, DPT19]; **(i)** not 0(*x*), hence: (**ex***o*f[*o*],*x*)=**k**, according to APT15; **(ii)** 0(*x*), hence by APT16: (**ex***o*f[*o*],*x*)= f[*x*]; hence: (**ex***o*f[*o*],*x*)=**k**; therefore: **all***x*(if f[*x*]=**k**, then (**ex***o*f[*o*],*x*)=**k**).

Therefore: allx(if not 0(x) or not 1(f[x]) or f[x]=k, then (exof[o],x)=k), hence: if allx(not 0(x) or not 1(f[x]) or f[x]=k), then allx((exof[o],x)=k) - what was to be proved.

•TPT146 allxally1((x,y)).

•TPT147 allxally[if allz(if 0(z), then (x,z)P(y,z)), then allz((x,z)P(y,z))] and allxally[if allz(if 0(z), then (x,z)=(y,z)), then allz((x,z)=(y,z))].

Proof: Assume allz(if 0(z), then (x,z)P(y,z)). Assume also: not 0(z), hence according to APT15: (x,z)=k and (y,z)=k; 1(k), hence by APT2: kPk; hence: (x,z)P(y,z). Therefore: allz(if not 0(z), then (x,z)P(y,z)). From the underlined sentence-forms: allz((x,z)P(y,z)). The proof of the second part of TPT147 is obvious now.

•TPT148 allx((exof[o],x)=f[x] or (exof[o],x)=k).

Proof: Assume 0(x) and 1(f[x]), hence by APT16: (exof[o],x)=f[x]. Assume on the other hand: not 0(x) or not 1(f[x]), hence according to APT15 and APT17: (exof[o],x)=k.

•TPT149 allxally((x,y)=(exo(x,o),y)).

Proof: According to TPT146: 1((x,y)); hence in case 0(y) by APT16: (exo(x,o),y)=(x,y); and in case not 0(y) by APT15: (exo(x,o),y)=(x,y).

•TPT150 allxally((exo(o,y),x)=k).

Proof: Assume for *reductio*: (exo(o,y),x)≠k, hence by APT15: <0>(exo(o,y)) and 0(x); according to TPT146: 1((x,y)); hence according to APT16: (exo(o,y),x)=(x,y); hence: (x,y)≠k; but because of 0(x) according to APT12: not <0>(x), hence by APT15: (x,y)=k - contradiction.

•TPT151 allx((exo′exof[o,o′],x)=k).

Proof: According to TPT148: allx((exo′exof[o,o′],x)=exof[o,x] or (exo′exof[o,o′],x)=k). Now: allx((exo′exof[o,o′],x)≠exof[o,x]), for according to TPT146: 1((exo′exof[o,o′],x)), but according to TPT144: <0>(exof[o,x]), hence by APT11: not 1(exof[o,x]). Therefore: allx((exo′exof[o,o′],x)=k).

•TPT152 allfallg(if f$P_{<0>}$g, then <0>(f) and <0>(g)).

•TPT153 allfallgallh(if f$P_{<0>}$g and g$P_{<0>}$h, then f$P_{<0>}$h).

•TPT154 allf(if <0>(f), then f$P_{<0>}$f).

Proof: Assume <0>(f); by APT14: allx(if 0(x), then 1((f,x)), hence by APT2: allx(if 0(x), then (f,x)P(f,x)); therefore by DPT41: f$P_{<0>}$f.

•TPT155 allfallg(if f$P_{<0>}$g and g$P_{<0>}$f, then f=g).

•TPT156 someh[<0>(h) and allf(if <0>(f) and A[f], then f$P_{<0>}$h) and allg(if <0>(g) and allf(if <0>(f) and A[f], then f$P_{<0>}$g), then h$P_{<0>}$g)].

Proof: (i) Assume: <0>(f) and A[f]; assume 0(z); hence: somek(<0>(k) and A[k] and (f,z)=(k,z)); 1((f,z)), according to APT14 (from the assumptions); hence: (f,z)Pconjysomek(<0>(k) and A[k] and y=(k,z)), according to TPT18 [that is: allx(if 1(x) and A′[x], then xPconjzA′[z]) and ally(if 1(y) and allx(if 1(x) and A′[x], then xPy), then conjzA′[z]Py); also a consequence of APT4, APT3 and DPT17: 1(conjzA′[z])]. p[z] := conjysomek(<0>(k) and A[k] and

y=(*k*,*z*)). 1(p[*z*]), hence - because of 0(*z*) - according to APT16: (**ex***o*p[*o*],*z*)=p[*z*]. Therefore from the first assumption: **all***z*(if 0(*z*), then (*f*,*z*)P(**ex***o*p[*o*],*z*)); by TPT144: <0>(**ex***o*p[*o*]); hence - because of <0>(*f*) - by DPT41: *f*$P_{<0>}$**ex***o*p[*o*]. We have now proved: **all***f*(if <0>(*f*) and A[*f*], then *f*$P_{<0>}$**ex***o*p[*o*]) and <0>(**ex***o*p[*o*]).
(**ii**) Assume: <0>(*g*) and **all***f*(if <0>(*f*) and A[*f*], then *f*$P_{<0>}$*g*). We have to deduce: **ex***o*p[*o*]$P_{<0>}$*g*; for this, according to DPT41, all that remains to be shown is: **all***z*(if 0(*z*), then (**ex***o*p[*o*],*z*)P(*g*,*z*)). Assume 0(*z*); by TPT18: (**x**) **all***y*′(if 1(*y*′) and **all***x*(if 1(*x*) and **some***k*(<0>(*k*) and A[*k*] and *x*=(*k*,*z*)), then *x*P*y*′), then p[*z*]P*y*′); (**xx**) 1((*g*,*z*)) by APT14 (from the assumptions); and assume: 1(*x*) and **some***k*(<0>(*k*) and A[*k*] and *x*=(*k*,*z*)); hence: *k*$P_{<0>}$*g*, according to the first assumption of (**ii**), and hence, because of 0(*z*), by DPT41: (*k*,*z*)P(*g*,*z*), hence: *x*P(*g*,*z*); therefore: (**xxx**) **all***x*(if 1(*x*) and **some***k*(<0>(*k*) and A[*k*] and *x*=(*k*,*z*)), then *x*P(*g*,*z*)). By (**x**), (**xx**), (**xxx**): p[*z*]P(*g*,*z*), hence by APT16: (**ex***o*p[*o*],*z*)P (*g*,*z*) [p[*z*] being a state of affairs, *z* an individual]. Therefore from the first assumption of (**ii**): **all***z*(if 0(*z*), then (**ex***o*p[*o*],*z*)P(*g*,*z*)) - what was to be shown. We have now proved: **all***g*(if <0>(*g*) and **all***f*(if <0>(*f*) and A[*f*], then *f*$P_{<0>}$*g*), then **ex***o*p[*o*]$P_{<0>}$*g*).
TPT156 is an immediate logical consequence of what was proved in (**i**) and (**ii**).
•TPT157 $\mathbf{conj}_{<0>}$*f*A[*f*]=**ex***o***conj***y***some***k*(<0>(*k*) and A[*k*] and *y*=(*k*,*o*)).
•TPT158 **all***z*[if 0(*z*), then ($\mathbf{conj}_{<0>}$*f*A[*f*],*z*)=**conj***y***some***k*(<0>(*k*) and A[*k*] and *y*=(*k*,*z*))].
•TPT159 $<0>_{CD}$($\mathbf{k}_{<0>}$).
•TPT160 **all***x*(if 1(*x*), then **all***z*(if 0(*z*), then (**b**(*x*),*z*)=*x*)).
Proof: Assume: 1(*x*), 0(*z*); 1(**conj***y*(*y*=*x* and *z*=*z*)) [APT4, APT3, DPT17], hence - because of 0(*z*) - by APT16: (**ex***o***conj***y*(*y*=*x* and *o*=*o*),*z*)=**conj***y*(*y*=*x* and *z*=*z*). Moreover: **conj***y*(*y*=*x* and *z*=*z*)=**conj***y*(*y*=*x*)=*x*, according to TPT29, TPT33 [in view of 1(*x*)]. Therefore, applying DPT44: (**b**(*x*),*z*)=*x*.
•TPT161 $<0>_{CD}$(**b**(**k**)).
•TPT162 **b**(**k**)=$\mathbf{k}_{<0>}$.
Proof: Because of <0>(**b**(**k**)) we have: **b**(**k**)$P_{<0>}\mathbf{k}_{<0>}$ (the role of $\mathbf{k}_{<0>}$ for properties being provably analogous to the role of **k** for states of affairs). Moreover: $\mathbf{k}_{<0>}P_{<0>}$**b**(**k**), according to DPT41, for we have: <0>($\mathbf{k}_{<0>}$) and <0>(**b**(**k**)) and **all***z*(if 0(*z*), then ($\mathbf{k}_{<0>}$,*z*)P(**b**(**k**),*z*)): **all***z*(if 0(*z*), then ($\mathbf{k}_{<0>}$,*z*)P**k**) by APT14 and T(**k**) [the latter by TPT34, **k** being a state of affairs], and **all***z*(if 0(*z*), then (**b**(**k**),*z*)=**k**) by TPT160, **k** being a state of affairs. From **b**(**k**)$P_{<0>}\mathbf{k}_{<0>}$ and $\mathbf{k}_{<0>}P_{<0>}$**b**(**k**) by TPT155: **b**(**k**)=$\mathbf{k}_{<0>}$.
•TPT163 **all***f***all***g*(if $<0>_{CD}$(*f*) and $<0>_{CD}$(*g*), then *f*=*g*).
Proof: Assume: $<0>_{CD}$(*f*) and $<0>_{CD}$(*g*), hence by DPT40: <0>(*f*) and **all***z*(if 0(*z*), then (*f*,*z*)=**k**) and <0>(*g*) and **all***z*(if 0(*z*), then (*g*,*z*)=**k**), hence: **all***z*(if 0(*z*), then (*f*,*z*)=(*g*,*z*)). Therefore by APT19: *f*=*g*.
•TPT164 $<0>_{TL}$(**b**(**t**)).
•TPT165 **b**(**t**)=$\mathbf{t}_{<0>}$.

•TPT166 <0>$_{TL}$(**t**$_{<0>}$).
•TPT167 **all***f***all***g*(if <0>$_{TL}$(*f*) and <0>$_{TL}$(*g*), then *f*=*g*).
•TPT168
(i) **all***x***all***x*′(if *x*=*x*′, then **conj***y*(*x*=*x*′ and *y*=**k**)=**k**);
(i′) **all***x***all***x*′(if *x*≠*x*′, then **conj***y*(*x*=*x*′ and *y*=**k**)=**t**).
(ii) **all***x***all***x*′(if **conj***y*(*x*=*x*′ and *y*=**k**)=**k**, then *x*=*x*′);
(ii′) **all***x***all***x*′(if **conj***y*(*x*=*x*′ and *y*=**k**)=**t**, then *x*≠*x*′).
Proof: (i) Assume *x*=*x*′; we have: 1(**k**) and **k**=**k**; hence by TPT18: **kPconj***y*(*x*=*x*′ and *y*=**k**); we also have: T(**k**) and 1(**conj***y*(*x*=*x*′and *y*=**k**)); hence: **conj***y*(*x*=*x*′ and *y*=**k**)P**k** [according to DPT5]. Therefore by APT3: **conj***y*(*x*=*x*′ and *y*=**k**)=**k**.
(i′) Assume *x*≠*x*′; hence: **all***y*(*x*=*x*′ and *y*=**k** iff *y*≠*y*), hence by TPT29: **conj***y*(*x*=*x*′ and *y*=**k**)=**conj***y*(*y*≠*y*), and **conj**(*y*≠*y*)=**t**.
(ii) Assume **conj***y*(*x*=*x*′ and *y*=**k**)=**k**; assume for *reductio*: *x*≠*x*′; hence by (i′): **conj***y*(*x*=*x*′ and *y*=**k**)=**t**; hence: **t**=**k** - contradicting TPT104.
(ii′) Assume **conj***y*(*x*=*x*′ and *y*=**k**)=**t**; assume for *reductio*: *x*=*x*′; hence by (i): **conj***y*(*x*=*x*′ and *y*=**k**)=**k**; hence **t**=**k** - contradicting TPT104.
•TPT169
(i) **all***x***all***z*′[if 0(*z*′), then ((**d**(*x*),*z*′)=**t** iff *z*′≠*x*)];
(ii) **all***x***all***z*′[if 0(*z*′), then ((**d**(*x*),*z*′)=**k** iff *z*′=*x*)].
Proof: Assume 0(*z*′); it is provable: 1(**conj***y*(*z*′=*x* and *y*=**k**)); hence by APT16: (**exoconj***y*(*o*=*x* and *y*=**k**),*z*′)=**conj***y*(*z*′=*x* and *y*=**k**), that is [by DPT47]: (**d**(*x*),*z*′)=**conj***y*(*z*′=*x* and *y*=**k**). Therefore, in case *z*′≠*x*, according to (i′) of TPT168: (**d**(*x*),*z*′)=**t**; in case (**d**(*x*),*z*′)=**t**, according to (ii′) of TPT168: *z*′≠*x*; in case *z*′=*x*, according to (i) of TPT168: (**d**(*x*),*z*′)=**k**; and in case (**d**(*x*),*z*′)=**k**, according to (ii) of TPT168: *z*′=*x*.
•TPT170
(i) **all***x***all***x*′(if *x*=*x*′, then **conj***y*(*x*≠*x*′ and *y*=**k**)=**t**);
(i′) **all***x***all***x*′(if *x*≠*x*′, then **conj***y*(*x*≠*x*′ and *y*=**k**)=**k**);
(ii) **all***x***all***x*′(if **conj***y*(*x*≠*x*′ and *y*=**k**)=**t**, then *x*=*x*′);
(ii′) **all***x***all***x*′(if **conj***y*(*x*≠*x*′ and *y*=**k**)=**k**, then *x*≠*x*′).
•TPT171
(i) **all***x***all***z*′[if 0(*z*′), then ((**i**(*x*),*z*′)=**t** iff *z*′=*x*)];
(ii) **all***x***all***z*′[if 0(*z*′), then ((**i**(*x*),*z*′)=**k** iff *z*′≠*x*)].
•TPT172 **all***f***all***z***all***y*[if <0>(*f*) and 0(*z*) and *y*P(*f*,*z*), then **some***h*(*h*P$_{<0>}$*f* and *y*=(*h*,*z*))].
Proof: Assume: <0>(*f*) and 0(*z*) and *y*P(*f*,*z*); hence by APT0: 1((*f*,*z*)) and 1(*y*), and hence by APT2: *y*P*y*; hence by TPT23: *y*P**disj**((*f*,*z*),*y*), and according to TPT26: **disj**((*f*,*z*),*y*)P*y*; therefore by APT3: *y*=**disj**((*f*,*z*),*y*). Consequently, in view of 0(*z*) and 1(**disj**((*f*,*z*),*y*)), by APT16: **(i)** *y*=(**exo****disj**((*f*,*o*),*y*),*z*). Moreover, **(ii)** **exo****disj**((*f*,*o*),*y*)P$_{<0>}$*f*, according to DPT41; for <0>(**exo****disj**((*f*,*o*),*y*))

[by TPT144] and <0>(*f*) [assumption] and **all***z*′[if 0(*z*′), then **(ex*o*disj((*f*,*o*),*y*),** *z*′**)**P**(*f*,*z*′)**]: assume 0(*z*′), hence, because of 1(**disj((*f*,*z*′),*y*)**), by APT16: **(ex*o*disj((*f*,*o*),*y*),*z*′)=disj((*f*,*z*′),*y*)**; but **disj((*f*,*z*′),*y*)**P**(*f*,*z*′)**, according to TPT26 [1(**(*f*,*z*′)**), hence APT2: **(*f*,*z*′)**P**(*f*,*z*′)**]; therefore: **(ex*o*disj((*f*,*o*),*y*),*z*′)**P **(*f*,*z*′)**. **(i)** and **(ii)** logically imply **some***h*(*h*$P_{<0>}$*f* and *y*=**(*h*,*z*)**).

•TPT173 **all***f*(if $QA_{<0>}$(*f*), then **all***z*[if 0(*z*), then QA(**(*f*,*z*)**)]).

Proof: Assume (**1**): $QA_{<0>}$(*f*), 0(*z*); it is to be deduced from this: QA(**(*f*,*z*)**), that is [according to DPT6]: **all***y*(if *y*P**(*f*,*z*)**, then *y*=**(*f*,*z*)** or M(*y*)) and 1(**(*f*,*z*)**). 1(**(*f*,*z*)**) from the assumption by APT14. Assume now (**2**): *y*P**(*f*,*z*)** and not M(*y*), hence by TPT172 and (**1**): **some***h*(*h*$P_{<0>}$*f* and *y*=**(*h*,*z*)**). According to the definition for properties that is parallel to DPT6, ''$QA_{<0>}$(*f*)'' is short for ''**all***h*(if *h*$P_{<0>}$*f*, then *h*=*f* or $M_{<0>}$(*h*)) and <0>(*f*)''. Therefore, in view of $QA_{<0>}$(*f*) and *h*$P_{<0>}$*f*: (*****) *h*=*f* or $M_{<0>}$(*h*). If $M_{<0>}$(*h*), then *h*=$\mathbf{t}_{<0>}$, according to the theorem for properties that is parallel to TPT32 (which parallel theorem we may use already); hence by TPT166: $<0>_{TL}$(*h*), hence, because of 0(*z*) in (**1**), according to DPT45: **(*h*,*z*)=t**, hence: *y*=**t** [because of *y*=**(*h*,*z*)**], hence by TPT32 [1(*y*) from *y*P**(*f*,*z*)** by APT0]: M(*y*) - contradicting (**2**). Therefore: not $M_{<0>}$(*h*); hence by (*****): *h*=*f*, hence: **(*h*,*z*)=(*f*,*z*)**, hence *y*=**(*f*,*z*)** [because of *y*=**(*h*,*z*)**], which needed to be deduced from (**2**) for yielding a deduction of QA(**(*f*,*z*)**) from (**1**).

•TPT174 **all***f*[if $QA_{<0>}$(*f*), then **all***z*(if 0(*z*), then **(*f*,*z*)=t**) or **some***z*(0(*z*) and **(*f*,*z*)≠t** and QA(**(*f*,*z*)**) and **all***z*′(if 0(*z*′) and *z*′≠*z*, then **(*f*,*z*′)=t**))].

•TPT175 **all***f*(<0>(*f*) and [**all***z*(if 0(*z*), then **(*f*,*z*)=t**) or **some***z*(0(*z*) and **(*f*,*z*)≠t** and QA(**(*f*,*z*)**) and **all***z*′(if 0(*z*′) and *z*′≠*z*, then **(*f*,*z*′)=t**))], then $QA_{<0>}$(*f*)).

Proof: Assume <0>(*f*); assume *g*$P_{<0>}$*f*.

Assume moreover: (**x**) **all***z*(if 0(*z*), then **(*f*,*z*)=t**); therefore: **all***z*(if 0(*z*), then **(*f*,*z*)**P**(*g*,*z*)**), for: **all***z*(if 0(*z*), then **t**P**(*g*,*z*)**), because **all***y*(if 1(*y*), then **t**P*y*) and **all***z*(if 0(*z*), then 1(**(*g*,*z*)**)) [APT14, <0>(*g*)]. From *g*$P_{<0>}$*f* according to DPT41: **all***z*(if 0(*z*), then **(*g*,*z*)**P**(*f*,*z*)**). Hence from the two underlined results by APT3: **all***z*(if 0(*z*), then **(*g*,*z*)=(*f*,*z*)**), hence by APT19: *g*=*f*, hence *a fortiori*: *g*=*f* or $M_{<0>}$(*g*).

Thus, <0>(*f*) and (**x**) together imply: $QA_{<0>}$(*f*).

Assume alternatively: (**xx**) **some***z*(0(*z*) and **(*f*,*z*)≠t** and QA(**(*f*,*z*)**) and **all***z*′(if 0(*z*′) and *z*′≠*z*, then **(*f*,*z*′)=t**)); assume *g*≠*f*, hence by APT19: **some***x*(0(*x*) and **(*g*,*x*)≠(*f*,*x*)**), hence by APT3: **some***x*(0(*x*) and [not **(*g*,*x*)**P**(*f*,*x*)** or not **(*f*,*x*)**P**(*g*,*x*)**]), hence, because of *g*$P_{<0>}$*f*, according to DPT41: **some***x*(0(*x*) and not **(*f*,*x*)**P**(*g*,*x*)**). Now: *x*=*z* or *x*≠*z*; in case *x*≠*z*, then, according to assumption, **(*f*,*x*)=t**, hence: **(*f*,*x*)**P**(*g*,*x*)** - contradiction. Therefore: *x*=*z*; hence by the underlined result: not **(*f*,*z*)**P**(*g*,*z*)**. Because of QA(**(*f*,*z*)**) and **(*g*,*z*)**P**(*f*,*z*)** [in view of *g*$P_{<0>}$*f*], according to DPT6: **(*g*,*z*)=(*f*,*z*)** or M(**(*g*,*z*)**); because not **(*f*,*z*)**P**(*g*,*z*)** and APT2: **(*g*,*z*)≠(*f*,*z*)**; hence: M(**(*g*,*z*)**), hence by TPT32: **(*g*,*z*)=t**; and we also have: **all***z*′(if 0(*z*′) and *z*′≠*z*, then **(*g*,*z*′)=t**), which follows by TPT36 from **all***z*′(if 0(*z*′) and *z*′≠*z*, then **(*f*,*z*′)=t**) [in assumption (**xx**)] and **all***z*′(if 0(*z*′), then **(*g*,*z*′)**P**(*f*,*z*′)**)

[since $gP_{<0>}f$]. Therefore: **all**z'(if 0(z'), then **(**g,z'**)=t**), hence by DPT45: <0>$_{TL}$(g), hence by TPT166, TPT167: g=$\mathbf{t}_{<0>}$, hence: $M_{<0>}$(g), according to the theorem for properties that is parallel to TPT32.
Thus, <0>(f) and (**xx**) together imply: $QA_{<0>}$(f).

•TPT176 **all**f**all**g(if <0>(f) and <0>(g) and **all**h(if $QA_{<0>}$(h) and $hP_{<0>}f$, then $hP_{<0>}g$), then $fP_{<0>}g$).

Proof: Assume: <0>(f), <0>(g), **all**h(if $QA_{<0>}$(h) and $hP_{<0>}f$, then $hP_{<0>}g$); assume also: 0(z). It has to be deduced: **(**f,z**)**P**(**g,z**)**. If this is deduced, then the first assumptions have been shown to imply **all**z(if 0(z), then **(**f,z**)**P**(**g,z**)**), hence, according to DPT41, to imply $fP_{<0>}g$ - and this proves TPT176.
Assume for *reductio*: not **(**f,z**)**P**(**g,z**)**, hence by APT5 [both **(**f,z**)** and **(**g,z**)** being states of affairs]: **some**y(QA(y) and yP**(**f,z**)** and not yP**(**g,z**)**), hence by TPT160 [1(y), 0(z)]: **some**y(QA(**(b(**y**)**,z**)**) and **(b(**y**)**,z**)**P**(**f,z**)** and not **(b(**y**)**,z**)**P**(**g,z**)**).
Consider **exo**o'**disj((b(**y**)**,o'**),(d(**z**)**,o'**))**. We have:
(**i**) QA(**(exo**o'**disj((b(**y**)**,o'**),(d(**z**)**,o'**))**,z**)**);
for - because of QA(**(b(**y**)**,z**)**) - by TPT53: QA(**disj((b(**y**)**,z**),k)**), hence: QA(**disj((b(**y**)**,z**),(d(**z**)**,z**)))**, since **(d(**z**)**,z**)=k** according to TPT169(b); according to APT16: **(exo**o'**disj((b(**y**)**,o'**),(d(**z**)**,o'**))**,z**)=disj((b(**y**)**,z**),(d(**z**)**,z**))**; hence (**i**).
(**ii**) **(exo**o'**disj((b(**y**)**,o'**),(d(**z**)**,o'**))**,z**)≠t**;
for **(b(**y**)**,z**)≠t** because not **(b(**y**)**,z**)**P**(**g,z**)** [1(**(**g,z**)**), **all**k(if 1(k), then **t**Pk)]; hence: **disj((b(**y**)**,z**),k)≠t**, etc. as above; hence (**ii**).
(**iii**) **all**z'(if 0(z') and z'≠z, then **(exo**o'**disj((b(**y**)**,o'**),(d(**z**)**,o'**))**,z'**)=t**);
for assume: 0(z') and z'≠z, hence by TPT169(a): **(d(**z**)**,z'**)=t**, hence: **disj((b(**y**)**,z'**),(d(**z**)**,z'**))=t** [applying TPT36], hence by APT16:
(exoo'**disj((b(**y**)**,o'**),(d(**z**)**,o'**))**,z'**)=t**.
Since [by TPT144] <0>**(exo**o'**disj((b(**y**)**,o'**),(d(**z**)**,o'**)))**, (**i**) - (**iii**) imply according to TPT175: (**1**) $QA_{<0>}$**(exo**o'**disj((b(**y**)**,o'**),(d(**z**)**,o'**)))**.
Moreover: (**2**) **exo**o'**disj((b(**y**)**,o'**),(d(**z**)**,o'**))**$P_{<0>}f$:
Assume 0(z');
in case z'≠z: according to (**iii**), **(exo**o'**disj((b(**y**)**,o'**),(d(**z**)**,o'**))**,z'**)=t**, hence: **(exo**o'**disj((b(**y**)**,o'**),(d(**z**)**,o'**))**,z'**)**P**(**f,z'**)**;
in case z'=z: **(exo**o'**disj((b(**y**)**,o'**),(d(**z**)**,o'**))**,z'**)=**
(exoo'**disj((b(**y**)**,o'**),(d(**z**)**,o'**))**,z**)=disj((b(**y**)**,z**),(d(**z**)**,z**))=disj((b(**y**)**,z**),k)=**
(b(y**)**,z**)**, and **(b(**y**)**,z**)**P**(**f,z**)**; hence: **(exo**o'**disj((b(**y**)**,o'**),(d(**z**)**,o'**))**,z'**)**P**(**f,z'**)**.
Therefore: **all**z'[if 0(z'), then **(exo**o'**disj((b(**y**)**,o'**),(d(**z**)**,o'**))**,z'**)**P**(**f,z'**)**], hence by DPT41: (**2**).
From (**1**) and (**2**) and the assumptions at the beginning of the proof: **exo**o'**disj((b(**y**)**,o'**),(d(**z**)**,o'**))**$P_{<0>}g$,
hence by DPT41: **(exo**o'**disj((b(**y**)**,o'**),(d(**z**)**,o'**))**,z**)**P**(**g,z**)**, hence: **(b(**y**)**,z**)**P**(**g,z**)** - contradicting the previous (underlined) result.
Therefore: **(**f,z**)**P**(**g,z**)** [the negation of the assumption for *reductio*] - what was to be deduced.

•TPT177 **all**_f_[if _f_ $P_{<0>}$**conj**$_{<0>}$_g_A[_g_] and not $M_{<0>}$(_f_), then **some**_h_(_h_ $P_{<0>}$ _f_ and not $M_{<0>}$(_h_) and **some**_k′_(_h_ $P_{<0>}$ _k′_ and A[_k′_]))].

Proof: Assume: _f_ $P_{<0>}$**conj**$_{<0>}$_g_A[_g_] and not $M_{<0>}$(_f_), hence: **all**_z_(if 0(_z_), then **(**_f_,_z_**)P(conj**$_{<0>}$_g_A[_g_],_z_**)**) and not $<0>_{TL}$(_f_) - according to DPT41, and according to TPT166, TPT167 and the theorem for properties which is parallel to TPT32; hence by DPT45 [because of <0>(_f_)]: **some**_z_(0(_z_) and **(**_f_,_z_**)P(conj**$_{<0>}$_g_A[_g_],_z_**)** and **(**_f_,_z_**)≠t**), hence by TPT32 and TPT158: **some**_z_[0(_z_) and **(**_f_,_z_**)P conj**_y_**some**_k′_(<0>(_k′_) and A[_k′_] and _y_=**(**_k′_,_z_**)**) and not M(**(**_f_,_z_**)**)], hence by APT6: **some**_r_[_r_P**(**_f_,_z_**)** and not M(_r_) and **some**_p_(_r_P_p_ and **some**_k′_(<0>(_k′_) and A[_k′_] and _p_=**(**_k′_,_z_**)**))], hence: **some**_r_[_r_P**(**_f_,_z_**)** and not M(_r_) and **some**_k′_(<0>(_k′_) and A[_k′_] and _r_P**(**_k′_,_z_**)**)].

Consider **exo**_o′_**disj((b(**_r_**),**_o′_**),(d(**_z_**),**_o′_**))**. We have:

(i) exo_o′_**disj((b(**_r_**),**_o′_**),(d(**_z_**),**_o′_**))**$P_{<0>}$_f_.

Assume 0(_z′_). In case _z′_≠_z_, then, according to the argumentation in **(iii)** of the proof of TPT176, **(exo**_o′_**disj((b(**_r_**),**_o′_**),(d(**_z_**),**_o′_**)),**_z′_**)=t**, hence: **(exo**_o′_**disj((b(**_r_**),**_o′_**),(d(**_z_**),**_o′_**)),**_z′_**)**P**(**_f_,_z′_**)**. In case _z′_=_z_, then because of _r_=**(b(**_r_**),**_z_**)** [by TPT160, 0(_z_), 1(_r_)], **(b(**_r_**),**_z_**)=disj((b(**_r_**),**_z_**),k)** [TPT53], **disj((b(**_r_**),**_z_**),k)= disj((b(**_r_**),**_z_**),(d(**_z_**),**_z_**))** [TPT169(b)], **disj((b(**_r_**),**_z_**),(d(**_z_**),**_z_**))=(exo**_o′_**disj((b(**_r_**),**_o′_**), (d(**_z_**),**_o′_**)),**_z_**)** [APT16], and because of _r_P**(**_f_,_z_**)**: **(exo**_o′_**disj((b(**_r_**),**_o′_**),(d(**_z_**),**_o′_**)),**_z′_**)** P**(**_f_,_z′_**)**. Hence we can conclude according to DPT41: **(i)**.

(ii) exo_o′_**disj((b(**_r_**),**_o′_**),(d(**_z_**),**_o′_**))**$P_{<0>}$_k′_.

For demonstrating this, one proceeds as in the case of (**i**), using _r_P**(**_k′_,_z_**)** instead of _r_P**(**_f_,_z_**)**, and <0>(_k′_) instead of <0>(_f_).

(iii) not $M_{<0>}$**(exo**_o′_**disj((b(**_r_**),**_o′_**),(d(**_z_**),**_o′_**)))**.

Since not M(_r_), _r_**≠t** by TPT32, and hence: **(exo**_o′_**disj((b(**_r_**),**_o′_**),(d(**_z_**),**_o′_**)),**_z_**)≠t**. Hence: **exo**_o′_**disj((b(**_r_**),**_o′_**),(d(**_z_**),**_o′_**))≠t**$_{<0>}$; for according to TPT166: $<0>_{TL}$(**t**$_{<0>}$), and consequently by DPT45: **(t**$_{<0>}$**,**_z_**)=t**. Therefore by the theorem for properties that is parallel to TPT32: **(iii)**.

From **(i)**, **(ii)** and **(iii)** we obtain: **some**_h_(_h_ $P_{<0>}$ _f_ and not $M_{<0>}$(_h_) and **some**_k′_(_h_ $P_{<0>}$ _k′_ and A[_k′_])) - which is what needed to be deduced from the first assumption for demonstrating TPT177.

•TPT178

all_f_**all**_g_[if <0>(_f_) and <0>(_g_), then **conj**$_{<0>}$**(**_f_,_g_**)=exo**_o_**conj((**_f_,_o_**),(**_g_,_o_**))**].

all_f_**all**_g_**all**_z_[if <0>(_f_) and <0>(_g_) and 0(_z_), then **(conj**$_{<0>}$**(**_f_,_g_**),**_z_**)= conj((**_f_,_z_**),(**_g_,_z_**))**].

Proof: Assume: <0>(_f_) and <0>(_g_); assume 0(_z_).

It is to be deduced: **(conj**$_{<0>}$**(**_f_,_g_**),**_z_**)=(exo**_o_**conj((**_f_,_o_**),(**_g_,_o_**)),**_z_**)**; then - the identity having been shown for all individuals _z_ - **conj**$_{<0>}$**(**_f_,_g_**)=exo**_o_**conj((**_f_,_o_**),(**_g_,_o_**))** by APT19 [<0>**(conj**$_{<0>}$**(**_f_,_g_**))**, and by TPT144 <0>**(exo**_o_**conj((**_f_,_o_**),(**_g_,_o_**)))**].

According to ParTPT20: **conj**$_{<0>}$**(**_f_,_g_**)=conj**$_{<0>}$_k_(_k_ $P_{<0>}$ _f_ or _k_ $P_{<0>}$ _g_), hence by TPT158:

(i) (conj$_{<0>}$(*f*,*g*),*z*)=**conj***y***some***k*(<0>(*k*) and (*k*P$_{<0>}$*f* or *k*P$_{<0>}$*g*) and *y*=(*k*,*z*)). By TPT20 [1((*f*,*z*)), 1((*g*,*z*))]: **conj**((*f*,*z*),(*g*,*z*))=**conj***y*(*y*P(*f*,*z*) or *y*P(*g*,*z*)); hence by APT16:
(ii) (exo conj((*f*,*o*),(*g*,*o*)),*z*)=**conj***y*(*y*P(*f*,*z*) or *y*P(*g*,*z*)).
We show:
(iii) conj*y***some***k*(<0>(*k*) and (*k*P$_{<0>}$*f* or *k*P$_{<0>}$*g*) and *y*=(*k*,*z*))=**conj***y*(*y*P(*f*,*z*) or *y*P(*g*,*z*)).
(x) Assume **some***k*(<0>(*k*) and (*k*P$_{<0>}$*f* or *k*P$_{<0>}$*g*) and *y*=(*k*,*z*)), hence by DPT41: *y*P(*f*,*z*) or *y*P(*g*,*z*). **(xx)** Assume: *y*P(*f*,*z*) or *y*P(*g*,*z*); in the first case by TPT172 [<0>(*f*), 0(*z*)]: **some***k*(*k*P$_{<0>}$*f* and *y*=(*k*,*z*)); in the second case by TPT172 [<0>(*g*), 0(*z*)]: **some***k*(*k*P$_{<0>}$*g* and *y*=(*k*,*z*)); hence from the assumption [of **(xx)**]: **some***k*(<0>(*k*) and (*k*P$_{<0>}$*f* or *k*P$_{<0>}$*g*) and *y*=(*k*,*z*)). From **(x)** and **(xx)** by applying TPT29: **(iii)**.
(i), **(ii)** and **(iii)** together logically imply what was to be deduced.
The corollary below TPT178 is easily seen to result from TPT178, applying APT16.
•TPT179 **all***f***all***g*[if <0>(*f*) and <0>(*g*), then **disj**$_{<0>}$(*f*,*g*)=**exo disj**((*f*,*o*),(*g*,*o*))].
all*f***all***g***all***z*[if <0>(*f*) and <0>(*g*) and 0(*z*), then **(disj**$_{<0>}$(*f*,*g*),*z*)=**disj**((*f*,*z*),(*g*,*z*))].
Proof: Assume: <0>(*f*) and <0>(*g*); assume 0(*z*). In view of APT19, it is to be deduced for obtaining TPT179: **(disj**$_{<0>}$(*f*,*g*),*z*)=(**exo disj**((*f*,*o*),(*g*,*o*)),*z*).
According to ParTPT22: **disj**$_{<0>}$(*f*,*g*)=**conj**$_{<0>}$*k*(*k*P$_{<0>}$*f* and *k*P$_{<0>}$*g*); hence by TPT158: **(disj**$_{<0>}$(*f*,*g*),*z*)=**conj***y***some***k*(<0>(*k*) and *k*P$_{<0>}$*f* and *k*P$_{<0>}$*g* and *y*=(*k*,*z*)). According to TPT22: **disj**((*f*,*z*),(*g*,*z*))=**conj***y*(*y*P(*f*,*z*) and *y*P(*g*,*z*)); hence by APT16: **(exo disj**((*f*,*o*),(*g*,*o*)),*z*)=**conj***y*(*y*P(*f*,*z*) and *y*P(*g*,*z*)). For the desired result it remains to be shown: **conj***y***some***k*(<0>(*k*) and *k*P$_{<0>}$*f* and *k*P$_{<0>}$*g* and *y*=(*k*,*z*))=**conj***y*(*y*P(*f*,*z*) and *y*P(*g*,*z*)).
(i) Assume **some***k*(<0>(*k*) and *k*P$_{<0>}$*f* and *k*P$_{<0>}$*g* and *y*=(*k*,*z*)), hence, according to DPT41, *y*P(*f*,*z*) and *y*P(*g*,*z*).
(ii) Assume: *y*P(*f*,*z*) and *y*P(*g*,*z*). Consider **exo′disj**((**b**(*y*),*o*′),(**d**(*z*),*o*′)).
(x) <0>(**exo′disj**((**b**(*y*),*o*′),(**d**(*z*),*o*′))), according to TPT144.
(xx) exo′disj((**b**(*y*),*o*′),(**d**(*z*),*o*′))P$_{<0>}$*f*: Assume 0(*z*′);
in case *z*′=*z*: (**exo′disj**((**b**(*y*),*o*′),(**d**(*z*),*o*′)),*z*′)=*y* [compare the proof of TPT177], hence because of *y*P(*f*,*z*): (**exo′disj**((**b**(*y*),*o*′),(**d**(*z*),*o*′)),*z*′)P(*f*,*z*′);
in case *z*′≠*z*: (**exo′disj**((**b**(*y*),*o*′),(**d**(*z*),*o*′)),*z*′)=**t** [compare the proof of TPT177], hence because of **t**P(*f*,*z*′): (**exo′disj**((**b**(*y*),*o*′),(**d**(*z*),*o*′)),*z*′)P(*f*,*z*′).
Since the underlined has been shown to hold for all individuals *z*′, one has obtained the desired result (according to DPT41).
(xxx) exo′disj((**b**(*y*),*o*′),(**d**(*z*),*o*′))P$_{<0>}$*g*: For showing this, one proceeds as under **(xx)**.
(xxxx) *y*=(**exo′disj**((**b**(*y*),*o*′),(**d**(*z*),*o*′)),*z*): See **(xx)**.
Hence according to **(x)** - **(xxxx)**: **some***k*(<0>(*k*) and *k*P$_{<0>}$*f* and *k*P$_{<0>}$*g* and *y*=(*k*,*z*)).
On the basis of **(i)** and **(ii)** and TPT29 one obtains what remained to be shown for proving TPT179.

The corollary below TPT179 is easily seen to result from it, applying APT16.

•TPT180 **all***f*[if <0>(*f*), then **neg**$_{<0>}$(*f*)=**exo*****neg**((*f*,*o*))].

all*f***all***z*[if <0>(*f*) and 0(*z*), then (**neg**$_{<0>}$(*f*),*z*)=**neg**((*f*,*z*))].

Proof: Assume <0>(*f*), and assume 0(*z*). For proving TPT180, (**neg**$_{<0>}$(*f*),*z*)=(**exo*****neg**((*f*,*o*)),*z*) needs to be deduced from these assumptions. According to ParTPT50 and ParTPT52: **neg**$_{<0>}$(*f*)=**conj**$_{<0>}$*k*(QA$_{<0>}$(*k*) and not *k*P$_{<0>}$*f*), hence by TPT158: (**neg**$_{<0>}$(*f*),*z*)=**conj***y***some***k*(<0>(*k*) and QA$_{<0>}$(*k*) and not *k*P$_{<0>}$*f* and *y*=(*k*,*z*)). According to TPT50 and TPT52: **neg**((*f*,*z*))=**conj***y*(QA(*y*) and not *y*P(*f*,*z*)), hence by APT16 (**exo*****neg**((*f*,*o*)),*z*)= **conj***y*(QA(*y*) and not *y*P(*f*,*z*)). For proving TPT180, it remains to be shown: **conj***y***some***k*(<0>(*k*) and QA$_{<0>}$(*k*) and not *k*P$_{<0>}$*f* and *y*=(*k*,*z*))=**conj***y*(QA(*y*) and not *y*P(*f*,*z*)).

(**i**) APT5 and TPT40 will be applied. Assume: QA(*p*) and *p*P**conj***y***some***k*(<0>(*k*) and QA$_{<0>}$(*k*) and not *k*P$_{<0>}$*f* and *y*=(*k*,*z*)).

In case (**1**) M(*p*), then *p*P**conj***y*(QA(*y*) and not *y*P(*f*,*z*)).

In case (**2**) not M(*p*), then by TPT40: **some***r*[*p*P*r* and **some***k*(<0>(*k*) and QA$_{<0>}$(*k*) and not *k*P$_{<0>}$*f* and *r*=(*k*,*z*))], hence by DPT41: **some***r***some***k*[*p*P*r* and QA$_{<0>}$(*k*) and **some***z*′(0(*z*′) and not (*k*,*z*′)P(*f*,*z*′)) and *r*=(*k*,*z*)], hence by TPT173:

some*r***some***k***some***z*′[*p*P*r* and QA$_{<0>}$(*k*) and 0(*z*′) and not (*k*,*z*′)P(*f*,*z*′) and QA((*k*,*z*′)) and *r*=(*k*,*z*)].

In case *z*≠*z*′, then - because of (*k*,*z*′)≠**t** - according to PPQ [the equivalent of TPT174; see III.5.(a)]: (*k*,*z*)=**t**, hence *r*=**t**, hence *p*=**t** [*p*P*r*, TPT36], hence: M(*p*) [by TPT32] - contradicting (**2**). Therefore: *z*=*z*′, hence: QA((*k*,*z*)) and not (*k*,*z*)P(*f*,*z*), hence: QA(*r*) and not *r*P(*f*,*z*), hence by TPT18: *r*P**conj***y*(QA(*y*) and not *y*P(*f*,*z*)), hence by APT1: *p*P**conj***y*(QA(*y*) and not *y*P(*f*,*z*)).

Thus we obtain by APT5: **conj***y***some***k*(<0>(*k*) and QA$_{<0>}$(*k*) and not *k*P$_{<0>}$*f* and *y*=(*k*,*z*))P**conj***y*(QA(*y*) and not *y*P(*f*,*z*)).

(**ii**) Assume: QA(*y*) and not *y*P(*f*,*z*). Consider once more **exo***o*′**disj**((**b**(*y*),*o*′), (**d**(*z*),*o*′)).

One obtains (compare the proof of TPT176):

<0>(**exo***o*′**disj**((**b**(*y*),*o*′),(**d**(*z*),*o*′))), 0(*z*), (**exo***o*′**disj**((**b**(*y*),*o*′),(**d**(*z*),*o*′)),*z*)≠**t**, QA((**exo***o*′**disj**((**b**(*y*),*o*′),(**d**(*z*),*o*′)),*z*)), **all***z*′(if 0(*z*′) and *z*′≠*z*, then (**exo***o*′**disj** ((**b**(*y*),*o*′),(**d**(*z*),*o*′)),*z*′)=**t**); and as a consequence of all this by TPT175: (**x**) QA$_{<0>}$(**exo***o*′**disj**((**b**(*y*),*o*′),(**d**(*z*),*o*′))).

Moreover: (**xx**) not **exo***o*′**disj**((**b**(*y*),*o*′),(**d**(*z*),*o*′))P$_{<0>}$*f*, because not (**exo***o*′**disj**((**b**(*y*),*o*′),(**d**(*z*),*o*′)),*z*)P(*f*,*z*), for: *y*=(**exo***o*′**disj**((**b**(*y*),*o*′),(**d**(*z*),*o*′)),*z*) and not *y*P(*f*,*z*).

Hence - according to (**x**), (**xx**) and the two underlined results - one obtains: **some***k*(<0>(*k*) and QA$_{<0>}$(*k*) and not *k*P$_{<0>}$*f* and *y*=(*k*,*z*)).

Thus we obtain by TPT28: **conj***y*(QA(*y*) and not *y*P(*f*,*z*))P**conj***y***some***k*(<0>(*k*) and QA$_{<0>}$(*k*) and not *k*P$_{<0>}$*f* and *y*=(*k*,*z*)).

What remained to be shown for proving TPT180 follows by APT3 from the the conjunction of the final results reached in **(i)** and **(ii)**.
The corollary below TPT180 is easily seen to result from TPT180, applying APT16.

•TPT181 **some***f*<0>$_{\mathrm{AC}}$(*f*) iff **some***y*(1(*y*) and *y*≠**t** and *y*≠**k**).

Proof: **(i)** Assume **some***f*<0>$_{\mathrm{AC}}$(*f*), hence by DPT50: **some***f*(<0>(*f*) and **all***z*(if 0(*z*), then **(***f*,*z***)≠t** and **(***f*,*z***)≠k**)), hence by APT13: **some***f***some***z*(<0>(*f*) and 0(*z*) and **(***f*,*z***)≠t** and **(***f*,*z***)≠k**), hence by APT14: **some***y*(1(*y*) and *y*≠**t** and *y*≠**k**).
(ii) Assume **some***y*(1(*y*) and *y*≠**t** and *y*≠**k**), hence by TPT160: **all***z*(if 0(*z*), then **(b(***y***),***z***)**=*y*), hence: **all***z*(if 0(*z*), then **(b(***y***),***z***)≠t** and **(b(***y***),***z***)≠k**), hence - since <0>(**b**(*y*)) by TPT144, DPT44 - according to DPT50: <0>$_{\mathrm{AC}}$(**b**(*y*)), hence: **some***f*<0>$_{\mathrm{AC}}$(*f*).

•TPT182 <0>$_{\mathrm{AC}}$(**b(w)**).

•TPT183 **all***f*(if <0>(*f*), then <0>$_{\mathrm{ES}}$(*f*)) iff **all***y*(if 1(*y*), then *y*=**t** or *y*=**k**).

Proof: **(i)** Assume **all***f*(if <0>(*f*), then <0>$_{\mathrm{ES}}$(*f*)), and assume 1(*y*). <0>(**b**(*y*)) by TPT144, DPT44. Hence: <0>$_{\mathrm{ES}}$(**b**(*y*)), hence by DPT49: **all***z*(if 0(*z*), then **(b(***y***),***z***)=t** or **(b(***y***),***z***)=k**), hence by APT13: **some***z*[0(*z*) and (**(b(***y***),***z***)=t** or **(b(***y***),***z***)=k**)], hence by TPT160: *y*=**t** or *y*=**k**.
(ii) Assume **all***y*(1(*y*), then *y*=**t** or *y*=**k**), and assume <0>(*f*). Assume 0(*z*); for <0>$_{\mathrm{ES}}$(*f*), according to DPT49, there needs to be deduced: **(***f*,*z***)=t** or **(***f*,*z***)=k**; this follows from <0>(*f*), 0(*z*), APT14 and the first assumption of **(ii)**.

•TPT184 **all***f*(if <0>(*f*), then <0>$_{\mathrm{ES}}$(*f*)) iff **no***f*<0>$_{\mathrm{AC}}$(*f*).

•TPT185 **all***f***all***g*[if <0>$_{\mathrm{ES}}$(*f*) and not <0>$_{\mathrm{CD}}$(*f*) and not <0>$_{\mathrm{TL}}$(*f*) and <0>$_{\mathrm{AC}}$(*g*), then not <0>$_{\mathrm{ES}}$(**conj**$_{<0>}$(*f*,*g*)) and not <0>$_{\mathrm{AC}}$(**conj**$_{<0>}$(*f*,*g*))].

Proof: Assume: <0>$_{\mathrm{ES}}$(*f*) and not <0>$_{\mathrm{CD}}$(*f*) and not <0>$_{\mathrm{TL}}$(*f*) and <0>$_{\mathrm{AC}}$(*g*); hence:
(*) <0>(*f*) and **all***z*(if 0(*z*), then **(***f*,*z***)=t** or **(***f*,*z***)=k**) and **some***z*′(0(*z*′) and **(***f*,*z*′**)≠t**) and **some***z*′′(0(*z*′′) and **(***f*,*z*′′**)≠k**) and <0>(*g*) and **all***z*(if 0(*z*), then **(***g*,*z***)≠t** and **(***g*,*z***)≠k**) [by DPT49, DPT45, DPT40, DPT50].
Consider *z*′ and *z*′′.
By **(*)** **(***f*,*z*′**)≠t**, hence by **(*)**: **(***f*,*z*′**)=k**, hence according to the ontology of states of affairs [and 1(**(***g*,*z*′**)**)]: **conj((***f*,*z*′**),(***g*,*z*′**))=k**, hence, because of 0(*z*′), by APT16: **(exo***o***conj((***f*,*o***),(***g*,*o***)),***z*′**)=k**, hence by TPT178: **(conj**$_{<0>}$**(***f*,*g***),***z*′**)=k** [<0>(*f*), <0>(*g*)], hence according to DPT50: **(1)** not <0>$_{\mathrm{AC}}$(**conj**$_{<0>}$(*f*,*g*)).
By **(*)** **(***f*,*z*′′**)≠k**, hence by **(*)**: **(***f*,*z*′′**)=t**, hence by TPT53: **conj((***f*,*z*′′**),(***g*,*z*′′**))=(***g*,*z*′′**)**, hence by **(*)**: **conj((***f*,*z*′′**),(***g*,*z*′′**))≠t** and **conj((***f*,*z*′′**), (***g*,*z*′′**))≠k**, hence, because of 0(*z*′′), by APT16: **(exo***o***conj((***f*,*o***),(***g*,*o***)),***z*′′**)≠t** and **(exo***o***conj((***f*,*o***),(***g*,*o***)),***z*′′**)≠k**, hence by TPT178: **(conj**$_{<0>}$**(***f*,*g***),***z*′′**)≠t** and **(conj**$_{<0>}$**(***f*,*g***),***z*′′**)≠k**, hence according to DPT49: **(2)** not <0>$_{\mathrm{ES}}$(**conj**$_{<0>}$(*f*,*g*)).

•TPT186 **all***z*[if 0(*z*) and **some***z*′(0(*z*′) and *z*≠*z*′), then <0>$_{\mathrm{ES}}$(**i**(*z*)) and not <0>$_{\mathrm{CD}}$(**i**(*z*)) and not <0>$_{\mathrm{TL}}$(**i**(*z*))].

Proof: Assume: 0(*z*) and **some***z*′(0(*z*′) and *z*≠*z*′). Hence: (**1**) <0>$_{ES}$(**i**(*z*)), according to TPT171, TPT144, DPT48, DPT49; (**2**) not <0>$_{CD}$(**i**(*z*)), according to DPT40, for (**i**(*z*),*z*)≠**k** by TPT171; (**3**) not <0>$_{TL}$(**i**(*z*)), according to DPT45, for **some***z*′(0(*z*′) and (**i**(*z*),*z*′)≠**t**) by TPT171 and the assumption.

•TPT187 **all***z*[if 0(*z*), then QC$_{<0>}$(**conj**$_{<0>}$(**b**(**w**),**i**(*z*)))].

Proof: Assume (**1**) 0(*z*); assume (**2**) **conj**$_{<0>}$(**b**(**w**),**i**(*z*))P$_{<0>}$*f*. For obtaining QC$_{<0>}$(**conj**$_{<0>}$(**b**(**w**),**i**(*z*))), according to ParDPT7, it is to be deduced from the assumptions: *f*=**conj**$_{<0>}$(**b**(**w**),**i**(*z*)) or T$_{<0>}$(*f*).

Assume also: (**3**) not T$_{<0>}$(*f*), hence [according to ParDPT5]: **some***g*(<0>(*g*) and not *g*P$_{<0>}$*f*) [since <0>(*f*)].

What remains to be deduced is *f*P$_{<0>}$**conj**$_{<0>}$(**b**(**w**),**i**(*z*)) (because of the second assumption above and TPT155).

Assume, therefore, (**4**) 0(*z*′); (**conj**$_{<0>}$(**b**(**w**),**i**(*z*)),*z*′)=**conj**((**b**(**w**),*z*′),(**i**(*z*),*z*′)) =**conj**(**w**,(**i**(*z*),*z*′)) [by the corollary of TPT178, and by TPT160, since 1(**w**)].

Now two cases have to be distinguished:

(**x**) *z*′≠*z*, then by TPT171: (**i**(*z*),*z*′)=**k**; hence: **conj**(**w**,(**i**(*z*),*z*′))=**conj**(**w**,**k**)=**k**.

Therefore: (*f*,*z*′)P(**conj**$_{<0>}$(**b**(**w**),**i**(*z*)),*z*′) [1((*f*,*z*′)), **all***y*(if 1(*y*), then *y*P**k**)].

(**xx**) *z*′=*z*, then by TPT171: (**i**(*z*),*z*′)=**t**; hence: **conj**(**w**,(**i**(*z*),*z*′))=**conj**(**w**,**t**)=**w**.

Because of (**2**) we have according to DPT41: **all***z*′′(if 0(*z*′′), then (**conj**$_{<0>}$(**b**(**w**),**i**(*z*)),*z*′′)P(*f*,*z*′′)). Hence (as we have seen): **all***z*′′(if 0(*z*′′) and *z*′′≠*z*, then **k**P(*f*,*z*′′)), hence: <u>**all***z*′′(if 0(*z*′′) and *z*′′≠*z*, then (*f*,*z*′′)=**k**)</u>. And hence also (because of (**4**)): (**conj**$_{<0>}$(**b**(**w**),**i**(*z*)),*z*′)P(*f*,*z*′), and therefore: **w**P(*f*,*z*′). QC(**w**) by APT8. Hence by DPT7: (*f*,*z*′)=**w** or T((*f*,*z*′)).

In the first case, because of **w**P**w** [1(**w**) by APT8, and APT2] and (**conj**$_{<0>}$(**b**(**w**),**i**(*z*)),*z*′)=**w**: (*f*,*z*′)P(**conj**$_{<0>}$(**b**(**w**),**i**(*z*)),*z*′).

The second case is excluded: from T((*f*,*z*′)) by TPT34: (*f*,*z*′)=**k**, hence: (*f*,*z*)=**k** [by the assumption of (**xx**)], hence by the underlined result and (**1**): **all***z*′′(if 0(*z*′′), then (*f*,*z*′′)=**k**), hence: **all***g*(if <0>(*g*), then *g*P$_{<0>}$*f*) [applying DPT41, APT14, **all***y*(if 1(*y*), then *y*P**k**)]; but this contradicts the corollary of assumption (**3**) above.

We have, therefore, deduced from assumptions (**1**) - (**3**): **all***z*′[if 0(*z*′), then (*f*,*z*′)P(**conj**$_{<0>}$(**b**(**w**),**i**(*z*)),*z*′)], hence by DPT41 [since also <0>(*f*), <0>(**conj**$_{<0>}$(**b**(**w**),**i**(*z*)))]: *f*P$_{<0>}$**conj**$_{<0>}$(**b**(**w**),**i**(*z*)) - what remained to be deduced.

•TPT188 **all***z*(if 0(*z*), then **conj**$_{<0>}$(**b**(**w**),**i**(*z*))≠**k**$_{<0>}$).

Proof: Assume 0(*z*); assume for *reductio*: **conj**$_{<0>}$(**b**(**w**),**i**(*z*))=**k**$_{<0>}$; hence: (**conj**$_{<0>}$(**b**(**w**),**i**(*z*)),*z*)=(**k**$_{<0>}$,*z*); therefore according to the argumentation in the proof of TPT187: **w**=(**k**$_{<0>}$,*z*); hence by TPT159, DPT40: **w**=**k** - contradicting AP7.

•TPT189 **all***z*[if 0(*z*), then MK$_{<0>}$(**conj**$_{<0>}$(**b**(**w**),**i**(*z*)))].

•TPT190 **all***z*[if 0(*z*), then EL$_{<0>}$(**neg**$_{<0>}$(**conj**$_{<0>}$(**b**(**w**),**i**(*z*))))].

•TPT191 **some***z*[0(*z*) and QA$_{<0>}$(**neg**$_{<0>}$(**conj**$_{<0>}$(**b**(**w**),**i**(*z*)))) and

neg$_{<0>}$(**conj**$_{<0>}$(**b**(**w**),**i**(*z*)))≠**t**$_{<0>}$].

•TPT192 **all***z***all***z*′[if 0(*z*) and 0(*z*′) and *z*≠*z*′, then **conj**$_{<0>}$(**b**(**w**),**i**(*z*)) ≠**conj**$_{<0>}$(**b**(**w**),**i**(*z*′))].

Proof: Assume: 0(*z*) and 0(*z*′) and *z*≠*z*′; hence we have: **(conj**$_{<0>}$**(b(w),i(***z***)),***z***)** =**w** and **(conj**$_{<0>}$**(b(w),i(***z*′**)),***z***)=k**, according to the proof of TPT187.
Therefore by APT7: **(conj**$_{<0>}$**(b(w),i(***z***)),***z***)≠(conj**$_{<0>}$**(b(w),i(***z*′**)),***z***)**, and hence by APT19: **conj**$_{<0>}$**(b(w),i(***z***))≠conj**$_{<0>}$**(b(w),i(***z*′**))**.

•TPT193 **all***x***all***f*(if *f*(*x*), then <0>(*f*) and 0(*x*)).

Proof: Assume *f*(*x*), hence by DPT55: O((*f*,*x*)), hence by DPT31: (*f*,*x*)**Pw**, hence: (*f*,*x*)≠**k** (for *otherwise*, because of **wPk** and (*f*,*x*)**Pw**, by APT3: **w=k** - contradicting APT7), hence by APT15: <0>(*f*) and 0(*x*).

•TPT194 **all***f***all***x*(if *f*(*x*), then not *x*(*f*)).

Proof: Assume: *f*(*x*) and *x*(*f*), hence by TPT193: <0>(*f*) and 0(*x*) and <0>(*x*) - contradicting APT12.

•TPT195 **all***z*(if 0(*z*), then [**conj**$_{<0>}$*g*A[*g*](*z*) iff **all***f*(if <0>(*f*) and A[*f*], then *f*(*z*))]).

Proof: Assume 0(*z*).

(i) Assume **(1)** **conj**$_{<0>}$*g*A[*g*](*z*); and assume: <0>(*f*) and A[*f*], hence by ParTPT18: *f*P$_{<0>}$**conj**$_{<0>}$*g*A[*g*], hence, because of 0(*z*), by DPT41: (*f*,*z*)P(**conj**$_{<0>}$*g*A[*g*],*z*). From (**1**) according to DPT55, DPT31: (**conj**$_{<0>}$*g*A[*g*],*z*) **Pw**. Hence by APT1: (*f*,*z*)**Pw**, hence by DPT31, DPT55: *f*(*z*).

(ii) Assume (**2**) **all***f*(if <0>(*f*) and A[*f*], then *f*(*z*)).
It is to be deduced: **conj***y***some***k*(<0>(*k*) and A[*k*] and *y*=(*k*,*z*))**Pw**; for from this results by TPT158 [in view of 0(*z*)]: (**conj**$_{<0>}$*g*A[*g*],*z*)**Pw**, hence by DPT31, DPT55: **conj**$_{<0>}$*g*A[*g*](*z*).
Assume **some***k*(<0>(*k*) and A[*k*] and *y*=(*k*,*z*)); hence by (**2**): *k*(*z*), hence by DPT55, DPT31: (*k*,*z*)**Pw**, hence: *y***Pw**. Therefore (applying TPT28): **conj***y***some***k*(<0>(*k*) and A[*k*] and *y*=(*k*,*z*))**Pconj***y*(*y***Pw**), hence by TPT30: **conj***y***some***k*(<0>(*k*) and A[*k*] and *y*=(*k*,*z*))**Pw**.

•TPT196 **all***z***all***f***all***g*{if 0(*z*) and <0>(*f*) and <0>(*g*), then [**neg**$_{<0>}$(*f*)(*z*) iff not *f*(*z*)] and [**conj**$_{<0>}$(*f*,*g*)(*z*) iff *f*(*z*) and *g*(*z*)] and [**disj**$_{<0>}$(*f*,*g*)(*z*) iff *f*(*z*) or *g*(*z*)]}.

Proof: Assume: 0(*z*) and <0>(*f*) and <0>(*g*); hence by APT14: 1((*f*,*z*)), 1((*g*,*z*)).

(i) **neg**$_{<0>}$(*f*)(*z*) iff [by DPT55, DPT31] (**neg**$_{<0>}$(*f*),*z*)**Pw** iff [by the corollary of TPT180] **neg**((*f*,*z*))**Pw** iff [by TPT106, TPT69] not (*f*,*z*)**Pw** iff [by DPT31, DPT55] not *f*(*z*).

(ii) **conj**$_{<0>}$(*f*,*g*)(*z*) iff (**conj**$_{<0>}$(*f*,*g*),*z*)**Pw** iff [by the corollary of TPT178] **conj**((*f*,*z*),(*g*,*z*))**Pw** iff [by TPT24] (*f*,*z*)**Pw** and (*g*,*z*)**Pw** iff *f*(*z*) and *g*(*z*).

(iii) **disj**$_{<0>}$(*f*,*g*)(*z*) iff (**disj**$_{<0>}$(*f*,*g*),*z*)**Pw** iff [by TPT179] **disj**((*f*,*z*),(*g*,*z*))**Pw** iff [by TPT109, DPT32, DPT31] (*f*,*z*)**Pw** or (*g*,*z*)**Pw** iff *f*(*z*) or *g*(*z*).

•TPT197 **all***z*[if 0(*z*), then **conj**$_{<0>}$*h*[*h*(*z*)]=**conj**$_{<0>}$(**b**(**w**),**i**(*z*))].

Proof: Assume 0(*z*).

(i) **b(w)**(*z*), for **(b(w)**,*z***)Pw**, because **wPw** and TPT160 [1(**w**), APT2]. **i**(*z*)(*z*), for **(i**(*z*),*z***)Pw**, because **tPw** and TPT171. Hence - since <0>(**b(w)**), <0>(**i**(*z*)) - by ParTPT18: **b(w)**P$_{<0>}$**conj**$_{<0>}$*h*[*h*(*z*)] and **i**(*z*)P$_{<0>}$**conj**$_{<0>}$*h*[*h*(*z*)], hence by ParTPT24: **conj**$_{<0>}$**(b(w),i**(*z*))P$_{<0>}$**conj**$_{<0>}$*h*[*h*(*z*)] **(1)**.

(ii) Assume *f*(*z*). We show: *f*P$_{<0>}$**conj**$_{<0>}$**(b(w),i**(*z*)). Assume, therefore, 0(*z′*).

(x) If *z′*≠*z*, then as in the proof of TPT187: **(conj**$_{<0>}$**(b(w),i**(*z*)),*z′***)=k**, hence: (*f*,*z′*)**P(conj**$_{<0>}$**(b(w),i**(*z*)),*z′*).

(xx) If *z′*=*z*, then as in the proof of TPT187: **(conj**$_{<0>}$**(b(w),i**(*z*)),*z′***)=w**. According to assumption: *f*(*z*), hence: (*f*,*z*)**Pw** [DPT55, DPT31]; hence (*f*,*z′*)**P(conj**$_{<0>}$**(b(w),i**(*z*)),*z′*).

On the basis of **(x)** and **(xx)** we can conclude according to DPT41: *f*P$_{<0>}$**conj**$_{<0>}$**(b(w),i**(*z*)) [<0>(*f*) by TPT193 because of *f*(*z*)].

We have now shown: **all***f*[if *f*(*z*), then *f*P$_{<0>}$**conj**$_{<0>}$**(b(w),i**(*z*))]; hence by ParTPT28: **conj**$_{<0>}$*h*[*h*(*z*)]P$_{<0>}$**conj**$_{<0>}$*h*[*h*P$_{<0>}$**conj**$_{<0>}$**(b(w),i**(*z*))], hence by ParTPT30: **conj**$_{<0>}$*h*[*h*(*z*)]P$_{<0>}$**conj**$_{<0>}$**(b(w),i**(*z*)) **(2)**.

From **(1)** and **(2)** by TPT155: **conj**$_{<0>}$*h*[*h*(*z*)]=**conj**$_{<0>}$**(b(w),i**(*z*)).

•TPT198 **all***z***all***z′*[if 0(*z*) and 0(*z′*), then (if *z′*=*z*, then **(conj**$_{<0>}$*h*[*h*(*z*)],*z′***)=w** and **conj**$_{<0>}$*h*[*h*(*z*)](*z′*)) and (if *z′*≠*z*, then **(conj**$_{<0>}$*h*[*h*(*z*)],*z′***)=k** and not **conj**$_{<0>}$*h*[*h*(*z*)](*z′*))].

•TPT199 **all***f*(if <0>(*f*) and [**all***z*(if 0(*z*), then (*f*,*z*)**=k**) or **some***z*(0(*z*) and (*f*,*z*)**≠k** and QC((*f*,*z*)) and **all***z′*(if 0(*z′*) and *z′*≠*z*, then (*f*,*z′*)**=k**))], then QC$_{<0>}$(*f*)).

Proof: Assume <0>(*f*).

(x) Assume **all***z*(if 0(*z*), then (*f*,*z*)**=k**), hence: **all***z*(if 0(*z*), then **neg(**(*f*,*z*))**=neg(k)**), hence by TPT54 and the corollary of TPT180: **all***z*(if 0(*z*), then **(neg**$_{<0>}$(*f*),*z***)=t**); hence by TPT175: QA$_{<0>}$(**neg**$_{<0>}$(*f*)), hence by ParTPT73: QC$_{<0>}$(*f*).

(xx) Assume **some***z*(0(*z*) and (*f*,*z*)**≠k** and QC((*f*,*z*)) and **all***z′*(if 0(*z′*) and *z′*≠*z*, then (*f*,*z′*)**=k**)).

From (*f*,*z*)**≠k** one obtains: **(1)** **(neg**$_{<0>}$(*f*),*z***)≠t**; for (*f*,*z*)**≠k** yields **neg(**(*f*,*z*))**≠t** [by TPT54, TPT55], and hence by the corollary of TPT180: **(neg**$_{<0>}$(*f*),*z***)≠t**.

From QC((*f*,*z*)) one obtains: **(2)** QA(**(neg**$_{<0>}$(*f*),*z*)); for QC((*f*,*z*)) yields QA(**neg(**(*f*,*z*))) [by TPT73], and hence: QA(**(neg**$_{<0>}$(*f*),*z*)).

From **all***z′*(if 0(*z′*) and *z′*≠*z*, then (*f*,*z′*)**=k**) one obtains: **(3)** **all***z′*(if 0(*z′*) and *z′*≠*z*, then **(neg**$_{<0>}$(*f*),*z′***)=t**).

By TPT175 one obtains from **(1)**, **(2)** and **(3)**: QA$_{<0>}$(**neg**$_{<0>}$(*f*)), hence by ParTPT73: QC$_{<0>}$(*f*).

•TPT200 **all***f*[if QC$_{<0>}$(*f*), then **all***z*(if 0(*z*), then (*f*,*z*)**=k**) or **some***z*(0(*z*) and (*f*,*z*)**≠k** and QC((*f*,*z*)) and **all***z′*(if 0(*z′*) and *z′*≠*z*, then (*f*,*z′*)**=k**))].

•TPT201 **all***f*[MK$_{<0>}$(*f*) iff <0>(*f*) and **some***z*(0(*z*) and MK((*f*,*z*)) and **all***z′*(if 0(*z′*) and *z′*≠*z*, then (*f*,*z′*)**=k**))].

Proof: **(i)** Assume MK$_{<0>}$(*f*), hence by ParTPT72: QC$_{<0>}$(*f*) and *f*≠**k**$_{<0>}$; hence by APT19: **some***z*(0(*z*) and (*f*,*z*)≠(**k**$_{<0>}$,*z*)), hence by TPT159 and DPT40:

some*z*(0(*z*) and **(***f*,*z***)≠k**). Hence - in view of QC$_{<0>}$(*f*) - by TPT200 and TPT72: <0>(*f*) and **some***z*(0(*z*) and MK((*f*,*z*)) and **all***z*′(if 0(*z*′) and *z*′≠*z*, then (*f*,*z*′)=**k**)).
(**ii**) Assume: <0>(*f*) and **some***z*(0(*z*) and MK((*f*,*z*)) and **all***z*′(if 0(*z*′) and *z*′≠*z*, then (*f*,*z*′)=**k**)). Hence by TPT72, TPT199: QC$_{<0>}$(*f*), and moreover: *f*≠**k**$_{<0>}$, for: (*f*,*z*)≠**k** [by TPT72 from the assumption], but **all***z*′(if 0(*z*′), then (**k**$_{<0>}$,*z*′)=**k**) [TPT159, DPT40]. Therefore by ParTPT72: MK$_{<0>}$(*f*).
•TPT202 **all***z***all***y*[if 0(*z*) and MK(*y*), then MK$_{<0>}$(**conj**$_{<0>}$(**b**(*y*),**i**(*z*)))].
•TPT203 **all***z***all***z*′**all***y***all***y*′[if 0(*z*) and 0(*z*′) and MK(*y*) and MK(*y*′) and (*z*′≠*z* or *y*′≠*y*), then **conj**$_{<0>}$(**b**(*y*),**i**(*z*))≠**conj**$_{<0>}$(**b**(*y*′),**i**(*z*′))].
Proof: Assume: 0(*z*) and 0(*z*′) and MK(*y*) and MK(*y*′).
(**x**) In case *z*′≠*z*: (**conj**$_{<0>}$(**b**(*y*),**i**(*z*)),*z*′)=**k** (compare the argumentation in the proof of TPT187), but (**conj**$_{<0>}$(**b**(*y*′),**i**(*z*′)),*z*′)=*y*′. Because of MK(*y*′) and TPT72: *y*′≠**k**. Hence: **conj**$_{<0>}$(**b**(*y*),**i**(*z*))≠**conj**$_{<0>}$(**b**(*y*′),**i**(*z*′)).
(**xx**) In case *y*′≠*y* and *z*′=*z*: **conj**$_{<0>}$(**b**(*y*),**i**(*z*))≠**conj**$_{<0>}$(**b**(*y*′),**i**(*z*′)), for (**conj**$_{<0>}$(**b**(*y*),**i**(*z*)),*z*)≠(**conj**$_{<0>}$(**b**(*y*′),**i**(*z*′)),*z*), because (**conj**$_{<0>}$(**b**(*y*),**i**(*z*)),*z*)=*y* and (**conj**$_{<0>}$(**b**(*y*′),**i**(*z*′)),*z*)=*y*′.
•TPT204 **all***f*[if MK$_{<0>}$(*f*), then **some***z***some***y*(0(*z*) and MK(*y*) and *f*= **conj**$_{<0>}$(**b**(*y*),**i**(*z*)))].
Proof: Assume MK$_{<0>}$(*f*), hence by TPT201: <u>**some***z*(0(*z*) and MK((*f*,*z*)) and **all***z*′(if 0(*z*′) and *z*′≠*z*, then (*f*,*z*′)=**k**))</u>.
Assume 0(*z*′′). If *z*′′≠*z*, then [according to the underlined result] (*f*,*z*′′)=**k**, and also: (**conj**$_{<0>}$(**b**((*f*,*z*)),**i**(*z*)),*z*′′)=**k** [corollary of TPT178, and TPT171, etc.]; hence: (*f*,*z*′′)=(**conj**$_{<0>}$(**b**((*f*,*z*)),**i**(*z*)),*z*′′). If *z*′′=*z*, then (*f*,*z*′′)=(*f*,*z*), and also: (**conj**$_{<0>}$(**b**((*f*,*z*)),**i**(*z*)),*z*′′)=(*f*,*z*) [corollary of TPT178, and TPT171, TPT53, TPT160, etc.]; hence: (*f*,*z*′′)=(**conj**$_{<0>}$(**b**((*f*,*z*)),**i**(*z*)),*z*′′).
Thus: **all***z*′′[if 0(*z*′′), then (*f*,*z*′′)=(**conj**$_{<0>}$(**b**((*f*,*z*)),**i**(*z*)),*z*′′)], hence by APT19: *f*=**conj**$_{<0>}$(**b**((*f*,*z*)),**i**(*z*)).
Therefore [applying the underlined result]: **some***z***some***y*(0(*z*) and MK(*y*) and *f*=**conj**$_{<0>}$(**b**(*y*),**i**(*z*))).
•TPT205 **all***z***all***y*[if 0(*z*) and MK(*y*), then **conj**$_{<0>}$*h*[*h*/in *y*/(*z*)]= **conj**$_{<0>}$(**b**(*y*), **i**(*z*))].
•TPT206 **all***f*[<0>(*f*) and *f*≠**k**$_{<0>}$ iff <0>(*f*) and **some***z***some***y*(0(*z*) and MK(*y*) and *f*/in *y*/(*z*))].
Proof: (**i**) Assume: <0>(*f*) and *f*≠**k**$_{<0>}$, hence by ParTPT91: **some***g*(MK$_{<0>}$(*g*) and *f*P$_{<0>}$*g*) [not **k**$_{<0>}$P$_{<0>}$*f* by TPT155, because *f*≠**k**$_{<0>}$ and *f*P$_{<0>}$**k**$_{<0>}$], hence by TPT204: **some***g*(MK$_{<0>}$(*g*) and **some***z***some***y*(0(*z*) and MK(*y*) and *g*=**conj**$_{<0>}$(**b**(*y*),**i**(*z*))) and *f*P$_{<0>}$*g*), hence: **some***z***some***y*[0(*z*) and MK(*y*) and *f*P$_{<0>}$**conj**$_{<0>}$(**b**(*y*),**i**(*z*))], hence by DPT41: **some***z***some***y*[0(*z*) and MK(*y*) and (*f*,*z*)P(**conj**$_{<0>}$(**b**(*y*),**i**(*z*)),*z*)], hence according to the argumentation in the proof of TPT187 (there we had "**w**" in place of "*y*"): **some***z***some***y*(0(*z*) and MK(*y*)

and (*f*,*z*)P*y*), hence by DPT56: <0>(*f*) and **some***z***some***y*(0(*z*) and MK(*y*) and *f*/in *y*/(*z*)).

(ii) Assume: <0>(*f*) and **some***z***some***y*(0(*z*) and MK(*y*) and *f*/in *y*/(*z*)), hence by DPT56: **some***z***some***y*(0(*z*) and MK(*y*) and (*f*,*z*)P*y*), hence: (*f*,*z*)≠**k** [for *otherwise* **k**P*y*, and hence, according to APT3, because of *y*P**k**: *y*=**k** - contradicting MK(*y*) in virtue of TPT72]; hence: not <0>$_{CD}$(*f*), according to DPT40. Therefore: <0>(*f*) and *f*≠**k**$_{<0>}$ [by TPT159].

•TPT207 **all***f***all***g*(if <0>(*f*) and <0>(*g*), then [*f*P$_{<0>}$*g* iff **all***y***all***z*(if MK(*y*) and 0(*z*) and *g*/in *y*/(*z*), then *f*/in *y*/(*z*))]).

Proof: Assume <0>(*f*), <0>(*g*).

(i) Assume *f*P$_{<0>}$*g*, and assume: MK(*y*), 0(*z*), *g*/in *y*/(*z*); hence according to DPT56: (*g*,*z*)P*y*; hence also (according to DPT41): (*f*,*z*)P(*g*,*z*). Therefore by APT1: (*f*,*z*)P*y*, and hence, because of MK(*y*), by DPT56: *f*/in *y*/(*z*).

(ii) Assume **(1)** **all***y***all***z*(if MK(*y*) and 0(*z*) and *g*/in *y*/(*z*), then *f*/in *y*/(*z*)). Assume **(2)** 0(*z*). According to DPT41 [*f* and *g* have been assumed to be properties], for showing *f*P$_{<0>}$*g*, <u>(*f*,*z*)P(*g*,*z*)</u> remains to be deduced. By **(1)**, **(2)** and DPT56: **all***y*(if MK(*y*) and (*g*,*z*)P*y*, then (*f*,*z*)P*y*); hence by TPT72: **all***y*(if QC(*y*) and *y*≠**k** and (*g*,*z*)P*y*, then (*f*,*z*)P*y*), hence: **all***y*(if QC(*y*) and (*g*,*z*)P*y*, then (*f*,*z*)P*y*) [since **all***y*(if *y*=**k**, then (*f*,*z*)P*y*), because of 1((*f*,*z*)) - like 1((*g*,*z*)) by APT14 - and **all***x*(if 1(*x*), then *x*P**k**)], hence by TPT73 and TPT59: **all***y*[if 1(*y*) and QA(**neg**(*y*)) and **neg**(*y*)P**neg**((*g*,*z*)), then **neg**(*y*)P**neg**((*f*,*z*))], hence by TPT55: **all***y*[if QA(*y*) and *y*P**neg**((*g*,*z*)), then *y*P**neg**((*f*,*z*))], hence by APT5: **neg**((*g*,*z*))P**neg**((*f*,*z*)), hence by TPT59: <u>(*f*,*z*)P(*g*,*z*)</u>.

•TPT208 **all***z*[if 0(*z*), then MK**w**$_{<0>}$(**conj**$_{<0>}$(**b**(**w**),**i**(*z*)))].

•TPT209 **all***f*[if MK**w**$_{<0>}$(*f*), then **some***z*(0(*z*) and *f*=**conj**$_{<0>}$(**b**(**w**),**i**(*z*)))].

Proof: Assume MK**w**$_{<0>}$(*f*), hence by DPT57: MK$_{<0>}$(*f*) and **b**(**w**)P$_{<0>}$*f*; hence by TPT204: **some***z***some***y*(0(*z*) and MK(*y*) and *f*=**conj**$_{<0>}$(**b**(*y*),**i**(*z*))), hence: **b**(**w**)P$_{<0>}$**conj**$_{<0>}$(**b**(*y*),**i**(*z*)), hence by DPT41: (**b**(**w**),*z*)P(**conj**$_{<0>}$(**b**(*y*),**i**(*z*)),*z*), hence, because (**b**(**w**),*z*)=**w** [by TPT160, 0(*z*), 1(**w**)] and (**conj**$_{<0>}$(**b**(*y*),**i**(*z*)),*z*) =*y*, **w**P*y*, hence, because MK(**w**) [by TPT106] and MK(*y*), by TP79: *y*=**w**. Therefore: **some***z*(0(*z*) and *f*=**conj**$_{<0>}$(**b**(**w**),**i**(*z*))).

•TPT210 **all***f*[MK**w**$_{<0>}$(*f*) iff **some***z*(0(*z*) and *f*=**conj**$_{<0>}$*h*[*h*(*z*)])].

•TPT211 **all***f*[MK$_{<0>}$(*f*) iff **some***z***some***y*(0(*z*) and MK(*y*) and *f*=**conj**$_{<0>}$*h*[*h*/in *y*/(*z*)])].

•TPT212 **all***f*[if <0>(*f*), then **some***g*(<0>$_{ES}$(*g*) and **all***z*(*g*(*z*) iff *f*(*z*)))].

Proof: Assume <0>(*f*). Consider **exo***o***conj***y*(not *f*(*o*) and *y*=**k**).

We have:

(1) **all***z*(if 0(*z*), then [*f*(*z*) iff (**exo***o***conj***y*(not *f*(*o*) and *y*=**k**),*z*)=**t**]), **all***z*(if 0(*z*), then [not *f*(*z*) iff (**exo***o***conj***y*(not *f*(*o*) and *y*=**k**),*z*)=**k**]).

The proof of **(1)** is *mutatis mutandis* like the proof of TPT171, substituting "**exo***o***conj***y*(not *f*(*o*) and *y*=**k**)" for "**i**(*x*)" [:= **exo***o***conj***y*(*o*≠*x* and *y*=**k**)]. (Replacing "*x*=*x*" and "*x*≠*x*" in TPT170 by "*f*(*x*)" and "not *f*(*x*)" [hence

"**conj***y*(*x*≠*x*′ and *y*=**k**)" by "**conj***y*(not *f*(*x*) and *y*=**k**)"] yields a principle which is provable in the same way as TPT170. The proofs of TPT170 and TPT171 are routine modifications of the proofs of TPT168 and TPT169.)
From **(1)** we immediately get by DPT49 and TPT144:
(2) <0>$_{\mathrm{ES}}$(**exo***o***conj***y*(not *f*(*o*) and *y*=**k**)).
And finally we have:
(3) all*z*(**exo***o***conj***y*(not *f*(*o*) and *y*=**k**)(*z*) iff *f*(*z*)):
(x) Assume **exo***o***conj***y*(not *f*(*o*) and *y*=**k**)(*z*); hence by DPT55, DPT31: **(exo***o***conj***y*(not *f*(*o*) and *y*=**k**),*z*)**Pw**, and by TPT193: <u>0(*z*)</u>. Hence: <u>**(exo***o***conj***y*(not *f*(*o*) and *y*=**k**),*z*)≠**k**</u>, for *otherwise* **kPw**, hence, because of **wPk**, by APT3: **w**=**k** - contradicting APT7. By applying **(1)** to the underlined results: *f*(*z*).
(xx) Assume *f*(*z*), hence by TPT193: 0(*z*). Hence by **(1)**: **(exo***o***conj***y*(not *f*(*o*) and *y*=**k**),*z*)=**t**, hence: **(exo***o***conj***y*(not *f*(*o*) and *y*=**k**),*z*)**Pw**, since **tPw**. Therefore by DPT31, DPT55: **exo***o***conj***y*(not *f*(*o*) and *y*=**k**)(*z*).
(2) and **(3)** logically imply: **some***g*(<0>$_{\mathrm{ES}}$(*g*) and **all***z*(*g*(*z*) iff *f*(*z*))).
•TPT213 **all***g***all***g*′(if <0>$_{\mathrm{ES}}$(*g*) and <0>$_{\mathrm{ES}}$(*g*′) and **all***z*(*g*(*z*) iff *g*′(*z*)), then *g*=*g*′).
Proof: Assume: <0>$_{\mathrm{ES}}$(*g*) and <0>$_{\mathrm{ES}}$(*g*′) and (*) **all***z*(*g*(*z*) iff *g*′(*z*)); hence according to DPT49: <0>(*g*) and <0>(*g*′) and **all***z*(if 0(*z*), then (*g*,*z*)=**t** or (*g*,*z*)=**k**) and **all***z*(if 0(*z*), then (*g*′,*z*)=**t** or (*g*′,*z*)=**k**). Assume 0(*z*). Hence: ((*g*,*z*)=**t** or (*g*,*z*)=**k**) and ((*g*′,*z*)=**t** or (*g*′,*z*)=**k**), hence: (*g*,*z*)=**t** and (*g*′,*z*)=**t**, or (*g*,*z*)=**t** and (*g*′,*z*)=**k**, or (*g*,*z*)=**k** and (*g*′,*z*)=**t**, or (*g*,*z*)=**k** and (*g*′,*z*)=**k**. In the first and fourth case: (*g*,*z*)=(*g*′,*z*). The second and third case, however, contradict assumption (*) [in view of DPT55, DPT31, APT7, etc.]: if (*g*,*z*)=**t** and (*g*′,*z*)=**k**, then *g*(*z*) and not *g*′(*z*); if (*g*,*z*)=**k** and (*g*′,*z*)=**t**, then not *g*(*z*), but *g*′(*z*).
We have now deduced from the assumptions other than 0(*z*): **all***z*(if 0(*z*), then (*g*,*z*)=(*g*′,*z*)), and hence - because of <0>(*g*), <0>(*g*′) - by APT19: *g*=*g*′.
•TPT214 **all***f***one***g*(<0>$_{\mathrm{ES}}$(*g*) and **all***z*(*g*(*z*) iff *f*(*z*))).
•TPT215 **all***g***all***g*′(if <0>$_{\mathrm{ES}}$(*g*) and <0>$_{\mathrm{ES}}$(*g*′) and **some***y*(MK(*y*) and **all***z*[*g*/in *y*/(*z*) iff *g*′/in *y*/(*z*)]), then *g*=*g*′).
Proof: Analogous to the proof of TPT213. In the second case, for example, we have: if (*g*,*z*)=**t** and (*g*′,*z*)=**k**, then *g*/in *y*/(*z*) and not *g*′/in *y*/(*z*) [by DPT56, since **t**P*y* and MK(*y*), but not **k**P*y* because of MK(*y*) by TPT72, etc.] - contradicting the assumption.
•TPT216 **all***f***all***y*[if <0>(*f*) and MK(*y*), then **some***g*(<0>$_{\mathrm{ES}}$(*g*) and **all***z*[*g*/in *y*/(*z*) iff *f*/in *y*/(*z*)])].
Proof: Assume: <0>(*f*) and MK(*y*). Consider **exo***o***conj***x*(not *f*/in *y*/(*o*) and *x*=**k**). The rest is analogous to the proof of TPT212. Neither the assumption <0>(*f*) nor the assumption MK(*y*) are really needed. Instead of DPT31 and DPT55, DPT56 is employed. *y*≠**k** because of MK(*y*) [which can be had by DPT56 both from **exo***o***conj***x*(not *f*/in *y*/(*o*) and *x*=**k**)(*z*) and from *f*/in *y*/(*z*)] and TPT72. 0(*z*)

both from **exo***o***conj***x*(not *f*/in *y*/(*o*) and *x*=**k**)(*z*) and *f*/in *y*/(*z*) by: DPT56, not **k**P*y* [MK(*y*)], APT15.

•TPT217 **all***f***all***y*[if MK(*y*), then **one***g*(<0>$_{ES}$(*g*) and **all***z*[*g*/in *y*/(*z*) iff *f*/in *y*/(*z*)])].

•TPT218 **all***f***all***g*(if <0>(*f*) and <0>(*g*) and **all***y*(if MK(*y*), then **rep**(*f*,*y*)=**rep**(*g*,*y*)), then *f*=*g*).

Proof: Assume: <0>(*f*), <0>(*g*), **all***y*(if MK(*y*), then **rep**(*f*,*y*)=**rep**(*g*,*y*)). Assume MK(*y*); hence by TPT217, DPT61: **all***z*(**rep**(*f*,*y*)/in *y*/(*z*) iff *f*/in *y*/(*z*)) and **all***z*(**rep**(*g*,*y*)/in *y*/(*z*) iff *g*/in *y*/(*z*)), and hence [because **rep**(*f*,*y*)=**rep**(*g*,*y*) on the basis of the assumptions]: **all***z*(*f*/in *y*/(*z*) iff *g*/in *y*/(*z*)). We have now deduced from the first three assumptions: **all***y*[if MK(*y*), then **all***z*(*f*/in *y*/(*z*) iff *g*/in *y*/(*z*))], and hence by TPT207: *f*$P_{<0>}$*g* and *g*$P_{<0>}$*f*, hence by TPT155: *f*=*g*.

•TPT219 if **all***z*(if A[*z*], then 0(*z*)), then **all***z*(**exo***o***conj***y*(not A[*o*] and *y*=**k**)(*z*) iff A[*z*]).

Proof: Assume **all***z*(if A[*z*], then 0(*z*)).

(**i**) Assume **exo***o***conj***y*(not A[*o*] and *y*=**k**)(*z*); hence by TPT193: 0(*z*), and moreover by DPT55, DPT31: (**exo***o***conj***y*(not A[*o*] and *y*=**k**),*z*)**Pw**. Therefore by APT16: **conj***y*(not A[*z*] and *y*=**k**)**Pw**, hence: **conj***y*(not A[*z*] and *y*=**k**)≠**k**, because **w**≠**k** (APT7); hence: A[*z*].

(**ii**) Assume A[*z*]; hence: 0(*z*) (according to main assumption); hence also: **conj***y*(not A[*z*] and *y*=**k**)=**t** (TPT35), and hence: **conj***y*(not A[*z*] and *y*=**k**)**Pw**. Therefore by APT16: (**exo***o***conj***y*(not A[*o*] and *y*=**k**),*z*)**Pw**, hence by DPT31, DPT55: **exo***o***conj***y*(not A[*o*] and *y*=**k**)(*z*).

•TPT220 if **all***z*(if A[*z*], then 0(*z*)), then **all***x*(if MK(*x*), then **all***z*[**exo***o***conj***y*(not A[*o*] and *y*=**k**)/in *x*/(*z*) iff A[*z*]]).

•TPT221 <0>$_{ES}$(**exo***o***conj***y*(not A[*o*] and *y*=**k**)).

•TPT222 **all***f***all***z***all***x*[if <0>(*f*) and 0(*z*) and MK(*x*), then [**nec**$_{<0>}$(*f*)/in *x*/(*z*) iff **all***y*(if MK(*y*), then *f*/in *y*/(*z*))]].

Proof: Assume: <0>(*f*), 0(*z*), MK(*x*).

(**i**) Assume **nec**$_{<0>}$(*f*)/in *x*/(*z*), hence by DPT56: (**nec**$_{<0>}$(*f*),*z*)P*x*, hence by APT16 and DPT62: **conj***y*((*f*,*z*)≠**t** and *y*=**k**)P*x*, hence: **conj***y*((*f*,*z*)≠**t** and *y*=**k**)≠**k** [because of MK(*x*)], hence: (*f*,*z*)=**t**, hence: **all***y*(if MK(*y*), then (*f*,*z*)P*y* and MK(*y*)), and hence by DPT56: **all***y*(if MK(*y*), then *f*/in *y*/(*z*)).

(**ii**) Assume **all***y*(if MK(*y*), then *f*/in *y*/(*z*)), hence: (*f*,*z*)=**t** [by DPT56, TPT90, TPT36], hence: **conj***y*((*f*,*z*)≠**t** and *y*=**k**)=**t** [by TPT35], hence by APT16, DPT62: (**nec**$_{<0>}$(*f*),*z*)=**t**, hence, because of MK(*x*) and **t**P*x*, by DPT56: **nec**$_{<0>}$(*f*)/in *x*/(*z*).

•TPT223 **all***f***all***z***all***x*(if <0>(*f*) and 0(*z*) and MK(*x*), then [**nec**$_{<0>}$(*f*)/in *x*/(*z*) iff (*f*,*z*)=**t**]).

•TPT224 **all***f***all***z*[if <0>(*f*) and 0(*z*), then ((**nec**$_{<0>}$(*f*),*z*)=**t** iff (*f*,*z*)=**t**) and ((**nec**$_{<0>}$(*f*),*z*)=**k** iff (*f*,*z*)≠**t**)].

•TPT225 **conj**x**some**z(A[z] and xPp[z])=**conj**x**some**z(A[z] and 1(p[z]) and x=p[z]).

Proof: Because of APT2 the predicate in the second conjunctive term implies for all x the predicate in the first; hence by TPT28: **(1) conj**x**some**z(A[z] and 1(p[z]) and x=p[z])**Pconj**x**some**z(A[z] and xPp[z]).

Assume now: QA(x′) and x′**Pconj**x**some**z(A[z] and xPp[z]); assume also: not M(x′). Hence by TPT40: **some**z′**some**z(x′Pz′ and A[z] and z′Pp[z]), hence by APT0, APT1: **some**z(x′Pp[z] and A[z] and 1(p[z]) and p[z]=p[z]), hence: **some**x**some**z(x′Px and A[z] and 1(p[z]) and x=p[z]), hence: **some**x(x′Px and **some**z(A[z] and 1(p[z]) and x=p[z])), hence by TPT40: x′**Pconj**x**some**z(A[z] and 1(p[z]) and x=p[z]). The same result follows trivially in case M(x′).

From the now established general statement we conclude by APT5: **(2)**·**conj**x**some**z(A[z] and xPp[z])**Pconj**x**some**z(A[z] and 1(p[z]) and x=p[z]).

From **(1)** and **(2)** we obtain by APT3 what was to be proved.

•TPT226 **all**f[V(∀(f)) iff **all**z(if 0(z), then f(z))].

Proof: **(i)** Assume V(∀(f)), hence by DPT32 and DPT31: ∀(f)**Pw**. Assume 0(z). According to TPT146: 1((f,z)), hence by APT2: (f,z)P(f,z). Therefore: **some**z′(0(z′) and (f,z)P(f,z′)), hence by TPT18: (f,z)**Pconj**x**some**z′(0(z′) and xP(f,z′)), hence by DPT64: (f,z)P∀(f). Hence from the underlined results by APT1: (f,z)**Pw**, and hence by DPT31, DPT55: f(z). Thus we have deduced from the first assumption: **all**z(if 0(z), then f(z)).

(ii) Assume **all**z(if 0(z), then f(z)); assume also: **some**z(0(z) and xP(f,z)). Hence by the first assumption, DPT55, DPT31, APT1: x**Pw**. Therefore from the first assumption: **all**x(if **some**z(0(z) and xP(f,z)), then x**Pw**), hence by TPT18 [1(**w**) by APT8]: **conj**x**some**z(0(z) and xP(f,z))**Pw**, hence by DPT64, DPT31, DPT32: V(∀(f)).

•TPT227 **all**y[if 1(y), then **all**f(∀(f)Py iff **all**z(if 0(z), then (f,z)Py))].

•TPT228 **all**f[**conj**x**all**z(if 0(z), then xP(f,z))=**disj**x**some**z(0(z) and x=(f,z))].

Proof: By logic alone:

allx[**all**z(if 0(z), then xP(f,z)) iff **all**y(if **some**z(0(z) and y=(f,z)), then xPy)].

Hence by TPT29:

conjx**all**z(if 0(z), then xP(f,z))=**conj**x**all**y(if **some**z(0(z) and y=(f,z)), then xPy)=**conj**x**all**y(if 1(y) and **some**z(if 0(z) and y=(f,z)), then xPy). But the latter is according to TPT63 no other state of affairs than **disj**x**some**z(0(z) and x=(f,z)).

•TPT229 **all**y**all**f(if **some**z(0(z) and (f,z)Py), then ∃(f)Py).

Proof: Assume **some**z(0(z) and (f,z)Py), hence [applying TPT146]: **some**x′[1(x′) and **some**z(0(z) and x′=(f,z)) and x′Py], hence by TPT65: **some**x′[**disj**x**some**z(0(z) and x=(f,z))Px′ and x′Py], hence by APT1: **disj**x**some**z(0(z) and x=(f,z))Py, hence by TPT228 and DPT65: ∃(f)Py.

•TPT230 **all**f[if **some**z(0(z) and f(z)), then V(∃(f))].

•TPT231 **all**y[if MK(y), then **all**f(if ∃(f)Py, then **some**z(0(z) and (f,z)Py))].

Proof: Assume MK(*y*), ∃(*f*)P*y*; hence by DPT26, DPT25, DPT65: **all***x*(if 1(*x*), then *x*P*y* or **neg**(*x*)P*y*) [MX(*y*)] and **conj***x***all***z*(if 0(*z*), then *x*P(*f*,*z*))P*y*, hence by TPT96: (**1**) **all***y*′(1(*y*′) and **all***z*(if 0(*z*), then *y*′P(*f*,*z*)), then *y*′P*y*). Assume now for *reductio*: **all***z*(if 0(*z*), then not (*f*,*z*)P*y*), hence by the underlined result: **all***z*(if 0(*z*), then **neg**((*f*,*z*))P*y*) [1((*f*,*z*)) by TPT146], hence by TPT60: (**2**) **all***z*(if 0(*z*), then **neg**(*y*)P(*f*,*z*)). By (**1**) and (**2**): **neg**(*y*)P*y* - contradicting K(*y*) [by DPT26 from MK(*y*)], since *y*P*y* by APT2 [consider DPT24].
Therefore: **some***z*(0(*z*) and (*f*,*z*)P*y*).

•TPT232 **all***f*[if V(∃(*f*)), then **some***z*(0(*z*) and *f*(*z*))].

•TPT233 **all***y*[if K(*y*) and **all***f*(if ∃(*f*)P*y*, then **some***z*(0(*z*) and (*f*,*z*)P*y*)), then MK(*y*)].

Proof: Assume: K(*y*) and **all***f*(if ∃(*f*)P*y*, then **some***z*(0(*z*) and (*f*,*z*)P*y*)). According to DPT26, MX(*y*) remains to be shown for obtaining MK(*y*). According to DPT25, MX(*y*) is shown, when **all***x*(if 1(*x*), then *x*P*y* or **neg**(*x*)P*y*) has been deduced from the assumption.
Assume, therefore, 1(*x*).
Strategy of proof: A property *f* has to be found which is such that its saturation by a certain individual is *x*, its saturation by a certain *other* individual, and by all other individuals, **neg**(*x*). Then we have ∃(*f*)=**t**, and hence: ∃(*f*)P*y*, therefore by assumption: **some***z*(0(*z*) and (*f*,*z*)P*y*). But, by construction of *f*, (*f*,*z*)=*x* or (*f*,*z*)=**neg**(*x*). Hence: *x*P*y* or **neg**(*x*)P*y*.

Lemma 1:
all*f*[if **some***y*′(1(*y*′) and **some***z*(0(*z*) and *y*′=(*f*,*z*)) and **some***z*(0(*z*) and **neg**(*y*′)=(*f*,*z*)), then **disj***x*′**some***z*(0(*z*) and *x*′=(*f*,*z*))=**t**].
Proof: Assume: 1(*y*′) and **some***z*(0(*z*) and *y*′=(*f*,*z*)) and **some***z*(0(*z*) and **neg**(*y*′)=(*f*,*z*)); hence by TPT65: **disj***x*′**some***z*(0(*z*) and *x*′=(*f*,*z*))P*y*′ and **disj***x*′**some***z*(0(*z*) and *x*′=(*f*,*z*))P**neg**(*y*′); hence by TPT46, TPT52: M(**disj***x*′**some***z*(0(*z*) and *x*′=(*f*,*z*))), hence by TPT32: **disj***x*′**some***z*(0(*z*) and *x*′=(*f*,*z*))=**t**.
Lemma 2:
all*f***all***z*(if 0(*z*) and *f*=**disj**$_{<0>}${**conj**$_{<0>}$(**b**(*x*),**i**(*z*)),**conj**$_{<0>}$(**b**(**neg**(*x*)),**d**(*z*))}, then (*f*,*z*)=*x* and **all***z*′(0(*z*′) and *z*′≠*z*, then (*f*,*z*′)=**neg**(*x*))).
Proof: Assume: 0(*z*) and *f*=**disj**$_{<0>}${... *x*,*z* ...}.
(**conj**$_{<0>}$(**b**(*x*),**i**(*z*)),*z*)=*x* [by the corollary of TPT178, and TPT160, TPT171, **conj**(*x*,**t**)=*x*].
(**conj**$_{<0>}$(**b**(**neg**(*x*)),**d**(*z*)),*z*)=**k** [by the corollary of TPT178, and TPT160, TPT169, **conj**(**neg**(*x*),**k**)=**k**].
Therefore: (*f*,*z*)=(**disj**$_{<0>}${... *x*,*z* ...},*z*)=**disj**(*x*,**k**)=*x* (applying the corollary of TPT179).
Assume now: 0(*z*′) and *z*′≠*z*. Hence:
(**conj**$_{<0>}$(**b**(*x*),**i**(*z*)),*z*′)=**k** [by the corollary of TPT178, and TPT160, TPT171, **conj**(*x*,**k**)=**k**].

(**conj**$_{<0>}$(**b**(**neg**(*x*)),**d**(*z*)),*z*′)=**neg**(*x*) [by the corollary of TPT178, and TPT160, TPT169, **conj**(**neg**(*x*),**t**)=**neg**(*x*)].
Therefore: (*f*,*z*′)=(**disj**$_{<0>}${... *x*,*z* ...},*z*′)=**disj**(**k**,**neg**(*x*))=**neg**(*x*).

By APT20, TPT193: **some***k***some***z*′(0(*k*) and 0(*z*′) and *z*′≠*k*). Consider the property **disj**$_{<0>}${**conj**$_{<0>}$(**b**(*x*),**i**(*k*)),**conj**$_{<0>}$(**b**(**neg**(*x*)),**d**(*k*))}, in short: f[*x*,*k*]. By *Lemma* 2: (f[*x*,*k*],*k*)=*x* and **all***z*′′(if 0(*z*′′) and *z*′′≠*k*, then (f[*x*,*k*],*z*′′)=**neg**(*x*)). Hence: 1(*x*) and **some***r*(0(*r*) and (f[*x*,*k*],*r*)=*x*) and **some***r*(0(*r*) and (f[*x*,*k*],*r*)=**neg**(*x*)), hence by *Lemma* 1: **disj***x*′**some***r*(0(*r*) and *x*′=(f[*x*,*k*],*r*))=**t**, hence by TPT228, DPT65: ∃(f[*x*,*k*])=**t**. Therefore according to the first assumption: ∃(f[*x*,*k*])P*y* and **some**(0(*z*) and (f[*x*,*k*],*z*)P*y*). (f[*x*,*k*],*z*)=*x* or (f[*x*,*k*],*z*)=**neg**(*x*), according to the underlined result, because 0(*z*) and (*z*=*k* or *z*≠*k*). Hence: *x*P*y* or **neg**(*x*)P*y*.

SYSTEM IOU

•AX-L0 if not **one**xA[x], then **the**xA[x]=**o**.
•AX-P0 - AX-P9: APT0 - APT9.
•AX-C0: APT13.
•AX-C1: APT10.
•AX-C2 **all**x(if 1(x), then E*(x)).
•AX-C3 **all**x(if 0(x), then E*(x)).
•AX-S0 **all**x[if 0(x) or 1(x) or not E*(x), then not E*((x,t_1,...,t_n))], for all natural numbers n with $n\geq 1$.
•AX-S1 if E*((t,t_1,...,t_n)), then not E*((t,t'_1,...,t'_k)), for all natural numbers k and n such that $n\geq 1$, and $k>n$ or $1\leq k<n$.
•AX-S2 if **some**x_1...**some**$x_k$$T$((t,$x_1$,...,$x_k$)), then **all**$x_1$...**all**$x_k$[if E*((t,$x_1$,...,$x_k$)), then T((t,x_1,...,x_k))], T being any generalized type.
•AX-S3 **all**f**all**g(if k-FUNC(f) and k-FUNC(g) and **all**y_1...**all**y_k((f,y_1,...,y_k)= (g,y_1,...,y_k)), then f=g).
•AX-E0 if **all**x_1...**all**x_k(if E*(f[x_1,...,x_k]), then T(f[x_1,...,x_k])) and E*(**ex**o_1...o_kf[o_1,...,o_k]),
then **all**x_1...**all**x_k(f[x_1,...,x_k]=(**ex**o_1...o_kf[o_1,...,o_k],x_1,...,x_k)), T being any generalized type.
•AX-I0 if E*(**that**A), then 1(**that**A).
•AX-I1 if 1(**that**A), then (O(**that**A) iff A).
•AX-R0 <0>1(**sr**).
•AX-R1: APT20.
•AX-A0 **all**x[if T(x), then (AE(x) iff AET(x))], for every generalized type T.
•AX-A1 not AE(**o**).
•AX-A2 if k-FUNC(t), then [AE(t) iff **some**x_1...**some**x_k(AE(x_1) and AE(x_k) and AE((t,x_1,...,x_k)))].

•DEF0 E*(t) := t≠**o**.
•DEF1 - DEF39: DPT1 - DPT39.
•DEF40 k-FUNC(t) := **some**x_1...**some**x_kE*((t,x_1,...,x_k)) [for all natural numbers k with $k\geq 1$, k being the Arabic numeral corresponding to k].
•DEF41 k-RELT(t) := **some**x_1...**some**x_k1((t,x_1,...,x_k)).
•DEF42 PROP(t) := 1-RELT(t).
•DEF43 <T_1,...,T_k>T_{k+1}(t) := **all**x_1...**all**x_k[T_{k+1}((t,x_1,...,x_k)) iff T_1(x_1) and ... and T_k(x_k)] and **some**x_1...**some**$x_k$$T_{k+1}$((t,$x_1$,...,$x_k$)), for all generalized types T_1, ..., T_k, T_{k+1}.

•DEF44 SET(t) := PROP(t) and **all**y(if E*((t,y)), then **(t,**y**)=t** or **(t,**y**)=k**).
•DEF45 t**(**$t_1,\ldots,t_k$**)** := O((t,$t_1,\ldots,t_k$)).
•DEF46 t′$\in_s$t := SET(t) and **(**t,t′**)=t**.
•DEF47 SSET(t) := SET(t) and **all**yE*((t,y)).
•DEF48 λxA[x] := **ex**o**conj**y(not A[o] and y=**k**).
•DEF49 $\lambda x_1\ldots x_k$R[$x_1,\ldots,x_k$] := **ex**$o_1\ldots o_k$**conj**y(not R[$o_1,\ldots,o_k$] and y=**k**).
•DEF50 <$t_1,\ldots,t_k$> := $\lambda x_1\ldots x_k$(x_1=t_1 and ... and x_k=t_k).
•DEF51 $\Diamond$A := 1(**that**A) and **that**A$\neq$**k**.
•DEF52
(i) AE0(t) := **sr**(t); AE1(t) := O(t).
(ii) AE<$T_1,\ldots,T_k$>T_{k+1}(t) := <$T_1,\ldots,T_k$>T_{k+1}(t) and **some**x_1...**some**x_k[AET_1(x_1) and ... and AET_k(x_k) and AET_{k+1}((t,$x_1,\ldots,x_k$))].

•THE1 **all**x(if k-FUNC(x), then E*(x) and not 1(x) and not 0(x)), for all Arabic numerals k, starting with "1".
•THE2 **all**x(if k-FUNC(x), then not n-FUNC(x)), for all Arabic numerals k and n - starting with "1" - that are different from each other.
•THE3 **all**x(if k-RELT(x), then k-FUNC(x)), for all Arabic numerals k, starting with "1".
•THE4 if k-RELT(t), then **all**x_1...**all**x_k[if E*((t,$x_1,\ldots,x_k$)), then 1((t,$x_1,\ldots,x_k$))].
•THE5 **all**x(if T(x), then E*(x)), for all *generalized types T*.
Proof: By induction on the length of T. For the generalized types of smallest length - those of length 1: the types "1" and "0" - THE5 is simply AX-C2 and AX-C3. Suppose now THE5 is proved for all generalized types with a length that is smaller or equal to the natural number n, with $n\geq 1$, and suppose the length of the generalized type T is n+1. Hence T has the form <$T_1,\ldots,T_k$>T_{k+1} (for some natural number $k\geq 1$). Assume T(x), hence according to DEF43: **some**y_1...**some**$y_k$$T_{k+1}$(($x$,$y_1,\ldots,y_k$)), hence by induction-assumption, since T_{k+1} is a generalized type of smaller length than T: E*((x,$y_1,\ldots,y_k$)), and hence by AX-S0: E*(x).
•THE6 **all**x(if <$T_1,\ldots,T_k$>(x), then k-RELT(x)), for all *ordinary types* $T_1,\ldots,T_k$.
Proof: Assume <$T_1,\ldots,T_k$>(x), $T_1,\ldots,T_k$ being ordinary types. Hence <$T_1,\ldots,T_k$> is an ordinary type, and therefore the abbreviation of a generalized type ending with ">1"; hence according to DEF43: **some**y_1...**some**y_k1((x,$y_1,\ldots,y_k$)), hence by DEF41: k-RELT(x).
•THE7 **all**x(if T(x), then not T'(x)), T and T' being *different ordinary types*.
Proof: By induction on the sum of the *type-degrees* of T and T'. The type-degree of "1" and "0" is zero; the type-degree of the ordinary type <$T_1,\ldots,T_k$> is the maximum of the type-degrees of $T_1,\ldots,T_k$ plus 1.
Inductionbasis: For the ordinary types "1" and "0" THE7 is simply a consequence of AX-C1.

Inductionassumption: Let THE7 be proved for all different ordinary types T and T' such that the sum of the type-degrees of T and T' is equal or less than the natural number n.
Inductionstep: Let T and T' be different ordinary types such that the sum of their type-degrees is n+1. Assume for *reductio*: $T(x)$ and $T'(x)$.
Consequently *both* T and T' must be *complex* ordinary types: that only one of them is a complex ordinary type contradicts the *assumption for reductio*: if, for example, T=<T_1,...,T_k> and T' is "0" or "1", then from the *assumption* by THE6: k-RELT(x) and (0(x) or 1(x)) - but this contradicts "**all**x(if k-RELT(x), then not 0(x) and not 1(x))" which is an immediate consequence of THE3 and THE1.
Therefore, T=<T_1,...,T_k> and T'=<T'_1,...,T'_m> for some natural numbers $k,m\geq 1$; and hence by THE6 and the *assumption for reductio*: k-RELT(x) and m-RELT(x). Hence: $k=m$; for *otherwise* k and m would be different Arabic numerals, and we would have a contradiction to the theorem for relations corresponding to THE2. (That theorem is a consequence of THE3 and THE2.)
Therefore: T=<T_1,...,T_k> and T'=<T'_1,...,T'_k>, for some natural number $k\geq 1$.
Hence, since both T and T' are abbreviations of 1-types, from "$T(x)$ and $T'(x)$" according to DEF43: **some**y_1...**some**y_k1((x,y_1,...,y_k)), and therefore, according to DEF43: (*) **some**y_1...**some**y_k($T_1(y_1)$ and ... and $T_k(y_k)$ and $T'_1(y_1)$ and ... and $T'_k(y_k)$). Since T is different from T', T_i must be *different* from T'_i for some natural number i with $1\leq i\leq k$. But both T_i and T'_i are ordinary types such that the sum of their type-degrees is at most n. Hence according to *inductionassumption*: **no**y($T_i(y)$ and $T'_i(y)$) - contradicting (*).
•THE8 **all**x(if <T_1,...,T_k>$T_{k+1}(x)$, then k-FUNC(x)), for all generalized types T_1,...,T_k,T_{k+1}.
Proof: Assume the antecedent and presupposition of THE8; hence by DEF43: **some**y_1...**some**$y_k$$T_{k+1}$(($x$,$y_1$,...,$y_k$)), hence by THE5: E*(($x$,$y_1$,...,$y_k$)), hence by DEF40: k-FUNC(x).
•THE9 **all**x(if $T(x)$, then not $T'(x)$), T and T' being *different generalized types*.
Proof: By induction on the sum of the lengths of T and T': l(T) and l(T').
THE9 is a consequence of AX-C1 for the generalized types "0" and "1"; hence THE9 is proved for all different generalized types T and T' such that l(T)+l(T')=2.
Let THE9 be proved for all different generalized types T and T' such that 2≤l(T)+l(T')≤n (n a natural number).
Let T and T' be different generalized types such that l(T)+l(T')=n+1. Assume for *reductio*: $T(x)$ and $T'(x)$.
Hence both T and T' must be complex generalized types; this is seen as in the proof of THE7, using THE1, and THE8 instead of THE6. Thus, T=<T_1,...,T_k>T_{k+1} and T'=<T'_1,...,T'_m>T'_{m+1}, for some natural numbers $k,m\geq 1$.
If $T_{k+1}=T'_{m+1}$, then the proof proceeds as in THE7, using THE2, and THE8 instead of THE6.

If $T_{k+1}\neq T'_{m+1}$, then by the *assumption for reductio* and DEF43: **(1)** $\mathbf{some}y_1...\mathbf{some}y_kT_{k+1}((x,y_1,...,y_k))$, and **(2)** $\mathbf{some}z_1...\mathbf{some}z_mT'_{m+1}((x,z_1,...,z_m))$. According to AX-S1 and THE5 we obtain from **(1)** and **(2)**: $k=m$. From **(1)** we obtain by AX-S2: $\mathbf{all}y_1...\mathbf{all}y_k[\text{if } E^*((x,y_1,...,y_k)), \text{ then } T_{k+1}((x,y_1,...,y_k))]$, hence - since we have $E^*((x,z_1,...,z_m))$ by THE5 from **(2)**, and since $k=m$ -: $T_{k+1}((x,z_1,...,z_m))$. Thus: the generalized types T_{k+1} and T'_{m+1}, although different, apply to a common entity. But this contradicts the *inductionassumption*, since $2\leq l(T_{k+1})+l(T'_{m+1})<n$.

•THE10 $\mathbf{all}x\mathbf{all}y(\text{if SET}(x) \text{ and SET}(y) \text{ and } \mathbf{all}z[E^*((x,z)) \text{ iff } E^*((y,z))]$ and $\mathbf{all}z(z\in_Sx \text{ iff } z\in_Sy), \text{ then } x=y)$.

Proof: Assume the antecedent of THE10; hence by DEF44, DEF46, DEF0: PROP(x) and PROP(y) and $\mathbf{all}z(\text{if } (x,z)\neq o, \text{ then } (x,z)=t \text{ or } (x,z)=k)$ and $\mathbf{all}z(\text{if } (y,z)\neq o, \text{ then } (y,z)=t \text{ or } (y,z)=k)$ and $\mathbf{all}z((x,z)=t \text{ iff } (y,z)=t)$ and $\mathbf{all}z((x,z)\neq o \text{ iff } (y,z)\neq o)$. If $(x,z)=t$, we have: $(x,z)=(y,z)$. Assume now: $(x,z)\neq t \text{ and } (x,z)\neq o$; hence: $(y,z)\neq t \text{ and } (y,z)\neq o$; therefore: $(x,z)=k \text{ and } (y,z)=k$, hence: $(x,z)=(y,z)$. Assume finally: $(x,z)\neq t \text{ and } (x,z)=o$; hence $(y,z)=o$, and therefore: $(x,z)=(y,z)$. Thus: $\mathbf{all}z((x,z)=(y,z))$. Therefore, since we also have 1-FUNC(x) and 1-FUNC(y) [by DEF42, THE3 from PROP(x), PROP(y)], according to AX-S3: $x=y$.

•THE11 $\mathbf{all}x\mathbf{all}y(\text{if SSET}(x) \text{ and SSET}(y) \text{ and } \mathbf{all}z(z\in_Sx \text{ iff } z\in_Sy), \text{ then } x=y)$.

•THE12 if $E^*(\lambda xA[x])$, then $\mathbf{all}z(\mathbf{conj}y(\text{not } A[z] \text{ and } y=k)=(\lambda xA[x],z))$.

•THE13 if SSET($\lambda xA[x]$), then $\mathbf{all}z(z\in_S\lambda xA[x] \text{ iff } A[z])$.

•THE14   if $E^*(\mathbf{exo}_1...o_k\mathbf{that}R[o_1,...,o_k])$ and $\mathbf{all}x_1...\mathbf{all}x_kE^*(\mathbf{that}R[x_1,...,x_k])$, then $\mathbf{all}x_1...\mathbf{all}x_k(\mathbf{exo}_1...o_k\mathbf{that}R[o_1,...,o_k](x_1,...,x_k) \text{ iff } R[x_1,...,x_k])$.

Proof: Assume the antecedent of THE14; from it by AX-I0: **(1)** $\mathbf{all}x_1...\mathbf{all}x_k1(\mathbf{that}R[x_1,...,x_k])$. Hence by AX-E0:
(2) $\mathbf{all}x_1...\mathbf{all}x_k((\mathbf{exo}_1...o_k\mathbf{that}R[o_1,...,o_k],x_1,...,x_k)=\mathbf{that}R[x_1,...,x_k])$.
According to AX-I1 because of **(1)**: O($\mathbf{that}R[x_1,...,x_k]$) iff $R[x_1,...,x_k]$; hence by **(2)**: O$((\mathbf{exo}_1...o_k\mathbf{that}R[o_1,...,o_k],x_1,...,x_k))$ iff $R[x_1,...,x_k]$; hence according to DEF45: $\mathbf{exo}_1...o_k\mathbf{that}R[o_1,...,o_k](x_1,...,x_k)$ iff $R[x_1,...,x_k]$.

•THE15 if $<0>1(\mathbf{exo}\mathbf{that}A[o])$ and $\mathbf{all}x(\text{if } A[x], \text{ then } 0(x))$, then $\mathbf{all}x(\mathbf{exo}\mathbf{that}A[o](x) \text{ iff } A[x])$.

Proof: Assume the antecedent of THE15.
(i) Assume $\mathbf{exo}\mathbf{that}A[o](x)$, hence by DEF45: O$((\mathbf{exo}\mathbf{that}A[o],x))$, and by DEF31, AX-P0: $1((\mathbf{exo}\mathbf{that}A[o],x))$. Because of $<0>1(\mathbf{exo}\mathbf{that}A[o])$ by THE5: $E^*(\mathbf{exo}\mathbf{that}A[o])$, and by AX-I0: $\mathbf{all}x(\text{if } E^*(\mathbf{that}A[x]), \text{ then } 1(\mathbf{that}A[x]))$. Therefore by AX-E0: $\mathbf{all}x((\mathbf{exo}\mathbf{that}A[o],x)=\mathbf{that}A[x])$, hence by the two underlined results and AX-I1: $A[x]$.
(ii) Assume $A[x]$, hence [according to the antecedent of THE15]: $0(x)$, and hence: $1((\mathbf{exo}\mathbf{that}A[o],x))$ [by $<0>1(\mathbf{exo}\mathbf{that}A[o])$ and DEF43]. As in **(i)** we have $\mathbf{all}x((\mathbf{exo}\mathbf{that}A[o],x)=\mathbf{that}A[x])$, hence by the two underlined results and AX-I1: O$((\mathbf{exo}\mathbf{that}A[o],x))$, hence by DEF45: $\mathbf{exo}\mathbf{that}A[o](x)$.

INDEX OF SUBJECTS

abstraction, 14
λ- (applied to predicates), 310f,313ff
abstractness, 14,21
accessibility-relation, 86f,294
accident, 139,143f,146,149,150
individual -, 12f,143f,149
universal -, 139,143f,149,165
actual existence, 15,37,84ff,88f,97,112f, 116,132f,140,145ff,148ff,154ff,157,161, 163f,169ff,172ff,176ff,179f,182ff,187, 193,211,217,65f,271,320ff,323f
at a time, 193,198,205,209ff,212,214ff, 217
of ("normal") individuals, 271ff,276ff, 290,320ff
of Leibniz-individuals, 272f,275f,278f (see in addition: **primary actuality**),
of properties of individuals, 271ff,321 (see in addition: **actuality of properties**),
of states of affairs, 320ff (see mainly: **obtaining of states of affairs**)
of typed functions, 320f
source/recipient of -, 323f
actualism, 85f,156
for individuals, 172,277f
for Leibniz-individuals, 278
for Meinongian objects, 182
actuality-determined individual(s), 199,262,268
actuality of properties (of individuals) (AP(*f*)), 145ff,148ff,154ff,157,160,163f, 170,172f, 178ff,182 (see in addition: **primary actuality)**
analytical implication (ontological concept), 28,35ff,38,42,47,53,68,75,80,87, 97,109,121,123f,291,295 (see in addition: intensional **part)**
and logical deducibility, 292,295
analytical implication(s) (semantical concept), 28,35,68,247
application, see: **exemplification**
atom(s), 29ff,32f,63,79,118,125,132,195
in a wider sense: quasi-atom(s), non-compositum(-a) (QA(x),QA$_{<0>}$(x)), 31ff, 51ff,54f,58,63,70,74ff,118,175,195f, 239,241,251,293 (see in addition: **element)**
in Tarski's sense, 62f,66
in the sence of physics, 195
atomism, 55,75
postulate of -, 66
attribute(s), 2f,11,22,35,39,116,304
algebra of (first-order monadic) -, 2
of individuals, 15
polyadic -, 213
bases of elements, 208f,211
bivalence,
ontological -, 36,90,98f,101,115
semantical -, 36,99,101,319
body(-ies), 202,215
(Boolean) algebra,
atomistic -, 66
extended (complete) -, 62,65f
ordinary -, 67
power-set -, 127,217
category(-ies) (ontological), 9,15,128, 134,199f,208f,221,223f,226,230,253,303, 324
class(es), 21f,233,310
as groups, 214
completeness (mereological), see under **whole**
compositum, 32f
compossibility, 83,176ff,179
concatenation, see: **saturation**
concept, 27,35,135,175
categorial -, 15
essentially applying -, 159f
in Frege's sense, 10,27,175,315
Leibnizian -, 162,175f,180
individual Leibnizian -, 143, 162f, 176, 178
objective -, 269
transcendental -, 15
conceptualism, 2,14
conjunction (conj,conj$_{<0>}$), 42,45,47f,58, 62,67,82,90,94,99,102ff, 105,111,115, 123,137,155,169ff,172,174,198,204,

209ff,240f,243,246,251,254ff,258,261,273ff,279,284,289,291ff,320
  big - (**conj**x,$\mathbf{conj}_{<0>}f$), 46ff,49,56ff,59f,62,69ff,72,86f,90,93,96,104f,115,126,137,141,143,150,155,171,175f,181,183,186,191,193f,202,205,208,210,232,235ff,241,243f,247,252,254,256,258f,261,264,283f,287,289f,309f,316,320,323
consistence, 73f,98,114,164,182,184,291f
  of one property with another, 170ff,173,184,273f
constituents, 51,79,128,143
contingency, 110,115,163,245,249
  for Leibniz, 162,175
  for Lewis, 162f
  -functor for properties, 289
continuant(s), 200,204,262
  modal, 262,270
counterpart(s), 163,183,259,261,265ff,268f,278f

definite description, 19,164,173,301
density, 125
designator(s), **rigid/non-rigid**, 28,88f,110,164,171,174,271,273f,279,318f,323
determinism, 161f,175
dimension (''boundedness''),
  modal -, 199,220,262f
  spatial -, 199ff,262f
  temporal -, 189f,199ff,203f,262f
dimensions (in the usual sense)
  in space (three), 194,200,263
  in space-time (four), 200,204f
discreteness, 123ff
disjunction (**disj**,$\mathbf{disj}_{<0>}$), 42,45,48,67ff,82,90f,99, 103ff,108,111,115,137,141f,155,240f,243,254,284,295
  big - (**disj**x,$\mathbf{disj}_{<0>}f$), 69ff,72,87,90f,104f,115,137,155,169,171,173,177,179f,272ff,279,283f,290,292
duration, 199ff

elementariness, see: **element(s)**
element(s) (*simpliciter* or *of something*),
  mereological -, 52,59f,62f,66,74ff,77ff,81,119ff,122f,124,126ff,156,175f,180,192f,195f,206,208ff,211,241,251f
  set-theoretical -, 3,63,65,126f,177f,206,208,233,280,308ff,313
ens successivum, 215f
entity(-ies),
  abstract -, 14,21,36f,40,107,157,208
  Boolean -, 67
  concrete -, 37,40,208
  fictional -, 183
  ''formal'' -, 312,314
  fundamental -, 321f
  genuine -, 301ff,305f,310f,314ff,319
  immanent -, 12
  linguistic/non-linguistic -, 301
  ontologically relative -, 208
  plural -, 208,214
  saturated (complete) -, 9,13,39,302
  transcendent -, 12,324
  typed -, 322f
  unified -, 213f
  unsaturated (incomplete) -, 3,10,13,39,225,229,302
essence (of an individual), 247ff,250f,254,270
essential property ***of***, 247,249,254,268,271,280,289
event, 12,40,136,149,200
exemplification (monadic: **of a property**), 2,133f,137ff,140,147f,158,162f,165,170,175,177,214,229,247,252ff,256,258f,268,271ff,280,283ff, 288,290f,293,308,317,320 (see in addition: **inherence**),
  existential -, 146,148
  in a possible world, 247f,256ff,259,261,264,268,270,272f,277f,281f,285,288
  <0>-, 253,257,259
  1- and 2-, 259,261, 272ff,275
exemplification (polyadic: **of a relation**), 308,317
existence,
  actual -, see: **actual existence**
  as more general than *actual existence*, 277
  expressed by a predicate, 12,19,86
  numerical -, 11f,86,116,119f,133,150,197,291,312ff
  proofs of (numerical) -, 291f,295
explanation, 323f
explication, 34f
extensionalism, 80,84,158,177f,297
  set-theoretical -, 297,312f
extension (spatial, temporal, modal), 190,199f,262f,270
extension(s) (**extensional entities**), 3,117
  of a predicate, 135,272,274,285,316,319
  of (*corresponding to*) a property (*simpliciter* or in a possible world), 135,158,280,282f
extraction, 13f,21,141,226ff,232,243,296,309ff

and predicates, 285f,310,314ff
bases of -, 14,141
in a wide/in a narrow sense, 14
monadic -, 226,300
objects of -, 13f,141
polyadic -, 300f
products of -, 13f,141
residue of -, 226f

fact(s),
as objects of science, 1,3
as obtaining states of affairs, 20,37,44, 73,88f
conjunctive -, 44
disjunctive -, 44
external -, 97
for us, 97,101
fundamental - about everything there is, 1f,7,9,36
linguistic -, 10,18
negative -, 44
ontological -, 18,323
the sum of them as the world, 73,80,88, 97f
Flux Argument, 198,204
function(s), 3,12ff,22,39,229,296f,300, 302ff,305ff,308ff,311,320ff,324
extensional -, 117
IS-, 296

geometry, 205
group, 198,206ff,209ff,212,214
-identity, 214
member of a -, 198,206ff,211,214

haecceity (of an individual), 248ff,251, 254
having of a property, see: **exemplification (of a property)**
human beings, 208ff,211

identity, 15,21,25,186f,190f,198f,202ff, 210f,225,231,233,236f,257,270,280ff,283, 296,308f,315,317f,322
laws of -, 2,165,317
of entities with complex types, 322
of individuals, 322
of properties of individuals, see under **properties of individuals**
of states of affairs, see under **states of affairs**
the property of self-, 307,313
implication (ontological functor), 68,99, 102
implication (sentence-connective), 68,102
independence,
-concepts for states of affairs, 78f
of AP5 from AP1 - AP4, 53f
of AP5 from AP1 - AP4 and AP6, 58
of AP5 from AP1 - AP4, AP6 and D′, 66
of AP6 from AP1 - AP5, 58
of AP5# from AP1 - AP4, AP6, 196
individuals, 2f,7f,13ff,21f,39,51,73,83ff, 86,116,128,133f,141ff,144,149,157f,189, 199,201,203f,213,229f,297,300,312,324
abstract (or non-concrete) -, 12,14,21, 156f,200f,216f,312
in a wide or global sense, 12,136,183f, 217,220,261f,324
in the Leibnizian (2-)sense, 134,137ff, 140,142ff,145f,150f,154,156,158,161ff, 169f,172f,175ff,178ff,182ff,185,187,220, 258f,261f,264f,267ff,271ff,274ff,278f, 296f,313,324
in the normal (**1**-)sense ($0(x)$), 133,185, 220,223ff,226f,231f,235,239f,243ff,246ff, 249,251ff,254ff,257ff,261f,264f,268ff, 271ff,274ff,277f,280f,285,289ff,292f, 296f,300,302,305,307,310,313ff,317,321f, 324
material (*simpliciter*) -, 198,202,211, 263
momentary (*simpliciter*) -, 191,203,216
momentary material, e.g. t_0-, 190ff, 193ff,196ff,199f,202ff,205,211f,216f
primary -, 117
temporally dimensioned material -, 204
time-free (*simpliciter*) -, 189,200f,216
time-free material -, 189ff,192f,198ff, 202ff,205f,208ff,211f,214ff,217
with and without spatial dimension, 200f
with and without temporal dimension, 199ff,203f
individuation, 183f,231,248
individuo-properties, 13,149,253
inference, 3,117
its logical form, 4
its ontological interpretation, 5f,102
inherence (*simpliciter*), 138ff,144,146ff, 149ff,152f,158ff,161ff,164f,169,174,176, 180,184,272ff,275
existential -, 146ff,150f,160f,184
inherence-theory of exemplification, 138,147,161,173,259

intending (semantically), 9,11f,20,34,36f, 39,105,133,213,285ff,291,295
intension(s) (intensional entities), 3,9,20f,34ff,37f,39f,75,93,117,135,159, 285,291,317
coarse-grained -, 37,39f,47,53,79,229, 231,250,282,296
fine-grained -, 37ff,40,250
first - (see also: **properties of individuals**), 139,145ff,148,150,154,156,162, 164f,167,173,175ff,178f,181f,314
of a predicate, 291f,316f,319
of a statement (sentence), 34ff,37,39,75, 93,292,295
intensional contexts, 286,317f
intensionalism, 281,314
intensional isomorphism, 8
intentionality, 183
interpretation,
of a logical form, 4f
of Boolean Algebra based on intensions, 45,175
of AP1 - AP6 based on numbers, 53f, 58,66
of AP1 - AP6 based on subsets of a set, 25,47,53,57f,82,166,189,206
of AP1 - AP6 based on groups, 206,209
of LP, 25,37f,134,138,189ff,192,206, 209,211,221
of LPT1 (and adaptation of previous results), 221ff
of extended PT1, 300
ontological - of truth-functional tautologies), 99
verifying AP1 - AP4 and AP6, but un-Boolean, 76
intuitionism, 291,295

language (natural, ordinary), 1,4,12 17f,20f,51,141,182,203f,285,287,319
as tool of cognition, 1,17
its core structures and ontology, 1ff,9, 12ff,14f,17
languages (formal and semi-formal),
L and LP, 24f,37f,99f,138
LP with "*L*", 159
LP with "$=^{w}$", 176
language for the mereology of material individuals, 211f
LPT1, 220,225f,288
that are extensions of LPT1, 300f
LIOU, 301
PL (of truth-functional propositional logic), 99f
MPL (of S5-modal propositional logic), 100
law,
logical -, 117
of formal validity, 3ff,6
of the reciprocity of intension and extension, 135
of truth and falsity, 90f,103ff,107f,115, 290,293
ontological -, 5f
ontological - of excluded middle, 98
ontological - of non-contradiction, 94
Löwenheim-Skolem Theorem, 127
logic,
and ontology, 5ff,293
and semantics, 4ff
as the science of the laws of truth, 107
classical -, 98,116,292,295
formal -, 3ff,6f
free -, 116
modal - (S5), 159ff,174
modern -, 3
philosophical -, 3

manifolds, 208,213f
maximal consistence (MK(x),$MK_{<0>}(x)$), 73ff,76f,80f,83f,98,104f,112f,119,121, 124,128,134,137ff,141ff,144f,151,156, 158,161,175f,181ff,187,248,251f,255ff, 258,261,264f,267f,279,291f,295f
(of a property) centered in a possible world y, 258
(of a property) centered in **w**, 257f,262
maximality, 73f,97,114,164,182,184,294f
meaning(s), 8,11,20f,27,37,39f
mereological essentialism, 215
mereology,
classical -, 196f
concepts of -, 29,31
extensional -, 32,197
Goodman's -, 129
in a general sense, 26,129,135
Leśniewskian -, 63
of groups, 209
of individuals, 51,189
of material t_0-individuals, 195f
of properties, 51
of states of affairs, 51
metaphysics, 2,94
minimality (M(x), **t**, $M_{<0>}(x)$, $\mathbf{t}_{<0>}$), 29ff, 33,42,48,68,80ff,86,93ff,96,99f,102, 108ff,112,114f,118,127f,137,155,172,

192,195,209,235ff,239,245ff,249,251,254,284,287ff,292,312ff,315,319,323f
monad, 178,180
mutabilia/immutabilia, 200f

name(s) (see in addition: **term(s)**, **designator(s)**), 7,9f,12ff,19f,151,153
  empty -, 64,213
  fundamental -, 12
  general -, 63f
  individual -, 63
  non-empty -, 63
necessity,
  -concept for properties of individuals, 155f
  -concept for states of affairs, 81f,87,93ff,110f,245,249
  conceptual - (expressed by the operator *L*), 159ff,162ff,173f,181,183,202,215,271,317,323f
  -functors for properties, 288f,294
  -functors for states of affairs, 86f,100,108,115,294
negation,
  first -, 42,48,60
  second -, 42,48,60
  simpliciter (**neg**,**neg**$_{<0>}$), 43,48,53,61,67ff,73ff,76,82,87,90f,94f,97,99,103f,110f,115,122,127f,137,141f,154f,170,175f,243,245,249,254,284,288f,293,319
  Tarskian -, 66
Neo-Platonic *One*, 164,324
nominalism, 2,9ff,19,32f,73,201,233,312
Nothing,
  (first sense), 206,209ff,212,216f
  (second sense: **o**), 301f,312f,321,324
null-element, 51,129,196f
null individual, 51,196
number(s), 3,10f,14,22,157,203,208,213,296f
  -properties: see under **property**

objects,
  as *individuals*, 277
  as *saturated entities*, 3,9ff,13,107
  as *entities*, 11
  Meinongian -, 19,181ff,184,186f,217,220,324
obtaining of states of affairs (O(*x*)), 82,88f,92ff,95ff,98,109f,113,115ff,126,154,170ff,174,247,253,271,277,287,308,313,316,320f,323
  in a possible world, 86,138,247,319
Ockham's Razor, 186,199
ontological argument(s), 150,152,169,171,272
ontological commitments, 312
ontological priority, 13,322
ontological square, 143f
ontology, 1
  aims of, 199
  and being *qua* being, 1
  and logic, 3,7,38,99f,105f,108,115ff
  and metaphysics, 2,94
  and natural science, 18
  and perception, 13f
  and philosophy, 15f
  and semantics, 3f,18f,90,105,141
  and scientific progress, 2
  and the Middle Ages, 2
  classical -, 98
  full -, 300
  intensional/extensional -, 117
  its field of reference, 1
  its history, 2f,144
  its language and logic, 7f,116
  its subject-matter, 1,7,94
  Leśniewskian, 63f
ordered pair(s), 225,256,262,264f,297,314f
ordered sequence(s), 315

part(s),
  as constituent, 51
  of a group, 208ff,211f
  central axioms for the concept, 24ff,43,190
  defined via elementhood, 209f
  extensional -, 132f,135,158ff
  globally conceived -, 135,220f
  intensional -, 6,40f,89,93,121,132ff,135ff,138,142,144ff,158ff,161,176f,181,184,186,221,231,235,239,241,247,255,257,262,289f,292
  proper -, 24f,32,38,51f,79,123f,139,144,193,195f,205,208,210,215f
  existence-essential spatial -, 215f
  spatial -, 144,189ff,192ff,195f,198,204,206,210ff,214ff
  temporal, 189,203f
  trivial - (of a group), 210
  trivial spatial -, 210f
part-whole structure, 242
person, 191,214,216
Platonic ideas, see: **individuo-properties**
Platonism, 33

medieval -, 164
points,
in modal space, 199,262
in space, 191f,200,202,205,210
in time, 200
possibilia, 18,85f,132
possibilism, 15,84,112,277
possibility, 2,80,83,85f,162,180
-concept for properties (of individuals), 139f,148
-concept for states of affairs, 80ff,83, 94f,110f,245,249
conceptual -, 161,177,183,215,323 (see in addition: conceptual **necessity**),
-functors for properties, 288f,294
-functors for states of affairs, 86f,90, 108,115
-operator (◊), 317f
possible individual(s), 2f,7f,83f,133,137, 139,156,158,177,182,184,187,257,271, 277,297,312,314
possible world(s), 2f,7f,28,68,73ff,78,80, 83ff,86f,98,112f,119,122,133,137,162f, 176ff,179f,247f,255ff,258f,261f,264ff, 267f,270,275ff,278,281f,286,288,292, 296f,312f,319
possible worlds ontology, 7f,75,78
precedence,
epistemological -, 13
ontological -, see: **ontological priority**
predicate(s), 1,4,7,8ff,11ff,18ff,21,27,93, 127,135,151,153,169,173,315ff
and extraction, 285f,310,314ff
as an ontological category, 230
categorial -, 220,225,300ff,304f,312,314
cumulative -, 92
dispositional -, 294
homoeomerous -, 92
non-linguistic -, 181f
non-ontological -, 285,301,315,319
of individuals, 285f
ontological -, 21,285
plural -, 207,213
predication,
analogous (derivative) -, 15,35,40
atemporal/temporal -, 203f
equivocal/univocal -, 15
ontological -, 181f,184
pre-eminence,
epistemological -, 15
ontological -, 15
primary actuality (PA(*x*)), 145ff,150, 152ff,155ff,161,163f,169,172ff,176,178, 180,182f,272ff,276,278 (see in addition: **actuality of properties**)
principle,
of allotment, 58
of anti-atomism, 196
of Cantor, 127
of connection for properties, 241
of exhaustion for properties, 241
of individuation for material individuals, 198f,202
of intensionalism, 314
of inversion (IP), 132,135,158ff
of nominalism, 312
of ontological unity, 213
of possible worlds ontology (PWO), 75
of predication, 249
of proper parts (PPP), 32
of property-quanta (PPQ), 239f
of real subsistence (RS), 150,169
of set-theoretical extensionalism, 312
of singular variation, 240f
of weak supplementation, 63,196
of the identity of indiscernibles, 142, 165ff,168,175
of the identity of properties, 231
of the type-uniformity of saturations, 305
privation, 141f
processes, 200
property(-ies), 3,7f,10,15,18f,39,132f, 135,151,157,189,233,303f,307f,310,313ff, 316f
accidental - (*simpliciter* or *with respect to*), 245f,249,262
conjunctive -, 141
contradictory -, 137,140,143,227f,234f, 246,257 (see in addition: **totality,**$\mathbf{k}_{<0>}$)
contradictory - *with respect to*, 246,268
disjunctive -, 135,141f,294
essential - (*simpliciter* or *with respect to*), 245f,249,268,280ff,284f,289,308
modal -, 198,288,294
natural -, 19
negative -, 135,141f,294
nuclear -, 186f
number-, 305,307
plural -, 214
of manifolds, 213
of properties, 225,300
of states of affairs, 127,253
relational -, 142
set-like -, 284

tautological -, 137,172,235f,246,251f
(see in addition: **minimality**,$\mathbf{t}_{<0>}$)
tautological - *with respect to*, 247,251, 268,271,280
the - of self-identity (**id**), 307,313
time-relative -, 271
transcendental -, 253
typed -, 313
type-transcendent (typeless) -, 306f,313, 317
property(-ies) of individuals (<0>(*x*)), 13,128,133f,136ff,139ff,142ff,145,150f, 154,156,158ff,161ff,164,169ff,172f,176f, 179ff,182ff,185,203,211,220,223ff,226f, 229ff,232ff,235ff,238ff,241ff,244ff,249ff, 252ff,255ff,258f,261,264f,267f,271ff,275, 280ff,283ff,286,288ff,291,294,296f,300, 304f,313ff,316,320,322,324
their identity, 158,231f,257,282
their intensional content, 239,284
their lower degrees, 156
their number, 156,167f,175,187,238, 294,296f
their parthood, 231
property-quantum(-a), 239,251f
property-yielding functors (not parallel to functors yielding states of affairs),
modalizers, 288f
the essential representative of *f*, 280,282
the essential representative of *f* in *w*, 281f
the Leibnizian representative of *x* in *w*, 261f,265ff,272,274ff,279
the property-image of *p*, 234ff,238, 241,244,251,255ff,258,261f,275,279,284
the property of being identical with *x* (see also: **haecceity**), 237,240f,245ff,248, 251,254ff,257ff,261,270
the property of differing from *x*, 236f,240f,245
the property specific to *x*, 251f,254ff, 258
the property specific to *x* in *y*, 256
the **w**-limitation of *f*, 284
property-yielding functors (parallel to functors yielding states of affairs), 232,243
proposition(s), 18,20f,35ff,39ff,87,107
propositional attitudes, 314

quality(-ies), 142,241
quantifiers (sentence- or term-forming), 24,288ff
numerically specific -, 119f,292f
quasi-atom(s), see under **atom(s)**
quasi-completeness (mereological), see under **whole**
quasi-individual, 181,187

realism,
modal -, 73,260,262
ontological -, 101f
semantic -, 20f
realism (with respect to **universals**), 2,9ff,19,314
weak/strong -, 14
reality,
of material t_0-individuals, 193ff,196
of material *t*-individuals, 216f
of parts of space, 192ff,205,210,217
realm of, see: **universe** of
real subsistence (rs and sr), 150,153,163, 169ff,172ff,179f,184,187,271ff,274f, 277ff,285f,320
receptacle, 194f,200,205
reduction (ontological), 117,184f,199, 281
relation(s), 2,7,10,15,18,22,39,213,303ff, 306ff,315,320
between individuals and states of affairs, 314
equivalence-, 267
extensional -, 315
non-extensional -, 314ff
of (between) individuals, 230,293,300, 304,314
restricted/unrestricted - (in its domain), 315f
similarity-, 267ff,279
relativism (ontological), 97,101
Russell's Antinomy, 151,310

saturation(s), 12,225ff,228f,231f,235, 239ff,243ff,247,251,253ff,284,288ff,291, 302f,305,308,313,315,321f
dyadic functor of - ((*x*,*y*)), 225,300
n-adic functors of - ($n \geq 2$), 229,300ff
schema, 46,50,226
science(s),
and explanation, 323
fundamental -, 15f
their field of reference, 1,3,88
their point of view, 1,3
semantics, 3
and logic, 4f
compositional -, 20f

intensional -, 87
of propositional logic, 90f,105f
sentence(s) (declarative), 1,4,6,9f,12,20, 24,27,34,40,287
non-ontological -, 287
sentence-connectives, 24,68,90,99f,320
infinitary -, 92
modal -, 159
sentence-form, 24,50,236,286,316
set(s), 3,8,25,28,45,117,126f,158,177, 180,186f,189,202,205f,208f,283,297,308f, 312ff,315ff
of individuals, 280ff,283ff,289
pure -, 14,157,312ff
Słupecki-, 283
super-, 309f,313ff,317
p-super-, 314
set theory, 3,5,7,18,28,47,84f,127,177, 281,300f,309f,312f
basic -, 7,281
axiom of comprehension, 47,158,280f
principle of abstraction, 47,56,60,309f
principle of extensionality, 47,158,233, 280f,308f
Ship of Theseus, 215f
simplicity,
epistemic -, 75,79
logical -, 14f
ontological -, 15,79
singular term(s), 11,19,24,50,141,203, 207,213,286,301,316
abstract -, 19f
eliminability of -, 44
solid(s), 205
space, 192f
modal -, 262
parts of -, 192ff,199f,202,205,210f
spatial coincidence, 190,193,198f,202, 204,206f,209ff,212,216f
spatial configuration(s), 191f,194f,200ff, 205f,210f,217
spatial location, 200f
spatial occupation, 192f,199,202
spatial region(s), see: **spatial configuration(s)**
standard theory of types, 7,17,300
statement(s), 12f,20,27,34ff,39,68,75,89, 92f,101,105ff,116f
elementary -, 75
existential -, 291f
modal -, 259,261
proofs of disjunctive -, 295
state(s) of affairs (1(*x*)), 2f,6ff,11ff, 14f,25,28,34ff,37ff,42f,45,47,51,53,58, 67f,73ff,78ff,83ff,86,88ff,91,93f,97f,105, 107,109f,112f,116ff,119ff,122ff,126ff, 132f,137,141,145,154,156f,170f,189,201, 211,220,223ff,226,229ff,232ff,235,238ff, 242,244f,248,251,255,258,275,277,286f, 289,291f,294ff,297,300,302ff,305,307, 310,312ff,316f,319,321ff,324
as sets of possible worlds, 45,58,78, 80,85,297,313
conjunctive -, 44
contradictory -, 48f,87,93,112,227,235, 245,254f,305,317 (see in addition: **totality,k**)
disjunctive -, 44,141
fundamental ontology of -, 25,88
negative -, 44f,141
primary -, 323
quantificational (existential, universal) - 288ff,291f,294
tautological -, 48,93,109,112,171,235, 239,245,289 (see in addition: **minimality,t**)
"that"-phrases as names of -, 3,12,20, 37,39f,44f,286 (see in addition: **that-functor**)
their identity, 37f
their intensional content, 121,123,239, 251
their lower and upper degrees, 118ff, 121f,128
their number, 82,101,109,112,114ff, 118,121f,124,126ff,129,238,296,312,314
their parthood (see also: ontological **analytical implication**), 37f,231,292,301
subject (non-linguistic), 181f,184
substance(s), 139,143ff,163,165,176ff, 179f
Aristotelian -, 200
sum, see: **conjunction**
superapplication, 163
superessentialism, 161ff
syllogistics, 2
system(s) (ontological),
P, PT1, IOU: see the Appendix
PT, 300
intensional -, 317

temporal configuration, 200
temporal indices, 203f
temporal occupation, 200
term(s) (see in additon: **name(s)**, **designator(s)**),

general -, 207f,214
plural -, 207f,213f
of extraction, 226,301,309f,314ff
singular -, see: **singular term(s)**
that-functor, 286,316ff,319f
the (actual) world (w), 28,36f,73,80,88ff, 93f,97f,101,103ff,108ff,112,114f,127f, 133,170ff,174,178ff,196,199,245,247,251, 254ff,257,259,262,272,274ff,278f,284, 286,312,323
thing(s),
ordinary -, 262f
with *n* dimensions (*0,1,2,3,4*), 200,204f
thought(s) (Fregean), 107,229
totality (T(x),**k**,$T_{<0>}(x)$,$\mathbf{k}_{<0>}$), 29ff,33, 42,48,80ff,86,93ff,96,100f,108ff,112, 114f,118,127f,137,140f,148,150f,164, 169f,192,209,211,225f,232,234ff,237, 245,249,251,254,273,284,287,289,291f, 312,314,319
totality of being, 1ff,7,9,12,17,122
transworld-individual, 262
truth/falsity (ontological concept), 28, 35ff,89ff,94,97ff,101f,103ff,107f,111, 117,170,290f
for Leibniz, 162
in a possible world, 138
truth(s)/falsity (semantical concept), 37, 89,92,101,105f,115,117,287,292,319
analytical, 27f,68,88f,93f,96f,101,105f, 108f,114,116,134,146,154,157,177,222, 225f,271,323
a priori, 94,171
correspondence theory of -, 10,11,19,37, 117
in all possible worlds, 28,68,93
in an interpretation, 4f
logical - (in the extended sense), 27,38, 97,221,225
logical - (for the formal language PL), 99
ontological - (of a sentence), 28,93
synthetic -, 94,105,116,171,179,278
truth-makers, 40f
truth value(s), 117,229,287,297,312
of a sentence, 287
type(s), 17,220
and tokens, 40,201
complex/simple -, 304,307,321f
generalized -, 301,303ff,306f,309ff, 312ff,320f,324
"natural" -, 314
of attributes, 3,10,12,300,304
1-, 304
ordinary -, 304,306,308
-restrictions for functions, 303,305

unity, 213
universal(s), 2,10f,12ff,15,18f,21f,73, 144,201,204,213,229f,314
universe,
as a mereologically total entity, 51,196
Boolean -, 70,255
of individuals, 244
of material t_0-individual, 196
of properties, 156,175f,234,242f,255, 296
of pure (super-)sets, 313f
of states of affairs, 75,82,88,98,101, 118,121f,126f,234,242f,296

validity,
formal -, 3ff,6
logical - (in an extended sense), 25,27
logical - (for the formal language PL), 102

whole,
complete -, 29,118
quasi-complete - (QC(x),$QC_{<0>}(x)$), 31, 70,74f,97f,101,103f,118,182,251
relative -, 33,214
world-equality, 176ff,180,258
worldways, 84f

INDEX OF NAMES

Abelard, 2
Angelelli, I., 143
Anselm of Canterbury, 157
Aristotle, 1f,13,98,143,149,200,203,322
Armstrong, D. M., 18ff,21,85,92,135, 141f,229,233,294,308

Barwise, J., 40
Bealer, G., 12,15,18,39
Beth, E. W., 295
Boethius, 144
Bolzano, 2
Borkowski, L., 17,295
Burkhardt, H., 143,175f,178

Cantor, 3,10,127
Carnap, R., 8,19,205,267,270,281,297
Cartwright, R., 190,192,194,202,204
Chisholm, R., 215f
Cresswell, M. J., 21,159

Dummett, M., 101

Ebbinghaus, H. D., 92

Findlay, J. N., 186
Fine, K., 187
Flum, J., 92
Frege, G., 3,9ff,12f,107f,117,135,225, 229,297,315

Geach, P. T., 199,203
Goodman, N., 32f,129
Gracia, J. J. E., 144

Henkin, 78
Hintikka, 267,270
Hobbes, 202
Hochberg, H., 44
Hodges, W., 129
Hughes, G. E., 159

Kanger, 267,270
Kant, 2,94
Kenny, A., 149
Kneale, W. and M., 180
Kripke, 87,267
Künne, W., 14,19,37
Küng, G., 63

Kutschera, F. v., 17,83,143,249

Leibniz, 2,80,83,87,138,142f,161ff, 165,167,175ff,178ff,261,278,324
Lejewski, C., 63f
Lenzen, W., 138
Leśniewski, 63f,283
Lewis, D., 18f,21,83ff,129,158,161ff,178, 180,229,260,262f,265ff,268ff,278f,297, 312f
Lewis Carroll, 149
Löwenheim, 127
Loux, M. J., 20

Mates, B., 83,87,143,162f,177
McTaggart, 205
Meinong, 19,181ff,186f,217,220,324
Minkowski, 203
Montague, R., 21,267
Mulligan, K., 39f

Neo-Platonists, 164

Ockham, 2,186,199

Parmenides, 2
Parsons, T., 186f
Perry, J., 40
Plantinga, A., 83,163,249f,267,277,294
Plato, 2,13,132,149,164
Protagoras, 101

Quine, W. V. O., 11,17,20ff,84,199,205, 213,233,312,318

Reinach, A., 39,116f
Rescher, N., 83
Russell, B., 10,19f,44,79,151,205,310

Sapir, 17
Simons, P., 32,40,51,63,92,196ff,207f, 213f
Skolem, 127
Słupecki, J., 283f
Smart, J. J. C., 203,205
Smith, B., 39,44,116
Sobociński, 64
Sophists, 101
Spinoza, 147f

Stenius, E., 79,230
Stoics, 3
Strawson, 203

Tarski, A., 4,62ff,65f,72,205
Tegtmeier, E., 314
Thomas Aquinas, 149,202,213,324
Thomas, W., 92

von Wright, G. H., 249

Whitehead, 205
Whorf, B. L., 17
Wittgenstein, L., 11,20,35,40,73,79,83,
88f,229f

Zemach, E., 201

LITERATURE

Angelelli, I.: *Studies on Gottlob Frege and Traditional Philosophy*, Reidel, Dordrecht 1967.
Anscombe, G. E. M.; Geach, P. T.: *Three Philosophers*, Basil Blackwell, Oxford 1967.
Armstrong, D. M.: *A Combinatorial Theory of Possibility*, Cambridge University Press, Cambridge 1989.
Armstrong, D. M.: *Universals and Scientific Realism*, 2 vols., Cambridge University Press, Cambridge 1978.

Barwise, J.; Perry, J.: *Situations and Attitudes*, MIT Press, Cambridge, Mass., 1983.
Bealer, G.: *Quality and Concept*, Clarendon Press, Oxford 1983.
Bealer, G.: "Foundations without Sets," *American Philosophical Quarterly* **18** (1981), pp. 347-353.
Beth, E. W.: *Mathematical Thought*, Reidel, Dordrecht 1965.
Borkowski, L.: *Formale Logik*, C.H. Beck, München 1977.
Burkhardt, H.: *Logik und Semiotik in der Philosophie von Leibniz*, Philosophia, München 1980.

Carnap, R.: *Meaning and Necessity*, University of Chicago Press, Chicago 1967.
Cartwright, R.: "Scattered Objects," in K. Lehrer (ed.), *Analysis and Metaphysics*, Reidel, Dordrecht 1975, pp. 153-171.
Chisholm, R. M.: "Mereological Essentialism," in R. M. Chisholm, *Person and Object*, Allen & Unwin, London 1976, pp. 145-158.
Cresswell, M. J.; Hughes, G. E.: *An Introduction to Modal Logic*, Methuen, London 1974.

Dummett, M.: *Truth and other Enigmas*, Duckworth, London 1978.

Ebbinghaus, H.-D.; Flum, J.; Thomas, W.: *Mathematical Logic*, Springer, New York/Berlin 1994.

Findlay, J. N.: *Meinong's Theory of Objects and Values*, Clarendon Press, Oxford 1963.
Fine, K.: "Critical Review of Parsons' *Nonexistent Objects*," *Philosophical Studies* **45** (1984), pp. 95-142.
Frege, G.: *Die Grundlagen der Arithmetik*, edited by C. Thiel, Meiner, Hamburg 1986.
Frege, G.: *Grundgesetze der Arithmetik*, 2 vols., reprint of the Jena 1893 edition, Olms, Hildesheim 1962.
Frege, G.: "Ausführungen über Sinn und Bedeutung," in *Schriften zur Logik und Sprachphilosophie*, edited by G. Gabriel, Meiner, Hamburg 1971, pp. 25-34.
(Translation in *Posthumous Writings*, edited by H. Hermes et al., Blackwell, Oxford 1979.)
Frege, G.: "Logische Untersuchungen I: Der Gedanke," in G. Frege, *Kleine Schriften*, edited by I. Angelelli, Wissenschaftliche Buchgesellschaft, Darmstadt 1967, pp. 342-362.
Frege, G.: "Über Begriff und Gegenstand," in *Kleine Schriften*, pp. 167-178.
Frege, G.: "Über Sinn und Bedeutung," in *Kleine Schriften*, pp. 143-162.
(Translations in *Collected Papers on Mathematics, Logic, and Philosophy*, edited by B. McGuinness, Blackwell, Oxford 1984.)

Goodman, N.: "A World of Individuals," in N. Goodman, *Problems and Projects*, Bobbs-Merrill, Indianapolis 1972, pp. 155-172.
Geach, P. T.: *Logic Matters*, Blackwell, Oxford 1972.

Gracia, J. J. E.: *Introduction to the Problem of Individuation in the Early Middle Ages*, Philosophia, München 1980.

Hochberg, H.: "Negation and Generality," in H. Hochberg, *Logic, Ontology, and Language.Essays on Truth and Reality*, Philosophia, München, 1984, pp. 296-312.

Hodges, W.; Lewis, D.: "Finitude and Infinitude in the Atomic Calculus of Individuals," *Noûs* **2** (1968), pp. 405-410.

Kenny, A.: *Aquinas*, Oxford University Press, Oxford 1980.

Kneale, W. and M.: *The Development of Logic*, Clarendon Press, Oxford 1988.

Küng, G.: *Ontologie und logistische Analyse der Sprache*, Springer, Wien 1963. (Translation by E. C. M. Mays, *Ontology and the Logistic Analysis of Language*, Reidel, Dordrecht 1967.)

Künne, W.: *Abstrakte Gegenstände*, Suhrkamp, Frankfurt a. Main 1983.

Kutschera, F. v.: *Einführung in die intensionale Semantik*, De Gruyter, Berlin 1976.

Kutschera, F. v.: *Sprachphilosophie*, Fink, München 1975.

Kutschera, F. v.: "Grundbegriffe der Metaphysik von Leibniz im Vergleich zu Begriffsbildungen der heutigen Modallogik," *Studia Leibnitiana* (1979), Sonderheft **8**, pp. 93-107.

Lejewski, C.: "Zu Leśniewskis Ontologic," *Ratio* **2** (1957/58), pp. 50-78. (English version: "On Leśniewski's Ontology," in J.T.J. Srzednicki, V.T. Rickey and J. Czelakowski (eds.), *Leśniewski's Systems, Mereology and Ontology*, M.Nijhoff, The Hague 1984.)

Lenzen, W.: "Zur extensionalen und 'intensionalen' Interpretation der Leibnizschen Logik," *Studia Leibnitiana* **15** (1983), pp. 129-148.

Lewis, D.: *On the Plurality of Worlds*, Basil Blackwell, Oxford 1986.

Lewis, D.: "Counterpart Theory and Quantified Modal Logic," in D. Lewis, *Philosophical Papers* I, Oxford University Press, Oxford 1983, pp. 26-46.

Lewis, D.: "New Work for a Theory of Universals," *Australasian Journal of Philosophy* **61** (1983), pp. 343-377.

Loux, M. J.: "The Existence of Universals," in M. J. Loux (ed.), *Universals and Particulars: Readings in Ontology*, University of Notre Dame Press, London 1976, pp. 3-24.

Mates, B.: *The Philosophy of Leibniz*, Oxford University Press, Oxford 1986.

Mates, B.: "Leibniz über mögliche Welten," in A. Heinekamp, F. Schupp (eds.), *Leibniz' Logik und Metaphysik*, Wissenschaftliche Buchgesellschaft, Darmstadt 1988, pp. 311-341.

Meixner, U.: "An Alternative Semantics for Modal Predicate-Logic," *Erkenntnis* **37** (1992), pp. 377-400.

Meixner, U.: "On Negative and Disjunctive Properties," in K. Mulligan (ed.), *Language, Truth and Ontology*, Kluwer, Dordrecht 1992, pp. 28-36.

Meixner, U.: "Ontologically Minimal Logical Semantics," *Notre Dame Journal of Formal Logic* **36** (1995), pp. 279-298.

Meixner, U.: "Propensity and Possibility," *Erkenntnis* **38** (1993), pp. 323-341.

Mulligan, K.; Simons, P.; Smith, B.: "Truth-Makers," *Philosophy and Phenomenological Research* **44** (1984), pp. 287-321.

Parsons, T.: *Nonexistent Objects*, Yale University Press, New Haven 1980.

Plantinga, A.: *The Nature of Necessity*, Clarendon Press, Oxford 1974.

Plantinga, A.: "essence and essentialism," in J. Kim, E. Sosa (eds.), *A Companion to Metaphysics*, Blackwell, Oxford 1995, pp. 138-140.

Quine, W. V. O.: "On what there is," in M. J. Loux (ed.), *Universals and Particulars: Readings in Ontology*, University of Notre Dame Press, London 1976, pp. 33-43.

Reinach, A.: "Zur Theorie des negativen Urteils," in A. Pfänder (ed.), *Münchener Philoso-*

phische Abhandlungen, Verlag Johann Ambrosius Barth, Leipzig 1911, pp. 196-254. (Translation by B. Smith: "On the Theory of the Negative Judgment," in B. Smith (ed.), *Parts and Moments*, Philosophia, München 1982, pp. 315 - 377.)

Rescher, N.: *A Theory of Possibility*, Basil Blackwell, Oxford 1975.

Russell, B.: "The Philosophy of Logical Atomism," in *The Philosophy of Logical Atomism and Other Essays: 1914 - 1919*, vol. 8 of *The Collected Papers of Bertrand Russell*, edited by J. G. Slater, Allen & Unwin, London 1986, pp. 160-244.

Simons, P.: *Parts. A Study in Ontology*, Clarendon Press, Oxford 1987.

Simons, P.: "Number and Manifolds," in B. Smith (ed.), *Parts and Moments*, Philosophia, München 1982, pp. 160-198.

Simons, P.: "Plural Reference and Set Theory," in *Parts and Moments*, pp. 199-260.

Słupecki, J.: "Towards a Generalized Mereology of Lesniewski," *Studia Logica* **8** (1958), pp. 131-154.

Smart, J. J. C.: "Space-Time and Individuals," in R. Rudner, I. Scheffler (eds.), *Logic and Art*, Bobbs-Merrill, Indianapolis 1972, pp. 3-20.

Smith, B.: "Introduction to Adolf Reinach 'On the Theory of the Negative Judgment'," in B. Smith (ed.), *Parts and Moments*, Philosophia, München 1982, pp. 289-313.

Spinoza, *The Collected Works*, vol. 1, edited and translated by E. Curley, Princeton University Press, Princeton, N.J., 1985.

Stenius, E.: *Wittgenstein's Tractatus*, Basil Blackwell, Oxford 1964.

Tarski, A.: "Foundations of the Geometry of Solids," in A. Tarski, *Logic, Semantics, Metamathematics*, Clarendon Press, Oxford 1956, pp. 24-29.

Tarski, A.: "On the Foundations of Boolean Algebra," in A. Tarski, *Logic, Semantics, Metamathematics*, pp. 320-341.

Tegtmeier, E.: *Grundzüge einer kategorialen Ontologie*, Alber, Freiburg/München 1992.

Thomas Aquinas: *Summa contra Gentiles*, edited by K. Allgaier et al., vol. III.1, Wissenschaftliche Buchgesellschaft, Darmstadt 1990.

Thomas Aquinas: *Summa Theologiae*, Editiones Paulinae, Milano 1988.

Wittgenstein, L.: *Tractatus logico-philosophicus*, English-German edition, Routledge & Kegan Paul, London 1960.

Wright, G. H. von: *An Essay in Modal Logic*, North-Holland Publishing Company, Amsterdam 1951.

Zemach, E.: "Four Ontologies," *The Journal of Philosophy* **67** (1970), pp. 231-247.

116. R. Tuomela, *Human Action and Its Explanation.* A Study on the Philosophical Foundations of Psychology. 1977 ISBN 90-277-0824-X
117. M. Lazerowitz, *The Language of Philosophy.* Freud and Wittgenstein. [Boston Studies in the Philosophy of Science, Vol. LV] 1977 ISBN 90-277-0826-6; Pb 90-277-0862-2
118. Not published
119. J. Pelc (ed.), *Semiotics in Poland, 1894–1969.* Translated from Polish. 1979 ISBN 90-277-0811-8
120. I. Pörn, *Action Theory and Social Science.* Some Formal Models. 1977 ISBN 90-277-0846-0
121. J. Margolis, *Persons and Mind.* The Prospects of Nonreductive Materialism. [Boston Studies in the Philosophy of Science, Vol. LVII] 1977 ISBN 90-277-0854-1; Pb 90-277-0863-0
122. J. Hintikka, I. Niiniluoto, and E. Saarinen (eds.), *Essays on Mathematical and Philosophical Logic.* 1979 ISBN 90-277-0879-7
123. T. A. F. Kuipers, *Studies in Inductive Probability and Rational Expectation.* 1978 ISBN 90-277-0882-7
124. E. Saarinen, R. Hilpinen, I. Niiniluoto and M. P. Hintikka (eds.), *Essays in Honour of Jaakko Hintikka on the Occasion of His 50th Birthday.* 1979 ISBN 90-277-0916-5
125. G. Radnitzky and G. Andersson (eds.), *Progress and Rationality in Science.* [Boston Studies in the Philosophy of Science, Vol. LVIII] 1978 ISBN 90-277-0921-1; Pb 90-277-0922-X
126. P. Mittelstaedt, *Quantum Logic.* 1978 ISBN 90-277-0925-4
127. K. A. Bowen, *Model Theory for Modal Logic.* Kripke Models for Modal Predicate Calculi. 1979 ISBN 90-277-0929-7
128. H. A. Bursen, *Dismantling the Memory Machine.* A Philosophical Investigation of Machine Theories of Memory. 1978 ISBN 90-277-0933-5
129. M. W. Wartofsky, *Models.* Representation and the Scientific Understanding. [Boston Studies in the Philosophy of Science, Vol. XLVIII] 1979 ISBN 90-277-0736-7; Pb 90-277-0947-5
130. D. Ihde, *Technics and Praxis.* A Philosophy of Technology. [Boston Studies in the Philosophy of Science, Vol. XXIV] 1979 ISBN 90-277-0953-X; Pb 90-277-0954-8
131. J. J. Wiatr (ed.), *Polish Essays in the Methodology of the Social Sciences.* [Boston Studies in the Philosophy of Science, Vol. XXIX] 1979 ISBN 90-277-0723-5; Pb 90-277-0956-4
132. W. C. Salmon (ed.), *Hans Reichenbach: Logical Empiricist.* 1979 ISBN 90-277-0958-0
133. P. Bieri, R.-P. Horstmann and L. Krüger (eds.), *Transcendental Arguments in Science.* Essays in Epistemology. 1979 ISBN 90-277-0963-7; Pb 90-277-0964-5
134. M. Marković and G. Petrović (eds.), *Praxis.* Yugoslav Essays in the Philosophy and Methodology of the Social Sciences. [Boston Studies in the Philosophy of Science, Vol. XXXVI] 1979 ISBN 90-277-0727-8; Pb 90-277-0968-8
135. R. Wójcicki, *Topics in the Formal Methodology of Empirical Sciences.* Translated from Polish. 1979 ISBN 90-277-1004-X
136. G. Radnitzky and G. Andersson (eds.), *The Structure and Development of Science.* [Boston Studies in the Philosophy of Science, Vol. LIX] 1979 ISBN 90-277-0994-7; Pb 90-277-0995-5
137. J. C. Webb, *Mechanism, Mentalism and Metamathematics.* An Essay on Finitism. 1980 ISBN 90-277-1046-5
138. D. F. Gustafson and B. L. Tapscott (eds.), *Body, Mind and Method.* Essays in Honor of Virgil C. Aldrich. 1979 ISBN 90-277-1013-9
139. L. Nowak, *The Structure of Idealization.* Towards a Systematic Interpretation of the Marxian Idea of Science. 1980 ISBN 90-277-1014-7

140. C. Perelman, *The New Rhetoric and the Humanities.* Essays on Rhetoric and Its Applications. Translated from French and German. With an Introduction by H. Zyskind. 1979 ISBN 90-277-1018-X; Pb 90-277-1019-8
141. W. Rabinowicz, *Universalizability.* A Study in Morals and Metaphysics. 1979 ISBN 90-277-1020-2
142. C. Perelman, *Justice, Law and Argument.* Essays on Moral and Legal Reasoning. Translated from French and German. With an Introduction by H.J. Berman. 1980 ISBN 90-277-1089-9; Pb 90-277-1090-2
143. S. Kanger and S. Öhman (eds.), *Philosophy and Grammar.* Papers on the Occasion of the Quincentennial of Uppsala University. 1981 ISBN 90-277-1091-0
144. T. Pawlowski, *Concept Formation in the Humanities and the Social Sciences.* 1980 ISBN 90-277-1096-1
145. J. Hintikka, D. Gruender and E. Agazzi (eds.), *Theory Change, Ancient Axiomatics and Galileo's Methodology.* Proceedings of the 1978 Pisa Conference on the History and Philosophy of Science, Volume I. 1981 ISBN 90-277-1126-7
146. J. Hintikka, D. Gruender and E. Agazzi (eds.), *Probabilistic Thinking, Thermodynamics, and the Interaction of the History and Philosophy of Science.* Proceedings of the 1978 Pisa Conference on the History and Philosophy of Science, Volume II. 1981 ISBN 90-277-1127-5
147. U. Mönnich (ed.), *Aspects of Philosophical Logic.* Some Logical Forays into Central Notions of Linguistics and Philosophy. 1981 ISBN 90-277-1201-8
148. D. M. Gabbay, *Semantical Investigations in Heyting's Intuitionistic Logic.* 1981 ISBN 90-277-1202-6
149. E. Agazzi (ed.), *Modern Logic – A Survey.* Historical, Philosophical, and Mathematical Aspects of Modern Logic and Its Applications. 1981 ISBN 90-277-1137-2
150. A. F. Parker-Rhodes, *The Theory of Indistinguishables.* A Search for Explanatory Principles below the Level of Physics. 1981 ISBN 90-277-1214-X
151. J. C. Pitt, *Pictures, Images, and Conceptual Change.* An Analysis of Wilfrid Sellars' Philosophy of Science. 1981 ISBN 90-277-1276-X; Pb 90-277-1277-8
152. R. Hilpinen (ed.), *New Studies in Deontic Logic.* Norms, Actions, and the Foundations of Ethics. 1981 ISBN 90-277-1278-6; Pb 90-277-1346-4
153. C. Dilworth, *Scientific Progress.* A Study Concerning the Nature of the Relation between Successive Scientific Theories. 3rd rev. ed., 1994 ISBN 0-7923-2487-0; Pb 0-7923-2488-9
154. D. Woodruff Smith and R. McIntyre, *Husserl and Intentionality.* A Study of Mind, Meaning, and Language. 1982 ISBN 90-277-1392-8; Pb 90-277-1730-3
155. R. J. Nelson, *The Logic of Mind.* 2nd. ed., 1989 ISBN 90-277-2819-4; Pb 90-277-2822-4
156. J. F. A. K. van Benthem, *The Logic of Time.* A Model-Theoretic Investigation into the Varieties of Temporal Ontology, and Temporal Discourse. 1983; 2nd ed., 1991 ISBN 0-7923-1081-0
157. R. Swinburne (ed.), *Space, Time and Causality.* 1983 ISBN 90-277-1437-1
158. E. T. Jaynes, *Papers on Probability, Statistics and Statistical Physics.* Ed. by R. D. Rozenkrantz. 1983 ISBN 90-277-1448-7; Pb (1989) 0-7923-0213-3
159. T. Chapman, *Time: A Philosophical Analysis.* 1982 ISBN 90-277-1465-7
160. E. N. Zalta, *Abstract Objects.* An Introduction to Axiomatic Metaphysics. 1983 ISBN 90-277-1474-6
161. S. Harding and M. B. Hintikka (eds.), *Discovering Reality.* Feminist Perspectives on Epistemology, Metaphysics, Methodology, and Philosophy of Science. 1983 ISBN 90-277-1496-7; Pb 90-277-1538-6
162. M. A. Stewart (ed.), *Law, Morality and Rights.* 1983 ISBN 90-277-1519-X

163. D. Mayr and G. Süssmann (eds.), *Space, Time, and Mechanics.* Basic Structures of a Physical Theory. 1983 ISBN 90-277-1525-4
164. D. Gabbay and F. Guenthner (eds.), *Handbook of Philosophical Logic.* Vol. I: Elements of Classical Logic. 1983 ISBN 90-277-1542-4
165. D. Gabbay and F. Guenthner (eds.), *Handbook of Philosophical Logic.* Vol. II: Extensions of Classical Logic. 1984 ISBN 90-277-1604-8
166. D. Gabbay and F. Guenthner (eds.), *Handbook of Philosophical Logic.* Vol. III: Alternative to Classical Logic. 1986 ISBN 90-277-1605-6
167. D. Gabbay and F. Guenthner (eds.), *Handbook of Philosophical Logic.* Vol. IV: Topics in the Philosophy of Language. 1989 ISBN 90-277-1606-4
168. A. J. I. Jones, *Communication and Meaning.* An Essay in Applied Modal Logic. 1983 ISBN 90-277-1543-2
169. M. Fitting, *Proof Methods for Modal and Intuitionistic Logics.* 1983 ISBN 90-277-1573-4
170. J. Margolis, *Culture and Cultural Entities.* Toward a New Unity of Science. 1984 ISBN 90-277-1574-2
171. R. Tuomela, *A Theory of Social Action.* 1984 ISBN 90-277-1703-6
172. J. J. E. Gracia, E. Rabossi, E. Villanueva and M. Dascal (eds.), *Philosophical Analysis in Latin America.* 1984 ISBN 90-277-1749-4
173. P. Ziff, *Epistemic Analysis.* A Coherence Theory of Knowledge. 1984 ISBN 90-277-1751-7
174. P. Ziff, *Antiaesthetics.* An Appreciation of the Cow with the Subtile Nose. 1984 ISBN 90-277-1773-7
175. W. Balzer, D. A. Pearce, and H.-J. Schmidt (eds.), *Reduction in Science.* Structure, Examples, Philosophical Problems. 1984 ISBN 90-277-1811-3
176. A. Peczenik, L. Lindahl and B. van Roermund (eds.), *Theory of Legal Science.* Proceedings of the Conference on Legal Theory and Philosophy of Science (Lund, Sweden, December 1983). 1984 ISBN 90-277-1834-2
177. I. Niiniluoto, *Is Science Progressive?* 1984 ISBN 90-277-1835-0
178. B. K. Matilal and J. L. Shaw (eds.), *Analytical Philosophy in Comparative Perspective.* Exploratory Essays in Current Theories and Classical Indian Theories of Meaning and Reference. 1985 ISBN 90-277-1870-9
179. P. Kroes, *Time: Its Structure and Role in Physical Theories.* 1985 ISBN 90-277-1894-6
180. J. H. Fetzer, *Sociobiology and Epistemology.* 1985 ISBN 90-277-2005-3; Pb 90-277-2006-1
181. L. Haaparanta and J. Hintikka (eds.), *Frege Synthesized.* Essays on the Philosophical and Foundational Work of Gottlob Frege. 1986 ISBN 90-277-2126-2
182. M. Detlefsen, *Hilbert's Program.* An Essay on Mathematical Instrumentalism. 1986 ISBN 90-277-2151-3
183. J. L. Golden and J. J. Pilotta (eds.), *Practical Reasoning in Human Affairs.* Studies in Honor of Chaim Perelman. 1986 ISBN 90-277-2255-2
184. H. Zandvoort, *Models of Scientific Development and the Case of Nuclear Magnetic Resonance.* 1986 ISBN 90-277-2351-6
185. I. Niiniluoto, *Truthlikeness.* 1987 ISBN 90-277-2354-0
186. W. Balzer, C. U. Moulines and J. D. Sneed, *An Architectonic for Science.* The Structuralist Program. 1987 ISBN 90-277-2403-2
187. D. Pearce, *Roads to Commensurability.* 1987 ISBN 90-277-2414-8
188. L. M. Vaina (ed.), *Matters of Intelligence.* Conceptual Structures in Cognitive Neuroscience. 1987 ISBN 90-277-2460-1
189. H. Siegel, *Relativism Refuted.* A Critique of Contemporary Epistemological Relativism. 1987 ISBN 90-277-2469-5

190. W. Callebaut and R. Pinxten, *Evolutionary Epistemology.* A Multiparadigm Program, with a Complete Evolutionary Epistemology Bibliograph. 1987 ISBN 90-277-2582-9
191. J. Kmita, *Problems in Historical Epistemology.* 1988 ISBN 90-277-2199-8
192. J. H. Fetzer (ed.), *Probability and Causality.* Essays in Honor of Wesley C. Salmon, with an Annotated Bibliography. 1988 ISBN 90-277-2607-8; Pb 1-5560-8052-2
193. A. Donovan, L. Laudan and R. Laudan (eds.), *Scrutinizing Science.* Empirical Studies of Scientific Change. 1988 ISBN 90-277-2608-6
194. H.R. Otto and J.A. Tuedio (eds.), *Perspectives on Mind.* 1988 ISBN 90-277-2640-X
195. D. Batens and J.P. van Bendegem (eds.), *Theory and Experiment.* Recent Insights and New Perspectives on Their Relation. 1988 ISBN 90-277-2645-0
196. J. Österberg, *Self and Others.* A Study of Ethical Egoism. 1988 ISBN 90-277-2648-5
197. D.H. Helman (ed.), *Analogical Reasoning.* Perspectives of Artificial Intelligence, Cognitive Science, and Philosophy. 1988 ISBN 90-277-2711-2
198. J. Wolenski, *Logic and Philosophy in the Lvov-Warsaw School.* 1989 ISBN 90-277-2749-X
199. R. Wójcicki, *Theory of Logical Calculi.* Basic Theory of Consequence Operations. 1988 ISBN 90-277-2785-6
200. J. Hintikka and M.B. Hintikka, *The Logic of Epistemology and the Epistemology of Logic.* Selected Essays. 1989 ISBN 0-7923-0040-8; Pb 0-7923-0041-6
201. E. Agazzi (ed.), *Probability in the Sciences.* 1988 ISBN 90-277-2808-9
202. M. Meyer (ed.), *From Metaphysics to Rhetoric.* 1989 ISBN 90-277-2814-3
203. R.L. Tieszen, *Mathematical Intuition.* Phenomenology and Mathematical Knowledge. 1989 ISBN 0-7923-0131-5
204. A. Melnick, *Space, Time, and Thought in Kant.* 1989 ISBN 0-7923-0135-8
205. D.W. Smith, *The Circle of Acquaintance.* Perception, Consciousness, and Empathy. 1989 ISBN 0-7923-0252-4
206. M.H. Salmon (ed.), *The Philosophy of Logical Mechanism.* Essays in Honor of Arthur W. Burks. With his Responses, and with a Bibliography of Burk's Work. 1990 ISBN 0-7923-0325-3
207. M. Kusch, *Language as Calculus vs. Language as Universal Medium.* A Study in Husserl, Heidegger, and Gadamer. 1989 ISBN 0-7923-0333-4
208. T.C. Meyering, *Historical Roots of Cognitive Science.* The Rise of a Cognitive Theory of Perception from Antiquity to the Nineteenth Century. 1989 ISBN 0-7923-0349-0
209. P. Kosso, *Observability and Observation in Physical Science.* 1989 ISBN 0-7923-0389-X
210. J. Kmita, *Essays on the Theory of Scientific Cognition.* 1990 ISBN 0-7923-0441-1
211. W. Sieg (ed.), *Acting and Reflecting.* The Interdisciplinary Turn in Philosophy. 1990 ISBN 0-7923-0512-4
212. J. Karpiński, *Causality in Sociological Research.* 1990 ISBN 0-7923-0546-9
213. H.A. Lewis (ed.), *Peter Geach: Philosophical Encounters.* 1991 ISBN 0-7923-0823-9
214. M. Ter Hark, *Beyond the Inner and the Outer.* Wittgenstein's Philosophy of Psychology. 1990 ISBN 0-7923-0850-6
215. M. Gosselin, *Nominalism and Contemporary Nominalism.* Ontological and Epistemological Implications of the Work of W.V.O. Quine and of N. Goodman. 1990 ISBN 0-7923-0904-9
216. J.H. Fetzer, D. Shatz and G. Schlesinger (eds.), *Definitions and Definability.* Philosophical Perspectives. 1991 ISBN 0-7923-1046-2
217. E. Agazzi and A. Cordero (eds.), *Philosophy and the Origin and Evolution of the Universe.* 1991 ISBN 0-7923-1322-4
218. M. Kusch, *Foucault's Strata and Fields.* An Investigation into Archaeological and Genealogical Science Studies. 1991 ISBN 0-7923-1462-X

219. C.J. Posy, *Kant's Philosophy of Mathematics*. Modern Essays. 1992 ISBN 0-7923-1495-6
220. G. Van de Vijver, *New Perspectives on Cybernetics*. Self-Organization, Autonomy and Connectionism. 1992 ISBN 0-7923-1519-7
221. J.C. Nyíri, *Tradition and Individuality*. Essays. 1992 ISBN 0-7923-1566-9
222. R. Howell, *Kant's Transcendental Deduction*. An Analysis of Main Themes in His Critical Philosophy. 1992 ISBN 0-7923-1571-5
223. A. García de la Sienra, *The Logical Foundations of the Marxian Theory of Value*. 1992 ISBN 0-7923-1778-5
224. D.S. Shwayder, *Statement and Referent*. An Inquiry into the Foundations of Our Conceptual Order. 1992 ISBN 0-7923-1803-X
225. M. Rosen, *Problems of the Hegelian Dialectic*. Dialectic Reconstructed as a Logic of Human Reality. 1993 ISBN 0-7923-2047-6
226. P. Suppes, *Models and Methods in the Philosophy of Science: Selected Essays*. 1993 ISBN 0-7923-2211-8
227. R. M. Dancy (ed.), *Kant and Critique: New Essays in Honor of W. H. Werkmeister*. 1993 ISBN 0-7923-2244-4
228. J. Woleński (ed.), *Philosophical Logic in Poland*. 1993 ISBN 0-7923-2293-2
229. M. De Rijke (ed.), *Diamonds and Defaults*. Studies in Pure and Applied Intensional Logic. 1993 ISBN 0-7923-2342-4
230. B.K. Matilal and A. Chakrabarti (eds.), *Knowing from Words*. Western and Indian Philosophical Analysis of Understanding and Testimony. 1994 ISBN 0-7923-2345-9
231. S.A. Kleiner, *The Logic of Discovery*. A Theory of the Rationality of Scientific Research. 1993 ISBN 0-7923-2371-8
232. R. Festa, *Optimum Inductive Methods*. A Study in Inductive Probability, Bayesian Statistics, and Verisimilitude. 1993 ISBN 0-7923-2460-9
233. P. Humphreys (ed.), *Patrick Suppes: Scientific Philosopher*. Vol. 1: Probability and Probabilistic Causality. 1994 ISBN 0-7923-2552-4
234. P. Humphreys (ed.), *Patrick Suppes: Scientific Philosopher*. Vol. 2: Philosophy of Physics, Theory Structure, and Measurement Theory. 1994 ISBN 0-7923-2553-2
235. P. Humphreys (ed.), *Patrick Suppes: Scientific Philosopher*. Vol. 3: Language, Logic, and Psychology. 1994 ISBN 0-7923-2862-0
Set ISBN (Vols 233–235) 0-7923-2554-0
236. D. Prawitz and D. Westerståhl (eds.), *Logic and Philosophy of Science in Uppsala*. Papers from the 9th International Congress of Logic, Methodology, and Philosophy of Science. 1994 ISBN 0-7923-2702-0
237. L. Haaparanta (ed.), *Mind, Meaning and Mathematics*. Essays on the Philosophical Views of Husserl and Frege. 1994 ISBN 0-7923-2703-9
238. J. Hintikka (ed.), *Aspects of Metaphor*. 1994 ISBN 0-7923-2786-1
239. B. McGuinness and G. Oliveri (eds.), *The Philosophy of Michael Dummett*. With Replies from Michael Dummett. 1994 ISBN 0-7923-2804-3
240. D. Jamieson (ed.), *Language, Mind, and Art*. Essays in Appreciation and Analysis, In Honor of Paul Ziff. 1994 ISBN 0-7923-2810-8
241. G. Preyer, F. Siebelt and A. Ulfig (eds.), *Language, Mind and Epistemology*. On Donald Davidson's Philosophy. 1994 ISBN 0-7923-2811-6
242. P. Ehrlich (ed.), *Real Numbers, Generalizations of the Reals, and Theories of Continua*. 1994 ISBN 0-7923-2689-X
243. G. Debrock and M. Hulswit (eds.), *Living Doubt*. Essays concerning the epistemology of Charles Sanders Peirce. 1994 ISBN 0-7923-2898-1
244. J. Srzednicki, *To Know or Not to Know*. Beyond Realism and Anti-Realism. 1994 ISBN 0-7923-2909-0
245. R. Egidi (ed.), *Wittgenstein: Mind and Language*. 1995 ISBN 0-7923-3171-0

246. A. Hyslop, *Other Minds*. 1995 ISBN 0-7923-3245-8
247. L. Pólos and M. Masuch (eds.), *Applied Logic: How, What and Why*. Logical Approaches to Natural Language. 1995 ISBN 0-7923-3432-9
248. M. Krynicki, M. Mostowski and L.M. Szczerba (eds.), *Quantifiers: Logics, Models and Computation*. Volume One: Surveys. 1995 ISBN 0-7923-3448-5
249. M. Krynicki, M. Mostowski and L.M. Szczerba (eds.), *Quantifiers: Logics, Models and Computation*. Volume Two: Contributions. 1995 ISBN 0-7923-3449-3
Set ISBN (Vols 248 + 249) 0-7923-3450-7
250. R.A. Watson, *Representational Ideas from Plato to Patricia Churchland*. 1995 ISBN 0-7923-3453-1
251. J. Hintikka (ed.), *From Dedekind to Gödel*. Essays on the Development of the Foundations of Mathematics. 1995 ISBN 0-7923-3484-1
252. A. Wiśniewski, *The Posing of Questions*. Logical Foundations of Erotetic Inferences. 1995 ISBN 0-7923-3637-2
253. J. Peregrin, *Doing Worlds with Words*. Formal Semantics without Formal Metaphysics. 1995 ISBN 0-7923-3742-5
254. I.A. Kieseppä, *Truthlikeness for Multidimensional, Quantitative Cognitive Problems*. 1996 ISBN 0-7923-4005-1
255. P. Hugly and C. Sayward: *Intensionality and Truth*. An Essay on the Philosophy of A.N. Prior. 1996 ISBN 0-7923-4119-8
256. L. Hankinson Nelson and J. Nelson (eds.): *Feminism, Science, and the Philosophy of Science*. 1997 ISBN 0-7923-4162-7
257. P.I. Bystrov and V.N. Sadovsky (eds.): *Philosophical Logic and Logical Philosophy*. Essays in Honour of Vladimir A. Smirnov. 1996 ISBN 0-7923-4270-4
258. Å.E. Andersson and N-E. Sahlin (eds.): *The Complexity of Creativity*. 1996 ISBN 0-7923-4346-8
259. M.L. Dalla Chiara, K. Doets, D. Mundici and J. van Benthem (eds.): *Logic and Scientific Methods*. Volume One of the Tenth International Congress of Logic, Methodology and Philosophy of Science, Florence, August 1995. 1997 ISBN 0-7923-4383-2
260. M.L. Dalla Chiara, K. Doets, D. Mundici and J. van Benthem (eds.): *Structures and Norms in Science*. Volume Two of the Tenth International Congress of Logic, Methodology and Philosophy of Science, Florence, August 1995. 1997 ISBN 0-7923-4384-0
Set ISBN (Vols 259 + 260) 0-7923-4385-9
261. A. Chakrabarti: *Denying Existence*. The Logic, Epistemology and Pragmatics of Negative Existentials and Fictional Discourse. 1997 ISBN 0-7923-4388-3
262. A. Biletzki: *Talking Wolves*. Thomas Hobbes on the Language of Politics and the Politics of Language. 1997 ISBN 0-7923-4425-1
263. D. Nute (ed.): *Defeasible Deontic Logic*. 1997 ISBN 0-7923-4630-0
264. U. Meixner: *Axiomatic Formal Ontology*. 1997 ISBN 0-7923-4747-X
265. I. Brinck: *The Indexical 'I'*. The First Person in Thought and Language. 1997 ISBN 0-7923-4741-2